C000010380

COLLINS GEM

Roget's

INTERNATIONAL®
THESAURUS

HarperCollins*Publishers*

First Edition 1995

© HarperCollins Publishers 1995

ISBN 0 00 470781-8

A catalogue record for this book is available from
the British Library

Typeset by Morton Word Processing Ltd
Scarborough, England

Printed and bound in Great Britain by
HarperCollins Manufacturing
PO Box, Glasgow G4 ONB

HOW TO USE THIS BOOK

The Gem Roget's Thesaurus is a tool for finding specific words or phrases
for general ideas. When you want a more accurate or effective way of saying
what you mean, it gives you possibilities and allows you to choose the one
you think is best. The book has a text of about 130,000 words and phrases,
arranged in categories by their meanings, and a comprehensive index.

The search for a word that you need begins with the index. Suppose
that you want a word to describe something odd.

1. In the index, look up the word
odd and pick the subentry closest
to the meaning you want.

odd
adj dissimilar 749.4
occasional 810.3
queer 832.11
sole 834.9
insane 881.22
eccentric 882.5

2. Follow its number into the text
and you will find a paragraph of
words meaning odd or queer.

832 ABNORMALITY

nouns

1 abnormality;.........

11 **odd, queer, peculiar, absurd,
    singular, curious,** quaint, **eccen-
    tric,** funny, rum; **strange,** surre-
    al, **weird,** unearthly

12 **fantastic,** fanciful, **unbelievable,**

To make good use of the book's structure, remember that it contains
many sequences of closely related categories. If you are not satisfied with
what you find in one place, glance at nearby categories too.

Terms within a category are organized into numbered paragraphs and
also subdivided by part of speech. Words in bold type are those most
commonly used. The words closest in meaning are grouped in clusters
separated by semicolons; the semicolon indicates a slight change in sense
or application. To help in choosing the right word, terms with restricted
uses are indicated by italic labels in brackets, such as nonformal (meaning
slang or informal), old, or Scots.

The Thesaurus offers invaluable help in all contexts that call for good
English, and, particularly when used in conjunction with one of the
Collins range of dictionaries, will actively promote a broader command of
the language.

1 BIRTH

nouns

1 **birth, childbirth, having a baby, giving birth,** the stork (*nonformal*); **confinement,** being brought to bed; **labour,** birth throes *or* pangs; **delivery,** happy event (*nonformal*); **hatching**

verbs

2 **be born,** have birth, come forth, issue forth, see the light of day, come into the world; **hatch**

3 **give birth, bear,** bear *or* have young, **have; have a baby,** bear a child; lie in, be confined, labour

adjectives

4 **born,** given birth; **hatched;** newborn; stillborn; **bearing, giving birth**

2 THE BODY

nouns

1 **body,** the person, anatomy, frame, physical self, physical *or* bodily structure, physique; organism

2 **the skeleton, the bones,** one's bones, framework, bony framework; rib cage; cartilage

3 **the muscles,** voluntary muscle, involuntary muscle; physique; **the skin, skin;** membrane

4 **member, external organ; head; arm;** forearm; wrist; elbow; upper arm, biceps; **leg,** limb, legs, pins (*nonformal*); shin; ankle; calf; knee; thigh, ham; **hand,** paw (*nonformal*); **foot**

5 **teeth, tooth,** fang, tusk; snaggletooth; canine tooth, canine; molar, grinder; wisdom tooth; milk tooth, baby tooth, deciduous tooth; permanent tooth

6 **eye,** visual organ, organ of vision, optic; clear eyes, bright eyes; saucer eyes, goggle eyes; naked eye; corner of the eye; eyeball; retina; lens; optic nerve; iris; pupil; eyelid, lid

7 **ear,** lug (*Scots*); external ear, **outer ear;** cauliflower ear; shell-like (*nonformal*); ear lobe, lobe; **middle ear;** eardrum; inner ear, labyrinth

8 **genitals,** sex organs, reproductive organs, private parts, privy parts; **crotch,** crutch, pelvis; **male organs; penis; testicles; bag** *and* **basket** (*both nonformal*), cod (*old*); **female organs; vagina;** clitoris; ovary; uterus, womb; secondary sex characteristic, beard, breasts

9 **nervous system, nerves,** central nervous system; **nerve;** nerve cell; **spinal cord; brain**

10 **internal organs, insides,** innards (*nonformal*); **heart; lung; lungs; liver; kidney,** kidneys

11 **digestion,** assimilation, absorption; metabolism; digestive system; gastric glands; liver; saliva, gastric juice, intestinal juice; bile

12 (*digestive system*) mouth; gullet, crop, **throat,** gorge; **abdomen, stomach,** belly (*nonformal*), diaphragm; paunch; **intestine, intestines;** entrails, **bowels;** small intestine; **appendix;** large intestine, colon, rectum; anus

13 (*nonformal terms*) tummy, **gut,** bulge, corporation, spare tyre, **potbelly,** beerbelly; love handles

14 **breathing**, **respiration**, aspiration; inspiration; **breath**, wind, breath of air; pant, puff; wheeze, asthmatic wheeze; broken wind; gasp, gulp; snoring, snore; sniff, snuff; sigh; sneeze; cough, hack; hiccup; **artificial respiration**, kiss of life

15 (*respiratory system*) **lungs**, bellows (*nonformal*), lights (*old*); **windpipe**; bronchial tube

16 **duct**, **vessel**, canal, passage; pore; **blood vessel**; artery; vein, jugular vein; varicose vein; **capillary**

17 (*body fluids*) humour (*old*); serum; **pus**, matter; discharge; **phlegm**; **saliva**, spit (*nonformal*); urine; perspiration, sweat (*nonformal*); tear; **milk**, mother's milk

18 **blood**, gore; **serum**; **plasma**; **blood cell** or **corpuscle**; **red corpuscle** or **blood cell**; **white corpuscle** or **blood cell**; **haemoglobin**; **blood pressure**; **circulation**; **blood group** or **type**, type O or A or B or AB; blood count; bloodstream

adjectives

19 **skeleton**, **skeletal**; **bone**, **bony**; **spinal**; **muscle**, **muscular**; cartilage, cartilaginous; **eye**, **optic**, visual; **ear**, **aural**; **genital**; **nerve**; **brain**, **cerebral**; **digestive**; **metabolic**; abdominal; **gastric**

20 **respiratory**, breathing; **nasal**; **bronchial**; **lung**; puffing, snorting, wheezing, asthmatic, snoring, panting

3 HAIR

nouns

1 **hair**, pile, **fur**, coat, pelt, **fleece**, wool, camel's hair; **mane**; tousled or matted hair, **mat of hair**; bristle

2 grey hair, silver or silvery hair, white hair, greying temples

3 **head of hair**, head; **crop**, crop of hair, mat, mop, **shock**, fleece; **mane**; **locks**, crowning glory

4 **lock**; flowing locks; **curl**, curly locks, ringlet; fringe

5 **plait**, braid; **pigtail**; coil, knot, French pleat; ponytail; bun

6 **beard**, **whiskers**; **sideburns**, muttonchops; **goatee**; stubble, designer stubble, bristles; five o'clock shadow

7 **moustache**, handlebar moustache, walrus moustache

8 **eyelashes**, lashes; **eyebrows**, brows

9 false hair, switch, fall, hair extensions; **wig**

10 **hairstyle**, hairdo, haircut; **perm**, permanent wave

11 **feather**, **plume**; **quill**; **plumage**, **feathers**, feather; breast feathers, flight feathers; down, fluff, **fuzz**, **fur**, pile; eiderdown

verbs

12 grow or sprout hair

13 cut or style the hair, trim; **barber**; wave, perm; **bob**, shingle

adjectives

14 **hairy**; **furry**; **woolly**; bushy, **shaggy**, matted; **bristly**, stubbly, **fuzzy**; **bearded**, unshaven

15 feathered; **downy,** fluffy, nappy, velvety, fuzzy, furry

4 CLOTHING MATERIALS

nouns

1 **material, fabric, cloth, textile,** textile fabric, texture, tissue, stuff, weave, web, **material, goods;** table linen; felt; silk; lace; rag, rags

2 **fur,** pelt, hide, fell, fleece; imitation fur, fake fur, synthetic fur, fun fur; skin; **leather;** imitation leather

5 CLOTHING

nouns

1 **clothing, clothes, wear, dress,** dressing, **garb, attire, array,** habit, fashion, style, guise, **costume,** gear, fig or full fig (both *nonformal*), trim; **garments,** robes, rags (*nonformal*), finery; work clothes, fatigues; linen; menswear, men's clothing, women's clothing

2 **wardrobe,** furnishings, things, trappings; **outfit;** wedding clothes, bridal outfit, trousseau

3 **garment,** robe, frock, gown, rag (*nonformal*)

4 **rags, tatters,** secondhand clothes, old clothes, worn clothes

5 **suit,** suit of clothes, **frock,** dress, rig (*nonformal*), **costume, habit**

6 **uniform,** civilian dress *or* clothes, **mufti,** civvies (*nonformal*), plain clothes

7 **costume,** fancy dress, masquerade, disguise; motley, cap and bells

8 **finery,** frippery, full fig (*nonformal*); **best clothes, Sunday best; glad rags** (*nonformal*), party dress

9 **formal dress, evening dress, full dress,** dress clothes, evening wear, white tie and tails; dinner clothes; dress suit, tails (*nonformal*); tuxedo; court dress; dress uniform, evening gown, dinner dress *or* gown

10 **coat, jacket; overcoat;** cloak; rain gear, raincoat, foul weather gear

11 **shirt,** waistcoat, linen, **blouse,** bodice; sweater

12 **dress, gown, frock; skirt**

13 **apron,** pinafore, bib; smock

14 **trousers,** pair of trousers, **breeches,** jeans, **slacks**

15 **waistband, belt; sash;** loincloth, G-string; **diaper,** napkin, nappies

16 **dishabille, undress,** something more comfortable; **negligee, wrap,** wrapper; sports clothes, casual clothes *or* dress

17 night clothes; **nightdress,** nightgown, pyjamas

18 **underclothes, underwear,** undies (*nonformal*), lingerie, linen, smalls (*nonformal*)

19 **corset,** stays, foundation garment, **girdle,** panty girdle; brassiere, bra

20 **headdress,** headgear; **cap, hat,** lid (*nonformal*); handkerchief

21 **footwear, shoes, boots;** wooden shoes, clogs

22 hose, **stockings; socks**

23 **bathing suit,** swim suit, swimming suit, two-piece; **trunks;** bikini, thong; wet suit

24 **children's wear;** rompers; baby clothes, baby linen, layette

25 garment making, **tailoring, dressmaking;** the rag trade (*nonformal*)

26 **clothier, haberdasher, draper,** outfitter; furrier

27 **tailor;** fitter, cutter; dressmaker, couturier, seamstress

verbs

28 **clothe, dress, garb, attire,** array, robe, invest, **deck;** drape, wrap, lap, envelop, sheathe, shroud; wrap or bundle or muffle up; swathe

29 **cloak,** coat, jacket; gown, frock; shirt; **hat,** bonnet, cap, hood; boot, shoe; stocking, sock

30 **outfit;** equip, uniform, rig, rig out or up, fit, **fit out,** turn out, **costume,** suit; **tailor,** make to order; order

31 **dress up, get up, doll** or **spruce up** (*nonformal*), pretty up (*nonformal*), deck out or up, trick out or up, fig out or up (*nonformal*); put on the style (*nonformal*); **dress down**

32 **don, put on,** slip on or into, get on or into, try on, dress in; change

33 **wear, have on,** be dressed in, affect, sport (*nonformal*)

adjectives

34 **clothing; dress,** sartorial; **clothed, clad, dressed,** attired, decked, vested, uniformed; in costume, cloaked, disguised; capped, hooded; **shod,** booted

35 **dressed up;** spruce, dressed to advantage, dressed to the nines, dressed to kill (*nonformal*); in Sunday best, in fine feather; in full dress, in full fig, in white tie and tails, in tails; **well-dressed, chic,** stylish; casual, casually dressed

6 UNCLOTHING

nouns

1 **removal; stripping;** baring, stripping or laying bare, uncovering, **exposure;** indecent exposure, exhibitionism, flashing (*nonformal*)

2 **undressing;** shedding, moulting, peeling

3 **nudity, nakedness; the nude, the buff** and **the raw** (*all nonformal*); **birthday suit** (*nonformal*); not a stitch

4 **baldness,** alopecia; slaphead (*nonformal*); shaving; hair remover, depilatory

verbs

5 **divest, strip, strip away, remove; uncover,** unveil, **expose,** lay open, bare, lay or strip bare; shear; pluck

6 **take off, remove, doff,** slip or step out of, slip off, cast off, throw off, drop; unwrap, undo

7 **undress; strip,** strip to the buff (*nonformal*)

8 **peel, skin, strip;** scalp

9 **husk, hull,** shell

10 **shed, cast,** moult

11 **scale, flake,** scale or flake off

adjectives

12 **divested, stripped, bared, exposed, uncovered,** stripped *or* laid bare, unveiled

13 **undressed, disrobed;** topless

14 **naked, nude; bare,** peeled, **in the raw** (*nonformal*); in one's birthday suit, **in the buff** (*nonformal*), with nothing on, without a stitch; **stark-naked,** naked as the day one was born, starkers (*nonformal*)

15 **bare-breasted,** topless, bare-chested

16 **hairless; bald;** bald as a coot; shaven, clean-shaven; smooth

7 NUTRITION

nouns

1 **nutrition, nourishment,** feeding, **food intake;** food chain *or* cycle

2 **nutrient,** food; growth factor; health food; roughage, fibre

3 **vitamin,** vitamin complex

4 **carbohydrate; sugar; starch**

5 **protein; amino acid**

6 **fat;** fatty acid; **cholesterol**

7 **digestion,** assimilation, absorption; digestive system; liver; saliva, gastric juice, intestinal juice, bile

8 **metabolism,** basal metabolism; assimilation

9 **diet, dieting; regimen,** regime; bland diet; balanced diet; diabetic diet, slimming diet; watching one's weight, counting the calories; liquid diet; vegetarianism, veganism; diet book, vitamin chart, calorie chart, calorie counter; fad diet

10 **fortification, enrichment,** restoration

11 **nutritionist,** dietician

12 (*science of nutrition*) dietetics

verbs

13 **nourish,** feed, sustain, nurture; **sustain,** strengthen

14 **digest, assimilate,** absorb

15 **diet,** go on a diet; watch one's weight, count the calories; fight the flab (*nonformal*)

16 **fortify, enrich,** restore

adjectives

17 **nutritious,** nutrient, **nourishing**

18 **digestive;** peptic

8 EATING

nouns

1 **eating, feeding, dining,** messing; consumption; **tasting,** relishing, savouring; **gourmet eating *or* dining;** nibbling, pecking, licking, **munching;** snacking, devouring, gobbling, wolfing, **gorging,** gluttony; **chewing; feasting, appetite, hunger;** nutrition; **dieting;** gluttony; grazing, cropping; vegetarianism, veganism; cannibalism

2 **bite, morsel, taste,** swallow; mouthful; nibble; cud; **chew;** munch; chomp (*nonformal*)

3 **drinking,** lapping, sipping, tasting; quaffing, gulping, swigging *and* swilling *and* guzzling *and* glugging (*all nonformal*); drunkenness

4 **drink,** potion; draught, **swig** (*nonformal*), swill *and* guzzle *and* glug (*all nonformal*); **sip,** tot,

snort (*nonformal*), gulp; nip; beverage

5 **meal**, mess, spread (*nonformal*), table, meat; **refreshment**, entertainment, treat; frozen meal

6 (*meals*) breakfast, continental breakfast, English breakfast, cooked breakfast; brunch, elevenses (*both nonformal*); **lunch**, luncheon; **tea**, teatime, high tea, cream tea; **dinner; supper;** buffet dinner; packed lunch; **picnic, barbecue;** coffee break, tea break

7 **snack**, light meal, refreshments, light lunch, spot of lunch (*nonformal*), **bite** (*nonformal*)

8 **hearty meal, full meal**, healthy meal, large *or* substantial meal, heavy meal, **square meal**

9 **feast, banquet**

10 **serving; portion, helping;** second helping; **course; dish, plate;** place

11 (*manner of service*) service, table service, waitress service, selfservice; table d'hôte; à la carte; service charge

12 **silver, silver plate; cutlery,** knives, forks, spoons; **table-spoon, dessertspoon, teaspoon; chopsticks; china, dishes,** plates, cups, glasses, saucers, bowls; **dish,** fruit dish; **bowl,** cereal bowl, fruit bowl, salad bowl; **tea service, tea set,** tea things, tea strainer; dinner set

13 **table linen,** tablecloth, table mat; **napkin,** table napkin, **serviette**

14 **menu, bill of fare**

15 **eater,** consumer; **diner;** mouth; **gourmet,** gastronome, epicure,

connoisseur of food *or* wine, bon vivant, foodie (*nonformal*); **glutton,** pig (*nonformal*); **carnivore; cannibal; vegetarian,** vegan

16 **restaurant,** dining room; **fast-food restaurant,** hamburger joint (*nonformal*); bistro; **coffee shop,** coffee bar; tea room; **pub,** tavern; grill; buffet; hamburger stand; **snack bar;** salad bar; pizzeria; **cafeteria;** mess hall, dining hall; canteen; **diner**

verbs

17 **feed, dine,** wine and dine; mess; nibble, snack, graze (*nonformal*); satisfy, gratify; board, sustain; put out to pasture, graze; forage

18 **nourish, nurture,** foster; **nurse, suckle,** breast-feed; fatten, fatten up, stuff

19 **eat, feed,** take, break bread, break one's fast; stuff one's face *and* pitch in (*both nonformal*); **taste,** relish, savour; **diet,** go on a diet, watch one's weight, count the calories

20 **dine;** breakfast; lunch; picnic; **eat out,** dine out; board; mess with, break bread with

21 **devour, swallow, consume,** take in, tuck in *and* tuck into (*both nonformal*), down, put away (*nonformal*); **eat up;** dispatch, dispose of (*nonformal*)

22 **gobble, gulp, bolt,** wolf

23 **feast, banquet;** eat heartily, have a good appetite, eat up, lick one's plate, do oneself proud (*nonformal*), do justice to, put it away (*nonformal*)

24 **stuff, gorge,** pig out (*nonformal*),

eat one's fill, stuff *or* gorge one-self

25 **pick, nibble; snack** (*nonformal*); pick at, peck at (*nonformal*), eat like a bird, have no appetite

26 **chew,** chew up, bite into; ruminate, chew the cud; **bite, grind; munch;** gnash; nibble, **gnaw;** mouth, mumble

27 **feed on** *or* **upon, feast on** *or* **upon,** fatten on *or* upon; prey on *or* upon, live on *or* upon, graze, crop

28 **drink,** wet one's whistle (*nonformal*); **sip; suck,** suckle; drink up; toss off *or* down, drain the cup; wash down; **toast,** drink to, pledge; tipple, **booze**

29 **lap up,** sponge *or* soak up, lick, lap

adjectives

30 **eating, feeding, dining; nourishing, nutritious; omnivorous, carnivorous;** cannibalistic; **vegetarian,** vegan

31 chewing; ruminating

32 **edible;** kosher; palatable, succulent, **delicious,** yummy (*nonformal*); **fine, fancy, gourmet**

9 REFRESHMENT

nouns

1 **refreshment, exhilaration, stimulation,** revival, renewal; **tonic,** breath of fresh air, pick-me-up *and* a shot in the arm (*both nonformal*)

verbs

2 **refresh, freshen,** freshen up; **revive; exhilarate, stimulate,** fortify, enliven, liven up, animate,

quicken; brace, buck up *and* pick up (*both nonformal*), set up; renew one's strength, put *or* breathe new life into, give a breath of fresh air, give a shot in the arm (*nonformal*); renew, recreate; **cheer**

adjectives

3 **refreshing, fresh,** brisk, crisp, **bracing, tonic; exhilarating, stimulating, invigorating,** rousing; cheering

4 **refreshed, restored, exhilarated,** stimulated, animated, **revived,** renewed, recreated

10 FOOD

nouns

1 **food,** foodstuff, food and drink, sustenance, **cuisine;** soul food; fast food, junk food; **fare;** provision; meat (*old*), bread, daily bread, bread and butter; health food; **board, feast, spread** (*nonformal*)

2 **grub** (*nonformal*), groceries, tuck (*nonformal*), victuals

3 **nourishment, nurture; refreshment; sustenance,** support, keep

4 **feed, fodder;** forage; pasture; grain; corn, oats, barley, wheat; meal, bran; **hay,** straw; mash; slops; pet food, dog food, cat food; bird seed

5 **provisions, groceries,** supplies, stores, larder, food supply; fresh foods, canned foods, frozen foods

6 **rations, board, meals, mess,** allowance; short commons; emergency rations

7 **dish,** culinary concoction; **course;** casserole; grill, roast; **main course, entree,** dish fit for a king; side dish

8 **delicacy, goody** (*nonformal*), treat, titbit; **morsel,** tasty morsel; dessert

9 **starter, appetizer, apéritif** (French); antipasto (Italian); **hors d'oeuvre;** dip; **pickle**

10 **soup,** broth

11 **stew;** casserole; Irish stew; goulash; curry

12 **meat,** red meat; butcher's meat; **cut of meat; game; roast,** joint; pot roast; barbecue; boiled meat; mince; sausage meat

13 **beef;** roast beef; hamburger, ground beef, mince; corned beef; beef extract, beef tea

14 **veal;** veal cutlet

15 **mutton, lamb;** leg of lamb

16 **pork**

17 **steak**

18 **chop, cutlet;** pork chop; lamb chop; veal cutlet

19 (*offal*) liver; kidney; heart; brain; tongue; tripe (*stomach*); giblets

20 **sausage,** banger (*nonformal*); **pâté**

21 **poultry,** fowl, bird

22 (*parts of poultry*) breast, leg, drumstick, thigh, wing; white meat, dark meat; giblets

23 **fish;** sole, lemon sole; cod, herring, whiting, mackerel; salmon, tuna; kipper; smoked salmon; smoked herring; jellied eel; roe, caviar; sushi; squid

24 **seafood, shellfish;** prawn, scampi; lobster, crab

25 **eggs;** fried eggs; boiled eggs; poached eggs; scrambled eggs; omelette; Scotch egg

26 **bread,** the staff of life; loaf; crust, crust of bread

27 **biscuit; cracker,** cream cracker, water biscuit; crispbread; wafer

28 **bun, roll, muffin;** bagel, croissant; scone, crumpet

29 **sandwich;** club sandwich; hamburger

30 **pasta, spaghetti, macaroni, noodles;** dumpling

31 **cereal,** breakfast cereal; porridge; **flour,** meal

32 **vegetables,** produce; **greens;** beans

33 **salad; greens**

34 **fruit;** produce; soft fruit; citrus fruit; fruit salad, fruit cocktail

35 **nut;** kernel

36 **sweets, confectionery; sweet;** chocolate; **jam, jelly;** preserve, conserve; marmalade; lemon curd; mousse; honey; icing, glaze; meringue; whipped cream

37 **pastry; Danish pastry;** turnover; **pie,** fruit pie, tart; puff pastry; cream puff; cream horn

38 **cake,** gâteau, cheesecake

39 **doughnut;** fritter

40 **pancake;** waffle; crêpe

41 **pudding,** custard, mousse, flan

42 **ice cream;** sorbet; banana split; ice-cream sundae

43 **dairy products; cheese;** tofu

44 **beverage,** drink, liquor, liquid; **soft drink;** cold drink; soda water, mineral water, tonic water; pop; milk shake, shake (*nonfor-*

mal); **alcohol,** hard drink, alcoholic drink

11 COOKING

nouns

1 **cooking, cookery, cuisine, culinary art;** food preparation; home economics, domestic science; catering; nutrition; baking, toasting, roasting, frying, boiling, grilling, simmering, stewing, poaching; **dish;** condiment, spice, herb; **sauce,** dressing

2 **cook, chef; baker**

3 **kitchen,** scullery; kitchenette; **galley; bakery; kitchen ware,** cooker, pots and pans

verbs

4 **cook,** prepare, rustle up (*nonformal*); boil, stew, simmer; poach; bake; **microwave;** roast; toast; fry; brown; grill; barbecue; steam; curry

adjectives

5 **cooking, culinary,** kitchen

6 **cooked,** stewed, fried, curried; toasted; roasted, roast; grilled; browned; boiled, simmered; steamed; poached; baked

7 **done, well-done; overcooked, overdone;** medium, medium-rare

8 **rare,** underdone, undercooked

12 EXCRETION

nouns

1 **excretion, discharge;** flow; ejaculation; **secretion**

2 **defecation,** evacuation; movement, bowel movement; number

two (*nonformal*), **stool, diarrhoea,** loose stools, trots *and* runs (*both nonformal*)

3 **excrement, discharge; waste,** waste matter

4 **faeces;** defecation, movement, bowel movement; **stool; manure, dung, droppings;** cow pats; sewage

5 **urine,** water, number one (*nonformal*); **urination,** micturition

6 **pus; matter; suppuration, festering,** running

7 **sweat, perspiration;** beads of sweat; cold sweat; **lather; body odour** *or* BO

8 **haemorrhage,** bleeding

9 **menstruation,** menstrual flow, **the curse** (*nonformal*); **period,** time of the month (*nonformal*)

10 **toilet, lavatory,** bathroom, loo (*nonformal*); WC (*nonformal*), washroom, public convenience, rest room; ladies' *or* little girls' room (*nonformal*), powder room; men's *or* little boys' room (*nonformal*); privy, outhouse; latrine

11 **toilet, WC** (*nonformal*); latrine; commode; **chamber pot,** potty (*nonformal*); **throne** (*nonformal*); chemical toilet; urinal; bedpan

verbs

12 **excrete,** discharge, emit, give off; relieve oneself, go to the toilet (*nonformal*); **exude;** weep; **secrete**

13 **defecate,** have a bowel movement

14 **urinate, pass water,** spend a penny (*nonformal*)

15 **fester,** suppurate, run, weep; come to a head

16 sweat, perspire; break out in a sweat, **get all in a lather** (*nonformal*); wilt

17 bleed, haemorrhage, lose blood; spill blood; bloody

18 menstruate, have one's period

adjectives

19 faecal; urinary

20 festering, suppurating

21 sweaty, sweating, perspiring; **sticky** (*nonformal*), **clammy;** bathed in sweat

22 bleeding, bloody

23 menstrual

13 SECRETION

nouns

1 secretion; weeping

2 digestive juice, gastric juice; bile, gall; semen, sperm; **hormone;** mucus; tears

3 saliva, spittle, spit; dribble; froth, foam

verbs

4 secrete, produce, give out; water; weep

5 salivate; slobber, slaver, **drool,** dribble; spit up; spew; clear the throat

adjectives

6 secretory; lymphatic; seminal; watery, watering; salivary

7 glandular; hormonal

14 BODILY DEVELOPMENT

nouns

1 physical development, growth, development, maturing, coming of age, growing up; vegetation, germination; sexual maturity, puberty; adulthood, manhood, womanhood; reproduction, procreation, sprouting; budding

verbs

2 grow, develop, increase; grow up, mature, spring up, ripen, come of age, **shoot up,** tower; **sprout,** blossom, reproduce, germinate; **flourish, thrive;** mushroom, balloon; outgrow

adjectives

3 grown, grown-up, developed, fully developed, **mature, adult; sprouting,** budding, flowering, **flourishing,** blossoming, blooming, thriving; overgrown

15 STRENGTH

nouns

1 strength, might; force, potency, power; **energy; vigour,** vitality; fortitude, **endurance, stamina,** staying power; **strength of will,** obstinacy

2 muscularity; brawn, beef (*nonformal*); **muscle;** build, physique; tone, elasticity

3 firmness, stability, solidity, **hardness**

4 impregnability, invulnerability

5 strengthening, fortification; **hardening,** toughening; reinforcement; refreshment

6 strong man, tower of strength, muscle man, hunk (*nonformal*); **giant;** Tarzan, Superman

7 (*nonformal terms*) **hunk, muscle man,** Rambo, man mountain, bully, tough, tough guy, gorilla

verbs

8 **be strong**, overpower, overwhelm; pack a punch

9 **not weaken**; bear up, hold up, stand up; **hold out**, see it out, not give up, **never say die**

10 (nonformal terms) **hang in**, stick it, sweat it out, stay the distance

11 put one's back into it (nonformal); use force, get tough (nonformal)

12 **strengthen, fortify**, beef up (nonformal), brace, shore up, support; steel, harden, stiffen, **toughen**, nerve; confirm, sustain; **reinforce**; refresh, revive

13 **proof**, insulate, soundproof, muffle, fireproof, waterproof, etc

adjectives

14 **strong, forceful, mighty, powerful, potent; stout, sturdy, stalwart, rugged**; hunky and beefy (both nonformal); strapping, hardy, hard; **robust**; obstinate; **vigorous, hearty, lusty**; bouncing

15 **well-built, athletic; muscular**, thickset, burly, **brawny**; wiry

16 gigantic, huge

17 **firm, stout, sturdy, tough, staunch, stable**, solid; rigid

18 **impregnable, invulnerable, invincible**, indomitable, unbeatable, more than a match for; overpowering, overwhelming

19 **resistant, proof; impervious**, foolproof; watertight; airtight; soundproof; fireproof

20 **undiminished**, unabated; **unflagging**; in full swing, **going strong** (nonformal)

21 (of sounds and odours) **intense, penetrating, piercing; loud**, deafening; **pungent, reeking**

adverbs

22 **strongly, stoutly, sturdily; powerfully, forcefully; vigorously, heartily, soundly, firmly; intensely; loudly**, at the top of one's voice

16 WEAKNESS

nouns

1 **weakness, softness; impotence; debility; dizziness; fatigue**, exhaustion, weariness, tiredness

2 **frailty, delicacy; fragility**; disintegration; cowardice

3 **infirmity**, incapacity; senility

4 **weak point, weakness**, chink in one's armour; feet of clay

5 **debilitation**, exhaustion; fatigue; relaxation, deadening, dulling; **dilution**, watering, thinning

6 **weakling**, big baby, mother's boy, teacher's pet; **wimp** (nonformal), nonentity

verbs

7 (be weak) **shake**, tremble, quiver, cringe, cower; be on one's last legs, have one foot in the grave

8 (become weak) **weaken**, go soft (nonformal); **languish, wilt**, faint, **droop**, drop, **sink, decline, flag, pine, tail off**, fail, fall by the wayside; crumble, go to pieces, disintegrate; go downhill, give way, break, collapse, cave in (nonformal), surrender; give out, have no staying power, run out of steam (nonformal); come apart at the seams; yield; wear thin

9 (*make weak*) **weaken,** undermine, soften up (*nonformal*), unnerve, rattle, shake up (*nonformal*); sap the strength of, exhaust, take it out of (*nonformal*); shake; mitigate, abate; deaden, dull, dampen, take the edge off; cramp, cripple

10 **dilute, thin;** water down, adulterate

adjectives

11 **weak, feeble;** listless; **impotent, powerless;** spineless, wimpy *and* gutless (*both nonformal*); cowardly; faint, dizzy; **soft, flabby; limp,** floppy, languid, **drooping**

12 **frail, slight, delicate, dainty, puny;** light; effeminate; **fragile, breakable,** brittle; **flimsy,** wispy

13 **unsound, infirm, unstable,** decrepit, crumbling, disintegrating; **unsteady, shaky, rickety,** spindly, spidery, ramshackle, dilapidated, rocky (*nonformal*), groggy, wobbly

14 **wishy-washy,** tasteless, bland, **insipid,** watery, milky; **indecisive,** irresolute, changeable

15 **weakened, disabled,** incapacitated; drained, exhausted, sapped, burned-out, used up, played out, spent; **fatigued; wasted, rundown,** worn-out

16 **diluted, thinned;** adulterated, watered-down

17 **debilitating;** exhausting, fatiguing, gruelling, trying, draining

18 **languishing,** flagging, pining, failing

adverbs

19 **weakly, feebly;** delicately, daintily; shakily, unsteadily

17 ENERGY

nouns

1 **energy, vigour, force, power, vitality, intensity, dynamism; potency; strength; energy source,** electrical energy, nuclear energy, solar energy

2 **vim, verve,** fire, adrenalin, **dash, drive; aggressiveness, enterprise,** initiative, thrust; **eagerness,** zeal, gusto

3 (*nonformal terms*) **pep,** kick, punch, push, zip

4 **animation, vivacity, ardour,** enthusiasm, **zest, gusto,** impetus, **life, spirit,** life force; activity

5 (*energetic disapproval or criticism*) **acrimony,** acidity, **bitterness;** harshness, roughness, **severity, vehemence,** violence; edge, point; bite, sting

6 **stimulus, stimulant, tonic;** human dynamo (*nonformal*); **life,** life and soul of the party

7 (*units of energy*) joule, calorie

8 **animation,** revival; **exhilaration, stimulation**

verbs

9 **animate, enliven, liven up,** jazz up (*nonformal*); **exhilarate, stimulate,** galvanize, electrify, fire, charge, charge up, rouse, arouse, be a shot in the arm (*nonformal*), **pep** *or* jazz *or* perk up (*nonformal*)

10 **be energetic, thrive,** flourish, be full of beans

11 **activate**, recharge

adjectives

12 **energetic, vigorous, strenuous, forceful, strong, dynamic,** intense, acute, keen, incisive, vivid, vibrant; **enterprising, aggressive; active, lively, animated, spirited, vivacious,** brisk, lusty, **robust,** hearty, enthusiastic, impetuous

13 **acrimonious,** acid, **bitter,** tart, **caustic, virulent, violent, vehement; harsh,** fierce, **rigorous,** severe, rough, stringent, **sharp, keen,** incisive, **cutting,** stinging, **scathing**

14 **enlivening;** tonic, bracing, rousing; **invigorating; exhilarating; stimulating**

adverbs

15 **energetically, vigorously, strenuously, forcefully,** intensely, lustily, heartily, keenly; **actively,** briskly

18 POWER, POTENCY

nouns

1 **power, force, might, vigour,** vitality, push, drive; vehemence; **strength; energy;** virility, machismo (*nonformal*); effect, impact, **effectiveness;** productivity, **influence,** pull; **authority,** weight; brute force, compulsion, duress; muscle power, full force, full blast; charisma

2 **ability, capability, capacity,** faculty, facility, talent, flair, genius, calibre, **competence,** efficiency; **proficiency**

3 **manpower;** horsepower; electric power; hydraulic power; solar power; atomic power, nuclear power; **thrust,** impulse

4 **work force,** hands, men; **fighting force,** troops, units, firepower; **personnel,** human resources; **forces**

verbs

5 **empower, enable;** invest, deputize; **authorize;** arm

6 **be able,** be up to; **can,** may; make it *or* make the grade (*nonformal*); hack it (*nonformal*); **wield power; take charge**

adjectives

7 **powerful, potent, mighty, forceful, dynamic; vigorous,** vital, **energetic,** ruling, in power; **cogent,** striking, telling, effective, operative, in force; **strong;** high-powered; **authoritative**

8 **omnipotent, almighty, all-powerful;** absolute, unlimited, **sovereign; supreme**

9 **able, capable, equal to,** up to, **competent,** adequate, effective, efficient; productive; **proficient**

adverbs

10 **powerfully, forcefully, vigorously, energetically,** dynamically; **cogently,** strikingly; **effectively;** with telling effect, to good account, with a vengeance

11 **ably, capably, competently,** adequately, effectively, **efficiently, well;** to the best of one's ability, as best one can; with all one's might

12 **by force,** by brute force; **forcibly**

19 IMPOTENCE

nouns

1 **impotence, powerlessness,** feebleness, **weakness**

2 **inability, incapacity, incompetence,** inadequacy, ineptitude, inefficiency

3 **ineffectiveness,** invalidity, **uselessness,** failure

4 **helplessness, defencelessness,** vulnerability

5 **emasculation,** castration

6 weakling, invalid, incompetent, wimp (*nonformal*); eunuch

verbs

7 be impotent, lack force; be ineffective, not work; **waste one's effort,** bang one's head against a brick wall

8 **cannot, not be able,** not have it *and* not hack it (*both nonformal*), not make it *and* not make the grade (*both nonformal*)

9 **incapacitate,** drain; **weaken;** cripple, maim, lame; disarm, put out of action, put *hors de combat*; put out of commission (*nonformal*); sabotage, wreck; put a spoke in one's wheels

10 (*put out of action*) paralyse, prostrate, shoot down in flames (*nonformal*), put *hors de combat,* knock out (*nonformal*), break the back of; strangle, get a stranglehold on; muzzle, gag, silence; deflate

11 **disqualify; invalidate**

12 exhaust; **emasculate;** castrate

adjectives

13 **impotent, powerless;** feeble, soft, flabby, **weak;** wimpy (*nonformal*)

14 **unable, incapable, incompetent,** inefficient; inept, **unfit;** out of one's depth, in over one's head

15 **ineffective, ineffectual,** feckless, not up to scratch *or* up to snuff (*nonformal*), **inadequate; vain,** futile, useless, fruitless

16 **disabled, incapacitated;** crippled; paralysed; prostrate

17 **out of action, out of commission** (*nonformal*); hors de combat (*French*)

18 **helpless, defenceless;** vulnerable

19 debilitated; **castrated,** emasculated

adverbs

20 **beyond one,** beyond one's capacity, out of one's depth, above one's head

20 REST, REPOSE

nouns

1 **rest, repose, ease, relaxation,** comfort; **tranquillity; inactivity**

2 **respite, rest, pause,** lull, **break,** interlude, **intermission; breathing space; breather; coffee break, tea break**

3 **holiday, vacation; time off; paid leave; leave, leave of absence,** shore leave; **sabbatical; weekend**

4 **holiday, day off;** gala day; statutory holiday, bank holiday; **feast day; half-day**

5 **day of rest; Sabbath**

verbs

6 **rest, take it easy** (*nonformal*); lie down, go to bed, curl up, doss down (*nonformal*), bed down, recline, lounge, sprawl, loll; put one's feet up

7 **relax,** unwind, chill out (*nonformal*); **ease up, let up, slow down**

8 **take a rest, take a break,** pause, **knock off** (*nonformal*), take five (*nonformal*); catch one's breath; stop work, suspend operations, call it a day

9 **go on holiday, take a holiday, holiday, get away from it all,** vacation; go on leave

adjectives

10 **holiday; comfortable; restful,** quiet

adverbs

11 **at rest, at ease;** in bed

12 **on holiday,** on vacation, on leave; off duty

21 FATIGUE

nouns

1 **fatigue, tiredness, weariness;** end of one's tether; weakness, debility; ME, postviral fatigue syndrome; **stress, strain**

2 **exhaustion; collapse, prostration,** breakdown

3 **breathlessness;** panting, gasping

verbs

4 **fatigue, tire, weary, exhaust,** wilt, flag; **wear down;** tire out, wear out, burn out; use up; do in

5 **burn out, get tired, grow weary, tire, weary, fatigue;** flag, droop,

faint, wilt; run down, burn out; gasp, wheeze, pant, puff; collapse, break down, crack up (*nonformal*), fall by the wayside, drop in one's tracks, succumb

adjectives

6 **tired, weary, fatigued,** jaded, run-down; ready to drop; feeling faint, **weak,** weakened; drooping, wilting, flagging

7 (*nonformal terms*) done in, dead beat, dead on one's feet; run ragged

8 **haggard,** ravaged, drawn, worn, wan

9 **burnt-out, exhausted,** drained, spent; **tired out, worn-out;** ready to drop, on one's last legs; prostrate

10 **breathless, winded;** wheezing, puffing, panting, **out of breath**

11 **fatiguing, wearying,** wearing, **tiring, stressful,** trying, **exhausting,** draining, gruelling, punishing, killing

22 SLEEP

nouns

1 **sleepiness, drowsiness,** lethargy, yawning, stretching

2 **sleep, slumber; repose;** shut eye (*nonformal*); **doze;** beauty sleep (*nonformal*); sleepwalking; hibernation; bedtime

3 **nap, snooze** and kip (*both nonformal*), **forty winks** (*nonformal*), wink of sleep; **siesta**

4 **deep sleep, sound sleep**

5 **stupor, coma, swoon; trance;** sedation

6 **hypnosis, trance;** hypnotherapy

7 **hypnotism; mesmerism**

8 **hypnotist;** hypnotherapist

9 **opium, opiate, morphine;** night-cap; sedative; anaesthetic

10 **sleeper;** sleepwalker

verbs

11 **sleep, slumber; doze, drowse; nap;** snore; have an early night; sleep in; oversleep

12 (*nonformal terms*) **snooze, kip,** doss, flake out, crash

13 **go to sleep, fall asleep, drop off,** drift off, **doze off,** nod off

14 **go to bed, retire;** bed down

15 (*nonformal terms*) **hit the hay, hit the sack,** crash, turn in, doss down

16 **put to bed,** put down; cradle; tuck in

17 **put to sleep;** rock to sleep; **hypnotize, mesmerize; entrance,** put in a trance; drug, dope (*nonformal*); anaesthetize, put under; sedate

adjectives

18 **sleepy, drowsy, dreamy;** half asleep, asleep on one's feet; yawning, **nodding; lethargic, in a stupor;** drugged, doped (*nonformal*); sedated; anaesthetized

19 **asleep, sleeping; unconscious, oblivious,** out like a light, out cold; **dead to the world**

20 **narcotic,** hypnotic; sedative

23 WAKEFULNESS

nouns

1 **wakefulness, wake; sleeplessness,** restlessness, tossing and turning; **insomnia,** vigil; consciousness; alertness

2 **awakening, wakening, rousing arousal;** reveille

verbs

3 **keep awake,** keep one's eyes open; keep alert, be vigilant; **toss and turn, not sleep a wink**

4 **awake, awaken, wake, wake up, get up,** rouse; stir (*nonformal*)

5 (*wake someone up*) **awaken, waken, rouse, arouse, wake wake up,** knock up

6 **get up, get out of bed, arise,** rise

adjectives

7 **wakeful, sleepless;** restless, watchful, vigilant

8 **awake, conscious, up; wide-awake;** alert

24 SENSATION

nouns

1 **sensation, sense, feeling;** perception; experience; **consciousness,** awareness

2 **sensibility;** receptiveness; **susceptibility**

3 **sensitivity, sensitiveness; tact,** courtesy, politeness; **compassion, sympathy;** empathy; **concern, solicitude; delicacy, tenderness; thin skin; irritability, touchiness;** nervousness; allergy

4 **sore point,** exposed nerve, raw nerve, the quick

5 **senses, five senses;** touch, taste smell, sight, hearing; sixth sense

verbs

6 **sense, feel, experience, perceive** be conscious or aware of; taste

smell, see, hear, touch; be sensitive to, have a thing *and* a complex about (*both nonformal*)

7 make sensitive; **sharpen, whet**, stimulate, excite, stir

8 **touch a raw nerve**, cut to the quick, strike home

adjectives

9 **sensory; sensitive**, receptive; sensuous

10 **neural, nervous;** neurological

11 sensible; **susceptible; receptive,** impressionable; **perceptive; conscious, aware**

12 **sensitive,** responsive, sympathetic, compassionate; delicate, tactful, considerate, courteous, solicitous, tender, refined; **thinskinned;** hypersensitive; **irritable, touchy,** prickly; nervous; allergic

13 (*keenly sensitive*) **exquisite,** poignant, **acute,** sharp, **keen**, vivid, intense, extreme, excruciating

25 INSENSIBILITY

nouns

1 **insensibility, insensitivity;** lack of concern; boorishness; **unfeeling, apathy;** thick skin, callousness; **numbness,** pins and needles

2 **unconsciousness;** oblivion; **faint, swoon, blackout; coma; stupor**

3 **anaesthetic,** general anaesthetic, local anaesthetic, analgesic, **pain killer;** tranquillizer, sedative, sleeping pill; drug, dope (*nonformal*), narcotic, opiate

verbs

4 **deaden, numb,** dull; paralyse; **anaesthetize, put to sleep;** drug, dope (*nonformal*); freeze; **stun;** knock unconscious, knock senseless, **knock out, KO** (*nonformal*)

5 **faint, swoon,** keel over (*nonformal*), **pass out, black out,** go out like a light

adjectives

6 **unfeeling, insensitive;** unsympathetic; unconcerned; tactless, boorish; thick-skinned; **numb, deadened;** unfeeling, apathetic; callous; anaesthetized

7 **stupefied, stunned,** dazed

8 **unconscious, senseless,** oblivious, comatose, asleep, **dead to the world, out cold;** drugged, doped (*nonformal*)

9 **deadening,** numbing, dulling; anaesthetic, analgesic, narcotic; anaesthetizing

26 PAIN

nouns

1 **pain; suffering, hurt, hurting;** discomfort, malaise; aches and pains

2 **pang,** throes; seizure, spasm, paroxysm; **twinge,** twitch, wrench; crick, cramp; **nip,** pinch, bite, prick, **stab,** stitch, **shooting pain**

3 smarting, stinging, tingling; burning

4 **soreness, irritation,** inflammation, tenderness; festering; sore; sore spot

5 **ache,** throbbing; **headache;** migraine; **backache; earache;**

toothache; stomachache; colic, gripe; heartburn; angina

6 **agony**, anguish, torment, torture

verbs

7 **pain, hurt, wound, afflict;** burn; sting; nip, bite, pinch; pierce, prick, stab, cut; **irritate;** chafe, fret, rasp, rub, grate; gnaw, grind; gripe; fester; **torture, torment,** rack, wring, twist, convulse; wrench, tear

8 **suffer; hurt; ache; smart,** tingle; throb, pound; **wince,** blanch, shrink, grimace; writhe

adjectives

9 **pained,** in pain, **hurt,** hurting, **suffering,** afflicted, wounded; **tortured, tormented, racked, agonized,** twisted, convulsed

10 **painful;** hurtful, **acute, sharp,** piercing, stabbing, shooting, stinging, biting, gnawing; **severe,** harsh, grave; griping, spasmodic; **agonizing, excruciating, harrowing**

11 **sore, raw;** smarting, tingling, **burning; irritated, inflamed, tender,** sensitive, fiery, angry, red; chafed; **festering**

12 **aching, throbbing;** griping

13 **irritating; chafing,** fretting, rasping, grating, stinging

27 VISION

nouns

1 **vision, sight, eyesight;** perception; field of vision

2 **observation; looking, watching, viewing, seeing,** witnessing; no-

tice, note, **regard;** watch, lookout; spying, espionage

3 **look, sight,** view; leer

4 **glance; glimpse,** flash; **peek,** peep

5 **gaze, stare; glare, glower;** evil eye

6 **scrutiny,** overview, **survey,** contemplation; **examination, inspection,** the once-over (*nonformal*), vetting (*nonformal*)

7 **viewpoint, standpoint, point of view,** vantage point; **outlook,** angle

8 **observation point; observatory;** tower; beacon, lighthouse; bridge, conning tower; **grandstand; gallery**

9 **eye; orb**

10 **sharp eye,** keen eye; **eagle eye,** watchful eye; **weather eye**

verbs

11 **see, behold, observe, view, witness, perceive, discern, spy; sight,** make out, pick out, spot (*nonformal*), discover, notice, distinguish, recognize, **catch sight of,** get a load of (*nonformal*), take in, look upon; **clap eyes on** (*nonformal*); **glimpse,** catch a glimpse of

12 **look, peer;** eye, gaze; **watch, observe,** view, **regard;** keep one's eyes peeled, be vigilant, keep one's eyes open; check *and* check out (*both nonformal*); keep under observation, spy on, keep an eye on, keep a weather eye on, follow, tail (*nonformal*), stake out; **peek, peep**

13 **scrutinize, survey,** eye, contemplate; **leer,** give one the glad eye

examine, vet (*nonformal*), inspect; pore over; size up (*nonformal*); take stock of

14 **gaze,** feast one's eyes on; **eye; stare,** look, **goggle, gape**

15 **glare, glower,** look daggers; give one the evil eye

16 **glance, glimpse,** take a squint at (*nonformal*)

17 give a sidelong look; squint; **look down one's nose** (*nonformal*)

18 **look away, avert the eyes,** look the other way; avoid one's gaze

adjectives

19 **visual,** eye; **sighted,** seeing; **optical;** visible

20 twenty-twenty;   sharp-eyed, **eagle-eyed**

adverbs

21 **at sight,** visibly, at a glance; by sight, visually; at first sight; out of the corner of one's eye

28 DEFECTIVE VISION

nouns

1 bad *or* poor eyesight, defect of vision, impaired vision, blurred vision; double vision; tunnel vision; **blindness;** partial sight

2 bleariness, redness

3 **short-sightedness,** myopia

4 **long-sightedness**

5 **squint,** strabismus

6 **winking, blinking,** twitching, fluttering the eyelids

verbs

7 barely see, be half-blind; be partially sighted; see double

8 **squint,** screw up the eyes

9 **wink, blink,** twitch

adjectives

10 visually impaired; **blind;** partially sighted; **short-sighted,** myopic; long-sighted

11 cross-eyed

12 half-blind; bleary-eyed

29 BLINDNESS

nouns

1 **blindness, sightlessness;** partial sight; **blind spot;** cataract; **blinding;** blindfolding

2 **colour blindness**

3 **the blind;** blind person

4 blindfold; eye patch; blinkers

verbs

5 **blind,** deprive of sight; darken, dim, obscure; **put one's eyes out,** gouge; **blindfold,** bandage; **dazzle,** daze; glare

6 **be blind,** not see, grope in the dark, feel one's way; go blind, lose one's sight; be blind to, close *or* shut one's eyes to, look the other way; have a blind spot

adjectives

7 **blind, sightless;** partially sighted; **blind as a bat;** colour-blind

8 **blinded,** darkened, obscured; **blindfolded,** blinkered; **dazzled,** dazed

9 **blinding,** obscuring; **dazzling**

30 VISIBILITY

nouns

1 **visibility;** exposure; **manifestation; revelation**

2 **distinctness, plainness,** obviousness; **clarity,** lucidity; definition; resolution; **prominence; exposure,** high profile, low profile; visibility

3 **field of view,** field of vision, **sight; vista, view, horizon, prospect, perspective, outlook,** range, scope; line of vision; naked eye; command; **viewpoint, observation point**

verbs

4 **show,** show up, shine through, **surface, appear, be visible,** be seen, be revealed, be evident, be noticeable, meet the gaze; **stand out,** loom large, glare, **stare one in the face,** hit one in the eye, **stick out like a sore thumb;** dominate; emerge, come into view, materialize

5 **be exposed,** be conspicuous, have high visibility, stick out; have a high profile

adjectives

6 **visible,** visual, **perceptible, discernible,** observable, noticeable, recognizable; **in sight,** in view, in full view, before one's eyes, exposed, showing; **evident,** in evidence; **manifest, apparent;** revealed, disclosed, unconcealed, undisguised

7 **distinct, plain, clear, obvious, evident, patent,** unmistakable, much in evidence, plain to be seen, for all to see; **definite, defined,** in focus; **clear-cut; conspicuous,** glaring, **prominent,** pronounced

adverbs

8 **visibly,** markedly, noticeably **manifestly, apparently,** evidently; **distinctly, clearl, plainly,** obviously, patently, definitely, unmistakably; conspicuously **prominently,** glaringly

31 INVISIBILITY

nouns

1 **invisibility;** disappearance; the invisible; **secrecy, concealment**

2 low profile; paleness, weakness darkness, obscurity, uncertainty blur, soft focus

verbs

3 be invisible, escape notice; disappear

4 **blur, dim, pale,** soften, film mist, fog

adjectives

5 **invisible; imperceptible; out of sight; secret; unseen,** unobserved, unnoticed; behind the scenes; disguised, camouflaged hidden, **concealed;** latent, submerged

6 **inconspicuous; indistinct, unclear, indefinite, faint,** pale, feeble, weak, **dim,** dark, **shadowy vague, obscure,** indistinguishable, unrecognizable; uncertain confused, out of focus, **blurred** bleary, **fuzzy, hazy,** misty, foggy

32 APPEARANCE

nouns

1 **appearance,** apparition, coming putting in an appearance; **emergence;** rise, occurrence; **materializing,** coming into being

manifestation, realization, incarnation; **presentation, disclosure, exposure**, unfolding, showing

2 **appearance**, exterior, **facade**, outside, **outward show, image**, display, front (*nonformal*), window dressing, cosmetics; whitewash

3 aspect, look, view; feature; **semblance, image**, likeness; effect, impression; **form, shape**, figure, configuration; **manner**, fashion, style; **respect, regard**, reference; **phase; facet, side**, angle, viewpoint, slant *and* twist (*both nonformal*)

4 **looks, features**, traits; **countenance**, face, feature; facial expression, cast; **look, air, demeanour, carriage, bearing, posture, stance, poise, presence; guise, complexion**

5 (*thing appearing*) **apparition**, phenomenon; **vision, image, shape, form**, figure, presence; mirage, spectre, **phantom**

6 view, scene, sight; prospect, outlook, **vista, perspective; scenery**; panorama, sweep; **landscape**

7 spectacle, sight; exhibit, **exhibition**, exposition, show, display, **presentation**; light show; **pageant; parade**

verbs

8 **appear, become visible; arrive**, put in an appearance, appear on the scene, catch the eye, **come into view, show**, show one's face, **show up** (*nonformal*), turn up, come, **materialize**, present oneself, **manifest oneself**, become manifest, **reveal oneself**,

expose *or* betray oneself; **come to light; emerge**, issue forth, come to the fore, come forward; enter; **rise, arise**, rear its head; peep out; loom, heave in sight, appear on the horizon

9 **burst forth**, erupt, explode; **pop up**, spring up; flare up, flash

10 **appear, seem, look**, feel, sound, have the appearance of, strike one as; have all the earmarks of, show signs of, have every sign *or* indication of

adjectives

11 **apparent**, appearing, **seeming, ostensible;** outward, surface, superficial; **visible**

adverbs

12 **apparently, seemingly, evidently, ostensibly**, by all accounts; on the face of it; on the surface, outwardly; at first sight

33 DISAPPEARANCE

nouns

1 **disappearance**, disappearing, **vanishing; going, passing, departure, loss;** dissolution, dissolving, melting, evaporation; fading, blackout; eclipse, blocking; elimination; extinction

verbs

2 **disappear, vanish**, do a vanishing act (*nonformal*), depart, fly, **flee**, go, be gone, **go away**, pass, exit, clear out; **perish, die**, die off; die out *or* away, dwindle, wane, **fade out** *or* away; sink, **dissolve, melt**, thaw, evaporate, **vanish into thin air**, go up in smoke; disperse, dispel, dissi-

pate; leave no trace, waste away, erode

adjectives

3 **vanishing, disappearing,** passing, fleeting, fugitive, transient, flying, fading, dissolving, melting, evaporating

4 **gone,** away, extinct, missing, no more, lost, long-lost, **out of sight**

34 COLOUR

nouns

1 **colour, hue; tint, tinge, shade, tone,** cast; colouring; colour scheme; **complexion,** skin colour or colouring or tone; pallor

2 **warmth,** warm colour; **blush, flush, glow**

3 **softness,** soft colour, pale colour, pastel

4 **colour, bright colour, brightness, brilliance,** intensity; **richness;** riot of colour

5 **garishness,** loudness, luridness, gaudiness; colour clash

6 brightness, purity; **hue,** lightness; tint, **tone;** warm colour; cold colour

7 **primary colour;** secondary colour; complementary colour; **spectrum,** halftone

8 *(colouring matter)* colour, pigment, stain; dye; paint, distemper; emulsion; coat; **undercoat,** primer; wash; medium, vehicle; thinner; turpentine, turps *(non-formal)*

9 *(persons according to hair colour)* **brunette; blonde;** bleached blonde, peroxide blonde; **redhead**

10 *(applying colour)* colouring, coloration; **staining, dyeing; tinting;** illumination

11 **painting,** paintwork; **enamelling,** glossing; emulsioning; **varnishing;** staining; fresco; undercoating, priming

verbs

12 **colour; tinge; tint; stain, dye,** dip; shade; illuminate; **paint, coat;** dab, **daub,** smear; enamel, gloss; emulsion; **varnish; whitewash;** wash; prime

13 *(be inharmonious)* **clash,** conflict

adjectives

14 **colouring;** multicoloured; rainbow; matching; toning, harmonious; warm, glowing; cool, cold

15 **coloured,** in colour; **tinged, tinted, painted, enamelled; stained, dyed;** full; deep

16 ingrained; colourfast, indelible

17 **colourful; bright, vivid,** intense, **rich,** exotic, **brilliant**

18 garish, lurid, loud, screaming, shrieking, glaring, gaudy

19 clashing, conflicting

20 **soft, subdued,** light, **pastel, pale,** subtle, delicate; pearly; sombre, simple, sober

35 COLOURLESSNESS

nouns

1 **colourlessness,** lack or absence of colour; dullness

2 **paleness,** weakness; lightness; fairness; **pallor; dullness; greyness;** anaemia

3 lightening; **fading, dimming; whitening; bleaching,** bleach

4 bleach, bleaching agent

verbs

5 discolour; fade, wash out; dim, dull, tarnish, tone down; **pale, whiten,** blanch, drain; **bleach**

6 lose colour, fade; bleach; pale, turn pale, change colour, **whiten,** blanch

adjectives

7 colourless; neutral; dull, flat, dingy; **faded,** dimmed, discoloured; **pale, dim,** weak, **faint; pallid, wan, sallow; white;** pasty; **ashen; grey;** anaemic; **ghastly,** livid, **haggard,** sickly

8 bleached, whitened, lightened; drained

9 light, fair; pastel

36 WHITENESS

nouns

1 whiteness, white; lightness, fairness; paleness; silver; albino

2 whitening; bleaching; whitewashing

3 whitening agent, whitener; **whitewash;** correction fluid

verbs

4 whiten; bleach; whitewash

adjectives

5 white, pure white, snowy, frosty; **hoary; silvery;** chalky; milky

6 light, fair; pale; off-white, pearly; alabaster; cream, **creamy;** ivory

7 blonde; fair-haired, flaxen-haired

37 BLACKNESS

nouns

1 blackness; inkiness; **black,** ebony; darkness

2 darkness, swarthiness; duskiness; sombreness, sadness; hostility, anger, black mood

3 dinginess, griminess

4 blackening, darkening; shading; smudge

5 blacking, blackening agent; charcoal; soot

verbs

6 blacken, denigrate; **darken,** shade, shadow; ink; **smudge,** blotch

adjectives

7 black; pitch-black; inky; ebony

8 dark, blackish; **swarthy; dusky; sombre, sober, grave,** sad; hostile, sullen, angry

9 dark-skinned; black

10 dingy, grimy, smoky, sooty, blotchy, dirty, **muddy,** murky

38 VARIEGATION

nouns

1 variegation; riot of colour

2 iridescence, opalescence

3 fleck, speck; spot, dot, blotch, patch, splash

4 check, checks; tartan; patchwork

5 stripe; streak; bar, band

verbs

6 variegate; fleck, speck, spot, dot, sprinkle, pepper; blotch; check; stripe, streak

adjectives

7 **variegated, multicoloured,** rainbow-coloured; colourful; psychedelic; shot

8 **iridescent; opalescent; pearly,** mother-of-pearl

9 **mottled; dappled;** marbled

10 **spotted, dotted,** sprinkled, peppered; **spotty,** dotty, patchy; **speckled; flecked;** spangled; blotchy

11 **checked;** tartan

12 **striped; streaked;** barred, banded

39 HEARING

nouns

1 **hearing;** ear; listening, attention

2 **audition,** hearing, **audience, interview,** conference; **listening; eavesdropping,** wiretapping, electronic surveillance, bugging (*nonformal*)

3 **good hearing,** acute sense of hearing, sensitive ear; **an ear for;** musical ear; no ear

4 **earshot,** hearing, range, reach, carrying distance, **sound of one's voice**

5 **listener; eavesdropper,** snoop; fly on the wall

6 **audience, house, congregation,** gallery, crowd; spectator

7 **ear;** external ear; **outer ear; middle ear**

8 **listening device; hearing aid;** ear trumpet; amplifier, megaphone; stethoscope

verbs

9 **listen, hark, heed, hear, attend,** pay attention, lend an ear; **listen to, sit in on; listen in; eavesdrop,** tap, intercept, bug (*nonformal*); be all ears (*nonformal*), strain one's ears; prick up the ears; hang on every word; hear out

10 **hear,** catch, get (*nonformal*), take in; **overhear; hear of,** hear tell of (*nonformal*); get wind of

11 **be heard,** reach the ear, register, make an impression, get across (*nonformal*); **have one's ear,** make oneself heard, get through to; ring in the ear; assail the ears

adjectives

12 **auditory,** audio, **hearing, aural;** audiovisual; audible; acoustic

13 **listening, attentive, all ears** (*nonformal*)

40 DEAFNESS

nouns

1 **deafness, hardness of hearing,** deaf ears; **tone deafness;** impaired hearing; loss of hearing, **hearing loss**

2 **the deaf;** the hard of hearing; lip reader

3 **sign language,** signing; lip reading

verbs

4 **be deaf;** lose one's hearing, go deaf; close one's ears; **turn a deaf ear;** fall on deaf ears

5 **deafen**

adjectives

6 **deaf,** hard of hearing, hearing-impaired; deafened; tone-deaf

41 SOUND

nouns

1 **sound,** acoustic; noise; sound wave

2 **tone, pitch, frequency,** audio frequency; monotone, monotony; overtone; intonation

3 **timbre,** tonality

4 **acoustics,** phonics

5 **sonics; supersonics;** speed of sound; sound barrier

6 (*sound unit*) **decibel**

7 **loudspeaker, speaker;** cone; horn (*nonformal*); **headphone, earphone**

8 **microphone, mike** (*nonformal*); **bug** (*nonformal*)

9 **amplifier, amp** (*nonformal*)

10 **hi-fi** (*nonformal*); sound system; **record player,** gramophone; **jukebox; stereo** (*nonformal*); stylus, needle; turntable; PA system; **intercom** (*nonformal*); **tape recorder,** tape deck, cassette recorder; **compact disc** or CD player

11 **record,** disc; album; vinyl; digital recording; **recording,** tape recording; digital disc; tape, cassette; compact disc or CD video

12 **distortion;** scratching; hum, hissing; feedback; static

verbs

13 **sound,** make a sound or noise; speak; resound; **record,** tape; play back

adjectives

14 **sounding,** sonorous; tonal; monotonic, toneless, droning

15 **audible; distinct, clear,** plain, definite, articulate; distinctive; hi-fi (*nonformal*)

16 **acoustic; supersonic**

adverbs

17 **audibly, aloud, out loud;** distinctly, clearly, plainly

42 SILENCE

nouns

1 **silence, stillness, quietness, quiet, still,** peace, **hush;** lull, rest; tranquillity

2 **muteness, dumbness;** speechlessness

3 **silencer,** muffle, mute; soft pedal; gag, muzzle; soundproofing

verbs

4 **be silent; keep one's mouth shut, hold one's tongue,** bite one's tongue, muzzle oneself, **not breathe a word, keep mum, hold one's peace,** not utter a word, not open one's mouth; keep to oneself; be mute

5 (*nonformal terms*) **shut up,** keep one's trap shut, button one's lip, save one's breath, clam up, say nothing, play dumb

6 **fall silent, hush,** quiet, quieten, pipe down (*nonformal*)

7 **silence, hush, quiet,** quieten; squash, stifle, choke, **gag, muzzle,** muffle

8 **muffle, mute, dull, soften, deaden,** deafen; subdue, stop, tone down

adjectives

9 **silent, still, quiet, hushed; in-audible**

10 **tacit, unspoken; implicit**

11 **mute, mum, dumb, speechless,** at a loss for words, choked up; inarticulate; **tongue-tied,** dumbstruck, **dumbfounded**

adverbs

12 **silently,** in silence, **quietly;** inaudibly

43 FAINTNESS OF SOUND

nouns

1 **faintness, lowness, softness,** gentleness

2 **pad, pat; patter; tap, click,** tick, pop; tinkle, clink, chink

3 **murmur; mutter; mumble; undertone; whisper;** breath, sigh

4 **ripple, splash;** titter, chuckle

5 **rustle,** rustling

6 **hum, humming, droning, buzzing,** whizzing, whirring, purring

7 **sigh, sighing, moaning, sobbing,** whining

verbs

8 **murmur, mutter, mumble;** coo; **whisper;** breathe, sigh

9 **ripple, babble,** bubble, **gurgle,** lap, **splash,** slosh

10 **rustle; swish**

11 **hum, drone, buzz,** whiz, whir, purr

12 **sigh, moan, sob, whine; whimper**

13 **patter; pad, pat; tap, click,** tick; pop; tinkle, clink, chink

adjectives

14 **faint, low, soft, gentle, dim, feeble, weak;** murmured, whispered; **distant;** indistinct, unclear

15 **muffled, muted, softened, dampened, smothered,** stifled, dulled, deadened

16 **murmuring, muttering, mumbling; whispering,** whisper; **rustling**

17 **rippling, babbling,** bubbling, **gurgling;** lapping, splashing, sloshing

18 **humming, droning, buzzing,** whizzing, whirring, purring

adverbs

19 **faintly, softly,** gently, weakly

20 **in an undertone,** *sotto voce (Italian),* **under one's breath,** in a whisper; aside

44 LOUDNESS

nouns

1 **loudness,** intensity, volume; surge, crescendo, swell

2 **noisiness,** obstreperousness; vociferousness

3 **noise, blast, racket, din, clamour; uproar,** hue and cry; howl; clatter, jangle, rattle; roar; **crash, boom; bang; tumult;** fracas, commotion; **pandemonium,** bedlam

4 *(nonformal terms for noisy occasions)* row, hullabaloo, rumpus, hoo-ha

5 **blare, blast,** shriek, peal; **toot, honk, whistle,** squeal; **fanfare;** tattoo

6 **cracker; rattle; horn; whistle,** siren

verbs

7 **din; boom, thunder; resound**, ring, peal; **deafen;** blast, **bang, crash;** surge, swell, rise; **shout**

8 **drown out,** shout down, overpower, overwhelm

9 **be noisy, make a racket,** raise a hue and cry, roar; raise the roof, whoop it up

10 **blare,** blast; shriek; **toot,** sound, peal; pipe, trumpet; bay, bray; **whistle,** squeal; **honk**

adjectives

11 **loud; resounding,** ringing, pealing; **deafening,** piercing; **thunderous; crashing, booming**

12 **noisy,** clanging, blaring; **tumultuous,** blustering, **boisterous,** rowdy, vociferous

adverbs

13 **loudly, aloud,** lustily; **noisily; at the top of one's voice**

45 RESONANCE

nouns

1 **resonance; vibrancy;** richness

2 **reverberation; rumble,** rumbling, thunder, boom, growl, grumble; **echo**

3 **ringing, pealing, chiming, tinkling, jingling; tolling;** clanking, clanging; **ring, peal, chime; tinkle, jingle;** clink, ping; **clank, clang; jangle**

4 **bell; gong,** triangle, **chimes**

verbs

5 **resonate, vibrate,** pulse, throb

6 **reverberate, resound, rumble,** boom, echo

7 **ring, peal; toll; chime; tinkle, jingle; clink; clank, clang; jangle**

adjectives

8 **resonant, vibrant;** mellow, rich; reverberating, echoing, vibrating, pulsing, throbbing

9 **deep; low; bass;** baritone; contralto

10 **reverberating, resounding, rumbling,** thundering, booming, growling; echoing

11 **ringing, pealing, chiming; tinkling, jingling**

46 REPEATED SOUNDS

nouns

1 **staccato; beat, roll;** drumming, beating, pounding, thumping; throbbing; sputter, splutter; **patter; tattoo**

2 **clicking, ticking**

3 **rattle; clatter**

verbs

4 **drum, beat, pound, thump;** sputter, splutter; patter; **throb,** pulsate

5 **tick, ticktock**

6 **rattle; clatter**

adjectives

7 **staccato; drumming, beating, pounding, thumping; throbbing;** sputtering, spluttering; clicking, ticking

8 **rattling, chattering,** clattering

47 EXPLOSIVE NOISE

nouns

1 **report, crash, crack, clap, bang,**

slam, clash, burst; **knock, rap, tap**, smack, whack, slap

2 **snap, crack; click; crackle**

3 **detonation, blast, explosion, bang, pop, crack; shot**, gunshot; volley

4 **boom, peal, rumble**, grumble, growl, **roll, roar**

5 **thunder, thunderclap**; thunderstorm

verbs

6 **crack, crash, slam, bang; knock, rap, tap**, smack, whack, slap

7 **snap, crack; click; crackle**

8 **blast, detonate, explode, burst**, go off, **bang, pop, crack**

9 **boom, thunder, peal, rumble**, grumble, growl, **roar**

adjectives

10 **snapping, cracking, crackling**

11 **banging**, crashing, bursting, exploding, **explosive, blasting**, cracking, popping; knocking, rapping, tapping; slapping

12 **thundering, thunderous; booming**, pealing, rumbling, roaring

48 SIBILATION

nouns

1 **hiss**; sizzle; fizz; swish, whoosh; whiz, buzz; zip; wheeze; whistle; **sniff**; spit, sputter, splutter; lisp

verbs

2 **hiss**; sizzle; fizz; whiz, buzz; zip; swish, whoosh; whistle; wheeze; sniff; spit, sputter, splutter; lisp

adjectives

3 **sibilant; hissing**; sizzling; **sniffing**; wheezing

49 STRIDENCY

nouns

1 **stridency; shrillness**

2 **raucousness, harshness**; discord, cacophony; coarseness, roughness, gruffness; **hoarseness**, huskiness, dryness; thickness, throatiness

3 **rasp, scratch, scrape**, grind; crunch; **jangle, clash**; clank, clang, twang; blare, bray; croak, cackle; growl, snarl

4 **screech, shriek, scream, squeal**, squeak, squawk, creak; **whistle; whine, wail, howl**

5 (*insect noises*) chirp, chirrup

6 (*high voices*) soprano, mezzo-soprano, treble; tenor, alto; falsetto

verbs

7 chirp, chirrup

8 **screech, shriek**, creak, squeak, squawk, **scream, squeal**, shrill, keen; **whistle**; pipe; **whine**, wail, howl

9 (*sound harshly*) **jangle, clash, jar**; blare, bray; croak, cackle; growl, snarl; clank, clang; twang

10 **grate, rasp, scratch, scrape**, grind; crunch

11 **grate on**, jar on

adjectives

12 **strident**

13 **high**, high-pitched; treble, soprano, tenor, alto, falsetto

14 **shrill, sharp, piercing**, penetrating; screeching, shrieking, **squeaky**, creaking; whistling, piping; whining, wailing, howling

15 **raucous, harsh;** coarse, rude, rough, gruff; **hoarse, husky,** dry; croaking; **squawking**

16 **grating, jarring,** grinding; **jangling; rasping;** scratching; scraping

50 CRY, CALL

nouns

1 **cry, call, shout, yell,** hoot; **cheer; howl;** bawl, bellow, roar; **scream, shriek,** screech, squeal; **yelp, yap, bark**

2 **exclamation,** ejaculation, outburst

3 **outcry, clamour;** hullaballoo, brouhaha, **uproar; hue and cry**

verbs

4 **cry, call, shout, yell, hoot; hail; cheer; howl;** squawk; **bawl, bellow,** roar; **scream, shriek,** screech, squeal; **yelp, yap, bark**

5 **exclaim,** burst out, blurt out; stammer out

6 **cry out,** call out, yell out, shout out; **sound off** (*nonformal*), pipe up

adjectives

7 **vociferous; noisy;** crying, shouting, yelling, bawling, screaming, yelping, yapping

51 ANIMAL SOUNDS

nouns

1 **call, cry;** grunt, howl, bark

verbs

2 **cry, call; howl;** wail, whine; **squeal,** screech, squeak; **roar; bellow, bawl; moo,** low; **bleat;**

bray; **neigh; bay; bark; yelp, yap; mew,** miaow

3 **grunt; snort**

4 **growl, snarl;** hiss, spit

5 (*birds*) **warble, sing,** call; whistle; **twitter; chirp, peep; quack, honk; croak; squawk; crow; cackle, cluck; gobble; hoot; coo; cuckoo**

adjectives

6 **howling,** crying, wailing, whining, bawling

52 DISCORD

nouns

1 **discord, cacophony**

2 **clash, jangle; noise;** harshness; clamour

verbs

3 **clash, jar, jangle,** conflict; grate

adjectives

4 **discordant;** strident, shrill, harsh, raucous, grating; off; flat, sharp

5 **clashing, jarring, jangling,** conflicting; **harsh, grating**

53 TASTE

nouns

1 **taste; flavour; smack, tang; savour, relish;** sweetness, sourness, bitterness; savouriness

2 **sip, sup, lick, bite**

3 **soupçon,** hint

4 **sample, specimen, taste,** taster; example

5 **taste bud; palate**

6 **tasting, savouring**

verbs

7 **taste,** taste of, sample; savour; sip, sup (*nonformal*); lick; smack

adjectives

8 **flavoured, savoury, flavourful; sweet, sour, bitter, bittersweet, salt**

54 SAVOURINESS

nouns

1 **savouriness, tastiness;** succulence

2 **relish, zest, gusto**

3 **flavouring; seasoning, relish, condiment, spice**

verbs

4 **savour, relish,** enjoy, appreciate; taste

5 **savour of,** taste of, smack of

6 **flavour; season,** salt, pepper, spice

adjectives

7 **tasty,** good, **palatable,** nice, agreeable, **delicious,** delectable, exquisite; delicate; juicy, succulent, **luscious;** gourmet

8 **nutty,** fruity; **rich**

9 **appetizing, tempting,** tantalizing, piquant

55 UNSAVOURINESS

nouns

1 **unsavouriness, distastefulness**

2 tartness, sharpness, **sourness,** pungency; **bitterness**

verbs

3 **disgust, repel,** nauseate

adjectives

4 **unsavoury, unpalatable, distasteful,** unpleasant

5 **bitter;** sharp, tart; sour; pungent

6 **nasty, offensive,** noxious, cloying, **foul, vile,** bad; **sickening, nauseating;** poisonous, rank, rancid, spoiled, high, rotten, stinking

7 **inedible, uneatable**

56 INSIPIDNESS

nouns

1 **insipidness, tastelessness,** blandness; **weakness,** mildness

adjectives

2 **insipid, tasteless, bland; weak,** mild, watery, diluted, dilute; indifferent

57 SWEETNESS

nouns

1 **sweetness; sugariness,** syrupiness

2 **sweetener;** sugar; saccharin, aspartame; treacle; syrup; **honey; nectar**

verbs

3 **sweeten; sugar;** glaze, candy

adjectives

4 **sweet,** sweetened; **sugary,** candied, syrupy

5 **saccharine, cloying;** sickly-sweet

58 SOURNESS

nouns

1 **sourness, tartness;** acidity; **dryness**

2 vinegar; pickle; lemon; sour
cream; acid
3 acidification; fermentation

verbs

4 sour, acidify; ferment

adjectives

5 sour, soured; tart; pickled; pungent; dry
6 acid

59 PUNGENCY

nouns

1 pungency, piquancy; sharpness;
bitterness; acidity, sourness
2 zest; tang, spice, relish; bite;
punch; kick
3 strength; rankness
4 saltiness; brackishness

verbs

5 nip, sting

adjectives

6 pungent, piquant; sharp, stinging, biting; bitter; acid, sour
7 nippy, tangy; spiced, seasoned;
spicy, curried, peppery, hot,
burning
8 strong; high; rank
9 salty, salt, saline; brackish; pickled

60 ODOUR

nouns

1 odour, smell, scent, aroma;
fume, breath, whiff, trace; fragrance; stink, stench
2 smelliness, pungency
3 smelling, scenting; sniffing
4 nose; nostrils

verbs

5 (*have an odour*) smell; reek,
stink
6 scent, perfume
7 smell, scent; sniff; whiff

adjectives

8 smelling, smelly, aromatic; fragrant; stinking
9 strong; pungent, penetrating;
reeking; suffocating, stifling

61 FRAGRANCE

nouns

1 fragrance, perfume, aroma,
scent, bouquet; odour
2 perfume, scent, essence; essential oil; musk
3 toilet water; rose water; lavender
water; cologne, eau de Cologne;
lotion
4 incense; joss stick; sandalwood
5 atomizer, spray; sachet; poman-
der; potpourri

verbs

6 be fragrant, smell sweet, smell
good
7 perfume, scent

adjectives

8 fragrant, aromatic, perfumed,
scented, sweet, sweet-smelling,
sweet-scented; flowery; fruity;
spicy

62 STENCH

nouns

1 stench, stink, niff *and* pong
(*both nonformal*), reek; body
odour *or* BO; halitosis; bad
breath

2 **smelliness, rankness, foulness,** offensiveness; **mustiness**

verbs

3 **stink,** smell, **reek**

adjectives

4 **fetid, stinking, reeking,** smelling, **smelly; foul,** vile, offensive, noxious; **rank,** high; **musty**

63 ODOURLESSNESS

nouns

1 **deodorizing,** fumigation

2 **deodorant;** antiperspirant

verbs

3 **deodorize;** fumigate

adjectives

4 unscented; inoffensive

5 **deodorant,** deodorizing

64 TOUCH

nouns

1 **touch; contact; feel,** feeling, **kiss, caress,** fondling; **brush,** graze, glance; **stroke,** rub; **tap,** flick

2 **touching, feeling, fingering, handling,** manipulation; petting, caressing, stroking, rubbing, friction; fondling; **pressure**

3 **tangibility;** tactility

4 **feeler; antenna**

5 **finger, digit;** forefinger; index finger; ring finger; middle finger; little finger; **thumb**

verbs

6 **touch, feel; finger, thumb; handle,** paw; **manipulate,** wield, ply; **twiddle;** poke at, prod; **tap,** flick

7 kiss, **brush,** sweep, graze, glance, scrape, skim

8 **stroke, pet, caress,** fondle; **nuzzle;** rub, rub against, massage, knead

9 **lick, lap**

adjectives

10 tactile

11 **palpable, tangible,** tactile

65 SENSATIONS OF TOUCH

nouns

1 **tingle,** thrill, buzz; **prickle; sting**

2 **tickle, ticklishness**

3 **itch,** itchiness

4 **creeps** (*nonformal*); goose pimples

verbs

5 **tingle,** thrill; **itch;** scratch; **prickle,** prick, sting

66 SEX

nouns

1 **sex,** gender; **maleness, masculinity, femaleness, femininity**

2 **sexuality,** love life; **love,** lovemaking; heterosexuality; homosexuality; bisexuality; lesbianism; **sensuality;** sexiness, flesh; **libido,** sex drive; impotence; frigidity

3 **sex appeal,** sexiness

4 **sex symbol, sex object;** sex goddess, sex kitten; stud *and* sex machine (*both nonformal*), sex god

5 **lust,** desire; **erection; passion;** lasciviousness; **eroticism;** nymphomania; **heat,** rut

6 aphrodisiac, love potion

7 copulation, **sex act**, coupling, mating, coition, **coitus, sex, intercourse, sexual intercourse,** sexual relations, marital relations, carnal knowledge; foreplay; **oral sex**, blow job (*nonformal*); **anal sex,** sodomy; **orgasm,** climax; adultery, fornication; group sex; gang bang (*nonformal*); wife swapping; casual sex, one-night stand; safe sex; sex shop; **lovemaking; procreation;** sperm, ovum

8 masturbation; sexual fantasy; wet dream

9 **sexlessness; impotence;** eunuch

10 **sexual preference; sexual orientation; heterosexuality; homosexuality; bisexuality; lesbianism;** sexism; heterosexism

11 perversion; bestiality; **sadomasochism; sadism; masochism;** pederasty, paedophilia; exhibitionism; voyeurism; transvestism; cross-dressing; **incest, sex crime; sexual abuse**

12 hermaphroditism; androgyny; transsexualism

13 **heterosexual, straight** (*nonformal*)

14 **homosexual, gay; bisexual; lesbian**

15 (*nonformal terms for homosexuals*) homo, queer, fairy, pansy, queen, poof, poofter; dyke, bull dyke

16 **pervert, deviant,** sex fiend; pederast; sadist; masochist; sadomasochist; transvestite; crossdresser; exhibitionist; voyeur; nymphomaniac; rapist

17 hermaphrodite; transsexual

verbs

18 sex

19 lust, **desire; be in heat,** rut

20 **copulate,** couple, **mate, have sex,** be intimate; sleep with, go to bed with; mount; commit adultery; fornicate; **make love**

21 masturbate; sodomize

22 **climax, come; ejaculate**

adjectives

23 **sexual,** sex; **erotic,** amorous; venereal; **carnal, sensual;** desirable; **sexy**

24 **aphrodisiac,** stimulating

25 **lustful, hot,** steamy, sexy, **salacious, passionate,** hot-blooded, randy; lascivious

26 **in heat, burning, hot;** rutting

27 **sexless,** asexual; **neuter,** neutral; castrated; **cold, frigid; impotent;** frustrated

28 **homosexual, gay,** queer *and* poofy (*both nonformal*); **bisexual; lesbian;** mannish, butch (*nonformal*); effeminate; transvestite; **perverted,** deviant

29 androgynous

67 MASCULINITY

nouns

1 **masculinity,** maleness; **manliness, manhood**

2 virility; machismo

3 **mankind, man, men, manhood,** menfolk

4 **male,** masculine; he, him, his; **man; gentleman,** gent (*nonformal*)

5 (*nonformal terms*) **guy**, fellow, lad, chap, joker, customer, party, character, body, dude, gent

6 **real man**, **he-man**, caveman (*nonformal*)

7 (*forms of address*) **Mister**, **Mr**, Messrs (*pl*), Master; **sir**

8 (*male animals*) cock; cockerel; drake; gander; peacock; dog; boar; stag; stallion, stud; tomcat; billy goat; ram; bull, bullock

9 (*mannish female*) **amazon**; lesbian, dyke (*nonformal*); **tomboy**

adjectives

10 **masculine**, **male**; **manly**, **manlike**; **gentlemanly**

11 **virile**; **macho**

12 **mannish**; **unwomanly**, **unfeminine**; **tomboyish**

68 FEMININITY

nouns

1 **femininity**; **womanliness**, **womanhood**; girlishness

2 **effeminacy**, **unmanliness**, **womanishness**; feminism

3 **womankind**, **woman**, **women**, femininity, **womanhood**, womenfolk

4 **female**; she, her

5 **woman**; **lady**; **wife**; **matron**, dame, **dowager**; spinster; lass, girl

6 (*nonformal terms*) dame, broad, doll, babe, chick, bird, bitch

7 (*forms of address*) **Ms**; Mistress (*old*); **Mrs**; **madam** *or* ma'am; dame (*old*); lady; **Miss**

8 (*female animals*) hen; peahen; bitch; sow; ewe; doe, hind, roe; mare; filly; cow; heifer; vixen; tigress; lioness

9 (*effeminate male*) **mummy's boy**, sissy; milksop; old woman

verbs

10 emasculate, castrate

adjectives

11 **feminine**, **female**; **womanly**, **womanish**, **womanlike**; **ladylike**; **matronly**; **girlish**; maidenly

12 **effeminate**, **womanish**, old-womanish, **unmanly**, **sissy**, sissyish

69 REPRODUCTION, PROCREATION

nouns

1 **reproduction**, **making**; **reconstruction**, rebuilding, restructuring, *perestroika* (*Russian*); **revision**; **reprinting**; **reorganization**; **redevelopment**; **rebirth**, resurrection, revival; **duplication**, **imitation**, **copy**, **repetition**; **restoration**; **birth rate**

2 **procreation**, **reproduction**, **generation**, **breeding**; **propagation**, **multiplication**, proliferation

3 **fertilization**; **impregnation**, **insemination**, **mating**, **servicing**; **pollination**; artificial insemination

4 **conception**

5 **pregnancy**, **gestation**, **incubation**; **brooding**

6 **birth**, **generation**, **genesis**; **development**; procreation

verbs

7 **reproduce**, **remake**, resurrect, revive, **reconstruct**, rebuild, re-

structure, **revise; reprint; reorganize; duplicate, copy, repeat, restore, renovate**

8 **generate, breed; propagate, multiply;** proliferate; mother; father

9 **lay** (*eggs*), deposit, spawn

10 **fertilize; impregnate, inseminate,** knock up (*nonformal*); **pollinate**

11 **conceive**

12 **be pregnant;** be knocked up (*nonformal*); breed, carry; **incubate, hatch; brood**

13 **give birth**

adjectives

14 **reproductive;** resurgent; **restorative**

15 **reproductive;** seminal, fertilizing

16 **genetic, generative;** genital

17 **impregnated,** inseminated

18 **pregnant,** knocked up (*nonformal*); expecting (*nonformal*)

70 CLEANNESS

nouns

1 **cleanness, cleanliness; purity; immaculateness; spotlessness;** whiteness; freshness; fastidiousness; sterility; tidiness

2 **cleansing, cleaning; purge,** cleanout, catharsis; **purification**

3 **sanitation, hygiene; disinfection, decontamination, sterilization;** fumigation, delousing

4 **refinement, clarification, purification; straining; filtering;** sifting, screening, sieving; distillation

5 **washing, ablutions; wash;** rinse; sponge; shampoo; flushing; enema; **scrub,** mopping, scouring; **washing up**

6 **laundry; wash, washing**

7 **bathing**

8 **bath; shower;** douche; bed bath; sponge; Turkish bath, sauna, hot tub, Jacuzzi (*trademark*)

9 **dip, bath;** acid bath; sheepdip

10 **baths,** public baths, sauna; spa; lavatory, washroom, bathroom; steam room; rest room

11 **laundry; Launderette** (*trademark*); car wash

12 **washbasin,** basin; **lavatory,** washstand; bath; bidet; **shower; sink,** kitchen sink; dishwasher; washing machine; finger bowl

13 **refinery; filter; strainer,** colander; **sieve**

14 **cleaner; janitor,** custodian; charwoman, charlady

15 **cleaner,** dry cleaner; **dishwasher;** scullery maid

16 **road sweeper; street sweeper; chimney sweep,** sweep

17 **cleanser;** cleaning agent; lotion, cream; cold cream, cleansing cream; **soap, detergent; shampoo; rinse; solvent;** mouthwash; **toothpaste;** enema

verbs

18 **clean, cleanse; purify;** freshen; whiten, bleach; clear out, sweep out; spruce, **tidy; wipe;** dust; **dry-clean**

19 **wash, bathe,** bath, shower; **launder;** rinse, flush; sponge; **scrub,** swab, mop; scour, soap, lather; shampoo

20 **groom,** dress, **brush up; preen;** manicure

21 **comb,** curry, card, rake

22 **refine, clarify,** clear, purify; **strain; filter; sift,** separate, sieve

23 **sweep, brush,** whisk; hoover, vacuum (*nonformal*)

24 **disinfect, sterilize; boil**

adjectives

25 **clean, pure; immaculate, spotless;** bleached, whitened; bright, shiny; unadulterated; **fresh;** fastidious

26 **cleaned, cleansed; purified;** refined; **spruce, tidy**

27 **sanitary, hygienic; sterile,** antiseptic; disinfected, sterilized; boiled; pasteurized

28 **cleansing, cleaning;** detergent; **purifying**

adverbs

29 **cleanly,** clean; **immaculately, spotlessly**

71 UNCLEANNESS

nouns

1 **impurity; dirtiness,** grubbiness, dinginess, griminess, muddiness

2 **filthiness, foulness**

3 **squalor, sordidness**

4 **defilement;** dirtying, soiling; **pollution, contamination, infection**

5 **soil; smudge,** smear, **spot,** blot, blotch, **stain**

6 **dirt, grime;** dust; **mud**

7 **filth, muck,** slime, mess; **excrement; mucus;** pus, decay, rot

8 **slime, slop,** scum, sludge, slush; **muck**

9 **offal; carrion; garbage,** slop, slops; **sewage; waste, refuse**

10 **pigsty; slum;** dump (*nonformal*); the ghetto, the slums; hovel

11 (*receptacle of filth*) **cesspit,** septic tank; **sewer,** drain; **dump,** rubbish dump; swamp, bog, marsh

12 **pig,** slut

verbs

13 **dirty;** muck up (*nonformal*); **muddy**

14 **soil; blacken; smudge,** smear, daub; **spot, stain**

15 **defile, foul; pollute, corrupt, contaminate, infect; taint,** tarnish

16 **spatter, splatter,** splash, spot

adjectives

17 **unclean, unwashed; impure; polluted, contaminated, infected, corrupted**

18 **soiled, dirtied,** smudged, spotted, **tarnished,** tainted, **stained, defiled,** fouled; bedraggled

19 **dirty, grimy, grubby,** dingy, messy (*nonformal*); scruffy, slovenly, untidy; **muddy; dusty;** sooty

20 **filthy, foul, vile;** rank, fetid; **rotten; nauseating, disgusting; odious, repulsive;** slimy

21 **squalid, sordid,** wretched, shabby

72 HEALTHFULNESS

nouns

1 **healthiness, wholesomeness**

2 **hygiene;** sanitation; **public health; preventive medicine; fitness**

verbs

3 **be good for; agree with**

adjectives

4 **healthy, wholesome, beneficial,** benign, **good for; hygienic,** sanitary; constitutional; bracing, refreshing, invigorating

73 UNHEALTHFULNESS

nouns

1 unhealthiness, unwholesomeness; health hazard; **contamination, pollution**

2 **poisonousness, toxicity, venomousness; virulence,** malignancy, noxiousness, destructiveness, deadliness; **infectiousness,** contagiousness, communicability; poison, venom

verbs

3 **disagree with,** not be good for

adjectives

4 **unhealthy, unwholesome, bad for;** noxious, noisome, injurious, harmful; **polluted,** contaminated, tainted, foul, septic; unhygienic, unsanitary

5 **poisonous, toxic; venomous; virulent, noxious, malignant,** destructive, deadly; **infectious,** contagious, communicable, catching

74 HEALTH

nouns

1 **health, well-being; fitness**

2 **healthiness,** wholesomeness; **good health**

3 **vitality,** strength, vigour; longevity

4 **immunity, resistance; immunization;** antibody

5 **health care;** preventive medicine; medical insurance; **health service;** health club

verbs

6 **feel fine, feel fit;** bloom, glow, flourish; keep fit

7 **get well, recover,** mend; recuperate

adjectives

8 **healthy, fine, fit**

9 (*nonformal terms*) **in the pink, fit as a fiddle;** bright-eyed and bushy-tailed

10 **well;** all right

11 **sound,** wholesome

12 **hearty, robust, vigorous, strong,** stout, sturdy, **rugged,** hardy, lusty, bouncing; **fit**

13 **fresh,** youthful, **blooming; rosy,** ruddy, pink

14 **immune, resistant;** health-conscious

75 FITNESS, EXERCISE

nouns

1 **fitness, condition, shape,** trim, tone; **gymnasium, gym** (*nonformal*), **health club; weight, barbell,** dumbbell, exercise machine, bench, exercise bike, rowing machine, treadmill; **Jacuzzi** (*trademark*), hot tub, spa

2 **exercise,** motion, movement, manoeuvre; routine, drill, **workout; warm-up, stretching,** cool-down; callisthenics; physical jerks, constitutional; **gymnastics; isometrics; aerobics;** Callanetics, **bodybuilding,** weightlifting,

weight training, pumping iron (*nonformal*); **running, jogging; walking; swimming**

verbs

3 **exercise, work out,** warm up, cool down, stretch, lift weights, pump iron (*nonformal*), jog, run, cycle, walk

76 DISEASE

nouns

1 **disease, illness, sickness, malady, ailment, indisposition, disorder,** complaint, **affliction, infirmity; disability,** defect, handicap; deformity; condition; **signs, symptoms, pathology,** syndrome; malaise; complication

2 **fatal illness, terminal illness; death; brain death;** cot death *or* sudden infant death syndrome *or* SIDS

3 **ill health,** poor health; **sickliness,** delicacy, fragility, **frailty; infirmity,** debility, exhaustion; invalidity

4 **infection, contagion,** contamination, virus; **contagiousness, infectiousness, communicability;** carrier

5 **epidemic, plague,** pandemic

6 **seizure, attack;** arrest; blockage, stoppage; **stroke; spasm, throes, fit, paroxysm, convulsion; epilepsy;** cramp

7 **fever, feverishness, temperature; heat;** flush; delirium

8 **collapse, breakdown, prostration,** exhaustion

9 (*symptoms*) anaemia; bleeding, haemorrhage; dizziness, vertigo;

chill; hot flush; morning sickness; fainting; fatigue; fever; indigestion; inflammation; itching; jaundice; vomiting, nausea; paralysis; rash; sore, abscess; tumour, growth; convulsion; seizure, spasm; pain; coughing, sneezing

10 **infectious disease,** infection

11 **germ, bug** (*nonformal*); **microbe; virus; bacteria;** fungus, mould; **carcinogen**

12 **sufferer, victim; invalid;** terminal case; **patient, case;** epileptic; **the sick, the infirm**

13 **disabled person, handicapped person,** cripple; amputee; paraplegic; the disabled, the handicapped, the lame

verbs

14 **ail, suffer,** complain of; **feel ill,** feel under the weather; look green about the gills (*nonformal*)

15 **take ill, sicken; catch, contract, get,** take, sicken for, **come down with** (*nonformal*); catch cold; break out in a rash, erupt; run a temperature; drop in one's tracks, **collapse;** overdose *or* OD (*nonformal*)

16 **fail, weaken, sink, decline,** dwindle, droop, flag, wilt, wither, fade, **languish,** waste away, pine

17 **afflict; sicken, indispose;** weaken, enfeeble; enervate, debilitate; **invalid,** incapacitate, **disable;** lay up, hospitalize

18 **infect, disease,** contaminate

adjectives

19 **unhealthy,** in poor health; **infirm, unsound,** debilitated, enervated, exhausted, drained;

housebound; **sickly; feeble, frail;** weakened, **run-down; dying; terminal,** languishing; failing; pale

20 unhealthy, unsound, morbid, diseased, pathological

21 ill, ailing, sick, unwell, indisposed, on the sick list; **seedy** (*nonformal*), **under the weather, out of sorts** (*nonformal*), below par (*nonformal*); not oneself; faint; sick as a dog (*nonformal*), laid low; in a bad way, critically ill, on the critical list, critical, in intensive care

22 nauseated, queasy, squeamish; seasick, carsick

23 feverish; flushed, inflamed, **hot, burning,** fiery, hectic; delirious

24 laid up, hospitalized, in hospital; **bedridden;** prostrate, flat on one's back; confined

25 diseased, infected, contaminated, poisoned, septic; ulcerated, gangrenous; **inflamed;** congested; **swollen**

26 anaemic; bilious; colicky; tubercular; rheumatic, arthritic; allergic; diabetic; epileptic; leprous; malarial; cancerous, malignant

27 contagious, infectious, catching, spreading; **communicable;** epidemic, pandemic

77 REMEDY

nouns

1 **remedy, cure; relief, help, aid, assistance,** succour; balm; restorative; specific; **prescription**

2 **patent medicine,** quack remedy

3 **panacea, cure-all;** elixir

4 **medicine, medicament, medication, drug,** preparation, mixture; medicinal herbs; drops; powder; elixir, syrup, linctus; **prescription drug;** over-the-counter drug; proprietary medicine *or* drug; **placebo**

5 **drug, narcotic drug, controlled substance**

6 **dose, draught, potion, shot,** injection, jab *and* jag (*both nonformal*)

7 **pill, tablet, capsule,** lozenge

8 **tonic, pick-me-up** (*nonformal*); **shot in the arm** (*nonformal*)

9 **stimulant;** adrenaline; amphetamine, upper (*nonformal*), caffeine, digitalis, smelling salts

10 **balm, lotion, salve, ointment,** oil; **liniment**

11 **sedative,** barbiturate, downer (*nonformal*), morphine; **sleeping pill; tranquillizer,** Librium (*trademark*), Valium (*trademark*); **analgesic, aspirin;** alcohol, liquor

12 **anaesthetic; gas, laughing gas**

13 **antiseptic, disinfectant;** alcohol

14 **toothpaste,** tooth powder; mouthwash, gargle

15 **contraceptive;** condom; oral contraceptive, **the pill** (*nonformal*), abortion pill; diaphragm; contraceptive foam

16 **antidote; serum; vaccination,** inoculation; vaccine; antibiotic, penicillin; **miracle drug, wonder drug**

17 **dressing, application;** plaster; **compress; bandage,** bandaging; sling; splint, brace; cast, plaster

cast; tape, **adhesive tape**; cotton, gauze, sponge

18 pharmacist, chemist, dispenser; pharmaceutical chemist; drugstore, pharmacy

verbs

19 remedy, cure; prescribe; treat

adjectives

20 remedial, therapeutic, healing, corrective; medicinal; soothing; **antibiotic;** preventive, protective; **antiseptic, disinfectant**

21 tonic, stimulating, bracing, invigorating, reviving, refreshing, strengthening

22 sedative, soothing, tranquillizing, quietening; narcotic; hypnotic; **anaesthetic,** deadening, numbing

78 SUBSTANCE ABUSE

nouns

1 substance abuse, drug abuse, drug use, solvent abuse; **addiction, drug addiction; habit,** drug habit; **alcoholism,** alcohol abuse; **smoking,** nicotine addiction, chain smoking; **tolerance; withdrawal, withdrawal symptoms;** drying out

2 drug, narcotic, dope (*nonformal*), dangerous drug, controlled substance, illegal drug, **hard drug;** soft drug; **sedative; stimulant**

3 dose; shot, injection; opium den

4 addict, drug addict, user, drug user, opium addict; **alcoholic; smoker,** heavy smoker, chain smoker, nicotine addict

verbs

5 use, be on; sniff, snort; **smoke marijuana, smoke opium;** inject, take pills, pop pills (*nonformal*); **withdraw,** dry out; **smoke, smoke tobacco,** puff, drag, chain-smoke

adjectives

6 intoxicated

7 (*nonformal terms*) **high,** smashed, stoned, tripping

8 addicted; using, on

79 INTOXICATION, ALCOHOLIC DRINK

nouns

1 intoxication, drunkenness; Dutch courage; hangover, morning after (*nonformal*)

2 alcoholism, problem drinking, heavy drinking, habitual drunkenness

3 drinking; social drinking; guzzling, gargling; hard drinking, serious drinking (*nonformal*)

4 spree, drinking bout, bout, celebration; binge, drunk (*both nonformal*)

5 drink, nip, draught, drop, spot, sip; swig, pull; shot; round

6 drink, cocktail, long drink, mixed drink; **punch; nightcap** (*nonformal*)

80 TOBACCO

nouns

1 tobacco; the weed (*nonformal*); smoke, tobacco smoke, cigarette smoke, cigar smoke, pipe smoke;

nicotine; smoker; tobacconist; smoking room

2 Cuban, Havana, Turkish, Russian; plug tobacco, leaf

3 **cigar**; Havana; cigar box, cigar case; cigar cutter

4 **cigarette; fag** (*nonformal*); cigarette case; cigarette end

5 **pipe**, tobacco pipe; clay pipe; water pipe; peace pipe; pipe rack, pipe cleaner, tobacco pouch

6 **smoking**, smoking habit, habitual smoking; chain-smoke; smoke, puff, drag (*nonformal*); passive smoking

verbs

7 (*use tobacco*) **smoke**; inhale, puff, draw, drag (*nonformal*), pull; chain-smoke

81 HEALTH CARE

nouns

1 **medicine, medical practice, health care, treatment, therapy**; health insurance; **care**

2 **surgery; operation**

3 **dentistry,** dental medicine, dental care

4 **doctor, physician, medical practitioner, medical man;** family doctor; country doctor; **intern; resident,** house physician, resident physician; **specialist;** coroner; **surgeon, quack** (*nonformal*)

5 **dentist; dental surgeon**

6 **veterinary, veterinarian, vet** (*nonformal*), veterinary surgeon, horse doctor, animal doctor

7 **physician, nurse, midwife, therapist,** practitioner

8 orderly, attendant; dresser; anaesthetist; X-ray technician; laboratory technician; physical therapist, physiotherapist; hospital administrator; ambulance driver

9 medical practice; general practice; group practice; family practice

verbs

10 **practise medicine,** doctor (*nonformal*); **treat; intern**

adjectives

11 **medical;** health; surgical; neurological; dental; homeopathic; clinical

82 THERAPY, MEDICAL TREATMENT

nouns

1 **therapy, treatment,** medication; healing; healing arts; psychotherapy; medicines; **faith healing**

2 **radiotherapy,** radiation therapy; radiology, radiography; X-ray

3 **diagnosis; examination, physical examination;** study, test; blood test, blood count

4 **prognosis; symptom, sign**

5 **treatment; cure; medication;** regime, protocol; first aid; hospitalization

6 **immunization; inoculation, vaccination; injection,** hypodermic; vaccine

7 **transfusion,** blood transfusion; serum; blood bank; blood donor

8 **surgery,** surgical treatment, **operation,** surgical operation, surgical intervention, the knife (*nonformal*)

9 **hospital, clinic,** treatment centre; hospice, infirmary; nursing home, rest home, sanatorium

10 **health resort, spa, watering place,** baths; mineral spring; pump room, pump house

verbs

11 **treat, doctor,** minister to, care for; **diagnose;** nurse; **cure, remedy, heal;** bandage, plaster, strap, splint; bathe; massage, rub; operate on; purge; **operate;** transplant,

12 drug, dope (*nonformal*), dose; X-ray

13 **immunize, inoculate, vaccinate**

14 **undergo treatment, take medicine**

83 PSYCHOLOGY, PSYCHOTHERAPY

nouns

1 **psychology;** psychological school, psychological theory; **psychiatry,** psychological medicine; social psychiatry; **psychotherapy**

2 **psychoanalysis, analysis,** the couch (*nonformal*); dream analysis

3 **intelligence testing;** psychological screening; psychological profile; IQ test (*nonformal*); lie detector

4 **psychotherapist, therapist; psychiatrist; psychoanalyst, analyst**

5 (*personality type*) **introvert, extrovert;** phlegmatic

6 **mental disorder, emotional disorder; reaction;** emotional instability; nervous breakdown; **insanity, mental illness;** schizophrenia; **paranoia; depression; neurosis;** nervous disorder

7 **psychological stress, stress, frustration;** conflict; **trauma**

8 delirium, delusion, disorientation, hallucination

9 **trance,** daze, stupor; dream state, daydreaming; sleepwalking; hypnotic trance; **amnesia**

10 multiple personality, split personality; **schizophrenia; paranoia**

11 **fixation, arrested development;** father fixation, mother fixation; **regression**

12 **complex,** inferiority complex, superiority complex, persecution complex; castration complex

13 **alienation; escapism; withdrawal; fantasy,** fantasizing, wishful thinking; sexual fantasy; **rationalization**

14 **suppression, repression, inhibition,** resistance, restraint, censorship; block, psychological block; **suppressed desire**

15 **conditioning;** conditioned reflex, conditioned response

16 **adjustment; readjustment, rehabilitation**

17 **psyche, personality, self; mind, subconscious, unconscious,** subliminal; motive force, vital impulse; pleasure principle, life instinct, death instinct; **ego,** conscious self; conscience; collective unconscious

**18 unconscious memory; arche-
type; image, father image, etc**

19 surrogate, substitute; father surrogate, father figure, father image; mother surrogate, mother
figure

20 association; free association;
identification

adjectives

**21 psychological; psychiatric; psy-
chotic;** psychiatric

22 neurotic, disturbed, disordered;
hysteric(al),   hypochondriac;
stressed

23 introverted, introvert, **subjective;** extrovert

24 subconscious, unconscious; subliminal

84 FEELING

nouns

1 feeling, emotion, sentiment, affection, affections; **feelings, sensibility,** thin skin; emotional life;
sense; sensation; impression;
hunch; foreboding; **reaction, response,** gut reaction (*nonformal*); **instinct; tone**

2 passion, strong feeling, powerful
emotion; **fervour; ardour,
warmth, heat, fire,** verve, **fury,**
vehemence; gusto, relish, savour;
spirit, heart, soul; **zeal; excitement; ecstasy**

**3 heart, soul, spirit, breast, bos-
om,** heart's core, being, innermost being; bones

4 sensibility, sensitivity, delicacy,
tenderness

5 sympathy, fellow **feeling,**
warmth, **caring,** concern; response, echo, chord; **empathy,**
identification; involvement, sharing; pathos

6 tenderness, tender feeling, softness,   gentleness,   delicacy;
warmth, **fondness, weakness**

7 bad feeling, hard feelings; immediate dislike, personality conflict, bad blood, **hostility,** animosity

8 sentimentality, sentiment; nostalgia; romanticism; bleeding
heart; soap opera

**9 making scenes; dramatics; melo-
drama;** yellow journalism; emotional appeal, human interest,
love interest

verbs

10 feel; feel deeply; **experience;
sense, perceive**

11 respond, react, be moved, be inspired, echo; care about, sympathize with, identify with, be involved, share; love; hate

**12 affect, touch, move, stir; melt,
soften; penetrate,** pierce; smart,
sting

13 impress, affect, strike, hit, rock;
sink in (*nonformal*), strike home;
tell, impress forcibly

14 impress upon; stamp, stamp on,
etch, engrave, engrave on

adjectives

15 emotional, emotive, **feeling;** of
soul, of heart, of feeling, of sentiment; gut (*nonformal*); demonstrative

**16 fervent,   passionate,   impas-
sioned,** intense, **ardent; hearty,
cordial,** enthusiastic, exuberant,
vigorous; keen, breathless, **excited; lively;** zealous; **warm, burn-**

ing, heated, hot, volcanic, red-hot, fiery, flaming, glowing, ablaze, on fire, boiling over, steaming, steamy; delirious, feverish, flushed; intoxicated, drunk

17 emotive, hysterical, sensational, melodramatic, theatrical, histrionic, dramatic

18 sensitive, sensible, delicate; responsive, sympathetic, receptive; susceptible, impressionable; tender, soft

19 sentimental, soft, cloying; romantic; nostalgic

20 affecting, touching, moving, emotive, pathetic

21 affected, moved, touched, impressed; seized with, imbued with, devoured by, obsessed; stricken, racked, torn, agonized, tortured; worked up, excited

22 heartfelt; deep, profound; indelible; pervasive, pervading, absorbing; penetrating, piercing; poignant, keen, sharp, acute

adverbs

23 emotionally; movingly, with feeling; sentimentally

24 fervently, passionately, intensely, ardently; keenly, breathlessly, excitedly; warmly, heatedly; heartily, cordially; enthusiastically, vigorously; kindly

85 LACK OF FEELING

nouns

1 unfeeling, lack of feeling; objectivity; coldness, coolness, chill; cold heart, cold blood; cold fish; withdrawal; straight face *and*

poker face (*both nonformal*), dead pan (*nonformal*); dullness

2 unconsciousness, oblivion

3 callousness, insensitivity; coarseness, hardness, heart of stone

4 apathy, indifference, disinterest; aloofness, detachment; lethargy, dullness; stupor; sloth; resignation, stoicism

verbs

5 not be affected by, remain unmoved, not turn a hair, not care less; have a heart of stone

6 callous, harden; brutalize

7 dull, blunt

8 numb, deaden, stun, anaesthetize

adjectives

9 unfeeling, unemotional; dispassionate, objective; heartless, cold-blooded; cold, cool, frigid; unsympathetic; impassive, immovable; dull, blunt

10 unconscious, unaware, oblivious, blind to, deaf to, dead to

11 unaffected, unmoved, untouched unruffled

12 callous, insensitive; thick-skinned; hard, hardened, coarsened, brutalized, as hard as nails

13 apathetic, indifferent, unconcerned, uncaring, disinterested, uninterested; withdrawn, aloof, detached; stoic, phlegmatic; nonchalant, listless, burned-out; lethargic, dull, sluggish, in a stupor, numb; resigned

adverbs

14 with a straight *or* poker face (*nonformal*), deadpan (*nonformal*); **dispassionately; heartlessly,** coldly, **in cold blood**

15 indifferently, heartlessly

86 PLEASURE

nouns

1 pleasure, enjoyment; well-being, contentment; ease, comfort; **gratification, satisfaction; self-indulgence; luxury; kicks** (*nonformal*), **fun,** entertainment; amusement; creature comforts

2 happiness, delight, joy; cheer, cheerfulness; **exhilaration, exuberance; high spirits, glee; gaiety; rapture,** elation, **ecstasy, bliss;** paradise, heaven, seventh heaven, cloud nine

3 treat; feast; festivity, celebration, revelry

4 pleasure principle, hedonism

verbs

5 please, pleasure, give pleasure, be to one's liking, take one's fancy; **warm the cockles of one's heart; suit,** suit one down to the ground

6 (*nonformal terms*) be just the ticket, be just what the doctor ordered

7 gratify, satisfy; appease, allay; regale, feed, feast

8 make happy, cheer

9 delight, tickle, thrill, **enthral,** fascinate, captivate, bewitch, **charm**

10 (*nonformal terms*) **give one a kick;** knock out, knock off one's feet, thrill to pieces, tickle

11 be pleased, feel happy, feel good, smile, laugh; **delight,** joy, take great satisfaction; be in heaven *or* seventh heaven, be on cloud nine

12 enjoy, be pleased with, derive pleasure from, take delight *or* pleasure in, get a kick out of (*nonformal*); **like, love,** adore (*nonformal*); **delight in; relish,** appreciate

13 enjoy oneself, have a good time, party, live it up (*nonformal*)

adjectives

14 pleased, delighted, glad, thrilled; tickled; euphoric, exhilarated; **gratified, satisfied;** taken with; pleased as Punch, in clover

15 happy, glad, joyful; radiant, beaming; laughing, smiling; **cheerful; gay; blissful; happy as a** sandboy

16 overjoyed, on top of the world; **rapturous, enchanted; carried away,** beside oneself; **ecstatic, in seventh heaven, on cloud nine** (*nonformal*); **elated,** exalted, jubilant

17 fun-loving, hedonistic

adverbs

18 happily, gladly, joyfully, delightedly

19 for fun

87 UNPLEASURE

nouns

1 lack of pleasure, discontent, displeasure, dissatisfaction, **discomfort; disquiet, uneasiness, anxiety, unhappiness;** anguish, dread; **dullness, boredom,** tedium; emptiness

2 **annoyance,** exasperation, **nuisance, bother, trouble, problem,** pain, pain in the neck (*nonformal*); bore, crashing bore (*nonformal*); **worry,** headache; persecution, hounding

3 **irritation, salt in the wound, irritant**

4 **chagrin, distress; embarrassment,** egg on one's face (*nonformal*), **humiliation, shame,** red face

5 **pain, distress, grief,** stress, suffering; wound, injury; shock, blow

6 **despair,** bitterness, misery, anguish, agony, woe; **melancholy, depression, sadness, grief,** despondency, desolation

7 **torment, torture; persecution,** martyrdom; purgatory, hell, hell on earth; nightmare, horror

8 **affliction, curse, woe,** distress, grievance, **sorrow; trouble, care;** burden, cross to bear, albatross around one's neck, thorn in the side

9 **trial,** trials and tribulations, ordeal

10 **tormentor,** torment; **nuisance, pest,** pain, pain in the neck (*nonformal*); nag, **tease, bully**

11 **sufferer,** victim, martyr; **wretch, poor devil** (*nonformal*)

verbs

12 **give no pleasure** *or* **joy, disquiet; bore,** be tedious, cheese off (*nonformal*)

13 **annoy, irk, vex, provoke, aggravate,** make a nuisance of oneself,

exasperate, try one's patience; **put one's back up, get one's goat,** brown off (*nonformal*); **torment, bother, harass,** drive up the wall (*nonformal*), **hound,** dog, nag, **persecute; rub it in** (*nonformal*), badger, bait, heckle; **bug** (*nonformal*), **pester, tease, needle,** pick on (*nonformal*); **plague,** beset

14 **irritate, aggravate,** exacerbate, worsen, rub salt in the wound, touch a raw nerve; provoke, gall, grate; **get on one's nerves, rub one up the wrong way**

15 **embarrass, disconcert, upset,** cast down, mortify

16 **distress, afflict, trouble,** burden, bother, disturb, disquiet, discomfort, agitate, upset

17 **pain, grieve; hurt, wound,** bruise, **hurt one's feelings**

18 **punish, torture, torment,** crucify, martyr

19 **suffer, hurt, ache; have a bad time of it, go through hell**

adjectives

20 **joyless, cheerless, depressed, grim; sad, unhappy** unfulfilled; **bored;** anguished, anxious, uneasy; **repelled,** revolted, **disgusted,** sickened

21 **annoyed, irritated;** bothered, troubled, disturbed, irked, vexed, aggravated, exasperated; resentful, angry

22 **distressed,** afflicted, beleaguered; troubled, bothered, disturbed, perturbed

23 **pained, grieved,** aggrieved; **wounded, hurt,** injured, aching, bruised, cut

24 **tormented, plagued, harassed,** dogged, **hounded, persecuted, heckled,** badgered, baited, **pestered, teased, needled, picked on** (*nonformal*)

25 **tortured,** savaged, crucified

26 **wretched, miserable,** woeful, **crushed, stricken; desolate, disconsolate, suicidal**

adverbs

27 to one's displeasure, to one's disgust

88 PLEASANTNESS

nouns

1 **pleasure, bliss,** sweetness; rapport, compatibility

2 loveliness **charm,** grace, **attractiveness, appeal**

3 **cheerfulness,** brightness; sunny side, bright side

verbs

4 make pleasant, brighten, sweeten

adjectives

5 **pleasant, pleasing, pleasurable; enjoyable, likable, desirable; agreeable,** harmonious, compatible; **gratifying,** satisfying, rewarding; genial, congenial, cordial, affable, amiable, amicable; good, nice, fine

6 delightful, exquisite, lovely; **charming, attractive,** endearing, engaging, appealing, sexy (*nonformal*), **enchanting,** bewitching, enthralling, intriguing, fascinating; captivating, irresistible; inviting, tempting, tantalizing; voluptuous, sensuous

7 (*nonformal terms*) **fun, sexy**

8 **blissful, divine, sublime, heavenly;** out of this world

9 **delectable, delicious,** luscious; tasty, juicy, succulent

10 **bright, sunny,** fair, mild

adverbs

11 **pleasantly,** pleasingly, pleasurably; genially, cordially, amiably, amicably, graciously, kindly, cheerfully

12 **delightfully, exquisitely, charmingly;** invitingly, sensuously

89 UNPLEASANTNESS

nouns

1 displeasure, unpleasantness; unattractiveness, ugliness

2 coarseness, obscenity, crudeness

3 atrocity, awfulness

4 **harshness,** agony, torture, torment

5 **distress, grief,** pain; harshness, bitterness; **woe, sadness,** pathos; **depression,** bleakness, desolation

6 **humiliation, embarrassment, egg on one's face** (*nonformal*)

7 annoyance, exasperation

8 **harshness, heaviness**

9 **intolerability,** insufferableness

verbs

10 **be unpleasant, displease,** be disagreeable

11 **offend,** give offence, **repel, revolt, disgust,** sicken, turn the stomach; **horrify, appal,** shock

12 **agonize, torture, torment**

13 **mortify,** humiliate, embarrass, disconcert

14 **distress, dismay**; grieve, mourn, lament

15 **vex, irk, annoy, aggravate**, exasperate, provoke, plague, harass, bother, hassle

16 **oppress, burden**; **tire, exhaust**, weary, wear out; **haunt, obsess**

adjectives

17 **unpleasant, displeasing, disagreeable**; abrasive, wounding, hostile, unfriendly; **undesirable**, unattractive; tacky (*nonformal*); unwelcome, thankless; **distasteful**, unsavoury; sour, **bitter**

18 **offensive, objectionable, odious, repulsive**, repellent, **repugnant, revolting**; disgusting, sickening; vile, foul, **nasty**, nauseating; stinking, fetid, noxious; coarse, crude, obscene; **obnoxious**, abhorrent, hateful, abominable, heinous, **contemptible, despicable**, detestable, beneath contempt, **base**

19 **horrid, horrible**, horrific, horrendous; **dreadful, atrocious, terrible**, awful; tragic; appalling, shocking

20 **distressing**, dismaying; afflicting, **painful, sore**

21 **mortifying**, humiliating, **embarrassing**

22 **annoying, irritating**, galling, provoking, **aggravating, exasperating**; irksome, tiresome; **troublesome**, troubling, disturbing

23 **agonizing, excruciating, harrowing, heartbreaking**

24 **oppressive, crushing**, trying, onerous; **harsh**, wearing, wearying, exhausting

25 **insufferable, intolerable, unbearable, more than flesh and blood can bear**

adverbs

26 **unpleasantly**; offensively, disgustingly

27 **horribly, dreadfully, terribly**, hideously; **tragically; appallingly; painfully**, sorely, **grievously**, ruefully, woefully, sadly, pathetically

90 DISLIKE

nouns

1 **dislike, distaste**; disfavour, disinclination; **displeasure, disapproval**

2 **hostility**, antagonism, **enmity**; hatred, hate; **aversion**, repulsion, antipathy; **horror; disgust, loathing**; nausea, shuddering, cold sweat

verbs

3 **dislike**, disfavour, be no love lost between, **not care for**, have no time for, not give the time of day to (*nonformal*), **disapprove of**; not stomach, not be one's cup of tea; be hostile to, have it in for (*nonformal*); **hate, abhor, detest, loathe**

4 **feel disgust**, be nauseated, choke on; gag, retch, vomit

5 **shudder at, shrink from**, recoil; grimace, turn up one's nose, raise one's eyebrows, take a dim view of, disapprove of

6 **repel, disgust; leave a bad taste in one's mouth**

adjectives

7 **distasteful, displeasing, unpleasant; not to one's taste,** not one's cup of tea; **abhorrent, odious**

8 **averse, allergic, disaffected, disenchanted, disinclined,** put off (*nonformal*); **disapproving; unfriendly, hostile**

9 **disliked,** undervalued, despised; **unpopular, out of favour,** misunderstood

10 **unloved,** loveless; **forsaken, rejected,** spurned

11 **unwanted, unwelcome,** uninvited, uncalled-for

91 DESIRE

nouns

1 **desire, wish, want, need, heart's desire; urge, drive;** wish-fulfilment, fantasy; **passion, ardour,** sexual desire

2 **liking, love, fondness, passion;** infatuation, crush; **affection; relish, taste**

3 **inclination, fancy, favour, preference,** leaning, bias, **affinity; mutual attraction; sympathy,** fascination

4 **nostalgia;** wishful thinking; longing, daydreaming

5 **yearning, yen** (*nonformal*); **longing,** hankering, pining; **nostalgia,** homesickness

6 **craving, coveting, lust; hunger, thirst, appetite;** sexual desire

7 **appetite,** stomach, taste; **hunger;** eyes bigger than one's stomach, empty stomach; **thirst,** drought

(*nonformal*), dryness; sweet tooth (*nonformal*)

8 **greed,** avarice, lust; **gluttony**

9 **aspiration, dream, ideals; idealism**

10 **ambition; social climbing; opportunism; desire,** heart's desire, **wish; hope;** catch, prize, trophy; **forbidden fruit, temptation**

11 **fancier, collector; addict, freak** (*nonformal*), devotee; **candidate; lover,** suitor

12 **desirability;** acceptability; **attractiveness,** attraction, magnetism, **appeal**

verbs

13 **desire, wish,** lust after, die for, give one's right arm for (*both nonformal*); **want; like,** have a taste for, fancy, take a fancy to, have designs on; **love, lust; prefer, favour**

14 **want to, wish to, like to,** love to, choose to

15 **wish for, hope for, yearn for,** have a yen for, lust for, **long for, pine for,** be dying for, thirst for; spoil for (*nonformal*)

16 **want with all one's heart, have one's heart set on**

17 **crave, covet, hunger after,** lust after, **hanker for** or **after** (*nonformal*); be consumed with desire

18 **hunger,** hunger for, feel hungry; starve (*nonformal*), be ravenous; **have a good appetite; thirst,** thirst for

19 **aspire, be ambitious;** aspire to; aim high, reach for the sky

adjectives

20 desiring, wanting, wishing, needing, hoping; dying to (*nonformal*); tempted; **eager;** lascivious, **lustful**

21 keen on, set on (*nonformal*); fond of, partial to; dying for, spoiling for (*nonformal*); mad on, crazy for (*both nonformal*)

22 wistful, wishful; **longing, yearning,** hankering (*nonformal*), pining

23 craving, coveting; hungry, thirsty; mad with lust, consumed with desire

24 hungry; empty (*nonformal*); **ravenous,** voracious; **starved, famished, starving** (*nonformal*); fasting

25 thirsty, dry, parched

26 greedy, avaricious, voracious, rapacious, **grasping,** mercenary; ravenous, devouring; **miserly,** covetous; omnivorous; insatiable

27 aspiring, ambitious; on the make (*nonformal*)

28 desired, wanted, coveted; **in demand, popular**

29 desirable, enviable, worth having; **likable, pleasing; agreeable,** acceptable; **attractive, sexy** (*nonformal*), seductive, provocative; appetizing, tempting; **lovable, adorable**

adverbs

30 wistfully, longingly

31 greedily, avidly

92 EAGERNESS

nouns

1 eagerness, enthusiasm, readiness, promptness, alacrity; **appetite; anxiety; zest,** gusto, verve, **life,** vitality, spirit, animation; impatience; keen interest, fascination

2 zeal, ardour, fervour, **spirit,** warmth, **passion,** intensity, **abandon; devotion, dedication, commitment;** seriousness, sincerity; loyalty, faith, fidelity

3 infatuation; fanaticism

4 enthusiast, zealot; addict, collector; **fanatic,** devotee, fancier, admirer; **follower, disciple**

5 (*nonformal terms*) **fan, buff, freak,** nut, great one for

verbs

6 jump at, fall all over oneself, get excited about; go to great lengths, bend over backwards

7 be enthusiastic, rave, enthuse, make a fuss over, rave about, gush about

adjectives

8 eager, anxious; avid, keen, forward, prompt, ready and willing; **lively,** full of life, vivacious, spirited, **animated**

9 zealous, ardent, fervent, spirited, intense, hearty, vehement, abandoned, **passionate,** impassioned, **warm,** heated, hot; **devout, devoted;** dedicated, committed; **earnest,** sincere, **serious;** loyal, faithful

10 enthusiastic, enthused, glowing, full of enthusiasm; enthusiastic about, infatuated with

11 (*nonformal terms*) **wild about,
crazy about, mad about,** nuts
about, hot for, steamed up
about, keen on

12 hectic, frenetic, furious, **frenzied,**
frantic, **wild,** hysterical, delirious,
fanatical

adverbs

13 eagerly, anxiously; **impatiently,**
breathlessly; **avidly,** readily; **enthusiastically,** with enthusiasm

14 ardently, fervently, vehemently,
passionately, intently, intensely;
earnestly, sincerely, seriously

93 INDIFFERENCE

nouns

1 **indifference, coolness,** coldness,
chill

2 **disinterest, detachment;** disregard, insensitivity; carelessness,
negligence, nonchalance, casualness; apathy, sloth

3 lack of appetite

verbs

4 **not care, not mind, not give a
damn,** not care less *or* two hoots
(*nonformal*), care nothing for;
take no interest in, have no desire for, have no taste for; be
half-hearted

5 **not matter to,** be all one to, take
it or leave it; make no difference

adjectives

6 **indifferent,** perfunctory; **cool,
cold; tepid, lukewarm;** neither
one thing nor the other, neither
fish nor fowl

7 **unconcerned, uninterested,** disinterested, dispassionate; careless, regardless, mindless, heed-

less, inattentive; reckless, negligent; **nonchalant,** casual; **listless,** sluggish; numb, **apathetic**

8 **loveless, passionless**

adverbs

9 **indifferently,** with indifference;
coolly, coldly

10 dispassionately, disinterestedly;
carelessly, recklessly, negligently; nonchalantly, **casually**

94 HATE

nouns

1 **hate, hatred; dislike; aversion,**
antipathy, **loathing;** spite, malice, malevolence; race hatred,
racism, xenophobia, **bigotry;**
scorn, despising, **contempt**

2 **enmity,** bitterness, **animosity**

3 aversion, antipathy, hate; phobia,
pet hate

4 **misanthrope, misogynist;** xenophobe, **racist,** bigot

verbs

5 **hate, detest,** loathe, abhor, not
stand the sight of, not stomach;
scorn, **despise**

6 **dislike,** have it in for (*nonformal*)

adjectives

7 **hating, abhorrent,** loathing, despising; averse to, disgusted;
scornful, **contemptuous**

8 **hateful,** detestable

95 LOVE

nouns

1 **love, affection, attachment, devotion, fondness,** like, **liking,**

fancy; **passion, ardour;** sexual love, sex; desire, yearning; charity, brotherly love; spiritual love, platonic love; **adoration,** worship, hero worship; **regard,** admiration

2 **affection, affectionateness; romantic love; ecstasy, rapture**

3 **infatuation, crush; puppy love** (*nonformal*); love at first sight

4 parental love, maternal love, paternal love

5 **love affair, affair, romance;** flirtation, hanky-panky; triangle, eternal triangle; adultery, infidelity

6 **sweetness, loveliness; attractiveness, desirability; charm, appeal**

7 Love, Eros

8 Cupid

9 **sweetheart,** loved one, **love,** beloved, **darling, dear,** light of one's life

10 **honey, baby, sugar**

11 **lover, admirer;** suitor, wooer; conquest, catch; escort, companion, **date**

12 swain, beau, **boyfriend; sugar daddy** (*nonformal*); Romeo, Prince Charming

13 lady, mistress, ladyfriend

14 (*nonformal terms*) **doll, angel,** baby, **girl, girlfriend;** old lady

15 **favourite, darling;** idol, apple of one's eye

16 betrothed, future, intended

17 **loving couple,** soul mates; Romeo and Juliet

verbs

18 **love, be fond of,** be in love with, **care for, like, fancy,** dote on, have a soft spot for, have a weakness for

19 (*nonformal terms*) have an eye for, only have eyes for, have a crush on, carry a torch for

20 **cherish, hold dear,** hold in one's affections, think the world of, treasure; **admire, regard,** esteem, revere; **adore, idolize,** worship, think the world of

21 **fall in love, lose one's heart;** take to, **take a fancy to,** take a shine to *and* fall for (*both nonformal*), become attached to; fall head over heels in love, be swept off one's feet

22 **endear;** win one's heart, take the fancy of; **charm, fascinate,** attract, allure, captivate, bewitch, carry away, sweep off one's feet, turn one's head; **seduce,** tempt

adjectives

23 **beloved, loved, dear, darling,** precious; adored, admired, revered; cherished, prized, treasured

24 **endearing, lovable, likable, adorable, lovely,** sweet, winning; **charming**

25 **amorous,** erotic; **sexual; passionate,** impassioned; lascivious

26 **loving,** fond, adoring, devoted, affectionate, **romantic,** sentimental, **tender;** conjugal, faithful; parental, paternal, maternal, filial

27 **charmed, fascinated, captivated,** bewitched, enchanted; **infatuated**

28 in love, head over heels in love

29 fond of, partial to, **in love with,** attached to, devoted to, taken with

30 (*nonformal terms*) **crazy about,** mad about

adverbs

31 lovingly, fondly, affectionately, tenderly, dearly

96 EXCITEMENT

nouns

1 excitement, emotion, arousal, stimulation, exhilaration

2 thrill, sensation, tingle; quiver, shiver, shudder

3 (*nonformal terms*) **kick, charge,** blast, hit, rush

4 agitation, ferment, turmoil, tumult, uproar, **commotion,** disturbance

5 trepidation; disquiet, unrest, restlessness; quivering, quavering, quaking, shaking, trembling; quiver, shiver, shudder

6 dither, fluster, fret, fuss, bother, flap

7 fever pitch, fever, heat, fire; sexual excitement, rut

8 ecstasy, rapture; intoxication, abandon; **passion, rage; frenzy,** orgy, orgasm; madness, craze, **delirium,** hysteria

9 outburst, outbreak, blaze, **explosion,** eruption; convulsion, spasm, seizure, fit, paroxysm

10 excitability, explosiveness; irritability, touchiness, sensitivity

11 excitement, arousal; stimulation, exhilaration, animation; **provocation, irritation, agitation, incitement**

verbs

12 excite, arouse, stir up, cause a stir; work up into a lather (*nonformal*); turn on (*nonformal*); awake, waken; **kindle,** light up, **fire;** fan the flames, add fuel to the fire; raise to a fever pitch, bring to the boil; **annoy,** incense, incite, enrage, infuriate

13 stimulate, whet, animate; exhilarate; galvanize, renew, give new life to, liven up, jazz up (*nonformal*)

14 agitate, disturb, trouble, disquiet, shake up, shock, upset, rock, rattle, disconcert

15 thrill, tickle, give one a kick (*nonformal*); fascinate, titillate

16 be excitable, excite easily; explode, flare up, go into hysterics, have a tantrum; rage, rave, rant; be angry, smoulder

17 (*nonformal terms*) **work oneself up,** have a short fuse, get hot under the collar; blow up, **blow one's top, flip one's lid, fly off the handle, hit the ceiling,** go bananas, lose one's cool

18 (*be excited*) **thrill,** tingle, glow; thrill to; tremble, shiver, quiver, flutter, **shake**

19 whiten, blanch, turn pale; darken, look black; **flush, blush, turn red**

adjectives

20 excited, impassioned; **thrilled,** tingling, exhilarated, high (*nonformal*); **moved,** aroused, turned on (*nonformal*), **worked up, carried away**

21 all of a flutter, in a fluster, in a sweat (*nonformal*), in a lather

22 **heated, passionate, hot,** burning; feverish, hectic, flushed; sexually excited, in rut; het up (*nonformal*), hot under the collar (*nonformal*); seething, boiling

23 **agitated,** perturbed, **disturbed, troubled, upset,** unsettled, flustered, **shaken**

24 **turbulent,** tempestuous, boisterous

25 **frenzied, frantic; ecstatic,** intoxicated; raging, raving, ranting; **wild, violent,** fierce, ferocious, **furious, mad,** rabid, demonic, possessed; **carried away,** beside oneself, hysterical

26 **overcome,** overwhelmed, overpowered

27 **restless,** restive, **uneasy,** unsettled, tense; **fidgety,** fussy

28 **excitable, emotional, highspirited; emotionally unstable,** volatile; **irritable, edgy, nervous,** sensitive, highly strung

29 **passionate, fiery; violent,** furious, fierce, **wild;** tempestuous, impetuous

30 **exciting, thrilling,** stirring, moving, breathtaking; disturbing, upsetting, unsettling; **impressive,** striking; **provocative,** tantalizing; **stimulating, exhilarating,** heady, intoxicating; **overwhelming,** overpowering

31 penetrating, **piercing,** stabbing, cutting, stinging; biting, keen, brisk, sharp

32 **sensational, lurid, melodramatic**

adverbs

33 **excitedly,** agitatedly; with heart in mouth

34 **heatedly, passionately,** fervently

35 **frantically,** furiously, fiercely, madly

36 **excitingly, thrillingly,** movingly

97 INEXCITABILITY

nouns

1 **stoicism;** even temper; **patience;** imperturbability; steadiness, evenness

2 **composure,** countenance; **calm, calmness,** serenity, tranquility, peace of mind; resignation, acceptance, fatalism; **coolness,** cool (*nonformal*)

3 **equanimity,** equilibrium, balance; level head; **poise,** aplomb, **self-control,** restraint, **presence of mind;** confidence, assurance, **self-confidence**

4 **seriousness,** gravity, solemnity, temperance, moderation

5 **nonchalance,** casualness; **indifference,** lack of concern

verbs

6 **not turn a hair,** keep one's cool (*nonformal*); calm, **set one's mind at ease** *or* rest

7 **compose oneself,** restrain oneself, get a grip on oneself (*nonformal*), regain one's composure; **calm down,** cool it (*nonformal*); relax, unwind, take it easy

8 (*control one's feelings*) **suppress,** repress, smother, stifle, hold back, inhibit

9 **keep cool,** keep one's cool (*nonformal*), **keep calm,** keep one's

head, keep one's shirt on (*nonformal*), not turn a hair; take things as they come, roll with the punches (*nonformal*); keep a stiff upper lip

adjectives

10 unflappable; dispassionate, objective; stoic, stoical; impassive, stolid

11 undisturbed, untroubled, unruffled

12 calm, placid, quiet, tranquil, serene, peaceful; **cool**, cool as a cucumber (*nonformal*)

13 composed, collected; poised, together (*nonformal*), balanced; **confident, assured, self-confident, self-assured**

14 sedate, staid, **sober, serious**, grave, solemn; temperate, moderate

15 nonchalant, **indifferent**, unconcerned; casual, **relaxed, easygoing**

adverbs

16 dispassionately, objectively; stoically; **calmly, quietly**, serenely, coolly

17 sedately, soberly, seriously

18 nonchalantly, casually

98 CONTENTMENT

nouns

1 **contentment, content; satisfaction**, fulfilment; ease, peace of mind; **comfort**, quality of life; happiness, well-being, euphoria; **acceptance**, resignation

2 **complacency, smugness**, self-satisfaction

3 adequacy, sufficiency; acceptability, viability

verbs

4 **content, satisfy**, gratify; put at ease, **set one's mind at rest**

5 **be content**, rest easy; accept one's lot, not complain, not worry, content oneself with; settle for less, cut one's losses

6 **be satisfactory, do, suffice**; suit, suit one down to the ground

adjectives

7 **content, contented, satisfied; pleased**; at ease; composed; **comfortable**; euphoric; carefree, without care; resigned, reconciled

8 **untroubled, undisturbed, unperturbed**

9 **well-pleased, well-satisfied**

10 **complacent, smug**, self-satisfied

11 **satisfactory, satisfying; sufficient, adequate, enough, ample**

12 **acceptable, agreeable**, viable; OK *and* **okay, alright** (*all nonformal*); **passable**, good enough

99 DISCONTENT

nouns

1 **discontent, dissatisfaction; resentment, envy; restlessness**, unease; disappointment; unhappiness, ill humour

2 **inadequacy, insufficiency**

3 malcontent, grumbler; reactionary; rebel

4 **moaning Minnie**, sourpuss, grump

verbs

5 **displease,** not fit the bill, disappoint, leave a lot to be desired

6 (*nonformal terms*) **moan,** beef, **bitch,** gripe

adjectives

7 discontented, **dissatisfied, disgruntled,** displeased, **let down, disappointed; resentful, envious; restless,** restive, uneasy; **complaining,** sour, grumbling, griping, petulant, sulky, querulous

8 (*nonformal terms*) **grouchy,** griping, bitching

9 **unsatisfactory,** displeasing; disappointing, disheartening; **inadequate, insufficient**

10 **unacceptable,** unsuitable, undesirable, intolerable, **objectionable,** impossible, untenable, indefensible

adverbs

11 **unsatisfactorily, inadequately, unsuitably**

100 CHEERFULNESS

nouns

1 **cheerfulness, cheer; happiness,** geniality; **brightness, radiance;** optimism

2 **good humour, high spirits,** exhilaration

3 **chirpiness, breeziness**

4 gaiety, **vivacity, vitality,** life, animation, spirit, high spirits, zest, verve, gusto, **exuberance**

5 **merriment, hilarity; joy,** glee; frivolity, mirth, **amusement, fun,** laughter

verbs

6 exude cheerfulness, **beam,** glow, sparkle; **sing,** lilt, whistle; walk on air, dance, skip, frolic, romp; **smile, laugh**

7 **cheer,** gladden; encourage, **hearten; inspire,** buoy up, boost; **exhilarate,** animate, liven; **rejoice,** do the heart good

8 **elate,** lift

9 **cheer up, take heart; brighten up,** perk up; snap out of it (*nonformal*); revive

10 bear up, keep one's chin up, keep a stiff upper lip, grin and bear it

adjectives

11 **cheerful, cheery;** in high spirits, exalted, elated, euphoric, **high** (*nonformal*), **glad, happy,** happy as a sandboy, on top of the world; **pleasant, genial; bright, sunny,** radiant, sparkling, beaming, smiling, laughing; optimistic, hopeful

12 **jaunty, carefree,** perky, breezy

13 **chirpy,** chipper (*both nonformal*)

14 **spirited,** sprightly, **lively,** animated, vivacious, exuberant, full of beans (*nonformal*); **playful,** kittenish

15 **merry, hilarious, joyful,** rejoicing; **jolly,** jovial, jocular

16 **cheering, encouraging, heartening; exhilarating,** enlivening, invigorating; **cheerful, cheery, glad, joyful**

adverbs

17 **cheerfully,** cheerily; **pleasantly,** genially, blithely; **gladly, happily, joyfully;** optimistically, hopefully

18 **gaily, heartily,** with zest, with verve, with gusto

19 **merrily,** gleefully

101 ILL HUMOUR

nouns

1 **ill humour, bad temper, ill nature; bile, gall; anger; discontent**

2 **irritability,** quick temper, short fuse (*nonformal*)

3 **grumpiness meanness**

4 **temper, quick temper,** hotheadedness

5 **touchiness,** sensitivity, thin skin

6 **petulance,** peevishness

7 **belligerence**

8 **moodiness;** dejection, **melancholy**

9 **scowl, frown,** lower, **glower, pout,** grimace; sullen looks, black looks, **long face**

10 **sulks,** dumps, **blues**

11 (*ill-humoured person*) grump, **bear with a sore head**

12 **bitch** (*nonformal*), shrew, vixen, **witch, she-devil; battle-axe,** scold

verbs

13 **have a temper, have a short fuse** (*nonformal*); be cross, get out on the wrong side of the bed

14 **sulk, mope**

15 look sullen, **frown, scowl,** lower, **glower, pout,** grimace

16 **sour,** exacerbate, **embitter**

adjectives

17 **out of humour, out of sorts, in a bad mood; abrasive,** caustic

18 **bad-tempered,** ill-natured

19 **irritable, irascible; cross,** cranky; spiteful, churlish; **gruff,** growling; perverse, bellicose

20 **crabby, grumpy, cantankerous,** shirty

21 **touchy,** ticklish, prickly, quick to take offence, **sensitive,** hypersensitive, highly strung, temperamental

22 **peevish, petulant,** querulous, fretful, resentful

23 **sour,** bilious, jaundiced; **bitter,** embittered

24 **sullen,** sulky, moody, surly; **morose, dour, glum,** grim; glowering, lowering, **scowling, frowning;** dark, black; dejected, **melancholy**

25 **passionate,** hot, fiery, **short-tempered;** hasty, quick, explosive

26 **contentious, quarrelsome, argumentative; controversial; belligerent, bellicose**

adverbs

27 irritably, testily

28 peevishly, petulantly

29 grumpily

30 **sullenly, moodily,** sulkily; **morosely,** glumly, grimly

102 SOLEMNITY

nouns

1 **solemnity, dignity, gravitas,** gravity, seriousness, **sobriety;** seriousness, earnestness

verbs

2 **honour the occasion, keep a straight face;** wipe the smile off one's face

adjectives

3 **solemn, dignified, sober, grave, sombre;** sedate, staid; serious, earnest

adverbs

4 **solemnly, soberly, gravely; sedately,** decorously; with dignity, **seriously, earnestly,** thoughtfully

103 SADNESS

nouns

1 **sadness;** weight; heavy heart; pathos, bathos

2 **unhappiness; displeasure,** discontent; **misery,** joylessness

3 **dejection, depression,** oppression; **despondency, hopelessness, despair, pessimism;** world-weariness

4 **hypochondria,** morbid anxiety

5 **melancholy; nostalgia,** homesickness

6 **blues, dumps** (*nonformal*), **doldrums**

7 **gloom,** darkness, **bleakness;** gravity, solemnity

8 **glumness,** sulkiness

9 **heartache, broken heart**

10 **sorrow, grief,** care, woe; anguish, misery, agony

11 **mournfulness, tearfulness**

12 **desolation**

13 moaning Minnie, mope; depressive, misery

14 **killjoy, spoilsport, wet blanket,** party pooper

verbs

15 hang one's head, pull *or* make a long face, have the blues (*nonformal*)

16 **lose heart, despair,** lose the will to live; **droop,** sink, languish; hit rock bottom

17 **grieve, sorrow; weep; mourn;** pine, pine away; **brood over, mope, fret;** break one's heart over; **agonize,** ache, bleed

18 **sadden,** darken, weigh heavy upon; **depress, oppress, crush, cast down,** lower, lower the spirits, get one down (*nonformal*), take the wind out of one's sails, **discourage;** damp, dampen; dash, knock down, beat down

19 **oppress, grieve, sorrow;** bring to tears; afflict, torment; **break one's heart;** prostrate, break down, crush, bear down; inundate, overwhelm

adjectives

20 **sad,** saddened; oppressed, weighed down, burdened with sorrow

21 **unhappy,** cheerless, joyless; humourless, mirthless; **wretched, miserable**

22 **dejected, depressed,** down, downcast, subdued; discouraged, **disheartened,** dispirited; down in the mouth, down in the dumps (*both nonformal*); **despondent,** despairing, suicidal

23 **melancholy, blue** (*nonformal*); **nostalgic,** homesick

24 **gloomy, dismal, bleak, grim;** sombre, solemn, grave

25 **glum, morose,** sullen; sulky, crestfallen; **moody, brooding**

26 **sorrowful, mournful,** rueful, woeful, doleful, plaintive; **anguished, tearful**

27 sorrow-stricken; grief-stricken, inconsolable

28 disconsolate, forlorn

29 overcome, crushed, cut up (*nonformal*); heartbroken, brokenhearted

30 depressing, oppressive; discouraging, disheartening

adverbs

31 sadly, gloomily, bleakly, grimly, solemnly, gravely

32 unhappily, cheerlessly

33 dejectedly, despondently; disconsolately, forlornly

34 wistfully, nostalgically

35 glumly, morosely; sullenly moodily

36 mournfully, ruefully, woefully, grievously, tearfully

104 REGRET

nouns

1 regret, regrets; remorse, shame, contrition; sorrow, grief; apologies

2 qualms, scruples, pangs of conscience

3 self-loathing; hair shirt; soul-searching

4 repentance, change of heart; apology; penance

5 penitent, confessor

verbs

6 regret, deplore, be sorry for; rue bemoan; kick oneself (*nonformal*), bite one's tongue; blame oneself, wear a hair shirt

7 repent, think better of; plead guilty, humble oneself, apologize, beg forgiveness

adjectives

8 regretful, full of remorse, ashamed, sorry, rueful, unhappy about

9 penitent, contrite, abject, humble, sheepish, apologetic

10 regrettable, much to be regretted; deplorable

adverbs

11 regretfully, ruefully, unhappily

12 humbly, sheepishly, abjectly, apologetically

105 UNREGRETFULNESS

nouns

1 remorselessness, shamelessness

2 heart of stone, callousness; hardness of heart; insolence, defiance

verbs

3 harden one's heart, steel oneself; have no regrets; have no shame

adjectives

4 remorseless, shameless, unashamed

5 unrepentant; untouched, callous; hard, hardened; insolent, defiant

106 LAMENTATION

nouns

1 lamenting, mourning, grieving, sorrow

2 weeping, sobbing, crying, greet (*Scots*); whimpering, snivelling; tears, flood of tears

3 lament, plaint; moan, groan;

whine, whimper; sob, cry; **howl**, bawl

4 **complaint**, **grievance**, moan (*nonformal*); dissent, protest; hard luck story (*nonformal*), tale of woe

5 (*nonformal terms*) **beef**, **gripe**, grouse, bitch

6 **dirge**, **requiem**, **elegy**, coronach, threnody, funeral march

7 (*mourning garments*) **mourning**, black, black tie, black armband

8 **mourner**, griever

9 **moaner**, moaning Minnie, grouch

verbs

10 **lament**, **mourn**, **moan**, **grieve**, sorrow, weep over, bemoan

11 wring one's hands, tear one's hair, gnash one's teeth, beat one's breast

12 **weep**, **sob**, **cry**, greet (*Scots*), bawl; **whimper**, **snivel**; **burst into tears**, burst out crying, break down and cry, cry one's eyes out

13 **wail**, **moan**, **groan**; howl cry, bawl, **yell**, **scream**, shriek

14 **whine**, whimper

15 **complain**, **groan**; **grumble**; murmur, mutter, fret, fuss, make a fuss about; air a grievance, lodge a complaint; **fault**, **find fault**

16 (*nonformal terms*) **beef**, **bitch**, gripe, grouse, moan

17 go into mourning, mourn

adjectives

18 **lamenting**, **grieving**, **mourning**; wailing, bemoaning

19 **plaintive**, **mournful**, **sorrowful**; whining, whimpering; querulous, petulant

20 (*nonformal terms*) **grouchy**, grousing, griping, bitching

21 **tearful**, weepy, lachrymose; weeping, sobbing, **crying**; whimpering, snivelling

22 elegaic, dirgelike

adverbs

23 **mournfully**, plaintively

107 REJOICING

nouns

1 **rejoicing**, jubilation; **elation**, **triumph**; the time of one's life; festivity, merriment, celebration

2 **cheer**, hooray; **cry**, **shout**, **yell**; hallelujah; applause

3 **smile**, **grin**; smirk, simper

4 **laughter**, **hilarity**; **laugh**; titter, giggle, chuckle; cackle, crow; snigger, snort; guffaw, belly laugh (*nonformal*)

verbs

5 **rejoice**, **exult**, **delight**, thank one's lucky stars; jump for joy, dance, skip, revel, frolic

6 **cheer**, **give three cheers**, cry for joy; **applaud**

7 **smile**, **crack a smile** (*nonformal*); grin, smirk, simper

8 **laugh**, **burst out laughing**; **titter**, **giggle**, **chuckle**; cackle, crow; snigger, snort; **guffaw**, belly laugh; roar with laughter; fall about (*nonformal*); crack up (*nonformal*), split one's sides, be in stitches (*nonformal*)

9 **make laugh**, kill (*nonformal*),

break, crack one up (*nonformal*), get a laugh

adjectives

10 **rejoicing,** delighting, exulting; **jubilant, exultant, elated,** flushed

adverbs

11 **jubilantly,** elatedly

108 DULLNESS

nouns

1 **dullness, dryness;** stiffness, woodenness; sterility, aridity

2 **unimaginativeness,** plainness

3 **banality,** sameness, repetition, staleness

verbs

4 **fall flat;** leave one cold, wear thin; go down like a lead balloon (*nonformal*), bomb

5 platitudinize, go through the motions

adjectives

6 **dull, dry,** dusty; **stuffy,** wooden, stiff; arid, barren, sterile; **insipid,** inane; **flat, stale; dead,** lifeless, pale, pallid; **slow,** pedestrian, plodding; **tedious, dreary,** dismal; **heavy,** leaden, ponderous

7 **uninteresting, uneventful,** unenjoyable

8 **prosaic, plain;** matter-of-fact, unimaginative

9 **trite, banal,** unoriginal, **stereotyped,** stock, **commonplace, common, familiar,** old hat (*nonformal*); hackneyed, **stale;** worn, moth-eaten, threadbare

adverbs

10 dully; heavily, ponderously

11 commonly, familiarly, unoriginally

109 TEDIUM

nouns

1 **tedium, monotony,** sameness; **the daily grind, the rat race** (*nonformal*)

2 **tediousness, dullness;** repetition

3 **weariness, tiredness; boredom,** ennui

4 **bore,** crashing bore (*nonformal*), trainspotter, anorak (*both nonformal*)

5 (*nonformal terms*) drip, wet blanket, party pooper, spoilsport

verbs

6 **be tedious, drag on,** go on forever; **weary, tire, irk,** wear, fatigue, weary, jade; **pall,** satiate

7 **bore,** send to sleep, **bore stiff**

8 **harp on,** dwell on

adjectives

9 **tedious, monotonous, humdrum,** uneventful; **dreary,** dry, dusty, **dull; protracted, prolonged, long-winded**

10 **wearying,** wearing, **tiring; tiresome,** irksome, **boring**

11 **weary, tired;** jaded, palled, fed up (*nonformal*); melancholy, tired of life; listless, dispirited

12 **bored, uninterested**

adverbs

13 tediously, monotonously, endlessly

110 AGGRAVATION

nouns

1 **worsening, souring, deterioration; heightening,** deepening, **increase,** amplification, enlargement, magnification; **exasperation, annoyance, irritation**

verbs

2 **aggravate, worsen; exacerbate,** embitter, sour; deteriorate; **intensify, heighten,** step up, sharpen, deepen, **increase,** enhance, amplify, enlarge, magnify; rub salt in the wound, twist the knife, add insult to injury; **exasperate, annoy, irritate**

3 **worsen, take a turn for the worse;** jump out of the frying pan and into the fire

adjectives

4 **aggravated, worsened, worse,** exacerbated, embittered, soured, deteriorated; **intensified, heightened, increased,** enhanced, amplified, magnified, enlarged; **exasperated, irritated, annoyed**

5 **aggravating, exasperating;** annoying, irritating; provocative, contentious

adverbs

6 **annoyingly, exasperatingly**

111 RELIEF

nouns

1 **relief, easing; relaxation; reduction,** lessening, remission; alleviation, softening, defusing; appeasement; dulling, deadening, numbing

2 **release, freeing,** removal; suspension, intermission; respite, reprieve; discharge; purging, purge, cleansing

3 **lightening,** unloading, a load off one's mind

4 sigh of relief

verbs

5 **relieve, ease; relax,** slacken; **reduce,** diminish, lessen, abate; **alleviate, mitigate,** soften, cushion; defuse, appease, mollify, subdue, **soothe; dull, deaden, numb**

6 **release, free, deliver,** reprieve

7 **lighten,** unload, unburden

8 **be relieved, breathe easy, rest easier**

adjectives

9 **relieving, easing,** alleviating, mitigating, subduing, **soothing, relaxing; dulling, deadening, numbing**

10 **relieved,** breathing easier, out of the woods (both nonformal)

112 COMFORT

nouns

1 **comfort, ease, well-being;** contentment

2 **peace, peacefulness; friendliness,** warmness; hospitality

3 **creature comforts, comforts, conveniences,** amenities

4 **consolation, solace, encouragement, assurance, reassurance, support; condolence, sympathy**

5 **comforter,** consoler

verbs

6 **comfort, console,** sympathize with; **bolster, support;** assure, reassure; **encourage, hearten**

7 **take comfort, take heart; pull oneself together, pluck up one's spirits**

8 **be at ease,** make oneself at home, put one's feet up, **relax**

9 **snug,** snug down

10 **snuggle, nestle, cuddle**

adjectives

11 **comfortable,** contented, easy; restful, peaceful, **relaxing;** soft, cushioned; **cosy, snug; friendly, warm; homely, lived-in,** roomy, commodious, convenient

12 **at ease,** easy, relaxed

13 **comforting, consoling; sympathetic,** assuring, reassuring, **supportive;** encouraging, heartening, cheering

adverbs

14 **comfortably, easily; cosily, snugly**

15 in clover, on a bed of roses

16 reassuringly, encouragingly

113 WONDER

nouns

1 **wonder, astonishment, amazement, surprise; awe, admiration,** bewilderment, puzzlement

2 **marvel, wonder, miracle;** astonishment, amazement; **rarity,** exception; **curiosity, sight, spectacle**

verbs

3 **wonder, marvel; gaze, gape**

4 **astonish, amaze, astound, surprise, startle, stagger,** confound, overwhelm, boggle, awe, **dazzle, daze, stun**

adjectives

5 **wondering,** marvelling, **astonished, amazed, surprised, astounded,** flabbergasted (*nonformal*), **bewildered,** puzzled, confounded, **dumbfounded,** staggered, overwhelmed; **aghast, wide-eyed; breathless; awestruck; awed; spellbound,** fascinated, captivated, **enthralled, enchanted,** entranced, bewitched, hypnotized, mesmerized

6 **wonderful, marvellous,** miraculous, **fantastic, fabulous, phenomenal,** prodigious, stupendous, unprecedented, **extraordinary, exceptional, rare, unique,** singular, remarkable, striking, **sensational;** beguiling, fascinating; **incredible, inconceivable,** unimaginable, incomprehensible, **bewildering, puzzling,** enigmatic

7 **awesome,** awful, awe-inspiring; transcending, surpassing; **mysterious;** weird, eerie, uncanny, bizarre

8 **astonishing, amazing, surprising,** startling, **astounding,** confounding, staggering, stunning (*nonformal*), breathtaking, overwhelming

9 **indescribable,** unspeakable, unmentionable

adverbs

10 **wonderfully**, marvellously, miraculously, fantastically, **fabulously**, extraordinarily, **exceptionally, remarkably,** strikingly; **strangely, incredibly,** enigmatically

11 awfully, **mysteriously,** weirdly, eerily

12 **astonishingly, amazingly, surprisingly**

13 unspeakably, indescribably

114 UNASTONISHMENT

nouns

1 **calm,** calmness, coolness, **cool** (*nonformal*), composure; poker face, straight face

verbs

2 **accept, take for granted, not turn a hair**

adjectives

3 unmoved, calm, **cool, composed**

115 HOPE

nouns

1 **hope, hopes; aspiration,** desire; prospect, expectation; **trust, confidence, faith;** conviction, assurance, security; assumption, presumption; **promise, prospect;** good prospects, high hopes

2 **optimism, rose-coloured spectacles; cheerfulness;** silver lining

3 glimmer of hope; faint hope

4 **dream,** pipe dream (*nonformal*)

5 **optimist;** perfectionist

verbs

6 **hope; look for, expect; trust,** confide, presume, feel confident, rest assured; hope in, rely on, count on, lean upon, bank on; hope for, **aspire to, desire**

7 **be hopeful,** take heart, keep hoping; touch wood

8 **be optimistic, look on the bright side**

9 **give hope,** inspire hope **raise expectations; cheer;** inspire; **assure, reassure,** support; **promise**

adjectives

10 **hopeful, hoping;** aspiring; expectant; **confident,** assured

11 **optimistic,** bright; **cheerful;** utopian, perfectionist

12 **promising,** of promise, **favourable,** looking up; inspiring, **encouraging,** cheering, reassuring, supportive

adverbs

13 **hopefully; expectantly; optimistically; cheerfully;** fondly; confidently

116 HOPELESSNESS

nouns

1 **hopelessness,** no hope; blank future, no future; futility; impossibility

2 **despair, desperation;** despondency; sloth; apathy

3 **blighted hope;** disappointment

4 **pessimism, cynicism;** gloomy outlook; defeatism

5 **pessimist, cynic;** defeatist

6 **lost cause, wild goose chase;**

hopeless case; dead duck (*nonformal*); terminal case

verbs

7 **be hopeless, look bleak; be pessimistic**

8 **despair,** despair of, falter, lose hope, **lose heart, abandon hope, give up**

9 disappoint, drive to despair

adjectives

10 **hopeless,** without hope, bleak, grim, dismal, cheerless; **desperate, despairing, in despair;** despondent; disconsolate; forlorn; apathetic

11 **futile, vain;** doomed

12 **impossible,** out of the question

13 **past hope, beyond recall; irretrievable;** incorrigible; irrevocable, **irreversible; irreparable, incurable,** beyond remedy, terminal; **ruined,** undone; lost, gone

14 **pessimistic, cynical; gloomy,** dismal, lugubrious; negative; defeatist

adverbs

15 **hopelessly, desperately,** forlornly; impossibly

16 **irretrievably;** irrevocably

117 ANXIETY

nouns

1 **anxiety; apprehension,** misgiving, foreboding, suspense, strain, tension, stress; **dread, fear; concern,** solicitude; **care; distress, trouble, unease; uneasiness, disturbance,** upset, agitation, disquiet; **nervousness;** malaise

2 **worry; worries,** troubles, concerns; worrying, fretting; harassment, torment

verbs

3 **concern, give concern, trouble, bother, distress, disturb, upset,** disquiet, agitate; keep on tenterhooks

4 (*make anxious*) **worry,** upset, vex, fret, agitate, get to (*nonformal*), **harass,** torment, dog, hound, plague, persecute, haunt, beset

5 (*feel anxious*) **worry,** worry oneself, lose sleep; **fret, fuss,** chafe, tense up

adjectives

6 **anxious, concerned, apprehensive,** foreboding, misgiving, strained, tense, tensed up (*nonformal*); **fearful; solicitous,** zealous; **troubled, bothered; uneasy,** perturbed, **disturbed, agitated;** nervous

7 **worried, vexed,** harassed, tormented, dogged, hounded, persecuted, haunted, beset, plagued; worried sick, worried stiff (*nonformal*)

8 **troublesome, distressing, disturbing, upsetting;** worrying; fretting; **harassing,** tormenting, plaguing; **annoying**

adverbs

9 **anxiously, apprehensively,** uneasily; solicitously

118 FEAR, FRIGHTENINGNESS

nouns

1 **fear, fright; scare, alarm, consternation, dismay; dread,** unholy dread, **awe; terror, horror; phobia; panic; stampede; cowardice**

2 **frightfulness, horror, grimness**

3 **timidity;** diffidence, stage fright

4 **apprehension, misgiving, qualm,** funny feeling; **anxiety;** doubt; **foreboding**

5 **trepidation; quaking, agitation; uneasiness, disquiet;** nervousness; goose bumps (*nonformal*); sweat, cold sweat; sinking stomach

6 **frightening, intimidation,** bullying, browbeating, cowing; psychological warfare, war of nerves

7 **terrorizing, scare tactics; terrorism**

8 **alarmist, scaremonger; terrorist,** bomber, assassin

9 **bogeyman, bugbear; horror, terror,** holy terror; **ogre, monster,** vampire; **nightmare; witch; ghost, spectre, phantom**

verbs

10 **fear, be afraid; have qualms; dread; sweat**

11 **take fright;** lose courage; pale; freeze

12 **start,** startle, **jump, shy,** fight shy; **panic, stampede**

13 **flinch, shrink, shy,** draw back, recoil, **quail, cringe, wince,** blink

14 **tremble, shake,** quake, shiver, quiver, quaver

15 **frighten, fright; scare; alarm,** disquiet; shake, stagger; **startle; unnerve**

16 **terrify, awe; horrify, appal, shock;** strike dumb, **stun, paralyse,** freeze

17 **daunt, deter,** shake, stop, set back; **discourage, awe, overawe**

18 **dismay, disconcert, appal, astound, confound, put out, take aback**

19 **intimidate, cow, browbeat, bulldoze** (*nonformal*), bludgeon; **bully, harass;** bluster; **terrorize;** threaten; **demoralize**

20 **frighten off, scare away**

adjectives

21 **afraid, scared**

22 **fearful,** fearing, fearsome, **in fear; cowardly; timid, shy;** shrinking, bashful, diffident; scary; jumpy; **tremulous,** trembling, shaky; **nervous**

23 **apprehensive,** misgiving, anxious

24 **frightened; alarmed; dismayed,** daunted; **startled**

25 **terrified;** awestruck; **horrified; appalled, astounded, aghast;** unnerved, unmanned, undone, cowed, awed, **intimidated; stunned, petrified, stupefied,** paralysed, frozen; deadly pale, blanched, pallid

26 **panicky, panic-stricken, terror-stricken**

27 **frightening, frightful; fearful,** fearsome, nightmarish, hellish; **scary,** scaring, chilling; **alarming, startling,** dismaying, disconcerting; **unnerving, daunting,** deter-

ring, deterrent, discouraging, disheartening; stunning

28 terrifying; hair-raising (*nonformal*); paralysing, stunning; **terrorizing**

29 terrible, terrific, tremendous; horrid, horrible, horrifying, horrific, horrendous; **dreadful, dread,** dreaded; **awful;** awesome, awe-inspiring; **shocking, appalling,** astounding; **dire,** fell; formidable; **hideous, ghastly,** morbid, grim, grisly, gruesome, macabre

30 creepy, spooky, eerie, weird, uncanny

adverbs

31 fearfully, apprehensively, diffidently; timidly, shyly, bashfully

32 in fear, in terror, in awe, in alarm, in consternation

33 frightfully, fearfully; alarmingly; appallingly; terribly, tremendously; dreadfully, awfully; horribly

119 NERVOUSNESS

nouns

1 nervousness, nerves, disquiet, uneasiness, apprehensiveness, malaise, qualm, qualms, misgiving; agitation, trepidation; fear; panic; fidgets; twitching, tic; stage fright

2 (*nonformal terms*) jumps, shakes, quivers, trembles, butterflies, shivers, cold shivers, creeps, sweat, cold sweat

3 tension, strain, stress, mental strain, nervous tension, pressure

4 frayed nerves, jangled nerves,

shattered nerves; neurosis; **nervous breakdown**

5 nervous wreck, wreck, bundle of nerves

verbs

6 fidget; have the jitters; tense up; tremble

7 lose self-control; lose courage; go to pieces, have a nervous breakdown, fall apart, come apart

8 (*nonformal terms*) crack, crack up, flip, flip one's lid, freak out

9 get on one's nerves, grate on, jar on, drive one crazy; irritate

10 unnerve, undo, demoralize, shake, upset, dash, crush, overcome

adjectives

11 nervous; highly strung, all nerves; uneasy, apprehensive; excitable; irritable, edgy, on edge, fearful, frightened

12 jittery (*nonformal*), jumpy; shaky; tremulous; fidgety, fidgeting; agitated; shaking, trembling, quivering, shivering

13 tense, uptight (*nonformal*), strained, taut

14 unnerved, unmanned, undone, demoralized, shaken, upset, dashed, stricken, crushed; shot to pieces; overcome

15 unnerving, nerve-racking; jarring, grating

adverbs

16 nervously, shakily

120 UNNERVOUSNESS

nouns

1 **calmness; steadiness,** steady nerves; no nerves, strong nerves, iron nerves, nerves of steel; cool head

adjectives

2 **nerveless; calm;** cool as a cucumber (*nonformal*); **steady,** rock-steady; unflinching **relaxed**

121 EXPECTATION

nouns

1 **expectation; predictability; anticipation, prospect,** thought; contemplation; probability; confidence; reliance; certainty

2 optimism, eager expectation, **hope**

3 **suspense; waiting,** hushed expectancy; uncertainty, nervous expectation; **anxiety, dread, pessimism,** apprehension

4 **expectations,** prospects, outlook, hopes, future prospects; probabilities

verbs

5 **expect,** be expectant, **anticipate,** face, think, **contemplate,** envisage; **hope,** presume; dread; foresee

6 **look forward to,** predict, foresee; **look for, watch for**

7 **be expected,** be in store

8 **await,** wait, wait for; watch; bide, **mark time;** hold one's breath

9 **expect to, plan on**

adjectives

10 **expectant,** expecting; anticipating; **waiting,** awaiting, waiting for; forewarned, forestalling, ready, prepared; looking for, watching for; gaping, **eager;** optimistic, hopeful; sure; certain; not surprised

11 **in suspense,** on tiptoe, **on edge,** tense, taut, quivering; anxious, **apprehensive**

12 **expected, anticipated, awaited, predicted, foreseen;** presumed; probable; **due, promised;** overdue; in prospect, prospective; in view; imminent

13 **as expected,** on schedule; **expected of,** counted on; in character

adverbs

14 **expectantly;** hopefully; with bated breath

122 INEXPECTATION

nouns

1 **surprise; blow,** eye-opener, revelation; **bolt from the blue, thunderbolt; bombshell;** surprise package; surprise party

2 **start, shock,** jar, jolt, turn

verbs

3 **not expect,** hardly expect, **not anticipate, not foresee**

4 **be startled,** be taken aback; **start,** startle, **jump; shy,** flinch

5 **be unexpected, come unawares,** appear unexpectedly, turn up, creep up on

6 **surprise; catch unawares,** take aback; ambush; **astonish**

7 **startle, shock,** electrify, jar, jolt, shake, stun, **stagger,** take aback; frighten

adjectives

8 **unsuspecting, unaware;** unprepared; off one's guard

9 **unexpected,** unprepared for, **unforeseen;** unpredictable; **improbable;** without warning, unannounced; sudden; out-of-theway, **extraordinary**

10 **surprising, astonishing; startling, shocking,** electrifying, staggering, stunning, jarring, jolting

11 **surprised; astonished;** taken unawares, caught short

12 **startled, shocked, electrified,** jarred, jolted, shaken, staggered, taken aback

adverbs

13 **unexpectedly, by surprise, unawares;** out of the blue; suddenly

14 **surprisingly; astonishingly**

123 DISAPPOINTMENT

nouns

1 **disappointment;** forlorn hope; **blow; frustration,** defeat; setback; failure, fiasco; **disillusionment;** mirage, tease; dissatisfaction

verbs

2 **disappoint; dash; balk, thwart, frustrate, baffle,** defeat, foil, cross; **let down,** cast down; **disillusion;** tantalize, tease

3 **be disappointing,** go wrong, turn sour, fall short

4 **be disappointed, be crestfallen;**

adjectives

5 **disappointed; let down,** betrayed; **dashed,** blighted, blasted, crushed; **balked, thwarted, frustrated,** baffled, crossed, defeated, foiled; disillusioned; crestfallen; soured; dissatisfied; regretful

6 **disappointing,** falling short; tantalizing, teasing; **unsatisfactory**

124 PREMONITION

nouns

1 **premonition; hunch;** prediction

2 **foreboding; apprehension,** misgiving

3 **omen, portent;** indication, **sign, token, promise;** foreshadowing, shadow

4 **warning, forewarning**

5 **forerunner, precursor, herald,** announcer

6 (*omens*) owl, raven; gathering clouds, clouds on the horizon, storm clouds; black cat; broken mirror; rainbow; shooting star

7 **portent,** significance, **meaning**

8 **benevolence; brightness,** cheerfulness; good omen, good auspices

verbs

9 presage; omen; **foreshadow,** shadow; **predict**

10 **bode,** portend; **threaten,** menace, **lower,** look black, spell trouble; **warn, forewarn**

11 **hint;** betoken, typify, **signify, mean** spell, **indicate,** point to, look like, show signs of

12 promise, suggest, hint, imply, make likely, raise expectation, show promise

13 herald, announce, proclaim; give notice, notify

adjectives

14 foreshadowed; indicated, signified; promised, threatened; predicted

15 forewarning, warning, indicative; **significant, meaningful,** speaking; foreshadowing; intuitive

16 ominous, portentous; foreboding, boding, looming; fateful; **unfavourable, unfortunate, unlucky; sinister,** dark, black, gloomy, sombre, dreary; **threatening, menacing, lowering;** bad, evil, ill, untoward; dire, baleful, **ill-fated**

17 favourable, favouring, fair, good; **promising,** of promise; **fortunate, lucky,** prosperous; benign, bright, happy, golden

adverbs

18 ominously; significantly, meaningfully; **threateningly, menacingly**

19 unfavourably, unfortunately, unluckily

20 favourably; fortunately, luckily, happily; brightly

125 PATIENCE

nouns

1 patience; tolerance, toleration, **acceptance; indulgence; forbearance; endurance; long-suffering;** stoicism, fortitude, self-control; waiting game; **perseverance**

2 resignation, humility; obedience; submission; acquiescence, compliance; **fatalism;** passivity

verbs

3 be patient, wait, play a waiting game, wait around; contain oneself; carry on

4 endure, bear, stand, support, sustain, **suffer, tolerate, abide,** bide, live with; persevere; **bear with, stand for,** tolerate, brook

5 (*nonformal terms*) **take it,** take it on the chin, take it like a man; swallow, stick, **hang in there, hang tough, stick it out;** lump it

6 accept, condone, countenance; overlook, let pass; obey; grin and bear it, shrug off; rise above

7 take, pocket, swallow, down, stomach, eat, digest, disregard, turn a blind eye, ignore; turn the other cheek

adjectives

8 patient, tolerant, tolerating, accepting; understanding, **indulgent,** lenient; philosophical; **long-suffering; enduring;** stoic, stoical; disciplined; persevering

9 resigned, reconciled; **meek,** humble; obedient, amenable; **submissive;** accommodating, adjusting, adapting; **passive;** uncomplaining

adverbs

10 patiently, stoically; **indulgently,** leniently, philosophically

11 resignedly, meekly, submissively, passively

126 IMPATIENCE

nouns

1 impatience; anxiety, eagerness; restlessness; disquiet, uneasiness, nervousness; fretting, chafing; haste; excitement

2 the last straw, the straw that breaks the camel's back, the limit

verbs

3 be impatient, hardly wait; hasten; itch to, burn to; chafe, fret, fuss, squirm; stew, sweat, get excited; wait impatiently

4 lose patience, have had it (nonformal)

adjectives

5 impatient; breathless; champing at the bit; dying, anxious, eager; excited; edgy, on edge; restless, restive, uneasy; fretful, fretting, chafing, squirming; impetuous; hasty

127 PRIDE

nouns

1 pride; self-esteem, self-respect, self-confidence, self-reliance, face, independence; vanity, conceit; arrogance

2 dignity, grandeur, nobility; majesty; worthiness; solemnity, gravity, sobriety

3 egoist; boaster

verbs

4 be proud, hold up one's head, hold one's head high

5 take pride, pride oneself, congratulate oneself; be proud of, glory in, exult in

6 make proud, gratify

7 save face, preserve one's dignity

adjectives

8 proud; self-confident, independent, self-sufficient

9 vain, conceited; haughty, arrogant; boastful

10 puffed up, swollen, bloated; elated, flushed

11 lofty, elevated; high-minded

12 dignified, stately, imposing, grand, aristocratic; noble; majestic, regal, royal; worthy, venerable; sedate, solemn, sober, grave

adverbs

13 proudly, with pride; independently

14 with dignity; nobly, grandly; majestically, regally, worthily; sedately, solemnly, soberly, gravely

128 HUMILITY

nouns

1 humility; lowliness, meanness, smallness; modesty

2 humiliation, chagrin, embarrassment; comedown, deflation; shame, disgrace

3 condescension, deigning, lowering oneself

verbs

4 humiliate, humble; mortify, embarrass; put out; shame, disgrace; deflate

5 debase, crush, degrade, reduce, diminish, demean, lower, bring low, bring down, trip up, take down, set down, put in one's place, put down

6 **humble oneself, demean oneself; eat humble pie,** eat one's words, swallow one's pride

7 **condescend, deign; stoop, descend,** trouble oneself; **patronize**

8 **be humiliated; be crushed, feel small,** look foolish; **be ashamed**

adjectives

9 **humble, lowly,** low, poor, mean, small, undistinguished; unimportant; innocuous; **modest; plain, simple,** homely; **humblest,** lowliest, lowest, least

10 **meek; abject,** submissive

11 **humbled,** diminished, lowered, brought low

12 **humiliated,** mortified, **embarrassed, crushed;** blushing, **redfaced, ashamed,** shamed; crestfallen

13 **humiliating,** chastening, mortifying, **embarrassing,** crushing

adverbs

14 **humbly, meekly;** modestly; submissively

129 SERVILITY

nouns

1 **servility, slavishness;** slavery

2 **obsequiousness;** sponging; **fawning,** grovelling, cringing, bootlicking (*nonformal*), back scratching; timeserving

3 **sycophant, flatterer,** courtier, flunky; lap dog, **tool,** dupe, instrument, slave

4 (*nonformal terms*) bootlicker, yes-man, stooge

5 **parasite,** leech; sponger, freeloader (*nonformal*)

6 **hanger-on, follower,** servant, henchman

verbs

7 **fawn; flatter; grovel,** crawl, creep, cower, cringe, crouch, stoop, kneel, prostrate oneself, bow, bow and scrape

8 **pander to, cater to, cater for,** wait upon; dance attendance, do the dirty work

9 **curry favour, court,** run after (*nonformal*); fawn upon

10 **ingratiate oneself,** insinuate oneself, get on the right side of

adjectives

11 **servile, slavish,** subservient, **menial, base,** mean; **submissive**

12 **obsequious, flattering,** sycophantic, fawning, flattering, ingratiating; **grovelling,** snivelling, cringing, cowering, crawling; **parasitic,** sponging (*nonformal*); abject

adverbs

13 **slavishly,** submissively

14 obsequiously, sycophantically, ingratiatingly

130 MODESTY

nouns

1 **modesty;** humility

2 **diffidence;** low self-esteem; inferiority complex

3 **reserve, restraint, constraint,** retiring disposition; low profile

4 **shyness, timidity, bashfulness;** coyness; self-consciousness, embarrassment; stammering

5 **blushing, flushing,** colouring; **blush, flush,** red face

6 shrinking violet, mouse

verbs

7 shrink, keep a low profile, take a back seat

8 blush, flush, colour, change colour, redden, turn red; stammer

adjectives

9 modest, meek; humble; unpretentious, unassuming, unobtrusive; unambitious

10 self-effacing; diffident

11 reserved, restrained, constrained; quiet; backward, retiring, shrinking

12 shy, timid, bashful; coy, demure; self-conscious, confused; stammering, inarticulate

13 blushing; flushed, red-faced; sheepish; embarrassed

adverbs

14 modestly, meekly; humbly; unobtrusively; quietly, without ceremony

15 shyly, timidly, bashfully, coyly, diffidently; sheepishly, with downcast eyes

131 VANITY

nouns

1 vanity; self-esteem, positive self-image, self-respect; ego trip (nonformal), smugness, complacency

2 pride; arrogance; boastfulness

3 egotism, egoism, ego, self-interest, individualism; selfishness

4 conceit, side; swollen head, big head

5 egotist, egoist, individualist; know-all, smart aleck

verbs

6 boast; give oneself airs

adjectives

7 vain; self-satisfied, smug, complacent, self-sufficient

8 proud; arrogant; boastful

9 egotistic, egoistic; selfish

10 conceited, immodest; cocky (nonformal); jumped-up; perky

adverbs

11 vainly; immodestly; cockily (nonformal)

132 ARROGANCE

nouns

1 arrogance; pride; high horse (nonformal); condescension

2 presumption; insolence

3 aloofness, coolness, remoteness

4 disdain, contemptuousness

5 snobbery, snobbishness; snootiness (nonformal)

6 snob, prig; elitist; highbrow (nonformal); name-dropper

verbs

7 give oneself airs; condescend, patronize, deign, stoop, descend, demean oneself, trouble oneself

adjectives

8 arrogant, overbearing, superior, domineering, proud, haughty; lofty; stuck-up (nonformal); condescending, patronizing

9 presumptuous, presuming, assuming, would-be, self-appointed; insolent

10 **imperious;** masterful, high-and-mighty; **elitist;** dictatorial

11 **aloof,** chilly, cool, distant, remote

12 **disdainful,** dismissive, **contemptuous, supercilious,** cavalier

13 **snobbish,** toffee-nosed (*nonformal*); **snooty** (*nonformal*)

adverbs

14 **arrogantly, haughtily, proudly; disdainfully,** contemptuously

133 INSOLENCE

nouns

1 **insolence; presumption; audacity, effrontery,** boldness, assurance; **contempt; disdain; arrogance**

2 **impertinence,** flippancy, **rudeness,** disrespect, derision, ridicule

3 (*nonformal terms*) **cheek,** face, **brass, nerve, gall**

4 **upstart; smart aleck,** wise guy (*nonformal*)

verbs

5 **have a nerve** (*nonformal*), **dare, presume,** take liberties, taunt, deride

6 **talk back,** answer back, provoke

adjectives

7 **insolent,** insulting; **presumptuous,** presuming; **audacious, bold,** assured; **contemptuous; disdainful, arrogant;** forward, pushy, familiar; cool, cold

8 **impudent, impertinent,** flip (*nonformal*), flippant, cocky, **cheeky;** uncalled-for, gratuitous;

rude, disrespectful, derisive, brash, bluff; **saucy**

9 **brazen, bold,** shameless; swaggering

adverbs

10 **arrogantly;** disdainfully

11 **rudely,** contemptuously, derisively

12 **brazenly, boldly,** shamelessly

134 KINDNESS, BENEVOLENCE

nouns

1 **kindness, kindliness,** kindly disposition; **goodness, decency;** warmth, **kind heart; brotherhood,** fellow feeling, **sympathy; pity, mercy, compassion;** humanity

2 **good nature, good humour,** good temper, sweetness; geniality; **gentleness,** mildness

3 **consideration, thoughtfulness,** solicitude, thought, regard, concern, delicacy, **sensitivity,** tact; indulgence, toleration; **helpfulness**

4 **benevolence,** benevolent disposition, **charity; altruism; goodwill,** grace, brotherly love, charity, love; **generosity; giving**

5 **social services,** social work; welfare state; relief, the dole, social security

6 **good works,** public service

7 **kindness, favour,** mercy, benefit, benevolence, blessing, **service,** turn, break (*nonformal*), **good turn,** courtesy, kindly act, labour of love

8 philanthropist, altruist, humanitarian, do-gooder; welfare worker

verbs

9 be kind, show kindness; treat well; favour, oblige, accommodate

10 be considerate, consider, respect, regard, think of

11 be benevolent, wish well

12 do a favour, do good, do a good turn; benefit, help

adjectives

13 kind, kindly; benign; good, nice, decent; gracious; warm, tender, loving, affectionate; **sympathetic,** sympathizing, **compassionate,** merciful; brotherly, fraternal; humane, human; charitable; Christian

14 good-natured, good-tempered, sweet; amiable, affable, genial, cordial; gentle, mild; easy, **agreeable**

15 benevolent, charitable, altruistic, humanitarian; **generous**

16 considerate, thoughtful, mindful, solicitous, attentive, delicate, tactful; **accommodating, helpful,** agreeable, **obliging,** indulgent, tolerant, lenient

17 well-meaning, well-intentioned

adverbs

18 kindly, benignly; **good,** nicely, well, favourably; **warmly;** humanely, humanly

19 sweetly; amiably, genially, cordially; graciously

20 benevolently, charitably

21 thoughtfully, tactfully, **sensitively,** solicitously, attentively

135 UNKINDNESS, MALEVOLENCE

nouns

1 unkindness; disagreeableness

2 thoughtlessness, forgetfulness

3 malevolence, ill will, bad will, bad blood, bad temper, ill nature; evil eye

4 malice; wickedness; evil intent

5 spite, spitefulness

6 rancour, venom, gall

7 acrimony, acidity, bitterness

8 harshness, roughness; severity, austerity, hardness

9 heartlessness, insensitivity, coldness; hardness; **callousness**

10 cruelty, sadism, wanton cruelty; **ruthlessness; inhumanity; brutality,** mindless brutality; vandalism; **savagery, violence; ferocity;** excessive force

11 atrocity, act of cruelty

12 bad deed, disservice, bad turn

13 beast, animal, brute, monster, devil

verbs

14 brutalize; torture, torment

adjectives

15 unkind, disagreeable, inhospitable; **unsympathetic**

16 inconsiderate, thoughtless, heedless, mindless, unthinking, forgetful; **tactless, insensitive;** unhelpful, uncooperative

17 malevolent, ill-natured

18 malicious; malignant, malign; hateful, nasty, baleful; **wicked,** iniquitous; **harmful, noxious**

19 spiteful; catty; snide

20 **virulent; venomous**

21 **caustic,** corrosive; **acrimonious,** acrid, acid, acidic; **bitter,** tart; **sharp,** keen, incisive, **cutting,** penetrating, piercing, biting, **stinging,** stabbing, **scathing, scorching,** withering, abusive

22 **harsh,** rough, rugged; **severe,** austere, **stringent,** astringent, hard, stern, dour, grim

23 **heartless, unfeeling,** unnatural, insensitive, **cold,** cold-blooded; hard, hardened, hard-hearted; callous

24 **cruel,** sadistic; **ruthless; brutal,** brutish, brute, bestial, beastly, animal; **mindless,** senseless, brutalized; **barbarous,** barbaric, uncivilized; **savage, ferocious, vicious,** fierce, **atrocious; inhuman,** inhumane; fiendish; diabolical, devilish, satanic, hellish; **bloodthirsty,** bloody; murderous; Draconian

adverbs

25 **inconsiderately,** thoughtlessly

26 **meanly,** nastily; **wickedly; spitefully,** in spite; with malice aforethought

27 **virulently;** venemously

28 **bitterly,** tartly; **sharply,** keenly

29 **harshly,** roughly; **severely,** sternly, grimly

30 **heartlessly, callously**

31 **cruelly, brutally; savagely, ferociously, viciously,** fiercely, atrociously; ruthlessly

136 PITY

nouns

1 **pity, sympathy,** feeling, **commiseration,** condolence, condolences; **compassion, mercy,** rue, humanity; **sensitivity; clemency,** quarter, reprieve, relief, favour, grace; gentleness; **kindness, benevolence;** pardon, **forgiveness;** self-pity; **pathos**

2 **tenderness,** gentleness; **bleeding heart**

verbs

3 **pity, feel sorry for; commiserate; sympathize, sympathize with,** feel for, weep for

4 **have pity, have mercy upon, take pity on;** melt, thaw; relent, relax, spare, soften; **reprieve, pardon, forgive**

5 (excite pity) **move, touch,** affect, reach, **soften,** melt; sadden, grieve

adjectives

6 **pitying, sympathetic,** sympathizing, understanding; **compassionate, merciful,** rueful, gentle, soft, tender; **humane,** human; lenient; charitable

7 **pitiful, pitiable, pathetic, piteous, touching, moving, affecting,** heartrending, grievous, doleful

adverbs

8 **pitifully,** sympathetically; **compassionately, mercifully,** ruefully, humanely

137 PITILESSNESS

nouns

1 **ruthlessness; hardness, harshness, cruelty**

verbs

2 **show no mercy,** harden one's
heart

adjectives

3 **pitiless; unsympathetic; merci-
less,** without mercy, **ruthless;**
unfeeling, relentless, inexorable;
heartless, hard, steely, harsh,
savage, **cruel**

adverbs

4 mercilessly, **ruthlessly,** relentlessly, inexorably; heartlessly,
harshly, savagely, cruelly; re-
morselessly

138 CONDOLENCE

nouns

1 **condolence, condolences, consolation,** comfort, soothing
words, **commiseration, sympathy**

verbs

2 **commiserate, sympathize with,**
send one's condolences; pity;
console, comfort

adjectives

3 comforting, commiserating, **sympathetic;** pitying

139 FORGIVENESS

nouns

1 **forgiveness; condoning,** overlooking, disregard; **patience; indulgence,** long-suffering; **kindness, benevolence; tolerance**

2 **pardon,** excuse, **amnesty,** exemption, immunity, reprieve,
grace; remission; redemption

verbs

3 **forgive, pardon, excuse,** spare;
hear confession, **absolve,** grant
remission; **exonerate**

4 **condone, overlook, disregard,
ignore,** pass over, connive at; allow for; bear with, endure

5 **forget;** write off

adjectives

6 **forgiving,** sparing, conciliatory;
**kind, benevolent; magnani-
mous, generous; patient;** long-
suffering; **tolerant**

7 **forgiven, pardoned, excused,**
spared, reprieved; overlooked,
disregarded, forgotten, wiped
away, cancelled, **condoned,** indulged; **absolved;** redeemed; exonerated, acquitted

140 CONGRATULATION

nouns

1 **congratulation, congratulations,**
blessing, **compliment;** good
wishes, best wishes; **applause,
praise,** flattery

verbs

2 **congratulate, bless, compliment;
applaud, praise,** flatter

adjectives

3 **complimentary,** flattering

141 GRATITUDE

nouns

1 **gratitude, appreciation;** obligation

2 **thanks,** praise; **acknowledg-ment, credit,** recognition

verbs

3 **be grateful, be obliged; be thankful,** thank God; **appreciate**

4 **thank, bless;** acknowledge, credit, recognize

adjectives

5 **grateful, thankful; appreciative; obliged, much obliged,** indebted to, under obligation

142 INGRATITUDE

nouns

1 **ingratitude,** ungratefulness, thanklessness

verbs

2 **be ungrateful, not appreciate**

adjectives

3 **ungrateful,** thankless, unappreciative

4 unrecognized, forgotten, neglected, ignored

143 RESENTMENT, ANGER

nouns

1 **resentment; displeasure,** disapproval, dissatisfaction, **discontent;** irritation, **annoyance,** exasperation

2 **offence, pique;** glower, scowl, angry look, dirty look (*nonformal*), glare, frown

3 **bitterness; rancour, acrimony;** gall, bile; hard feelings, **animosity**

4 **indignation,** righteous indignation

5 **anger, wrath**

6 **temper;** bad temper

7 **huff,** pique, ferment

8 **fit of temper,** rage, **tantrum,** temper tantrum; paroxysm, convulsion

9 **outburst, explosion,** flare-up (*nonformal*); storm, scene

10 **rage, passion; fury;** vehemence, violence

11 **provocation, affront, offence,** red rag, sore point, raw nerve

verbs

12 **resent,** be resentful, feel hurt, smart; bear a grudge

13 **take amiss, mind; take offence**

14 (*show resentment*) colour, flush; **growl, snarl, snap,** spit; **glower,** lour *or* lower, scowl, **glare,** frown, look daggers; **stew**

15 (*be angry*) **burn, seethe, simmer,** smoulder, steam; be livid, **fume,** stew (*nonformal*), boil, fret, chafe; **rage, storm, rave,** rant, bluster; rant and rave

16 **snap at, bite one's head off**

17 (*become angry*) become irate, forget oneself; bridle, bristle; boil over

18 (*nonformal terms*) see red, get hot under the collar, flip out

19 **flare up, blaze up,** fire up

20 **fly off the handle; explode, blow up** (*nonformal*)

21 **offend, give offence,** affront, outrage; grieve; wound, hurt, cut

22 **anger, make angry, make mad**

23 **provoke, incense,** arouse, embitter; **vex, irritate, annoy,** aggravate (*nonformal*), **exasperate**

nettle, chafe; **pique; ruffle,** bristle; **stir up**

24 **enrage, infuriate, madden**

adjectives

25 **resentful,** resenting; **bitter,** embittered, virulent, **acrimonious;** caustic; acidic; **sore** (*nonformal*)

26 **provoked, vexed; irritated,** annoyed, aggravated (*nonformal*), exasperated

27 **angry,** angered, **incensed, indignant, irate; livid,** beside oneself, **cross,** worked up

28 **burning, seething,** simmering, smouldering, boiling

29 (*nonformal terms*) **mad, sore;** stroppy, het up, boiling, hopping mad

30 **infuriated; furious,** wild; **fuming; enraged, raging,** raving, ranting, storming

adverbs

31 **angrily, indignantly,** furiously, heatedly; **in anger**

144 JEALOUSY

nouns

1 **jealousy, jaundice; envy**

2 **suspicion,** doubt, mistrust, distrust

verbs

3 **suspect, distrust,** mistrust, doubt

adjectives

4 **jealous, jaundiced; envious; suspicious,** distrustful

145 ENVY

nouns

1 **envy;** grudging; resentment; **jealousy;** rivalry; meanness

verbs

2 **envy, covet;** resent; **grudge, begrudge**

adjectives

3 **envious,** envying; **jealous; covetous;** resentful; **grudging, begrudging;** mean

146 RESPECT

nouns

1 **respect, regard,** consideration, appreciation, favour; approval; **esteem,** estimation, prestige; **reverence,** awe; **deference; honour, homage,** duty; high regard, **admiration;** adoration, worship, hero worship; idolatry

2 **reverence, homage; bow, nod,** curtsy; kneeling; salute; **submission**

3 **respects, regards**

verbs

4 **respect, regard, esteem,** favour, **admire;** appreciate, value, prize; **revere, reverence, honour,** defer to, **bow to, worship,** idolize, adore

5 **pay homage to, show respect for;** salute

6 **bow,** bow down, curtsy, bend, scrape; **kneel,** prostrate oneself

7 **command respect,** inspire respect, have prestige, rank high

adjectives

8 **respectful**, attentive; **deferential**, dutiful; **courteous**

9 **reverent**; admiring, **adoring**, worshipping, **idolizing**; awestruck, awed, in awe; solemn

10 prostrate, on bended knee; **submissive**; **obsequious**

11 **respected, revered**, adored, worshipped, admired, appreciated, valued, prized, highly considered, prestigious

12 **venerable, honourable**, awe-inspiring, awesome

adverbs

13 **respectfully**; dutifully

147 DISRESPECT

nouns

1 **disrespect**, dishonour; **ridicule**; **disparagement**; insolence

2 **indignity, affront, offence, injury**, humiliation; contempt, flouting, mockery, jeering, jeer, scoff, gibe, taunt; **insult; outrage**, atrocity, enormity

3 (*nonformal terms*) **put-down, dig**, shot

verbs

4 **disrespect**, not respect; **be disrespectful**; trifle with; **ridicule; disparage**

5 **offend, affront**, outrage; dishonour, humiliate; flout, mock, jeer at, scoff at, gibe at, taunt; **insult**, call names

6 (*nonformal terms*) **put down, trash**, rubbish, roast, slam

adjectives

7 **disrespectful, irreverent; insolent, impudent**; ridiculing, derisive; disparaging

8 **insulting, insolent, abusive, offensive**, humiliating, degrading; contemptuous; **outrageous**, atrocious, unspeakable

148 CONTEMPT

nouns

1 **contempt, disdain, scorn**; airs; arrogance; **insult**; disparagement

2 **snub, rebuff; slight**, humiliation; spurning, disregard; sneer, snort; **dismissal; rejection**

verbs

3 **disdain, scorn, despise**, hold cheap, be above; deride, **ridicule; insult; disparage**; sniff at, sneeze at, sneer at

4 **spurn**; spit upon

5 **snub, rebuff**; give the cold shoulder (*nonformal*)

6 **slight, ignore**, dismiss, disregard, overlook, neglect

7 **avoid**, shun, dodge, steer clear of (*nonformal*)

adjectives

8 **contemptuous**, **disdainful**, supercilious, snooty, **scornful**, sneering, withering; snobbish, exclusive; **conceited; haughty**, **arrogant**

adverbs

9 **contemptuously, scornfully**, disdainfully

149 SPACE

nouns

1 **space, extent,** extension, continuum; **expanse,** expansion; spread, breadth; depth; height; **measure,** volume; **dimension,** proportion; **area,** tract, surface; field, arena, sphere; **void,** empty space, emptiness; outer space, deep space

2 **range, scope, compass, reach,** stretch, sweep; **gamut, scale,** register; **spectrum**

3 **room, latitude, margin;** breathing space; **headroom,** clearance

4 **open space; clearing,** clearance, glade; open country, **terrain,** prairie, plain; wilderness, outback (*Australia*), desert; **territory;** living space

5 capacity, extent, expanse

verbs

6 **extend, reach, stretch,** sweep, spread, run, cover, carry, **range,** lie; span, straddle, take in, hold, encompass, surround

adjectives

7 **spatial;** proportional; twodimensional, flat, spherical, cubic

8 **spacious, sizeable, roomy, capacious,** ample; **extensive,** expansive, extended, wide-ranging; far-reaching, extending, spreading, **vast,** broad, **wide,** deep, high, voluminous; widespread; **infinite**

adverbs

9 **extensively, widely,** broadly, vastly; infinitely

10 **everywhere, here, there, and everywhere; all over,** all round; **universally**

150 LOCATION

nouns

1 **location, situation, place, position,** spot; **whereabouts; area,** district, region; locality; abode; site; **spot, point; bearings**

2 **station, status, stand, standing,** standpoint; **viewpoint,** angle, perspective, distance; **seat, post,** base, footing, ground, venue

3 **navigation,** guidance; **position, orientation,** lie; **fix**

4 **place,** stead

5 **map, chart;** contour line; **scale;** grid line, latitude, longitude

6 (*act of placing*) **placement, positioning, situation, location, siting, locating, placing,** putting; **allocation, disposition,** assignment, **deployment,** posting, **stationing,** spotting; **deposit,** disposal, dumping; storage; loading, packing

7 **establishment, foundation,** settlement, settling, population, plantation; fixation; mooring; **installation,** instalment, inauguration, initiation

8 geography; surveying, navigation

verbs

9 **have place,** be there; **belong, go, fit,** fit in

10 **lie, be found,** stand, rest, repose; lie in

11 **locate, site, place, position; install; allocate, deploy,** assign;

map, chart; **fix; pinpoint;** navigate

12 **place, put, set, lay,** pose, site, seat, stick (*nonformal*), **station, post;** park; dump

13 (*put violently*) **clap,** slap, **thrust, fling, hurl,** throw, cast, chuck, toss

14 **deposit,** repose, rest, **lay,** lodge; **put down,** set down, lay down

15 **load,** burden; fill; stow, store; **pack,** pack away; dump, heap, heap up, stack, mass; bag, pocket

16 **establish, fix, plant, site,** pitch, seat, **set; found, base,** ground; **build,** put up, set up; build in; **install, invest,** vest, put in

17 **settle, settle down,** sit down, locate; **reside, inhabit; move,** locate, relocate, move in; place oneself, plant oneself, stand; **anchor,** drop anchor, moor; **squat;** camp; perch, roost, burrow; keep house; **colonize, populate,** people

adjectives

18 **located, placed, sited, situated, positioned,** installed, spotted, **set, seated; stationed, posted,** deployed, assigned, positioned; **established,** fixed, in place, **settled,** planted

19 **geographic; regional**

adverbs

20 **in place,** in position

21 **where,** whereabouts

22 **wherever;** anywhere

23 **here;** aboard, on board

24 **there;** thereabouts

25 **here and there, in places**

26 **somewhere, someplace**

151 DISPLACEMENT

nouns

1 **displacement; shift, removal;** eviction; **uprooting,** ripping out

2 **unseating;** upset

3 misplacement, mislaying

4 **homeless person,** exile, drifter, vagabond

verbs

5 **dislocate, displace**

6 **dislodge;** evict; **uproot;** depose, unseat; dismount; throw off

7 **misplace, mislay**

adjectives

8 **dislocated, displaced; disjointed,** unhinged; out, **out of joint**

9 **unsettled; uprooted;** evicted; homeless, exiled, outcast

10 **misplaced, mislaid; out of place**

11 **eccentric,** unbalanced

152 DIRECTION

nouns

1 **direction; line,** point, quarter, **aim, way,** track, range, **bearing, course;** current; tendency, trend, inclination, bent, tenor, drift; **orientation,** lay, lie; steering, piloting; navigation

2 **points of the compass,** cardinal points, degrees; magnetic north, true north; **north; south; east,** orient, sunrise; **west,** sunset

3 **orientation, bearings;** adaptation, adjustment, accommodation, alignment; disorientation, deviation

verbs

4 **direct, point, aim, turn, bend, train,** fix, set, determine; fix on; take aim, aim at

5 **direct to,** give directions to, show the way, show, steer, set straight

6 **head, turn, point, aim,** lead, go, steer, direct oneself; **incline, tend, trend,** set, dispose, verge

7 go west, go east, go north, go south

8 **head for, go for, make for, steer for;** sail for

9 **go directly, go straight,** make a beeline for

10 **orient,** orientate; adapt, adjust, accommodate

adjectives

11 **direct, straight,** straightforward, straightaway; uninterrupted, unbroken; one-way, irreversible

12 **directed,** guided, aimed; well-placed, on the mark

13 **northern,** north, northernmost, northerly, **arctic; southern,** south, southerly; **eastern,** east, easterly, **oriental; western,** west, westerly

adverbs

14 **north,** northward, northwards

15 **south,** southward, southwards

16 **east,** eastward, eastwards

17 **west,** westward, westward

18 **directly, direct, straight; straight ahead,** dead ahead; due, dead, due north; straight across

19 **clockwise; anticlockwise;** homeward

20 **everywhere,** around, all round, round about

153 PROGRESSION

nouns

1 **progression, progress,** going, going forward; **go-ahead** (*nonformal*), onward course; **advance,** advancing, **advancement, promotion;** forward motion; **headway,** way; **leap, jump,** spring; **passage,** course, march, career; travel; improvement

verbs

2 **progress, advance, proceed,** go, step forward, go on, **go ahead,** go along, push ahead; **move,** travel; **make progress,** come on, **get along,** get ahead; further oneself; **make headway;** gain ground

3 **march on,** run on, **jog on, roll on;** drift along

4 **make** *or* **wend one's way, work** *or* **weave one's way,** inch forward, feel one's way, muddle along *or* through; go *or* swim against the current; come a long way, move up in the world; **forge ahead, push** *or* **press on**

5 **advance, further, promote,** forward, hasten, contribute to, foster, aid, facilitate

adjectives

6 **progressive,** progressing, advancing, **ongoing,** oncoming, onward, forward, go-ahead (*nonformal*)

adverbs

7 **in progress,** in mid-course; by leaps and bounds

8 **forward, forwards, onward,
forth, on,** along, **ahead;** on the
way to, on the road or high road
to, en route to or for

154 REGRESSION

nouns

1 **regression,** recession; return;
backward motion, backward
step; lapse, relapse

2 **retreat, withdrawal; retirement;
backing down** or **off** or **out**
(*nonformal*)

3 **reversal;** U-turn; back track

verbs

4 **regress,** go backwards, **recede,**
return, revert; pull back; fall or
get or go behind, lose ground;
backslide, lapse, relapse

5 **retreat,** beat a hasty retreat,
withdraw, retire, pull out or
back, disengage; **fall back,** go
back; **draw back; back out;** defer, **take a back seat, play second
fiddle**

6 **reverse; back, back up,** back off
or away; have second thoughts,
cut one's losses

7 **turn back,** double back, retrace
one's steps; turn one's back
upon; **return,** go or come back

8 **turn round,** turn, make a U-
turn, turn tail; veer around; **swivel,** pivot, swing round; wheel
about, whirl round, spin round

adjectives

9 **regressive,** retrogressive; retrograde

10 **backward, reverse,** reflex; counter

adverbs

11 **backwards,** backward; **back,**
away; **in reverse;** anti-clockwise

155 DEVIATION

nouns

1 **deviation, departure, digression,**
diversion, **divergence,** branching
off, aberration, **variation; detour,
bias, slant; wandering,** rambling,
straying; drift, drifting; turning,
shifting, swerving, swinging;
turn, corner, bend, curve, zigzag, twist, warp, swerve; shift;
wandering

2 **bending; distortion, contortion,**
twisting, warping; **scatter,** diffusion, dispersion

verbs

3 **deviate, depart from,** vary, **diverge,** branch off; **digress,** turn
aside, detour; **swerve, veer,**
curve, shift, **turn, bend; alter
one's course,** change one's bearing

4 **stray,** go astray, lose one's way,
err; take a wrong turning; drift,
go adrift; **wander; ramble;** meander, wind, twist, snake, twist
and turn

5 **deflect,** deviate, **divert,** diverge
bend, curve; **warp,** bias, twist
distort, contort; **scatter, diffuse,**
disperse

6 **avoid, evade, dodge,** duck (*nonformal*), **avert; head off;** turn
back; swing aside, sidestep, sidle
go or fly off at a tangent

adjectives

7 **deviating, deviant, shifting,
turning; step aside,** veering; dis-

cursive, **circuitous**; **indirect**,
out-of-the-way; **erratic**, **zigzag**,
wandering, rambling, roving,
winding, twisting, meandering

8 **deflected**, scattered, diffuse, dispersed

9 **evasive**, dodging

156 LEADING

nouns

1 **the lead**; precedence; priority;
front, point, cutting edge, forefront; herald, precursor

verbs

2 **lead, head,** spearhead; take the
lead, **lead the way; be the point;**
show the way; guide; get ahead
of, lap, outstrip, pace, set the
pace; **precede,** go before

adjectives

3 **leading, heading,** precedent,
foregoing; **first, foremost; preceding,** antecedent; **prior; chief**

adverbs

4 **before, in front,** in the vanguard,
in the forefront, in advance

157 FOLLOWING

nouns

1 **following, trailing,** tailing (*nonformal*); **hounding, dogging,**
chasing; **pursuit; sequence; sequel; series**

2 **follower,** successor; **attendant,**
hanger-on, dependent, parasite,
stooge (*nonformal*); **henchman,**
partisan, supporter; fan *and* buff
(*both nonformal*); courtier; **public; entourage, following; disciple**

verbs

3 **follow,** come after, move behind;
pursue, shadow *and* **tail** (*both
nonformal*), trail after, follow in
the steps *or* footsteps of, breathe
down the neck of, bring up the
rear; tag along (*nonformal*); **dog,
hound,** chase, **pursue**

4 **lag behind, straggle,** drag, trail,
trail behind, loiter, linger, fall
behind

adjectives

5 **following,** trailing; succeeding;
consecutive

adverbs

6 **behind, after,** in the rear, in the
wake of

158 APPROACH

nouns

1 **approach,** coming *or* going toward, coming *or* going near,
nearing; advance, oncoming; **advent, coming**

2 **access,** openness

verbs

3 **approach, near;** close in, close
in on; **accost,** encounter, confront; **advance, come, come forward;** sidle up to; bear down on,
gain upon, narrow the gap

adjectives

4 **approaching, nearing,** advancing; **coming,** oncoming, forthcoming; near; imminent

5 **accessible,** open

159 RECESSION

nouns

1 recession; retreat, retirement, withdrawal

verbs

2 recede; retreat, retire, withdraw; move off or away; go away; die away, fade away; diminish, decline, sink, shrink, dwindle, fade, ebb, wane; tail off

3 retract, withdraw, pull out; defer, take a back seat, play second fiddle; shrink, wince, cringe, flinch, fight shy, duck

adjectives

4 receding, retreating, retiring, withdrawing; shy; diminishing, declining, sinking, shrinking, eroding, dwindling, ebbing, waning; fading, dying

160 CONVERGENCE

nouns

1 convergence, meeting, congress; concentration, focus; meeting point; union, merger; crossroads, crossing; hub, spokes; radius; tangent

verbs

2 converge, come together, approach, meet, unite, connect, merge; cross, intersect; link up with; go toward, narrow the gap, close up, close in; centre; centre on or around, concentrate, come to a point

adjectives

3 converging; meeting, uniting, merging; concurrent, approaching; crossing, intersecting; focal; tangent

161 CROSSING

nouns

1 crossing, intersection; cross section

2 crossing; intersection; level crossing; interchange, spaghetti junction

3 network, weaving, net, netting; mesh; web; weave; lace; wickerwork; lattice; grate, grating; grille; grid

4 cross, crux; crucifix

5 traverse; diagonal; crossbar

verbs

6 cross; intersect; cut across; traverse, lie across; bar

7 net, web, mesh; lattice; grate, grid

adjectives

8 cross, crossed; intersecting

9 traverse, across, cross; oblique

10 cross-shaped, cross, crossed

11 netted; meshed; laced, lacy; grated; barred; streaked, striped

12 webbed, woven, interwoven

adverbs

13 cross, across; traverse

162 DIVERGENCE

nouns

1 aberration, deviation; separation, division; spread, splaying, fanning out

2 radiation, ray, radius; radiance, diffusion; scattering

3 **fork, prong; branch**, stem, offshoot; **crotch; fan, delta**

verbs

4 **diverge; separate**, divide, separate off, split off; spread, **spread
out**, splay, fan out; go off or
away

5 **radiate**, beam out, diffuse, emanate, spread, disperse, scatter

6 **fork; branch**, stem, branch off or
out

adjectives

7 **divergent;** splayed; radiating, ra-
diated

8 **forked, forking;** V-shaped;
branched, branching

163 MOTION

(motion in general)

nouns

1 **motion; movement, momentum;** unrest, restlessness; **operation, working, ticking; activity;
dynamics;** motivation; mobilization

2 **course, career,** set, **passage, progress,** trend, **advance,** forward
motion, **momentum; travel;
flow,** flux, flight; stream, current,
run, rush; drift; backward motion, **regression;** downward motion, **descent;** upward motion,
rising, ascent

3 **velocity,** rate, pace, tread, step,
stride, gait

verbs

4 **move, budge, stir;** go, run, flow,
stream; **progress;** advance; **back,**
regress; ebb, subside, wane; **descend,** sink, plunge; **ascend,**
mount, rise, climb, soar; circle,

rotate, spin, whirl; travel; **speed;
hurry**

5 **set in motion, move,** motivate,
push, shove, nudge, **drive,** impel,
propel; mobilize

adjectives

6 **moving, stirring, in motion;
mobile;** impelling, driving; travelling; **active**

7 **flowing,** fluent, passing, streaming, flying, **running, progressive,**
rushing; drifting; **regressive,
backward;** descending, sinking,
plunging; **ascending,** mounting,
rising, soaring; **rotary**

adverbs

8 **under way,** on one's way, **in
motion**

164 QUIESCENCE

nouns

1 **stillness,** silence, quietness, **quiet, calmness, tranquillity,** serenity, **peace;** contemplation; **rest,
repose; sleep, slumber**

2 **immobility,** inactivity, inaction

3 **standstill, stop,** halt, cessation;
subsidence, waning, ebbing,
wane, ebb

4 **inertia,** apathy, indifference;
stagnation, vegetation

5 **calm, lull;** doldrums

verbs

6 **be still, keep quiet,** lie still; **stop
moving, come to a standstill;
rest, repose; remain, stay;** freeze
(*nonformal*); **stand, stand still;**
stand firm, stay put (*nonformal*);
not stir, not move a muscle;
hold one's breath; bide one's
time; mark time, tread water

7 quiet, quieten, **lull, soothe, calm,** tranquillize, pacify; **stop, halt, bring to a standstill; cease, wane, subside, ebb, die off, dwindle**

8 stagnate, vegetate; **sleep,** slumber; **idle**

9 sit, sit down; perch, roost

adjectives

10 quiet, still, hushed; waning, subsiding, ebbing, dwindling; restful, relaxed; cloistered, isolated, secluded, sheltered; **calm, tranquil, peaceful; placid; smooth; unruffled, untroubled,** cool, undisturbed, unmoved; stoic, impassive

11 motionless, unmoved, **immobile; still, fixed, stationary, static; idle,** unemployed

12 inert, inactive, static, dormant, passive, sedentary; **latent,** suspended; **sleeping, slumbering; stagnant, languid,** apathetic; phlegmatic, **sluggish,** groggy, heavy, leaden, **dull, flat, dead,** lifeless

13 stuffy, airless; close, oppressive, stifling, suffocating

adverbs

14 quietly, still; **calmly, peacefully;** smoothly, **coolly**

15 passively; heavily, dully, coldly; stoically

165 SWIFTNESS

nouns

1 velocity, speed; rapidity, swiftness; haste, hurry, rush; **dispatch,** expedition, promptness; **flight; lightning speed**

2 speed of sound, speed of light

3 run, sprint; dash, rush, plunge, **race, spurt, burst, burst of speed;** canter, **gallop, trot, full speed;** fast track *or* lane

4 acceleration, quickening; thrust, drive, impetus; sprinter; **speed demon** *or* merchant *(nonformal);* runner

5 *(comparisons)* lightning, thunderbolt, flash, bat out of hell *(nonformal),* light, wind, shot, bullet, rocket, arrow, dart, mercury, jet plane, swallow, antelope, greyhound, hare

verbs

6 speed, fly; zoom; rush, tear, dash, dart, shoot, hurtle, bolt, scamper, scurry, scramble, **race; hasten, hurry; run, sprint, trip,** spring, **bound,** leap; gallop, canter; trot

7 *(nonformal terms)* tear along, breeze, tear up the road, scorch, zip, whiz, make tracks, run like mad, go flat out, step on it, get a move on

8 accelerate, speed up, hurry up, quicken; hasten; pick up speed, gain ground

9 spurt, dash, rush ahead, put on a burst of speed

10 overtake, outstrip, overhaul, catch up with, gain on, pass, lap; outrun; **leave behind**

11 keep up with, run neck and neck

adjectives

12 fast, swift, speedy, rapid; quick, express, hasty, rushing, dashing, flying, galloping, running, **agile, nimble,** lively, light-footed; quick as lightning, swift as an arrow, **breakneck**, reckless, headlong, precipitate; **prompt**

adverbs

13 **swiftly, rapidly, quickly, speedily, fast, quick; at a great rate, with rapid strides, by leaps and bounds, hastily,** promptly, **with great** *or* **all haste, hand over fist;** in double time, **like a shot, like a flash,** like a blue streak, like lightning, **like greased lightning, like a bat out of hell, like mad** *and* **crazy** *and* **fury**

14 **in no time,** instantaneously, in less than no time, before you can say Jack Robinson, **in a flash**

15 **at full speed, for all one is worth** (*nonformal*), as fast as one's legs will carry one; **at full pelt; all out** (*nonformal*), flat out; full speed ahead

166 SLOWNESS

nouns

1 **slowness;** sloth, laziness, idleness, inertia

2 **slow motion,** snail's pace; **creep, crawl;** trudge, waddle, saunter, stroll; slouch, shuffle, plod; limp, hobble; slow march, dead *or* funeral march

3 **dawdling, lingering, loitering,** lag, **lagging**

4 **slowing, slackening,** flagging, slowing down; **delay, detention, setback,** hold-up, check, obstruction

verbs

5 **go slow** *or* **slowly, take it slow; drag,** drag out; **creep, crawl;** laze, idle; go dead slow, get nowhere fast; shuffle *or* stagger *or* totter *or* toddle along; drag one's feet, **saunter, stroll, amble,** waddle, toddle (*nonformal*); limp, hobble

6 **plod, trudge,** lumber; plod along

7 **dawdle, linger, loiter, delay,** waste time, **take one's time,** lag, drag, trail; flag, falter, halt

8 **slow, slow down** *or* **up, let down** *or* **up, ease off** *or* **up, slack off** *or* **up, slacken,** relax, moderate, taper off; **delay, detain,** impede, obstruct, arrest, stay, **check,** curb, **hold up, hold back,** keep back, set back, hold in check; take one's foot off the gas; idle

adjectives

9 **slow, leisurely,** slack, moderate, gentle, **easy,** deliberate, unhurried, relaxed, gradual, circumspect, tentative, cautious, reluctant; **creeping, crawling; tottering, staggering, toddling, trudging, lumbering,** ambling, **waddling,** shuffling, **sauntering,** strolling; **sluggish,** languid, lazy, indolent; idle; **slow-moving; limping, hobbling; halting; faltering, flagging**

10 **dawdling, lingering, loitering,** delaying, **lagging,** dragging

11 **retarded,** eased, slackened; **delayed, detained,** checked, **arrested,** impeded, set back, backward, behind; late

adverbs

12 **slowly, slow, leisurely,** unhurriedly, easily, moderately, gently; lazily, idly, deliberately, tentatively, cautiously, reluctantly; in

slow motion, at a funeral pace, with faltering or halting steps

13 **gradually,** little by little

167 TRANSFERRAL, TRANSPORTATION

1 **transfer; interchange; translation; migration; import, importation; export;** deportation, extradition, expulsion, **transit,** transition; **passage; communication,** spread, dissemination, diffusion; transfusion

2 **transportation, transport, carrying,** bearing, **carriage,** haulage, freight, **shipping; delivery; travel**

3 **moving, removal, movement,** relocation, shift; **displacement**

4 moving pavement; conveyor belt; lift, escalator

5 **freight, consignment,** goods; **cargo,** load, pack; **baggage, luggage**

verbs

6 **transfer, transmit,** switch; **transplant,** translate; **pass,** pass over, **hand over,** consign, assign; **deliver; pass on,** pass the buck (*nonformal*), hand on, relay; **import, export;** deport, extradite, expel; communicate, diffuse, disseminate, spread, impart

7 **remove, move, relocate, shift;** displace, dislodge; take away, cart off or away, carry off or away; set or lay or put aside, put or set to one side

8 **transport, convey,** freight, conduct; **take; carry, bear,** lift, haul

9 **send,** send off or away, send forth; **dispatch,** transmit, consign, forward; **ship,** ship off,

freight, embark, pass along, send on; **post, mail,** airmail, drop a letter; **export**

10 **fetch, bring,** go and get, **go after, go for,** call for, pick up; **get,** obtain, procure, secure; **bring back, retrieve;** chase after, run after, fetch and carry

11 **ladle, dip, scoop;** dish out or up; cup; **shovel,** spade, fork; **spoon; pour,** decant

adjectives

12 **movable; portable;** interchangeable

adverbs

13 from hand to hand, from door to door; by freight, by express, by rail, by bus, by ship, by aeroplane, by mail, by special delivery, by messenger, by hand

14 **on the way,** along the way, on the road; **en route,** in transit; in passing

168 TRAVEL

nouns

1 **travel,** travelling, going, journeying, touring, **movement, motion, transit, progress, passage,** course, crossing; **tourism**

2 **travels,** journeys, migrations

3 **wandering, roving, roaming, rambling,** traipsing (*nonformal*), flitting, straying, drifting, pilgrimage; ramble; the open road; **migration,** passage, trek; **immigration; emigration**

4 **journey, trip,** trek; progress, course, run; **tour,** grand tour; travel agency or bureau, holiday company; **conducted tour,** pack-

age tour *or* holiday; **excursion**, **jaunt**, **outing**; round trip, circuit; **cruise**; **expedition**, campaign; safari, hunting expedition, **pilgrimage**, **voyage**

5 riding, **driving**; **motoring**, cycling; **horseback riding**

6 ride, **drive**; spin *and* whirl (*both nonformal*)

7 walking, going on foot; strolling, sauntering, ambling; **tramping**, **marching**, **hiking**, trudging; treading; lumbering, waddling; toddling, staggering, tottering

8 walk, ramble, amble, **hike**, traipse (*nonformal*); slog, trudge; **stroll**, **saunter**; **promenade**; jaunt; **constitutional** (*nonformal*); **march**; **parade**

9 step, **pace**, **stride**; **footstep**, tread; hop, jump; skip

10 gait, **pace**, **walk**, **step**, **stride**, **tread**; saunter, stroll; shuffle, hobble, limp, waddle; totter, stagger, lurch; slouch, droop, drag; mince, scuttle, prance, flounce, stalk, strut, swagger; slink, slither, sidle; jog; amble, trot, gallop; velocity; slowness

11 leg, **limb**; **pins** (*nonformal*); hind leg; shin; ankle; calf; knee; thigh; ham

12 gliding, **sliding**, slipping, slithering, sweeping, flowing, sailing; **skating**, **skiing**; glide, slide, slither, sweep

13 creeping, **crawling**, going on all fours; sneaking, stealing, slinking, sidling, padding, prowling; worming, snaking; creep, crawl, scramble, scrabble

verbs

14 travel, **go**, **move**, **pass**, cover ground; **progress**; **move on** *or* **along**; **wend one's way**; run, flow, stream

15 (*go at a given speed*) **go**, **go at**, reach, **make**, **do**, hit (*nonformal*)

16 traverse, **cross**, travel **over** *or* **through**, pass through, **go** *or* **pass over**, **cover**; patrol, scout; make one's rounds; scour the country; voyage

17 journey, **travel**, make *or* take *or* go *or* go on a journey, **take** *or* **make a trip**, get around *or* about, trek, jaunt; **tour**; hit the trail (*nonformal*), go on the road; **cruise**, **go on a cruise**, **voyage**; go abroad, go to foreign places *or* shores; go on *or* make a pilgrimage; campaign, go overseas, go on an expedition, go on safari

18 migrate; **emigrate**, expatriate

19 wander, **roam**, **rove**, range, flit, traipse (*nonformal*), knock around *or* about (*nonformal*); prowl, **drift**, **stray**, float around, meander, ramble, stroll, saunter, jaunt, go *or* run about; take to the road, **hit the road** *or* **trail**

20 go for an outing; **get some air**; **go for a walk**; **go for a ride**

21 go to, **repair to**, make one's way to, set foot in, **visit**, drop in *or* by

22 creep, **crawl**, scramble, scrabble, grovel, **go on hands and knees**, go on all fours; worm one's way, inch along; **sneak**, **steal**, slink, sidle, pad, prowl; **tiptoe**, **go on tiptoe**

23 walk, traipse (*nonformal*); **step, tread, pace, stride,** pad; foot it; leg it; hoof it, peg *or* jog *or* shuffle on *or* along

24 (*ways of walking*) **stroll,** saunter; shuffle, scuffle, straggle, slouch; stride, straddle; **trudge, plod,** peg, traipse (*nonformal*); clump, drag, **lumber;** stamp, stomp (*nonformal*); hobble, halt, limp, lurch; totter, stagger; toddle; waddle, wobble, wiggle; slither, sidle; stalk; **strut, swagger;** mince, prance, flounce; trip, skip, foot; hop; jump; bundle along; **amble**

25 go for a walk, take a walk, take one's constitutional (*nonformal*), stretch the legs; **promenade,** parade

26 march, tramp, hike, backpack; file, **parade,** go on parade; do the goose step

27 hitchhike *or* hitch; hitch *or* bum *or* cadge *or* thumb a lift (*nonformal*)

28 sleepwalk, somnambulate, walk in one's sleep

29 drive, go for a drive; go for a spin (*nonformal*); **drive, chauffeur; motor,** taxi; bus; bike *and* cycle *and* wheel *and* pedal (*all nonformal*); **motorcycle, bicycle;** go by rail, catch a train (*nonformal*)

30 go on horseback, ride, ride bareback; mount; trot, amble, pace, canter, gallop, lope; prance, frisk

31 glide, coast, skim, sweep, flow; **sail, fly,** flit; **slide, slip,** skid, slither; skate, ice-skate, rollerskate, skateboard; ski; toboggan, sledge, sleigh

adjectives

32 travelling, moving, trekking, passing; **itinerant; journeying,** strolling; **walking, pedestrian, touring,** on tour

33 wandering, roving, roaming, rambling, meandering, strolling, **straying;** nomadic, floating, drifting; fugitive; **vagrant,** vagabond

34 creeping, crawling, on hands and knees, on all fours; **on tiptoe**

35 travelled, cosmopolitan

adverbs

36 on the move *or* **go,** en route, in transit, on the fly; on the run, on the road

37 on foot, by foot

38 on horseback, horseback, by horse, mounted

169 TRAVELLER

nouns

1 traveller, tourist; travel *or* **tourist guide; visitor; sightseer; voyager, cruiser, sailor; jet set; pilgrim; passenger;** adventurer, climber, mountaineer; explorer, pioneer; camper; astronaut

2 itinerant, rolling stone

3 vagabond, vagrant; tramp, knight of the road; beggar; stray; urchin, street urchin

4 nomad, gypsy, Bohemian

5 migrant; immigrant; expatriate; displaced person, exile

6 pedestrian, walker

7 rider, equestrian, horseback rider, cavalier, knight; mounted policeman; cowboy; **jockey;** circus rider

8 driver, motorist; chauffeur; lorry driver; bus driver; road hog (*nonformal*)

9 cyclist; motorcyclist

10 engine driver, train driver

11 conductor, guard; stationmaster; baggage man; porter

170 VEHICLE

nouns

1 vehicle, carrier, means of transport, carriage; aircraft

2 wagon; van, caravan; covered wagon

3 cart, barrow, wheelbarrow

4 baby buggy (*nonformal*), pram; walker, push chair

5 wheel chair, Bath chair

6 cycle, bicycle, bike (*nonformal*); **tricycle; motorcycle,** bike (*nonformal*)

7 automobile, car, auto, motor, motor vehicle

8 (*nonformal terms*) **jalopy,** banger, wheels

9 police car, patrol car; squad car; police van; wagon *and* paddy wagon *and* Black Maria (*all nonformal*)

10 lorry, truck

11 (*public vehicles*) **commercial vehicle; bus,** chartered bus, motor coach; express bus, local bus; **cab, taxi, rental car; hired car**

12 train, passenger train; express train, express; freight train, goods train; subway, tube, underground; rolling stock

13 railway car, car; coach; buffet car *or* compartment; smoking compartment

14 tram *or* tramcar; horse box; cable car

15 tractor, bulldozer

16 trailer, mobile home; caravan

17 sledge, sleigh; toboggan

18 skates, ice skates, hockey skates, figure skates, roller skates, skateboard; **skis**

171 SHIP, BOAT

nouns

1 ship, cargo ship, container ship, cruise ship, dredge, freighter, liner, paddle boat *or* steamer, tanker, trawler, **boat,** canoe, lifeboat, motorboat, shell; vessel, craft, bottom, bark, hull, hulk, keel

2 sailing vessel, sailing boat, cruiser, sailing ship, tall ship, **galley; yacht**

3 motorboat; cruiser, power cruiser, **cabin cruiser**

4 liner, ocean liner, luxury liner; **cruise ship**

5 warship, war vessel, naval vessel; ship of war, armoured vessel; battle cruiser, battleship, communications ship, cruiser, destroyer, heavy cruiser, hospital ship, mine layer, mine ship

6 carrier, aircraft carrier

7 submarine, underwater craft

8 ships, shipping, merchant navy *or* fleet; **fleet;** line; fishing fleet, whaling fleet, etc; **navy**

9 float, raft; life raft; buoy, life buoy; bob

10 rigging, rig, tackle, tackling, **gear;** roping

11 timber; **mast,** pole

12 **sail, canvas,** muslin, cloth

13 **oar, paddle,** sweep, pole; steering oar

14 **anchor,** mooring, moorings; **berth,** slip; mooring buoy

adjectives

15 **rigged,** decked, trimmed

16 fit for sea; watertight, waterproof

172 AIRCRAFT

nouns

1 **aircraft,** aeroplane, **plane, ship, shuttle, space shuttle; flight instrument, aircraft engine**

2 **propeller plane,** tractor plane; piston plane

3 **jet plane, jet;** jumbo jet; supersonic jet, Concorde

4 **rocket plane;** rocket ship, spaceship; rocket

5 **rotor plane; helicopter**

6 **military aircraft,** combat plane; dive bomber, fighter, jet bomber, jet fighter, jet tanker, night fighter, torpedo bomber; air fleet; air force

7 **airship,** ship, **balloon**

8 **glider**

9 **parachute, chute** (nonformal); parachute jump; sky dive

173 WATER TRAVEL

nouns

1 **water travel,** travel by water, marine or ocean or sea travel, **navigation,** navigating, **sailing,** steaming, **cruising; boating,** canoeing, rowing

2 **voyage,** ocean or sea trip, **cruise,** sail; course, **run, passage; crossing**

3 **wake,** track; wash

4 (submarines) **surfacing,** breaking water; **dive;** crash dive

5 **way,** progress; headway

6 **waterway,** road, channel, ocean or sea lane, ship route, steamer track or lane; approaches

7 **swimming, bathing, swim, bathe;** crawl, freestyle, Australian crawl, breaststroke, butterfly, backstroke; treading water; floating; diving; wading; fin; flipper; surfing; windsurfing

8 **swimmer;** mermaid; bathing beauty; frogman

verbs

9 **navigate, sail, cruise,** steam, run, voyage, go by ship, go on or take a voyage, go to sea, sail the sea; **boat, yacht,** motorboat, canoe, row; surf; bear or carry sail; cross, traverse, make a passage or run; sail round; coast

10 **pilot, steer,** guide, direct, manage, handle, run, operate; **navigate,** shape or chart a course

11 **anchor,** come to anchor, lay anchor, **cast anchor,** let go the anchor, drop the hook; **dock, tie up; moor,** pick up the mooring; run out a warp or rope; lash, lash and tie; disembark

12 **weigh anchor,** drop the mooring, cast off or loose or away

13 **get under way,** put or have way upon, **put** or **push** or **shove off; put to sea,** go to sea; **sail,** sail away; embark

14 **set sail**, hoist sail, **make sail**, trim sail

15 **make way**, gather way, **make headway**; make knots; **go full speed ahead**; **go** or run or steam at flank speed

16 **shipwreck**, wreck, beach, run on the rocks

17 **list, heel**, tip

18 **capsize, upset, overturn**, turn over, keel, keel over or up; somersault; **sink, founder**, be lost, go down; scuttle

19 (*submarines*) **surface**, break water; **submerge, dive**, go below

20 **row, paddle**, ply the oar, **pull**, punt

21 **float, drift**; **sail**; skim; ghost, glide, slip; ride the sea, plough the deep

22 **pitch, toss, tumble**, toss and tumble, pitch and toss, **plunge**, rock, reel, sway, lurch, heave, **flounder**

23 **swim, bathe**, tread water, **float**, float on one's back; **wade; dive**

adjectives

24 **nautical, marine, maritime, naval**

25 **aquatic, swimming**; shore, seashore; tidal; deep-sea

26 **floating**, afloat

27 **adrift**, afloat, untied, loose

adverbs

28 **on board**, on board ship, **aboard**, all aboard, afloat; **on deck**; in sail

29 **under way**, making way; **at sea**, on the high seas, in blue water; **under sail** or **canvas**, with sails spread; under press of sail or

canvas or steam; on or off the heading or course; homeward bound

30 **overboard**, over the board or side

174 MARINER

nouns

1 **seaman, sailor, navigator**, sea or water dog (*nonformal*), jack, **tar, salt** (*nonformal*), hearty; common or ordinary seaman, able-bodied seaman; deep-sea man; fisherman; pirate

2 **navy man, marine**, Royal Marine; cadet, naval cadet; frogman

3 **oar**, oarsman, punter; galley slave

4 **hand**; cabin boy; purser; steward, stewardess, mess steward, hospital steward; mail orderly; navigator; radio operator, gunner; watch

5 **skipper** (*nonformal*), **commander**; navigator, navigating officer, sailing master; deck officer; watch officer; **mate**, first or chief mate, second mate, third mate; pipes (*nonformal*); chief engineer; naval officer

6 wharf hand, docker

175 AVIATION

nouns

1 **aviation, flying, flight**; powered flight, jet flight; **gliding**, soaring, sailing; ballooning; **air traffic**; airline traffic; commercial aviation, general aviation, private aviation, private flying; air show

2 **takeoff**; taxiing, takeoff run

3 **flight**, trip, run; powered flight; solo flight; supersonic flight; test flight

4 **air travel**, air transport; **air cargo; airline travel**, airline service, scheduled airline, charter airline, **shuttle**, shuttle service

5 (*Air Force*) **mission**, flight operation; training mission; combat rehearsal, **dry run** (*nonformal*); reconnaissance, observation flight, search mission; combat flight; scramble (*nonformal*); **air raid**; bombing mission; bombing; **air support** (*for ground troops*), **air cover**

6 **landing**, coming in (*nonformal*), touching down; arrival; crash landing

7 **crash**; crash landing; collision, mid-air collision; near collision

8 **airport, airfield**, port, aviation field, **landing field; air terminal; air base**

9 **runway**, strip, landing strip; **flight deck**, landing deck

10 (*air, atmosphere*) **weather, weather conditions;** cloud layer *or* cover; visibility; **overcast;** fog; trough; front; **air pocket** *or* **hole; turbulence;** head wind, **unfavourable wind; tail wind, favourable wind; cross wind**

11 **air lane, air line**, air route, corridor, flight path

verbs

12 **fly**, be airborne, wing, take *or* make a flight, take to the air; **jet; aeroplane;** travel by air, go by plane *or* air, ride the skies; **soar**, drift, hover; **cruise; glide**

13 **pilot**, control, be at the controls, **fly**, manipulate, drive (*nonformal*)

14 **take off**, hop *or* jump off (*nonformal*), become airborne, get off *or* leave the ground, take to the air

15 **ascend**, climb, gain altitude, mount

16 (*manoeuvre*) perform aerobatics; **spin; loop**, loop the loop; **roll**, spiral, dip, nose down, nose up

17 **dive**; lose altitude

18 **land, alight, light**, touch down; **descend**, come down; come in, come in for a landing

19 **parachute, bail out, jump**, make a parachute jump

adjectives

20 **aviation**, aerial; aerodynamic

21 **flying, airborne**, soaring; hovering, fluttering; gliding

adverbs

22 **in flight, on the wing** *or* fly, while airborne

176 AVIATOR

nouns

1 **pilot**, air pilot, licensed pilot, private pilot, airline pilot, commercial pilot; captain, chief pilot; second officer; flight engineer, third officer; jet pilot; instructor; test pilot; bush pilot; astronaut; stunt pilot

2 **military pilot**, naval pilot, combat pilot; fighter pilot; bomber pilot; observer; **aviation cadet**, air *or* flying cadet, pilot trainee; ace; air force

3 **crew**, flight crew; **navigator;** gunner; crew chief; aerial photographer; **flight attendant, steward, stewardess,** hostess

4 **ground crew**, landing crew

177 ARRIVAL

nouns

1 **arrival, coming, advent,** approach, appearance, **reaching;** attainment, accomplishment, achievement

2 **landing;** docking, mooring, tying up, dropping anchor; **getting off,** coming or going ashore

3 **return,** homecoming

4 **welcome,** greetings

5 **destination, goal;** port, haven, harbour; end of the line, terminus, **terminal;** stop, last stop; **airport, air terminal**

verbs

6 **arrive, arrive at, come, come or get to,** approach, access, **reach, hit** (nonformal); find, gain, attain, accomplish, achieve, make, **make it** (nonformal), get there, reach one's destination, end up; **come to rest,** settle, settle in; **make or put in an appearance, show up** (nonformal), turn up, surface, pop up (nonformal); **get in, come in, roll in; check in;** clock or punch or ring or time in (all nonformal), sign in; hit town (nonformal); come to hand, be received

7 **arrive at,** get at, **reach,** arrive upon, **come upon, hit upon,** stumble on or upon

adjectives

8 **arriving,** approaching, entering, **coming,** incoming; homeward

adverbs

9 **arriving,** on arrival or arriving

178 RECEPTION

nouns

1 **reception, taking in,** receipt, receiving; **welcome,** open or welcoming arms; refuge

2 **admission,** admittance, acceptance; **installation,** inauguration, initiation; baptism, ordination; enrolment

3 **in** (nonformal), entry, **entrance, access, opening, open door, open arms;** a foot in the door

4 **eating; drinking; swallowing,** gulping, swallow, gulp

5 (drawing in) **suction,** suck, sucking; inspiration, aspiration; sniff

6 **absorption,** digestion, assimilation, infiltration; **sponging, blotting; sponge,** blotting paper

7 (bringing in) **introduction;** import, **importation**

8 welcoming, welcome, openness, hospitality

verbs

9 **receive, take in; admit, let in,** give entrance or admittance to; **welcome,** bid welcome, roll out the red carpet; open the door to, give refuge or shelter or sanctuary to, throw open to

10 **eat, put away; drink; swallow, devour, engulf; gulp, gulp down,** wolf down, gobble

11 **draw in, suck,** suck in or up; **inhale,** breathe in; sniff

12 **absorb, assimilate,** digest, **drink,** take up or in, drink up or in; **blot up, soak up,** sponge; infiltrate; **soak in,** seep in

179 DEPARTURE

nouns

1 **departure, leaving, going,** passing, **parting; exit,** walkout (*nonformal*); **withdrawal,** removal, retreat, retirement; evacuation, abandonment, desertion; escape, flight, getaway (*nonformal*); exodus; migration

2 **start,** starting, takeoff and getaway (*both nonformal*); the starting gun or pistol; the green light

3 **boarding;** takeoff

4 **leave, parting, departure; farewell,** good-bye; parting words; swan song; one for the road

5 **point of departure, starting place** or **point, start,** base; starting line or post or gate, starting blocks

verbs

6 **depart,** make off, be off, take oneself off or away, take leave or take one's leave, **leave, go, go away, go off, get off** or **away, come away, go one's way, go** or get along, go on, get on; move off or away, move out; exit; take or break or tear oneself away, take wing or flight

7 (*nonformal terms*) **beat it, split,** up and off, trot, toddle, stagger along, buzz off, pull up stakes, clear out, hit the road or trail, get lost, get going, shove off,

push off, get out, clear out, get the hell out, make oneself scarce, take off

8 **set out, set forth,** go forth, issue forth, **set off,** be off, be on one's way, **start, start out** or **off, strike out,** get off, get away; get the green light; break; set sail

9 **quit, vacate,** evacuate, abandon, desert, turn one's back on, walk away from, leave to one's fate, leave high and dry; leave or desert a sinking ship; **withdraw,** retreat, **beat a retreat,** retire, remove; walk away, disappear, vanish; **bow out** (*nonformal*), make one's exit

10 **hurry away; dash off, nip** and nip off (*both nonformal*), tear off or out

11 **run off** or **away,** run along, flee, take to flight, fly, take to one's heels; run for one's life; beat a retreat or a hasty retreat

12 **check out;** clock and ring and punch out (*all nonformal*), sign out

13 say or bid good-bye or farewell, take leave; see off or out

14 **leave home,** go from home; leave the country, emigrate, expatriate, defect; vote with one's feet; burn one's bridges

adjectives

15 **departing, leaving; parting,** last, final, farewell

16 **departed, left, gone,** gone off or away

adverbs

17 **hence,** thence, whence; off, **away,** forth, out

180 ENTRANCE

nouns

1 **entrance, entry,** access; **admission, reception; incoming,** income; **importation,** import, importing; **input, intake; penetration,** injection; infiltration, leakage; introduction

2 **influx,** incursion

3 **immigration,** incoming population, foreign influx

4 **entrant,** arrival; **visitor; immigrant,** newcomer; settler; **intruder**

5 **entrance,** entry, gate, door, portal; **inlet,** intake, approach, **access,** means of access, way in; a foot in the door; **opening; passageway,** corridor, hall, hallway, passage, way; gangway

6 **porch; portal, threshold, door, doorway, gate, gateway; hatch**

verbs

7 **enter, go in** or **into,** access, cross the threshold, **come in;** be admitted, gain admission or admittance; **set foot in,** walk in; **get in,** jump in; **drop in,** look in, visit, drop by or in, pop in (*nonformal*); **breeze in; break** or **burst in; barge in** or come barging in and wade in (all *nonformal*); push or press in, crowd in, pack in, squeeze in; slip or creep in, wriggle or worm oneself into, get one's foot in the door, insinuate oneself; intrude; take in, admit; insert

8 **penetrate, pierce,** pass or go through, get into, make an entrance; crash (*nonformal*)

9 **flow in, pour in**

10 **filter in, infiltrate, seep in,** soak in

adjectives

11 **entering, incoming;** in, inward; intrusive

adverbs

12 **in,** inward, inwards, inwardly

181 EMERGENCE

nouns

1 **emergence,** coming out, coming forth, coming into view, surfacing; issue; **emission,** giving out; venting, discharge

2 **exit,** exodus; going out; **departure; extraction**

3 **discharge; outpouring,** gush

4 **leakage; leak; drip,** dribble, drop, trickle; distillation

5 **exuding;** filtering; straining; seep; **oozing;** weeping

6 **emigration;** exile, deportation

7 **outlet, exit,** way out; loophole, escape; **opening;** estuary; chute, weir; **vent,** port; safety valve; avenue, channel; spout, tap; **exhaust;** door; pore

verbs

8 **emerge, come out,** issue, come into view, extrude; surface; come to the fore; emanate, arise, come; jump out, leap out; **burst forth, erupt;** break cover, **come out in the open;** protrude

9 **exit, make one's exit; go out,** get out, walk out, bow out (*nonformal*); walk out on; **depart**

10 **run out,** empty; **exhaust, drain; flow out, pour out,** spew, flow,

pour, well, surge, gush, jet, spout, spurt

11 leak, leak out, drip, dribble, drop, trickle, distil

12 exude; emit, discharge, give off; filter; strain; seep, ooze; bleed; weep; excrete

13 emigrate; exile, expatriate, defect; deport

14 export, send abroad

adjectives

15 emerging, emergent; issuing, arising, surfacing, coming, forthcoming

16 outgoing; effusive, effluent

17 exuding; porous, leaky

adverbs

18 forth; out, outward, outwards, outwardly

182 INSERTION

nouns

1 introduction, injection; entrance; penetration; interjection; graft, transplant

2 insert, graft

verbs

3 insert, introduce, insinuate, inject; enter; penetrate; put in, stick in, throw in, slip in; interject

4 install, inaugurate, initiate, invest, ordain; enlist, enrol, sign up, sign on

5 graft, implant

6 thrust in, drive in, force in, push in, ram in, squeeze in, cram in, pack in

7 implant, transplant; fit in

183 EXTRACTION

nouns

1 extraction, withdrawal, removal; eradication, uprooting; excavation, mining, quarrying, drilling; dredging

2 unearthing, uncovering, digging out

3 drawing, drafting, sucking, suction, aspiration; pumping, siphoning, tapping; milking; drainage, draining, emptying; bleeding

4 drawing out or forth, bringing out or forth; evocation, calling forth; arousal

5 extortion, claim, demand; wresting, wrenching, wringing, tearing, ripping

6 (obtaining an extract) squeezing, pressing; distillation; rendering; soaking; concentration

7 extract; essence, spirit; distillation; concentrate

8 extractor; siphon; pump, vacuum pump; press; corkscrew; forceps, pliers, pincers, tweezers; crowbar

verbs

9 extract, take out, get out, withdraw, remove; pull, draw; pull out, draw out, tear out, rip out, wrest out, pluck out, pick out, weed out, prise out; pull up, root up or out, uproot, eradicate; cut out, excise; gouge out; extricate, disentangle, unravel; dig up or out, excavate, unearth, mine, quarry, dredge, dredge up or out

10 exhume, dig up, uncover

11 draw off, draft off, draft, draw, draw from; **suck,** suck out *or* up, **siphon off;** pump; tap, broach; let, let out; bleed; milk; **drain,** decant; exhaust, empty

184 ASCENT

nouns

1 ascent, rise, rising, uprising; **taking off,** leaving the ground, takeoff; **jump,** vault, spring, leap; mount, **mounting; climb, climbing,** clamber; surge, upsurge; upgrade; elevation; **increase**

2 stairs, stairway, staircase, flight of stairs; **steps;** spiral staircase, winding staircase; stile; ramp, incline

3 ladder, scale; stepladder, rope ladder

4 step, stair, footstep, rest, stepping-stone; **rung, round,** spoke, stave, scale; doorstep; string

5 climber; mountain climber, **mountaineer,** rock climber

6 (*comparisons*) rocket; lark, skylark, eagle

verbs

7 ascend, rise, mount, arise, up, **go up,** rise up, come up; go onwards and upwards, go up and up; **surge;** spiral; stand up, **rear,** rear up, **tower,** loom; grow up

8 shoot up, spring up, jump up, **leap up,** start up, fly up, pop up, bob up; float up, surface, break water; rocket

9 take off, leave the ground, leave the earth behind, gain altitude; become airborne; **soar,** zoom,

fly; **hover,** hang, poise, float, float in the air

10 climb, climb up, **mount, clamber up,** scramble up, claw one's way up, struggle up, inch up, shin, work *or* inch one's way up, climb the ladder; **scale,** scale the heights; climb over, surmount

11 mount, get on, climb on; **board,** go aboard, go on board; **get in,** jump in, hop in, pile in (*nonformal*)

12 upturn, turn up, slope up

adjectives

13 ascending, in the ascendant, **mounting, rising,** uprising; ascendant; **leaping, springing,** spiralling; **upward;** uphill; rearing, rampant; climbing

adverbs

14 up, upward, upwards; skyward; uphill; upstream; upstairs; up north

185 DESCENT

nouns

1 descent; drop, fall, downfall, debacle, **collapse,** crash; **swoop,** stoop; cascade, waterfall, cataract, **downpour;** downturn, downward trend; gravitation; downgrade; **decrease**

2 lowering, decline, slump, subsidence, lapse; cadence; **droop,** sag

3 tumble, fall, flop (*nonformal*); **sprawl; stumble;** trip; **dive,** plunge

4 slide; slip; landslide, subsidence; **avalanche**

verbs

5 **descend, go** or **come down,** dip down, lose altitude; gravitate; **fall, drop,** precipitate, rain, rain or pour down, fall or drop down; **collapse,** crash; **swoop,** stoop; **pitch, plunge, plummet;** cascade, cataract; parachute; come down a peg (*nonformal*); **fall off,** drop off; go downhill

6 **sink, go down,** submerge; **set, settle,** settle down; **decline,** lower, **subside,** give way, lapse, cave in; **droop,** slouch, **sag; slump,** slump down; flop *and* flop down (*both nonformal*); plop or plop down; founder

7 **get down, alight,** touch down, **light; land,** settle, perch, come to rest; **dismount, get off;** climb down

8 **tumble, fall, fall down,** take a fall or tumble; fall over, tumble over, trip over; **sprawl,** sprawl out, measure one's length; fall headlong, fall flat, fall on one's face; topple down or over; capsize; **topple,** lurch, ·pitch, **stumble,** stagger, totter, list, tilt, trip, flounder

9 **slide, slip,** slip or slide down; avalanche

10 **light upon,** alight upon, settle on; **descend upon,** come down on, **fall on,** hit or strike upon

adjectives

11 **descending,** descendant, on the descendant; **down,** downward; **dropping, falling, plunging, plummeting; sinking,** foundering, submerging, setting; declining, **subsiding;** collapsing, tottering; drooping, sagging; downhill

12 **downcast;** hanging

adverbs

13 **down, downward, downwards,** from the top down; below; downhill; downstream; downstairs; down south

186 CONTAINER

nouns

1 **container, receptacle;** holder, vessel, utensil; basin, pot, pan, cup, glass, ladle, bottle; **cask; box, case; basket; luggage, baggage;** cabinet, cupboard

2 **bag, sack,** poke (*nonformal*); **pocket,** fob; **balloon,** bladder

187 CONTENTS

nouns

1 **contents, content; insides,** guts; **components, constituents, ingredients,** elements, **items, parts, divisions,** subdivisions; **inventory,** index, census, list

2 **load, cargo, freight, charge, burden**

3 **lining, liner; filling, packing,** padding, **stuffing**

4 (*essential content*) **substance, sum** and **substance, stuff, material, matter,** medium, building blocks, fabric; **gist, heart, soul, meat; core,** kernel, marrow, pith, sap, spirit, **essence,** distillation

5 **enclosure,** the enclosed

verbs

6 **fill, pack, load; line; pad,** wad, **stuff;** feather, fur

188 ROOM

nouns

1 **room, chamber,** four walls

2 **compartment,** chamber, enclosed space; **cavity,** hollow, hole; **cell; booth,** stall, crib; box, pew; **crypt, vault**

3 **nook, corner, cranny, niche,** recess, cove, bay, alcove; cubicle

4 **hall;** assembly hall; gallery; meeting room; **auditorium; concert hall; theatre,** music hall; stadium, dome, **arena;** lecture hall; operating theatre; dance hall; ballroom; **chapel**

5 **parlour, living room, sitting room, morning room, drawing room, front room,** best room (*nonformal*), **salon**

6 **library; study,** studio; **office,** workplace; **loft**

7 **bedroom,** chamber, master bedroom, guest room; nursery; dormitory

8 **den,** retreat, closet, cabinet

9 **dining room,** dining hall, refectory, commons; dining car *or* diner; **restaurant, cafeteria**

10 **playroom,** recreation room, family room, game room; **gymnasium**

11 **utility room,** laundry room, sewing room

12 **wardrobe, cloakroom; dressing room, fitting room**

13 **attic,** attic room, **garret, loft;** junk room

14 **cellar, basement;** wine cellar; coal cellar, coal hole, hold, hole, bunker

15 **corridor, hall,** hallway; passage, **passageway; gallery;** arcade, cloister

16 **portal, portico,** entry, entrance, **entrance hall, threshold; lobby, foyer**

17 side room; **waiting room; reception room,** presence chamber *or* room; throne room; lounge

18 **porch, veranda,** patio, gallery

19 **balcony,** gallery, terrace

20 **showroom,** display room, exhibition room, gallery

21 **hospital room; ward,** maternity ward, fever ward, etc; private room; examining *or* examination room, consulting *or* consultation room; treatment room; **operating room** *or* **OR,** operating theatre, surgery; delivery room; recovery room; emergency, emergency room; intensive care unit *or* **ICU;** pharmacy; clinic, nursery; laboratory *or* blood bank

22 **bathroom, lavatory, water closet** *or* **WC,** rest room, **toilet**

23 (*for vehicles*) **garage;** coach *or* carriage house; hangar

189 TOP

nouns

1 **top,** top side, upper side, upside; surface; upper storey, top floor; **roof;** rooftop

2 **summit, top; peak, pinnacle; crest, brow;** ridge, edge; **crown,** cap, **tip,** point, spire, pitch; **apex, zenith, climax,** pole; **culmination; extremity, maximum, limit,** upper extremity, highest point, very top, top of the world, extreme limit, **sky,** heaven *or*

heavens, seventh heaven, cloud nine (*nonformal*); noon, high noon

3 **topping**, icing

4 (*top part*) **head**, heading, cap, **crown, crest**

5 **head**, pate, poll (*nonformal*), crown, bonce *or* noggin (*both nonformal*); brow, ridge

6 **skull**, cranium; brain box *or* case

verbs

7 **top**, top off, **crown, cap**, crest, **head**, tip, peak, surmount; have the top place *or* spot; **culminate**, consummate, climax; ice (*a cake*); fill, top up

adjectives

8 **top**, topmost, **uppermost, highest; maximum**, ultimate; vertical, **consummate; head**, capital, chief, paramount, supreme

9 **topping, crowning, capping**, heading, surmounting; **culminating**, consummating, perfecting

10 **topped**, headed, **crowned, capped**, tipped, peaked

adverbs

11 **on top**, at *or* on the top; at the top of the tree *or* ladder, on top of the heap; on the crest *or* crest of the wave; at the head

190 BOTTOM

nouns

1 **bottom, underside, underneath; belly; rock bottom, bedrock**, bed; **grass roots;** lowest level *or* layer *or* stratum; **nadir,** the pits (*nonformal*)

2 **base, basement, foot,** footing, sole, toe; **foundation;** skeleton; bare bones; frame

3 ground covering, **ground,** earth; **floor,** flooring; parquet; **deck; pavement,** paving, surfacing, asphalt; concrete; **cover,** carpet, floor covering; artificial turf

4 **bed, bottom, floor,** ground, **basin, channel;** seabed, ocean bottom

5 **foot,** extremity; **hoof; paw,** pad; **toe; heel; sole;** instep, arch

verbs

6 **base on, found on, build on; root in; underlie**

adjectives

7 **bottom,** deepest, **lowest;** bedrock; ground

8 **basic; underlying, fundamental, essential, elementary, elemental, primary, primitive, rudimentary, original; radical**

9 **pedal;** footed, clawed; toed

191 VERTICALNESS

nouns

1 **verticality; erectness, uprightness;** steepness, sheerness, **perpendicularity**

2 **vertical, upright, perpendicular,** plumb, normal; right angle

3 **precipice, cliff,** sheer drop, steep, bluff, wall, face, scar; crag

4 **erection, erecting, elevation; rearing,** raising; uplifting

5 **rising, uprising,** ascending, ascent; vertical height *or* dimension; **gradient,** rise

verbs

6 **stand, stand erect, stand up, stand upright, stand up straight,** be erect, be on one's feet; hold oneself straight *or* stiff

7 **rise, arise,** ascend, mount, **rise up, get up,** get to one's feet; **stand up, stand on end; stick up,** cock up; bristle; **rear,** ramp; sit up, sit bolt upright; jump up, spring to one's feet

8 **erect, elevate, rear, raise,** pitch, **set up,** raise *or* lift up; **upend,** stand upright *or* on end

adjectives

9 **vertical, upright,** bolt upright, **erect,** standing up; rearing, rampant; **upended**

10 **perpendicular, plumb,** sheer, steep, precipitous, plunging

adverbs

11 **vertically,** upright, up; **on end**

192 HORIZONTALNESS

nouns

1 **horizontalness,** horizontality; **levelness, flatness,** evenness, smoothness, flushness

2 **prostration; repose; sprawl, loll**

3 **horizontal, plane, level, flat;** horizontal projection; horizontal axis; water level, sea level; **plain,** prairie, bowling green, table, billiard table; floor, platform

4 **horizon, skyline;** sea line

verbs

5 **lie, lie down, recline, repose,** lounge, sprawl, loll, splay; **grovel, crawl**

6 **level, flatten, even,** align, level out, smooth out, flush; roll out; **lay; raze,** lay out; **fell**

adjectives

7 **horizontal, level, flat,** flattened; **even,** smooth, smoothed out; **flush; plane,** rolled, trodden, squashed

8 **prostrate,** flat; **lying, reclining;** sprawling, lolling, lounging; sprawled, spread, splay, splayed; grovelling, crawling

adverbs

9 **horizontally, flat,** flatly; **evenly,** flush; **level**

193 PENDENCY

nouns

1 **pendency;** hanging, suspension

2 **hang, droop, dangle; sag,** bag

3 **overhang,** overhanging, **projection,** jutting

4 **pendant, hanger; hanging,** drape

5 **suspender, hanger,** supporter; braces, suspenders

verbs

6 **hang,** hang down, fall; **dangle,** swing, flap; flow, drape, cascade; **droop; sag,** bag; **trail, drag**

7 **overhang,** hang over, hang out, **project,** jut

8 **suspend, hang, hang up,** put up

adjectives

9 **suspended,** hung; **hanging,** pending, dependent; **falling; dangling,** swinging, falling loosely; weeping; flowing, cascading

10 **drooping,** limp, loose, floppy (*nonformal*); **sagging;** baggy

11 **overhanging,** overhung, lowering, **pending; projecting; jutting**

194 PARALLELISM

nouns

1 **parallelism;** alignment; **analogy**

2 **parallel;** parallel line, parallel bar

verbs

3 **parallel,** be parallel; run parallel, go alongside, go beside, run abreast; match, equal

4 line up, align; match; correspond, follow, equate

adjectives

5 **parallel; equidistant,** collateral, concurrent; lined up, aligned; equal, even; analogous

adverbs

6 **in parallel;** alongside, abreast

195 OBLIQUITY

nouns

1 **obliquity; deviation,** divergence, digression, excursion, aberration, squint

2 **inclination, leaning,** lean; **slant,** rake, **slope; tilt, tip,** pitch, list, sway

3 **bias, bend,** bent, **crook, warp, twist, turn, veer, sheer, swerve,** lurch

4 **incline,** inclination, **slope, grade,** gradient, pitch, **ramp,** bank, chute; hillside, side

5 **descent,** dip, drop, fall, **decline**

6 **ascent,** climb, **rise,** rising

7 **diagonal,** oblique, bias, slash, **slant**

verbs

8 **deviate, diverge,** deflect; **angle off, swerve, veer,** sheer, sway, twist, turn, bend, bias

9 **incline, lean; slope, slant,** rake, pitch, grade; **tilt, tip,** keel, sway; **ascend, rise, go uphill; descend, decline,** dip, **go downhill**

10 **cut,** slash

11 **zigzag, stagger**

adjectives

12 **oblique;** deviant, divergent; **indirect,** side, sidelong; left-handed, sinister; backhand; circuitous

13 **askew; awry;** squinting; **crooked**

14 **inclining,** inclined; **leaning, sloping,** sloped; raking, pitched; **slanting,** slanted; biased; **tilting,** tilted, tipped; sidelong

15 (sloping downward) **downhill; descending,** falling, dropping, dipping; **declining**

16 (sloping upward) **uphill; rising,** uprising, **ascending,** climbing

17 **steep, precipitous, bluff,** plunging, abrupt, **sheer,** sharp

18 **across; diagonal; slant, bias, biased**

19 **crooked, zigzag;** hairpin; staggered

adverbs

20 **indirectly,** sidelong

21 **askew, awry**

22 **diagonally;** across

196 INVERSION

nouns

1 **inversion;** turning inward; **reversing, reversal;** revulsion

2 overturn, upset, overthrow, upturn, **turnover,** spill (*nonformal*); subversion; **revolution; somersault**

3 inverse, reverse, converse, opposite

verbs

4 invert; introvert; turn down; turn out; **revert,** relapse, lapse; convert; turn about; rotate, revolve

5 overturn, turn over, upturn, **upset, overthrow,** subvert; **turn turtle; tip over,** keel over, topple over; **capsize**

adjectives

6 inverted, backwards, reversed; inside out, outside in; reverted, lapsed; **capsized; introverted**

adverbs

7 vice versa, backwards, turned around; **upside down,** over

197 EXTERIORITY

nouns

1 appearance, outward appearance, front, manner; cosmetics

2 exterior, outside; surface, covering, skin, envelope, crust, rind, shell; plating; top; **periphery, fringe,** circumference, outline, border; **face,** facade, **front**

3 outdoors, outside, the open

4 show, display; realization

verbs

5 bring out, show, display, exhibit; project, realize

adjectives

6 exterior, external; outer, outside, outward, outlying; **outermost; surface, superficial;** cosmetic; **peripheral, fringe,** roundabout; apparent, seeming; open, public

7 outdoor, out-of-doors, **outside; open-air**

8 foreign, alien

adverbs

9 externally, outwardly; without, outside, outwards, out; apparently; openly, publicly

10 outdoors, outside, abroad

198 INTERIORITY

nouns

1 interiority, internality, internalness, **inwardness,** internalization; depth

2 interior, inside, inner, inward, internal; recesses; bosom, heart, soul; inner self, inner life; core, centre

3 inland, interior; heartland

4 insides, inwards; guts (*nonformal*); giblets; entrails, bowels, guts

verbs

5 put in, keep within; enclose, surround, contain, comprise, include, enfold, assimilate

adjectives

6 interior, internal, inner, inside, inward; **innermost, intimate,** private; gut (*nonformal*); **intrinsic;** deep; central; indoor

7 inland, interior

adverbs

8 **internally, inwardly, intimately,**
deeply, profoundly; intrinsically;
centrally

9 **in, inside, within;** therein,
wherein

10 **inward, inwards, inwardly;** inland, inshore

11 **indoors,** indoor

199 CENTRALITY

nouns

1 **centre; middle, heart, core, nucleus;** kernel; pith, marrow; **hub,**
axis, pivot; **navel; bull's-eye;
dead centre**

2 **focus,** focal point, prime focus

3 **nerve centre; control centre**

4 **headquarters** *or* **HQ,** central station, central office, main office,
central administration, seat,
base; company headquarters

5 **metropolis, capital;** shopping
centre, tourist centre, trade centre, etc

6 **centralization,** centring; focus;
convergence; **concentration**

verbs

7 **centralize, centre,** middle; centre round

8 **focus, concentrate, channel,** direct; converge

adjectives

9 **central, middle; equidistant;**
centralized, concentrated; key

10 **focal;** converging

11 **concentric; coaxial**

adverbs

12 **centrally,** in the centre of, at the
heart of

200 ENVIRONMENT

nouns

1 **environment, surroundings,**
ambience, entourage, circle; **precincts, milieu; neighbourhood,
vicinity; suburbs;** outskirts, out-
posts; borders, boundaries, limits, periphery, perimeter; **context, situation;** habitat

2 **setting, background,** ground,
surround, field, scene, arena,
theatre; back, rear, distance;
stage, stage set

3 **ambience, atmosphere, climate,
air,** aura, spirit, feeling, feel,
quality, colour, local colour,
sense, note, tone, overtone,
undertone

4 **surrounding,** environment; **enclosure;** inclusion, involvement

verbs

5 **surround, encompass,** enclose;
envelop, enfold, lap, wrap, embrace, involve, invest

6 **encircle, circle; girdle;** ring,
band; loop

adjectives

7 **surrounding,** encompassing, enclosing; **enveloping,** wrapping,
enfolding, embracing; **encircling,**
circling; bordering, peripheral;
suburban, neighbouring

8 **environmental;** ecological

9 **surrounded, enclosed; enveloped,** wrapped, enfolded,
wreathed

10 **encircled, circled,** ringed, belted

adverbs

11 **around**, round, **about**, round about; close

12 **all round**, all about

201 CIRCUMSCRIPTION

nouns

1 **limiting**, circumscribing, **bounding, demarcation**, definition, determination, specification

2 **limitation, restriction**, confinement, prescription, restraint, discipline, moderation; qualification, **hedging**; bounds, boundary, limit

3 **patent, copyright; trademark**, registered trademark, trade name

verbs

4 **circumscribe, bound**; stake out, rope off; hedge in; **define**, determine, fix, specify; surround; enclose

5 **limit, restrict, restrain, bound**, confine; narrow, tighten; specialize; **condition**, qualify, hedge; discipline, moderate, contain; restrain oneself; **patent, copyright**, register

adjectives

6 **circumscribed; defined**, definite, determined, specific, stated, set, fixed; surrounded, encircled

7 **limited, restricted**, bound, finite, confined, prescribed, cramped, strait, narrow; conditioned, qualified; disciplined, moderated; **deprived**, pinched, strapped, patented, registered, protected

8 **restricted**, out of bounds, off-limits

9 **limiting, restricting**, defining, determining, confining; restrictive, exclusive

202 BOUNDS

nouns

1 **bounds, limits**, boundaries, limitations, **confines, pale**, marches, verges, edges, outlines, outskirts, **fringes**, periphery, **perimeter**; parameters; **circumference**

2 **outline, contour**, lines, shapes, figure, **configuration; features; profile, silhouette**; skeleton, framework

3 **boundary, bound, limit**, limitation, extremity; **barrier**, block; time limit, deadline, target date; finish, **end, tail end; start**; threshold; upper limit, ceiling; lower limit, floor, nadir; **confine**, march; **boundary line, border line**, frontier, break, boundary

4 **border, edge, verge, brink**, brow, **brim, rim, margin, skirt**, fringe, hem; forefront, cutting **edge**, front line, vanguard; sideline; shore, bank, coast

5 **frontier, border**, march, marches; outskirts, outpost

6 **edging, bordering, trimming**, binding, skirting; fringe; **hem**; frill

verbs

7 **bound**, circumscribe, surround, limit, enclose, divide, separate

8 **outline, contour**; silhouette, profile

9 **border, edge, bound, rim, skirt**, hem, lap, margin, march, verge; **adjoin; frame**; trim, bind

adjectives

10 **bordering,** skirting; extreme, terminal; **marginal, borderline,** frontier; coastal

11 **bordered,** edged; **fringed,** trimmed, skirted

12 outlining; peripheral; outlined, **in outline**

203 ENCLOSURE

nouns

1 **enclosure; confinement; imprisonment,** incarceration, jailing; **siege,** blockade, cordoning, quarantine; inclusion

2 **packaging, packing; boxing; canning; bottling; wrapping**

3 (*enclosed place*) **enclosure, confine,** precinct, enclave; **cloister; pen,** fold; **yard,** park, court, courtyard; square; **field, arena,** theatre; **container**

4 **fence, wall,** boundary, **barrier; railing; balustrade**

verbs

5 **enclose,** close in, bound, include, **contain;** encompass; **surround,** encircle; **fence in,** wall in, curtain off; box in, pocket; pen, cage, impound; **imprison,** incarcerate, jail, lock up; **besiege,** beset, cordon off, quarantine, blockade; **wrap**

6 **confine,** cramp, encase

7 **fence, wall,** fence in; bar; hem in, hedge in

8 **package, pack, parcel;** box, case, encase; **wrap**

adjectives

9 **enclosed; confined,** bound, cloistered; **imprisoned,** incarcerated, jailed; caged, cramped, restrained; besieged, beleaguered, beset, cordoned off, blockaded; pent-up, **penned, cooped,** fenced, walled, barred

10 enclosing, confining, **cloistered,** surrounding; limiting

11 **packed, packaged,** boxed, canned, tinned, encased; bottled; **wrapped**

204 INTERPOSITION

nouns

1 **intervention, intrusion**

2 **interjection,** introduction, **injection; remark,** aside; episode; insert

3 **intermediary,** medium; link, tie, connection, **go-between,** liaison; middleman, broker, agent; **mediator**

4 **partition, dividing wall,** division, separation, **wall, barrier; border,** dividing line; **buffer,** bumper

verbs

5 **interject; mediate,** go between, liaise; **intervene;** put between, sandwich; stick in, slip in; squeeze in; **intrude**

6 **partition,** set apart, separate, divide; **wall off,** fence off, screen off

adjectives

7 **intervening; intermediate,** intermediary, **middle**

8 partitioned, walled

205 INTRUSION

nouns

1 **intrusion**, imposition, **interference**, intervention, interruption, injection, interjection; **encroachment**, trespass, unlawful entry; **infringement**, invasion, incursion, influx, **infiltration**; entrance

2 **meddling**; impertinence, presumption

3 **intruder**, **trespasser**; gatecrasher (*nonformal*)

4 **busybody**, **pry**

verbs

5 **intrude**, come between, **intervene**, interfere, insinuate, impose; **encroach**, **infringe**, impinge, **trespass**, **invade**, **infiltrate**; break in, burst in; **barge in** (*nonformal*), **cut in**, **push in**, **crowd in**, **elbow in**, **muscle in** (*nonformal*); **get in**, creep in, sneak in, slip in

6 **interrupt**, put in, cut in; jump in

7 **meddle**, busybody, **meddle with**, **tamper with**; **pry**, snoop

adjectives

8 **intrusive**, obtrusive, **interfering**

9 meddling; **officious**, impertinent, presumptuous; **busybody**; forward; **prying**, inquisitive

206 CONTRAPOSITION

nouns

1 **opposition**; **antithesis**, contrast; **confrontation**; contention; hostility

2 **opposites**, polar opposites; **poles**, opposite poles, North Pole, South Pole

3 opposite side, other side; **reverse**, **inverse**, **converse**; heads, tails (*of a coin*)

verbs

4 **oppose**, contrast, match; **confront**, face, front, meet head-on; counteract; contend; **polarize**

adjectives

5 **opposite**, opposing, **facing**, confronting; **opposed**, at loggerheads; **reverse**, **inverse**, **converse**; **polar**, up against

adverbs

6 **opposite**, **poles apart**; contrary, counter

207 FRONT

nouns

1 **front**, **fore**, forefront, forehand; **priority**; **frontier**; **foreground**; frontage; front page; **preface**, front matter, foreword; prefix; front view, front elevation; **head**, heading; **face**, facade, frontal; **false front**, window dressing, display; brave face; facet; head (*of a coin*); lap

2 **vanguard**, van, point, point man; **spearhead**, advance guard, **forefront**, cutting edge, avant-garde; scout; **pioneer**; **precursor**; leader; **front**, front line; outpost

3 **bow**, rostrum, figurehead, nose, beak

4 **face**; **countenance**, features

5 **forehead**, brow

verbs

6 **lead, head,** head up; forge
ahead; **pioneer;** lead, be first;
front, front for, represent, speak
for

7 **confront, face, meet, encounter,**
breast, stem, brave, meet squarely, stand fast; **confront with, face
with,** present to, lay before;
bring up, bring forward; **challenge,** dare, defy, start something

8 **front on, face upon,** look over,
overlook

adjectives

9 **front, frontal; fore, forward,**
forehand; **foremost; first, earliest,**
pioneering, advanced; leading,
first, chief, head, prime, primary;
confronting, head-on; **ahead, in**
front

10 **fronting, facing,** opposite

adverbs

11 **before, ahead, in front,** in advance; **foremost, first**

12 **forward,** forwards, **onward,** onwards; **facing**

208 REAR

nouns

1 **rear, rear end, hind end,** hind
part, **behind,** stern, tail, tail end;
heel; **back,** tail (*of a coin*); back
door; back seat

2 rear guard, rear, rear area

3 **back,** ridge

4 **buttocks,   rump,** bottom;
haunches

5 (*nonformal terms*) arse, bum, behind, backside, cheeks, hind end,
rear, rear end

6 **tail;** scut (*of a hare, rabbit, or*
deer); brush (*of a fox*); dock,
stub; queue; **pigtail**

7 **stern,** heel; counter

verbs

8 **come last, follow,** come after;
trail, trail behind, lag behind,
straggle; fall behind, fall back;
back up, back, go back, go backwards, regress, get behind; revert

adjectives

9 **rear, back,** backward, retrograde;
tail; **hind**

adverbs

10 **behind,** in the rear; in the background; behind the scenes; tan-
dem

11 **backward,** backwards

209 SIDE

nouns

1 **side, flank, hand;** border; bank,
shore, coast; siding; beam; quarter; hip, haunch; cheek, chop;
temple; **profile**

verbs

2 **side, flank;** edge, skirt, border

3 **go sideways, sidle,** lateral, **edge,**
veer, angle, slant, sidestep

adjectives

4 **side, lateral;** flanking, skirting;
beside; alongside, parallel; side-
long, **sideways**

5 **sided, flanked,** handed; lateral;
one-sided, unilateral; **many-**
sided, multilateral

adverbs

6 **sideways,** sidelong, aside

7 **aside**, sidelong; **alongside**, in parallel

210 PRESENCE

nouns

1 **presence; immediacy;** availability; **occurrence**, existence

2 **omnipresence, ubiquity;** continuum; infinity

3 penetration; transfusion; diffusion; absorption; **overrunning**, ripple effect, overwhelming

4 **attendance**, number present, turnout (*nonformal*)

5 **visitor; patron;** supporter; spectator; audience

verbs

6 **be present**, be there; **occur**, exist; lie, stand, remain

7 **pervade, permeate**, penetrate; diffuse, imbue; **fill**, extend throughout; occupy; **overrun**, run through, overwhelm; teem with

8 **attend, be at; appear**, turn up, show up (*nonformal*), **visit;** watch, see; witness, look on

9 **revisit**, return to, come again

10 **frequent, haunt**, hang around *and* hang about (*both nonformal*)

11 **present oneself**, report

adjectives

12 **present**, attendant; **on hand**, on deck (*nonformal*); **immediate, available, accessible, at hand,** in view, in place

13 **omnipresent**, ubiquitous, everywhere; continuous, uninterrupted, infinite

14 **pervasive**, pervading

15 **permeated**, saturated, shot through, filled with; crawling, swarming, teeming

adverbs

16 **here, there**

17 **in person**, personally, **in the flesh**

211 ABSENCE

nouns

1 **absence; want, lack,** deprivation; subtraction

2 **vacancy, emptiness,** bleakness; job vacancy, opening, vacant post

3 **void, vacuum,** blank, emptiness, empty space; clean slate; **nothing**

4 **absence, leaving,** taking leave, **departure; running away,** fleeing; **disappearance,** escape; **truancy,** French leave; **leave; vacation,** holiday, day off, sick leave

5 **absentee,** truant

verbs

6 **be absent, stay away,** keep away, not come

7 **absent oneself;** slip out, bow out, exit, **depart, disappear,** escape

8 **play truant,** go AWOL

9 (*nonformal terms*) **split,** make tracks, push off, **beat it,** shove off

adjectives

10 **absent,** not present, **away, gone,** departed, disappeared, vanished; **missing,** wanting, lacking, not

found, omitted, taken away, subtracted, deleted; long-lost

11 **away from home:** on tour;
abroad, overseas

12 **vacant, empty,** hollow, inane,
bare, void, devoid; **blank,** clear,
white, bleached; bland, insipid;
barren

13 **available, open,** free, **unoccupied, uninhabited,** unmanned;
deserted, abandoned, forsaken

adverbs

14 **absently;** hollowly, blankly

15 **away, elsewhere,** somewhere
else, not here

212 NEARNESS

nouns

1 **closeness, proximity,** intimacy,
immediacy; approach, convergence; **vicinity, neighbourhood,**
surroundings, setting, grounds,
confines; **foreground**

2 **short distance, short way,** step,
short step, a little; short range;
middle distance; **stone's throw,**
spitting distance (*nonformal*);
earshot, **hair,** an inch; hair's
breadth

3 junction, connection, union;
conjunction

4 **meeting,** joining up, **encounter;**
confrontation; collision course,
near thing

5 **contact, touch;** caress, brush,
glance, nudge, kiss, rub, graze

6 **neighbour;** bystander, onlooker

verbs

7 **near, come near, approach;**
converge

8 **approximate, approach,** get
warm (*nonformal*), come near

9 **adjoin,** join, **connect; neighbour,** border

10 **contact, touch, feel, impinge;**
hit; **graze,** caress, kiss, nudge,
rub, brush, glance, scrape, skim,
shave

11 **meet, encounter; come across,
run across,** meet up; **come
upon;** come among; **meet with,**
confront; run into

12 **stay near;** stand by; hover over;
cling to, clasp, hug, huddle

13 **join, adjoin,** butt against, neighbour

adjectives

14 **near, close,** intimate; **approaching,** nearing

15 **nearby, handy, convenient,**
neighbouring

16 **adjacent, next,** immediate, **ad-
joining; neighbouring, neighbour;** bordering, connecting;
joined

17 **in contact,** contacting, **touching,
meeting,** impinging; grazing,
kissing, glancing, brushing, rubbing, nudging

18 **nearer, closer**

19 **nearest, closest,** next, immediate

adverbs

20 **near, close;** hard; **nearby, close
by,** at hand; **about, around**
(*nonformal*); next-door

21 **in conjunction;** beside

22 **nearly, near, close, closely;** almost, all but, not quite; **just
about**

23 **approximately,** practically (*non-

formal); roughly, roundly; **generally**, generally speaking, say

213 INTERVAL

nouns

1 **interval, gap, space; clearance,** margin, **room; jump, leap, interruption; hiatus; time interval, interim**

2 **crack,** cranny, chink, **crevice,** fissure, incision, notch, score, cut, gash, slit, split, **rift,** rent; **opening,** cavity, hole; **gap, abyss, gulf, chasm,** void; **breach, break,** fracture, rupture; fault, flaw; slot, groove, furrow, moat, ditch, trench; joint, seam; **valley**

verbs

3 **space,** dot, scatter, **space out, separate,** split off, part

4 **crack, cut, cut apart,** gash, slit, **split,** rent, rip open; **open;** breach, break, fracture, rupture

adjectives

5 **spaced, spaced out,** dotted, scattered, **separated, parted**

6 **cleft, cut, cracked,** rift, rent; **slit, split;** gaping

214 HABITATION

nouns

1 **habitation, tenancy,** occupation, **living, dwelling,** lodging, staying, stopping, staying over; squatting; cohabitation, living together; **abode, habitat**

2 **peopling, population,** inhabiting; **settlement,** plantation

3 **housing; lodging,** hospitality; living quarters; **housing development; housing problem, housing bill**

4 **camping;** camp

5 temporary stay; **stay, stop; stopover**

verbs

6 **inhabit, occupy;** rent, lease; **reside, live, live in, dwell, lodge, stay,** remain, abide; **room,** crash (*nonformal*); berth, squat (*both nonformal*); cohabit, live together

7 stop, stay, **stop over,** stay over

8 **people, populate, inhabit;** colonize, **settle,** settle in

9 **house;** shelter, harbour; **lodge, quarter, put up**

10 **camp;** pitch, **pitch camp;** go camping, camp out, sleep out, rough it

adjectives

11 **inhabited, occupied; peopled,** populated, colonized

12 **resident, in residence;** residing, **living, dwelling,** lodging, **staying;** cohabiting, live-in

13 **housed,** lodged

14 **habitable, fit to live in**

215 NATIVENESS

nouns

1 **nativeness, nationality,** citizenship

2 **naturalized citizenship, nationalization, adoption, assimilation;** papers; culture shock

verbs

3 adopt, admit, **assimilate;** go native (*nonformal*)

adjectives

4 **native, indigenous,** endemic; mother, maternal, original, primitive

5 **naturalized,** adopted, **assimilated**

216 INHABITANT, NATIVE

nouns

1 **population, inhabitants,** dwellers, **populace, people, folk, souls, body; public;** general public; **community, society, nation,** constituency, electorate; **census,** head count; population statistics

2 **inhabitant; occupant,** occupier, **dweller, tenant,** inmate; **resident;** incumbent

3 **native,** earliest inhabitant, primitive settler; primitive; aboriginal

4 **citizen, national,** subject; **naturalized citizen,** immigrant

5 **fellow citizen,** fellow countryman, **compatriot, countryman**

6 **townsman, townswoman, villager,** city dweller

7 **householder,** proprietor

8 **lodger,** paying guest; **tenant**

9 **settler; colonist,** colonial, immigrant; **pioneer; precursor**

217 ABODE, HABITAT

nouns

1 **abode, habitation, place, dwelling,** dwelling place, roof, **residence; lodging; seat, nest, living space; home turf; address,** permanent residence; **housing;** public housing, public-sector housing; council house; private housing

2 **home, fireside, hearth,** fireplace; **household;** ancestral halls

3 **domesticity; housekeeping**

4 **quarters, living quarters; lodgings,** lodging; room; **rooms,** berth, roost; **housing, shelter**

5 **house,** dwelling, dwelling house; **building, structure, edifice,** erection; **hall; lodge; manor house; town house;** country house, country seat; ranch house, farmhouse, farm; prefabricated house; penthouse; **rectory,** vicarage, manse; official residence, Downing Street, White House; presidential palace; embassy, consulate

6 **estate; mansion,** stately home; **villa, castle,** tower; **palace,** court

7 **cottage, bungalow; cabin,** log cabin; **second home, holiday home;** chalet, lodge

8 **hut, shack, shanty, shed; booth,** stall; sentry box; **outhouse;** privy; **pavilion,** kiosk

9 wigwam, tepee; igloo (*Eskimo*)

10 **hovel, dump** (*nonformal*), hole, pigsty

11 kiosk, alcove, retreat; **conservatory, greenhouse,** glasshouse

12 **apartment, flat,** tenement, chambers, rooms; bedsitter, granny flat; **suite; penthouse**

13 **flats, tenement;** block of flats, high rise

14 **inn, hotel,** hostel, **tavern;** guest house, bed and breakfast; youth hostel, hospice; **dormitory; motel**

15 **trailer, mobile home,** caravan

16 **habitat**, home, **range**, stamping grounds, locality, native environment

17 **zoo**, menagerie

18 **barn**, **stable**, stall; mews

19 **kennel**; pound

20 **aviary**, bird cage; pigeon loft; roost, perch; coop, henhouse

21 **aquarium**; fishpond

22 **nest**; **beehive**, hive, wasp's nest

23 **lair**, **den**, cave, **hole**, covert, mew, form; **burrow**, tunnel, earth, run, couch, lodge

24 **resort**, **haunt**, stamping ground (*nonformal*); meeting place, club; casino; health farm; **spa**, baths, springs

25 (*disapproved place*) **dive** (*nonformal*), **den**, **lair**

26 **camp**, detention camp, concentration camp

verbs

27 **keep house**, run a household

adjectives

28 **residential**; domestic; **home**, **household**; palatial

29 homely; — comfortable, friendly, cheerful, peaceful, cosy, snug, intimate; simple, plain

30 **domesticated**, **tame**, tamed, broken in

218 FURNITURE

nouns

1 **furniture**, furnishings, home furnishings, household effects, household goods, office furniture, school furniture, church furniture; chair, sofa, bed, table, desk, cabinet, mirror, clock, screen; **suite**, decor

219 TOWN, CITY

nouns

1 **town**, township; **city**, **metropolis**, greater city, conurbation; **borough**; **suburb**, suburbia, outskirts; market town; small town; twin town; boom town, ghost town

2 **village**, **hamlet**; **country town**

3 **capital**, capital city, **seat**

4 **town hall**, **city hall**, **municipal building**; courthouse; fire station, police station; county building; community centre

5 **city centre**, **inner city**; suburbs, suburbia, outskirts; residential area; shopping centre; **ghetto**

6 **square**, market, forum

7 **circle**, circus; crescent

adjectives

8 **urban**, **metropolitan**, **municipal**, **civic**; city, town, village; suburban; **inner-city**, ghetto

220 REGION

nouns

1 **region**, **area**, **zone**, belt, **territory**, terrain; **place**; **space**; **country**, **land**, ground, soil; territorial waters; air space; heartland; **district**, **quarter**, **section**; part, parts; **neighbourhood**, vicinity; premises, confines, precincts, milieu

2 **sphere**, hemisphere, **orbit**, circle; **circuit**, **beat**, **round**, walk; **realm**, **domain**, dominion, jurisdiction; border; march; **province**,

precinct, department; **field,** pale, arena

3 **zone; longitude; latitude,** parallel; equator, the line; tropics

4 **plot, patch, tract, field;** lot; air space; block, square; section; close, enclave, pale

5 (*territorial divisions*) **state, territory, province,** region, electorate, government, principality; **county; borough, ward,** riding; **township; metropolis, city, town; village,** hamlet; **district;** diocese, parish

6 **Northern Hemisphere; Southern Hemisphere; Western Hemisphere,** Occident; **Eastern Hemisphere,** Orient; America, Asia, Europe, Africa, Oceania

adjectives

7 **regional, territorial, geographical**

8 **local, localized,** parochial, provincial, insular, limited, confined

221 COUNTRY

nouns

1 **country,** land; **nation,** nationality, **state; power,** superpower, world power; **republic,** people's republic; **kingdom; empire;** realm, dominion, domain; **principality;** county; **province,** territory, possession; colony, settlement; mandate; buffer state; **ally,** military ally, treaty partner; satellite; developed nation; underdeveloped nation

2 **fatherland, motherland,** mother country, **native land,** native soil, **birthplace; cradle; home, homeland**

3 nationhood, **nationality; sovereignty,** independence, self-government; **nationalism**

222 THE COUNTRY

nouns

1 **the country,** agricultural region, farmland, arable land, rural district, countryside, woodland, **the soil,** grass roots; highlands, moors, uplands, foothills; lowlands, plains

2 hinterland, outback (*Australia*); **the bush,** bush country, **woods,** woodlands, forests, timbers, brush; wilderness, wilds; **wasteland; frontier,** outpost

3 **rusticity,** simplicity, unspoiledness

adjectives

4 **rustic, rural,** country, provincial, farm, pastoral **agrarian; agricultural**

5 **country,** outback (*Australia*), wild, virgin; **waste;** woodland

223 LAND

nouns

1 **land, ground,** earth, clod, **soil,** dirt, dust, clay; terrain; **dry land;** arable land; grassland, woodland; earth's crust; **real estate,** real property, acres, **territory**

2 **shore, coast; strand, beach,** sands; waterside, **waterfront;** shoreline, coastline; bank, embankment; riverside; **seashore, coast, seaside; bay**

adjectives

3 terrestrial, earthly

4 earthy, earthen

5 **coastal, seaside, shore;** riverside; seaside, seafront, beachfront; tidal

adverbs

6 **on land;** ashore; by land, overland

7 **on earth;** under the sun, **here below**

224 STREAM

nouns

1 **stream, waterway, channel;** river; **brook,** branch; rivulet

2 **head; source**

3 **tributary, branch, fork,** affluent; effluent

4 **flow, flux; stream, current,** set, trend, tide, water flow; drift; **course, surge, gush, rush,** spate, run, race; undercurrent; affluence; downpour

5 **torrent, river, flood,** flash flood, **deluge;** spate

6 **overflow,** spill, **flood, deluge,** cataclysm

7 **trickle, dribble, drip,** drop; distillation, condensation, sweating; seeping

8 **lap, wash, slosh, splash**

9 **jet, spout, spurt,** squirt, spit, spew, spray; rush, **gush, flush; fountain, font; geyser**

10 **rapids, rapid,** white water, wild water; chute

11 **waterfall, cataract,** fall, **falls,** cascade

12 **eddy,** back stream; **whirlpool,** gulf; backwater

13 **tide;** tide gate; high tide, high water, full tide; **low tide,** low water; lunar tide, solar tide; **flood tide, ebb tide;** flux, flow, flood; ebb

14 **wave, billow, surge, swell;** trough, peak; **sea,** heavy swell, ocean swell, ground swell; **roller;** surf, **breakers; ripple; tidal wave; bore;** white horse; rough water

verbs

15 **flow, stream, issue, pour, surge, run, course, rush, gush, flush, flood;** empty into, flow into, join; set, make, trend; flow out; flow back, surge back, ebb, regurgitate

16 **overflow,** flow over, wash over, **run over, brim over,** lap, overrun, **spill, slop; cascade; inundate, engulf,** swamp, sweep, overwhelm, **flood,** deluge, submerge

17 **trickle, dribble, drip,** drop; **filter;** distil, condense, sweat; seep, weep; gurgle

225 CHANNEL

nouns

1 **channel, conduit, duct,** canal, course; **way, passage, passageway;** trough; tunnel, ditch, trench; entrance; exit; **stream**

2 **waterway, aqueduct,** water channel, water gate, **canal; bed,** river bed; **gully;** race; irrigation ditch, water furrow

3 **gutter, trough;** flume, chute, guide

4 **drain; sink; gutter; sewer**

5 **tube; pipe; tubing, piping;** reed, stem, straw; **hose,** garden hose, fire hose; pipeline; **siphon;** tap; funnel

6 **main,** water main, gas main

7 **spout,** beak

8 **nozzle,** pressure nozzle, spray nozzle, nose, snout; shower head, sprinkler head

9 **valve,** gate; **faucet, tap;** cock, draw cock, sea cock, drain cock, ball cock

10 **gate, head gate,** water gate; tide gate; weir; **lock,** lock gate

11 **hydrant,** fire hydrant, **plug,** water plug

12 air passage, air duct, **air hole;** breathing hole; nostril; **vent; ventilator,** ventilating shaft; wind tunnel

13 **chimney, flue,** flue pipe, funnel, **stack,** smoke pipe

verbs

14 **channel, conduct, convey,** put through; pipe, funnel, siphon; direct

adjectives

15 **tubular;** cylindrical; piped; valved

226 SEA, OCEAN

nouns

1 **ocean, sea,** tide, salt sea, salt water, blue water, deep water, open sea, **the brine, the deep, high seas**

2 **ocean; sea,** tributary sea, gulf, bay

3 sea devil, sea god; **mermaid,** siren; seaman

4 oceanography; marine biology

adjectives

5 **marine, maritime;** nautical; deep-sea

adverbs

6 **at sea;** afloat; by water, by sea

7 **overseas,** beyond seas, over the water, across the sea

8 **oceanward, seaward;** offshore

227 LAKE, POOL

nouns

1 **lake,** landlocked water, loch (*Scots*), mere, freshwater lake; glacial lake; volcanic lake; inland sea; **pool, pond,** still water, dead water; **oasis; puddle; lagoon; reservoir,** artificial lake; dam; **well, cistern,** tank, flowing well, **spring**

228 INLET, GULF

nouns

1 **inlet, cove,** creek, arm, canal, reach, loch (*Scots*), **bay; cove; gulf; estuary,** firth, mouth; **harbour,** natural harbour; straits, **narrows; sound**

229 MARSH

nouns

1 **marsh, swamp, morass, bog, mire, quagmire,** wash; glade; wallow; **moor, moorland,** peat bog; salt marsh; quicksand; **mud**

verbs

2 **mire**, sink in, **bog**

adjectives

3 **marshy; swampy;** boggy, miry; **muddy**

230 QUANTITY

nouns

1 **quantity**, quantum, amount, **whole; mass; bulk**, substance, matter, magnitude, **extent, sum; measure**, measurement; strength, force, numbers

2 **amount**, quantity, large amount, small amount, **sum, number**, count, group, total, reckoning, **measure, portion**, clutch, ration, share, issue, allotment, lot, deal; **batch**, bunch, heap (*nonformal*), pack, dose

3 **some**, somewhat, something; any, anything

verbs

4 **count**, enumerate, **number**, rate, fix; mete out, issue, allot, divide; **increase, decrease, reduce; measure**

adjectives

5 **quantitative**, quantified, measured; **some**, certain, one; a, an; **any**

adverbs

6 **approximately**, nearly, some, about, circa

231 DEGREE

nouns

1 **degree, grade, step**, leap; round, rung, tread, stair; **point**, mark, peg, tick; **notch, cut; plane**, level,

plateau; **period**, space, interval; **extent, measure**, amount, ratio, proportion, standard, height, pitch, reach, compass, range, scale, scope, calibre; **shade**, shadow, nuance

2 **rank, standing, level**, footing, **status**, station; **position**, place, sphere, orbit, echelon; **order**, estate, precedence, condition; rate, rating; **class**, caste; **hierarchy**

3 **gradation, graduation**, grading, staging, phasing, shading

verbs

4 **graduate, grade;** phase in, phase out, taper off; **increase, decrease**

adjectives

5 **gradual**, graduated, phased, staged; regular, progressive; hierarchical

adverbs

6 **by degrees; gradually;** a little, fractionally; by inches; slowly

7 **somewhat, kind of** (*nonformal*), sort of (*nonformal*), rather, pretty, quite, fairly; a little, a bit; slightly, scarcely; very, extremely

232 MEAN

nouns

1 **mean, middle; golden mean; medium**, happy medium; middle course; **average**, balance, norm, rule, generality; **mediocrity**, adequacy; **centre**

verbs

2 **average**, average out; avoid extremes; **do**, just do, pass

adjectives

3 **medium**, mean, **intermediate**, intermediary; **average**, normal, standard; middle-of-the-road, moderate; **ordinary**, usual, routine, common, mediocre, banal, so-so; **central**

adverbs

4 midway; **centrally**

5 all in all, on the whole, on balance; **generally**

233 GREATNESS

nouns

1 **greatness, magnitude**; fullness; **grandeur; immensity, vastness**, expanse, infinity; **might**, strength, power, intensity; bulk; **superiority**

2 **glory, eminence, prominence**, distinction; nobility; **fame**, renown, celebrity; heroism

3 **quantity, much, abundance**, profusion, plenty; **volume**, mass, mountain, load; bag, barrel, ton; world, acre, ocean, sea; flood, spate; **multitude**

4 **lot, lots**, deal, **heap, pile, stack**, loads, **raft**, spate, **wad, batch**, mint

verbs

5 **loom, bulk**, loom large, stand out; **tower**, rear, soar; **tower above**, rise above; **exceed, transcend**, outstrip

adjectives

6 **great, grand, considerable**; **mighty**, powerful, strong, irresistible, intense; maximum, **total**, **full**, comprehensive, exhaustive; grave, **serious**, heavy, deep

7 **large, immense, enormous, huge; gigantic**, mountainous, colossal, mammoth, monster, outsize, sizable, overgrown, monumental; **massive**, weighty, bulky, voluminous; **vast**, boundless, **infinite, immeasurable, cosmic, astronomical; spacious**, extensive; **tremendous**, stupendous, awesome

8 **much, many**, ample, **abundant**, copious, generous, overflowing, plentiful, **numerous, countless**

9 **eminent, prominent**, outstanding, high, elevated, towering, exalted, **lofty, sublime**; majestic, noble, distinguished; **magnificent**, heroic, superb; famous, renowned, glorious

10 **remarkable**, **outstanding**, extraordinary, **superior**, noteworthy; **marvellous**, notable, wonderful, formidable, exceptional, astonishing, fabulous, fantastic, incredible

11 *(nonformal terms)* **terrific; whacking, thumping, rousing**

12 **downright, outright, out-and-out; absolute, utter, perfect, consummate**, superlative, positive, decided; **thorough, complete**, total; **unmitigated**, unqualified, undeniable, unquestionable

13 **greatest, furthest, most, utmost**

adverbs

14 **greatly, largely; much**, very much, so, ever so; **considerably**, abundantly, plenty *(nonformal)*, no end, galore *(nonformal)*, **a lot; highly**

15 **vastly, immensely, enormously, hugely, tremendously**

16 **by far,** far

17 **very, exceedingly, quite,** so, **really, pretty,** only too

18 **decidedly, clearly,** manifestly, patently, **obviously,** visibly, unmistakably, unquestionably, **noticeably,** demonstrably; **certainly,** actually, **really, truly, undeniably,** without doubt, assuredly, **indeed, seriously**

19 **acutely, exceptionally,** eminently; **remarkably, markedly,** notably, **strikingly, emphatically,** prominently, conspicuously; **particularly, singularly,** peculiarly, uncommonly, extraordinarily, **unusually; wonderfully,** amazingly, marvellously, incredibly; **abundantly,** richly, amply, **generously; magnificently,** splendidly

20 **terribly, awfully, dreadfully, frightfully; excessively,** extravagantly, **inordinately**

21 **utterly, most; immeasurably,** indefinitely; **infinitely; perfectly, absolutely; purely, totally,** completely; unconditionally, unequivocally, **downright**

234 INSIGNIFICANCE

nouns

1 **insignificance,** meanness, triviality; **smallness**

2 **modicum; minimum; little, bit,** bite, **particle,** fragment, spot, **speck,** fleck, dot; pittance, dole; pinch, dribble, drop; grain, granule, pebble; **molecule, atom;** spoonful, handful, trivia

3 **scrap,** patch, **stitch, shred,** splinter, sliver; **morsel, crumb**

4 **hint, suspicion, suggestion,** intimation; **trace, touch, dash, smattering,** sprinkling; tinge; **taste, lick,** sip, **smell; shade,** shadow; gleam, spark

5 **trifle, a drop in the ocean**

adjectives

6 **insignificant, small, inconsiderable, inconsequential,** negligible; unimportant, **trivial,** trifling, petty, mean, niggling; shallow, cursory, superficial; **little, tiny, miniature, meagre; few; short**

7 **dainty, delicate; subtle,** tenuous, thin

8 **mere, sheer,** stark, bare, plain, simple

adverbs

9 **hardly, barely,** only just, **slightly,** lightly, fractionally, minimally, **little;** faintly, weakly, feebly; **a little, a bit**

10 **moderately,** mildly, **somewhat,** modestly, **fairly, partially,** partly; **comparatively, relatively; merely,** simply, purely, only; **at least,** at worst; **at most,** at best

11 not much; not nearly, **nowhere near**

235 SUPERIORITY

nouns

1 **superiority, greatness, lead,** prestige, favour; precedence, **priority,** prerogative, privilege; **excellence; seniority;** precedence; **success, accomplishment, skill**

2 **advantage; upper hand; start; edge**

3 **supremacy, first place,** height, zenith, summit, top spot (*nonformal*); **sovereignty, rule,** control; **kingship, dominion; command,** sway; **leadership,** presidency; **authority,** management, jurisdiction, **power; influence; maximum,** highest, most; **championship,** crown, laurels, first prize, blue ribbon, record

4 **superior, chief, head, boss, commander, ruler, leader, master;** senior, principal, big shot (*nonformal*); **genius;** paragon, virtuoso, ace, **star,** champion, winner

5 **nobility; aristocracy,** barons, top people (*nonformal*), **elite,** upper crust, upper class; **establishment,** ruling class

verbs

6 **excel, surpass, exceed, transcend,** overcome, **better,** improve on, perfect; **cap,** trump; top; **outweigh**

7 **beat, defeat; triumph; win**

8 **overshadow, eclipse, top,** extinguish; show up (*nonformal*), put down (*nonformal*)

9 **outdo,** edge out; **outstrip;** outwit; **outrun**

10 **distance; pass, surpass; get ahead; leave behind**

11 **rule, command, lead,** possess authority; **take precedence;** rank; **lead; star**

adjectives

12 **superior, greater,** better, finer; **higher,** upper, over, super, above; **eminent,** outstanding, distinguished, of choice; **surpassing, exceeding, excellent, excelling; ahead**

13 **superlative, supreme, greatest, best, highest,** maximum, most, utmost, outstanding; **top, uppermost, first-rate,** first-class

14 **chief, main, principal, foremost, leading, dominant;** great, arch, master; central, focal, prime, **primary,** first; **predominant; ruling, sovereign; star**

15 **matchless, champion;** immortal, inimitable, **incomparable; unbeatable,** invincible

adverbs

16 **exceedingly;** eminently, prominently; **supremely, the most;** incomparably

17 **chiefly, mainly, in chief; predominantly, mostly; principally, especially, particularly,** peculiarly; **primarily,** above all; indeed

18 **incomparably; uniquely; unbeatably**

236 INFERIORITY

nouns

1 **inferiority; subservience,** humility

2 **inferior, subordinate, junior;** secondary; follower, pawn; masses

3 **inadequacy, mediocrity,** deficiency, **imperfection; incompetence; failure; smallness;** meanness, triviality, **vulgarity**

verbs

4 **be inferior, fail;** want; not compare; serve, follow

5 **bow to;** give in (*nonformal*), lose face

adjectives

6 **inferior, subordinate,** small-scale, **secondary; junior, minor; subservient,** subject, servile, low, lowly, humble, modest; **lesser,** less, lower; **common,** vulgar, **ordinary;** underprivileged, disadvantaged; demeaning

7 **inadequate, mediocre,** deficient, imperfect, **insufficient, incompetent;** small, little, mean, base, petty, trivial, shabby

8 **least, smallest,** slightest, **lowest,** shortest; minimum, minimal; few

adverbs

9 **poorly, inadequately,** badly

237 INCREASE

nouns

1 **increase, gain, enlargement, amplification, growth,** development, widening, spread, broadening, elevation, **extension, increment; addition; expansion; proliferation; accumulation; upturn,** upsurge; **leap, jump**

2 **heightening, deepening; strengthening, magnification,** blowing up, exaggeration; **concentration; reinforcement,** redoubling; **acceleration; boom, explosion,** baby boom, population explosion

3 **gains, winnings, profits**

verbs

4 **increase, enlarge, amplify, augment, extend; expand, inflate;** lengthen, broaden, fatten, thicken; **raise,** put up, **up** (*nonformal*); **build up**

5 **intensify, heighten, deepen,** enhance, **strengthen,** beef up (*nonformal*); **exaggerate, magnify; reinforce,** double, redouble; triple; **concentrate; step up** (*nonformal*), accelerate

6 **grow, increase; spread, widen,** broaden; wax, swell, balloon, mount, **rise,** go up, crescendo, snowball; **intensify, strengthen;** accumulate; **multiply, proliferate,** breed; **boom, explode**

adjectives

7 **increased, heightened,** raised, elevated; **intensified,** deepened, reinforced, strengthened, fortified; **enlarged, extended,** augmented, amplified; broadened, widened, spread; **magnified, inflated, expanded,** swollen, bloated; **accelerated**

8 **increasing, rising; growing,** fast-growing, flourishing, blossoming, swelling, lengthening, **multiplying,** proliferating, spreading, expanding; intensifying; snowballing; mushrooming

adverbs

9 **increasingly,** more, ever more

238 DECREASE

nouns

1 **decrease, reduction, lessening, lowering,** waning, scaling down; depression, dampening; easing off; **alleviation,** relaxation; weakening, dying, tailing off; depreciation; **deflation; deduction;** subtraction; contraction

2 **decline, subsidence,** slump (*nonformal*), lapse, **drop; collapse,** crash; wane, ebb; down-

turn, retreat, remission; **fall, plunge,** dive

3 **waste, loss,** erosion, depletion, corrosion, consumption, exhaustion; dissolution

4 **curtailment,** cut, cutback

5 devaluing, undervaluing, **belittling**

verbs

6 **decrease, diminish, lessen;** abate; **decline, subside,** shrink, wane, wither, ebb, dwindle, languish, sink, wind down; **drop,** dive, plummet, plunge, fall; **waste,** wear, crumble, erode, corrode, consume; melt away

7 **reduce, decrease, diminish, lessen; lower, depress,** dampen; **downgrade;** depreciate, **deflate; cut; deduct; shorten; compress, shrink**

8 **abate,** ease; **weaken,** dilute, water down; alleviate, mitigate, slacken

9 **minimize, belittle,** detract from; play down

adjectives

10 **reduced, decreased, diminished, lowered; deflated,** contracted, shrunken; **eroded, worn; weakened;** miniaturized; **minimized, belittled; lower,** lesser, smaller, shorter

11 **decreasing, diminishing, lessening, subsiding, declining,** dwindling

adverbs

12 **decreasingly,** less, ever less

239 ADDITION

nouns

1 **addition,** attachment, junction, **joining,** uniting; **increase; adjunct**

2 (*maths terms*) plus sign, plus; sum, total

3 **adding,** computation

verbs

4 **add,** attach, adjoin, tag on; glue on; **complicate,** ornament, decorate

5 **add to, augment, supplement; increase; reinforce,** strengthen, fortify

6 **compute,** add up; total, total up, tally

adjectives

7 **additive,** additional; **cumulative**

8 **added, attached; adjunct**

9 **additional, supplementary; extra,** further, farther, fresh, **more,** new, **other,** another, ulterior; **surplus,** spare

adverbs

10 **additionally, in addition, also,** even more, more so, **as well,** too, else, **besides, to boot;** over, above; **plus; extra; moreover, furthermore,** then, again, yet; similarly, likewise; all included, altogether

240 ADJUNCT

(*thing added*)

nouns

1 **adjunct, addition,** increase, increment; **reinforcement; accessory,** attachment; **supplement,**

complement, continuation, extension; offshoot, side issue, corollary, side effect, spin-off (*nonformal*), **accompaniment, additive**

2 (*written text*) postscript, appendix; **epilogue; note, commentary;** prefix, suffix

3 (*building*) wing, **addition,** extension

4 **extra, bonus, premium; padding,** stuffing, filling; trimming, **frill,** flourish, decoration, ornament

241 SUBTRACTION

nouns

1 **subtraction, deduction, removal;** erosion, abrasion, wearing away; refinement

2 **reduction,** decrease, curtailment, shortening; depletion, remission; **depreciation,** disparagement; **extraction**

3 **elimination,** exclusion, extinction, eradication, destruction, annihilation; cancellation; writeoff; **amputation**

4 cancellation, omission; abbreviation

5 negative; minus sign, minus

6 (*thing subtracted*) **deduction,** minus

7 (*result*) **difference, remainder,** discrepancy, net, balance, deficit

verbs

8 **subtract, deduct,** take away, **remove,** withdraw; **reduce,** shorten, curtail, lessen, **diminish, decrease;** depreciate, disparage, detract; erode; **extract,** drain,

wash away; thin out, weed; **refine,** purify

9 **excise,** cut out; **cancel,** write off; **eradicate,** root out, **eliminate,** kill, kill off, annihilate, destroy, extinguish; **exclude,** except, take out, cancel out, censor out, bar, ban; **amputate;** prune, peel, clip, crop, dock, lop, shear, shave, strip

10 (*written text*) **delete,** erase, **cancel,** omit; edit out; cut; **censor;** abbreviate

242 REMAINDER

nouns

1 **remainder, remains, remnant, residue, rest, balance; leftovers, oddments; refuse,** scraps, **rubbish, waste;** shavings, sawdust; chaff, straw, stubble, husks; **debris,** ruins; end, fag end; vestige, trace, hint, shadow; **fossil,** relics

2 **dregs, grounds,** slag; **sediment, deposits; silt; scum, froth; ash, ember, cinder;** soot

3 **survivor,** heir, successor; **widow,** widower, **orphan**

4 **excess, surplus**

verbs

5 **remain, survive,** subsist

6 **leave,** leave behind

adjectives

7 **remaining, surviving, extant,** left, **leftover, still around, remnant; spare,** to spare; unused; **surplus,** superfluous; **outstanding**

243 SIZE, LARGENESS

nouns

1 **size, greatness, vastness, magnitude; mass, bulk, volume; dimensions, proportions; measure**, measurement, gauge; **scale; extent**, expanse, **scope**, reach, range, spread, coverage, area; length, height; depth, breadth, width

2 **capacity, volume, content, accommodation**, room, space, measure, limit, burden; tonnage; **quantity**

3 **full size**, life size

4 **large size, family size, king size**, giant size

5 **oversize**, outsize; **overweight**

6 greatness, grandeur

7 **vastness; enormity, immensity; monstrosity**

8 **corpulence, obesity, stoutness; fatness, plumpness**

9 **bulkiness;** clumsiness, awkwardness

10 **lump, clump; mass, piece; batch, wad**, block, loaf, pat *(of butter)*; clod; **quantity**

11 *(corpulent person)* **heavyweight, pig; fat person, fatty** *and* **fatso** *(both nonformal)*; tub

12 **giant**, colossus

13 **monster;** mammoth; elephant, jumbo; whale; hippopotamus; **dinosaur**

verbs

14 **size, adjust, grade**, rank, graduate, sort; **gauge, measure, proportion; enlarge;** fatten

adjectives

15 **large, sizable, big, great, grand,** tall *(nonformal)*, **considerable,** healthy, tidy *(nonformal)*, **substantial,** bumper; numerous; large-scale

16 **voluminous, capacious, generous, ample,** copious, **broad,** wide, **extensive, expansive,** comprehensive; **spacious**

17 **stout, fat, overweight, obese,** fleshy, **beefy, hefty;** bloated, puffy, distended, swollen; **plump, buxom; full; thickset, chubby,** chunky *(nonformal)*, **stocky,** squat, dumpy; **brawny, burly;** lusty, strapping *(nonformal);* **portly**

18 **bulky,** lumpy, lumbering; **massive; ponderous,** cumbersome; **clumsy,** awkward, **unwieldy**

19 **huge, immense, vast, enormous,** astronomical, tremendous, stupendous; great big, mighty, **colossal, monumental,** heroic, epic, towering, mountainous; **monster,** monstrous; **mammoth, gigantic, giant;** jumbo *(nonformal);* **infinite**

20 **walloping, whacking,** spanking, thumping, thundering

21 **full-sized, full-scale; full-blown; life-sized**

22 oversized; **outsize,** too big; **overgrown; overweight; obese**

244 LITTLENESS

nouns

1 **littleness, smallness,** diminutiveness, shortness

2 **imperceptibility; invisibility**

3 (*small person or creature*) **runt,
shrimp** (*nonformal*); slip, shorty,
small fry (*nonformal*); minnow,
mouse

4 **dwarf, midget,** midge; elf,
gnome

5 **miniature;** microcosm; baby;
doll, puppet

6 **drop, mite, point,** pinpoint, **dot;**
fleck, **speck,** jot, trace; **particle,**
crumb, scrap, bite, snip, snippet;
grain; midge; gnat; microbe, bacteria, germ, virus

7 **atom; molecule;** electron, proton

verbs

8 **make small, contract; shorten;
miniaturize,** scale down; **reduce**

adjectives

9 **little, small; slight,** puny, trifling; cramped, limited; short

10 **tiny; minute,** fine

11 **miniature, diminutive, minus-
cule,** mini, micro, miniaturized,
small-scale, minimal; **baby;**
pocket; toy; handy, compact

12 **dwarf, midget;** squat, dumpy;
stunted; shrunken, wizened,
shrivelled; meagre; rudimentary

13 **infinitesimal, microscopic;** thin,
intangible; imperceptible, invisible; atomic; molecular; micro-
cosmic(*al*); embryonic

adverbs

14 **small,** little, **slightly, fractionally; in miniature**

245 EXPANSION, GROWTH

nouns

1 **expansion, extension, enlargement, increase, magnification,
amplification, broadening, widening; spread,** spreading; **flare,**
splay; **addition**

2 **stretching; inflation,** blowing up;
dilating; **swelling,** swell; puffing

3 **growth, development;** maturing,
growing up; reproduction, procreation, germination

verbs

4 (*make larger*) **enlarge, expand,
extend, widen, broaden,** build
up, **magnify, increase,** augment,
add to; raise; develop; **stretch,
dilate, swell, inflate, blow up,**
puff up; pump up

5 (*become larger*) **enlarge, expand,
extend, increase, develop, wid-
en, broaden,** bulk; **stretch, dilate, swell, swell up, puff out,**
balloon, fill out; snowball

6 **spread,** spread out; **expand, extend,** widen; open up, unfold;
flare, broaden out, splay; sprawl;
branch out; fan out, disperse

7 **grow, develop, increase; grow
up,** mature, spring up, ripen,
shoot up, tower; **sprout,** blossom, reproduce, grow, germinate; **vegetate; flourish;** mushroom; outgrow

8 **fatten; gain weight,** become
overweight

adjectives

9 **expansive, extensive;** elastic; in-
flatable; inflationary

10 expanded, extended, enlarged, increased, raised, amplified, widened, broadened

11 spreading; sprawling; **outstretched;** open, unfolded, gaping; widespread; flared, splayed

12 grown, grown-up, mature, developed, fully developed; growing, sprouting, budding, flowering, **flourishing,** blossoming, blooming, fast-growing

13 distended, dilated, inflated, puffed up, swollen, **bloated; puffy;** fat

246 CONTRACTION

nouns

1 contraction; compression; compacting; condensation, concentration; narrowing, reduction, **decrease;** abbreviation, curtailment, shortening; constriction, **choking;** neck, narrow place

2 squeezing, compression, tightening; **pressure,** press, crush; **pinch, squeeze**

3 shrinking; shrivelling, withering; searing; thinning; wasting, consumption

4 collapse; deflation

verbs

5 contract, compress, cramp, compact, condense, concentrate; **reduce, decrease, abbreviate,** curtail, shorten; **constrict, narrow;** strangle, choke; **pucker, purse;** knit, wrinkle

6 squeeze, compress, clamp, cramp, tighten; **press,** pressurize, crush; **pinch, nip**

7 shrink, shrivel, wither; consume, waste away, thin

8 collapse, cave in, fall in; **fold,** fold up; **deflate; puncture**

adjectives

9 contracted, compressed, cramped, concentrated, condensed; **constricted,** strangled, choked, **squeezed;** puckered, pursed; knitted, wrinkled

10 shrunken; shrivelled; withered, parched, dried-up; wasted away, emaciated, thin; **wizened**

11 deflated, punctured, flat

247 DISTANCE, REMOTENESS

nouns

1 distance, remoteness; separation, divergence; **extent, length,** space, **reach,** stretch, range, compass, span, stride; perspective; deep space, infinity; **mileage,** light-years

2 long way, great distance, far cry; long range

3 the distance, offing; horizon, vanishing point, background

4 the back of beyond, Timbuktu, Siberia, North Pole, South Pole; outpost, outskirts; **nowhere;** frontier, outback (*Australia*); the moon; outer space

verbs

5 reach out, stretch out, extend

6 extend to, stretch to, lead to, go to, get to, run to

7 distance oneself, keep away, steer clear of (*nonformal*)

adjectives

8 **distant, remote,** removed, far, far-off, **faraway,** exotic; long-distance, long-range

9 **out-of-the-way;** godforsaken, **inaccessible**

10 **yonder; farther, further,** remoter, more distant

11 overseas; transatlantic

12 **farthest, furthest,** extreme, remotest, most distant

adverbs

13 **yonder, in the distance,** on the horizon

14 **away, off;** distantly, remotely

15 **far, far off,** far away, **afar**

16 wide, widely, broadly, abroad

17 **apart, away,** wide apart, beyond reach, out-of-the-way

18 **wide, clear;** abroad, astray, far afield

248 FORM

nouns

1 **form, shape, figure;** configuration; formation; structure; **build,** frame; **arrangement; format, layout; composition; cut, set, type, turn, cast, mould, impression, pattern, model, mode; style, fashion; art form, genre**

2 **contour;** broad lines, silhouette, profile, **outline;** organization

3 **appearance;** features

4 *(human form)* **figure, form,** shape, frame, anatomy, **physique,** build; body

5 **forming, shaping,** moulding, modelling, fashioning, making;

formation, configuration; sculpture; creation

verbs

6 **form,** formalize, **shape, fashion,** tailor, figure; work, knead; set, fix; **forge; mould,** model; cast, found; stamp, mint; carve, cut, chisel; lay out, sketch out; create; organize

7 *(be formed)* **form,** take form, shape, **shape up, take shape;** materialize

adjectives

8 **formative,** formal, plastic; **formed, shaped,** patterned, fashioned, tailored, framed; **forged, modelled; cast, founded; stamped, minted; carved, cut, whittled, chiselled; made, produced**

249 FORMLESSNESS

nouns

1 **chaos,** confusion, mess, muddle, **disorder;** anarchy; obscurity

2 raw material

verbs

3 **deform, distort;** disorder, jumble, mess up, muddle, confuse; obscure, fog up, blur

adjectives

4 **formless, shapeless,** nondescript, lumpy; amorphous, **chaotic,** disorderly, confused, anarchic; **indeterminate, indefinite,** indecisive, vague, misty, hazy, fuzzy, unclear, obscure; unstructured

250 SYMMETRY

nouns

1 **symmetry, proportion, balance,** equilibrium; **regularity,** uniformity; equality; finish; harmony, consistency, conformity, **correspondence,** keeping

2 balancing, evening, integration; **compensation**

verbs

3 **balance,** compensate; harmonize; **proportion,** proportionate; even, even up; coordinate, integrate

adjectives

4 **symmetrical, balanced,** harmonious; **regular,** uniform, even, equal, fifty-fifty (*nonformal*), square; coordinated; **well-balanced;** finished

5 **shapely, well-shaped,** well-made; trim, neat, spruce, clean

251 DISTORTION

nouns

1 **distortion,** twistedness; imbalance, irregularity, **deviation;** twist, quirk, turn, screw; **warp,** buckle; knot

2 **perversion, corruption,** misrepresentation, misinterpretation; **falsification; twisting,** false colouring, **spin,** slanting, straining, torturing; misuse

3 **deformity,** monstrosity; mutilation

4 **grimace, wry face,** wry mouth, snarl; mow, pout

verbs

5 **distort, contort,** turn awry; **twist,** turn, screw, wring, wrench, wrest; writhe; **warp,** buckle, crumple; knot; **crook,** bend

6 **pervert,** falsify, **twist,** colour, varnish, slant, strain, torture; **bias;** misrepresent, misinterpret; misuse

7 **deform,** twist, torture; **disfigure,** deface; mutilate; blemish, mar

8 **grimace,** mouth, pout

adjectives

9 **distorted, contorted, warped, twisted, crooked;** tortuous, buckled, bent, bowed; crazy; crunched, crumpled; asymmetrical; irregular; one-sided, lop-sided; askew, off-centre

10 **falsified, perverted, twisted, garbled, slanted, doctored, biased, crooked; strained, tortured;** misrepresented

11 **deformed,** misshapen; dwarfed, stumpy; bloated; **disfigured,** defaced, blemished, marred; mutilated; grotesque, **monstrous;** bandy-legged, bandy; rickety

252 STRUCTURE

nouns

1 **structure, construction,** architecture, **frame,** make, **build,** fabric, tissue, web, weave, texture, mould, **shape, pattern, plan,** fashion, arrangement, **organization;** organism, organic structure, **constitution, composition; formation, format; arrangement,** configuration; **composition;** making, building, creation, production, forging, fashioning,

moulding, fabrication, manufacture, shaping, structuring; anatomy, physique; form

2 **structure, building, edifice, construction,** construct, erection, establishment, fabric; house; tower, pile, pyramid, skyscraper

3 **frame, framework,** skeleton, fabric, shell; case, casing; window frame, picture frame

verbs

4 **construct, build;** structure; organize; form

adjectives

5 **structural,** formal; anatomical, **organic; structured, patterned,** shaped, formed; **architectural**

253 LENGTH

nouns

1 **length,** overall length; **extent,** extension, **measure, span, reach, stretch; distance;** infinity; long time; linear measures; longitude

2 a length, **piece, portion,** part; **strip,** bolt, roll; run

3 **line, strip,** bar; stripe; string

4 **lengthening,** extension, stretching

verbs

5 **be long, be lengthy, extend,** be prolonged, **stretch; stretch out,** reach out, crane; sprawl, straggle

6 **lengthen, prolong, extend,** produce, continue; **stretch,** draw, pull

adjectives

7 **long, lengthy; tall; extensive, far-reaching,** far-flung; interminable, without end

8 **lengthened, prolonged,** elongated, extended, protracted; long-winded; drawn-out, dragged out, straggling; **stretched, drawn,** pulled

adverbs

9 extensively, at length, along, in length, at length

254 SHORTNESS

nouns

1 **shortness, briefness, brevity;** transience, short time,

2 **shortening, abbreviation; reduction; condensation,** compression, epitome, summary, abstract, precis

3 **shortcut,** shortest way; beeline

verbs

4 **shorten, abbreviate, cut; reduce; condense,** compress, contract, **boil down,** abstract, sum up, summarize, epitomize, encapsulate, precis; curtail, cut short; **dock,** bob, shear, shave, trim, clip; mow, reap, **crop; prune,** poll; stunt; telescope

5 cut across, cut through; cut corners

adjectives

6 **short, brief, abbreviated, concise; curt, succinct, summary,** compact; **little; low;** transient, instantaneous

7 **shortened, abbreviated; abridged,** compressed, condensed, epitomized, digested, abstracted, precised, encapsulated; **curtailed,** cut short, **docked,** bobbed, sheared, shaved, trimmed, clipped, snub; mowed,

mown, reaped, **cropped; pruned**, polled

8 **stubby**, stumpy (*nonformal*), **thickset, stocky, chunky** (*nonformal*), **fat, chubby**, dumpy; **squat**

adverbs

9 **shortly, briefly**, summarily, *tout court* (*French*), in brief, economically, curtly, succinctly, **concisely**, in a nutshell

10 **short, abruptly**, suddenly

255 BREADTH, THICKNESS

nouns

1 **breadth, width**, fullness, latitude, extent, **span, expanse, spread**; beam

2 **thickness**, distance through, depth; **mass, bulk, body**; fatness

3 **diameter, bore, calibre**

verbs

4 **broaden, widen**, deepen; **expand, extend; spread**

5 **thicken**, grow thick, thick; fatten

adjectives

6 **broad, wide**, deep; wide-ranging, exhaustive, comprehensive, extensive; **expansive**, spacious, **roomy**; ample, full; widespread

7 **thick**, thickset; massive, bulky; coarse, heavy, gross, fat; full; dense

256 NARROWNESS, THINNESS

nouns

1 **narrowness; closeness;** restriction, limitation, confinement; tight squeeze; hair, hairsbreadth; narrow gauge

2 **narrowing, tapering**, taper; **contraction;** constriction

3 (*narrow place*) narrow, **narrows, strait;** bottleneck; channel, canal; pass, defile; neck, throat

4 **thinness, slimness**, frailty, lightness, delicacy

5 **skinniness**, skin and bones; underweight

6 (*comparisons*) paper, wafer, **rake**, slip, shaving, streak; shadow; skeleton

7 (*thin person*) slim, lanky; **shadow, skeleton**, stick, walking skeleton; corpse; beanpole

8 reducing, slimming, weight-watching, calorie-counting

verbs

9 **narrow**, constrict, diminish, draw in, go in; restrict, limit, confine; **taper; contract**

10 **thin**, thin down, dilute, water down, weaken

11 **reduce**, count calories, diet, slim

adjectives

12 **narrow, slender; close**, near; **tight, strait;** close-fitting; **restricted**, limited, circumscribed, **confined**, constricted; **cramped**, crowded; meagre, scant, scanty; **tapered**, tapering

13 **thin, slender, slim**; slight; frail, delicate, light, airy, wispy, lacy,

gossamer, insubstantial, misty, vague, flimsy, **fine**; tenuous; watery, weak, diluted

14 lean, **skinny** (*nonformal*), spare, scrawny, gaunt, lanky; spindly; **bony**, skeletal; undernourished

15 **haggard, poor**, puny, pinched; shrivelled, withered; wizened; **emaciated**, wasted, skeletal; **starved; undernourished**, underfed

16 **dieting**, reducing, slimming; diet, light, lite

adverbs

17 **narrowly**, closely, nearly, **barely**, hardly, only just

18 **thinly**, thin; sparsely, sparingly

257 FILAMENT

nouns

1 **filament; fibre; thread; strand; hair**; synthetic fibre, natural fibre; **tendril; web**, cobweb, gossamer, spider's web

2 **cord**, line, rope, wire, cable; **yarn**, spun yarn, skein, hank; **string, twine**; braid; ligature

3 **tackle**, tack, gear, rigging; ship's ropes

4 **strip, strap; lace**, thong; **band**, bandage, fillet; **belt**, girdle; ribbon; tape

5 **spinster**; spider; spinning wheel, spinning jenny

verbs

6 (*make threads*) **spin; braid**, twist

adjectives

7 **stringy**, ropy, wiry; hairy; fibrous; capillary; gossamer, silky

258 HEIGHT

nouns

1 **height, altitude, elevation**; eminence, prominence; **stature**

2 **height, elevation**, eminence, **rise**, lift, rising ground, vantage point; heights; zenith, apex

3 **highlands**, upland, uplands, moorland, moors, downs, rolling country

4 **plateau**, table, table mountain; **hill**; ridge; **mountain; peak; mountain range**

5 **tower; turret**; bell tower, belfry; **spire; lighthouse**; dome; pole; windmill; observation post, fire tower; **mast**, aerial; water tower; pinnacle; **steeple; pyramid; pylon**; shaft, **pillar, column**; monument; skyscraper

6 **high tide**, high water, flood tide, spring tide, flood; storm level

verbs

7 **tower, soar**, spire, **rise, ascend**, **mount, rear**

8 **rise above**, clear, top, surmount; overlook; **command**, dominate, overshadow

9 (*become higher*) **grow**, grow up; mount

10 **heighten, elevate**

adjectives

11 **high**, lofty, elevated, eminent, exalted, prominent, superlative, sublime; towering, soaring, aspiring, mounting, ascending; overlooking, dominating; airy, aerial; monumental, colossal; high-rise

12 **giant**, gigantic, colossal; **tall**, **lengthy**; lanky

13 **highland,** upland; **hilly,** rolling; **mountainous,** alpine

14 **higher,** superior, greater; **over, above;** upper

adverbs

15 **on high,** high up, high; **aloft; up,** upward, upwards, straight up; **above, over,** overhead

259 SHAFT

nouns

1 **shaft, pole, bar, rod, stick;** stalk, stem; **telephone** or **telegraph pole;** tent pole

2 **staff,** stave; **cane, stick, walking stick;** baton, swagger stick; pastoral staff, crook; crutch

3 **beam, timber,** pole, spar

4 **post, standard, upright;** king post, queen post; crown post; banister, balustrade; gatepost, doorpost; signpost

5 **pillar, column,** post, pier; arcade, portico

6 **leg; stake,** peg; picket, pale

260 LOWNESS

nouns

1 **lowness;** lying, lying down, reclining; depression

2 **low tide,** low water, ebb tide, neap tide

3 **lowland, lowlands;** water meadow

4 **base, bottom,** lowest point, nadir; the lowest of the low; lower strata, bedrock

verbs

5 **lie low, squat, crouch;** crawl, grovel; lie under, underlie

6 **lower,** debase, depress

adjectives

7 **low, flat, low-lying;** short, squat, stumpy; **lowered,** debased, depressed; demoted; **reduced;** prone, crouched, stooped; laid low, knocked flat

8 **lower,** inferior, **under;** down; less advanced; earlier; lowest

adverbs

9 **low; below,** down below, **under;** downstairs, below deck; underfoot

261 DEPTH

nouns

1 **depth,** deepness

2 **pit, deep, depth, hole,** hollow, **cavity, shaft, well, gulf, chasm, abyss,** yawning abyss; crater; valley

3 **depths,** bowels; hell, underworld, **ocean depths, the deep,** the depths, inner space, abyss; **seabed**

4 **sounding** or **soundings,** depth sounding; **echo sounding,** echolocation

5 **draft,** displacement

6 **deepening, lowering, depression;** sinking; excavation, digging, mining, drilling, probing

verbs

7 **deepen, lower, depress, sink; dig,** excavate, tunnel, mine, **drill**

8 **sound,** fathom, plumb

adjectives

9 **deep, profound;** deep-seated, deep-rooted

10 **abysmal,** yawning, cavernous, gaping, plunging; bottomless

11 **underground, subterranean,** buried

12 **underwater;** submarine; submerged, immersed, buried, engulfed, inundated, flooded, drowned, sunken

adverbs

13 **deep;** out of one's depth

262 SHALLOWNESS

nouns

1 **shallowness;** no water, no depth; **superficiality,** triviality; **surface,** skin; veneer, gloss; scratch, mere scratch

2 **shoal, shallow,** shallows, shelf; bank, bar, sandbank; **reef,** coral reef; ford; tidal flats

verbs

3 **shoal,** shallow; silt up

4 **touch upon,** hardly touch, skim, skim over, scratch the surface

adjectives

5 **shallow,** shoal, not deep; **surface,** merely surface; **superficial,** cursory, slight, light, cosmetic, thin, trivial

263 STRAIGHTNESS

nouns

1 **straightness,** directness

2 **straight line,** straight, direct line; straightaway; streamline; edge, side, diagonal, chord, tangent, perpendicular, normal, segment, diameter, axis, radius

3 **rule,** ruler; square, T square, triangle

verbs

4 **be straight;** arrow; go straight

5 **straighten,** rectify; straighten up, square up; straighten out, extend; flatten, smooth; streamline

adjectives

6 **straight;** dead straight, even, right, true; linear; **direct;** uninterrupted, unbroken; upright, vertical; flat, level, smooth, horizontal

adverbs

7 **straight,** directly

264 ANGULARITY

nouns

1 **angle,** point; apex; **corner,** coin, nook; crook, curve, swerve, veer; L; cant; fork; zigzag; elbow, knee; crank

verbs

2 **angle, crook, hook, bend,** elbow; crank; curve, swerve, veer, veer off, slant off; branch, fork; zigzag

adjectives

3 **angular;** cornered, **crooked, hooked, bent;** V-shaped; **forked;** sharp, pointed; zigzag, jagged

4 **rectangular, square;** oblong: triangular; hexagonal etc; multilateral

265 CURVATURE

nouns

1 **curving; arching, vaulting**

2 **curve; bow, arc; crook, hook;** ellipse; circle; curl

3 **bend,** bending; **bow,** bowing; **turn,** turning, sweep, meander, U-turn

4 **arch, span, vault,** vaulting; **dome,** igloo; cove; arched roof; **arcade**

5 **crescent, semicircle,** scythe, sickle; crescent moon; horseshoe

verbs

6 **curve, turn,** arc, sweep; **crook, hook,** loop; bend back; sag; **bend,** flex; deflect; reflect, reflex; **bow; arch,** vault; dome; **hump,** hunch; wind, curl; round

adjectives

7 **curved,** curve, **curving;** wavy, billowing; sinuous, tortuous, meandering; **bent,** flexed

8 **hooked, crooked, bowed,** bandy; **convex, concave,** arched, vaulted; **humped,** hunched

9 **crescent-shaped,** crescent; meniscoid; S; **semicircular;** lunar

266 CIRCULARITY

nouns

1 **circle,** circus, **ring, O, circumference,** radius; **round; cycle, circuit;** orbit; vicious circle; magic circle, charmed circle; fairy ring; circular reasoning; **wheel; disc,** discus, saucer; **loop;** noose; crown, coronet; garland, wreath; halo, glory

2 *(thing encircling)* **band, belt,** girdle, girth, zone, fillet; collar; necklace, bracelet; ring, earring, nose ring, finger ring; hoop; zodiac, equator, great circle; **rim; tyre**

3 **oval;** ellipse; **semicircle,** half circle; crescent; sector

verbs

4 **circle, round;** orbit; **encircle,** surround, encompass, girdle

adjectives

5 **circular, round,** rounded; cyclic, cyclical; planetary; **oval,** eggshaped

267 CONVOLUTION

nouns

1 **winding, twisting, turning;** meander, meandering; crinkle, crinkling; wave, waving; **complexity**

2 **coil,** roll, **curl, spiral,** scroll; **twist, twirl;** screw, corkscrew, tendril; whirl, swirl

3 **curler,** curling iron, tongs, rollers

verbs

4 **wind, twine,** twirl, **twist, turn,** meander, crinkle; snake, slink, worm; screw, corkscrew; whirl, swirl; wring; contort

5 **curl, coil;** crisp, crimp

adjectives

6 **winding, twisting, turning;** meandering; roundabout, circuitous; sinuous; tortuous

7 **coiled, spiral,** corkscrew; **curly, curled;** frizzy; crisp; **wavy,** undulating; billowing, rolling

adverbs

8 in waves; in and out, round and round

268 ROTUNDITY

nouns

1 **sphere; ball,** orbit, **globe;** globule; pellet; bulb; knob, knot; blob; pill; **balloon,** bladder, bubble, **drop;** raindrop; bead, pearl

2 **cylinder,** pillar, column; barrel, drum, cask; pipe, tube; roll, roller, rolling pin

verbs

3 **round; round out, fill out**

4 **ball, snowball;** sphere, globe; roll; bead; balloon, mushroom

adjectives

5 **round,** rounded, rounded out; convex, bulging, bulbous; **spherical;** global; beady; **cylindrical,** tube-shaped

269 CONVEXITY, PROTUBERANCE

nouns

1 **projection;** prominence, eminence, boldness, **bulging;** salient; relief, high relief, low relief

2 **bulge,** bow, convex; **bump;** speed hump, sleeping policeman; hill, mountain; **hump; lump,** clump, bunch, blob; **mole,** wart; knob, boss, button, bulb; stud, peg; lip; tab, ear, flap, loop, ring, handle; **knot,** gall; blister; bubble

3 **swelling;** rising, lump, bump, pimple; boil; corn; tumour; cyst; nodule

4 **breast, bosom, bust, chest;** breasts, teats; **nipple;** udder, bag

5 **nose;** snout, muzzle; trunk; beak, rostrum; neb

6 *(point of land)* **point,** hook, spur, **cape,** tongue, bill; **headland,** head, mull *(Scots);* **peninsula;** spit; **reef,** coral reef; breakwater

verbs

7 **protrude, project, stick out,** jut out, poke out, stand out, shoot out; **stick up**

8 **bulge,** belly, bag, balloon, pouch; pout; **goggle, pop; swell, swell up,** dilate, billow; swell out, belly out, round out

9 **emboss,** chase, raise

adjectives

10 **convex,** bowed, arched; humped

11 **protruding;** projecting, jutting, outstanding; prominent, eminent, salient, bold

12 **bulging, swelling,** distended, bloated; baggy; rounded; billowing, ballooning, pneumatic; **bumpy,** bunched; bulbous; swollen; goggle-eyed

13 **studded;** knotted, gnarled; in relief, bold, raised; chased, bossed, embossed

270 CONCAVITY

nouns

1 **hollowness;** depression; emptiness

2 **cavity,** concave; **hollow,** hollow shell, shell; **hole, pit, depression,** dip, sink, fold; scoop, pocket; **basin,** trough, **bowl,** punch bowl, cup, container

3 pit, well, shaft; chasm, gulf, abyss; **excavation,** dig, workings; mine, quarry

4 cave, cavern, hole, grotto; lair; **tunnel, burrow,** warren; subway; bunker; sewer

5 indentation, dent; gouge, **furrow,** dimple; pit; impression, imprint, print; honeycomb; Swiss cheese; **notch**

6 recess, niche, nook, corner; cove, alcove; bay

7 valley, vale; **glen,** bottom, gill; gap, pass, ravine

8 digger; miner; steam shovel; dredge

9 excavation, digging; mining; indentation, **engraving**

verbs

10 hollow, hollow out, concave, **dish,** cup, bowl; cave, cave in; sink

11 dent, depress, press in, stamp, punch, punch in, impress, imprint; **pit;** dimple; **recess,** set back; set in; **notch;** engrave

12 excavate, dig, dig out, **scoop,** scoop out, **gouge,** gouge out, grub, shovel, spade, delve, scrape, scratch; dredge; **trench,** furrow, groove; **tunnel, burrow,** drive (*min*), sink, lower; **mine,** sap; quarry; drill, bore

adjectives

13 concave; sunk, sunken; **hollow,** hollowed, empty; dished, **cupped,** cup-shaped; **cavernous**

14 dented, depressed; dimpled; pitted; engraved

271 SHARPNESS

nouns

1 (*sharp edge*) edge, cutting edge; fine edge; edge tool

2 point, tip; nib; needle; hypodermic needle, hypodermic syringe; **drill,** bit; **prick, prickle;** sting; **tooth**

3 (*pointed projection*) projection, spur, **snag;** horn, antler; crag, peak; spire, steeple

4 thorn, bramble, nettle, prickle, burr, sticky willow; **spike,** spine; bristle; quill; **needle,** pine needle; **thistle,** goose grass, cactus

verbs

5 prick, sting, stick, bite; be keen, cut; bristle with

6 sharpen, edge, taper; **whet,** file, grind; strop; set; **point;** barb, spur

adjectives

7 sharp, keen, edged, acute, fine, **cutting;** sharpened, set

8 pointed, acute; tapered, tapering; **spiked,** spiky; **barbed**

9 prickly, pricking, stinging; **thorny,** bristly

272 BLUNTNESS

nouns

1 bluntness, dullness

verbs

2 blunt, dull; turn; weaken, repress

adjectives

3 blunt, dull; rounded, smoothed, streamlined; blunted, dulled

273 SMOOTHNESS

nouns

1 **smoothness,** uniformity, regularity

2 **polish, gloss, glaze,** shine, lustre, finish

3 (*smooth surface*) smooth, **plane, level, flat;** tennis court; slide; glass; ice; marble, alabaster, ivory; silk, satin, velvet; mahogany

4 **smoother;** roller; sleeker; **polish, abrasive**

verbs

5 **smooth, flatten, plane,** level, even; dress, dab; lay; plaster, plaster down; roll, roll smooth; drag; grade; mow, shave; lubricate, oil, grease

6 **press, iron,** mangle; roll

7 **polish, shine,** sleek, slick, slick down, gloss, glaze, glance, lustre, **rub,** scour, **buff;** wax, varnish, finish

8 **grind, file, sand, scrape,** sandpaper

adjectives

9 **smooth,** even, level, plane, flat, regular, uniform, unbroken; unruffled; downy; silky, velvety

10 **sleek, slick, glossy,** shiny, gleaming; silky, silken, velvety; **polished,** burnished, rubbed, finished; varnished, lacquered, glazed, glassy

11 **slippery,** slick, oily, greasy, soaped; lubricated, oiled, greased

adverbs

12 **smoothly, evenly,** regularly, uniformly; **like clockwork,** on wheels

274 ROUGHNESS

nouns

1 **roughness,** irregularity, inequality; abrasion, harshness; rough air, turbulence

2 (*rough surface*) **rough,** broken ground; broken water, ripple; goose bumps, goose pimples; sandpaper

3 **bristle,** barb; **stubble;** whisker

verbs

4 rough, rough up; coarsen; knob, stud, boss; pimple

5 **ruffle,** wrinkle, crinkle, crumple, **rumple; bristle**

adjectives

6 **rough, uneven,** broken, irregular, **bumpy,** pitted; corrugated; **choppy;** ruffled, unkempt; **shaggy;** coarse, rank; grainy, granulated

7 **rugged,** ragged, harsh; wrinkled, crinkled, crumpled, corrugated; abrasive; **jagged;** serrated; craggy; **rocky,** gravelly, stony

8 **gnarled,** knotted, knobbly, studded, lumpy

9 **bristly, bristling,** bristled; studded; hairy

adverbs

10 **roughly,** rough; irregularly

275 NOTCH

nouns

1 **notch, nick, cut,** cleft, incision, gash, hack, blaze, scotch, **score,** depression; indentation

verbs

2 notch, nick, cut, **gash**, slash, chop, saw; **score**, blaze; pink, mill, tooth

adjectives

3 **nicked**, gashed, scored, chopped, blazed; serrated, scalloped; **jagged**

276 FURROW

nouns

1 **furrow**, groove, scratch, crack, cranny, chase, chink, score, **cut**, gash, streak, **gouge**, slit, incision, **rut**, well-worn groove; wrinkle; flute; rifling; engraving

2 **trench**, trough, channel, **ditch**, dike (*old*), **canal**, cut, gutter, kennel; moat; sunk fence; pleat

verbs

3 **furrow**, groove, score, scratch, cut, carve, chisel, gash, streak, gouge, slit, crack, plough; rifle; **channel**, **trough**, **flute**; trench, canal, **ditch**, dike (*old*), gully, **rut**; wrinkle; pleat; **engrave**

adjectives

4 **furrowed**, grooved, scratched, scored, cut, gashed, gouged, slit; channelled, ditched; fluted; rifled; **corrugated**; wrinkled, pleated; **engraved**

277 FOLD

nouns

1 **fold**, double, doubling; ply; **crease**, creasing; **tuck**, **gather**; ruffle, frill, flounce; lapel

2 **pleat**, accordion pleat, box pleat, knife pleat

3 **wrinkle**, ridge, **furrow**, **crease**, pucker, cockle; **crinkle**, ripple; crumple, rumple

4 **folding, creasing**

verbs

5 **fold**, fold up; **double**, ply; fold over, double over, lap over; **crease**; crisp; **pleat**; **tuck**, **gather**, tuck up; ruffle, frill; flounce; quill, flute; **fold in**, wrap, lap

6 **wrinkle**, ridge, **furrow**, **crease**, cockle, cocker, **pucker**, **purse**; **knit**; **crumple**, rumple, **crinkle**, ripple

adjectives

7 **folded, doubled**; pleated, plaited; **creased**; tucked, gathered; flounced, ruffled; fluted; folding, flexible, pliable

8 **wrinkled**; corrugated; **creased**, furrowed; puckered, pursed; knitted, knotted; rugged; **crinkled**, rippled; **crumpled**, rumpled

278 OPENING

nouns

1 **opening**, aperture, hole, hollow, **cavity**; slot; split, crack, leak; opening up, uncorking, clearing, throwing open, laying open, broaching, cutting through; passageway; inlet; outlet; **gap**, hiatus, space, interval; **chasm**, **gulf**; cleft; pore; **disclosure**

2 **gaping**, yawning, gape, yawn; the gapes

3 **hole**, **penetration**, **piercing**, **puncture**, goring, boring, puncturing, punching, pricking,

broach; skewering; bore, drill hole

4 **mouth; muzzle,** jaw, lips; jaws, chops, chaps

5 **door, doorway; entrance, entry**

6 **window;** window glass, pane, light; window frame, window ledge, window-sill

7 screen, sieve, strainer, riddle, net; honeycomb; sponge

279 CLOSURE

nouns

1 **closure, closing, shutting,** shutting up; **shutdown; exclusion,** shutting out; **ruling out;** blockade, embargo

2 **obstruction, block,** blockade, sealing off, **blockage,** choking, **stoppage,** stop, **bar, barrier, obstacle,** impediment; **congestion,** jam, traffic jam, rush hour; **blind alley,** blank wall, **dead end,** cul-de-sac, dead-end street, impasse; blind gut

3 **stopper,** stop; **plug, cork,** bung, tap, faucet, valve, check valve, cock, sea cock, peg, pin; lid

4 wadding, **stuffing,** padding, **packing,** pack, tampon

verbs

5 **close, shut;** close up, shut up, contract, constrict, strangle, choke, squeeze; **exclude, shut out; rule out; fasten,** secure; **lock,** lock up, padlock, latch, bolt, bar, barricade; **seal,** seal up, seal off; button, button up; snap; zipper, zip up; **cover;** contain; **slam, clap, bang**

6 **stop, stop up; obstruct, bar,** stay; **block,** block up; **clog,** clog up, foul; **choke; fill,** fill up; **stuff,** pack, jam; **plug;** stopper, cork, bung; cover; **dam,** dam up; blockade, embargo; bind

7 **shut up shop,** shut down, close down; cease trading

adjectives

8 **closed, shut;** excluded; ruled out; barred; contracted, constricted, choked, choked up; blank; blind, dead; dead-end; **exclusive,** private

9 **stopped; obstructed, blocked;** plugged; clogged up, foul, fouled; **choked,** strangled; **full, stuffed,** packed, jammed, like sardines; **congested,** stuffed up; constipated, bound

10 **close, tight, compact,** fast, shut fast, **snug,** staunch, firm; **sealed;** airtight; impervious, impenetrable; impassable

280 TEXTURE

nouns

1 **texture,** surface texture; **surface; finish,** feel; grain, weave, nap, pile; **structure**

2 **roughness,** irregularity; coarseness, hardness

3 **smoothness,** refinement, delicacy; down, fluff, velvet, fuzz, peach fuzz; satin, silk; softness

verbs

4 **coarsen;** grain; roughen; smooth

adjectives

5 **rough,** coarse; **grainy,** granulated, gritty, gravelly

6 nappy, shaggy, hairy; bumpy, lumpy, textured; studded; pitted

7 smooth; fine, refined; delicate, dainty; gossamer, downy, fluffy, velvety, fuzzy; satin, silky

281 COVERING

nouns

1 (*act of covering*) **covering,** coverage; **coating,** cloaking; **screening,** shielding, hiding, obscuring, masking, shrouding, blanketing; blocking, blotting out, eclipse, eclipsing; **wrapping,** sheathing

2 cover, covering, coverage, covert, housing, hood, **shelter; screen,** shroud, shield, veil, pall, curtain, hanging, drape; **coat,** cloak, mask, guise

3 skin; rind; **flesh;** the buff; pelt, hide **coat,** cast, fell, fleece, fur, hair; **peel,** peeling, rind; **bark;** cork

4 lap, overlap; **flap,** fly

5 cover, lid, top, cap; stopper

6 roof, rooftop; roof garden, penthouse; slates, tiles; eaves; **ceiling;** skylight

7 umbrella, parasol, beach umbrella

8 tent, canvas; big top

9 rug, carpet, mat; groundsheet; **flooring,** floorboards; pavement

10 blanket, space blanket, cover, covers, rug; **bedspread; duvet, continental quilt,** feather bed, eiderdown; patchwork quilt; **bedding, bedclothes,** clothes; **linen,** bed linen; **sheet,** fitted sheet; **pillowcase,** pillow slip, case, slip; duvet cover

11 blanket, coating, coat; **veneer;** facing; **film, scum,** skin, scale; slick, oil slick; varnish, enamel, lacquer, paint

12 plating, plate; nickel plate, silver plate, gold plate, chromium plate

13 crust, shell; scale, scab

14 shell, armour, mail, **shield;** plate; **protective covering,** elephant skin

15 hull, shell, pod, capsule, case, **husk;** bark, jacket; chaff, bran

16 case, casing; **sheath,** sheathing

17 wrapper, wrapping, gift wrapping, wrap; wrapping paper, waxed paper, aluminium foil, tin foil, plastic wrap; **binder,** binding; **bandage,** bandaging; **envelope; jacket;** dust jacket

verbs

18 cover, cover up; apply to, **put on,** lay on; superimpose; **lay over; spread over;** clothe, cloak, muffle, blanket, canopy, **veil,** curtain, **screen, shield,** screen off, mask, cloud, obscure, fog; block, eclipse; **film,** film over, scum

19 wrap, wrap up; **envelop, sheathe;** surround, encompass, lap, smother, enfold, embrace, invest; shroud, swathe; **box, case,** encase, **crate,** pack; **package,** encapsulate

20 top, cap, tip, crown; cork, stopper, plug; hood, hat, bonnet; roof, dome

21 floor; carpet; pave, cobblestone, flag, pebble; cement, concrete; **pave, surface;** tar, asphalt

22 face, veneer; board, plank; shingle; tile, brick, slate; glaze; paper, wallpaper

23 **coat**, spread on; smear, **smear on**, slap on, dab, daub, plaster; pour on; lay on; prime; enamel, gloss, lacquer; butter; tar

24 **plaster**, cement, concrete, mortar; face, line

25 **plate**, electroplate; **galvanize**

26 **crust**; scab, scab over

27 lie over; **overlap**, lap, lap over, jut; extend over, span, bridge, arch over, hang over, overhang

adjectives

28 **covered**, covert, under cover; **cloaked**, blanketed, muffled, hooded, **shrouded, veiled**, clouded, obscured; eclipsed; **screened**; shielded, masked; **housed**; under canvas; roofed; walled; **wrapped**, enveloped, sheathed, swathed; **boxed**, encased, **packaged**; **coated**, filmed; shelled; armoured; **floored**; paved, surfaced; plastered

29 **plated**, gold-plated, silver-plated; galvanized

30 **covering, coating**; cloaking, blanketing, shrouding, obscuring, **screening**, shielding, sheltering, wrapping, **enveloping**, sheathing, **overlapping**, lapping, spanning

282 LAYER

nouns

1 **layer**, thickness; **level, tier**, stage, storey, floor, gallery, step, ledge, deck; **stratum**, seam, belt, band, **bed, course**, measures; zone; shelf; floor, bedding

2 **sheet**, leaf, foil; wafer, disc; **plate**, plating; covering, **coat**, coating, veneer, film, scum, membrane, peel, skin, rind, hide; slick, oil slick; **slice**, cut, rasher; **slab**, plank, panel, pane; **fold**, lap, flap, **ply**; plywood

3 **flake**, scale, dandruff; chip; shaving

verbs

4 **layer**, lay down; flake, scale

adjectives

5 **layered**, in layers; plated, coated; faced; single storey, etc

6 **flaky**; scaly, scabby

283 WEIGHT

nouns

1 **weight**; body weight, fatness; tonnage; live weight; gross weight, **net weight**, net, nett; overweight; **solemnity, gravity**

2 (*sports*) bantamweight, featherweight, flyweight, heavyweight, light heavyweight, lightweight, middleweight, cruiser weight, welterweight

3 (*physics terms*) **gravity, gravitation**, G; specific gravity; gravitational field; G suit; **mass**; atomic weight, molecular weight, molar weight

4 **weight**, paperweight; lead, plumb, plummet, bob; sash weight

5 **burden**, pressure, **oppression**; burdening, saddling, charging, taxing; charge, **load**, loading, freight, cargo, bale; encumbrance; handicap, drag; overload

6 **pound, ounce, gram**, etc

7 **weighing**, balancing; **scale**, weighing instrument

verbs

8 **weigh**, weight; **balance**; counterbalance; weigh in; be heavy, weigh heavy, have weight, carry weight; lie on, press, press down

9 **weight**, weigh *or* weigh down; **ballast**

10 **burden**, load, encumber, charge, freight, tax, handicap, hamper, saddle; **oppress; overload**

11 **gravitate**, descend, drop, plunge, precipitate, sink, settle, subside; tend, **incline**, point, head, lead, lean

adjectives

12 **heavy, ponderous, massive**, weighty, hefty (*nonformal*), fat; **leaden**; heavyweight; overweight; **solemn**

13 **onerous, oppressive**, cumbersome; massive; **unwieldy**

14 **weighted; burdened, oppressed**, laden, encumbered, charged, loaded, fraught, taxed, saddled, hampered; overloaded

15 **gravitational**, mass

adverbs

16 **heavily**, heavy; oppressively; **ponderously**

284 LIGHTNESS

nouns

1 **lightness; buoyancy; softness**, gentleness, delicacy, tenderness; light touch, gentle touch

2 (*comparisons*) air, feather, down, fluff, fuzz, sponge, gossamer, cobweb, fairy, straw, chaff, dust, cork, chip, bubble, froth, foam

3 **lightening**, easing, **alleviation, relief**; unloading

verbs

4 **lighten**, reduce weight; **ease**, alleviate, relieve; unload; **be light**, weigh lightly

5 raise, **ferment**, leaven

6 **buoy**, buoy up; float, float high, ride high, waft; **sustain, hold up**, bear up

7 **rise**, ascend; hover, **float**

adjectives

8 **light**; weightless; airy; volatile; frothy, bubbly; downy, feathery, fluffy

9 **lightened, eased**, relieved, alleviated; mitigated

10 **light, gentle, soft, delicate**, dainty, tender, **easy**

11 **lightweight**, bantamweight, featherweight; underweight

12 **buoyant;** floating

13 **lightening, easing**, alleviating, relieving

285 RARITY

nouns

1 **rarity**, thinness, tenuousness; **subtlety, fineness**, flimsiness, **insubstantiality**

2 **diffusion**, dispersion, scattering; **thinning**, dilution, watering

verbs

3 **thin**, thin out; dilute, adulterate, water down; diffuse, disperse, scatter; expand

adjectives

4 **rare, rarefied; subtle; thin,** dilute; diluted, adulterated, watered; **tenuous, fine,** flimsy, slight, **insubstantial; airy,** gaseous; **diffuse,** dispersed, scattered

286 MEASUREMENT

nouns

1 **measurement, measure; gauging; estimation,** estimate, rough measure, approximation; **appraisal, stocktaking; assessment,** determination, rating, valuation, evaluation; **survey,** surveying; metric system; computation, calculation

2 **measure,** measuring instrument, **meter, instrument, gauge,** barometer, **rule, yardstick, standard,** norm, criterion, test, check; **pattern, model, type; scale;** reading, value, degree, quantity; parameter

3 **extent,** quantity, degree, size, distance, length, breadth; **weight**

4 **co-ordinates; latitude, longitude; altitude**

5 **measurability,** computability, determinability

6 **surveyor,** quantity surveyor; topographer, cartographer, mapmaker; **assessor**

verbs

7 **measure, gauge; estimate; assess, rate, appraise, value,** evaluate, appreciate, prize; **weigh,** weigh up; survey; plumb, probe, sound, fathom; span, pace, step; graduate; divide; meter; compute, calculate

8 **measure off, mark off,** rule off; **measure out,** mark out; put at

adjectives

9 **measuring, metric; quantitative,** numerative

10 **measured, gauged; appraised,** assessed, valued, rated, ranked; surveyed, plotted, mapped

11 **measurable, quantifiable, determinable,** calculable; appreciable, perceptible, noticeable

287 YOUTH

nouns

1 **youth,** tenderness, tender age, early years, school age, salad days

2 **childhood; boyhood; girlhood**

3 **immaturity,** inexperience, **callowness,** freshness; minority, **infancy**

4 **childishness,** childlikeness; **boyishness, girlishness**

5 **infancy,** the cradle, the crib

6 **adolescence, puberty; teens**

verbs

7 **make young, rejuvenate**

adjectives

8 **young, juvenile, youthful,** blooming, flowering, fresh-faced

9 **immature; inexperienced,** ripening, **raw, green,** budding, tender, innocent, naive, ingenuous, **undeveloped,** growing; **minor**

10 **childish,** childlike; **boyish; girlish**

11 **infant, infantile, babyish,** baby; **newborn;** in nappies, in arms

12 **adolescent,** pubescent; **teenage**

13 junior; younger

288 YOUNGSTER

nouns

1 **youngster, young person, youth,
juvenile;** sprig; sapling; fledgling;
**minor; infant; adolescent; teen-
ager; junior, younger, youngest,
baby**

2 **young people, youth,** young,
younger generation, young
blood; **children,** tots

3 **child; little one, tot,** innocent;
darling, lamb, kitten, **offspring**

4 **brat, urchin;** little monkey, little
terror; spoiled brat; juvenile delinquent

5 **boy, lad, youth,** young man,
schoolboy; fellow; master;
schoolboy

6 **girl, maid, maiden, lass,** young
lady, miss

7 **schoolgirl,** junior miss; **tomboy**

8 **infant, baby, babe,** bouncing
baby; **toddler; suckling**

9 (*animals*) **fledgling,** nestling;
**chick; duckling; gosling; kitten;
pup,** puppy; **cub; calf; colt,** foal;
piglet; **lamb;** kid; fawn; **tadpole;**
litter, nest

10 (*plants*) **sprout, seedling;** shoot;
twig, sprig, sapling

11 (*insects*) **larva, chrysalis, cocoon;**
caterpillar, maggot, grub

289 AGE

(*time of life*)

nouns

1 **age,** years; lifespan, life expectancy

2 **maturity, adulthood, majority;**
full growth; ripe age, **prime;**
manhood, virility; masculinity;
womanhood, femininity

3 **middle age,** middle life

4 **old age;** senior citizenship; infirmity, debility; second childhood;
senility; **longevity,** long life

5 **development,** growth, ripening,
blooming, blossoming, flourishing; **mellowing,** seasoning; **aging**

6 **menopause,** change of life

verbs

7 **mature, grow up,** grow, **develop,
ripen,** flower, flourish, bloom,
blossom; settle down; **mellow,**
season, temper

8 **age, grow old; decline,** wane,
fade, waste away; totter, shake;
wither, wrinkle, shrivel

adjectives

9 **adult, mature, of age,** big,
grown, **grown-up**

10 **mature, ripe,** ripened, **developed,** fully developed, full-
blown; seasoned, tempered, aged

11 **aged, elderly, old, ancient,** geriatric; **venerable;** hoary, **grey,**
white; wrinkled

12 **aging,** growing old; **declining,**
waning, fading, wasting, doting

13 **decrepit, infirm,** weak, feeble,
geriatric; tottering, rickety, shaky;
wizened, withered, shrivelled,
senile

290 ADULT OR OLD PERSON

nouns

1 **adult; man, woman;** major

2 **old man, elder;** senior citizen, geriatric; old chap, **old gentleman,** veteran; grandfather; Father Time

3 **old woman, old lady,** granny, dame, hag, witch, old wife; grandmother

4 **senior, elder;** dean; father; **eldest,** oldest

verbs

5 **mature;** grow old

adjectives

6 **mature;** middle-aged; aged, older

291 ORGANIC MATTER

nouns

1 **organic matter,** living nature matter; **biology; flesh, tissue,** fibre

2 **organism,** organization, organic being, being, creature, **individual,** genetic individual; virus; microbe

3 **cell;** plant cell, animal cell; germ cell; corpuscle; germ layer; cellular tissue; cell wall; nucleus

4 **chromosome;** sex chromosome; W chromosome; X chromosome, accessory chromosome; Y chromosome; Z chromosome

5 **genetic material, gene;** structural gene, operator gene; altered gene; messenger RNA; transfer RNA; gene pool, gene complex; **hereditary character,** heredity; gene mapping; gene transfer; **genetic engineering**

6 **germ cell,** reproductive cell

7 **sperm, seed, semen; sperm cell;** pollen

8 **ovum, egg, egg cell**

9 **embryo; fetus,** germ; **larva**

10 **egg;** bird's egg; **roe,** fish eggs, caviar, spawn; **yolk; white, egg white**

adjectives

11 **organic;** organized; **animate, living,** vital; **biological;** physiological

12 **genetic,** hereditary

13 **cellular;** corpuscular

14 **nuclear; chromosomal**

15 **embryonic, germinal;** larval, fetal

292 LIFE

nouns

1 **life, living, vitality,** animation; breath; vivacity; long life, longevity; life expectancy, life-span; viability; lifetime; immortality; birth; existence

2 **life force, soul,** spirit; **breath,** life breath; blood, heart's blood; **heart,** heartbeat; **life process;** biological clock, life cycle

3 **the living,** the quick

4 animation; quickening

verbs

5 **live,** have life, exist, breathe, subsist

6 **quicken; revive, come to,** come alive; **awake, awaken;** rise again, live again, resuscitate

7 **animate, quicken; conceive; give birth**

8 **keep alive,** endure, survive, persist, last, last out, hang on, hang in (*nonformal*), be spared; cheat death

adjectives

9 **living**, **alive**, live, conscious, breathing, **animate**, animated, **vital**, enlivened; viable

10 **life-giving**, quickening, energizing

293 DEATH

nouns

1 **death**, **dying**, clinical death, biological death, **demise**; brain death; release, **passing away**, passing, passing over, departure, going, exit, **end**; dissolution, extinction, annihilation; doom, final summons; **sleep**, **rest**; **grave**; curtains (*nonformal*)

2 (*personifications and symbols*) **Death**, **Grim Reaper**; **skull**, skull and crossbones

3 Styx; Heaven; Hell

4 early death, early grave, premature death; sudden death

5 **violent death**; killing; suffocation, smothering; choking, strangling; drowning, watery grave; starvation

6 **natural death**; euthanasia

7 dying day, dying hour, final hour

8 **extremity**; **deathbed**; death struggle, last agony, death throes; dying breath; **death rattle**, death groan

9 **deathliness**; **wierdness**, eeriness; ghostliness; ghastliness; paleness; pallor

10 **death rate**, death toll; **mortality**; transience

11 **obituary**; casualty list; **death toll**, body count

12 **corpse**, dead body, **carcass**, **body**; **stiff** (*nonformal*); **the dead**, **the deceased**, the departed; late lamented; **remains**, bones, skeleton, relics; dust, ashes, earth, clay; **carrion**; **mummy**

13 **autopsy**, postmortem, inquest, medical examiner, coroner

verbs

14 **die**, **succumb**, **expire**, **perish**, depart, go, go out, pass, **pass away**, be lost, **give up the ghost**, breathe one's last

15 (*nonformal terms*) **croak**, kick the bucket, push up daisies, bite the dust, cash in one's chips; turn up one's toes

16 **meet one's Maker**, go to a better place, go to one's rest, join the choir invisible

17 **drop dead**, fall down dead

18 be killed; **starve**, smother, **suffocate**; asphyxiate; choke, strangle; **drown**, go to a watery grave; catch one's death of cold

19 **lay down one's life**, **make the supreme sacrifice**

20 die out, become extinct

adjectives

21 **deathly**, **deathlike**, deadly; weird, eerie, uncanny, unearthly; ghostly; **ghastly**, grisly, gruesome, macabre; pale, wan, haggard

22 **dead**, lifeless, **deceased**, departed, gone, passed on, gone the way of all flesh, dead and gone, **at rest**, gone to a better world or place, joined the choir invisible; in the grave, six feet under *and*

pushing up daisies (*both nonformal*); stillborn; late

23 **dying, terminal**, sinking fast, not long for this world, done for (*nonformal*); **on one's last legs** (*nonformal*), with one foot in the grave; on one's deathbed

24 **mortal**, perishable

25 **bereaved**, bereft; widowed; **orphaned**, fatherless, motherless

adverbs

26 **deathly, deadly**

294 KILLING

nouns

1 **killing, slaying, slaughter, extermination, destruction; bloodshed**, blood, gore; euthanasia; lynching; stoning; shooting; poisoning; execution

2 **homicide, manslaughter; murder**; foul play; **assassination**

3 **butchery, slaughter**, holocaust

4 **carnage, massacre, bloodbath; mass murder, genocide**

5 **suicide**, hara-kiri (*Japanese*)

6 **suffocation**, smothering, **asphyxiation**; strangling, throttling, stifling; **choking; drowning**

7 **fatality, casualty**, disaster, calamity

8 **killer, butcher; murderer; assassin**; thug; **hatchet man**; homicidal maniac; serial killer; executioner

9 **slaughterhouse**, butchery, abattoir; concentration camp, killing fields

verbs

10 **kill, slay, put to death, do away with**, put to sleep, **put an end to**, end the life of, **dispatch, do to death**, do for, finish off, kill off, **dispose of, exterminate, destroy**, annihilate; **liquidate**, purge; put down, put one out of one's misery; send to kingdom come (*nonformal*); **martyr;** sacrifice; lynch; cut down, nip in the bud; poison; starve; **execute**

11 (*nonformal terms*) **waste**, rub out, croak, snuff, bump off, knock off, lay out, polish off, blow away, blot out, erase, wipe out, blast, do in, hit, ice, gun down, pick off, take care of, take out, take for a ride, get, fix, settle

12 **shed blood**, spill blood, have blood on one's hands

13 **murder; assassinate**; remove, purge, liquidate, eliminate, get rid of

14 **slaughter, butcher, massacre, decimate**; commit mass murder, commit genocide

15 **strike dead**, fell, bring down, lay low; drop; **shoot**, shoot down, gun down, riddle; cut down, cut to pieces or ribbons, **put to the sword**, stab to death, cut the throat; silence; brain, blow or knock or dash one's brains out; blow up, blow to bits or pieces or kingdom come; disintegrate; incinerate, burn at the stake

16 **strangle, throttle, choke;** suffocate, stifle, smother, asphyxiate; drown

17 **condemn to death**, sign one's death warrant, give the kiss of death to

18 **be killed**, get killed, **come to a violent end**

19 **commit suicide, take one's own life, kill oneself**, die by one's own hand, do away with oneself; blow one's brains out, take an overdose (*of a drug*), overdose *or* OD (*nonformal*)

adjectives

20 **deadly, deathly, killing, destructive**; savage, brutal; **fatal, mortal, lethal, malignant**, malign, **virulent, pernicious; terminal**

21 **murderous; homicidal;** suicidal; **soul-destroying;** cruel; **bloodthirsty; bloody, gory**

295 INTERMENT

nouns

1 **interment, burial,** burying

2 **cremation, incineration, burning**

3 embalming; mummification

4 **last rites,** funeral rites, funeral service; burial service; requiem; eulogy; **wake**

5 **funeral, burial,** burying; funeral procession, cortege; dead march, last post; burial at sea

6 **knell,** passing bell, death bell

7 **mourner,** griever; **pallbearer,** bearer

8 **undertaker,** funeral director; gravedigger

9 **mortuary, morgue; funeral parlour; crematorium**

10 **hearse,** funeral car

11 **coffin,** box; wooden overcoat (*nonformal*); **urn**

12 **bier,** litter

13 **shroud,** winding sheet; **pall**

14 **graveyard, cemetery, burial ground** *or* **place,** necropolis; **churchyard**

15 **tomb; grave,** pit; resting place; **crypt, vault,** burial chamber; **mausoleum;** pyramid, mummy chamber; burial mound, barrow

16 **monument,** gravestone

17 **epitaph,** inscription

verbs

18 **bury, lay to rest**

19 **cremate, incinerate, burn,** reduce to ashes

20 **lay out; embalm;** lie in state

adjectives

21 **funereal,** funeral; **dismal; mournful**

adverbs

22 **underground,** six feet under (*nonformal*), at rest, resting in peace

296 PLANTS

nouns

1 **plants, vegetation; flora, plant life;** greenery, greens; botany

2 **growth, crop; plantation,** planting; **clump,** tuft

3 **plant; vegetable; weed;** seedling; cutting; flowering plant; fungus; annual, perennial; evergreen, deciduous plant; aquatic plant

4 **pulse, bean, pea, lentil; herb;** succulent; **vine,** creeper, ivy, climber; **fern,** bracken; **moss; seaweed; fungus,** mould, rust, mushroom, toadstool

5 **grass; cereal, grain, corn;** rush, reed, cane, bamboo

6 **turf, sod**

7 **green, lawn;** grounds; **common, park, village green;** golf course or links; bowling green, putting green

8 **grassland,** grass; parkland; **meadow,** water meadow; **pasture; range; prairie**

9 **shrubbery; shrub, bush;** scrub, bramble

10 **tree,** timber; sapling, seedling; conifer, evergreen

11 **woodland, wood, woods; timber, forest;** forestry; **bush,** scrub; parkland, chase

12 **grove; orchard;** copice, copse

13 **thicket,** copse, covert; **brake**

14 **brush, scrub,** bush, **brushwood**

15 **foliage,** leafiness

16 **leaf, frond;** leaflet; **blade; needle;** petal

17 **branch,** fork, limb, bough; **twig, sprig;** spray; **shoot,** offshoot, frond; **sprout; sucker; runner;** tendril

18 **stem, stalk, stock; trunk;** straw; reed; cane

19 **root; taproot; bulb**

20 **flower, posy, blossom, bloom; gardening,** horticulture

21 **bouquet, posy,** flower arrangement; buttonhole; **spray; wreath;** garland

22 **flowering, blossoming, blooming; blossom, bloom; full bloom**

23 **seed vessel;** husk; **capsule, pod,** seed pod

24 **seed;** stone, pit, nut; pip; fruit; **grain, kernel, berry**

25 **vegetation, growth;** germination; sprouting; budding

verbs

26 **vegetate, grow;** germinate; root, take root; sprout up, shoot up; burst forth; **sprout, shoot; bud; leaf,** put forth leaves; flourish, luxuriate, riot; overrun

27 **flower,** be in flower, **blossom, bloom,** be in bloom

adjectives

28 **vegetable,** herbal; cereal; fruity; botanic, botanical

29 **floral; flowery; flowering,** blossoming, **blooming,** in flower, in bloom, in blossom

30 **woodland, forest, wooded; woody,** bushy

31 **mossy; grassy**

32 **luxuriant,** flourishing, **rank, lush;** dense, impenetrable, thick, heavy; overgrown, overrun; gone to seed

33 **perennial,** ephemeral; hardy; **deciduous,** evergreen

297 HUMANKIND

nouns

1 **mankind, man, human race, humanity,** human beings, mortals, mortality, flesh; **race,** strain, stock; **culture; society, ethnic group;** community, **the people, the populace; nationality, nation**

2 **the people,** the populace, the population, the public

3 **person, human, human being, man, woman, child,** member of the human race; **mortal,** life, **soul; being;** creature; **individual;** personage, **personality; body;**

somebody, one, someone; fellow (*nonformal*)

4 **humanity**, mortality; **human nature**; human frailty

5 **anthropology, sociology, psychology**; anatomy; anthropologist

verbs

6 make human, civilize

adjectives

7 **human**; frail, mortal; only human

8 **personal, individual**, private, peculiar, idiosyncratic

9 **public, general, common**; communal, **social**; civic, civil; **national**; state; international, cosmopolitan

298 SEASON

(*time of year*)

nouns

1 **season**, time of year, **period**; dry *or* rainy *or* cold season, monsoon

2 **spring**, springtime

3 **summer**, summertime; midsummer; **dog days**; the silly season

4 **autumn, fall**, harvest, harvest time

5 **Indian summer**, St Martin's summer

6 **winter**, wintertime; midwinter; Christmastime, Yuletide

7 **equinox**; solstice

adjectives

8 **seasonal**; **spring**, vernal; **summer**; midsummer; **autumn**, autumnal; **winter**, wintry, arctic, snowy, icy

299 MORNING, NOON

nouns

1 **morning**, morn, AM

2 **dawn**, the dawn of day, **daybreak, sunrise**, light, first light, daylight; **break of day, crack of dawn**

3 **noon, high noon**, midday, twelve o'clock

adjectives

4 **morning**; dawn, dawning

5 **noon**, midday

adverbs

6 **in the morning**, before noon; at sunrise, at dawn, at first light, **at the crack of dawn**; with the lark

7 at noon, at midday

300 EVENING, NIGHT

nouns

1 **afternoon**, PM

2 **evening**, eve; **nightfall, sunset**, sundown

3 **dusk, twilight**, gloaming

4 **night**, night-time, bedtime, darkness

5 eleventh hour, curfew

6 **midnight**, dead of night

adjectives

7 **afternoon**

8 **evening**; twilight; dusk

9 **nocturnal**, night, **nightly**; all-night; midnight

adverbs

10 **nightly**, nights (*nonformal*), at *or* by night; **overnight**, all night

301 RAIN

nouns

1 **rain, rainfall,** moisture, wet, rainwater; **shower,** flurry; **drizzle; mist,** Scotch mist; raindrop

2 **rainstorm; cloudburst,** torrential rain or downpour; **downpour,** pouring rain, **deluge, flood,** heavy rain, driving rain

3 **wet weather,** stormy or dirty weather, wet; rainy day; **rains,** rainy season, **monsoon**

verbs

4 **rain, precipitate,** rain down, fall; **shower;** spatter, patter; **drizzle; pour,** stream down, pour with rain, **pelt,** pelt down, come down in torrents or sheets or buckets, **rain cats and dogs** (nonformal)

adjectives

5 **rainy;** drizzling; **misty;** torrential, pouring, streaming, pelting, drumming, driving

302 AIR, WEATHER

nouns

1 **air;** ozone (nonformal); thin air

2 **weather, climate; the elements,** forces of nature; fair weather, halcyon days, good weather; heat wave, hot weather; cold weather

3 weather map; high; low; front; cold front; warm front

4 **meteorology,** forecasting

5 **meteorologist; weatherman, weather report,** weather forecast

6 **barometer,** glass; weather vane

7 **ventilation, airing;** air conditioning

8 **ventilator;** air filter, cooling system; fan

verbs

9 **air, air out, ventilate,** refresh, freshen; **fan**

adjectives

10 **airy,** exposed, roomy; light; breezy; open-air; **atmospheric**

11 **elemental;** meteorological

303 WIND

nouns

1 **wind,** current, **air current, draught;** undercurrent; head wind, tail wind, following wind; jet stream

2 **puff,** puff of wind, breath, breath of air

3 **breeze,** light or gentle wind or breeze, air; stiff breeze; cool or cooling breeze; sea breeze

4 **gust, blast,** blow, flurry

5 **winter wind, cold wind,** icy blast; wind chill or wind chill factor

6 **north wind; east wind,** easterly; **west wind,** westerly; **south wind**

7 prevailing wind; trade wind; doldrums; roaring forties

8 (naut terms) **head wind, tail wind,** following wind, fair or favourable wind

9 strong or stiff or high or howling wind, ill wind; storm; blow; squall; **gale; hurricane,** typhoon, tropical storm, blizzard

10 dust storm, sandstorm

11 whirlwind; cyclone, tornado, typhoon

12 weather vane, weathercock, wind sock

13 fan; ventilator

verbs

14 blow, waft; puff; breeze; freshen; bluster, squall; storm, rage, blast; blow over

15 sigh, whisper, mutter, murmur, **sob, moan,** groan, growl, **wail, howl,** scream, screech, shriek, **roar,** whistle, sing

adjectives

16 windy; breezy, draughty, airy; brisk, fresh; blustery

17 stormy, tempestuous, raging, storming, angry; turbulent; dirty, foul; rainy; cloudy

18 windblown; windswept, bleak, raw, exposed

304 CLOUD

nouns

1 cloud; cloud bank, cloud cover

2 fog; smog; mist; haze, gauze, film; vapour

verbs

3 cloud, cloud over, overshadow, shadow, shade, **darken,** obscure; **smoke; fog;** mist over, mist up

adjectives

4 cloudy, nebulous; **clouded, overcast;** dirty, heavy, dark; **gloomy;** stormy

5 foggy; hazy, misty

305 BUBBLE

nouns

1 bubble, globule; **blister,** blood blister; balloon, bladder; air bubble, soap bubble

2 foam, froth; spray, surf, breakers, white water; **suds, lather;** head; **scum;** mousse, meringue

3 bubbling, sparkle, frothing, foaming; fizz; fermentation, ferment

verbs

4 bubble, bubble up; **fizz, fizzle;** hiss, **sparkle; ferment; foam, froth,** froth up; foam over; **boil,** seethe, simmer; plop; gurgle; bubble over, **boil over**

5 foam, froth, cream; **lather;** whip, beat, whisk

adjectives

6 bubbly, bubbling, **fizzy, sparkling;** ebullient; puffed, beaten, whipped; **blistered**

7 frothy; soapy

306 BEHAVIOUR

nouns

1 behaviour, conduct, deportment, manner, manners, demeanour, carriage, bearing, poise, posture, guise, **air,** presence; tone, style, lifestyle; way of life; **way, ways;** behaviour trait; methods, **method; practice;** procedure, proceeding; **actions,** acts, goings-on, doings, what one is up to; movements, moves, tactics; action, doing; activity; motions, gestures; pose, affectation; behaviour pattern; **custom**

2 good behaviour; good manners, **etiquette; courtesy;** sociability, bad behaviour

verbs

3 behave, act, do, go on; **behave oneself, conduct oneself, handle oneself,** carry oneself; acquit oneself; proceed, move, swing into action; **misbehave**

4 behave oneself, behave, act well, clean up one's act (*nonformal*), act one's age, **be good,** be nice, **do right,** do the right *or* proper thing, keep out of mischief, be on one's best behaviour, play one's cards right

5 treat, use, do by, behave toward, act with regard to; **deal with,** cope with, **handle;** respond to

adjectives

6 behaved, mannered

307 MISBEHAVIOUR

nouns

1 misconduct, misdemeanour; **disorderly conduct,** disorder, disruption, hooliganism; vandalism; vice; delinquency

2 mischief; playfulness, high spirits, youthful spirits; foolishness

3 mischief-maker, rogue, devil, rascal, scamp; wag; joker, practical joker, life and soul of the party; **rowdy, ruffian,** hooligan; bad boy, little devil, little monkey

verbs

4 misbehave; get into mischief; act up *and* make waves *and* carry on (*all nonformal*), sow one's wild oats; horse around (*nonformal*), play the fool

adjectives

5 misbehaving; naughty, bad; improper; **disorderly,** disruptive, **rowdy**

6 mischievous, full of mischief; arch; **devilish; playful,** high-spirited; foolish

adverbs

7 mischievously; playfully, in fun

308 WILL

nouns

1 will, volition; **choice,** determination, **decision; wish, mind, fancy,** discretion, pleasure, **inclination,** disposition, liking, **desire;** half a mind *or* notion, idle wish; **appetite, passion, lust,** sexual desire; **objective, intention; command; free choice,** one's own discretion *or* initiative, **free will;** will power, **resolution**

verbs

2 will, wish, see *or* think fit, think good, think proper, **choose to, have a mind to;** have half a mind *or* notion to; **choose,** determine, **decide; resolve;** command, decree; **desire**

3 have one's will, **have *or* get one's way,** have it all one's way, do as one pleases, please oneself; take charge of one's destiny; take the law into one's own hands; have the last word, impose one's will

adjectives

4 willing, voluntary

adverbs

5 at will, at one's pleasure, at one's discretion; ad lib; as one wishes, as one thinks best; of one's own free will, of one's own accord, on one's own; without coercion

8 **favourably;** nothing loath

9 **voluntarily, freely, gratuitously, spontaneously;** by choice; without reservation; independently

309 WILLINGNESS

nouns

1 **willingness,** readiness; **acquiescence, consent; compliance; eagerness,** promptness, alacrity, zeal, ardour, enthusiasm; goodwill; willing heart, favourable disposition, willing ear

2 **volunteering; spontaneity;** autonomy, independence; volunteer

verbs

3 **be willing, be game** (nonformal), be ready; **incline, lean;** bring oneself, **agree; acquiesce, consent;** be eager, be keen; plunge into; **cooperate,** collaborate

4 **volunteer,** do voluntarily

adjectives

5 **willing, ready, game** (nonformal); **disposed, inclined;** predisposed; **favourable, agreeable;** content, **consenting; eager;** keen, prompt, quick, forward, zealous, ardent, enthusiastic; receptive, responsive; amenable, docile

6 **voluntary;** gratuitous; spontaneous, **free;** offered, proffered; **discretionary,** optional; arbitrary; autonomous, independent; **unsolicited, uninvited,** uncalled-for

adverbs

7 **willingly; eagerly,** with relish, without question, ardently, enthusiastically; **readily,** promptly

310 UNWILLINGNESS

nouns

1 **refusal, unwillingness, disinclination, reluctance;** slowness; sulk, sulks; disobedience; aversion, antipathy, distaste; **obstinacy;** opposition; **resistance; disagreement;** dissent

2 **demur, qualm,** reservation; **hesitation,** pause, **falter; faltering;** shrinking, shyness, **diffidence,** modesty; recoil; **protest, objection**

verbs

3 **refuse, be unwilling; mind,** object to, **balk at;** grudge, begrudge

4 **demur;** strain; falter; waver; **hesitate,** pause, be half-hearted, **hang back,** hold off; shy, shrink, recoil, flinch, wince, quail, pull back

adjectives

5 **unwilling, disinclined,** averse; **resistant; disagreeing,** differing, at odds; disobedient, sullen, sulky, mutinous; cursory, perfunctory; **involuntary, forced**

6 **reluctant,** grudging, loath; backward, slow; indifferent, apathetic, perfunctory; balking, restive

7 **demurring,** hedging, squeamish, **scrupulous; diffident,** shy, modest, bashful; **hesitant,** hesitating, faltering; shrinking

adverbs

8 unwillingly, involuntarily

9 reluctantly, grudgingly, sullenly, sulkily; under protest

311 OBEDIENCE

nouns

1 **obedience,** compliance; acquiescence, consent; **deference,** submission; **service,** homage, **allegiance, loyalty,** faith; conformity

verbs

2 **obey, mind, heed, keep, observe;** comply, conform; fall in; defer to; take orders; **submit**

adjectives

3 **obedient,** compliant; consenting, **submissive,** deferential; willing, **dutiful;** loyal, faithful, devoted; uncritical; conforming; law-abiding

adverbs

4 **obediently; submissively;** willingly, **dutifully;** loyally, faithfully

312 DISOBEDIENCE

nouns

1 **disobedience;** wilful disobedience; **insubordination; disrespect; lawlessness;** violation, infringement; civil disobedience, passive resistance; deliberate negligence, default, delinquency

2 **defiance; obstinacy**

3 **revolt, rebellion, revolution, mutiny,** insurrection, uprising, outbreak, **riot,** civil disorder, **strike,** general strike

4 **rebel;** maverick (*nonformal*), troublemaker; nonconformist;

agitator; extremist; revolutionary; traitor, subversive; freedom fighter

verbs

5 **disobey, ignore, disregard, defy,** scoff at; flout; **violate;** break the law

6 **revolt, rebel; rise up; mutiny; riot,** run riot; revolutionize, subvert, overthrow; strike; break away

adjectives

7 **disobedient,** lawless, wayward, naughty; wilful, obstinate; **defiant**

8 **uncooperative,** intractable

9 **defiant, unruly,** restive; feisty (*nonformal*); wild, untamed

10 **rebellious,** rebel, breakaway; **mutinous,** riotous, turbulent; revolutionary; subversive; extreme

313 ACTION

nouns

1 **action, activity,** act; **acting, doing;** practice; **exercise,** drill; **operation,** working, function, functioning; play; **operations,** affairs, **workings; business,** employment, work, occupation; **behaviour**

2 **performance, execution,** carrying out; **transaction; discharge, dispatch;** conduct, **handling,** management, administration; **achievement, accomplishment, implementation;** completion

3 **act, action, deed, doing,** thing; turn; **feat;** master stroke, **exploit,** adventure, **enterprise,** initiative, achievement, accomplishment, **performance**, production, track record (*nonformal*); effort, endeavour, job, undertaking; **transaction**; dealing, deal; **operation, proceeding, step, measure, manoeuvre, move, movement**; coup, stroke; blow, go (*nonformal*); *fait accompli* (*French*); **dealings; works**; work, handiwork

verbs

4 **act, serve, function; operate, work, move**, practise; proceed; make, play, **behave**

5 **take action, take steps; proceed**, proceed with; do something; **manoeuvre**

6 **do, effect, make; bring about, bring off, produce, deliver** (*nonformal*); **achieve, accomplish**, realize; render, pay; inflict, wreak; commit, perpetrate; pull off (*nonformal*)

7 **carry out**, fulfil, work out; **bring off**, carry off; **implement**

8 **practise, exercise, employ, use; conduct, prosecute, wage; follow, pursue; engage in**, work at, **do; take up**, take to, undertake, tackle; specialize in

9 **perform, execute, enact; discharge, dispatch;** conduct, **manage, handle;** dispose of, **deal with,** cope with; **make, accomplish,** complete

adjectives

10 **acting**, performing, practised, serving, functioning, functional, operating, operative, operational, working; in action

314 INACTION

nouns

1 **inaction; passive resistance; pacifism; neutrality;** waiting game; **inertia, immobility,** stagnation, vegetation, paralysis; **idleness,** sloth; immobility; equilibrium; **inactivity; serenity;** contemplation, meditation; contemplative life

verbs

2 **do nothing, sit back; delay,** lie low; hang fire; **rest, be still;** drift, coast; **stagnate,** vegetate, lie dormant, hibernate; idle

3 **refrain, abstain, spare, forgo,** keep from

4 **let alone,** leave alone; **let be,** leave be (*nonformal*)

5 **let go,** let pass, **let slip**

adjectives

6 **passive; neutral; inert,** immobile, dormant, stagnant, stagnating, vegetable, static, stationary, motionless, immobile, paralysed; **inactive, idle;** contemplative, meditative

315 ACTIVITY

nouns

1 **activity, action; movement,** motion, **stir; proceedings, doings,** goings-on; militancy; business

2 **animation, vivacity; life, spirit, verve,** energy, adrenalin

3 **swiftness, alacrity,** readiness; **promptness; dispatch,** expedition; **agility**

4 **bustle, fuss, flurry, flutter,** fluster, scramble, ferment, stew,

sweat, whirl, swirl, **stir**, ado, bother; tumult, commotion, **agitation; restlessness; spurt, burst,** fit, spasm

5 **industry, diligence, application,** concentration, ardour, fervour, vehemence; **energy**

6 **enterprise, dynamism, initiative,** aggression, aggressiveness, killer instinct, force, **push, drive, hustle, go,** go-ahead; spirit

7 **beaver, busy bee, eager beaver** (*nonformal*); **activist,** political activist, **militant;** enthusiast; new broom

verbs

8 **be busy; work, labour; busy oneself**

9 **stir,** take hold

10 **bustle, fuss,** stir, tear around, hurry about

11 **hustle** (*nonformal*), **drive,** drive oneself, **push,** step lively (*nonformal*); press on, drive on; forge ahead

12 **keep going, keep on, carry on,** keep moving; keep busy

adjectives

13 **active, lively, animated, spirited,** bubbly, ebullient, **vivacious, sprightly;** spry, breezy, brisk, **energetic,** eager, keen; alive, live; **militant**

14 **quick, swift, speedy, prompt,** ready, smart, sharp; **agile, nimble, spry,** springy

15 **stirring,** afoot; in full swing

16 **bustling,** fussing, fussy, **fidgety,** restless, fretful, jumpy, unsettled; **agitated, turbulent**

17 **busy; occupied, engaged, employed, working; at work,** on duty, in harness

18 **industrious, assiduous, diligent,** laborious; hard, unremitting, relentless, zealous, ardent, fervent, vehement; **energetic, strenuous;** tireless, indefatigable

19 **enterprising, aggressive, dynamic,** driving, forceful, pushy; adventurous; **ambitious**

20 **hectic, frenzied, frantic, frenetic;** intrusive, officious

adverbs

21 **actively, busily; briskly, energetically,** with gusto; full tilt, all out (*nonformal*)

22 **quickly, swiftly, readily, promptly**

23 **assiduously, diligently,** laboriously; relentlessly, ardently, fervently, vehemently; **energetically,** strenuously

316 INACTIVITY

nouns

1 **inactivity, inaction;** lull, suspension; suspended animation; hibernation; immobility; **inertia**

2 **idleness,** unemployment; **leisure; relaxation,** unwinding

3 **unemployment;** seasonal unemployment

4 **idling,** lazing; trifling; dawdling; loitering, lingering; lounging, lolling

5 **laziness, sloth;** slowness; inertia

6 **slowness, dullness, sluggishness, lethargy;** apathy, indifference; stupor; **sloth;** yawning, drowsi-

ness; **weariness, fatigue;** boredom

7 **idler,** layabout (*nonformal*);
slouch; time waster; dawdler

8 derelict; drifter, vagrant, tramp;
beggar

9 **drone;** lounge lizard (*nonformal*), parasite

verbs

10 **idle,** do nothing, **laze, loaf,
lounge; lie around,** lounge
around, moon, sit around,
slouch around; **shirk,** avoid work

11 **waste time, kill time; trifle,** dabble, potter

12 **dally, dawdle, loiter,** linger, lag,
take one's time

13 **take it easy, drift,** coast

14 **lie idle, lie fallow;** hibernate, lie
dormant

adjectives

15 **inactive,** stationary, static; sedentary; motionless

16 **idle,** fallow; **unemployed, unoccupied, jobless;** free, available, at
liberty, at leisure; off duty, off
work, off

17 **indolent, lazy;** slow, slack, lax;
easy; parasitic, cadging, sponging, scrounging

18 **languid, listless,** lifeless, inanimate, slow, **lethargic,** apathetic,
sluggish, drugged, nodding, **dull,**
heavy, leaden, stultified; **inert,**
stagnant, stagnating, dormant;
phlegmatic; dead; sleepy; weary;
jaded, sated; bored

317 ASSENT

nouns

1 **assent, acquiescence, concurring, compliance, agreement,
acceptance;** welcome; general
agreement; support; **consent**

2 **affirmative; yes,** aye, amen; nod

3 **acknowledgment, recognition,
acceptance;** appreciation; **admission,** confession, concession, allowance; avowal, profession,
declaration

4 **ratification, endorsement, acceptance, approval, sanction,
permission, confirmation,**
authorization, warrant; stamp,
rubber stamp; seal of approval;
signature; visa

5 **unanimity;** total agreement;
understanding, mutual understanding; **consent,** general consent, **accord,** accordance, **concord, agreement,** general agreement; **consensus;** unison, harmony, **chorus, concert**

6 **subscriber;** signatory; party

verbs

7 **assent, acquiesce, consent, comply, accede, agree;** accept, receive, buy (*nonformal*); **subscribe to,** acquiesce in, abide by;
nod, vote for; welcome, hail,
cheer, acclaim, applaud

8 **concur, accord, coincide, agree,
agree with;** go with, meet, conform to, side with; **echo**

9 **come to an agreement, agree,
settle on,** agree on, shake on it
(*nonformal*)

10 **acknowledge, admit, own,** con-

fess, allow, **grant**, warrant, concede; accept, recognize

11 ratify, endorse, second, support, **certify, confirm, validate, authenticate, accept,** permit, give permission, **approve;** sanction, **authorize,** warrant, accredit; **pass;** subscribe to; sign, initial; rubber stamp (*nonformal*)

adjectives

12 assenting, agreeing, acquiescing, compliant, consenting, submissive, **agreed, content**

13 accepted, approved, received; acknowledged, admitted, allowed, granted, conceded, recognized, professed, confessed, avowed, warranted; self-confessed; **ratified, endorsed, certified,** confirmed, validated, authenticated; **signed,** sealed; stamped; affirmed

14 unanimous, solid; unchallenged; **concurrent; agreeing, in agreement, like-minded**

adverbs

15 unanimously, concurrently, without contradiction, in chorus, in concert, in unison, **together,** all together, all agreeing, **as one**

318 DISSENT

nouns

1 dissent; disagreement, difference, variance, diversity, disparity; **dissatisfaction, disapproval;** repudiation, **rejection; refusal, opposition;** dissension; **alienation,** withdrawal

2 objection, protest; protestation; **challenge; demur; reservation,** qualm; **complaint, grievance;**

exception; demonstration, rally, march, sit-in, boycott, strike, picketing; **rebellion**

3 dissenter, dissident; nonconformist

verbs

4 dissent, disagree, differ, not agree, disagree with; **take exception,** withhold assent, **take issue;** oppose; withdraw, drop out

5 object, protest; remonstrate; **complain; dispute; challenge; demur; demonstrate, demonstrate against,** rally, march, boycott, strike, picket; **rebel**

adjectives

6 dissenting, dissident; disagreeing, differing; opposing, in opposition; alienated; underground; rebellious

7 protesting; objecting; under protest

319 AFFIRMATION

nouns

1 affirmation, assertion, declaration, allegation; **avowal; position, stand,** stance; **statement, word,** say, saying; manifesto; **creed; pronouncement, proclamation,** announcement; proposition, conclusion; protest, protestation; utterance

2 assertiveness; speaking out

3 affidavit; vouching, swearing; testimony

4 oath, vow, word, assurance, guarantee, warrant; pledge

verbs

5 **affirm, assert,** protest, **declare,** say, **sound off** (*nonformal*), speak, **state,** set down, express; **allege,** profess; announce, **pronounce,** enunciate, **proclaim; maintain,** contend, argue, **insist, hold,** submit

6 **testify,** witness; **warrant, attest,** certify, **guarantee, assure; vouch, vouch for, swear; vow**

adjectives

7 **affirmative,** affirming, certifying; **assertive; positive,** absolute, emphatic, decided, unmistakable

8 **affirmed, asserted,** avowed, **declared; alleged,** professed; **stated,** pronounced, announced, enunciated; warranted, **attested, certified,** vouched, **vouched for,** vowed, pledged, **sworn**

adverbs

9 **positively,** absolutely, decidedly, loudly, loud and clear; emphatically, with emphasis; under oath

320 NEGATION, DENIAL

nouns

1 negation; perversity, **negative, no**

2 **denial;** renunciation, repudiation; **contradiction,** contravention; **refutation; reversal**

verbs

3 **negate,** say 'no'; shake the head

4 **deny,** not admit, not accept; **disown,** renounce, retract, take back; revoke, **repudiate; contradict,** cross, contravene, **dispute,** oppose, **counter,** contest; belie; **refute, disprove;** defect

adjectives

5 **negative; denying, disclaiming,** disowning; **contradictory,** contradicting, **opposing, contrary,** repugnant; perverse

321 IMITATION

nouns

1 **imitation, copying,** counterfeiting, repetition; following, mirroring; **simulation,** modelling; forgery; **impersonation, impression;** parody

2 **mimicry, mockery**

3 **reproduction, duplication,** imitation, **copy,** dummy, mock-up, **replica,** facsimile, representation, paraphrase, approximation, model, version; parody, travesty

4 **impostor, mimic;** parrot, ape, monkey; echo; forger; hypocrite, phoney (*nonformal*); conformist, sheep

verbs

5 **imitate, copy, repeat;** mirror, reflect; **echo,** chorus; **simulate;** counterfeit, fake (*nonformal*), forge, crib, lift (*nonformal*); **parody; paraphrase,** approximate

6 **mimic, impersonate,** mime, **ape, parrot;** take off

7 **emulate, follow,** follow suit; model on, take after

adjectives

8 **imitation, mock, sham,** copied, counterfeit, forged, unoriginal; synthetic

322 NONIMITATION

nouns

1 **originality, novelty,** newness, innovation, freshness, uniqueness; **authenticity;** inventiveness, creativity

2 **original, model,** archetype, prototype, **pattern, mould; innovation,** new departure

verbs

3 **originate, invent; innovate; create;** revolutionize

adjectives

4 **original, novel, unprecedented; unique;** new, fresh; **authentic, imaginative, creative; avant-garde,** revolutionary; pioneering

5 unprecedented; **archetypal; prime,** primary, primitive

323 COMPENSATION

nouns

1 **compensation,** repayment; **amends; redress,** satisfaction; substitution; **offsetting,** balancing, **counterbalancing; retaliation,** revenge

2 **counterbalance; balance,** ballast

verbs

3 **compensate,** make compensation, make good, set right, pay back, rectify; **make amends,** do penance, atone; pay back, repay, cover; **trade off; retaliate**

4 **offset,** set off, **counteract, counterbalance, balance,** set against; **square**

adjectives

5 **compensating, compensatory;** rectifying; **offsetting;** balancing, **counterbalancing; retaliatory**

adverbs

6 **in compensation,** in return, back; in consideration

324 CAREFULNESS

(close or watchful attention)

nouns

1 **carefulness, care, heed, concern, regard; attention; thoughtfulness; consideration,** solicitude, caring, loving care, TLC (*nonformal*); forethought, anticipation; **caution**

2 **pains; diligence,** industry; **thoroughness**

3 **exactness, accuracy, precision,** correctness; **strictness;** nicety, delicacy, detail, subtlety, refinement

4 **vigilance,** prudence, **watching, observance, surveillance; watch,** vigil, lookout; monitoring; custody; **guard; sharp eye, weather eye,** watchful eye, eagle eye

5 **alertness; attention;** sleeplessness; **readiness,** promptness

verbs

6 **care, mind, heed,** think, consider, regard; be concerned; **pay attention**

7 **be careful,** take heed, take care; **be cautious;** take pains, take trouble, **be painstaking;** go out of one's way, bend over backwards (*nonformal*)

8 **be vigilant,** be watchful, be on the lookout; keep watch; watch, look sharp, be on one's guard; be on the alert; **look out, watch out**

9 look after, nurture, foster, **tend, take care of**

adjectives

10 **careful, mindful, thoughtful, considerate, caring,** solicitous, loving, tender; circumspect; **attentive; cautious**

11 **painstaking, diligent, assiduous, thorough,** industrious, elaborate

12 **meticulous, exacting, scrupulous, conscientious,** punctual, **particular, fussy, critical, attentive,** scrutinizing; **thorough; exact, precise, accurate, correct;** close, narrow; **strict, rigid, rigorous,** demanding; nice, delicate, subtle, fine, refined, minute, detailed, exquisite

13 **vigilant, wary,** prudent, **watchful,** sleepless, **observant; on guard,** guarded; sharp-eyed

14 **alert, on the alert, on one's toes, on the ball** (*nonformal*), **attentive; awake, wide-awake,** sleepless, alive, ready, prompt, quick, quick on the uptake (*nonformal*); **smart, bright, keen, sharp**

adverbs

15 **carefully,** thoughtfully, solicitously, tenderly, lovingly; **cautiously; with care;** painstakingly, **diligently,** assiduously, thoroughly

16 **meticulously, scrupulously, conscientiously,** punctually, strictly, rigorously, exactly, **accurately, precisely, with precision;** nicely, minutely, in detail, exquisitely

17 **warily,** prudently, watchfully

325 NEGLECT

nouns

1 **neglect, negligence;** slackness; permissiveness; disregard; **oversight; omission,** lapse, failure

2 **carelessness; blindness; uncaring, thoughtlessness;** oblivion, forgetfulness; **recklessness; indifference; laziness;** casualness; abandon

3 **untidiness, messiness;** loose ends; bad job, botch; bungling

4 inaccuracy, imprecision

5 slacker, shirker, idler

verbs

6 **neglect, overlook, disregard,** not heed, **ignore; pass over,** gloss over; **be negligent, fail,** lapse, default; **be caught napping**

7 **leave undone,** leave, skip, jump, **miss, omit,** pass over, pass up (*nonformal*), **shirk,** malinger

8 **slight;** turn one's back on; leave undone; skimp (*nonformal*); pass over, skate over, dodge, waffle (*nonformal*), fudge; **skim over; cut corners**

9 **do carelessly; botch; bungle;** dash off; rough out; throw together, patch together, patch up

adjectives

10 **negligent, neglectful,** neglecting; **inattentive;** unwary; slack, lax, relaxed, loose, permissive; skimping (*nonformal*)

11 **careless, heedless, regardless, uncaring,** tactless, **thoughtless, unthinking, inconsiderate,** for-

getful, oblivious; **unprepared; reckless; indifferent; lazy;** perfunctory, cursory, casual; airy, flippant

12 **slovenly,** untidy; **clumsy, bungling; haphazard; deficient,** botched

13 **unscrupulous, uncritical;** inaccurate

14 **neglected,** unattended to; **disregarded, overlooked, missed,** omitted, passed over, gathering dust, **ignored, slighted;** unsolicited; left undone; deserted, abandoned; shelved

15 **unheeded, unobserved, unnoticed, unseen,** unmarked

adverbs

16 **negligently,** inadvertently; loosely; lightly

17 **carelessly, thoughtlessly; recklessly;** casually, airily; clumsily, haphazardly

326 INTERPRETATION

nouns

1 **interpretation, construction, reading; diagnosis; definition,** description; **meaning**

2 **rendering; version;** variant; **edition**

3 **translation; paraphrase;** decoding; **glossary;** key

4 **explanation,** unfolding, illumination, enlightenment, light, **clarification,** simplification; **exposition,** expounding; **illustration, demonstration;** decoding, cracking, unlocking, **solution**

5 (*explanatory remark*) **comment;**

notation, **note,** footnote, gloss; commentary

6 **interpreter; commentator;** critic; exponent; **translator; guide**

verbs

7 **interpret, diagnose;** understand; **read into; define, describe**

8 **explain, expound,** make of; **spell out,** unfold; **account for; clarify, elucidate,** clear up, make clear, make plain; **simplify,** popularize; **illuminate,** enlighten; rationalize; **demonstrate, show, illustrate,** exemplify; **decipher,** crack, unlock, unravel, read into, **solve;** explain away

9 **comment upon,** remark upon

10 **translate, render,** transcribe; paraphrase

adjectives

11 **explanatory,** explaining; **clarifying; illuminating,** enlightening; critical

12 explicable, accountable

327 MISINTERPRETATION

nouns

1 **misinterpretation, misunderstanding, misapprehension, misreading, mistaking, misconception; perversion, distortion,** twisting, contorting; reversal; **error**

verbs

2 **misinterpret, misunderstand, mistake; misread,** get wrong, take amiss; **get backwards,** reverse; **pervert, distort,** contort, **misjudge**

adjectives

3 **misinterpreted, misunderstood, mistaken, misread,** misconceived; **garbled, perverted, distorted;** backwards

328 COMMUNICATION

nouns

1 **communication,** communion, congress, **commerce; speaking, speech,** utterance, talking, **conversation; contact, touch, connection; interplay,** interaction; **exchange,** interchange; answer, response, reply; **dealings, traffic, truck** (*nonformal*); information; message; ESP, telepathy; correspondence

2 **informing, telling,** imparting, **telling, transmission,** transfer, sharing, giving, sending, signalling; notification, alerting, **announcement, publication, disclosure**

3 **sociability;** candour, **frankness, openness,** outspokenness

4 **communications,** media; telecommunication

verbs

5 **communicate,** hold communication; interchange, commune with; **deal with, traffic with; speak, talk,** converse

6 **communicate, impart, tell, convey, transmit,** transfer, send, send word, disseminate, broadcast, pass on, **hand on; report, render, make known; signal;** share, share with; tell

7 **communicate with, contact,** reach, get to; **make advances, make overtures, approach; relate to; answer; question,** interrogate; **correspond**

adjectives

8 **communicating; verbal,** linguistic, oral; **conversational;** interactive, interacting, responsive, answering; questioning, interrogative; telepathic

9 **communicative, talkative; sociable;** unrestricted; demonstrative, expansive, effusive; candid, **frank; open,** free, outspoken; **accessible;** outgoing

adverbs

10 verbally, orally

329 UNCOMMUNICATIVENESS

nouns

1 **taciturnity; silence;** quietness; brevity

2 **reticence; reserve,** restraint; discretion; suppression, repression; low profile; **aloofness, distance,** remoteness, **detachment,** withdrawal; **coolness,** coldness; modesty

3 **evasion,** dodging, parrying, waffling

verbs

4 **clam up** (*nonformal*); refuse to comment; **stand aloof**

5 **prevaricate,** waffle (*nonformal*), evade, dodge, sidestep, parry, duck; **mince words**

adjectives

6 **uncommunicative, unsociable,** secretive

7 **taciturn; silent, speechless,** mum; mute, dumb, quiet; close;

tongue-tied; curt, brief, terse, brusque, short, concise

8 reticent, **reserved**, restrained, low-key, constrained; **suppressed**, repressed; subdued; guarded, discreet; **retiring**, shrinking; **aloof, distant**, remote, **detached**, withdrawn; impersonal; **cool**, cold, frosty; **inaccessible**, forbidding; **introverted**; modest, bashful; expressionless, blank, impassive

9 prevaricating, **equivocal**, waffling (*nonformal*), **evasive**

330 SECRECY

nouns

1 secrecy; the dark; **concealment**; discretion; evasion, subterfuge

2 privacy; isolation, seclusion; anonymity; confidentiality

3 veil, curtain, wraps; **suppression**, repression, stifling, smothering; **censorship, cover-up**; security

4 stealth, furtiveness, clandestine behaviour, underhand dealing

5 secret, confidence; trade secret; classified information; inside information; **mystery, enigma**; the occult

6 code, cipher; secret language; code word, code name

verbs

7 keep secret, keep mum, veil, keep dark; secrete, **conceal**; **keep back, keep from**, withhold; not tell, clam up (*nonformal*); play dumb

8 cover up; hush up; suppress, repress, stifle, smother, squash,

quash, kill; **censor**, black out (*nonformal*)

9 tell confidentially, whisper, breathe

10 encode, encipher

adjectives

11 secret, closed, closet; cryptic, dark; unspoken, untold; **top secret**, classified, restricted, under wraps (*nonformal*); **censored**, suppressed, stifled, smothered; latent, ulterior, concealed, hidden; esoteric, occult; enigmatic, mysterious

12 covert, clandestine, quiet, unobtrusive, **surreptitious, undercover**, underground, cloak-and-dagger, underhand; **furtive, stealthy, sly, shifty, sneaky**

13 private, privy; intimate, innermost, **personal**; **privileged**, protected; **secluded**, isolated, withdrawn, retired; anonymous

14 confidential, inside (*nonformal*), esoteric; sealed; sensitive, privileged

15 secretive, close, dark; discreet; evasive, shifty; **uncommunicative**

16 coded, encoded

adverbs

17 secretly, in secret; covertly, undercover

18 surreptitiously, furtively, stealthily, slyly; by stealth

19 privately, in private, apart, aside

20 confidentially, in confidence; between ourselves

331 CONCEALMENT

nouns

1 **concealment, hiding, secretion;** burial, burying; **cover, covering,** covering up, masking, screening; clouding; **secrecy;** invisibility; **subterfuge, deception**

2 **veil,** curtain, **cover, screen;** fig leaf; **cover, disguise**

3 **ambush;** booby trap, trap

4 **hiding place,** hiding, concealment, **cover;** safe house; **recess, corner,** dark corner, nook, cranny, niche; **hole,** lair, den; **asylum, sanctuary, retreat, refuge; cache,** stash (nonformal)

5 **secret passage; back way, back door, side door;** escape route, escape hatch; **back stairs**

verbs

6 **conceal, hide; cover, cover up,** cloak, veil, screen off, shroud, envelop; **disguise, camouflage, mask;** whitewash (nonformal); **paper over,** gloss over, varnish, **obscure,** cloud, shade; **eclipse**

7 **secrete, hide away,** keep hidden, put away, store away, stow away, bottle up, lock up, seal up; **keep secret;** stash (nonformal), deposit, plant (nonformal); **bury**

8 (hide oneself) **hide, conceal oneself, take cover, hide out, hide away,** lie low (nonformal), **go underground; disappear;** disguise oneself, masquerade, remain anonymous

9 **lurk;** sneak, skulk, slink, prowl, steal, creep, tiptoe; stalk, shadow

10 **ambush, waylay;** stalk

adjectives

11 **concealed, hidden; covered;** covert, under cover, under wraps (nonformal); **obscured,** clouded, clouded over; eclipsed; buried; underground; secluded; **obscure,** mysterious; **secret;** unknown, latent

12 **invisible, unseen,** undetected; undiscovered, unexplored; unsolved

13 **disguised, camouflaged, in disguise;** masked, masquerading

14 **in hiding, under cover;** lurking, skulking, prowling, sneaking, stealing; on tiptoe; stealthy, furtive, surreptitious

15 **concealing, hiding,** obscuring, covering

332 COMMUNICATIONS

nouns

1 **communications,** signalling, telecommunication; satellite communication; wireless communication; media; communication

2 **telegraph;** Telex (trademark); code; transmitter, sender; receiver

3 **radio,** wireless; **television**

4 **telephone, phone;** receiver; mouthpiece, transmitter; telephone extension; telephone booth, telephone box, call box, pay phone; mobile phone, cellular telephone

5 **telephone operator, operator,** switchboard operator, telephonist

6 telephone number, **phone number; telephone directory, phone book** (*nonformal*); telephone exchange, exchange; area code

7 telephone call, **phone call, call;** local call, long-distance call; dial tone; conference call; hot line, chat line

8 telegram, telegraph, **wire** (*nonformal*), telex; **cable**

9 facsimile, fax

10 line, telephone line; direct line; party line; cable, telegraph cable

verbs

11 telephone, phone (*nonformal*), call, call up, ring, ring up; hang up, ring off

12 wire, telex; **cable**; radio

333 MANIFESTATION

nouns

1 manifestation, appearance; expression; indication, evidence, proof; embodiment, incarnation; revelation, disclosure; dissemination, publication

2 display, demonstration, show, showing; presentation, exhibition, exhibit, exposition, retrospective; production, performance, representation, projection; opening, unfolding; **showcase**, unveiling; exposure

3 obviousness, distinctness; openness; visibility

4 prominence, boldness; notoriety; ostentation

verbs

5 manifest, show, exhibit, demonstrate, display, unfold, develop; present; indicate, betoken,

mean; **express,** set forth; show off, showcase; **make plain, make clear;** produce, bring out, trot out (*nonformal*), bring forth; reveal, divulge, disclose; illuminate, highlight, spotlight, feature; flaunt, dangle, wave, flourish, brandish, parade; perform, enact, dramatize

6 (*manifest oneself*) come out, come forth, **surface;** speak up, speak out, assert oneself; **appear, materialize**

7 be manifest, **surface;** glare, shout; come across, project; stand out, stick out

adjectives

8 manifest, apparent, evident, self-evident, indisputable, obvious, plain, clear, distinct, palpable, patent, tangible; **visible,** perceptible, discernible, observable, **noticeable;** express, explicit, unmistakable

9 manifesting, showing, displaying, demonstrating, **demonstrative, expressive; indicative;** appearing, materializing

10 open, overt; **revealed, disclosed,** exposed; bare, bald, naked

11 unconcealed; undisguised

12 conspicuous, noticeable, notable, ostensible, prominent, **bold,** pronounced, salient, striking, outstanding, highlighted, featured; obtrusive; **flagrant,** blatant, notorious; **glaring,** staring

13 manifested, demonstrated, exhibited, shown, displayed; demonstrable

adverbs

14 manifestly, apparently, evidently, obviously, patently, plainly, clearly, distinctly, unmistakably, expressly, explicitly; **visibly, noticeably**

15 openly, overtly; publicly, in public

16 conspicuously, prominently, noticeably, ostensibly, **notably, markedly, strikingly, boldly, outstandingly;** blatantly, notoriously; glaringly

334 REPRESENTATION, DESCRIPTION

nouns

1 representation, drawing, portrayal, depiction, rendering; illustration, demonstration; projection, **realization;** imagery; **art; drama;** plan, diagram, **blueprint, chart, map;** notation; score; **writing,** script, written word, text; **writing system; alphabet;** letter; printing; **symbol**

2 description, portrayal, depiction, rendering, **representation,** imagery; **picture, portrait, image,** photograph, evocation, impression; **sketch,** cameo; character, profile; specification, details, catalogue; **narration**

3 account, recounting, statement, report, word; case study

4 impersonation, mimicry, mime, pantomime, dumb show; **imitation;** embodiment, incarnation; portrayal; **acting, playing,** performance; **posing,** masquerade

5 image, likeness; resemblance, semblance; **effigy, icon, idol; copy; picture; portrait,** likeness; **photograph; duplicate, double;** match, fellow, mate, companion, **twin; image, picture; miniature, model; reflection,** shadow; trace, tracing; rubbing

6 figure; doll; puppet; model, dummy, lay figure; wax figure, waxwork; scarecrow, snowman; **sculpture, bust, statue, statuette; death mask, life mask;** carving; **figurehead**

7 representative, representation, **type, specimen,** embodiment; example

verbs

8 represent, depict, render, characterize, hit off, **portray, picture,** draw, paint; **register; write,** print, map, chart; trace, trace out; **symbolize**

9 describe, portray, picture, render, **depict, represent, paint,** draw; evoke; outline, sketch; **characterize; express,** set forth; write

10 mirror, reflect, figure; **embody, personify,** impersonate; **illustrate, demonstrate, exemplify;** project, realize

11 impersonate; mimic, mime, pantomime, take off, mock; ape, copy; **pose as, masquerade as,** pass for; **act,** enact, perform, do; **play, act as,** act out

adjectives

12 representative; pictorial, graphic, vivid; **representing, portraying,** illustrating; **typifying, symbolizing,** personifying, embodying

13 descriptive, representative; expressive, vivid, graphic; realistic, lifelike, faithful

14 typical; exemplary, sample; **characteristic,** distinctive, distinguishing; **realistic; natural,** normal, usual

adverbs

15 expressively, vividly, graphically; faithfully, realistically

335 MISREPRESENTATION

nouns

1 **misrepresentation, perversion, distortion,** twisting, slanting; inaccuracy; **falsification; injustice; exaggeration; understatement**

2 bad likeness, **daub,** botch; scribble; distortion; **travesty,** parody, **caricature,** gross exaggeration

verbs

3 **misrepresent, belie; pervert, distort, twist,** warp, wrench, slant; **colour,** falsify; **disguise,** camouflage; overstate, exaggerate, blow up; understate; **travesty,** parody, **caricature**

4 daub, botch, butcher, scribble

336 DISCLOSURE

nouns

1 **disclosure,** disclosing; **revelation,** revealing, making public, publicizing, broadcasting; discovery, discovering; manifestation; unfolding, **uncovering,** unwrapping, **unveiling; exposure,** exposition; baring, stripping; **showing up**

2 **divulging,** letting out; **betrayal,**

indiscretion; leak; telltale, telltale sign

3 **confession,** confessing, **admission,** concession, avowal, owning

verbs

4 **disclose, reveal, let out, show,** impart, **leak;** manifest; unfold, unroll; **open,** open up, lay open; **expose, show up; bare; uncover,** unveil, ventilate, unwrap

5 **divulge; reveal, make known,** tell, breathe, utter, vent, ventilate, air, **give out, let out; confide; publish**

6 **betray,** inform; leak (*nonformal*), spill (*nonformal*); tell secrets; babble, tell tales; let slip; **blurt, blurt out**

7 **confess, admit, acknowledge,** tell all, concede, grant, **own, own up,** let on, come clean (*nonformal*); reveal oneself

8 **be revealed, become known,** surface, appear, manifest itself, transpire, **leak out, get out, come out**

adjectives

9 **revealed, disclosed;** admitted, confessed, self-confessed

337 PUBLICATION

nouns

1 **publication, publishing, dissemination, diffusion, broadcast, broadcasting, spread, spreading, circulation,** ventilation, airing; **display;** issue; printing; **book,** periodical

2 **announcement; proclamation,** pronouncement; **report, declaration, statement; programme,** no-

tice, **notification, public notice;**
circular; manifesto; rationale;
white paper; edict; **bulletin
board, notice board**

3 press release, release, handout;
bulletin, notice

4 publicity, notoriety, fame, notice, **celebrity,** glare, **exposure,
currency;** report; cry; press (*nonformal*); **puff** (*nonformal*), **plug**
(*nonformal*)

5 promotion, publicizing, promoting, advocating; **advertising**

6 advertisement, ad (*nonformal*),
advert (*nonformal*), notice; **commercial; spread, testimonial**

7 poster, bill, placard, sign; billboard, hoarding; sandwich board

8 advertising matter; leaflet, folder, bill, handout, **circular**

9 publicist, PR man, **press agent;
advertiser; promoter**

verbs

**10 publish, propagate, circulate,
diffuse, disseminate,** distribute,
broadcast, televise, air, **spread,
advertise,** repeat, retail, put
about, bandy about; whisper,
buzz

**11 make public; display, make
known; divulge; ventilate,** air,
open up, broach

12 announce, enunciate; **declare,
state,** affirm, pronounce, give
notice; **say; report**

13 proclaim, cry; **herald,** blaze,
blare, thunder, shout, trumpet

14 issue, bring out, put out, emit

15 publicize; advertise, promote,
build up, cry up, sell, puff (*nonformal*), **plug** (*nonformal*); **write
up; post bills,** post

16 (*be published*) **come out, appear,**
break, **issue,** find vent, become
public; **circulate, spread,** have
currency, get exposure

adjectives

17 published, public, made public,
circulated, in circulation, propagated, **disseminated,** issued,
spread, diffused, distributed; in
print; **broadcast,** televised; **announced,** proclaimed, declared,
stated, affirmed; **reported;** common knowledge, current; **open,**
accessible

adverbs

18 publicly, in public; openly; reportedly

338 MESSENGER

nouns

1 messenger, courier, carrier, **runner; go-between; emissary;** Mercury; post office, courier service;
answering service

2 herald, harbinger, forerunner;
announcer

3 postman, mail carrier, letter carrier; postmaster, postmistress;
postal clerk; errand boy, office
boy

4 (*mail carriers*) carrier pigeon,
carrier, homing pigeon; pigeon
post; post coach, mail coach;
post boat, mail boat, mail packet; mail train

339 FALSENESS

nouns

1 falsehood, untruth; fallacy; artificiality

2 **sham,** faking, feigning, pretending; pretext, **pretence;** humbug; **bluff,** bluffing; cheating, fraud; deception, delusion; acting; **simulation;** seeming, semblance, appearance, face, **show,** outward show, front, gloss, varnish; gilt; masquerade, facade, disguise; posture, pose; affectation

3 **double-dealing; double** standard; **dishonesty,** bad faith; treachery

4 **insincerity;** emptiness; mockery; hypocrisy; cant; lip service; token gesture, empty gesture; smooth talk; crocodile tears

5 **dishonesty,** falsehood; credibility gap; **lying,** fibbing

6 **deliberate falsehood, falsification,** falsifying; **perversion, distortion, bending; misrepresentation,** slanting; tampering; stretching, **exaggeration; perjury,** false swearing, oath breaking

7 **fabrication, invention,** concoction; **forgery; fiction,** figment, **myth,** fable, romance

8 **lie,** falsehood, untruth, fib; **fiction; story** (*nonformal*), **yarn** (*nonformal*), **tale,** fairy tale (*nonformal*), tall tale, tall story (*both nonformal*); exaggeration; white lie; **slander, libel**

9 **fake, phoney** (*nonformal*), **sham, mock, imitation,** dummy; paste, tinsel, shoddy, junk; **counterfeit, forgery; hoax, cheat, fraud, swindle;** whitewash; impostor

verbs

10 **falsify,** belie, **misrepresent;** overstate, understate; **pervert, distort,** strain, warp, **slant, twist;**

gloss, gloss over, whitewash, varnish, paper over (*nonformal*); fudge (*nonformal*), dress up, embellish, embroider; **disguise,** camouflage, mask; ring false

11 **tamper with,** manipulate, fake, **juggle,** rig; pack, stack; **adulterate**

12 **fabricate, invent, manufacture,** trump up, make up, hatch, concoct, fudge (*nonformal*), fake; counterfeit, **forge;** fantasize

13 **lie,** tell lies, falsify, speak falsely, **fib; exaggerate; prevaricate;** deceive, mislead; **swear falsely**

14 **sham, fake** (*nonformal*), **feign, counterfeit, simulate; pretend, make believe,** make like (*nonformal*); let on; **affect,** profess, **assume,** put on; cover up; **act, play; bluff**

15 **pose as, masquerade as,** impersonate, pass for

adjectives

16 **false, untrue,** not true, in error, **erroneous;** unfounded

17 **spurious,** bastard, **fake** (*nonformal*), **phoney** (*nonformal*), **sham, mock, counterfeit, bogus,** dummy, **make-believe,** so-called; **imitation; falsified;** dressed up, embellished, embroidered; garbled; twisted, distorted, warped, perverted, slanted; **simulated, faked, feigned,** fictitious, affected, assumed; artificial, synthetic; unreal; unnatural, man-made; illegitimate; quack

18 gilded, tinsel, **seeming,** apparent, plausible, **ostensible**

19 **fabricated,** invented, manufactured, **concocted,** hatched;

forged; fictitious, fictional, mythical, fabulous, legendary; fantastic, fancied

20 tampered with, **manipulated**, juggled, **rigged**, engineered

21 false; double, **double-dealing**; **dishonest**; crooked, **deceitful**; artful, cunning, crafty; **treacherous**; **insincere**; dishonest; **empty**, hollow

22 dishonest, lying; prevaricating, equivocal

adverbs

23 falsely; **erroneously**; artificially; unnaturally; seemingly, apparently, ostensibly; nominally

340 EXAGGERATION

nouns

1 exaggeration, exaggerating; big talk (*nonformal*), **hyperbole**; **superlative**; **extravagance**; magnification, enlargement, inflation, expansion, blowing up, puffing up; **stretching, heightening**; exaggerated lengths, extreme, excess; travesty, caricature

verbs

2 exaggerate; **overstate**; overdo, carry too far, go to extremes; overestimate; **stretch**, stretch the truth; **magnify, inflate**; build up; talk big (*nonformal*), make much of; caricature, travesty

adjectives

3 exaggerated, magnified, inflated; **stretched**, disproportionate, blown up out of all proportion; **overstated**; **overdone**, overwrought; overestimated; extreme, exorbitant, inordinate, **excessive**; **superlative**, **extravagant**, profuse, **prodigal**

4 exaggerating, hyperbolic

341 DECEPTION

nouns

1 deception, subterfuge; **falseness**; fallacy; wishful thinking; vision, hallucination, mirage, **delusion**, illusion; deceiving; hoodwinking; swindling, conning; **fooling**, tricking, **kidding** (*nonformal*); bluffing; outwitting

2 misleading; misinformation

3 deceit, guile, falseness; **hypocrisy**; craft, **cunning**

4 trickery; **underhand dealing**; connivance, collusion, conspiracy

5 juggling, trickery; hocus-pocus

6 trick, device, ploy, gambit, stratagem, **scheme**, design, subterfuge, blind, **ruse**, dodge; **bluff**; gimmick, **catch**; **dirty trick**, dirty deal, scurvy trick; **bag of tricks**, tricks of the trade

7 hoax, deception, humbug, **sham**

8 fraud, fraudulence, dishonesty; **imposition**, cheat, cheating, **swindle**, dodge; **racket** (*nonformal*); **graft** (*nonformal*)

9 (*nonformal terms*) double cross, fiddle

10 confidence game, con game (*nonformal*)

11 cover, disguise, camouflage; **false colours**, false front; smoke screen; **masquerade**; mask, visor, false face

12 trap, gin; pitfall; mousetrap; booby trap, mine; decoy

13 snare; net; bait; lure

verbs

14 deceive, trick, hoax, dupe, gull, humbug, take in, string along, pull a fast one on; **delude,** mock; **betray,** let down, leave in the lurch, play one false, **double-cross** (*nonformal*); juggle, conjure; **bluff;** cajole, forestall; **outwit**

15 fool, make a fool of, **pull one's leg; trick; play a trick on,** play a practical joke upon

16 mislead, lead astray, lead up the garden path; feed one a line (*nonformal*), throw off the scent; misinform

17 hoodwink, blindfold, blind, blind one's eyes, **pull the wool over one's eyes**

18 cheat, gull, swindle, con, fleece, cheat out of, do out of; obtain under false pretenses

19 (*nonformal terms*) **clip, rook,** sting, do

20 trap, catch, catch out, catch in a trap; net, tangle; trip, trip up; **set** or **lay a trap for; lure, allure, decoy**

adjectives

21 deceptive, deceiving, misleading, beguiling, **false; illusory;** tricky

22 deceitful; false; fraudulent, sharp, shifty, tricky; underhand, furtive, surreptitious, indirect; **treacherous;** sneaky; **cunning,** artful, **wily, crafty;** calculating, scheming

adverbs

23 deceptively, falsely, with intent to deceive

24 fraudulently, furtively, surreptitiously, indirectly,

342 DECEIVER

nouns

1 confidence man; **forger;** charmer; **joker,** practical joker; trickster

2 juggler, magician, illusionist, conjurer

3 cheat; swindler, two-timer (*nonformal*); **sharper, sharp; confidence man, confidence trickster**

4 impostor; sham, humbug, fraud, phoney (*nonformal*), **quack,** ringer; **wolf in sheep's clothing**

5 hypocrite, phoney (*nonformal*); false friend

6 liar, fibber; consummate liar, dirty liar; pathological liar, confirmed or habitual liar; false witness

7 traitor, quisling, rat (*nonformal*), **snake in the grass;** double agent; informer, stool pigeon; conspirator

8 subversive; fifth columnist; security risk; collaborator; fifth column, underground

343 DUPE

nouns

1 dupe, gull; victim; trusting or simple soul, innocent; **fool;** stooge

2 (*nonformal terms*) **sucker,** fall guy, mug, easy mark, sitting duck

344 RESOLUTION

nouns

1 **resolution, resolve, determination, decision,** fixed *or* firm resolve, **will,** purpose; **seriousness,** devotion, dedication, commitment, total commitment; persistence, tenacity, perseverance; obstinacy

2 **firmness,** firmness of mind *or* spirit, constancy, **staunchness, steadfastness; stability;** concentration; rigidity; loyalty

3 **pluck, backbone** (*nonformal*), **grit,** spirit, **stamina;** courage

4 **will power, will,** power, strength of mind, strength, fortitude; iron will, will of iron *or* steel; a will *or* mind of one's own; the courage of one's convictions

5 **self-control, self-restraint,** self-discipline, control, restraint, discipline; composure, possession, aplomb; **independence**

verbs

6 **resolve, determine, decide, will, make up one's mind,** make *or* take a resolution; **settle,** settle on, fix; conclude, come to a conclusion *or* decision

7 **be determined,** be resolved; **have a mind** *or* **will of one's own,** know one's own mind; **be in earnest, mean business** (*nonformal*), mean what one says; steel oneself, brace oneself, grit one's teeth, never say die, die hard, die fighting, die with one's boots on

8 **remain firm, stand fast** *or* **firm, hold out,** hold fast, **take one's stand, stand** *or* **hold one's ground,** hold one's own, dig in, dig one's heels in; **stick to one's guns,** stick, stick with it, stick fast, stick to one's colours, adhere to one's principles; **put one's foot down** (*nonformal*), stand no nonsense

9 **not hesitate,** think nothing of, think little of, **make no bones about** (*nonformal*), **stick at nothing,** stop at nothing; not look back; carry through

adjectives

10 **resolute, resolved, determined, bound, decided,** decisive, **purposeful;** definite; **earnest, serious,** sincere; **devoted,** dedicated, committed, wholehearted; single-minded, relentless, persistent, tenacious, persevering; **obstinate**

11 **firm, staunch,** fixed, settled, steady, steadfast, constant, steely; immovable, inflexible; true, loyal

12 **plucky,** dauntless, **game,** game to the last *or* end; **courageous**

13 **strong-willed,** controlled, forward; **independent**

14 **determined upon,** resolved upon, decided upon, intent upon, fixed upon, settled upon, set on, bent on

adverbs

15 **resolutely, determinedly, decidedly,** decisively, **purposefully;** firmly, steadfastly, steadily; **seriously, earnestly,** in earnest, sincerely; hammer and tongs, tooth and nail; heart and soul, with all one's heart *or* might, whole-

heartedly; relentlessly, persistently

16 manfully, like a man; **courageously, heroically**

17 unhesitatingly, unflinchingly

345 PERSEVERANCE

nouns

1 **perseverance; resolution; stability; constancy; loyalty, fidelity;** concentration, undivided *or* unswerving attention, preoccupation; **endurance,** staying power, **tenacity, doggedness,** plodding, plugging, slogging; **obstinacy; diligence,** application, industry; **stamina; patience**

verbs

2 **persevere, persist, carry on,** go on, **keep on, keep up, keep at, keep at it,** keep going, try and try again, **keep up the good work; endure,** last, **continue**

3 **plod,** drudge, slog *or* slog away, soldier on, peg away

4 **stay with it, hold on,** hold fast, **hang on, stick to one's guns;** not give up, **never say die; stick out, hold out;** hold up, last out, **bear up,** stand up; **stay the distance** *or* the course

5 **go through with it,** follow through, **see it through,** see it out; go through with it, go to the bitter end, go the distance, go all the way; **leave no stone unturned**

6 **die trying, die with one's boots on** *or* die in one's boots, die in the attempt, die hard

7 (*nonformal terms*) **stick with it, stick it, stick it out, hang on for** dear life, go all out, go for broke, go through hell and high water

adjectives

8 **persevering, persistent,** persisting, insistent; **enduring,** permanent, **constant, lasting;** continuing; **stable, steady, steadfast;** immutable; **resolute; diligent, assiduous,** industrious, **dogged,** plodding; **tenacious; loyal, faithful;** unremitting, uninterrupted; single-minded; relentless; **unrelenting; obstinate, stubborn;** unfailing, **tireless, indefatigable,** sleepless; undaunted, indomitable, invincible; **patient**

adverbs

9 **persistently,** insistently; resolutely; loyally, faithfully; **diligently,** assiduously; **doggedly;** relentlessly; **patiently**

10 **through thick and thin,** come hell or high water, rain or shine; **come what may, all the way,** to the bitter end

346 OBSTINACY

nouns

1 **obstinacy; mind** *or* will of one's own, inflexible will; **perseverance, determination,** tenacity; fanaticism; intolerance, bigotry

2 **obduracy, firmness,** stiffness, **rigidity**

3 **perversity, contrariness**

4 **defiance;** resistance

5 (*obstinate person*) **mule** and donkey (*both nonformal*); **intransigent,** hard-liner; maverick; bigot, fanatic, purist

verbs

6 balk; hold one's ground, not budge, not yield an inch, stick to one's guns; hold out; die hard; **persevere**

adjectives

7 obstinate, stubborn; wilful, headstrong; dogged, tenacious; stubborn as a mule; **set, set in one's ways; sullen, sulky;** uncooperative; **bigoted, intolerant, fanatic, fanatical;** dogmatic, **opinionated**

8 inflexible, hard, firm, stiff, rigid, rigorous, stuffy; **adamant;** unmoved, unaffected; **immovable,** not to be moved; **unalterable, immutable; uncompromising,** intransigent, irreconcilable; **implacable, inexorable, relentless,** unrelenting; **stern, grim, dour;** steely

9 obdurate, tough, **hard,** hard-nosed (*nonformal*)

10 perverse, contrary, wayward, difficult; **sullen, sulky**

11 unmanageable, uncontrollable, indomitable, intractable; incorrigible; irrepressible; unruly, wild; beyond control, out of hand; **resistant, resisting; defiant**

12 positive; dogmatic

adverbs

13 stubbornly; wilfully; doggedly

14 firmly, stiffly, rigidly, rigorously; inexorably, relentlessly; sternly, grimly

15 perversely, sullenly, sulkily

347 IRRESOLUTION

nouns

1 irresolution, indecision; uncertainty; instability; change of mind, second thoughts

2 vacillation, wavering, blowing hot and cold

3 hesitation, hesitancy, hesitating, holding back, dragging one's feet; faltering; diffidence, caution

4 weak will; weakness, frailty, infirmity; fear; cowardice

5 waverer; wimp, weakling

verbs

6 not know one's own mind, be in *or* **of two minds,** have mixed feelings; stagger, stumble

7 hesitate, pause, falter, hang back, hover; think twice about, stop to consider, ponder; debate, deliberate; be divided; yield, back down; retreat, withdraw; pull back, drag one's feet; **flinch,** shy away from, shy; **fear; not face up to**

8 vacillate, waver, fluctuate, dither; blow hot and cold; change one's mind; vary, **alternate;** shift, change

adjectives

9 irresolute; undecided, indecisive, unsettled; dubious, **uncertain; in** *or* **of two minds,** ambivalent; changeable; capricious, fickle

10 vacillating, wavering, fluctuating

11 hesitant, hesitating; faltering; diffident, tentative, timid, cautious

12 **weak**, feeble, **frail**, **faint**, **infirm**;
spineless; afraid, cowardly

adverbs

13 **indecisively**; **uncertainly**; hesitantly

348 CHANGING OF MIND

nouns

1 **reverse**, **reversal**, U-turn (nonformal), about turn; **change of mind**; second thoughts

2 **treason**, betrayal, turning traitor, turning one's coat; bolt, breakaway; **desertion**; relapse; **disloyalty**

3 **withdrawal**, denial, repudiation, disowning, **renunciation**

4 **opportunist**, timeserver

5 **turncoat**, renegade; defector; deserter, fifth columnist, collaborator, **traitor**

verbs

6 **change one's mind** or **tune**; come round, do a U-turn (nonformal); think better of it, have second thoughts

7 **go over**, change sides, switch, **defect**; turn one's coat; desert a sinking ship; **break away**, bolt; desert

8 **retract**, repudiate, withdraw, **take back**, **disown**, deny, disclaim; **renounce**, **eat one's words**, eat humble pie; **back down**, climb down

9 **change with the times**; sit on or straddle the fence

adjectives

10 **apostate**, renegade; **disloyal**

11 **separatist**, breakaway (nonformal); **opportunistic**

349 CAPRICE

nouns

1 **whim**, humour; **fancy**, fantasy, notion, crazy idea; **fad**, **craze**, passing fancy; **quirk**; bee in one's bonnet (nonformal)

2 **lightness**, volatility; **mood swing**

verbs

3 **blow hot and cold**, chop and change, **fluctuate**, vacillate; act on impulse

adjectives

4 **capricious**, whimsical; **fanciful**, harebrained, quirky; wayward, vagrant; **arbitrary**, **unreasonable**; **moody**, **temperamental**; petulant

5 **fickle**, **flighty**, skittish, **light**; flirtatious; **changeable**; volatile; unpredictable; **impulsive**; unreliable

adverbs

6 **lightly**; arbitrarily; without rhyme or reason

350 IMPULSE

nouns

1 **impulse**; natural impulse, blind impulse, **instinct**, urge, drive; reflex; gut reaction (nonformal); inspiration, brain wave

2 **haste**, suddenness; **recklessness**; impatience

3 **thoughtlessness**, carelessness; negligence

4 spontaneity, snap judgment *or* decision

5 improvisation, improvising, **impromptu, ad-lib,** ad-libbing (*nonformal*); **stopgap, makeshift**

verbs

6 act on the spur of the moment; blurt out, come out with, let slip out

7 improvise, speak off the cuff, think on one's feet, play it by ear (*nonformal*); **dash off; make up**

adjectives

8 impulsive, impetuous, hasty, quick, sudden; **precipitate,** headlong; **reckless, rash; impatient**

9 unthinking, thoughtless, heedless, careless, inconsiderate; arbitrary, capricious

10 spontaneous, unintentional, unintended; involuntary, reflex, automatic; unconscious; casual; **ill-considered,** ill-advised

11 impromptu, improvised; ad-lib, stopgap, makeshift; **offhand,** off-the-cuff (*nonformal*)

adverbs

12 impulsively, hastily, suddenly, quickly, headlong; **recklessly,** rashly

13 on impulse, on the spur of the moment; thoughtlessly, carelessly; unintentionally, inadvertently, involuntarily

14 impromptu, ad lib, offhand, out of hand; off the top of one's head *and* off the cuff (*both nonformal*); at short notice

351 LEAP

nouns

1 leap, jump, hop, spring, skip, bound, bounce; **pounce; hurdle; vault,** pole vault; long jump, broad jump; high jump

2 frisk, cavort; **prance**

3 leaping, jumping, bouncing, bounding, hopping, prancing, skipping, **springing; vaulting,** pole vaulting; hurdle race

4 jumper; broad jumper, high jumper; hurdler; jumping bean; kangaroo, gazelle, frog, grasshopper, flea

verbs

5 leap, jump, vault, spring, skip, hop, bound, bounce; leap over, jump over, etc; **hurdle,** clear, negotiate; start; **pounce,** pounce on *or* upon

6 cavort, frisk, trip, skip, bob, bounce; **romp;** prance

adjectives

7 leaping, jumping, springing, hopping, skipping, prancing, bouncing, bounding

352 PLUNGE

nouns

1 plunge, dive, pitch, drop, fall; swoop, pounce; nose dive, power dive; parachute jump, sky dive; bungee jump; crash dive

2 immersion, burial; **dipping, ducking, dousing, sinking; dip, duck, diving,** plunging; high diving; skin diving, deep-sea diving

3 diver, parachute jumper, paratrooper, jumper; scuba diver, deep-sea diver, frogman

4 (*diving equipment*) diving bell; submarine; Scuba; diving mask; wet suit; diving suit; diving helmet; periscope

verbs

5 **plunge, dive, pitch, plummet, drop, fall;** plump, plop; swoop, **pounce,** pounce on *or* upon; parachute

6 **submerge, immerse,** merge, **sink,** bury, engulf, **inundate,** deluge, drown, overwhelm; **dip, duck,** douse, plunge in water; baptize

7 **sink, scuttle,** send to the bottom; **founder, go down,** go to the bottom, sink like a stone

353 AVOIDANCE

nouns

1 **avoidance, shunning;** refraining; **evasion;** prevention, forestalling; **escape;** evasive action; zigzag, slip, dodge, duck, side step

2 **shirking; clock-watching, malingering,** skulking; **dodging,** ducking; ~~skiving~~, ~~truancy~~

3 **shirker, slacker;** clock watcher; truant

4 **flight,** exit, quick exit, bolt, hasty retreat; **running away;** disappearance; French leave, absence without leave; **desertion**

5 **fugitive,** person on the run, **runaway; refugee;** illegal immigrant

verbs

6 **avoid, shun,** shy away from, keep from, **keep away from,** keep clear of, avoid like the plague, **steer clear of** (*nonformal*), keep *or* get out of the way of, **give a wide berth, keep one's distance,** stand aloof; have nothing to do with, leave alone; turn away from, turn one's back upon

7 **evade, elude, get out of,** skirt; shake off (*nonformal*), get away from; throw off the scent

8 **dodge, duck; take evasive action;** shy, shy off *or* away; swerve, sheer off; pull away *or* clear; pull back, shrink, recoil, sidestep, step aside; parry, ward off; **hedge,** sit on the fence, beat around *or* about the bush, beg the question

9 **shirk, slack, lie,** not pull one's weight; **malinger;** get out of, dodge, duck

10 **flee, fly, take flight,** take wing, **run, cut and run** (*nonformal*), run off *or* away, run away from, take to one's heels, make off, **depart, turn tail; run for it, bolt,** run for one's life; make a run for it; **take French leave,** go AWOL; **desert;** ~~clear~~ ~~run~~ ~~away~~ with

11 (*nonformal terms*) beat it, make tracks, cut and run, **skip,** skip out, duck out, **clear out,** make oneself scarce, make a break for it

12 **slip away, steal away, sneak off,** slink off

13 **not face up to,** hide one's head in the sand, not come to grips with, put off

adjectives

14 **avoidable;** preventable

15 **evasive, elusive; shifty,** slippery; shirking, malingering

16 **fugitive, runaway,** in flight

354 ESCAPE

nouns

1 **escape; getaway; release,** freeing, **liberation, rescue;** emergence, issue, outlet, vent; **leakage,** leak; **break;** evasion; **flight;** escapism

2 **narrow escape, close call** or **shave** (*nonformal*), **near miss,** near thing (*nonformal*), narrow squeak (*nonformal*)

3 **escape hatch,** fire escape, lifeboat, life raft, life buoy, lifeline, emergency exit

4 **loophole, way out,** escape hatch, escape clause

5 **escape artist;** escapologist; **fugitive;** escapist

verbs

6 **escape,** make or effect one's escape, make good one's escape; **get away, make a getaway** (*nonformal*); **free oneself, get free, get clear of, get out, get out of, break loose,** break away; **evade;** flee

7 **go free, get off scot free,** win freedom; **get away with** (*nonformal*), get away with murder (*nonformal*), **get off lightly**

8 scrape or squeak through, squeak by, escape by the skin of one's teeth, have a close call or close shave (*nonformal*)

9 **slip away, give one the slip,** sneak out of, wriggle or worm out of, find a loophole

10 come forth, exit, **emerge, issue,** erupt, break out, break through, come out, run out, **leak out,** ooze out

adjectives

11 **escaped, loose,** on the loose, disengaged, out of; fled, flown; fugitive, runaway; free as a bird, at large, **free**

355 ABANDONMENT

nouns

1 **abandonment, forsaking, leaving;** casting away or aside; **withdrawal,** evacuation, pulling out; cessation; disuse

2 **desertion, defection;** bolt, breakaway, walkout; betrayal

3 **surrender, resignation,** renunciation, abdication, handing over, standing or stepping down, **yielding; withdrawing**

4 **derelict; rubbish, junk,** trash, refuse, waste, waste product; **dump,** garbage dump, scrap heap; orphan; reject, **discard**

verbs

5 **abandon, desert, forsake; leave,** leave behind, take leave of, depart from, say goodbye to, walk away, **walk** or **run out on** (*nonformal*), leave in the lurch (*nonformal*); **withdraw, back out, drop out** (*nonformal*), pull out, stand down (*nonformal*), **go back on; vacate; evacuate;** maroon; **jettison; junk, discard**

6 **defect, bolt,** break away; pull out (*nonformal*), **betray;** turn one's back on

7 give up, relinquish, surrender, yield, waive, **forgo, resign, renounce,** abdicate, **have done with,** give up as a bad job, cede, hand over, lay down, wash one's hands of, **write off,** drop; **cease, desist from,** leave off, give over; acknowledge defeat, **throw in the towel** or **sponge**

adjectives

8 abandoned, forsaken, deserted, left; disused; **derelict,** jettisoned; marooned; discarded

356 CHOICE

nouns

1 choice, selection, election, preference, decision, **pick, choosing; will,** volition, **free will; first choice;** the pick

2 option, discretion, pleasure, alternative

3 dilemma; no choice

4 adoption, acceptance

5 preference, affinity, inclination, leaning, bias, tendency, taste; favour, fancy; prejudice; style, type

6 vote, voting, **suffrage;** franchise; **voice, say; poll;** exit poll; **ballot,** balloting, secret ballot; **referendum;** show of hands; proxy; casting vote, deciding vote

7 elector, **voter; electorate**

8 nomination, designation, naming, proposal

9 election, appointment

10 eligibility, qualification, fitness, suitability, acceptability, desirability

11 elect, elite, the chosen

verbs

12 choose, elect, pick, opt, opt for, pick and choose

13 select; pick, pick out, single out, seize on; extract; **decide between;** cull, glean, sift

14 adopt; approve, ratify, pass, carry, endorse; **take up, go in for** (*nonformal*); accept, embrace

15 decide upon, determine upon, settle upon, fix upon; make or take a decision, **make up one's mind**

16 prefer, favour, like better or **best; had** or **have rather,** had rather or sooner; see or think fit, think best; incline or lean or tend toward

17 vote, cast one's vote, ballot, cast a ballot; have a say or a voice; plump for

18 nominate, name, designate; put up, propose, submit; run, run for office

19 elect, vote in, place in office; appoint

20 put to vote, have a show of hands

adjectives

21 voluntary; **optional; alternative**

22 selective, selecting, choosing; **electoral;** appointing; exclusive, discriminating; **choosy** (*nonformal*), particular

23 eligible, qualified, fit, fitted, **suitable,** acceptable, worthy, desirable

24 preferable, better, preferred, **to be preferred,** more desirable, favoured

25 chosen, selected, picked; select, elect; **adopted**, accepted, approved, ratified, passed, carried; **elected**; **appointed**; **nominated**, designated, named

adverbs

26 at choice, at will, at one's pleasure; alternatively

27 preferably, by choice *or* **preference,** in preference; by vote, by election; **rather than,** sooner than, first, sooner, rather, before

357 REJECTION

nouns

1 rejection, repudiation; exclusion, exception; **disapproval, refusal;** contradiction, denial; ignoring, discounting, dismissal, disregard; throwing out *or* away; rebuff; contempt; scorn, disdain

verbs

2 reject, repudiate, renounce, disown, disclaim; vote out; except, **exclude,** cut out; **disapprove, decline, refuse;** contradict, **deny;** waive, ignore, discount, **dismiss; disregard;** throw out *or* away, **discard;** repel, rebuff, send packing, spurn, disdain, scorn, despise

adjectives

3 rejected, repudiated; renounced, disowned; denied, refused; excluded, excepted; **declined;** ignored, discounted, **dismissed, discarded;** rebuffed; **spurned, disdained, scorned,** despised

4 dismissive; contemptuous, **scornful,** disdainful

358 CUSTOM, HABIT

nouns

1 custom, convention, way, tradition, the done thing, manner, **practice, observance,** ritual; **fashion;** manners, etiquette; way of life, lifestyle; conformity

2 culture, society, civilization; ethos

3 habit, custom; usage, way, practice; stereotype; pattern; peculiarity, characteristic

4 rule, norm, procedure, **common practice,** form; drill

5 routine, beat, track, beaten path *or* track; **rut, groove; red tape,** bureaucracy

6 accustoming; conditioning, seasoning, training; orientation; adjustment, accommodation

7 addiction; addict

verbs

8 accustom; condition, season, **train;** familiarize, orient, orientate; acclimatize; adapt, adjust, accommodate; confirm, fix, establish

9 become a habit, grow on one, take hold of one

10 be used to; get used to, **take to,** accustom oneself to

11 get in a rut, be in a rut

adjectives

12 customary; traditional; familiar, everyday, ordinary, **usual; established,** accepted; set, prescribed; **normal; standard;** prevalent, prevailing, widespread, popular, **current; conventional**

13 habitual, regular, frequent, constant, persistent; repetitive, recurring, recurrent; stereotyped; **routine;** trite, hackneyed

14 accustomed, used to; conditioned, trained, seasoned; experienced, **familiarized,** oriented, orientated; acclimatized; hardened; adapted

15 used to, familiar with, conversant with, **at home with**

16 in the habit of, used to; **in a rut**

17 confirmed, chronic, established, fixed, settled, rooted, thorough; incorrigible, irreversible; **deep-rooted; ingrained**

adverbs

18 customarily, conventionally; normally, **usually**

19 habitually, regularly, routinely, frequently, persistently; **chronically**

359 UNACCUSTOMED-NESS

nouns

1 newness; newness to; inexperience; ignorance

verbs

2 cure, break off, stop, wean

3 break the habit, cure oneself of, wean oneself from; **give up,** abandon, drop, stop, discontinue; swear off

adjectives

4 unaccustomed, new; rusty; **unused to, unfamiliar with,** new to, a stranger to; inexperienced; ignorant

360 MOTIVATION, INDUCEMENT

nouns

1 motive, reason, cause, source; matter, consideration; **ground, basis;** sake; **aim, goal;** end; **ideal,** principle, **ambition,** aspiration, inspiration; calling, vocation; intention

2 motivation, prompting, stimulation, animation; direction; **influence**

3 inducement, persuasion; preaching; **lobbying;** coaxing, wheedling, conning

4 incitement, instigation, stimulation, excitement, agitation, stirring; **provocation,** irritation

5 urging, pressure, encouragement; insistence; goading, spurring

6 urge, urgency; impulse, compulsion; **pressure, drive,** constraint, stress

7 incentive, inducement, encouragement, invitation, provocation, incitement; stimulus; reward, payment; bait, **lure;** bribe

8 goad, spur; whip, lash

9 inspiration; fire, spark; **animation, exhilaration;** genius; muse; moving spirit

10 instigator; agitator; trouble-maker; ringleader

verbs

11 motivate, move, impel, propel; **stimulate,** galvanize, animate, animate, **spark;** promote, foster; force, compel

12 **prompt, provoke, evoke, elicit, call up,** summon up, muster up, **inspire;** bring about; **cause**

13 **urge, press, push; insist, nag, pressure; lobby; coax,** wheedle, cajole, plead with; **exhort,** advocate, recommend

14 **goad, prod,** nudge, **spur, prick,** sting; whip; lash

15 **urge on, egg on** (*nonformal*), hasten on, hurry on **spur on**

16 **incite, instigate, put up to** (*nonformal*); **agitate, arouse, excite,** stir up, work up, whip up; **rally;** incense, **fire; provoke;** nettle; fan

17 **kindle, fire, spark off, trigger, touch off,** set off

18 **rouse, arouse,** raise, **waken, awaken,** wake up, stir, **stir up**

19 **inspire;** fire; **animate, exhilarate,** enliven

20 **encourage, hearten,** give encouragement; **invite,** ask for; **abet; foster, nurture,** nourish, feed

21 **induce, prompt, influence,** sway, incline, bring, lead; **lure;** tempt; determine, decide

22 **persuade, prevail on** *or* **upon,** sway, convince, **bring round; win over; talk into; charm, captivate; bribe**

23 **persuade oneself,** make up one's mind; be persuaded

adjectives

24 **motivating, motive, moving, driving; urgent, pressing, driving**

25 **inspiring;** exhilarating, enlivening

26 **provocative, provoking,** piquant, **exciting,** challenging, **rousing, stirring, stimulating; encouraging,** inviting, **alluring**

27 **inciting, incentive; incendiary**

28 **persuasive,** persuading; wheedling, cajoling

29 **moved, motivated, impelled;** stimulated, animated; inclined

30 **inspired, fired**

361 PRETEXT

nouns

1 **pretext, pretence, show;** facade, **sham, excuse,** apology, poor excuse, **lame excuse; occasion; subterfuge;** refuge, **device, stratagem, trick;** smoke screen, **screen, cover, blind;** guise, semblance; **mask, cloak, veil; cosmetics,** gloss, varnish; **cover,** alibi

2 **claim,** profession, allegation

verbs

3 **make a pretext of, take as an excuse, pretend,** make a pretence of; put up a front *or* false front; **allege, claim,** profess

4 **hide behind** *or* **under,** shelter under, take refuge in; **cover,** cover up, gloss over

adjectives

5 **pretended, alleged, claimed, professed,** avowed; **ostensible;** so-called

adverbs

6 **ostensibly, allegedly; as a pretext,** as an excuse, as a cover *or* a cover-up *or* an alibi

362 ALLUREMENT

nouns

1 **allure,** invitation; inducement; **temptation; seduction; fascination; attraction, interest, charm, glamour, appeal,** magnetism; charisma; flirtation

2 **attractiveness, allure,** winning ways; sex appeal

3 **lure,** charm, **attraction; decoy; bait; snare,** trap

4 **charmer;** flirt; **siren; vamp**

verbs

5 **lure, allure, entice, seduce, decoy, lead on;** flirt; **woo;** coax, cajole

6 **attract, interest, appeal, engage,** impress, be attractive, take or tickle one's fancy; **invite,** summon, beckon; **tempt, tantalize, titillate**

7 **fascinate, captivate, charm,** cast a spell, **intrigue, enthral, entrance, bewitch;** sweep off one's feet, turn one's head; hypnotize, mesmerize

adjectives

8 **alluring, fascinating, captivating, charming, glamorous,** exotic, **enchanting, entrancing,** ravishing, **intriguing, enthralling, bewitching; attractive, interesting, sexy** (nonformal), winning; exciting; charismatic; **seductive, beguiling, enticing, inviting;** flirtatious, **tempting, tantalizing,** teasing, titillating; **provocative;** appetizing, piquant; hypnotic

adverbs

9 charmingly; **tantalizingly;** irresistibly

363 BRIBERY

nouns

1 **bribery,** bribing, **corruption,** graft

2 **bribe,** bribe money; hush money (nonformal); protection

verbs

3 **bribe; purchase;** pay off (nonformal); **corrupt,** tamper with; **fix**

adjectives

4 **venal, corrupt**

364 DISSUASION

nouns

1 **warning, caution,** cautioning; intimidation, deterrence, scaring or frightening off

2 **deterrent; discouragement;** damp, damper, **wet blanket**

verbs

3 **dissuade,** convince otherwise, **talk out of** (nonformal); cry out against; **warn, warn off, caution; intimidate,** scare or frighten off, daunt

4 **deter,** repel, turn from, turn away; divert, deflect; distract, put off (nonformal); **discourage; throw cold water on,** damp, dampen, **cool, chill,** quench, blunt

adjectives

5 **dissuading, discouraging; deterrent,** off-putting; cautionary; intimidating

365 INTENTION

nouns

1 **intention, intent, aim,** meaning, point, purpose, function; sake; **design, plan, project,** idea, notion; **quest,** pursuit; **proposal,** prospectus; **resolve,** resolution, mind, will; **motive;** determination; **ambition,** aspiration, **desire**

2 **objective, object, aim, end, goal,** destination; **target,** bull's-eye; quarry, prey, game

3 **deliberation; premeditation,** calculation, forethought

verbs

4 **intend, plan, mean,** think, propose; resolve, determine; **design; aim,** aim at, set one's sights on, go for, drive at, aspire to, be after; **desire**

5 **contemplate, meditate; envisage, have in mind;** have a mind or notion

6 **plan, plan on,** plan for, count on, calculate, calculate on, reckon, reckon or bargain on, bargain for, bank on or **upon**

7 **calculate;** plan; plot; scheme

adjectives

8 **intentional, intended,** proposed, **designed,** meant; **purposeful wilful, voluntary, deliberate;** considered, studied, **calculated, contemplated, envisaged, conscious,** knowing; planned

9 **premeditated,** predetermined

adverbs

10 **intentionally, purposely,** purposefully, pointedly, **on purpose, deliberately, wilfully, voluntarily,** of one's own accord or one's own free will; **consciously, knowingly**

366 PLAN

nouns

1 **plan, scheme, design,** method, device, conception, enterprise, **idea, notion;** organization; **planning,** calculation; approach, plan of attack; **way,** procedure; **arrangement,** system, disposition, layout; **schedule,** timetable; blueprint, **guidelines;** tactics, **strategy; intention;** forethought, foresight

2 **project, scheme; proposal,** prospectus, proposition; **scenario**

3 **diagram, plot, chart, blueprint,** graph; design, pattern; **sketch, draft, drawing,** rough; outline, skeleton, figure, profile; projection; **map, chart**

4 **policy,** principles; **procedure,** course, line, plan of action; **platform**

5 **intrigue, plot, scheme,** game (nonformal), trick, stratagem; **conspiracy; complicity, collusion; contrivance,** contriving; **scheming,** plotting; manipulation, **manoeuvring**

6 **planner, designer;** organizer, promoter, developer, engineer; **architect, strategist**

verbs

7 **plan, devise, contrive, design,** frame, shape; organize, rationalize, sort out; **arrange,** make arrangements, set up, work out; **schedule; calculate; project,** plan ahead; intend

8 **plot, scheme, intrigue; conspire, connive, collude; hatch,** cook up (*nonformal*), **brew,** concoct; **manoeuvre,** engineer, wangle (*nonformal*)

9 **plot; map, chart; sketch;** map out, plot out, **lay out,** set out, mark out; mark off

10 **outline; sketch, draft,** trace; block in *or* out; rough in, rough out

adjectives

11 **planned, devised, designed,** charted, **contrived; plotted;** arranged; **organized;** worked out, **calculated; projected; scheduled; tactical, strategic**

12 **scheming, calculating, designing, contriving, plotting, intriguing; manipulative; conniving,** conspiring

367 PURSUIT

nouns

1 **pursuit,** pursuing, **quest,** seeking, hunting, searching; **following,** follow-up; tracking, trailing, tracking down, dogging, stalking; **chase; hue and cry**

2 **hunting,** shooting, sport; **hunt, chase;** stalking

3 **fishing,** fishery; **angling**

4 **pursuer,** follower; hunter, tracker

5 **hunter,** sportsman; sportswoman; big game hunter

6 **fisherman, angler;** trawler, drifter, etc

7 **quarry, game, prey,** victim, the hunted; kill; big game

verbs

8 **pursue, follow,** follow up, **go after,** run after; **chase, give chase;** hound, dog; **seek,** seek out, hunt, **search**

9 **hunt,** go hunting, hunt down, chase; **shoot; track,** trail; **stalk;** hound, dog; hawk, falcon; fowl; flush

10 **fish,** go fishing, **angle;** shrimp, whale; reel in

adjectives

11 **pursuing,** following, **seeking, searching; in pursuit; hunting, fishing**

368 ROUTE, PATH

nouns

1 **route, path, way, itinerary, course,** track, line, road; circuit, tour, orbit; walk, beat, round; **sea lane, air lane,** flight path

2 **path, track, trail,** footpath; walkway; **walk;** promenade, parade; cycle path; runway

3 **passageway, pass, passage, defile; avenue; corridor, aisle, alley, lane; channel;** ford, opening, aperture; access, inlet; exit, outlet; connection, communication; covered way, gallery, arcade; cloister; flyover; tunnel; junction, interchange

4 **side road, side street; bypass, detour,** roundabout way; back way, back stairs, back door, side door; back road, back street

5 **road,** highway, **carriageway, street**

6 **pavement,** paving; asphalt, tarmac; **cement, concrete;** tile,

brick; stone, paving stone, flag, flagstone; cobblestone; gravel; kerb; gutter

7 **railway, railroad,** rail, line, track; junction; terminus, terminal; embankment; bridge

8 **bridge, span, viaduct;** rope bridge, suspension bridge; stepping-stone

369 MANNER, MEANS

nouns

1 **manner, way, wise, means, mode,** form, **fashion, style,** tone; **method, system; approach,** tack; **technique, procedure, process,** proceeding, course, practice; order; lines, line; modus operandi; **routine**

2 **means,** ways; funds; **resources,** capital; stock, supply; power, capacity, ability; constituency, backing, support; devices; method

3 **agency;** machinery, **mechanism;** service; **expedient,** recourse, resort, device

4 **instrument, tool, implement, appliance,** device; contrivance, lever, mechanism; **vehicle, organ; agent;** medium, mediator, intermediary, intermediate, liaison, go-between; servant, slave, **puppet, dummy, pawn,** creature; toy, plaything; dupe

verbs

5 **use, utilize,** adopt, effect; **approach;** proceed, practise, go about

6 be instrumental, **serve,** come in handy; minister to, act for, **promote, advance, forward, assist,** facilitate; mediate, go between; liaise

adjectives

7 **instrumental; useful,** handy, **serviceable; helpful,** conducive, favouring, assisting, facilitating; subservient; intermediary

adverbs

8 **how; thus, so,** just so; as, like

9 **anyhow, anyway; nevertheless,** nonetheless, however, regardless; **at all; somehow, in some way**

10 **herewith;** whereby, thereby, hereby

370 PROVISION, EQUIPMENT

nouns

1 **provision,** providing; **equipment,** fitting out; **supply,** supplying; **furnishing; logistics;** investment, endowment, subsidy; catering; **preparation**

2 **provisions, supplies, merchandise**

3 **accommodation,** facilities; **lodgings;** bed, board, full board; **subsistence,** keep

4 **equipment,** munitions; **furniture, furnishings; fixtures, fittings, appointments,** installations, plumbing; **appliances,** utensils; **outfit, apparatus, rig,** machinery; **plant,** facility, facilities; paraphernalia, things, **gear, stuff** (*nonformal*); **tackle,** rigging; **kit,** personal effects

5 **harness,** trappings, tackle

6 **supplier;** donor; patron; **caterer;** retailer, merchant; steward

verbs

7 **provide, supply,** find, **furnish;**
accommodate; invest, endow,
fund, subsidize; donate, give, afford, contribute, yield, present;
stock, store; provide for; prepare;
support, maintain, keep; fill, fill
up; replenish

8 **equip, furnish, outfit, prepare,**
fit, fix up (*nonformal*), **rig, turn**
out, appoint, clothe, dress; man,
staff

9 **provision,** cater; **board,** feed;
forage; fuel, fill up, top off, oil;
sell

10 **accommodate;** house, lodge; **put**
up, board

11 **make a living,** earn a living,
earn one's keep

12 **support oneself;** keep afloat;
survive, subsist, cope, eke out,
scrape along, manage, get by

adjectives

13 **provided, supplied, furnished,**
catered; invested, endowed;
equipped, fitted, fitted out,
rigged; armed; staffed, manned;
prepared

371 STORE, SUPPLY

nouns

1 **store, hoard, treasure,** treasury;
plenty, abundance; heap, mass,
stack, pile; **collection, accumula-**
tion, stockpile, backlog; repertoire; **inventory, stock; stores,**
supplies, provisions, rations; larder; munitions; material, materials

2 **supply, fund, resource, re-**
sources; means, assets, balance,
capital; holdings, property

3 **reserve, reserves,** reservoir, resource; **stockpile, cache,** nest
egg, savings

4 source, resource; well, fountain,
spring; mine, **gold mine, bonan-**
za; quarry, vein; oilfield, oil well,
oil rig

5 **storage;** preservation, conservation; cold storage, storage space

6 store, storage, **repository,** reservoir, depot, magazine, warehouse; dock; hold; attic, cellar,
basement; closet, cupboard; wine
cellar; **treasury,** treasure house,
treasure room; bank, vault; **ar-**
chives, library, dump; drawer,
shelf; bin, bunker; vat, tank;
crate, box; chest, **locker;** bookcase, stack

7 **larder, pantry;** dairy

8 **museum; gallery,** art gallery,
picture gallery; salon

verbs

9 **store, stow;** lay in, store away,
stow away, **put away,** pack away,
bundle away, lay down, salt
away; **deposit,** lodge; **cache,**
stash (*nonformal*); **bank;** file, file
away

10 **store up, stock up, save up,**
hoard up, heap up, pile up, **ac-**
cumulate, collect, amass, stockpile; garner; **hoard,** treasure,
save, keep, hold, squirrel away;
hide, secrete

11 **reserve, save, conserve, keep,**
retain, husband, withhold; **pre-**
serve; put by; save up

adjectives

12 **stored, accumulated,** amassed,
laid up; gathered, garnered, col-

lected; **stockpiled; hoarded,** treasured

13 **reserved, preserved, saved,** conserved, put by, kept, retained, held, withheld, held back; spare

adverbs

14 **in store,** in stock, in supply, **on hand**

15 **in reserve,** back, aside, by

372 USE

nouns

1 **use, employment,** utilization, usage; **exercise, exertion,** active use; good use; ill use, misuse; hard wear, heavy duty; **application,** appliance; expenditure, expending, using up, exhausting, dissipating, **consumption**

2 **usage, treatment, handling,** management; care

3 **utility, usefulness, use,** avail, good, **helpfulness,** profitability, availability, practicality, **effectiveness,** efficiency

4 **benefit, use, service, avail, profit, advantage,** point, convenience; interest, behalf; **value, worth**

5 **function, use, purpose, role,** part, operation; work, duty

6 **utilization,** using; **employment,** employing; **management,** manipulation, handling, working, operation, **exploitation,** recruiting, recruitment; mobilization, mobilizing

7 **user,** employer; **consumer**

verbs

8 **use, utilize,** do with; **employ,** practise, work, manage, handle, manipulate, operate, **wield,** play; exercise, **exert**

9 **apply,** carry out, enforce

10 **treat, handle,** manage, use, **deal with, cope with,** take on, tackle (*nonformal*), contend with, do with; care for

11 **spend,** consume, expend, **pass,** employ, **put in;** devote, bestow; while, while away; dissipate, **exhaust, use up**

12 **resort to, turn to,** look to, refer to, take to (*nonformal*); revert to, impress, **call upon,** recruit, muster

13 **improve,** turn to advantage; **profit by, benefit from; exploit,** capitalize on, trade on

14 **exploit, use; manipulate; impose upon,** presume upon; abuse, misuse; milk, bleed, bleed white (*nonformal*); drain, suck dry

15 **avail,** serve, **suffice,** do, answer, be handy; **profit, benefit,** pay *and* pay off (*both nonformal*)

adjectives

16 **useful,** of use, of service, **serviceable;** good for; **helpful,** of help; **advantageous, profitable,** beneficial; **practical, functional, utilitarian;** fitting, proper, appropriate, expedient

17 exploitative, manipulative

18 **handy, convenient; available,** accessible, **ready, at hand,** to hand, **on hand,** on tap, on call; versatile, adaptable

19 **effective,** active, efficient, operative

20 **valuable,** of value, **profitable, worthwhile,** rewarding; gainful

21 **usable; applicable;** practical

22 **used, employed,** exercised, exerted, **applied;** secondhand

23 **in use, in practice,** in force, in effect, in service, in operation, in commission

adverbs

24 **usefully,** to good use; **profitably, to advantage;** effectively, efficiently; **practically;** conveniently

373 CONSUMPTION

nouns

1 **consumption, consuming;** burning up; absorption, assimilation, digestion, **expenditure,** expending, spending; squandering; finishing; **depletion,** drain, exhausting, **exhaustion,** impoverishment; **waste,** wastage, erosion, wearing down, wearing away; throwing away

verbs

2 **consume, spend, expend, use up;** absorb, assimilate, digest, eat, **eat up,** swallow, swallow up, gobble, gobble up; burn up; **finish,** finish off; **exhaust, deplete,** impoverish, drain; suck dry, bleed white (*nonformal*); wear away, erode; **throw away, squander**

3 **be consumed,** waste; **run out, give out,** peter out (*nonformal*); run dry, dry up

adjectives

4 **used up, consumed,** eaten up, burnt up; finished, done, gone; **spent,** exhausted, dissipated, depleted, impoverished, drained, worn-out; worn away, eroded; **wasted**

5 **consumable, expendable;** disposable, throwaway

374 MISUSE

nouns

1 **misuse, abuse;** mismanagement; **embezzlement;** prostitution; violation, pollution, fouling, desecration; malpractice, misconduct

2 **abuse; molesting; violation,** outrage, violence, injury, atrocity

3 **persecution,** oppression, hounding, tormenting, harassment, victimization; witch-hunt

verbs

4 **misuse, abuse;** mismanage; embezzle; pervert, prostitute; profane, violate, pollute, foul, desecrate, defile, debase

5 **maltreat, ill-treat, abuse,** injure, molest; manhandle; batter, bruise, **savage,** maul, knock about, rough, rough up

6 **persecute,** oppress, **torment,** victimize, **harass,** hound; pursue, hunt

375 DISUSE

nouns

1 **disuse; abstinence, abstention, obsolescence;** retirement

2 **cessation,** desisting; **abdication,**

resignation, renunciation; suspension; **abandonment**

3 **discarding,** disposal, dumping,
waste disposal; scrapping; removal, elimination; **rejection; reject; refuse**

verbs

4 **abdicate, relinquish; discontinue, disuse,** stop, drop (*nonformal*), give up, give over, **phase
out,** let go, cut out, desist; resign, renounce

5 **not use, do without,** dispense
with, **let alone,** not touch; **abstain, refrain,** forgo, spare,
waive; reserve, save, save up,
hoard

6 **put away, put aside,** salt away;
stow, store; **shelve;** postpone,
delay

7 **discard, reject, throw away,**
throw out; shrug off, **dispose of,
dump, ditch** (*nonformal*), **jettison;** part with, give away; write
off, **abandon;** remove, **eliminate;
scrap;** retire, pension off

adjectives

8 **disused, abandoned,** deserted,
discontinued, done with; old;
outworn, worn-out; **obsolete;**
superseded, outdated, out-of-
date, outmoded; antique, antiquated, old-fashioned

9 **discarded,** rejected, cast-off

10 **unused, unemployed;** in abey-
ance, suspended; waived; held
back, put by, put aside, saved, in
hand, in reserve, spare, to spare,
extra, reserve; stored; **new,** original, fresh, mint

376 USELESSNESS

nouns

1 **futility,** vanity, emptiness;
worthlessness; triviality; **impotence;** absurdity

2 **wasted effort, wasted breath,
waste of time**

3 **refuse, waste,** effluent, sewage,
sludge; **offal;** dust, **scraps; garbage,** slop, slops; **dregs;** shavings; **scum;** chaff, stubble, husks;
rags, bones; scrap iron; slag; **rubbish, rubble, trash, junk** (*nonformal*), dust, **debris, litter;** rubbish heap, scrap heap; **dump,**
garbage dump; wastepaper basket; litter basket, litter bin; garbage can, dustbin, trash can;
skip

verbs

4 **be useless, be futile, make no
difference;** waste one's breath

adjectives

5 **useless; aimless,** meaningless,
pointless, feckless, failed; ineffective, **ineffectual;** impotent;
superfluous

6 **needless, unnecessary,
uncalled-for;** unrecognized

7 **worthless, valueless,** not worthwhile; trivial; **cheap,** shoddy,
shabby

8 **fruitless, unprofitable;** abortive,
barren, sterile, unproductive

9 **vain, futile,** hollow, empty, stale,
flat, idle; absurd; inane, fatuous

adverbs

10 **needlessly,** unnecessarily; **vainly;
aimlessly, pointlessly**

377 IMPROVEMENT

nouns

1 **improvement, betterment;** mending, amendment; **progress,** headway; breakthrough **advance, advancement; promotion; rise,** ascent; **increase,** upgrading; **enrichment; restoration,** revival, recovery

2 **development, refinement,** elaboration, **perfection;** embellishment; ripening, evolution

3 **cultivation, culture, refinement, polish,** civility; **civilization;** enlightenment, education

4 **revision;** revised edition; **amendment,** correction; editing; **rewrite,** rewriting; **polishing,** touching up, finishing, finishing touches, perfecting, tuning

5 **reform, reformation; transformation; conversion;** extremism; revolution

6 **reformer;** utopian; **progressive; radical, extremist; revolutionary**

verbs

7 *(get better)* **improve, grow better, look better, mend;** develop; **advance, progress, make progress, make headway, gain,** gain ground, go forward, come on

8 **rally,** come round, get over *(nonformal),* gain strength; **recuperate, recover**

9 **improve, better;** transform; refine, **mend, amend; advance,** promote, foster, favour, nurture, forward, bring forward; **lift,** elevate, raise; **upgrade; enhance, enrich,** fatten; better oneself; **reform;** go straight *(nonformal);*

civilize, socialize; enlighten, edify; **educate**

10 **develop,** elaborate; beautify, embellish; **cultivate;** mature, ripen, evolve, season

11 **perfect, touch up,** finish, polish, **brush up,** spruce, **spruce up,** freshen, brighten up, polish; **revive, renovate; repair, fix**

12 **revise, rewrite,** redraft; **amend,** rectify, correct; **edit**

adjectives

13 **improved;** advanced, enhanced, enriched; developed, perfected; beautified, embellished; upgraded; **reformed; transformed,** converted; **cultivated,** cultured, refined, polished, civilized; **educated**

14 **better,** better off, better for

15 **improving,** progressive, progressing, advancing, ongoing; mending; looking up *(nonformal)*

16 **corrective;** progressive; utopian; radical; revolutionary

378 IMPAIRMENT

nouns

1 **damage, injury, harm,** mischief, **hurt, detriment,** loss, weakening; **worsening;** disablement; breakage; **breakdown; collapse; malfunction;** sabotage; mayhem, mutilation, crippling, hamstringing, maiming; destruction

2 **corruption, pollution, contamination,** fouling; **poisoning;** infection, festering, perversion, prostitution; misuse

3 **deterioration, degradation;** degeneration; regression; decline,

descent, downturn, depreciation, **decrease, drop, fall, plunge,** lessening, slump, lapse, fading, failure, wane, ebb

4 **waste,** wastage, **consumption;** withering, wasting, wasting away, wilting

5 **wear,** use, hard wear; **erosion, weathering**

6 **decay, decomposition, disintegration, dissolution,** degradation, **corruption; corrosion,** rust; mildew, mould

7 **rot,** decay, decomposition; carrion; dry rot, wet rot

8 **wreck, ruins, ruin, total loss;** hulk, carcass, skeleton

verbs

9 **impair, damage, injure, harm, hurt,** irritate; **worsen,** make worse, deteriorate, aggravate, exacerbate, embitter; **weaken**

10 **spoil, mar,** botch, **ruin,** wreck, blight; **destroy;** screw up, balls up, bugger up, mess up, muck up (*all nonformal*)

11 **corrupt, debase, degrade, defile,** violate, desecrate; **contaminate, pollute, poison, infect, taint; pervert,** warp, twist, distort; prostitute, misuse; devalue; coarsen; adulterate, water

12 (*inflict an injury*) **injure, hurt;** draw blood, wound; stab, stick, pierce, puncture; cut, slit, slash, gash, scratch; scuff, scrape, chafe, gall, bark, skin; break, fracture, rupture; crack, chip; claw, tear, rip; fray; burn, scorch, scald; mutilate, maim, rough up (*nonformal*), maul, batter, savage; sprain, strain, wrench;

bruise, batter, bash (*nonformal*), beat

13 **cripple, lame,** maim; **hamstring;** castrate; incapacitate

14 **deteriorate, sicken, worsen;** slip back, regress, relapse, fall back; slacken

15 **decline, sink, fail, fall,** slip, fade, die, wane, ebb, subside, lapse, **run down,** go down, **go downhill, fall away, fall off,** go off (*nonformal*), slide, slump

16 **languish,** pine, droop, **flag, wilt;** fade; **wither, shrivel,** shrink, diminish, **dry up,** wrinkle

17 **waste, waste away, wither away,** consume, erode, pine away; wear, wear away, wear down; rub off; fray; **wear out;** weather

18 **corrode, erode,** eat, gnaw, eat away; **rust**

19 **decay, decompose, disintegrate;** break up, crumble; **spoil,** corrupt, **go bad; rot;** fester; mould, rot away, mildew

20 **break, break up,** fracture, **come apart,** come unstuck, **disintegrate;** burst, rupture; crack, split; snap

21 **break down, founder, collapse;** topple; totter, sway

22 **malfunction;** go wrong; give out, **break down,** pack up

adjectives

23 **impaired, damaged, hurt, injured, harmed; worsened,** aggravated, exacerbated; **worse,** worse off; imperfect; mangled, cut, split, rent, torn, slit, slashed, mutilated; **broken, shattered, smashed,** in bits, in pieces, burst, ruptured; cracked,

chipped; burned, scorched, scalded; **damaging**, traumatic

24 **spoiled, spoilt, marred,** botched, blighted, **ruined,** wrecked; **destroyed**

25 **screwed up, fouled up,** snarled up, **messed up,** mucked up, botched up; finished, done for, sunk

26 **crippled,** bad, handicapped, maimed; **lame,** hobbling, limping; hamstrung; **disabled, incapacitated;** castrated

27 **worn,** well-worn, dog-eared; timeworn; **threadbare,** bare

28 **shabby, shoddy, seedy,** scruffy, **tacky** (*nonformal*), dowdy, tatty; **ragged, tattered, torn;** patchy, **frayed;** in rags, in tatters

29 **dilapidated, ramshackle,** decrepit, **broken-down, run-down,** in ruins, ruinous, ruined, derelict; **battered**

30 **weather-beaten, weathered,** eroded; **faded,** bleached, blanched

31 **wasted,** shrunken; **withered,** shrivelled, wilted, wizened, dried-up; wrinkled; brittle; **emaciated;** starved

32 **worn-out, used up** (*nonformal*); exhausted, tired, fatigued, **spent,** played out, jaded; **run-down**

33 **decayed, decomposed;** spoiled, **corrupt,** bad, **gone bad; rotten,** rotting, **foul;** festering; rotting; septic

34 **tainted, off,** blown; **stale; sour,** soured, turned; **rank, rancid, high**

35 **corroded, eroded,** eaten; **rusty;**

corrosive, corroding; eroding; **damaging**

36 **deteriorating, worsening,** disintegrating, crumbling, cracking; **decadent, degenerate;** retrograde, regressive; **declining, sinking, failing,** falling, waning, subsiding; **slipping,** slumping; tottering; **languishing, pining,** drooping, flagging, wilting; ebbing, draining, dwindling; **wasting,** fading, **withering,** shrivelling

379 RELAPSE

nouns

1 **relapse, lapse,** falling back; **reversion, regression; reverse, reversal, setback; return,** recurrence; throwback; **fall**

verbs

2 **relapse, lapse,** slide back, lapse back, **slip back,** sink back, **fall back, return to, revert to,** recur to; revert, **regress; fall**

380 DESTRUCTION

nouns

1 **destruction, ruin, ruination, rack and ruin; damnation;** wreck; devastation, havoc, holocaust, carnage, shambles, slaughter, **desolation; waste; dissolution, disintegration,** disruption, undoing; vandalism

2 **end, fate, doom,** death, death warrant, final blow

3 **fall, downfall; overthrow, upset, upheaval;** convulsion, **subversion,** sabotage

4 **debacle, disaster, cataclysm, catastrophe;** breaking up; **break-**

down, collapse; crash, smash; wreck, wrack, shipwreck; total loss

5 **demolition**; wrecking, wreckage, levelling, razing, flattening, smashing, tearing down

6 **extinction**, **extermination**, **elimination**, **eradication**; rooting out, uprooting; **annihilation**; **abolition**; **liquidation**, **purge**; **suppression**; choking off, suffocation, stifling; silencing

7 **obliteration**, **erasure**, **blotting out**, wiping out; cancellation

8 **destroyer**; **vandal**; terrorist; **bomber**; burner

9 **eraser**, rubber, sponge

verbs

10 **destroy**; **ruin**; **wreck**, shipwreck; damn, **condemn**, confound; **devastate**, **desolate**, waste, **lay waste**, **ravage**, havoc, wreak havoc; vandalize; **decimate**; devour, consume, gobble up, swallow up; gut, incinerate; dissolve

11 **do for**, **fix** (*nonformal*), settle, sink, scuttle, do in, **undo**, knock out; **defeat**

12 **end**, **finish**, finish off (*nonformal*), dispose of, do in (*nonformal*); cut off; **slaughter**, kill off, strike down, **kill**; cut short

13 **abolish**, annihilate, annul, tear up, repeal, revoke, negate, invalidate, **undo**, cancel

14 **exterminate**, **eliminate**, **eradicate**, **annihilate**; **wipe out**; **cut out**, uproot; **liquidate**, **purge**; remove, sweep away, wash away

15 **extinguish**, quench, **snuff out**, put out; **smother**, choke, stifle,

strangle, suffocate; silence; **suppress**, **quash**, **quell**, put down

16 **obliterate**, **efface**, **erase**, raze, blot, **wipe out**, rub out, **blot out**, sponge out, wash away; cancel, strike out, cross out, scratch, scratch out, delete, kill

17 **demolish**, **wreck**, undo, **dismantle**; **take apart**, **tear apart**; **split**; disintegrate, fragment, pulverize, **smash**, shatter

18 **blow up**, blast, explode, bomb, bombard; mine

19 **raze**, fell, level, flatten, smash; steamroller, bulldoze; **pull down**, **tear down**, bring down, break down, beat down; cut down, chop down, mow down; blow down; burn down

20 **overthrow**, **overturn**; **upset**, upend, **subvert**; undermine, weaken

21 **overwhelm**, swamp, engulf; inundate

22 (*be destroyed*) **fall**, tumble, topple; **break up**, crumble, disintegrate, fall apart

23 **perish**, **expire**, **succumb**, **die**, cease, end, go, pass, **pass away**, **vanish**, **disappear**, fade away, run out

adjectives

24 **destructive**, destroying; **ruinous**, ruining; demolishing; **disastrous**, calamitous, cataclysmic, catastrophic; fatal, fateful; **deadly**; consuming, withering; **devastating**, ravaging, wasting; suicidal

25 **ruined**, **destroyed**, **wrecked**, broken, bankrupt; spoiled; fallen, overthrown; **devastated**, rav-

aged, blighted, wasted; ruinous, in ruins

26 (*nonformal terms*) **done for,** done in, finished; belly up, washed up

381 RESTORATION

nouns

1 **restoration;** replacement; **rehabilitation,** redevelopment; improvement

2 **reclamation, recovery, retrieval,** salvage; redemption, salvation

3 **revival, renewal;** resurrection, resurgence; **refreshment;** second wind; renaissance, **rebirth,** new birth

4 **renovation, renewal;** refreshment; refurbishment

5 **reconstruction, remaking, rebuilding;** reassembling; restructuring

6 **repair,** repairing, **fixing, mending;** servicing, **maintenance;** overhaul, overhauling; correction, remedy; redress, amends, satisfaction, compensation

7 **cure, curing, healing, remedy,** therapy

8 **recovery, rally, comeback** (*nonformal*), return; **recuperation, convalescence**

verbs

9 **restore, put back, replace, return; reinstate; rehabilitate;** refill, replenish; give back

10 **redeem, reclaim, recover, retrieve;** ransom; rescue; salvage; recycle; win back

11 **remedy, rectify, correct,** patch up, amend, **redress, put right,**

set right, heal up, knit up; give satisfaction, compensate

12 **repair, mend, fix,** fix up (*nonformal*), do up; ready; **service, overhaul;** patch, **patch up;** tinker; sew up, darn

13 **cure, remedy, heal,** heal up, knit up, make better, make well, fix up

14 **revive, renew; rejuvenate, revitalize; refresh; resuscitate,** bring to; **resurrect,** bring back, call back

15 **renovate, renew;** refit, revamp

16 **remake,** reconstruct, **rebuild,** reassemble

17 **recuperate, gain strength, get better; improve;** rally, pick up; convalesce

18 **recover,** rally, revive, get well, get over, pull through; survive; come to

19 **heal,** heal over, close up; **knit, set**

adjectives

20 **tonic, restorative;** remedial

21 **convalescent;** buoyant, resilient, elastic

382 PRESERVATION

nouns

1 **preservation, conservation, saving, salvation,** salvage, **keeping,** maintenance, upkeep, support; protection

2 **curing,** seasoning, salting, pickling, marinating; **drying;** evaporation; **smoking;** freezing; canning; bottling; **embalming;** stuffing

3 **preservative;** salt, brine, vinegar, embalming fluid

4 **keeper;** saviour; **conservationist; ranger, forest ranger,** fire warden, game warden

5 life jacket, life belt; life buoy; water wings; breeches buoy; lifeboat, life raft, rubber dinghy; lifeline; safety belt; **parachute**

6 **preserve, reserve, reservation; park;** national park; **refuge, sanctuary,** bird sanctuary; museum, library, archives, bank, store

verbs

7 **preserve, conserve, save,** spare; **keep,** keep safe; **guard, protect; maintain, sustain,** uphold, support, **keep up,** keep alive

8 **preserve, cure,** season; salt, brine, pickle, **dry;** dehydrate, evaporate; **smoke;** freeze; **can,** tin; **bottle, pot; embalm;** stuff

adjectives

9 **preservative,** conservative, conservatory; custodial; conservationist; preserving, conserving, saving, keeping; **protective**

10 **preserved,** conserved, **kept,** saved, spared; protected; **unspoiled;** intact

383 RESCUE

nouns

1 **rescue,** delivery, **saving; release, freeing, liberation; salvation,** salvage, **redemption,** ransom; **recovery, retrieval**

2 **lifeguard;** coast guard; **saviour;** lifeboat

verbs

3 **rescue, deliver, save, redeem,** ransom, **salvage; recover, retrieve; free,** set free, **release, extricate,** extract, **liberate;** bail one out (*nonformal*)

384 WARNING

nouns

1 **warning, caution; notice,** notification; **hint,** broad hint; tip-off (*nonformal*); **lesson,** object lesson, **example;** moral; **alarm;** ultimatum; **threat**

2 **forewarning, premonition, foreboding; portent**

3 **warning sign, danger sign; symptom, precursor; omen;** red light, red flag; warning signal, **alert,** red alert; siren, alarm bell

verbs

4 **warn, caution, advise, admonish; give warning; notify; threaten; alert,** warn against; sound the alarm; **forewarn**

adjectives

5 **warning,** cautioning, **cautionary;** admonishing, exemplary, deterrent; **precautionary**

385 ALARM

nouns

1 **alarm, alert;** red light, danger signal; **alarm button;** alarm bell; SOS, flare; storm warning, gale warning, burglar alarm; fire alarm; siren, whistle, horn; alarm clock; lighthouse, beacon; flashing light; **false alarm**

verbs

2 **alarm, alert, arouse; warn; cry
wolf; frighten,** startle

adjectives

3 **alarmed, aroused;** alerted;
frightened; startled

386 HASTE

nouns

1 **haste, hurry, scurry, rush, race,
dash, drive, scuttle, scamper,
scramble, bustle, flutter, flurry**

2 **swiftness, alacrity, promptness;
speed; suddenness, abruptness;
eagerness**

verbs

3 **hasten, hurry, accelerate, speed,
rush,** quicken, hustle (*nonformal*), bustle, bundle, precipitate,
forward; **dispatch;** whip, spur,
urge; **push, press; crowd, stampede**

4 **make haste, hasten, hurry, race,
run, rush, chase, tear, dash,**
spurt, plunge, **scurry, scamper,
scramble, scuttle, hustle** (*nonformal*), bundle, **bustle; rush
through, romp through, hurry
through; dash off**

adjectives

5 **hasty, hurried, quick,** flying,
prompt; **immediate, instant;
swift, speedy; urgent;** furious, feverish; **cursory,** passing, snap
(*nonformal*), superficial; last-
minute

6 **precipitate,** precipitous; **sudden,**
abrupt; **impetuous, impulsive,
rash;** headlong, breakneck;
breathless, panting

7 **hurried, rushed,** pushed,
pressed, crowded

adverbs

8 **hastily, hurriedly, quickly,**
promptly, with dispatch, post-
haste; **immediately,** instantly, at
once; **swiftly, speedily; in haste;
with haste; furiously, feverishly**

9 **suddenly,** abruptly; **impulsively,
rashly; headlong**

387 LEISURE

nouns

1 **leisure, ease, convenience,** freedom; retirement; **rest, repose;
free time, spare time; time; inactivity; slowness; deliberation**

verbs

2 **have time,** be in no hurry; **take
one's time;** go slow

adjectives

3 **leisure;** idle, unoccupied, free,
open, spare; retired

4 **leisurely, unhurried,** easy, relaxed; deliberate; inactive; **slow**

388 ENDEAVOUR

nouns

1 **endeavour,** effort, striving, struggle, strain; **all-out effort,** best effort; **exertion; determination,
resolution; enterprise**

2 **attempt, trial, effort, essay;** endeavour, undertaking; **approach,
move;** step; offer; **bid;** experiment

3 (*nonformal terms*) **try, whack,
fling, shot, crack,** bash, belt, go,
stab

verbs

4 endeavour, strive, struggle,
strain, sweat, labour, **exert one-**
self, apply oneself; seek, aim; resolve, be determined

5 attempt, try, essay, offer; **under-**
take, approach; venture, chance;
tackle, take on (*both nonformal*)

6 try for, strive for, struggle for,
contend for, bid for

7 trouble oneself, take trouble,
take pains

adjectives

8 trial, tentative, experimental;
willing; determined, resolute;
utmost

389 UNDERTAKING

nouns

1 undertaking, enterprise, opera-
tion, work, venture, project;
programme, plan; affair, busi-
ness, matter, task, concern, interest; **initiative,** effort, attempt;
action; engagement, contract,
obligation, commitment

2 adventure, mission; quest, pilgrimage; expedition, exploration

verbs

3 undertake, assume, accept, **take**
on, take up, go with, **tackle,** attack; **engage in;** busy oneself;
take up, move into, go into, proceed to, **venture upon;** set
about, go about; **set to, turn to,**
buckle to, fall to; pitch into
(*nonformal*), plunge into; **en-**
deavour, attempt

adjectives

4 undertaken, assumed, accepted,
taken on (*nonformal*), **ventured,**
attempted; **in hand, in progress,**
under way

5 enterprising, adventurous, keen,
eager

390 PREPARATION

nouns

1 preparation, preparing,
readying, warm-up; mobilization; **run-up;** lead time, advance
notice, warning, advance warning, alerting; **planning;** trial, dry
run; **provision, arrangement;**
preliminaries; grounding; training, briefing; prerequisite; processing; treatment; equipment;
manufacture; groundwork, foundation

2 fitting, fit; conditioning; adaptation, **adjustment,** tuning; **quali-**
fication; equipment, furnishing

3 (*a preparation*) **concoction,**
brew; composition, **mixture,**
combination

4 readiness; fitness, suitability;
condition, trim; **qualification,**
credentials, record, track record
(*nonformal*); **ability, capability,**
proficiency, mastery

5 trainer, coach, instructor, mentor, teacher

verbs

6 prepare, ready, fix (*nonformal*);
arrange; mobilize, marshal, deploy; plan; dress; treat; process

7 make up, get up; concoct, brew;
compound, compose, put to-
gether, mix; make

8 fit, condition, adapt, adjust, suit, tune; **qualify,** enable; **equip, furnish**

9 prime, load, charge, cock; set; wind, wind up; warm up

10 prepare for, provide for, arrange for, look to; see to; provide against, forearm

11 prepare oneself, brace oneself, **get ready, get set** (*nonformal*), limber up, warm up; gear up

12 be prepared, be ready, stand by, stand ready

adjectives

13 prepared, ready; eager, keen; alert, vigilant; **ripe, mature;** about to; **planned; primed,** loaded, cocked; familiarized, briefed, informed; groomed, coached; in arms, **armed;** mobilized; **provided, equipped;** dressed; treated, processed; **readied,** available

14 fitted, adapted, adjusted, suited; **qualified, fit, competent, able,** capable, proficient

15 prepared for, ready for, alert for; loaded for, primed for; up for (*nonformal*); equal to, up to

16 ready-made; prefabricated

17 preparatory; prerequisite; provisional

adjectives, adverbs

18 in readiness, in store, in reserve; in anticipation

19 in preparation, under way, **going on,** in embryo, **in production,** on stream, under construction, **in hand;** brewing, forthcoming

391 UNPREPAREDNESS

nouns

1 vulnerability; improvisation, ad-lib (*nonformal*); **disqualification;** negligence

2 natural state, nature; virginity; natural man

3 immaturity; rudeness, coarseness, roughness, the rough

4 raw material; crude; ore; rough diamond; **virgin soil**

verbs

5 be surprised; improvise, ad-lib, play by ear (*both nonformal*)

adjectives

6 unprepared; surprised, caught short, caught napping, taken aback, taken unawares, tripped up; haphazard; makeshift, improvised; impromptu, snap (*nonformal*); unmade; hasty, precipitate

7 unfit, unsuited, unqualified, disqualified, incompetent, incapable; **unfurnished,** unarmed, ill-equipped

8 raw, crude; uncooked; rare, red

9 immature, raw, green, cub, fledgling; adolescent, juvenile, boyish, girlish

10 undeveloped, unfinished; untreated; **underdeveloped;** backward, arrested, stunted; **crude, rude, coarse; rough; rudimentary;** embryonic, in embryo; **simplistic**

11 native; virgin, virginal, untouched; fallow

392 ACCOMPLISHMENT

nouns

1 **accomplishment, achievement, fulfilment, performance, execution,** implementation, **discharge, dispatch, consummation, realization, attainment,** production, fruition; **success;** *fait accompli* (*French*); mission accomplished

2 **completion,** completing, **finish,** finishing, **conclusion, end,** ending, **termination,** terminus, **close,** topping off, wrapping up; **perfection,** culmination; maturity, full development

3 **finishing touch,** final touch, last touch, last stroke; **crown;** climax

verbs

4 **accomplish, achieve, effect, compass, consummate, do, execute, produce, deliver, make, enact, perform, discharge, fulfil, realize, attain; work,** work out; **dispatch, dispose of,** polish off (*nonformal*), **deal with,** put away; succeed, manage

5 **bring about; implement, carry out, carry through; bring off, carry off, pull off** (*nonformal*); **put through,** get through

6 **complete, perfect, finish, finish off, conclude, terminate, end; get through, get done; finish up; wind up** (*nonformal*), **top off;** top out, **crown, climax, culminate; finalize**

7 **ripen, mature;** bloom, blow, blossom, **flourish;** bear fruit; **mellow;** grow up, reach maturity

adjectives

8 **completing, finishing,** culminating, conclusive, **concluding,** fulfilling, finalizing, crowning; ultimate, **last, final,** terminal

9 **accomplished, achieved,** effected, implemented, **consummated, executed, discharged, fulfilled, realized, attained; dispatched, disposed of;** wrought

10 **completed, done, finished, concluded, terminated, ended,** finished up; signed, sealed, and delivered; washed up (*nonformal*), **through,** done with

11 **complete, perfect, consummate,** polished; exhaustive, thorough; fully realized

12 **ripe, mature,** matured, seasoned; blooming; **mellow,** fully developed

393 NONACCOMPLISH-MENT

nouns

1 omission; **neglect;** loose ends, rough edges; **disappointment; failure**

verbs

2 neglect, leave undone; be disappointed

adjectives

3 unfulfilled; **unfinished, undone,** open-ended; **neglected; disappointed**

394 SUCCESS

nouns

1 **success; prosperity;** accomplishment; **victory**

2 **great success, triumph**, resounding triumph, brilliant success; **stardom; success story;
best seller**

3 (*nonformal terms*) **smash, hit**,
smash hit

4 **score, hit, bull's-eye; goal; grand
slam; strike; home run**

5 (*successful person*) **winner, star,
success; victor**

verbs

6 **succeed, prevail**, be successful,
deliver; **come off; prosper;** do
well, fare well, work well; pass,
graduate, qualify; score

7 **make good, come through,
achieve success, make it** (*nonformal*); **advance, progress,**
make headway, **get on, come on**
(*nonformal*), **get ahead** (*nonformal*); go places, **go far; rise, step
up; arrive, get there** (*nonformal*);
break through

8 **succeed with; accomplish,
achieve; bring off, carry off, pull
off** (*nonformal*)

9 **manage, contrive, succeed in;
make out**, go on; **scrape along,
muddle through, get by**, manage somehow; **make it** (*nonformal*); **clear; negotiate** (*nonformal*), **engineer; swing** (*nonformal*)

10 **win through**, come through
(*nonformal*); **triumph; live
through**; persevere

adjectives

11 **successful**, succeeding; **prosperous**, fortunate; **triumphant, winning**

adverbs

12 **successfully**, well

395 FAILURE

nouns

1 **failure; no go** (*nonformal*); futility; **defeat; losing game; bankruptcy**

2 (*nonformal terms*) **flop, dud**,
non-starter, **loser, turkey, total
loss**

3 **collapse, crash**, smash, breakdown, **fall**, stumble, tumble,
downfall; disappointment

4 **miss; slip; error, mistake**

5 **abortion, miscarriage**, miscarrying, abortive attempt, vain attempt; **misfire, malfunction; dud**
(*nonformal*)

6 **fiasco, botch, bungle, hash,
mess, muddle**

7 (*unsuccessful person*) **failure;
bankrupt; loser, non-starter,
flop** (*all nonformal*)

verbs

8 **fail**, be unsuccessful, **lose;** not
pass; **go bankrupt; lose out, flop**
(*both nonformal*); **fold** (*nonformal*)

9 **sink, founder**, go down, go under (*nonformal*); **slip, go downhill**

10 **fall, fall down** (*nonformal*), fall
flat; **fall short, fall through; collapse; crash**

11 **misfire**, hang fire; **blow up, explode**

12 **miss; slip**, slip up (*nonformal*);
blunder, err; botch, bungle

13 **miscarry, abort**, be stillborn; **go
amiss**, go astray, **go wrong**

14 **stall**, stick, die, go dead

adjectives

15 **unsuccessful, failing; failed; un-fortunate; abortive**, miscarrying, miscarried, stillborn; fruitless, futile, useless; **lame, ineffectual**, ineffective; malfunctioning

adverbs

16 **unsuccessfully, without success;** ineffectually, lamely; **in vain**

396 VICTORY

nouns

1 **victory, triumph, conquest;** total victory, grand slam; **championship**, crown, laurels, cup, trophy, blue ribbon; lap of honour; win (*nonformal*); runaway victory; landslide; moral victory; **winning streak** (*nonformal*); **winning ways; success**; mastery

2 **victor, winner; conqueror;** top dog (*nonformal*); master; hero, conquering hero; champion; easy winner, sure thing (*nonformal*); runner-up

verbs

3 **triumph, prevail, be victorious,** clean up (*nonformal*); **win, gain, capture, carry; win through,** succeed

4 **win hands down** (*nonformal*); walk off with (*nonformal*); take by storm

5 **defeat, triumph over, prevail over, best, beat; get the better of; surmount, overcome,** rise above

adjectives

6 **victorious, triumphant, winning, prevailing;** conquering, vanquishing, defeating; ascendant, dominant; successful

7 **undefeated, unbeaten, uncon-quered,** unsubdued, unbowed

adverbs

8 **triumphantly,** victoriously

397 DEFEAT

nouns

1 **defeat; beating,** thrashing; **con-quest**, mastery, subjugation, sub-duing; **overthrow,** overcoming; **fall, downfall,** collapse, crash, undoing, ruin, debacle; **destruction**; Waterloo; failure

2 **rout,** rebuff; **frustration,** confusion; **checkmate,** check; reversal, setback

3 **utter defeat,** total defeat, crush-ing defeat, decisive defeat; no contest; **pasting** *and* **clobbering** (*both nonformal*)

4 **loser;** the vanquished; good loser, **good sport;** bad loser; **under-dog, also-ran;** victim

verbs

5 **defeat, get the better of; outdo,** outrun, etc; **triumph over;** ruin, destroy

6 **overcome, surmount; overpow-er; overthrow, overturn; upset,** trip up; silence, floor, deck

7 **overwhelm,** snow under (*nonfor-mal*); **rout,** scatter, stampede, panic; confound

8 (*nonformal terms*) **clobber, skin alive, beat,** massacre, lick, whip, thrash, run rings round, trounce,

5 bungle, blunder, botch; slip, trip, stumble; hash *and* mess (*both nonformal*); bad job; off day; **error, mistake**

6 mismanagement, mishandling, misconduct; malpractice; omission, **negligence,** neglect

7 incompetent; duffer (*nonformal*)

8 bungler, blunderer, fumbler; bull in a china shop; **oaf,** boor, **clown; clod,** clot, dolt

verbs

9 bungle, blunder, muff, fumble, flounder, muddle, lumber; stumble, **slip,** trip; **botch,** mar, **spoil, butcher, murder**

10 (*nonformal terms*) blow it, **mess up, make a mess** *or* hash of, foul up; **screw up, louse up**

11 mismanage, mishandle; be negligent

adjectives

12 inexpert; inefficient; **inept,** hopeless, poor; mediocre, pedestrian

13 unskilled, unaccomplished, untrained, uninitiated, unprepared; **untalented; amateurish,** unprofessional

14 inexperienced, unpractised; immature, green, untried; unskilled in, unaccustomed to, unused to, new to, uninitiated in; ignorant

15 out of practice, stiff, **rusty;** slipping

16 incompetent, incapable, unable, inadequate, unequipped, unqualified, unfit, unfitted; **ineffectual,** ineffective; maladjusted

17 bungling, blundering, bumbling, fumbling; **clumsy, awkward,** heavy-handed, all thumbs; stiff; **ungainly, uncouth,** graceless, gauche; **gawky;** boorish; **sloppy, careless, ponderous,** cumbersome, lumbering; **unwieldy**

18 botched, bungled, fumbled, spoiled, **butchered,** murdered; mismanaged; ill-advised; negligent

adverbs

19 inexpertly; inefficiently; **incompetently,** inadequately; poorly

20 clumsily, awkwardly

400 CUNNING

nouns

1 cunning, craftiness, artfulness, wiliness, wiles, guile, **slyness; canniness, shrewdness; resourcefulness,** inventiveness; subtlety, finesse

2 politics, diplomacy

3 stratagem, wile, strategy, **device, contrivance, expedient, design, scheme, trick, gimmick** (*nonformal*), **ruse, tactic, manoeuvre,** master stroke, **move, coup,** gambit, **ploy, dodge; game; plot,** conspiracy, **intrigue; subterfuge;** deceit, trickery

4 machination, manipulation, wire-pulling (*nonformal*); influence; **manoeuvring,** manoeuvres; **tactics,** devices, expedients

5 evasion, the slip (*nonformal*); **frustration,** foiling, **thwarting, outwitting,** outmanoeuvring

6 fox, charmer; shady character; swindler

7 strategist, tactician; manipulator; schemer

8 diplomat, politician

verbs

9 live by one's wits; dodge; trick, deceive

10 manoeuvre, manipulate; contrive, jockey, engineer; play games *(nonformal)*; plot, scheme, intrigue; finagle, wangle

11 outwit, outfox, outsmart, outmanoeuvre; evade, elude, frustrate, foil; deceive, victimize

adjectives

12 cunning, crafty, artful, wily, sly, insidious, shifty, arch, smooth, slippery, foxy; canny, shrewd, knowing, sharp, acute, astute, clever; resourceful, ingenious, inventive; subtle; tricky; Machiavellian; strategic, tactical; sneaky, wary, cagey *(nonformal)*; scheming, designing; manipulative; deceitful

adverbs

13 cunningly, craftily, artfully, smoothly, slyly; cannily, shrewdly, knowingly, cleverly; warily

401 ARTLESSNESS

nouns

1 artlessness, ingenuousness, guilelessness; simplicity; naivety; innocence; openness, sincerity, candour; integrity, directness, bluntness

2 naturalness; unaffectedness; genuineness

3 ingenue, innocent, child, infant, baby, lamb; noble savage; primitive; lout

adjectives

4 artless, simple, guileless; unsophisticated, naive, ingenuous; childlike; innocent; trusting, unwary, confiding; open, frank, sincere, candid; direct, bluff, blunt, outspoken

5 natural; unspoiled; unaffected, unassuming, genuine

adverbs

6 artlessly, guilelessly; ingenuously; simply, plainly; naturally, genuinely; openly

402 AUTHORITY

nouns

1 authority, prerogative, right, power, faculty, mandate; legitimacy; divine right

2 authority, power, potency, strength, might, clout *(nonformal)*

3 masterfulness; imperiousness, high-handedness

4 prestige, authority, influence; weight, consequence, moment; eminence, stature, rank, seniority, priority, precedence; greatness; importance, prominence

5 governance, authority, jurisdiction, control, command, power, rule, reign, dominion, sovereignty, empire, sway; government; administration; control, grip, claws, clutches, hands

6 dominance, domination, dominion; pre-eminence, supremacy, superiority; ascendance or ascendancy; upper hand, sway; sovereignty; predominance

7 **mastery; leadership; hierarchy,** nobility, aristocracy, ruling class; presidency; premiership; principality; consulate; **dictatorship**

8 **sovereignty, royalty, monarchy,** empire, imperialism; the throne, the Crown

9 **sceptre, rod, staff**

10 (*seat of authority*) **saddle** (*nonformal*), **helm, driver's seat** (*nonformal*); **chair,** bench

11 (*acquisition of authority*) **accession; succession; usurpation,** assumption, taking over, seizure, coup; coronation; **appointment,** assignment, delegation; **election; authorization,** empowerment

verbs

12 **have power;** have clout (*nonformal*); **rule, control;** supervise

13 **take command, take charge, take over;** assume command, usurp; seize power

adjectives

14 **authoritative, commanding, governing, controlling, ruling; pre-eminent, supreme, superior,** leading; **powerful, potent,** mighty; **dominant; influential, prestigious,** weighty, momentous, **eminent; great; important, prominent, senior, authorized, empowered; official;** authoritarian; **absolute, autocratic; totalitarian**

15 **imperious, masterful,** authoritative, feudal, aristocratic, lordly, arrogant; **dictatorial, authoritarian; bossy** (*nonformal*), **domineering, high-handed, overbearing;** autocratic, **despotic, tyran-**nical; **oppressive; repressive,** strict, severe

16 **sovereign; regal, royal, majestic;** imperial

adverbs

17 **authoritatively,** with authority; commandingly; **powerfully; officially**

18 **imperiously, masterfully; peremptorily; high-handedly,** domineeringly, overbearingly, dictatorially, tyranically

19 **in authority, in power, in charge, in control, in command,** at the helm

403 LAWLESSNESS

nouns

1 **lawlessness; licence; insubordination, mutiny, disobedience;** permissiveness; irresponsibility; wilfulness

2 **anarchy; disorderliness, unruliness, disorder,** disruption, confusion, turmoil, chaos; nihilism; lynch law, revolution; rebellion

3 **anarchist;** nihilist; rebel

adjectives

4 **lawless;** permissive; mutinous, disobedient; **uncontrolled,** unchecked, rampant; **irresponsible,** unaccountable; wilful, headstrong

5 **anarchic,** anarchistic; **unruly, disorderly,** disorganized, chaotic; nihilistic

404 PRECEPT

nouns

1 **precept, prescription, teaching; instruction, direction, charge,** commission, injunction, dictate; **order,** command

2 **rule, law, canon, maxim,** moral; norm, standard; formula, form; commandment; **tradition; regulation, principle,** imperative, tenet, convention; **guideline,** ground rule, protocol; golden rule; **code**

3 **formula, recipe; prescription**

adjectives

4 **prescriptive,** didactic, instructive, moralistic; prescribed, mandatory, binding; standard, regulation, official, authoritative, statutory; **conventional;** traditional

405 COMMAND

nouns

1 **command, commandment, order, bidding,** imperative, dictate, dictation, will, pleasure, word; **authority**

2 **injunction, charge,** commission, **mandate**

3 **direction, directive, instruction, rule, regulation;** prescription, precept

4 **decree, edict; law; rule, ruling; proclamation,** pronouncement, declaration

5 **summons, bidding, beck and call**

6 **court order,** injunction

verbs

7 **command, order, dictate, direct, instruct,** bid, charge, commission; **decree, rule, ordain; proclaim, declare,** pronounce

8 **prescribe, require, demand, dictate,** impose, lay down, set, fix, appoint; authorize

9 **summon, call,** demand; call for; **cite, summons** (*nonformal*), subpoena, serve; page; convene, call together; call away; muster, invoke; summon up, muster up, conjure up; evoke; recall; requisition

adjectives

10 **mandatory, imperative, compulsory, obligatory;** imposed, required; decisive, final, peremptory, absolute, conclusive, binding, irrevocable

11 **commanding,** imperious, imperative, peremptory, abrupt; compelling, prescriptive; **authoritative**

adverbs

12 **commandingly, imperatively,** peremptorily

13 **by order;** mandatorily, compulsorily, obligatorily

406 DEMAND

nouns

1 **demand, claim, call;** requisition, requirement, order; levy, tax; duty, contribution; rush; extortion, blackmail; **ultimatum; notice,** warning

2 **stipulation, provision,** proviso, condition; **terms;** exception, reservation; **qualification**

3 (*nonformal terms*) **catch**, snag; strings

4 **insistence**; **urgency**, pressure, exigency; **persistence**

verbs

5 **demand**, **ask**, **ask for**; **call for**; clamour for; **claim**, challenge, **require**; **impose**, levy; **exact**, **extort**, squeeze, screw; blackmail; **requisition**; order

6 **claim**, pretend to, lay claim to; **challenge**

7 **stipulate**; **qualify**

8 **insist**, stick to (*nonformal*); **put one's foot down** (*nonformal*); **maintain**, **contend**, assert; urge, press; **persist**

adjectives

9 **demanding**, **exacting**; draining, taxing, grasping; **insistent**, urgent, pressing, loud, crying; persistent

10 **claimed**, spoken for; requisitioned

adverbs

11 **insistently**, **urgently**, loudly

12 **on demand**, **on call**

407 ADVICE

nouns

1 **advice**, **counsel**, **recommendation**, **suggestion**; proposal; **direction**, **instruction**, guidance, briefing; **exhortation**; **sermon**, preaching; **warning**, admonition, caution; **idea**, thought, opinion; **consultation**; **counselling**

2 **hint**, **tip** (*nonformal*), intimation, insinuation

3 **adviser**, **counsel**, **counsellor**, **consultant**, expert; **instructor**, guide, mentor; confidant

verbs

4 **advise**, **counsel**, **recommend**, **suggest**, advocate, propose, submit; **instruct**, coach, guide, direct, brief; prescribe; hint at, intimate, insinuate; meddle; confer, consult with

5 **admonish**, exhort, preach; **charge**; caution; **warn**, urge, incite, encourage, **induce**, persuade, move, prompt; **implore**

adjectives

6 **advisory**; instructive; **warning**, cautionary; **didactic**, moralistic

408 COUNCIL

nouns

1 **council**, **assembly**; chamber, house; **board**, court, bench; **congress**, senate; **legislature**; **cabinet**; privy council; brains trust (*nonformal*), inner circle; **association**, **syndicate**; **conference**; **assembly**; **tribunal**

2 **committee**; select committee

3 **forum**, **conference**, round table, panel; powwow (*nonformal*)

4 **chapter**, conference, congregation, convention, session

adjectives

5 **council**; advisory

adverbs

6 **in conference**, **in consultation**, **in a huddle** (*nonformal*); **in session**, sitting

409 COMPULSION

nouns

1 **compulsion, obligation, command; necessity; inevitability;** enforcement; command performance; constraint; restraint

2 **force, brute force,** physical force; tyranny

3 **coercion, intimidation,** scare tactics, duress; **pressure;** violence

verbs

4 **compel, force, make;** have, cause; **constrain, bind,** tie; **restrain;** enforce, drive, impel

5 **oblige, necessitate, require,** exact, demand, dictate, impose, call for

6 **press; put pressure on,** bring pressure to bear upon

7 **coerce,** use violence, intimidate, bully, bludgeon; hijack

8 (nonformal terms) **twist one's arm,** steamroller, bulldoze, **pressure,** lean on, squeeze; pull rank

9 **be compelled, be coerced,** have to

adjectives

10 **compulsory, compulsive, compelling, pressing, driving,** imperative; constraining; **restraining; irresistible**

11 **obligatory, compulsory,** imperative, mandatory, required, binding; involuntary; **necessary; inevitable**

12 **forcible;** violent

adverbs

13 **compulsively, compellingly**

14 **forcibly, by force,** at gunpoint

15 **compulsorily;** of necessity

410 STRICTNESS

nouns

1 **strictness, severity, harshness,** stringency, hard line; **discipline; austerity,** sternness, toughness (nonformal)

2 **firmness, rigour, rigorousness,** rigidity, stiffness, hardness, inflexibility; relentlessness; obstinacy; fundamentalism, orthodoxy

3 **firm hand,** heavy hand, tight rein

verbs

4 regiment, discipline

adjectives

5 **strict, exacting,** demanding, stringent; disciplined; **severe, harsh,** dour; stern, grim, austere, rugged, tough (nonformal); authoritarian

6 **firm, rigorous,** rigid, stiff, hard, steely, inflexible, dour, relentless, unrelenting; **uncompromising;** stubborn, obstinate; fundamentalist, orthodox

adverbs

7 **strictly, severely, harshly;** sternly, grimly

8 **firmly, rigorously,** rigidly, stiffly, inexorably; relentlessly

411 LAXNESS

nouns

1 **laxness, slackness, looseness;** loosening, relaxation; imprecision, sloppiness (*nonformal*), carelessness; negligence; indifference; weakness; impotence

2 **leniency; permissiveness, softness;** flexibility

adjectives

3 **lax, slack, loose,** relaxed; imprecise, sloppy (*nonformal*), careless; negligent; indifferent; weak; impotent

4 **undemanding; lenient; permissive, soft;** flexible, yielding

412 LENIENCY

nouns

1 **leniency; clemency, mercy,** humaneness, humanity, pity, compassion; mildness, gentleness, tenderness, softness; patience; **tolerance,** acceptance

2 **compliance;** decency; **benevolence,** kindness, kindliness

3 **indulgence, humouring;** gratification, pleasing; **pampering, spoiling,** cosseting; permissiveness

verbs

4 **tolerate,** bear with

5 **indulge, humour, oblige;** favour, gratify, please, cater to; yield to; **pamper, spoil,** cosset

adjectives

6 **lenient, mild, gentle,** tender, humane, compassionate, merciful; soft, moderate; lax; forgiving; patient; **tolerant,** accepting

7 **indulgent, compliant, obliging, accommodating,** amiable, gracious, generous, affable, decent, kind, kindly, benign, benevolent; permissive

8 **indulged, pampered, spoiled,** spoiled rotten (*nonformal*)

413 RESTRAINT

nouns

1 **restraint, constraint; inhibition;** injunction; **control, curb, check,** rein, arrest; curtailment; self-control; **hindrance;** rationing; monopoly, protection; **prohibition**

2 **suppression, repression;** quelling, smashing, crushing; quashing; smothering, stifling, suffocating, strangling, throttling; quenching; **censorship,** censoring

3 **restriction, limitation, confinement;** zero option; cramping; qualification

4 **shackle,** restraint, manacle, bonds, irons, chains; stranglehold; **handcuffs;** stocks; **tether,** lead; **rein;** yoke, collar; bridle; **muzzle, gag**

5 **lock,** bolt, bar, padlock, catch, safety catch; barrier

verbs

6 **restrain, constrain, control, govern,** contain; **inhibit,** prohibit; **curb, check,** arrest; slow down; curtail; withhold; hinder; **hold back, keep back;** rein in; hold fast; restrain oneself

7 **suppress, repress; keep down,** hold down, keep under; **subdue, quell,** smash, crush; quash; ex-

tinguish, quench, damp down; smother, stifle, suffocate, strangle, throttle, **muzzle, gag; censor,** silence; bottle up

8 **restrict, limit, confine,** tighten; ground; circumscribe; **cage in,** hem in, box in; **cramp,** stint; qualify

9 **bind, restrain, tie, strap,** lash, fasten, secure, make fast; **hamper; rope; chain; shackle, fetter, manacle; handcuff;** tether, moor, anchor; tie down, pin down

adjectives

10 **restraining, constraining; inhibiting; repressive;** controlling

11 **restrictive, restricting, limiting, confining;** cramping

12 **restrained, constrained; inhibited;** guarded; **controlled, curbed;** grounded; slowed down, retarded, arrested, in remission

13 **suppressed, repressed; subdued, quelled,** smashed, **crushed;** quashed; smothered, stifled, suffocated; censored

14 **restricted, limited, confined;** circumscribed; hemmed in, boxed in; landlocked; snowbound; **cramped;** qualified

15 **bound, tied,** strapped; **hampered; shackled, fettered;** handcuffed; tethered

414 CONFINEMENT

nouns

1 **confinement, restraint,** restriction, penning, **constraint,** check

2 **quarantine, isolation,** cordoning off, segregation, separation, seclusion; cordon

3 **imprisonment, jailing,** incarceration, internment, detention, captivity, duress; house arrest

4 **commitment,** committal, consignment; remand

5 **custody, care, charge, ward,** guarding, hold; protection, safekeeping

6 **arrest; capture,** apprehension, seizure

7 **close quarters;** limbo, hell, purgatory; pound; **cage; enclosure,** pen

8 **prison,** penitentiary; detention centre; **jail,** gaol; **stockade; dungeon;** youth custody centre; **prison camp, concentration camp,** internment camp, forced-labour camp, gulag; prisoner-of-war camp; cell; solitary confinement, the hole (nonformal); death row; penal colony

9 (nonformal terms) nick, **slammer,** can, cooler, stir, clink; **joint**

10 **jailer,** gaoler; **keeper, warder, warden,** prison guard, governor, commandant; custodian, guardian; **guard**

11 **prisoner, captive; convict, con** (nonformal); **jailbird** (nonformal); **internee; prisoner of war** or **POW;** political prisoner; chain gang

verbs

12 **confine, shut in,** hem in; **coop up, pen up,** seal up, impound; pen, cloister, cage; **enclose; hold, keep in, detain, restrain,** constrain, ground; check, inhibit; restrict; shackle

13 **quarantine, isolate, segregate,**

separate; **cordon off**, seal off, rope off

14 **imprison, incarcerate, intern,** jail, gaol; **lock up;** hold captive, hold prisoner

15 **arrest**, pick up; **take captive, take prisoner, apprehend, capture**, seize

16 (*nonformal terms*) nick, bust, pull in, **run in,** collar

17 **commit**, consign; remand

adjectives

18 **confined**, in confinement; impounded; cloistered; **enclosed;** kept in, detained, under restraint; grounded; restricted

19 **quarantined, isolated**, segregated, separated; **cordoned off**

20 **jailed, imprisoned, incarcerated, interned;** in prison, in captivity, behind bars, locked up, inside (*nonformal*)

21 **under arrest, in custody**, nicked (*nonformal*)

415 FREEDOM

nouns

1 **freedom, liberty;** licence; civil liberty

2 **right, rights**, civil liberties, constitutional rights, legal rights; **human rights,** liberty

3 **exuberance; abandon;** permissiveness

4 **latitude, scope, room; margin; space**, breathing space, clearance, leeway (*nonformal*), wide berth; **tolerance; free hand; carte blanche**, blank cheque

5 **independence, self-government,** autonomy, home rule; individualism; self-reliance

6 **free will, discretion**, option, choice, say

7 **own free will, own account, own accord, own initiative,** own volition; own way

8 **exemption, immunity**, exception; **release**, discharge; **franchise, licence,** charter, liberty; diplomatic immunity; **privilege;** permission

9 **nonintervention**, deregulation; liberalism, free enterprise; capitalism; free trade

10 **liberalism**, tolerance; free thought; **liberation**, liberalization

11 **free agent, independent; individualist;** free spirit; **liberal;** neutral

verbs

12 **liberalize**, ease; **free, liberate**

13 **exempt, free, release**, discharge; **excuse**, spare, except; grant immunity; **dispense from;** absolve

14 **not interfere, leave alone, let be**, not tamper, not meddle

15 (*nonformal terms*) get off one's back, back off, leave be, get lost

16 **be free**, feel free; breathe free; be exonerated, walk

17 **let oneself go**, open up; run wild

18 **suit oneself**, please oneself (*nonformal*)

adjectives

19 **free; at liberty, at large, loose**, unattached, uncommitted, clear; **freed, liberated, emancipated**, released

20 **independent, individualistic**,

autonomous, sovereign; self-sufficient, self-contained; neutral

21 outspoken, open, frank, direct, candid, blunt

22 uninhibited, exuberant; unchecked; uncontrolled, unruly; abandoned, incontinent, loose, wanton, riotous, wild; irrepressible; lax

23 permissive; indulgent; lax; liberal; open-minded, tolerant

24 unimpeded; clear

25 unrestricted; unlimited, limitless; unconditional, unqualified; absolute, perfect, unequivocal, full; open-ended, open

26 untied, unfettered

27 exempt, immune; released, excused, excepted, let off (nonformal), spared; privileged, licensed, favoured; permitted; unaccountable

28 quit, clear, free, rid

adverbs

29 freely, free; without restraint, unreservedly, with abandon; outright

30 independently, alone, by oneself, on one's own; of one's own free will, of one's own accord

416 LIBERATION

nouns

1 liberation, freeing; deliverance, delivery; rescue; emancipation

2 release, freeing; unleashing, untying; unlocking; discharge, dismissal; parole

3 extrication, freeing, releasing, clearing; disengagement, disen-

tanglement, untangling, unravelling

verbs

4 liberate, free; deliver, set free; rescue; emancipate

5 release, let go, let loose, turn loose, let out; discharge, dismiss; parole

6 loose, loosen, let loose, untie; unleash; unlock

7 extricate, free, release, clear, get out; disengage, disentangle, untangle, unravel

8 extricate oneself; throw off, shake off; escape, break out

9 go free, get off, walk (nonformal)

adjectives

10 liberated, freed; delivered, rescued; emancipated; released; untied; on parole; extricated, free

417 SUBJECTION

nouns

1 subjugation; domination; restraint, control; bondage, captivity; slavery, enslavement; servitude, serfdom; feudalism; tyranny

2 subservience, subordination, inferiority

3 quelling, crushing, humiliation; breaking, taming; conquering; suppression

4 subordinate, inferior, junior, lieutenant; underling, errand boy; assistant, helper; right-hand man; servant, employee

5 dependent, charge, ward

6 subject, captive; slave, servant, labourer; serf

verbs

7 **subjugate; dominate; enslave;** take captive

8 **subdue, quell, crush,** beat down, break, overwhelm; trample underfoot; **suppress; conquer; humble,** humiliate

9 **domesticate, tame, break,** break in

adjectives

10 **subject, dependent; subservient, subordinate, inferior;** servile; feudal

11 **subjugated, enslaved, captive; oppressed, suppressed;** in captivity; subordinated

12 **subdued, quelled, crushed,** broken; humiliated; **domesticated, tamed**

13 **downtrodden,** ground down, trampled, oppressed; **abused,** misused; **browbeaten;** slavish, servile, submissive

418 SUBMISSION

nouns

1 **submission, yielding; compliance, acquiescence, acceptance; assent; consent; obedience; resignation,** stoicism; **deference,** homage; **passivity;** quietness

2 **surrender, capitulation;** renunciation, abandonment, retreat

3 **submissiveness, docility;** flexibility; **servility,** subservience

4 **meekness, gentleness,** tameness, mildness; humility

verbs

5 **submit, comply, take, accept,** suffer, bear, brook, acquiesce, be agreeable, accede, assent; consent; **relent, succumb,** resign oneself; shrug off

6 **yield, cede, give way, give ground, back down, give in,** cave in (*nonformal*)

7 **surrender, give up, capitulate;** renounce, abandon, relinquish, cede, give over, hand over

8 **submit to, yield to, defer to,** bow to, succumb to

9 **bow down,** stoop, crouch; curtsy; **bow to,** bend to, knuckle to (*nonformal*); **kowtow,** grovel

10 **eat dirt, eat humble pie**

adjectives

11 **submissive, compliant, acquiescent,** consenting; **assenting,** accepting, agreeable; subservient, abject, obedient; servile; **resigned; passive,** long-suffering

12 **docile, yielding,** pliable, flexible

13 **meek, gentle, mild,** quiet; **subdued, chastened, tame,** broken, domesticated; humble

14 **deferential; subservient, obsequious,** servile; crouching, prostrate, prone

adverbs

15 **submissively; obediently; resignedly,** with resignation; **passively**

16 **meekly, gently, mildly,** quietly

419 OBSERVANCE

nouns

1 **observance,** observation; **keeping,** adherence; compliance, conformity, accordance; **faith,** fidelity; **respect, deference; performance, practice,** execution, dis-

charge; acquittal, fulfilment, satisfaction; heed, care

verbs

2 **observe, keep, heed, follow;** defer to, respect, attend to, comply with, conform to; **abide by,** adhere to; fulfil, fill, meet, satisfy

3 **perform, practise,** do, execute, discharge

adjectives

4 **observant,** respectful, mindful; **faithful,** devout, devoted, true, loyal, constant; dutiful; practising, active; conforming; punctual, scrupulous, meticulous, conscientious

420 NONOBSERVANCE

nouns

1 **indifference, disregard; failure, delinquency,** omission, default, slight, oversight; **negligence; neglect;** abandonment

2 **violation, breach,** breaking; **infringement, trespass,** contravention; offence

verbs

3 **disregard; neglect;** abandon; defect

4 **violate, break, breach; infringe, trespass,** contravene, trample on, outrage; **defy,** flout

adjectives

5 **inattentive; negligent;** unfaithful

421 PROMISE

nouns

1 **promise, word,** pledge; **oath, vow;** assurance, guarantee

2 **obligation, commitment, agreement, engagement, undertaking;** understanding; contract

3 **engagement,** betrothal

verbs

4 **promise,** pledge, plight; **vow; swear;** vouch, **warrant,** assure, guarantee

5 **commit, engage,** undertake, bind, agree to, answer for; contract

6 **be engaged,** be betrothed; contract

adjectives

7 **promised, pledged, bound, committed,** compromised; **sworn,** warranted, guaranteed, assured; contracted; **engaged,** betrothed, intended

422 COMPACT

nouns

1 **compact, pact, contract, covenant,** convention, transaction, accord, agreement, undertaking; adjustment; **understanding, arrangement, bargain, settlement;** bond; promise

2 **treaty,** entente cordiale (French), concord, convention, capitulation; **alliance, league**

3 signing, signature, sealing, closing, conclusion; handshake

4 **execution, completion;** transaction; carrying out, fulfilment; enforcement; observance

verbs

5 **contract, bargain, agree, engage,** undertake, commit, stipulate; **promise;** subcontract, outsource

6 **negotiate, bargain**

7 **sign,** seal, formalize

8 **arrange, settle; adjust,** fix, make up, straighten out, work out; **conclude,** close

9 **execute, complete, make;** make out, fill out; **discharge, fulfil,** render, administer; **carry out,** carry through; effect, implement; enforce; **abide by, honour,** adhere to, live by, observe

adjectives

10 contractual, conventional

11 **contracted,** agreed, stipulated; engaged, undertaken; **promised;** arranged, settled; **signed,** sealed

423 SECURITY

nouns

1 **security, guarantee, insurance,** warrant, assurance; **obligation; bond,** tie

2 **pledge;** undertaking; **earnest;** pawn; **bail, bond; hostage**

3 **collateral;** deposit, stake, forfeit

4 **mortgage,** lien

5 guarantee; sponsor; godparent, godfather, godmother

6 godchild, godson, goddaughter

verbs

7 **secure, guarantee, warrant, assure,** insure, certify; sponsor, sign for, back; **endorse;** sign, subscribe to; confirm, attest

8 **pledge, deposit, stake,** post, put up, pawn; mortgage, bond; bail out

adjectives

9 **secured, covered, guaranteed, warranted, assured, insured,** certified; certain, sure

10 **pledged, deposited, staked,** posted, put up, pawned, in hock *(nonformal)*

424 OFFER

nouns

1 **offer,** offering, presentation, bid, submission; **advance, overture,** approach, invitation; asking price

2 **proposal, proposition, suggestion; motion,** resolution; pass *(nonformal)*; request

3 **ultimatum,** sticking point

verbs

4 **offer, proffer, present,** tender, put up, submit, extend, hold forth

5 **propose, submit; suggest,** recommend, advance, pose, put forward; **bring up, broach,** introduce, open up, launch, start, kick off *(nonformal)*; **move**

6 **bid,** bid for

7 **make advances,** approach; **solicit**

8 *(nonformal terms)* proposition, make a pass

9 **urge upon, press upon,** force upon; **press, ply;** insist

10 **volunteer,** come forward

425 REQUEST

nouns

1 **request,** asking; desire, wish; **petition, address; application;** requisition; demand

224

2 **appeal, plea, bid,** suit, call, cry, clamour; **prayer**

3 **urgency, pressure,** urging, pressing, plying; buttonholing; **teasing,** pestering, plaguing, nagging; **coaxing,** wheedling

4 **invitation,** bidding, call, summons

5 **canvass, canvassing; suit,** addresses; **wooing**

6 **begging,** cadging, scrounging

7 **applicant,** claimant; suitor; wannabe (*nonformal*); **candidate;** bidder

8 **beggar;** tramp

verbs

9 **request, ask, desire,** wish, crave; **ask for,** order, call for; **requisition;** apply for, file for; **demand**

10 **petition; pray,** sue; **apply to**

11 **implore, beseech, beg,** crave, plead, appeal, pray; invoke, appeal to, run to; **plead for,** clamour for, cry for

12 **urge, press,** pressure (*nonformal*), prod, push, ply; buttonhole, besiege; **tease,** pester, plague, nag, bug (*nonformal*); **coax,** wheedle, cajole

13 **invite, ask,** call, summon, call in

14 **solicit, canvass; court, woo;** seek, bid for, look for; **fish for,** angle for

15 **beg,** cadge, scrounge

adjectives

16 **begging,** cadging, scrounging

17 **imploring, beseeching, begging,** pleading, appealing

18 **teasing,** pestering, plaguing, nagging; **coaxing,** wheedling, cajoling; **insistent, demanding,** urgent

426 CONSENT

nouns

1 **consent, assent, agreement,** acceptance, approval, blessing, sanction, endorsement, ratification, backing; affirmative; **leave, permission; willingness,** readiness, promptness, eagerness, connivance; **acquiescence, compliance;** submission

verbs

2 **consent, assent,** be willing, be amenable, accede to, nod; **accept, agree to; approve of,** hold with; **approve, okay** *or* **OK** (*nonformal*); **sanction, endorse,** ratify; **wink at, connive at; be willing;** deign, condescend; permit

3 **acquiesce, comply,** be persuaded, come round; **submit**

adjectives

4 **consenting, assenting,** affirmative, amenable, persuaded, approving, agreeing, favourable, sanctioning, endorsing, ratifying; submissive; **willing, agreeable,** content; ready, prompt, eager; permissive

adverbs

5 approvingly, favourably, positively; willingly; yes

427 REFUSAL

nouns

1 **refusal, rejection,** turning down; declining, denial, repudiation; disagreement, dissent; contradiction; negative, no; unwillingness;

disobedience; withholding, holding back, retention, deprivation

2 **repulse, rebuff**

verbs

3 **refuse, decline, reject, turn down** (*nonformal*), **not have,** not buy (*nonformal*); **say no,** side against, disagree, dissent; negate; vote down; be unwilling; **repudiate,** disclaim

4 **deny, withhold,** hold back; grudge, begrudge

5 **repulse, rebuff, repel;** cut, snub

adjectives

6 **negative; unwilling;** uncooperative; disobedient; deaf to

428 PERMISSION

nouns

1 **permission, leave, allowance, consent;** admission, ticket; licence, liberty; dispensation, release

2 **tolerance, indulgence;** overlooking, connivance; permissiveness

3 **authorization, authority, sanction, licensing, warrant;** empowerment, enabling, entitlement; clearance; ratification

4 **carte blanche,** blank cheque (*nonformal*), full authority, free hand

5 **grant, concession;** charter, franchise, liberty, diploma

6 **permit, licence, warrant;** building permit, driving licence, marriage licence, fishing permit

7 **pass, passport,** safeguard, protection; visa; **clearance**

8 **validity,** legitimacy, legality

verbs

9 **permit, allow, admit, let,** make possible; consent; **grant, accord;** dispense, release, waive

10 **suffer, countenance,** have, tolerate, condone, brook, endure, stomach, bear, stand for; indulge; **wink at,** overlook, connive at

11 **authorize, sanction, warrant;** validate, legalize; empower, enable, entitle; license; **privilege;** enfranchise; accredit, certificate, certify; ratify; **legalize**

12 **may,** can, have permission

adjectives

13 **permissive,** permitting, allowing; consenting; **tolerant,** tolerating, obliging; **indulgent, lenient;** lax

14 **permissible, allowable,** justifiable; **lawful, legitimate, legal,** legalized

15 **permitted, allowed,** admitted, tolerated; unchecked

16 **authorized,** empowered, entitled; **warranted, sanctioned;** licensed, **privileged;** accredited

adverbs

17 **permissively; tolerantly; indulgently**

18 with permission; legally

429 PROHIBITION

nouns

1 **prohibition, forbidding; ruling out,** denial, rejection; refusal; **repression, suppression; ban, embargo, injunction; taboo;** law, statute; exclusion; prevention; forbidden fruit, contraband

2 **veto; thumbs-down** (*nonformal*)

verbs

3 prohibit, forbid, rule out, deny, reject; refuse; ban, embargo, outlaw; **bar,** preclude, exclude, shut out, prevent; **repress, suppress**

4 not have, not endure, not stomach, not bear, not countenance, not brook, not condone, not accept

5 veto, kill

adjectives

6 prohibitive, forbidding, repressive; exclusive, preventive

7 prohibited, forbidden; ruled out; banned, outlawed, contraband; **barred; vetoed; off limits; taboo; illegal,** unlawful, illicit

430 REPEAL

nouns

1 repeal; reversal; suspension; waiving, setting aside; withdrawal; **cancellation,** cancelling, write-off; **abolition; recall**

verbs

2 repeal, revoke, reverse; suspend; waive, set aside; **cancel,** write off; **annul,** withdraw, invalidate, void; **overrule,** override; **abolish; recall,** retract

adjectives

3 repealed, revoked; set aside; invalid, void

431 PROMOTION

nouns

1 promotion, advancement, advance, rise, elevation, upgrading, jump, step up; **boost** (*nonformal*); graduation; pay rise

verbs

2 promote, advance, elevate, upgrade, jump; **raise;** pass, graduate

432 DEMOTION, DEPOSITION

nouns

1 demotion, degrading, degradation, downgrading; humiliation; reduction

2 deposition, deposal, removal, displacement, supplanting, replacement, deprivation, ousting; **firing** (*nonformal*), **dismissal;** kicking upstairs (*nonformal*); **retirement; suspension;** purge, liquidation; **overthrow;** expulsion

verbs

3 demote, degrade, downgrade; debase, humble, humiliate; **lower, reduce**

4 depose, remove, displace, supplant, replace, oust; **dismiss;** kick upstairs (*nonformal*); **retire,** pension off; **suspend;** purge, liquidate; **overthrow;** expel

433 RESIGNATION, RETIREMENT

nouns

1 resignation, withdrawal; **retirement;** abdication

verbs

2 resign, quit, leave, vacate, withdraw from; **retire;** relinquish, give up; stand down, abdicate; pension off

adjectives

3 **retired**, in retirement

434 AID

nouns

1 **aid, help, assistance, support, relief, comfort**, ease, remedy; **service, benefit**; ministry, offices; therapy; protection; **rescue**

2 **helping hand, hand, lift; support group**, self-help group

3 **support, maintenance, sustenance, subsistence**, provision, meal ticket (*nonformal*); **keep, upkeep; livelihood, living**, daily bread; **nurture, fostering**, nourishment, mothering, rearing, care, caring; subsidy, endowment; **social services**

4 **patronage, sponsorship, backing, auspices**, care, guidance, championing, championship, seconding; interest, encouragement, backing; **favour, goodwill**, charity, **sympathy**

5 **furtherance, helping along, advancement, promotion, forwarding**, speeding, expedition, rushing

6 **self-help**, self-improvement; independence

7 **helper, assistant**; benefactor

8 **reinforcements, support, relief**, auxiliaries, reserves, reserve forces

9 **facility, accommodation, appliance, convenience**, amenity; advantage

10 **helpfulness; usefulness**, utility; profitability

verbs

11 **aid, help, assist**, comfort, relieve, ease, doctor, remedy; do good, benefit; **favour, befriend**; cater for; **save**, redeem, bail out (*nonformal*); rescue; protect; resuscitate, rally, revive, restore

12 **support; maintain, sustain, keep; uphold**, hold up, bear, bear up; reinforce, bolster, buttress, shore up, prop; **finance, fund**, subsidize

13 **back, back up; stand by, champion**; second, side with

14 **abet, encourage**, hearten; advocate, countenance, endorse; subscribe, favour, go for (*nonformal*)

15 **patronize, sponsor**, take up

16 **foster, nurture**, nourish, mother, care for, feed, rear, cherish; pamper, cosset; **nurse**, suckle, cradle

17 **be useful, further, forward, advance, promote**, encourage, boost (*nonformal*), favour, facilitate

18 **serve, work for; minister to**, cater to; attend; pander to

19 **oblige, accommodate**, favour

adjectives

20 **helping**, assisting, serving; **assistant, auxiliary**, subservient, subsidiary, ancillary, accessory; fostering; caring

21 **helpful, useful, profitable, salutary**, good for, beneficial; remedial, therapeutic; **serviceable, useful; contributory**, contributing, conducive, constructive, positive

22 **favourable;** kind, kindly, well-intentioned, well-meaning; be-

nevolent, benign; friendly, amicable, neighbourly

adverbs

23 **helpfully**; favourably, profitably, to advantage; **usefully**

435 COOPERATION

nouns

1 **cooperation, collaboration; consensus; community**, harmony, concord, fellowship, fellow feeling, solidarity, teamwork; pooling; team spirit, morale; **collusion, complicity**

2 **affiliation, alliance, allying, alignment, association**, combination, union, unification, coalition, fusion, merger, amalgamation, league, federation, confederation, consolidation, incorporation, inclusion, integration; **partnership; fraternity; fellowship;** camaraderie

verbs

3 **cooperate, collaborate,** concur; harmonize; **join, associate,** ally,combine, unite, fuse, merge, coalesce, amalgamate, confederate, consolidate; partner; **join together,** club together, band together; **work together, pull together; hang together; close ranks,** join in; reciprocate; **conspire,** collude

4 **side with, unite with; join,** align with, range with; act with, rally round, flock to

adjectives

5 **cooperative; collaborative; fellow;** concurrent, concurring, concerted, in concert; agreeing,

in agreement; harmonious; **common, communal,** collective; **mutual,** reciprocal; **joint, combined;** communist; **conniving**

adverbs

6 **cooperatively,** concurrently; in consensus; **jointly;** harmoniously; **together,** communally, collectively; **as one,** unanimously, in chorus, in unison, en masse

7 **in cooperation, in collaboration, in partnership, in cahoots** (nonformal), in collusion, in league

436 OPPOSITION

nouns

1 **opposition, opposing, crossing, standing against; resistance; contention; rejection,** refusal; **contradiction,** challenge, contravention, denial; undercurrent

2 **hostility, antagonism, antipathy,** enmity, bad blood; **obstinacy; friction, conflict,** clashing, collision, cross-purposes, dissension, rivalry, vying, competition

verbs

3 **oppose, counter, cross, go against; protest,** make waves (nonformal); **obstruct,** sabotage; side against, vote against, veto; not abide; counteract; **resist,** withstand

4 **contend against, contest, combat, battle, clash with, take on** (nonformal), grapple with, fight, buck (nonformal), counter; buffet, beat against, breast, stem; rival; fight back, resist

5 **confront, affront,** front, meet, face, meet head-on; **encounter**

6 contradict, cross, contravene, deny, challenge, contest; **belie,** negate; **reject**

adjectives

7 opposing, opposed; at odds, at loggerheads; **adverse, adversary,** repugnant; **contrary, counter; negative; opposite; contradictory;** unfavourable; **hostile, antagonistic,** unfriendly, enemy, inimical, alien; uncooperative; obstructive; perverse, obstinate; **conflicting, clashing;** rival, competitive

adverbs

8 in opposition, in confrontation, head-on, at variance, at cross-purposes, at odds, at issue, at daggers drawn

437 OPPONENT

nouns

1 opponent, adversary, antagonist, assailant, foe, enemy; the opposition, opposite camp; combatant

2 competitor, contestant, contender, player, entrant; **rival**

3 protester, dissident, plaintiff, defendant; intransigent

438 RESISTANCE

nouns

1 resistance, withstanding, countering; **defiance; opposing, opposition; stand; repulsion,** rebuff; **objection, protest, dispute,** challenge, demur; **complaint; dissent;** reaction; revolt; **reluctance; obstinacy;** passive resistance

verbs

2 resist, withstand; **defy; stand; endure;** stand up, bear up, hold up, hold out; **repel, repulse,** rebuff

3 offer resistance, fight back, withstand; confront, meet head-on; **object, protest, dispute,** challenge, complain; **dissent;** make waves (*nonformal*); kick against; **revolt; oppose; contend with; strive against**

4 stand fast, remain firm, hold out

adjectives

5 resistant, resisting, up against, withstanding, repellent; obstructive; rebellious; **proof against; objecting, protesting,** disputing, complaining, dissenting; **reluctant;** uncooperative

439 DEFIANCE

nouns

1 defiance, defying; daring, audacity, boldness, bold front, bravado, insolence; **arrogance;** impertinence; **contempt,** derision, disdain, disregard

2 challenge, dare, double dare; **fighting words; war cry,** battle cry

verbs

3 defy, dare, challenge, cross swords; beard, face, stare down, stare out, **confront; brave**

4 flout, disregard, slight; **disdain, despise, scorn;** laugh at; scoff at, deride

5 bluster, strut, crow, look big

adjectives

6 defiant, defying, challenging; **daring, bold,** brash, brazen, audacious, insolent; arrogant; saucy, cheeky (*nonformal*), impudent, impertinent; cocky; **contemptuous,** disdainful, derisive

440 ACCORD

nouns

1 accord, accordance, concord, harmony; **rapport; sympathy,** empathy, identity, fellow feeling, fellowship, kinship, affinity; **agreement, understanding; compatibility;** unity, unison, union; **community,** communion; solidarity, team spirit; sharing; peace; **love,** charity, brotherly love

verbs

2 get along, harmonize, agree with, harmonize with; **sympathize,** identify with, respond to; **accord;** reciprocate

adjectives

3 in accord, harmonious, in harmony, in tune, attuned, agreeing, amicable; **sympathetic, understanding; like-minded,** akin, at one, united, together; corresponding; agreeable, congenial, compatible; **peaceful**

441 DISACCORD

nouns

1 discord; generation gap; **conflict, friction; jarring,** jangle, clash, clashing; strained relations, tension; bad blood; mischief; **contention; enmity**

2 disagreement, difficulty, misunderstanding, difference, variance, division; cross-purposes; **disparity**

3 dissension, dissent, flak (*nonformal*); bickering; faction; **aggressiveness; irritability**

4 falling-out; alienation, estrangement, disaffection, disfavour; **breach, break, rupture, split, rift,** cleft, disruption, separation, divergence, division

5 quarrel, dispute, argument, controversy, fight, squabble, contention, strife, tussle, wrangle, fuss; **fracas;** words, sharp words; **feud,** blood feud, vendetta; brawl

6 (*nonformal terms*) **row, rumpus,** ructions, hoo-ha, barney, set-to, run-in, scrap, hassle

7 bone of contention, sore point

verbs

8 disagree, differ; conflict, clash, collide, jostle, jangle, jar

9 fall out, break with, split, separate, diverge, divide, part company

10 quarrel, dispute, fight, squabble, bicker, wrangle, have words, set to, join issue; cross swords, feud, battle; **brawl**

11 (*nonformal terms*) **row, scrap, hassle;** lock horns

12 sow dissension, alienate, estrange, separate, divide, come between; **irritate, provoke; set against,** pit against, set on

adjectives

13 discordant, dissident, disagreeing, differing; **conflicting,** clash-

ing, colliding; **divided**, fragmented

14 **at odds, at variance, at loggerheads**, at cross-purposes; at war

15 **partisan, divisive; quarrelsome**,
bickering, wrangling; **aggressive**,
belligerent; touchy, irritable

442 CONTENTION

nouns

1 **contention, contest, combat,
fighting, conflict**, strife, war,
struggle; **warfare**, hostility, enmity; **quarrel, controversy, debate, argument, dispute**; litigation; words; **fighting; quarrel-
ling**, bickering, wrangling,
squabbling; **competitiveness**, vying

2 **competition, rivalry**, vying

3 **contest, engagement, encounter, match**, meet, meeting, trial,
test; fight, bout; tournament, rally; **game; games**, Olympic
Games, Olympics, gymkhana

4 **fight, battle, fray**, combat, action, conflict; **clash; brush, skirmish**; tussle, scuffle, struggle;
quarrel; pitched battle; street
fight; hand-to-hand combat; **internal struggle**

5 **brawl, fracas**, riot

6 **boxing, fighting, fisticuffs**, the
ring; **boxing match**, spar, bout

7 **wrestling**, grappling, sumo; **martial arts**; wrestling match

8 **racing, track; horse racing**, the
turf; dog racing; **motor racing**

9 **race, horse race; motor race;
heat, lap**, lap of honour; run; ob-

stacle race, sack race; walk; boat
race, yacht race

verbs

10 **contend, contest**, jostle; **fight,
battle, combat, war**; wage war;
**strive, struggle; tussle, scuffle;
quarrel**; clash, collide; **wrestle**,
grapple, grapple with; **come to
blows, box**, spar; **cross swords,
fence; duel**; feud; skirmish;
brawl; riot

11 **attack**; jump

12 **engage, take on** (*nonformal*)

13 **contend with, engage with, fight
with, strive with, struggle with**,
wrestle with, grapple with; exchange shots

14 **compete, contend, vie**, jockey
(*nonformal*); **challenge; rival**,
emulate

15 **race**, race with

16 **contend for, strive for, struggle
for, fight for**, vie for

17 **dispute, contest; fight over,
quarrel over, wrangle over,
squabble over**, bicker over

adjectives

18 **contending**, contesting; striving,
struggling, fighting, battling; **warlike; quarrelsome**

19 **competitive**, competing, vying,
rivalling, rival

443 WARFARE

nouns

1 **war, warfare, combat, fighting**,
armed conflict, armed combat,
military operations, the sword,
bloodshed; **hostilities; all-out
war; wartime; battle; attack;
war zone**; trouble spot

2 **deployment;** close formation; echelon

3 **campaign, war, drive, expedition; crusade,** holy war, jihad

4 **operation,** action; **mission; operations;** logistic; war game, manoeuvres; **strategy, tactics; battle**

5 **military science;** war, arms; chivalry, knighthood

6 **declaration of war;** challenge; defiance

7 **call-up, rally; mobilization; muster;** conscription, recruitment; **rallying cry, slogan; battle cry,** war cry; **bugle call**

8 **service, military service;** national service

9 **mobilization;** national emergency; **war effort;** martial law; military dictatorship; arms race

10 **ferocity; hard line; hostility, antagonism; aggression, aggressiveness;** aggro (*nonformal*); **belligerence, truculence,** fight (*nonformal*); **militarism, militancy;** sabre rattling; **chauvinism, jingoism, warmongering**

11 (*rallying devices and themes*) battle flag, banner, colours; fiery cross; battle hymn, national anthem; foreign threat; independence

verbs

12 **war, wage war, make war;** battle, fight

13 **attack; declare war, challenge;** defy; open hostilities

14 **serve; soldier, bear arms,** shoulder arms

15 **call up, rally; mobilize; muster;** conscript, recruit

16 **militarize, activate, mobilize**

adjectives

17 **warlike, militant,** fighting, battling; **martial, military;** contentious; **belligerent, truculent; aggressive,** offensive; fierce, ferocious, savage, bloody, bloodthirsty; **hostile, antagonistic, enemy,** inimical; unfriendly; **quarrelsome**

18 **militaristic, warmongering,** sabre-rattling; **chauvinistic, jingoistic; hard-line**

19 **embattled, engaged,** in combat; **deployed; militarized; armed;** war-torn

444 ATTACK

nouns

1 **attack, assault; offence, offensive; aggression; onset, onslaught; strike;** first strike; **charge, rush; drive, push** (*nonformal*); **sally, sortie;** infiltration; breakthrough; **counterattack;** diversion; assault and battery, mugging (*nonformal*); **pre-emptive strike; blitzkrieg, blitz;** shock tactics

2 **thrust, pass, lunge, swing,** cut, stab, jab; **feint**

3 **raid, foray; invasion, incursion; air raid, air strike;** scaling, boarding

4 **siege;** blockading, blockade; **pincer movement**

5 **storm,** storming, overrunning

6 **bombardment, bombing**

7 **gunfire, fire, firing, shooting;** gunfight; **firepower**

8 volley, salvo, burst, spray, **fusillade, broadside; barrage**

9 stabbing, piercing; **knifing;** the sword

10 assailant, attacker; mugger (*nonformal*); aggressor; invader, raider

11 zero hour; D-day

verbs

12 attack, assault, assail; strike, hit, pound; come at; pounce upon; surprise, ambush

13 (*nonformal terms*) **pitch into, lambaste,** wade into, lay into; **land on; mug** (*nonformal*); jump; **go for**

14 lash out at, hit out at, let fly at, strike out at; thrust at, swing at, lunge at; feint

15 push, thrust, drive; infiltrate; strike; flank

16 charge, rush, rush at, fly at, run at, dash at

17 besiege, encompass, surround, encircle, envelop; **blockade; beset, beleaguer, harass;** soften up

18 raid, foray, **invade;** scale, board; storm, overwhelm, inundate

19 fire at, shoot at; open fire; aim at, level at; snipe at; **bombard, blast,** strafe, **shell;** pepper; rake; cannon; **torpedo; shoot**

20 stab, stick (*nonformal*), **pierce,** plunge in; **run through, impale,** spit; **spear,** bayonet; **knife;** spike

21 pelt, stone

22 hurl at, throw at, cast at, heave at, chuck at (*nonformal*), fling at, sling at, toss at, shy at, fire at, let fly at; hurl against

adjectives

23 attacking, assailing, assaulting, charging, driving, thrusting, advancing; **invading**

24 offensive; aggressive

adverbs

25 under attack, under fire; under siege

445 DEFENCE

nouns

1 defence, guard, ward; **protection;** resistance; self-defence; self-protection, self-preservation; the defensive; **defences,** defence mechanism

2 military defence, national defence; civil defence

3 armour; armour plate; harness; mail, chain mail; **protective covering, thick skin,** shell; spines, needles

4 fortification, work, defence work, bulwark, rampart, fence, barrier; enclosure

5 trench, ditch; moat; bunker; tunnel; mine

6 stronghold, hold, strong point, keep, ward, bastion, citadel, castle, tower; **fort, fortress, post; bunker;** peel

7 defender, champion, advocate; guardian angel, supporter; protector; guard; guard dog, attack dog

verbs

8 defend, guard, shield, screen, secure, guard against; **safeguard, protect;** flank; **advocate, champion; defend oneself**

9 **fortify, arm; armour, man; barricade, blockade;** wall, fence; bank; **dig in;** mine

10 **fend off, ward off, stave off, hold off, fight off,** keep off, beat off, parry, fend, counter, turn aside; stop, check, block, hinder, obstruct; **repel, rebuff, drive back,** put back, push back

adjectives

11 **defensive,** defending, guarding, shielding, screening; **protective**

12 **armoured;** in armour

13 **armed;** under arms; **manned**

446 COMBATANT

nouns

1 **combatant, fighter, contestant, contender, competitor, rival;** militant; gladiator; **knight;** swordsman, blade; **tough, rowdy, ruffian,** thug, hoodlum, hood (*nonformal*), hooligan, bully

2 **boxer, pugilist;** street fighter

3 **bullfighter,** toreador; picador, matador

4 **militarist, warmonger, hawk** (*nonformal*), **chauvinist,** jingoist

5 **serviceman, servicewoman; soldier, warrior,** brave, fighting man; **cannon fodder;** Amazon

6 **enlisted man,** noncommissioned officer; **private**

7 **infantryman, foot soldier;** rifleman; marksman; **sniper**

8 **artilleryman, gunner,** machine gunner; **bomber**

9 **cavalryman, trooper;** dragoon

10 **engineer,** sapper

11 **elite troops, storm troops;** commandos, marines, paratroops; guardsmen, guards

12 **irregular,** casual; **guerrilla,** partisan; underground, resistance, maquis

13 **mercenary, soldier of fortune,** adventurer; gunman, gun, hired gun, hired killer, professional killer

14 **recruit, rookie** (*nonformal*), **conscript,** drafted man, trainee; **raw recruit;** draft

15 **veteran, vet** (*nonformal*), campaigner, old campaigner, old soldier

16 **defence forces, services, armed forces, the forces,** fighting machine; **the military**

17 **branch, corps; service,** Air Force, Army, Navy, Marine Corps

18 (*military units*) **unit, organization, outfit** (*nonformal*); **army,** corps, division; **regiment, battalion, company,** troop, brigade, legion, platoon, section; **task force; squad,** squadron; detachment, detail

19 **army, forces, troops, host,** legions; ranks; regulars; ground forces, ground troops; storm troops; **airborne troops,** paratroops; occupation force

20 **militia;** home guard

21 **reserves,** territorial army

22 **navy, naval forces; fleet,** flotilla, armada, squadron, division, task force; marine, merchant navy, merchant fleet; naval reserve; coast guard

23 **marines,** Marine Corps, Royal Marines

24 air force; squadron, flight, wing

447 ARMS

nouns

1 arms, weapons, military hardware, weaponry, munitions; conventional weapons; nuclear weapons, atomic weapons; biological weapons

2 armoury, arsenal, magazine, dump

3 ballistics, artillery

4 fist, clenched fist; knuckle-dusters; club, blunt instrument

5 sword, blade; steel; knife; dagger; axe

6 arrow, shaft, dart, bolt; barb; flight, volley

7 bow, longbow; crossbow

8 spear, javelin

9 sling; catapult

10 gun, firearm; stun gun; automatic, machine gun, pistol, revolver, rifle, shotgun

11 artillery, cannon; anti-aircraft artillery, flak (nonformal); battery

12 ammunition, ammo (nonformal)

13 explosive; dynamite, gelignite, gunpowder, powder, trinitrotoluene or TNT

14 fuse, detonator; cap, percussion cap; primer

15 charge, load; blast; warhead

16 cartridge, shell

17 missile, projectile, bolt; stone, rock; boomerang; ballistic missile, cruise missile; rocket; torpedo

18 shot; cannonball; bullet, slug, pellet; shell, shrapnel

19 bomb; atomic bomb or atom bomb, hand grenade, hydrogen bomb, letter bomb, Molotov cocktail, neutron bomb, nuclear warhead, plutonium bomb, smart bomb, stink bomb, time bomb; mine

20 rocket launcher, mortar; bazooka

448 ARENA

nouns

1 arena, site, scene, setting, background, field, ground, terrain, sphere, place, locale, milieu, precinct; course, range; campus; theatre, stage, set, scenery; platform; public square; amphitheatre, circus, stadium; hall, auditorium; gymnasium, gym (nonformal); floor, pit; ring, boxing ring, canvas, mat, bull ring; parade ground; field, playing field; stamping ground; turf

2 battlefield, battleground, battle site, combat area; the front, front line, line, firing line; combat zone; theatre

3 camp, encampment, bivouac

449 PEACE

nouns

1 peace; peacetime; harmony, accord

2 peacefulness, tranquillity, serenity, calmness, quiet, quietness; order, orderliness

3 pacifism; nonviolence

4 civilian, citizen

5 pacifist, peace lover, dove (nonformal); conscientious objector

verbs

6 **keep the peace;** defuse

adjectives

7 **peaceful; tranquil, serene;** idyllic, pastoral; halcyon, soft, calm, quiet, restful, untroubled, orderly, at peace; bloodless

8 **civilian; antiwar, peaceable;** meek; pacifist; **nonviolent;** conciliatory

450 PACIFICATION

nouns

1 **conciliation, appeasement;** calming, soothing

2 **peace offering; olive branch; white flag;** peace pipe; outstretched hand; cooling-off period

3 **reconciliation, reunion**

4 **adjustment,** accommodation, resolution, compromise, arrangement, settlement, terms

5 **truce, armistice, peace; ceasefire;** buffer zone, neutral territory

6 **disarmament;** unilateral disarmament; **demilitarization, demobilization,** disbanding; civilian life, civvy street (*nonformal*)

verbs

7 **pacify, placate, appease, mollify; calm, settle, soothe,** tranquillize; smooth; allay; cool (*nonformal*), defuse

8 **reconcile, bring together,** reunite; **harmonize,** restore harmony; adjust, settle, compose, accommodate, settle differences, resolve, compromise; fix up (*nonformal*); mediate

9 **make peace,** cease hostilities, cease fire, stand down

10 **shake hands,** come round, come together, meet halfway

11 **disarm; demilitarize, demobilize,** disband

adjectives

12 **conciliatory,** mollifying, appeasing; **pacifying, soothing**

451 MEDIATION

nouns

1 **mediation,** mediating, intercession; **intervention,** stepping in, involvement

2 **arbitration;** mediatorship

3 **mediator, intermediary; medium; go-between, middleman;** connection (*nonformal*); deputy, agent; **spokesman, spokeswoman,** spokesperson; **mouthpiece; negotiator**

4 **arbiter,** third party; **umpire, referee, judge;** magistrate

5 **conciliator;** marriage guidance counsellor

verbs

6 **mediate, intermediate, intercede; intervene,** step in, involve oneself; represent; **negotiate,** bargain, treat with, meet halfway; **arbitrate, moderate; umpire, referee,** judge

7 **settle, arrange,** compose, patch up, adjust, straighten out; make peace

adjectives

8 **mediating;** intermediary; intermediate, middle, intervening

452 NEUTRALITY

nouns

1 **neutrality; independence; evasion, cop-out** (*nonformal*), abstention; **impartiality**

2 **indifference;** apathy

3 **middle ground,** centre; meeting ground; grey area; **happy medium;** mean, golden mean; moderation; compromise; half measures

4 **neutral; independent**

verbs

5 **remain neutral; evade, cop out** (*nonformal*), abstain

adjectives

6 **neutral;** uncommitted; **indifferent;** passive; apathetic; even, fifty-fifty (*nonformal*); **moderate,** midway; **independent; impartial**

453 COMPROMISE

nouns

1 **compromise,** composition, adjustment, accommodation, settlement, mutual concession, give-and-take; bargain, deal (*nonformal*), arrangement, understanding, **concession,** giving way, yielding; surrender

verbs

2 **compromise,** compound, compose, accommodate, adjust, settle; **meet halfway,** go fifty-fifty (*nonformal*); play politics; steer a middle course; **make concessions,** give way, yield; **surrender,** evade responsibility, sidestep

454 POSSESSION

nouns

1 **possession; owning; title;** squatting; **claim, legal claim;** occupation; **hold, holding, tenure; tenancy, lease;** feud; colony; mandate; preoccupation; **property**

2 **ownership, title; dominion, sovereignty;** land tenure

3 **monopoly,** monopolization

verbs

4 **possess, have, hold, occupy, fill, enjoy,** boast; **command;** claim; squat

5 **own, have title to**

6 **monopolize;** tie up; **corner the market** (*nonformal*)

7 **belong to,** pertain to; vest in

adjectives

8 **possessed, owned, held; own; in hand;** on hand, in stock

9 **possessing, having, holding, occupying, owning; possessed of,** master of; **endowed with, blessed with;** worth; landed

10 **possessive, proprietory**

455 POSSESSOR

nouns

1 **possessor, holder,** keeper

2 **proprietor, owner; master, mistress, lord; landlord, landlady;** squire, country gentleman; householder

3 **landowner,** property owner; landed gentry; absentee landlord

4 **tenant, occupant,** occupier, incumbent, resident; **lodger,** paying guest

456 PROPERTY

nouns

1 **property, possessions, holdings,** goods, chattels, effects, one's all; acquisitions, receipts; **inheritance**

2 **belongings,** trappings, paraphernalia, accessories; **things,** material things; consumer goods; **personal effects**

3 **luggage, baggage,** tackle, apparatus, truck, gear, kit

4 **estate, interest, stake,** part, percentage; **right, title, claim,** holding; use, trust, benefit; settlement

5 **real estate; land, lands,** property, grounds, acres; lot, parcel, plot; manor

6 **assets, means, resources;** stock; **worth;** circumstances, funds; wealth; **material assets,** tangible assets; frozen assets, liquid assets

adjectives

7 **propertied; landed**

8 **real;** feudal

457 ACQUISITION

nouns

1 **acquisition,** gaining, getting, coming by, attainment, winning; addition; **earnings,** making

2 **collection,** gathering, gleaning, bringing together, assembling, accumulation, heaping up

3 **gain, profit,** percentage (*nonformal*); **gains, profits, earnings,** winnings, return, returns, proceeds, bottom line (*nonformal*); makings; **income; receipts;**

fruits; **booty, spoils;** net profit; gross profit; capital gains; interest, dividends; hoard, store; wealth

4 **profitability,** gainfulness

5 **yield, output,** make, production; **proceeds,** produce, product; **crop, harvest,** fruit, vintage

6 **find,** finding, discovery; buried treasure; **windfall, bonus**

7 **godsend, boon, blessing**

verbs

8 **acquire, get, gain, obtain, secure, procure; win;** score; **earn,** make; **reap, harvest;** contract; take, catch, capture; **net; come into, come by;** draw, derive

9 (*nonformal terms*) **grab,** bag, catch, collar, cop, dig up, grub up, round up, drum up, scratch together, hook, land, throw together, pick up, nail; take home

10 **take possession, appropriate, take up,** take over

11 **collect, gather, glean, pick, pluck,** cull, take up, pick up, scrape together; heap up, amass, assemble, accumulate

12 **profit, make money;** gain by, capitalize on; **gross, net;** realize, clear

13 **be profitable,** pay, repay, pay off (*nonformal*)

adjectives

14 **obtainable, available,** accessible

15 **acquisitive;** grasping; **greedy**

16 **gainful, productive, profitable, lucrative,** fat, paying, high-yielding, advantageous, worthwhile

adverbs

17 **profitably, gainfully;** for money; to advantage

458 LOSS

nouns

1 **loss, losing, privation; deprivation,** bereavement, taking away, stripping, robbery; **sacrifice, forfeit,** denial; **expense, cost, debit;** detriment, injury, damage; **destruction, ruin;** losing streak (*nonformal*); **loser**

2 **waste, wastage, exhaustion, depletion,** sapping, depreciation, diffusion, wearing away, erosion; moulting, shedding; **using up, consumption, expenditure, drain;** stripping, impoverishment; leakage, evaporation; decrease

3 **losses;** net loss, bottom line (*nonformal*)

verbs

4 **lose,** incur loss, suffer loss; **forfeit,** default; **sacrifice; miss,** wander from; **mislay; lose everything**

5 **waste, deplete, depreciate,** dissipate, wear away, erode, consume, drain, shrink, dribble away; **moult, shed;** decrease; squander

6 **dissipate, leak, leak away**

adjectives

7 **lost, gone;** forfeited, forfeit; long-lost; wasted, consumed, depleted, dissipated, diffused, expended; **worn away, eroded,** used up, shrunken; stripped;

clear-cut; squandered; irretrievable

8 **bereft, bereaved,** divested, deprived of, shorn of, parted from, stripped of, dispossessed of, robbed of; **out of,** minus (*nonformal*), wanting, lacking; cut off; **penniless, destitute, broke** (*nonformal*)

adverbs

9 **at a loss, unprofitably**

459 RETENTION

nouns

1 **retention, keeping, holding, maintenance, preservation;** locking in, suppression, repression, inhibition; **tenacity**

2 **hold, purchase, grasp, grip, clutch, clamp, clinch, clench;** seizure; bite, nip; clinging; foothold, footing; **clasp, hug, embrace,** bear hug

3 (*wrestling holds*) half-nelson, full nelson, stranglehold, lock, scissors, bear hug

4 **clutches, claws, talons; nails,** fingernails; **pincers; tentacles; fingers,** digits; **hands,** paws (*nonformal*); **jaws; teeth,** fangs

verbs

5 **retain, keep, save;** maintain, preserve; lock in, suppress, repress

6 **hold, grip, grasp, clutch, clinch, clench;** bite, nip; grapple; **clasp, hug, embrace;** cling to, stick to, adhere to; **hold on, hang on** (*nonformal*); **seize**

7 **hold, keep, harbour,** bear, have; **cherish,** entertain, treasure; **fos-**

ter, **nurture, nurse;** embrace, hug, cling to

adjectives

8 **retentive,** gripping, grasping; **tenacious,** clinging; vicelike

adverbs

9 **for keeps** (*nonformal*), **to keep, for good,** for always; forever

460 RELINQUISHMENT

nouns

1 **relinquishment, release,** giving up, letting go, dispensation; **disposal,** disposition, dumping; **renunciation,** swearing off, resignation, abandonment; **surrender,** turning over, yielding; sacrifice

verbs

2 **relinquish, give up, surrender, yield,** render up, cede; spare; resign, vacate; drop, waive, dispense with; **forgo,** do without, renounce, swear off; **abandon;** retract; **part with,** give away, dispose of, dump; **sacrifice;** sell off

3 **release,** let go

adjectives

4 **relinquished, released, surrendered, yielded,** ceded; waived, dispensed with; renounced; **abandoned;** retracted; disposed of; **sacrificed**

461 PARTICIPATION

nouns

1 **participation, sharing,** contribution, association; **involvement,** engagement; complicity; **voting,**

suffrage; partnership, joint control; joint ownership

2 **communion, community,** cooperation; **social life,** socializing; collective enterprise, kibbutz; **democracy;** state ownership, communism, socialism; profit sharing

3 **participant, player;** party, accomplice, accessory; **partner;** shareholder

verbs

4 **participate, take part, contribute,** chip in, get involved; **join in,** figure in; **join up,** sign on, enlist; **vote; enter into,** go into; sit in, sit on

5 **share, share in, divide with,** halve, go halves; cooperate

6 **socialize, nationalize**

adjectives

7 **participating, participant;** involved, engaged; implicated, accessory; **sharing**

8 **communal, common,** general, public, collective, popular, social; **mutual,** reciprocal, associated, joint, in common

462 APPORTIONMENT

nouns

1 **apportionment, division, partition,** partitioning, budgeting, rationing, dividing, sharing, sharing out, splitting, cutting, slicing

2 **distribution, disposal,** disposition; doling out, giving out, passing round; **dispensation,** administration; paying out; redistribution

3 **allotment, assignment, appoint-**

ment, setting aside, earmarking;
allocation

4 **dedication, commitment,** devotion, consecration

5 **portion, share, interest, part,**
stake, stock, piece, bit, segment;
**lot, allotment, proportion, per-
centage,** measure, quota, helping; **contingent; dividend; commission; equal share, half; lion's
share;** modicum; **allowance, ration, budget; load,** work load;
fate, destiny

verbs

6 **apportion, portion, parcel, partition, part, divide;** share; **split,**
carve, cut, slice

7 **proportion,** divide *pro rata*

8 **parcel out, portion out,** measure
out, serve out, deal out, dole out,
hand out, mete out, ration out,
give out, hand round, pass
round; **distribute,** disperse; **dispense,** issue, administer; pay out

9 **allot, assign, appoint, set;** detail;
allocate, earmark; set
off, mark off, portion off; assign
to; reserve, restrict to; **ordain,
destine, fate**

10 **budget, ration**

11 **dedicate, commit, devote, consecrate,** set apart

adjectives

12 **apportioned,** portioned out, par-
celled, allocated, etc; **divisible,**
dispensable

13 **proportionate,** proportional; *pro
rata;* **half; equal; respective,** particular, per head, per capita

adverbs

14 **proportionately, in proportion,**
pro rata; **respectively,** severally

463 GIVING

nouns

1 **giving, donation, endowment;
presentation; award;** grant,
granting; accordance; **delivery,**
surrender; **concession,** communication; **contribution,** subscription; accommodation, supplying,
provision; **offer**

2 **commitment, consignment,** assignment, delegation, commendation

3 **charity; philanthropy**

4 **gift, present,** presentation, offering; **award,** tribute; **free gift,**
freebie (*nonformal*); peace offering

5 **gratuity, bounty; perks** (*nonformal*); **tip,** sweetener, inducement, consideration; **premium,
bonus;** incentive pay, time and a
half, double time; bribe

6 **donation; contribution, subscription; charity; handout**
(*nonformal*), pittance; **offering,**
collection

7 **benefit,** benevolence, blessing

8 **subsidy,** support; **grant; allowance, stipend,** allotment; **aid,** assistance; **help;** scholarship, fellowship; **welfare,** dole; alimony;
pension, social security; unemployment benefit; income support; Family Credit

9 **endowment,** investment, settlement, foundation; **dowry**

10 **bequest, legacy;** inheritance; **will, testament**

11 **giver, donor,** presenter; fairy godmother, Santa Claus, sugar daddy (*nonformal*); **contributor, subscriber,** supporter, backer; patron; **philanthropist**

verbs

12 **give, present, donate,** slip (*nonformal*); **bestow, confer, award, allot;** impart, communicate; **grant,** accord, allow, yield, afford, make available; **tender,** proffer, offer, extend; **issue, dispense,** administer; serve, help to; **distribute;** deal, dole, mete; pour, shower, rain, snow, heap, lavish

13 **deliver, hand, pass,** reach, forward; transfer; **hand over, turn over;** hand out, give out, pass out, distribute, circulate; hand in, give in; **surrender**

14 **contribute, subscribe;** pledge; give to, donate to

15 **furnish, supply, provide, afford;** accommodate with, favour with, indulge with; **heap upon,** pour on, lavish upon

16 **commit, consign, assign, delegate,** relegate; **entrust,** trust

17 **endow with,** favour with, bless with, grace with, vest with

18 **bequeath, will, leave,** hand down, hand on, pass on

19 **subsidize, finance, fund; aid, assist,** support, help; **pension off**

20 **thrust upon, force upon,** press upon

21 **give away,** dispose of, part with, sacrifice, spare

adjectives

22 **charitable,** philanthropic; giving, liberal, generous

23 **presentable;** allowable

24 **given,** allowed, accorded, granted, bestowed, etc; gratuitous

25 contributory; testate; intestate

26 **endowed,** invested

adverbs

27 on one, on the house, free

464 RECEIVING

nouns

1 **receiving, reception, receipt, getting, taking; acquisition;** derivation; **assumption, acceptance;** admission, admittance

2 **inheritance, heritage, legacy,** bequest; **succession; heirloom**

3 **recipient, receiver,** taker; holder, trustee; **viewer,** beholder, audience, listener, spectator

4 **beneficiary;** pensioner

5 **heir; heiress;** heir apparent; **successor**

verbs

6 **receive, get, gain, secure,** have, come by; **obtain, acquire; admit, accept, take; take in;** assume, take on, take over; **derive, draw;** take home

7 **inherit, come into;** succeed to

8 **be received, come in**

adjectives

9 **receiving; receptive**

465 TAKING

nouns

1 **taking,** possession, taking possession, taking away; **claiming; acquisition; reception; theft**

2 **seizure, seizing,** grabbing, snatching; **kidnapping, abduction; coup; hold; catching; capture; apprehension; arrest**

3 **rape,** violation, indecent assault, sexual assault, date rape; taking; statutory rape

4 **appropriation, taking over, takeover** (*nonformal*), **adoption, assumption;** requisition; preoccupation; **conquest,** occupation, subjugation, enslavement

5 **attachment, annexation; confiscation; commandeering;** nationalization, socialization

6 **deprivation,** privation, bereavement

7 **dispossession; repossession,** reclaiming; **eviction**

8 **extortion, blackmail; protection racket**

9 **pillaging, looting**

10 **catch,** capture, seizure, haul; booty

11 **taker;** catcher, captor

12 **extortionist, blackmailer; predator; vulture,** shark

verbs

13 **take,** possess, take possession; **get;** pocket; **claim; acquire; receive;** steal

14 **seize; grab, grasp, grip, grapple, snatch, clutch,** claw, clench; **clasp, hug, embrace;** loot; **kidnap, abduct,** snatch (*nonformal*), carry off

15 **rape,** ravish, violate, assault sexually; **take**

16 **seize on; catch at, snatch at,** jump at, scramble for

17 **catch, take,** hook, snag, snare, spear, harpoon; entangle; **net; bag; trap;** trap

18 **capture, apprehend, collar** (*nonformal*), **grab** (*nonformal*), take prisoner; **arrest**

19 **appropriate, adopt, assume;** requisition; **take over;** hog (*nonformal*), monopolize; **conquer,** overrun, occupy, subjugate, enslave

20 **confiscate,** impound; **commandeer,** press; **expropriate,** nationalize, socialize

21 **take from, deprive of,** relieve of; **deprive, divest;** tap, milk, mine, drain, bleed

22 **wrest,** wring, wrench; **extort, exact,** blackmail, squeeze, screw

23 **dispossess,** expropriate; **evict; disinherit, disown,** cut off

24 **strip, fleece** (*nonformal*), divest, pick clean; **milk; bleed white;** exhaust, drain, suck dry; **impoverish**

adjectives

25 **taking, catching;** private

26 **rapacious, ravenous, predatory;** parasitic; **grasping, insatiable**

466 RESTITUTION

nouns

1 **restitution, restoration,** restoring, giving back, return; extradition; repatriation

2 **reparation, recompense,** paying back, repayment, refund, compensation; retribution, redress, amends

3 **recovery,** regaining; **retrieval;** recapture; resumption; reclaiming; **redemption,** salvage; **restoration**

verbs

4 **restore, return, give back;** take back, bring back; repatriate; extradite

5 **make amends,** atone, redress, pay back, repay, reimburse, refund, compensate; pay damages

6 **recover, regain, retrieve, recoup, get back; redeem; reclaim; repossess,** resume; recapture, take back

adjectives

7 compensatory; reimbursable

adverbs

8 in compensation, in retribution

467 THEFT

nouns

1 **theft, stealing,** thieving; **filching;** shoplifting; poaching; **graft; embezzlement; fraud, swindle**

2 **larceny,** petit or petty larceny

3 **theft, robbery,** robbing; **mugging; pickpocketing; hijacking;** extortion

4 (*nonformal terms*) **heist,** job; **ripoff**

5 **burglary,** break-in, unlawful entry

6 **plundering, pillaging, looting, sacking,** ransacking, rifling; **raiding, ravaging; sack; marauding,** foraging; raid, foray

7 **piracy; buccaneering;** hijacking

8 **plagiarism, piracy,** borrowing, cribbing

9 **abduction, kidnapping,** snatching (*nonformal*)

10 **booty, spoils, loot, swag** (*nonformal*), **plunder,** prize, haul

11 sticky fingers; kleptomania

verbs

12 **steal, appropriate, take,** snatch, abstract; **filch;** poach; rustle; **embezzle;** swindle; **extort**

13 **rob;** pick pockets; hold up

14 burgle (*nonformal*); crack a safe

15 (*nonformal terms*) **swipe, pinch,** lift, rip off, nick; **stick up; mug;** hijack

16 **plunder, pillage, loot, sack,** ransack, rifle, raid, ravage, ravish; **fleece;** foray, forage

17 **plagiarize, pirate,** borrowing, cribbing

18 **abduct,** spirit away, magic away; **kidnap, snatch** (*nonformal*)

adjectives

19 **thieving, light-fingered;** fraudulent

20 **plundering, looting,** ravaging, marauding; predatory

21 **stolen;** pirated, plagiarized; **hot** (*nonformal*)

468 THIEF

nouns

1 **thief, robber, crook** (*nonformal*); shoplifter; poacher; **swindler,** con man; grave robber, body snatcher; embezzler

2 **burglar;** housebreaker, cat burglar; **safecracker**

3 **bandit**, brigand; **gangster; thug,**
hoodlum

4 **robber**; highwayman; **mugger**
(*nonformal*); **hijacker**

5 **marauder, raider**

6 **pirate, buccaneer**

7 **plagiarist, pirate,** cribber (*non-*
formal)

8 **abductor, kidnapper**

469 PARSIMONY

nouns

1 **parsimony;** frugality; **stinting,**
scrimping, skimping; **economy**

2 **niggardliness, meanness**

3 **stinginess,** tight-fistedness, mi-
serliness, hoarding; **avarice**

4 **miser, skinflint**

verbs

5 **stint, scrimp,** skimp, starve;
grudge, begrudge

6 **withhold,** hold back

adjectives

7 **parsimonious, sparing, stinting,**
scrimping, skimping; frugal

8 **niggardly, grudging, mean,**
shabby, sordid

9 **stingy,** tight-fisted, miserly; **ava-**
ricious

470 LIBERALITY

nouns

1 **liberality,** freedom; **generosity,**
unselfishness; bounty; **hospital-**
ity, welcome

verbs

2 **give freely; spare no expense;**
heap upon, lavish upon

adjectives

3 **liberal, free; generous,** large,
handsome; **unselfish; lavish,**
profuse; **hospitable,** gracious;
giving; magnanimous

adverbs

4 **liberally, freely; generously,**
handsomely; **unselfishly; lavish-**
ly, profusely; graciously; without
stint

471 PRODIGALITY

nouns

1 **extravagance;** profusion; **waste;**
squandering

2 **prodigal;** prodigal son

verbs

3 **squander, lavish,** blow (*nonfor-*
mal); **dissipate,** scatter (*old*), sow
broadcast; **run through,** go
through; **throw away;** gamble
away

4 **waste,** consume, spend, expend,
use up, exhaust; spill

5 **fritter away,** fool away, dribble
away, trifle away, potter away,
muddle away; idle away, while
away

adjectives

6 **prodigal, extravagant, lavish,**
profuse, **wasteful;** incontinent;
easy come, easy go

7 **wasted, squandered, dissipated,**
consumed, spent, used, lost

472 CELEBRATION

nouns

1 **celebration,** celebrating; **obser-**
vance, remembrance, memory;
jubilee; **holiday;** anniversaries;

festivity; revel; rejoicing; **ceremony;** religious rites; ovation, triumph; **tribute;** testimonial; toast; **salute;** fanfare; dressing ship

verbs

2 **celebrate, observe, keep, mark,** honour; commemorate; hold jubilee; **make merry;** dress ship

adjectives

3 celebrating; commemorating; memorial; solemn

adverbs

4 in honour of, in commemoration of, in memory of

473 HUMOROUSNESS

nouns

1 hilarity; wittiness; **absurdity,** eccentricity, incongruity; the funny side; slapstick quality

adjectives

2 **humorous, funny, amusing, witty;** whimsical; ludicrous, ridiculous, hilarious, absurd, quaint, eccentric, incongruous, bizarre; priceless, rich, hysterical; farcical, slapstick, broad

adverbs

3 **humorously, amusingly,** funnily, broadly; ludicrously, ridiculously, absurdly, incongruously

474 WIT, HUMOUR

nouns

1 **wit, humour,** pleasantry, salt; ready wit, quick wit, nimble wit, agile wit, pretty wit; dry wit, subtle wit; **comedy;** black humour, sick humour, gallows humour;

satire, sarcasm, irony; **parody,** travesty, **caricature; farce,** mere farce; **slapstick,** slapstick humour, broad humour; visual humour

2 pleasantry, **joking;** frivolity, flippancy, merriment; trickery; clowning, clowning around; fooling, **banter**

3 **joke, jest, wheeze, fun, sport, play; story, yarn, funny story,** good story; sick joke (*nonformal*); ethnic joke; capital joke, good one, laugh, belly laugh, scream, riot; visual joke; **point,** punch line

4 **witticism,** pleasantry, **quip,** conceit, smart saying, retort; gibe; **pun; old joke,** chestnut (*nonformal*)

5 **prank,** trick, practical joke

6 **wit, comic, joker;** wag; zany; **comedian,** clown; gag writer (*nonformal*)

verbs

7 **joke, jest, quip,** make fun; pun; sparkle; gibe at, mock, scoff at; ridicule

8 trick, **play a joke** *or* trick on; clown around

adjectives

9 **witty, amusing, humorous, comic, comical,** farcical; **funny; jocular, joking,** tongue-in-cheek; facetious, whimsical; smart, clever, brilliant, sparkling; keen, sharp, pungent, pointed, biting; **satirical, sarcastic, ironic,** ironical; salty, salt; **playful**

adverbs

10 **wittily, humorously;** in fun, in sport, in play, in jest, in joke, jokingly; for fun, for sport

475 BANTER

nouns

1 **banter,** pleasantry, fooling, fooling around, rallying, **sport,** good-natured banter, harmless teasing; ridicule; exchange, give-and-take

2 **joking, fooling, teasing**

3 (*nonformal terms*) **kidding,** joshing, fooling around; ribbing

verbs

4 **banter,** twit, chaff, rally, **joke, jest, tease**

5 (*nonformal terms*) **kid,** jolly, fool around, rib; needle

adjectives

6 **bantering;** kidding (*nonformal*), **fooling, teasing**

476 COWARDICE

nouns

1 **cowardice; fear;** weakness, softness; **timidity**

2 **cold feet** (*nonformal*), weak knees, chicken heart, **yellow streak** (*nonformal*), white feather

3 **coward,** invertebrate, **weakling,** weak sister (*nonformal*), mouse, baby, **big baby, chicken** (*nonformal*); white feather

verbs

4 **dare not, lose one's nerve,** lose courage, falter, boggle, **chicken out** (*nonformal*); back out; turn

tail, **run scared** (*nonformal*), scuttle

5 **cower, quail, cringe, crouch, skulk, sneak, slink**

adjectives

6 **cowardly, coward; afraid, fearful;** timid, **chicken** (*nonformal*); weak, soft; daunted, dismayed, unmanned, cowed, intimidated

7 **cowering, cringing;** skulking, sneaking, slinking, sneaky

adverbs

8 **cowardly,** spiritlessly; wimpishly

477 COURAGE

nouns

1 **courage, nerve,** pluck, **bravery,** boldness, gallantry, conspicuous gallantry, prowess, virtue; **heroism;** chivalry; manhood, virility; Dutch courage (*nonformal*)

2 (*nonformal terms*) **balls, guts,** spunk, backbone

3 **daring,** bravado, audacity, tightrope walking; enterprise

4 **fortitude,** grit, **stamina,** pith (*old*), bottom; **heart,** spirit, stout heart; **resolution,** tenacity, bulldog tenacity

5 **exploit, feat, deed, enterprise, achievement, adventure, bold stroke; heroic deed**

6 (*brave person*) **hero, heroine;** brave, stalwart, gallant, valiant, a man, valiant knight, good soldier; the brave; decorated hero; David; lion, **tiger,** bulldog, fighting cock

7 **encouragement, heartening, inspiration,** assurance, reassurance

verbs

8 **dare, venture,** take risks; defy

9 **brave, face, confront,** front, meet; set at; speak up, speak out; head into, face up, grapple with; **brazen;** beard

10 face down, face out; brazen out; stare down, outstare

11 **steel oneself,** nerve oneself; take courage, take heart, bear up

12 **encourage, hearten, nerve,** assure, reassure, bolster, support, cheer on, root for; **inspire;** cheer

adjectives

13 **courageous, brave, bold,** valiant, gallant, intrepid, hardy, stalwart, stout; **heroic,** chivalrous, manly, virile, macho

14 **resolute, tough,** game; spirited, tenacious

15 **confident, fearless,** undaunted

16 **daring, audacious, adventurous,** enterprising; foolhardy

adverbs

17 **courageously, bravely, boldly, heroically, gallantly,** stoutly; resolutely

478 RASHNESS

nouns

1 brazen boldness, **indiscretion,** insolence; **temerity**

2 **recklessness,** carelessness; **haste,** hotheadedness

3 **audacity,** boldness, presumption, **daring**

4 **daredevil,** devil, wild man, **adventurer**

verbs

5 be rash, be reckless, court danger, risk all

adjectives

6 **rash,** brash, imprudent, indiscreet, unwary; impudent, insolent, brazen

7 **reckless;** careless; impetuous, hasty, hurried; furious, desperate, mad, wild, wanton; precipitate, precipitous; headlong, breakneck

8 **foolhardy,** harebrained, wild, **audacious;** forward, bold, presumptuous; daring, adventurous

adverbs

9 **rashly,** brazenly; **recklessly,** carelessly; hastily, hurriedly; furiously, desperately, wildly, madly, **headlong**

479 CAUTION

nouns

1 **caution;** care, heed, solicitude; thoroughness; hesitation, hesitancy; deliberate stages, **prudence, discretion,** coolness; calculation, deliberation, careful consideration, prior consultation; safety first; hedge, hedging

2 **suspicion, distrust,** mistrust

3 **precaution, forethought, foresight,** providence, provision; precautions, steps, measures; **safeguard,** protection, preventive measure, safety net, safety valve, sheet anchor; **insurance**

verbs

4 **be cautious, be careful;** think twice; tiptoe

5 **take precautions,** forearm; guard against, make sure, **play safe** (*nonformal*); shorten sail, reef down, hedge

6 **beware, take care,** take heed; mind; **look out, watch out** (*nonformal*); **look sharp;** stop, look, and listen; lie low; hold one's tongue

adjectives

7 **cautious, careful,** mindful, thorough; prudent, circumspect, noncommittal, uncommitted; sly, crafty, scheming; **discreet,** judicious; gingerly; **guarded,** on guard; uncommunicative; **tentative,** cool; **deliberate;** safe

8 **wary, cagey** (*nonformal*), **suspicious,** suspecting, **distrustful,** shy

9 **precautionary, preventive,** foreseeing; provisional

adverbs

10 **cautiously, carefully,** prudently, discreetly, judiciously; **gingerly,** easy (*nonformal*), with caution, with care; warily, suspiciously

480 FASTIDIOUSNESS

nouns

1 **fastidiousness, particularity;** scrupulousness; precision; **meticulousness,** conscientiousness; **taste; sensitivity,** discrimination; **selectiveness,** choosiness; **strictness,** perfectionism; puritanism, prudishness, propriety

2 **nicety, delicacy,** daintiness, refinement, **subtlety**

3 **exclusiveness,** selectness; cliquishness; snobbery

4 **perfectionist,** nitpicker (*nonformal*); fusspot (*nonformal*), fuss

verbs

5 **fuss,** fuss over; disdain, scorn, spurn

adjectives

6 **fastidious, particular,** scrupulous, meticulous, conscientious, exacting, precise; **sensitive,** discriminating; **selective,** choosy; critical, **strict;** puritanical, prudish, proper

7 **finicky, fussy, squeamish,** difficult

8 **nice, dainty, delicate,** fine, refined, exquisite, **subtle**

9 queasy; hypercritical; hypersensitive; **compulsive,** anal

10 **exclusive,** selective, **select,** elect, elite; **snobbish**

adverbs

11 **fastidiously,** scrupulously, meticulously, conscientiously, critically; selectively; **fussily;** subtly

481 TASTE, TASTEFULNESS

nouns

1 **taste, good taste,** quality, excellence, elegance, grace; **refinement,** finesse, polish, **culture, cultivation;** delicacy, **subtlety,** sophistication; discrimination

2 **decorum,** decency, propriety, right thinking, fitness, suitability; civility

3 **restraint, understatement,** unobtrusiveness; simplicity

4 **connoisseur, judge, critic, expert,** authority, arbiter, **gourmet;**

virtuoso; amateur; culture vulture (nonformal)

adjectives

5 **tasteful; excellent; aesthetic,** artistic, pleasing, choice; pure, chaste; restrained, understated, unobtrusive, quiet, subdued, simple, unaffected

6 **elegant,** graceful, gracious; **refined, polished, cultivated,** civilized, **cultured;** fine, delicate, dainty, **subtle, sophisticated, discriminating,** fastidious

7 **decorous,** decent, proper, right, **becoming,** fitting, appropriate, suitable, meet; genteel; civil, urbane

adverbs

8 **tastefully,** in good taste; aesthetically, artistically; elegantly, gracefully; decorously, decently, properly; quietly; simply

482 VULGARITY

nouns

1 **vulgarity,** commonness, meanness; **inelegance,** indelicacy, impropriety, **indecency;** inappropriateness, unsuitableness; tastelessness, tackiness (nonformal), bad taste

2 **coarseness, rudeness,** crudity, roughness, **obscenity**

3 **unrefinement, uncouthness;** wildness; impoliteness, ill breeding; **barbarism,** philistinism, savagery; **brutality, mindlessness**

4 boorishness; hooliganism

5 **commonness,** ordinariness, homeliness; **lowness, meanness**

6 Philistine; **boor, lout,** peasant; **ruffian,** rowdy, hooligan

7 **barbarian, savage,** animal, brute

adjectives

8 **vulgar, inelegant, indelicate, indecent, improper, unseemly,** inappropriate, unsuitable, undignified; tasteless, tacky (nonformal), offensive

9 **coarse, rude, crude,** crass, rough, earthy; **obscene;** loud (nonformal), gaudy

10 **unrefined, uncouth;** uncivilized; impolite, ill-bred; **wild,** barbarous; primitive; **savage,** brutal, mindless

11 **boorish,** loutish; rowdy

12 **common,** commonplace, ordinary; homely; **general, public, popular**

13 **low, base, mean,** ignoble, vile

adverbs

14 **vulgarly, inelegantly,** indelicately, indecently, improperly, offensively; **coarsely, rudely, crudely,** roughly

483 ORNAMENTATION

nouns

1 **ornament; decoration,** decor; **adornment, embellishment,** embroidery, elaboration; garnish; trimming; flourish; illumination; colour, colour scheme; **arrangement,** flower arrangement; window dressing

2 **ornateness, elegance, elaborateness;** ostentation; luxuriousness; floridity; gaudiness, flashiness; flamboyance

3 **finery,** frippery, trappings; **frills,** fuss (*nonformal*)

4 **trinket,** bauble; bric-a-brac; **jewellery**

5 **jewel, gem,** precious stone; pin, brooch; **ring,** earring, nose ring; bracelet, anklet; chain, necklace; locket; beads; bangle; charm; fob; crown, tiara

6 **motif, figure, detail,** form, touch; **pattern, theme,** design; **background,** setting, foil, style

verbs

7 **ornament, decorate, adorn,** dress, trim, garnish, array, **deck,** beautify; **embellish,** embroider, enrich; paint, colour; **dress up;** preen; smarten up

8 **spangle;** bead; tinsel; jewel; flounce; garland; feather, plume; illuminate; paint; engrave

adjectives

9 **ornamental, decorative,** adorning, embellishing

10 **adorned, decorated, embellished,** decked out, garnished, trimmed; figured; flowered; festooned, wreathed; spangled; jewelled; studded; feathered

11 **ornate, elegant, fancy,** fine; picturesque; **elaborate, ostentatious; rich, luxurious,** luxuriant; flowery; florid; flamboyant, fussy, frilly, busy; cluttered

484 PLAINNESS

nouns

1 **plainness, simplicity, ordinariness, commonness, homeliness, purity, chasteness**

2 **naturalness; unaffectedness, unpretentiousness;** directness, straightforwardness; innocence, naivety

3 **bareness,** baldness, nakedness, nudity, undress

4 **austerity,** severity, starkness

verbs

5 **simplify;** chasten, purify; spell out

adjectives

6 **simple, plain, ordinary,** nondescript, common, commonplace, prosaic, **matter-of-fact,** homely, everyday, household; pure, chaste

7 **natural; unaffected,** unassuming, direct, straightforward, honest, candid; innocent, naive

8 **unadorned, undecorated;** nononsense, uncomplicated, **unsophisticated,** unadulterated; **undressed;** bare, bald, blank, naked, nude

9 **unelaborate,** austere, severe, stark

adverbs

10 **plainly, simply,** ordinarily, commonly

11 **naturally,** directly, straightforwardly

485 AFFECTATION

nouns

1 **affectation; pretension,** pretence, airs, **show;** front, **facade, image,** public image; **hypocrisy;** sham; artificiality, insincerity

2 **mannerism, quirk,** habit, peculiarity, idiosyncrasy, trademark

3 **posing, pose, posturing**

4 preciousness; formality, pedantry; euphemism

5 **prudishness, primness, stuffiness** (*nonformal*); sanctimony, puritanism; **false modesty,** demureness

6 **fake** *and* **fraud** (*both nonformal*); actor, performer

7 **poser, poseur, posturer;** prude, puritan

verbs

8 **affect,** assume, put on, wear, **pretend,** simulate, counterfeit, sham, fake (*nonformal*), **feign,** play

9 **pose, posture;** mince; simper

adjectives

10 **affected, pretentious; mannered, artificial, unnatural,** insincere; theatrical, histrionic; conceited

11 **assumed, pretended,** simulated, feigned, counterfeited; spurious, sham; hypocritical

12 precious, mincing, simpering, pedantic, euphemistic

13 **prudish, prim, smug, stuffy** (*nonformal*), demure, straitlaced, sanctimonious, **puritanical**

adverbs

14 **affectedly, pretentiously;** for effect, for show

15 **prudishly,** primly

486 OSTENTATION

nouns

1 **ostentation, pretension, pretence;** loftiness

2 **pretensions; airs,** airs and graces

3 **showiness,** flamboyance, panache, dash, glitter, dazzle; **gaudiness, razzmatazz** (*nonformal*), tawdriness; **garishness, blatancy,** brazenness, extravagance

4 **display, show, demonstration,** manifestation, **exhibition,** parade, **pageantry, spectacle;** blazon, flourish, flaunting; **exhibitionism,** showing off; theatrics, histrionics, dramatics

5 **grandeur, magnificence, splendour,** resplendence, brilliance, glory; nobility, **stateliness,** majesty; **elegance,** lavishness, luxuriousness; **luxury**

6 **pomp,** circumstance, solemnity, formality

7 **pomposity, stuffiness** (*nonformal*), self-importance

8 **swagger, strut,** swaggering, strutting; swashbuckling

9 **show-off** (*nonformal*), **exhibitionist;** swaggerer

verbs

10 **come forward,** attract attention

11 **cut a dash;** shine, glitter, dazzle

12 **put on airs,** put on; strut, swagger, prance

13 **show off** (*nonformal*); **flaunt, parade,** display, demonstrate, **exhibit,** air, put forward; advertise; **flourish,** brandish, wave; trumpet

adjectives

14 **ostentatious, pretentious; ambitious, lofty, fancy,** classy (*nonformal*)

15 **showy, flashy,** flashing, glittering, **jazzy** (*nonformal*); jaunty,
dashing; gallant, brave, daring;
frilly, flouncy, frothy

16 **gaudy, tawdry; garish,** loud
(*nonformal*), **blatant,** flagrant,
brazen, lurid, extravagant, sensational, **spectacular,** glaring,
screaming (*nonformal*)

17 **grandiose, grand, magnificent,
splendid, glorious,** superb, fine,
fancy; **imposing, impressive,**
awesome; **noble,** stately, majestic, sumptuous, elegant, elaborate, luxurious, extravagant

18 **pompous,** self-important; **bombastic;** solemn, formal

19 **strutting, swaggering;** swashbuckling

20 **theatrical, dramatic,** histrionic;
spectacular

adverbs

21 **ostentatiously,** pretentiously

22 **showily;** dashingly; gallantly,
bravely

23 **blatantly, flagrantly,** shamelessly, **brazenly,** sensationally, **spec-
tacularly,** glaringly

24 **grandly, magnificently, splendidly,** gloriously, superbly; nobly,
proudly, majestically; impressively; elaborately, luxuriously, **extravagantly**

25 **pompously,** bombastically

487 BOASTING

nouns

1 **boasting, bragging; boastfulness; boast, brag;** bombast, bravado; bluster, swagger; vanity,

conceit; big talk *and* hot air
(*both nonformal*)

2 **crowing,** elation, triumph, jubilation; **gloating**

3 **braggart, boaster;** blusterer

verbs

4 **boast, brag,** blow one's own
trumpet; bluster, swagger

5 (*nonformal terms*) blow, mouth
off, sound off

6 **flatter oneself, congratulate
oneself,** pat oneself on the back

7 **exult,** triumph, glory, delight;
crow; **gloat**

adjectives

8 **boastful, bragging;** vain, conceited

9 **self-approving,** self-praising,
self-advertising, self-promoting

10 **inflated,** swollen, **bombastic,**
pretentious

11 **crowing,** exultant, jubilant, **triumphant, gloating**

adverbs

12 **boastfully;** self-approvingly

13 **jubilantly,** triumphantly, in triumph

488 BLUSTER

nouns

1 **bluster,** blustering, bullying,
swagger; bravado, rant; fuss,
bustle, flurry; bluff; intimidation;
boastfulness

2 **blusterer, swaggerer, bully;**
ranter, hector; bluff; **braggart**

verbs

3 **bluster, swagger;** bully; sputter,

splutter; rant, rage, rave, storm;
bluff; intimidate; sound off, **brag**

adjectives

4 **blustering**, hectoring, **bullying**,
swaggering, boisterous; ranting,
raging, raving, storming; tumultuous; noisy

489 COURTESY

nouns

1 **courtesy, politeness, civility;**
graciousness; thoughtfulness,
tact, consideration; respect, deference; civilization

2 **gallantry, chivalry**

3 **manners,** good manners; correctness, **etiquette**

4 **good breeding; refinement,** finish, polish, culture, cultivation;
gentility, gentleness, elegance

5 **suaveness, smoothness;** oiliness,
smarminess (*nonformal*); **glib-**
ness; sweet talk

6 **amenities, courtesies, civilities;**
graces; formalities, ceremonies,
rites, rituals, observances

7 **regards, compliments, respects,**
best wishes, love; greetings; re-
membrances

8 **gallant, cavalier, knight**

verbs

9 mind one's manners, mind one's
P's and Q's (*nonformal*)

10 **extend courtesy,** do the honours, pay one's respects

adjectives

11 **courteous, polite, civil, urbane,**
gracious, agreeable, affable, fair;
obliging,   accommodating;
thoughtful, considerate, tactful,

solicitous; respectful, deferential,
attentive

12 **gallant, chivalrous; formal,** cer-
emonious; old-fashioned

13 **well-mannered,**   well-behaved,
correct

14 **well-bred; cultivated, cultured,**
polished, refined, genteel; gentlemanly, ladylike

15 **suave, smooth,** glib, oily, ingratiating, disarming

adverbs

16 **courteously, politely, civilly; gal-**
lantly, chivalrously; **graciously;**
respectfully, attentively

490 DISCOURTESY

nouns

1 **discourtesy; impoliteness; rude-**
ness, bad *or* ill manners, **ill**
breeding; inconsiderateness,
tactlessness, **insensitivity; vul-**
garity, coarseness, crudeness, offensiveness

2 **disrespect; insolence**

3 **gruffness, brusqueness, curt-**
ness, abruptness, bluntness;
harshness, roughness, severity;
aggressiveness; surliness, churl-
ishness

adjectives

4 **discourteous, impolite; rude,**
uncivil, ungracious; disrespectful;
insolent

5 **unmannerly, ill-mannered**

6 **vulgar,** boorish, unrefined, **in-**
considerate, tactless, insensitive;
offensive, crass, **coarse, crude**

7 **gruff, brusque, curt,** short, abrupt, **blunt,** bluff; brash; **harsh,**

rough, severe; aggressive; **surly**, churlish

adverbs

8 **discourteously, impolitely, rudely;** inconsiderately, tactlessly, insensitively

9 **gruffly, brusquely, curtly,** sharply, abruptly, bluntly; harshly

491 RETALIATION

nouns

1 **retaliation, reciprocation,** exchange, interchange, give-and-take; **retort, reply,** return, comeback *(nonformal)*; counter, counterblast, recoil, backlash

2 **reprisal, requital,** retribution; compensation, reward, comeuppance *(nonformal)*, **just deserts, revenge; punishment**

verbs

3 **retaliate, retort,** counter, **strike back; reciprocate**

4 **requite,** recompense, compensate, reward, redress, make amends, **repay, pay back**

5 **get even with** *(nonformal)*, settle the score *(nonformal)*, take revenge; **punish**

adjectives

6 **retaliatory; retributive;** reparative, compensatory, reciprocal; punitive

adverbs

7 **in retaliation,** in exchange, **in return,** in reply; **in revenge**

492 REVENGE

nouns

1 **revenge,** vengeance; **wrath;** retaliation, reprisal; vendetta, feud

2 **vindictiveness,** rancour, grudgefulness, implacability

verbs

3 **revenge,** avenge; **retaliate, get even with**

adjectives

4 **vengeful,** avenging; **vindictive; punitive;** wrathful, grudgeful, irreconcilable, implacable; **retaliatory**

493 RIDICULE

nouns

1 **ridicule, derision, mockery;** scoffing, jeering, sneering, sniggering, smirking, grinning, leering, flippancy, fooling, taunting, booing, hooting, hissing; **banter**

2 **gibe, scoff, jeer,** flout, mock, barracking; **taunt,** quip, jest, **insult; caustic remark;** cutting remark; parting shot

3 **boo,** booing, **hoot,** catcall; **hiss**

4 snigger, **smirk,** leer, **sneer,** snort

5 **sarcasm, irony, cynicism, satire,** invective, innuendo

6 **lampoon, parody, satire, farce,** mockery, imitation, pastiche, takeoff *(nonformal)*, **travesty, caricature**

7 **laughing stock,** derision, mockery, figure of fun, jest, joke, **butt,** target, game, **fair game,** victim, dupe, fool, monkey, mug

verbs

8 **ridicule,** deride; **roast** (*nonformal*), **insult;** make fun of, poke fun at; **laugh at**

9 **scoff, jeer,** gibe, barrack, **mock,** rail at, **taunt;** dig at; sneer

10 **boo, hiss, hoot,** catcall, whistle at

11 **lampoon, satirize,** parody, caricature

adjectives

12 **ridiculing,** derisory; **mocking, scoffing,** jeering, sneering, sniggering, smirking, grinning, leering, flippant, fooling, taunting, booing, hooting, hissing, kidding, teasing

13 **satirical; sarcastic, ironic,** sardonic, cynical, dry; caustic

14 **burlesque, farcical,** broad, slapstick

adverbs

15 **derisively,** mockingly

494 APPROVAL

nouns

1 **approval; sanction,** acceptance, countenance, favour; admiration, esteem, respect; endorsement, vote, adherence, blessing, seal of approval, nod, OK

2 **applause, acclaim;** clap, clapping, **cheer; hand,** big hand; **ovation,** standing ovation

3 **commendation,** good word, acknowledgement, recognition, appreciation; **boost** *and* **buildup** (*both nonformal*); promotion; **blurb** *and* **plug** *and* **hype** (*all nonformal*)

4 **recommendation;** advocacy, patronage; **reference, credential, testimonial;** character reference

5 **praise; laudation;** glorification, exaltation, honour; eulogy; accolade; **tribute,** homage; congratulation; flattery; idolatry, adulation, hero worship

6 **eulogist;** praiser, promoter; **applauder; fan** *and* **buff** (*both nonformal*), adherent; **flatterer**

verbs

7 **approve, approve of, sanction, accept; admire, esteem, respect;** endorse, bless, OK; hold with, uphold; favour

8 **applaud,** acclaim, hail; **clap, cheer;** root for (*nonformal*), cheer on

9 **commend;** boost (*nonformal*), promote; plug *and* tout *and* hype (*all nonformal*); **recommend, advocate,** support, back

10 **praise;** eulogize, pay tribute, salute; **extol, glorify,** exalt, bless; blow up, puff up; boast of, brag about (*nonformal*); celebrate, trumpet; flatter; idolize, deify

11 **espouse,** take up; **campaign for,** push for (*nonformal*)

12 **compliment,** pat on the back, congratulate

13 **meet with approval,** pass muster, recommend itself

adjectives

14 **commendatory, complimentary,** eulogistic, **appreciative;** admiring, respectful; flattering

15 **approving, favourable,** favouring, **pro,** well-disposed, supporting, backing, **advocating;** promoting, promotional

16 uncritical; adulatory, fulsome

17 approved, favoured, backed, advocated, supported; favourite; **accepted,** received, admitted; **recommended,** admired, applauded, **acclaimed; popular**

18 praiseworthy, worthy, **commendable,** admirable, creditable; exemplary, model; deserving; **good**

495 DISAPPROVAL

nouns

1 disapproval, disfavour, disrespect; **displeasure,** distaste, **dissatisfaction,** discontent, indignation, **unhappiness,** disillusionment, disenchantment, disappointment; disagreement, **opposition;** rejection, exclusion, ban; **complaint, protest,** objection, **dissent**

2 deprecation, denegration; **ridicule;** disparagement; **contempt**

3 censure, blame, denunciation, decrying, indictment, **condemnation,** damnation; castigation

4 criticism, flak (*nonformal*), bad press, **aspersion;** niggle, quibble, exception; **censoriousness,** reproachfulness; **faultfinding,** carping, quibbling, niggling, nitpicking, pestering, nagging

5 reproof, rebuke, reprimand, reproach, **scolding,** chiding; admonishment; **correction,** castigation, chastisement; lecture, lesson, sermon

6 berating; revilement, vilification, **abuse,** invective; **tirade,** diatribe; **attack, assault,** onslaught; abusiveness, acrimony

7 dirty look (*nonformal*), frown, scowl

8 faultfinder, critic, nitpicker (*nonformal*), censor; **complainer**

verbs

9 disapprove; disfavour, frown on, turn up one's nose at; **object to, oppose, reject,** disallow; vote down, veto, exclude, ostracize, ban; **dissent from,** protest

10 deprecate, denigrate, **fault,** put down (*nonformal*), pick holes in; **ridicule;** deprecate, disparage; disdain, **despise**

11 censure, blame, reproach, **condemn,** damn; **denounce, accuse,** decry, indict

12 criticize; pan and **knock** and **slam** and **hit** (*all nonformal*), snipe at

13 find fault, take exception, pick holes; carp, quibble, nitpick

14 nag, niggle, carp at, **pester,** pick on (*nonformal*), bug and hassle (*both nonformal*)

15 reprove, rebuke, reprimand, scold, chide, admonish, upbraid, **lecture;** correct, **chastise;** take to task, bring to book

16 (*nonformal terms*) **dress down,** tell off, come down on, **bawl out,** give hell

17 berate, rail at, fulminate against, bark at; **revile,** vilify, execrate, abuse

18 attack, assail; castigate, flay, lash, **roast** (*nonformal*)

adjectives

19 disapproving, displeased, dissatisfied, discontented, disgruntled, indignant, **unhappy;** disillusioned, disenchanted, disappointed; unfavourable, low, poor, **opposed, opposing,** against, down on, dissenting; **uncomplimentary;** unappreciative

20 **condemnatory,** censorious, reproachful; deprecatory; **derisive,** ridiculing, scoffing; **disparaging; contemptuous; abusive**

21 **critical, faultfinding,** quibbling, cynical; nagging, niggling

22 **uncommendable; objectionable,** exceptionable, unacceptable

23 **blameworthy,** to blame, at fault; **reprehensible; culpable**

adverbs

24 **disapprovingly,** unfavourably; critically, reproachfully

496 FLATTERY

nouns

1 **flattery, adulation; praise;** blandishment, cajolery, wheedling; blarney *and* soft soap (*both nonformal*); sweet talk, honeyed words; **compliment;** fawning, **sycophancy**

2 **flatterer, adulator;** cajoler, wheedler; brown-nose, **sycophant**

verbs

3 **flatter;** cajole, wheedle; **praise, compliment;** fawn upon

4 honey, **butter up,** soften up; blarney; lay it on thick (*nonformal*); play up to, get around

adjectives

5 **flattering, adulatory; complimentary;** cajoling, wheedling; fulsome, slimy, gushing, smarmy (*nonformal*); insincere; **fawning, sycophantic, obsequious**

497 DISPARAGEMENT

nouns

1 **disparagement, faultfinding, detraction,** deprecation, **belittling;** sour grapes; slighting, discrediting, decrying; **disapproval; contempt;** indignity, disgrace, comedown (*nonformal*)

2 **defamation; vilification,** revilement, blackening, denigration; **smear,** character assassination; muckraking, mudslinging

3 **slander, scandal, libel;** backbiting, cattiness *and* bitchiness (*both nonformal*)

4 **aspersion,** slur, **remark,** insinuation, suggestion, innuendo

5 **lampoon, send-up** (*nonformal*), **satire,** burlesque; hatchet job

6 **disparager,** detractor, **knocker** (*nonformal*), **critic; slanderer,** muckraker, mudslinger; **cynic**

verbs

7 **disparage, belittle,** slight, degrade, debase, **put down** (*nonformal*); **discredit,** disgrace; detract from; decry; disapprove of; hold in contempt

8 **defame, malign,** bad-mouth (*nonformal*); cast aspersions on; **slur**

9 **vilify, revile,** defile, sully, soil, smear, tarnish, **blacken,** denigrate; **call names,** give a bad name, stigmatize

10 **slander, libel**

11 **lampoon, satirize;** parody, send up (*nonformal*)

adjectives

12 disparaging, derogatory, depre-catory, pejorative, catty *and* bitchy (*both nonformal*), con-temptuous, derisory, ridiculing; **snide,** insinuating; **defamatory, slanderous,** libellous

498 CURSE

nouns

1 **curse,** damnation, denunciation; blasphemy

2 **vilification,** abuse, invective; **dis-paragement**

3 **cursing, swearing,** profanity, ob-scenity, filth

4 **oath, curse; swearword** (*nonfor-mal*), expletive, obscenity

verbs

5 **curse, damn,** blast; excommuni-cate; blaspheme

6 **curse, swear**

7 **vilify, abuse,** call names; **swear at,** damn

adjectives

8 **cursing; abusive;** blasphemous, profane, foul, vile, **dirty** (*nonfor-mal*), **obscene**

9 **cursed,** bloody (*nonformal*), **damned, damn;** blasted, dashed; ruddy

499 THREAT

nouns

1 **threat, menace;** powder keg, timebomb; **foreboding; warning;** scare tactics, **intimidation**

verbs

2 **threaten, menace,** bludgeon; ter-rorize, **intimidate;** loom; fore-bode; **warn**

adjectives

3 **threatening,** menacing; immi-nent; **ominous,** foreboding; abu-sive; **intimidating,** bludgeoning, bullying, terrorizing

adverbs

4 under duress *or* threat, at gun-point *or* knifepoint

500 FASTING

nouns

1 **fasting; starvation; hunger strike**

2 **fast,** starvation diet, bread and water

3 **fast day;** Lent; Yom Kippur; Ramadan

verbs

4 **fast,** not eat, go hungry

501 SOBRIETY

nouns

1 **sobriety,** soberness; temperance

verbs

2 **sober up;** sleep it off; dry out

adjectives

3 **sober;** clearheaded; dry, temper-ate

4 **nonalcoholic,** soft

502 SIGNS, INDICATORS

nouns

1 **sign,** telltale sign, sure sign, **in-dex, indicator,** measure; **symp-**

tom; note, **mark**, hallmark, **badge, banner, stamp, signature, seal, trait, characteristic,** peculiarity, idiosyncrasy, **property;** image, picture, **representation; insignia**

2 **symbol, emblem, icon, token; allegory; symbolism; logo** (*nonformal*)

3 **indication,** identification, differentiation, **designation,** denomination; highlighting; **specification,** naming, pointing, selection; hint, suggestion; **expression, manifestation;** show, disclosure

4 **pointer,** index, **lead; direction, guide; arrow;** hand, hour hand, minute hand, **needle,** compass needle; **signpost**

5 **mark, marking;** scratch, scratching, **score,** cut, hack, gash; bar code; nick, notch; **scar; brand, earmark; stigma; stain;** blemish, **spot,** blotch, patch, splash; **dot,** point; **speck, speckle,** fleck, freckle, mole; **birthmark,** strawberry mark; beauty spot; prick, puncture; tattoo

6 **line,** score, **stroke,** slash, diagonal, **dash, stripe, strip, streak,** bar, band; dotted line; **underline,** underscore; hatching

7 **print, imprint, impression,** dent, indentation; **stamp, seal; fingerprint,** thumbprint; **footprint,** footstep; paw print; **bump, stud,** pimple, lump

8 **track, trail,** path, course, **line,** wake; signs, traces, **scent**

9 **clue, key, tip-off** (*nonformal*); **trace, vestige,** scent, whiff; lead; **evidence; hint,** intimation, suggestion

10 **marker, mark;** bookmark; **landmark;** bench mark; **milestone; lighthouse,** tower; platform, watchtower; **buoy; monument**

11 **identification,** identification mark; **badge,** identification tag, dog tag (*military*), personal idenitfication number *or* PIN, **identity card** *or* **ID card; card,** business card, calling card, visiting card, press card; signature, initials; credentials; serial number; DNA print, genetic fingerprint; fingerprint

12 **password, watchword;** token

13 **label, tag;** ticket; **stamp, sticker; seal;** stub, counterfoil; **brand, brand name,** trade name; **trademark,** registered trademark; **hallmark;** price tag; bookplate; imprint, title page; letterhead

14 **gesture, gesticulation; motion,** movement; carriage, bearing, posture, poise, pose, stance; body language; shrug; charade; **pantomime;** sign language; hand signal

15 **signal, sign;** wink, glance, leer; nod; nudge, poke, kick, touch; **alarm; beacon; flare; rocket,** Roman candle; **traffic signal,** traffic light

16 **call,** summons; whistle; **bugle call,** trumpet call; last post; **alarm; battle cry,** war cry

verbs

17 **signify,** stand for, identify, differentiate, speak of, talk of, **indicate,** argue, **characterize, mark,** highlight, **denote, mean;** testify, give evidence; **show, express, display, manifest, hint,** suggest, reveal, **disclose;** entail, involve

18 **designate, specify;** name, denote; **symbolize, stand for,** typify; **point to,** refer to, allude to; pick out, select; **point out,** point at

19 **mark;** pencil, chalk; mark out, define; **mark off, check off,** tick, chalk up; punctuate; point; **dot, spot,** blotch, dash, **speck,** fleck; blemish; **brand, stain, discolour;** stamp, seal, punch, impress, imprint, **print, engrave; score,** scratch; gash, scar; nick, notch; **line, seam,** trace, **stripe, streak;** hatch; **underline;** prick, puncture, tattoo, riddle, pepper

20 **label, tag,** tab, ticket; stamp, seal; **brand, earmark;** hallmark

21 **gesture, gesticulate; motion,** motion to; beckon; shrug; mime, ape, take off

22 **signal, sign;** speak; nod; nudge, poke, kick, touch; wink, glance, leer; **wave, flag; salute;** hail

adjectives

23 **indicative;** indicating, signifying; **significant,** meaningful; symptomatic, diagnostic; **suggestive,** demonstrative; representative; identifying; individual, peculiar, idiosyncratic; **emblematic, symbolic;** typical; metaphorical

24 **marked, designated,** flagged; signed; individualized, personal

503 MEANING

nouns

1 **meaning, significance,** point, **sense,** idea; **reference;** extension; denotation; undertone, overtone, colouring; relevance, bearing, relation; **substance, gist,** pith, spirit, essence; **drift,** tenor; sum; **literal meaning; secondary meaning, connotation;** effect, force, impact, consequence, response; implied meaning, **implication**

2 **intent, intention,** purpose, aim, object, design, plan

3 **explanation,** definition, **interpretation**

4 **meaningfulness, suggestiveness,** expressiveness, pregnancy; **significance;** intelligibility, readability

verbs

5 **mean, signify, denote, connote,** import, spell; **stand for, symbolize; imply,** suggest, argue, **indicate; refer to;** mean something, have impact, come home

adjectives

6 **meaningful, significant; symbolic, metaphorical,** figurative, allegorical; intelligible, readable; **suggestive,** indicative, **expressive; pregnant, pithy,** substantial; pointed

7 **meant,** implied, **intended**

8 **semantic;** symbolic, verbal, phrasal, lexical

adverbs

9 **meaningfully, significantly;** suggestively; **expressively**

504 LATENT MEANINGFULNESS

nouns

1 latency; **potentiality,** possibility

2 implication, connotation, import, implied meaning; **suggestion,** allusion; tinge, undertone, overtone, undercurrent, intimation, touch, nuance, innuendo; **hint; inference, supposition,** assumption, presumption; **symbolism, allegory**

verbs

3 be latent, underlie, lurk, lie beneath, hibernate, lie dormant

4 imply, implicate, involve, import, entail; mean; **suggest, hint,** insinuate, infer, intimate; **allude to; suppose, presuppose,** assume, presume

adjectives

5 latent, lurking, hidden, obscured, veiled, muffled, covert, cryptic; **underlying,** submerged; hibernating, sleeping, dormant; **potential,** virtual, possible

6 suggestive, allusive, indicative; insinuating; ironic; implicative

7 implied; meant, indicated; **suggested, intimated,** insinuated, hinted; inferred, supposed, assumed, presumed, presupposed; hidden, esoteric, **cryptic**

8 tacit, implicit, implied, understood

9 unspoken, undeclared, wordless, silent; **unmentioned, untold;** unwritten, unrecorded

10 symbolic, allegorical, figurative, metaphorical

adverbs

11 latently; potentially, virtually

12 suggestively, allusively, insinuatingly

13 tacitly, implicitly, wordlessly, silently

505 MEANINGLESSNESS

nouns

1 meaninglessness, senselessness; insignificance; noise, static; inanity, emptiness; purposelessness, aimlessness, futility

2 nonsense, rubbish; humbug; rant, claptrap, absurdity; **babble,** gabble, jabber; **gibberish,** jargon

3 (*nonformal terms*) bull, rubbish, rot, double Dutch, balls, tripe, hot air, gas, wind, waffle

verbs

4 be meaningless, mean nothing, signify nothing; not figure (*nonformal*), not compute; **not register**

5 talk nonsense, waffle, babble, gabble, jabber, prattle, rattle

adjectives

6 meaningless, senseless, insignificant; empty, inane; garbled, scrambled; **aimless**

7 nonsensical, silly; **foolish,** absurd

adverbs

8 meaninglessly, senselessly, nonsensically; insignificantly; aimlessly

506 INTELLIGIBILITY

nouns

1 intelligibility, comprehensibility; articulateness

2 clarity; plainness, distinctness, explicitness, definition; **lucidity,** transparency; **simplicity,**

straightforwardness, directness; **coherence**, consistency, structure

3 **legibility**, readability

verbs

4 **be understandable, make sense;** be obvious, be self-evident

5 **get over** or **across, register** (*nonformal*), **penetrate,** sink in

6 **make clear; simplify,** spell out (*nonformal*); elucidate, **explain, clarify;** decode, decipher

7 **understand,** comprehend, **know,** conceive, realize, appreciate; **fathom,** follow; grasp, seize, **take in, catch on; master, learn; assimilate,** absorb, digest

8 **perceive, see,** discern, **make out;** see daylight (*nonformal*), wake up to; **see through,** penetrate, pierce

adjectives

9 **intelligible, comprehensible; understandable;** readable; articulate

10 **clear, plain,** distinct, **definite,** defined, **clear-cut,** crisp; **direct, literal;** simple, **straightforward;** explicit; unmistakable, unequivocal, unambiguous; **lucid,** transparent, translucent; **coherent,** connected, consistent

11 **legible, readable;** clear

adverbs

12 **intelligibly, understandably, comprehensibly; clearly,** lucidly, **simply,** plainly, distinctly; **coherently; explicitly; unmistakably,** unequivocally, unambiguously

13 **legibly,** readably

507 UNINTELLIGIBILITY

nouns

1 **unintelligibility, incomprehensibility, impenetrability; incoherence;** inarticulateness; **ambiguity**

2 **complexity,** intricacy, **complication;** hardness, difficulty

3 **obscurity;** unclearness, opacity; **vagueness,** indistinctness, fuzziness, shapelessness; mist, fog, darkness

4 **illegibility;** scribble, scrawl

5 **expressionlessness,** impassivity; straight face

6 **inexplicability;** mystery, strangeness

7 **enigma,** mystery, puzzle; **problem; question;** riddle

verbs

8 **be incomprehensible,** lose one, not penetrate; **baffle, perplex,** riddle; babble, ramble, drivel

9 **not understand,** not get (*nonformal*); be lost; escape one; give up, pass (*nonformal*)

10 **make unintelligible,** scramble, jumble; **obscure,** mystify; **complicate**

adjectives

11 **unintelligible,** incomprehensible, inscrutable, impenetrable; **ambiguous; incoherent,** unconnected, rambling; **inarticulate**

12 **difficult, hard,** tough (*nonformal*); intricate, **complex, complicated; scrambled,** jumbled, garbled; obscure

13 **obscure, vague, indistinct,** indeterminate, fuzzy, shapeless, amorphous; **unclear, opaque,**

muddy, **dark**, dim; **murky**, cloudy, foggy, hazy, misty

14 abstract; **profound**, deep; hidden; **secret**

15 enigmatic, cryptic; **perplexing**, puzzling

16 inexplicable, indefinable, funny, **unaccountable;** mysterious, mystical

17 illegible, unreadable, **unclear;** indecipherable

18 impassive; uncommunicative; **expressionless; vacant, empty,** blank; glassy, glazed, fishy, wooden; deadpan

adverbs

19 unintelligibly, incomprehensibly

20 obscurely, vaguely, indistinctly; **unclearly;** illegibly

21 inexplicably, unaccountably, enigmatically; mysteriously

22 vacantly, blankly, emptily

508 LANGUAGE

nouns

1 language, speech, tongue, spoken language, natural language; **talk,** parlance, phraseology, **idiom, lingo** (*nonformal*); dialect; **usage**

2 dead language, ancient language, lost language; classical language; living language

3 mother tongue, native tongue, vernacular, first language

4 standard language; national language, official language; literary language, written language

5 nonformal *or* informal language *or* speech, spoken language, colloquial language *or* speech; vernacular; **slang;** colloquialism

6 dialect, idiom; patois; regional accent

7 jargon, lingo (*nonformal*), slang, cant, patois, patter, vernacular; vocabulary, phraseology; taboo language, vulgar language; obscene language

8 lingua franca, jargon, pidgin, trade language; creole

9 polyglot, linguist, **bilingual,** multilingual

verbs

10 speak, talk, communicate verbally; cant; patter

adjectives

11 linguistic; philological; lexicological; syntactic, **grammatical;** semantic; phonetic

12 vernacular, colloquial, **conversational,** nonformal, informal, spoken, vulgar; familiar, common, everyday; **substandard,** uneducated

13 taboo

14 idiomatic; dialectal; provincial, regional, local

509 SPEECH

nouns

1 speech, talk, talking, speaking, **discourse,** communication; **words, accents;** chatter; conversation; elocution; **language**

2 utterance, speaking; speech act; **voice,** tongue; **word**

3 remark, statement, word, say, utterance, observation, reflection, expression; thought, **mention;** assertion, allegation, pro-

nouncement; **declaration;** interjection, exclamation; question; answer; address, greeting; sentence, phrase

4 articulateness, **eloquence**

5 **articulation,** uttering, voicing, vocalization; pronunciation, utterance; **delivery,** attack

6 **intonation, inflection;** tone, pitch

7 manner of speaking; **tone of voice, voice, tone;** voice quality, **timbre**

8 **accent,** regional accent, brogue, twang, burr, drawl, broad accent; **foreign accent**

9 **accent; emphasis, stress, word stress;** beat; rhythm, rhythmic pattern; **cadence; stress pattern**

10 **speech sound,** phone; articulation; **consonant;** semivowel; **vowel;** diphthong; **syllable**

11 **talker, speaker;** chatterbox; conversationalist

12 tongue; vocal cords, vocal folds; voice box, larynx, Adam's apple; lips, teeth, palate; nasal cavity, oral cavity, pharynx, throat

verbs

13 **speak, talk; mouth; chatter;** converse

14 yap, gab, jaw, rattle away, natter, sound off

15 **speak up, speak out,** speak one's mind, **pipe up,** sound off, break silence

16 say, utter, breathe, sound, **voice,** vocalize, **articulate,** enunciate, pronounce; whisper; **express,** verbalize; **word,** formulate, couch, phrase; **present,** deliver; **emit,** give, raise, let out; chorus,

chime; **tell, communicate; convey,** impart, disclose

17 **state, declare, assert,** affirm, allege; **say, announce, relate, recite;** quote; proclaim

18 **remark, comment, observe, note; mention;** refer to, allude to, touch on; muse, reflect; interject; blurt out, exclaim

19 murmur, mutter, mumble, whisper, breathe, sigh; gasp, pant; exclaim, yell; sing, lilt, warble, chant, coo, chirp; squeak; cackle, crow; bark, yelp, yap; growl, snap, snarl; hiss; grunt, snort; roar, bellow, bawl, boom; scream, shriek, screech, squeal; whine, wail, sob; drawl, twang

20 **address,** speak to, talk to, **appeal to,** invoke; **approach; accost,** call to, hail, greet, salute

21 inflect, modulate, intonate

adjectives

22 **speech; language, linguistic, spoken,** uttered, said, **voiced,** verbalized, pronounced, sounded, articulated, enunciated; vocal; **oral, verbal,** unwritten

23 **phonetic;** articulatory, acoustic; pitched, tonal, tonic; accented, stressed; unaccented, unstressed; articulated; muted, nasal, twangy; soft; hard; **consonant; vowel;** syllabic

24 **speaking, talking;** articulate, talkative; **eloquent,** well-spoken; plain-speaking, loud-speaking, **outspoken,** soft-spoken

adverbs

25 **orally, vocally, verbally,** by word of mouth

510 IMPERFECT SPEECH

nouns

1 **speech defect,** speech impediment; **broken speech;** indistinct *or* blurred speech; loss of voice, muteness; **nasalization, twang;** falsetto, artificial voice; **shake, quaver,** tremor; **lisp; hiss; croak,** choked voice; harshness, hoarseness

2 **inarticulateness,** inarticulacy

3 **stammering, stuttering,** hesitation, faltering; stammer, stutter

4 **mumbling, muttering;** drone; mumble, mutter; jabber, gabble; whispering, whisper; mouthing; murmuring

5 **mispronunciation,** misspeaking; corruption, language pollution

verbs

6 **speak poorly; croak; lisp; shake, quaver; drawl;** lose one's voice

7 **stammer, stutter;** hesitate, falter, halt, stumble; **hum and haw**

8 **mumble, mutter;** drone on; jabber, gabble; splutter, sputter; sob; whisper; murmur; mouth

9 nasalize, whine, twang

10 **mispronounce,** misspeak

adjectives

11 (*imperfectly spoken*) inarticulate, indistinct, blurred; mispronounced; **shaky, quavering,** tremulous; **drawling; throaty, guttural,** thick; stifled, choked, strangled; **nasal,** breathy; croaking; harsh, hoarse

12 **stammering, stuttering,** halting, hesitating, faltering, stumbling; dumb, **mute**

511 WORD

nouns

1 **word, term,** expression, lexeme; content word, function word; utterance, articulation; syllable, polysyllable; monosyllable; synonym; antonym

2 **root,** primitive; derivative, derivation

3 **morpheme; inflection,** conjugation; derivation; root; stem; combining form; **suffix, prefix**

4 **word form,** formation, construction; back formation; **compound;** acronym

5 **technical term;** jargon word

6 **corruption,** taboo word, dirty word *and* four-letter word (*both nonformal*); **colloquialism, slang**

7 **loan word,** borrowing

8 **neologism,** new word; **coinage**

9 **catchword,** catch phrase, slogan, cry; byword, cliche; **buzzword,** in-word; euphemism; **code word**

10 hybrid word, portmanteau

11 **vocabulary, lexis, words; phraseology;** lexicon

12 **lexicology; meaning,** semantics

13 **etymology, derivation, origin,** word history

adjectives

14 **verbal;** lexical; etymological, derivational

15 **morphological;** inflectional, derivational

512 NOMENCLATURE

nouns

1 **nomenclature, terminology; taxonomy,** classification; class, order, family, genus, species

2 **naming, calling, denomination,** designation, terming, definition, identification; **christening,** baptism; dubbing; nicknaming

3 **name, denomination, designation; title; label, tag; epithet;** scientific name; middle name; eponym

4 **first name,** forename, Christian name, given name, baptismal name

5 **surname, last name,** family name; **maiden name;** married name

6 **nickname, sobriquet;** epithet; **pet name,** diminutive

7 **alias, pseudonym,** assumed name, **pen name,** nom de plume; stage name, professional name

8 **misnomer,** wrong name

9 **signature, autograph, hand;** initials; subscription; endorsement; monogram, cipher; seal

verbs

10 **name, nominate, designate, call, term, dub;** specify; define, identify; **title, entitle; label, tag; nickname; christen,** baptize

11 **misname,** misterm

12 **be called,** be known as, go by the name of

adjectives

13 **named, called,** titled, **known as,** designated, termed, dubbed,

identified as; christened, baptized

14 **nominal; titular, in name only; so-called,** quasi; would-be; **self-styled;** by name; **alias,** aka (*also known as*)

513 ANONYMITY

nouns

1 **anonymity, namelessness; incognito;** cover name; code name

2 **what's-his-name** *and* what's-his-face (*both nonformal*); so-and-so

adjectives

3 **anonymous,** anon; **nameless,** unnamed, unidentified, **unknown; incognito**

514 DICTION

nouns

1 **diction,** words, verbiage, **usage,** formulation; **rhetoric,** speech, talk (*nonformal*); **language,** dialect, expression, **grammar; idiom;** composition

2 **style; mode, manner,** vein; fashion, way; **rhetoric; manner of speaking,** literary style; personal style; mannerism, trick; affectation; inflation, exaggeration, grandiloquence

verbs

3 **phrase, express, word,** state, **frame,** conceive, style, couch; put, present, set out; **formulate;** paragraph

adjectives

4 **phrased,** expressed, worded, for-

mulated, styled, put, presented, couched; stylistic

nered, **artificial**, **unnatural**, studied; precious

515 ELEGANCE
(of language)

nouns

1 **elegance, grace, taste,** good taste; **correctness, propriety, aptness; refinement,** precision; **discrimination,** choice; **restraint;** polish, neatness; smoothness, **fluency; ease;** clarity, lucidity; distinction, dignity; **purity,** chastity; plainness, straightforwardness, directness, **simplicity,** naturalness; fittingness, appropriateness

2 **harmony, proportion,** symmetry, **balance,** equilibrium, order, measure; rhythm; sweetness, beauty

3 *(affected elegance)* **affectation, pretentiousness, mannerism, artificiality,** unnaturalness; preciousness

adjectives

4 **elegant, tasteful, graceful, polished,** finished, round, terse; neat, **refined,** exact, **restrained; clear,** lucid; **simple,** unaffected, natural, fluent, flowing, **easy; pure,** chaste, **plain,** straightforward, direct

5 **appropriate, fitting, proper, correct,** seemly; **apt,** well-chosen; well-put, well-expressed, inspired

6 **harmonious, balanced,** symmetrical, orderly, ordered, measured; sweet; **smooth,** tripping, fluent, flowing

7 *(affectedly elegant)* **affected;** elaborate; **pretentious,** man-

516 INELEGANCE
(of language)

nouns

1 **inelegance; clumsiness;** stiltedness, **ponderousness;** turgidity, pompousness; gracelessness; **tastelessness, impropriety,** unseemliness; incorrectness, impurity; **vulgarity, coarseness,** rudeness, crudeness; · cacophony, harshness

adjectives

2 **inelegant, clumsy,** heavy-handed, graceless; **tasteless, incorrect,** improper; unseemly, undignified; impure; **vulgar,** rude, crude; low; coarse; harsh

3 **stiff, stilted, formal, laboured,** ponderous, turgid, bombastic, pompous; **forced,** awkward, halting

517 PLAIN SPEECH

nouns

1 **plain speech,** plain speaking, plain style, **plain English,** vernacular; plainness, simplicity; spareness, leanness, baldness, bareness, starkness, naturalness; unaffectedness; **directness,** straightforwardness; candour, frankness, openness

verbs

2 **speak plainly,** call a spade a spade

adjectives

3 **plain-speaking; plain,** common;
simple, unadorned, pure; austere, spare, lean, bald, bare,
stark; **natural, unaffected;** direct,
straightforward; **candid,** frank,
open; **prosaic;** unimaginative,
dull, dry, **matter-of-fact**

adverbs

4 **plainly, simply,** naturally,
matter-of-factly; **directly,** to the
point; candidly, frankly

518 FIGURE OF SPEECH

nouns

1 **figure of speech, figure, image,**
ornament, device, flourish; imagery, figurativeness; floridity

verbs

2 figure (*old*); personify; symbolize

adjectives

3 **figurative; metaphorical;** allusive, referential; mannered, orna-
mented, **flowery**

adverbs

4 **figuratively, metaphorically;**
symbolically; so to speak, as it
were

519 CONCISENESS

nouns

1 **conciseness, brevity; curtness,**
brusqueness, **terseness;** taciturnity, reserve; pithiness, senten-
tiousness

2 **aphorism,** epigram, abridgement

3 **abbreviation,** shortening, clipping, cutting

verbs

4 **be brief;** shorten, condense, **abbreviate**

adjectives

5 **concise, brief, short, condensed,**
compressed, tight, close, compact; **curt,** brusque; **terse;** taciturn; reserved; **pithy, succinct;**
abridged, abbreviated, shortened, clipped, cut, contracted;
sententious; epigrammatic;
aphoristic(al), **pointed**

adverbs

6 **concisely, briefly,** shortly; **curtly,**
brusquely, tersely; **succinctly,**
pointedly

7 **in brief, in short,** for short; in
outline; in a nutshell; in a word

520 DIFFUSENESS

nouns

1 **diffuseness,** diffusion; **shapelessness,** formlessness, unstructured-
ness; obscurity

2 **wordiness, verbosity; prolixity;**
profuseness, profusion; effusive-
ness, gush; tirade; **talkativeness;**
exuberance, extravagance, prodi-
gality, fertility, productivity,
abundance, overflow; superfluity,
inundation; **redundancy**

3 discursiveness, desultoriness;
rambling, meandering, wandering

4 **digression, departure,** deviation,
excursion, sidetrack

5 **circumlocution,** circuitousness;
obliqueness

6 **amplification,** enlargement, expansion, dilation; **elaboration;**
development, unfolding

verbs

7 **amplify, dilate, expand, enlarge
on,** expand on, **elaborate;** detail;
develop, fill in, flesh out, evolve,
unfold; work out

8 **protract, extend, spin out,** draw
out, drag out; **pad, fill out**

9 **digress,** wander, get sidetracked,
ramble, stray; depart, **deviate**

adjectives

10 **diffuse, formless, unstructured;
profuse, effusive,** gushing; copious, exuberant, extravagant,
prodigal, teeming, prolific, productive, abundant, overflowing;
redundant, repetitive

11 **wordy, verbose; talkative; long-
winded,** protracted, extended,
lengthy, long, endless; padded,
filled out

12 **discursive, aimless,** loose; **rambling, wandering;** digressive,
desultory

13 **circumlocutory, roundabout,**
circuitous, oblique, indirect

14 enlarging, amplifying, expanding;
developmental

adverbs

15 **at length,** at large, in full, in detail

521 AMBIGUITY

nouns

1 **ambiguity; double meaning;**
punning; **double entendre;** grey
area; inexplicitness, uncertainty;
irony, contradiction, oxymoron

2 **ambiguity;** equivocation, double
entendre; pun

verbs

3 equivocate; be uncertain

adjectives

4 **ambiguous, equivocal;** two-
sided; bitterswweet, mixed; inex-
plicit, uncertain; ironic; obscure,
mysterious, funny, enigmatic

522 TALKATIVENESS

nouns

1 **talkativeness, loquacity;** loose
tongue, big mouth *(nonformal);*
garrulousness; prolixity, verbosity; **fluency;** openness, candour,
frankness; gushiness, effusive-
ness; **communicativeness;** gregariousness, sociability

2 **chatter, jabber, babble,** chat,
gabble, blether; guff *and* hot air
(both nonformal); gossip

3 **chatterbox,** blab; **windbag** *(nonformal)*

verbs

4 **chatter, chat, prate, prattle,
babble, gab** *(nonformal),* **jabber,**
blether, natter, haver, **gush;** talk
away, **go on** *(nonformal),* rattle
on; ramble on; gossip

5 **outalk,** outspeak, talk down

adjectives

6 **talkative, loquacious,** garrulous,
chatty; longwinded, **voluble, fluent; glib; candid, frank; effusive;**
expansive, **communicative;** conversational; gregarious, sociable

7 **chattering, prattling,** gabbling,
jabbering, babbling

adverbs

8 **talkatively, loquaciously; vol-
ubly, fluently,** glibly; effusively

523 CONVERSATION

nouns

1 **conversation; exchange; discourse;** repartee, backchat; communion, intercourse, communication

2 **talk, speech, words;** confab (*nonformal*); chinwag (*nonformal*); **dialogue, interview**

3 **chat,** heart-to-heart; pillow talk

4 **chitchat, small talk,** idle chat, gossip

5 **conference, congress, convention,** confab (*nonformal*), conclave, powwow, **consultation, meeting;** session, sitting; **council; discussion; interview, audience;** news conference, press conference; high-level talk, summit; negotiations, bargaining; confrontation; negotiating table

6 **discussion, debate, deliberation,** ventilation, airing, review, consideration, investigation, **examination, study, analysis; panel,** open discussion, joint discussion, conference, seminar; **forum,** open forum

verbs

7 **converse, talk together,** discourse with, **commune with,** communicate with; bandy words

8 **chat;** prattle; **gossip**

9 **confer,** deliberate, counsel; **discuss,** talk over; **consult,** refer to, call in; **compare notes;** negotiate, bargain

10 **discuss, debate, reason, deliberate,** talk, talk over, comment upon, **consider,** treat, handle, deal with, take up, **go into,** ex-

amine, investigate, talk out, **analyse,** sift, **study,** review, ventilate, air, thrash out

adjectives

11 conversational, colloquial; **communicative;** chatty

adverbs

12 conversationally, colloquially

524 PUBLIC SPEAKING

nouns

1 **public speaking, speaking, speechmaking,** lecturing; **oratory;** the stump, the hustings; the soap box; **elocution; rhetoric; eloquence; debating; preaching,** Bible-thumping (*nonformal*), the pulpit; demagoguery, rabble-rousing

2 **speech, talk, oration, address,** declamation, harangue; say; **tirade, diatribe,** invective; eulogy; recital, reading

3 **lecture,** discourse; **sermon,** homily; preaching; **evangelism**

4 **speaker, public speaker, speechmaker;** after-dinner speaker; **spokesman, spokeswoman;** demagogue; rabble-rouser; panellist, debater

5 **lecturer,** reader; **preacher; evangelist**

6 **orator, public speaker;** rhetorician

verbs

7 **make a speech; speak, talk, discourse; address;** take the floor

8 **orate,** spout (*nonformal*); **harangue, rant, recite,** read; debate

9 **lecture; preach,** sermonize

adjectives

10 **rhetorical;** eloquent; demagogic

525 ELOQUENCE

nouns

1 **eloquence, rhetoric; articulateness;** smoothness; **expressiveness,** gift of the gab (*nonformal*)

2 **fluency; glibness, smoothness,** ease; **grace,** poetry; **elegance**

3 **vigour, force,** power, strength, vitality, drive, effectiveness, impressiveness; incisiveness, poignancy

4 **spirit,** liveliness, sparkle, vivacity, dash, verve; poignancy

5 **vehemence, passion,** enthusiasm, ardour, fervour, fire, glow, warmth

6 **loftiness,** elevation; grandeur, **nobility,** gravity, solemnity, **dignity**

adjectives

7 **eloquent,** silver-tongued; well-spoken, **articulate; glib, smooth, slick;** spellbinding

8 **fluent, flowing,** tripping; **smooth,** pleasing, **easy, graceful, elegant**

9 **expressive, graphic, vivid,** suggestive, imaginative; **meaningful**

10 **vigorous,** strong, **powerful,** imperative, **forceful,** vital, driving, **striking, telling, effective,** impressive; incisive, cutting, biting, piercing, poignant, penetrating; sensational

11 **spirited, lively,** racy, sparkling, vivacious; piquant, poignant

12 **vehement,** emphatic, **passionate, impassioned,** enthusiastic, **ardent,** fiery, **fervent,** burning, glowing, warm; urgent, stirring, exciting, stimulating, provoking

13 **lofty, elevated, sublime, grand, majestic,** noble, stately, grave, solemn, dignified; serious, weighty; moving, inspiring

adverbs

14 **eloquently; fluently,** smoothly, glibly; **expressively,** vividly, graphically; **meaningfully;** powerfully, forcefully; strikingly, effectively, impressively; **vehemently, passionately,** ardently, fervently, warmly

526 GRANDILOQUENCE

nouns

1 **grandiloquence,** pomposity; **rhetoric; loftiness;** pretentiousness, **affectation;** ostentation; **inflatedness,** turgidity

2 **bombast, rant;** hot air (*nonformal*)

3 **ornateness,** floridity; flourish; **ornament,** adornment, embellishment

verbs

4 **pontificate;** inflate, lay it on thick (*nonformal*)

5 **ornament,** decorate, adorn, embellish, embroider; elaborate

adjectives

6 **grandiloquent, pompous; grandiose;** lofty, elevated, stilted; pretentious, affected; **showy, flashy, ostentatious,** gaudy, flamboyant, garish; high-flown; high-

sounding; **rhetorical;** convoluted, tortuous

7 **bombastic, inflated, swollen,** turgid; fulsome

8 **ornate, fancy;** adorned, **embellished,** embroidered, lavish; **flowery, florid,** lush, luxuriant; figured

adverbs

9 **grandiloquently,** pompously, loftily; **ostentatiously; ornately;** floridly

527 LETTER

nouns

1 **letter, character, sign, symbol,** graph; diacritic; cipher; device; writing

2 phonetic symbol; pictograph; hieroglyphic; rune; **character; shorthand**

3 **writing system, script, letters;** alphabet; phonetic alphabet

4 **spelling,** orthography; phonetics

5 **lettering,** initialling; **inscription**

verbs

6 **letter, initial, inscribe,** sign, mark; **capitalize;** transcribe

7 **spell;** spell out, write out

adjectives

8 **literal, lettered; alphabetical; capital,** capitalized, upper-case; lower-case; transcribed

528 WRITING

nouns

1 **writing,** inscription, lettering; pen; **typing**

2 **authorship, writing, composition; creative writing;** journalism, rewriting, automatic writing; writer's cramp

3 **handwriting, hand, script, calligraphy; manuscript; autograph**

4 **printing,** block letter, **lettering; stationery; writing materials,** paper, note paper, pad, parchment, tracing paper, typing paper

5 **calligraphy,** fine writing, fair hand

6 **scribble, scrawl, scratch**

7 **stenography, shorthand;** contraction

8 (*written matter*) **writing, the written word; piece;** text, screed; **copy, matter;** printed matter, literature, reading matter; nonfiction; fiction; **composition, work,** opus, production, artefact; essay, article; poem; play; letter; **document; paper,** parchment, scroll; **script; typescript; manuscript,** autograph; draft; **version;** transcript; printout, hard copy

9 **literature, letters; literary work, text; complete works; canon; classics,** ancient literature; national literature; contemporary literature; underground literature; folk literature; popular literature

10 **writer, scribbler** (*nonformal*); penpusher (*nonformal*); scribe, **secretary, clerk;** calligrapher

11 graphologist, handwriting expert

12 **author, writer,** composer; **creative writer;** wordsmith; ghostwriter; short story writer, novelist; poet; dramatist; essayist; critic; columnist

13 **typist;** printer

verbs

14 **write, pen; inscribe; draw up,**
draft, write out; **write down,** record; **type; transcribe,** copy out,
copy; trace; **rewrite,** revise, edit

15 **scribble, scrawl,** doodle

16 **write, compose,** formulate, produce; dash off, churn out; ghost-
write

adjectives

17 **written,** penned; **inscribed; in
writing,** on paper; graphic;
manuscript; **longhand; shorthand,** in shorthand; italic; cursive; typewritten; printed

18 **scribbled, scrawled;** scribbly,
scrawly

529 PRINTING

nouns

1 **printing,** publishing; lithography;
book printing; photography;
printmaking

2 **composition, typesetting, setting;** imposition; justification;
layout

3 **print, imprint,** stamp, impression; reprint; reissue; offset

4 **copy,** manuscript, typescript

5 **proof,** trial impression

6 **type, print, stamp, letter;** type
size; lower case; upper case;
capital, small capital; **font; face**

7 **space,** spacing, justifying space

8 **printing surface, plate,** printing
plate

9 **press, printing press**

10 **press,** print shop, printers; publishers, **publishing house**

11 **printer,** printworker; **typesetter;**
keyboarder

12 **proofreader,** reader; **copyreader,**
copy editor

verbs

13 **print; imprint,** impress; stamp;
engrave; run, run off; **publish,** issue, bring out; reprint, reissue

14 **compose,** set; impose; justify

15 **copy-edit; proofread,** read

adjectives

16 **printed, in print;** typeset

530 RECORD

nouns

1 **record, recording,** documentation; **chronicle,** history; story;
roll, **rolls; account; register, registry,** rota, roster, scroll, catalogue, inventory, table, list; letters, correspondence; **vestige,
trace,** memorial, token, relic, remains

2 **archives,** public records, historical documents, memorabilia;
biographical material; papers;
parish register

3 registry, registry office; archives,
files

4 **memorandum, memo** (*nonformal*), memoir, memorial; **reminder; note,** marginal note,
footnote; **entry,** item; **minutes**

5 **document,** official document, legal document, writ; **paper,**
parchment, scroll, roll, **writing,**
script; **papers; file, dossier**

6 **certificate,** ticket; authority,
authorization; credential, **voucher, warrant,** testimonial;
affadavit, sworn statement; **visa;**

diploma; birth certificate, death certificate

7 report, bulletin, brief, **statement, account; minutes,** proceedings, transactions

8 (*recording media*) notice board, bulletin board; scoresheet, scoreboard; **tape,** magnetic tape, videotape; **computer disk,** floppy disk *or* floppy, hard disk; memory; compact disc *or* CD; phonograph disc; film; slip, card, index card, filing card; library catalogue; microfiche, microdot, microfilm; **file**

9 (*record books*) **notebook, pocketbook; address book;** workbook; blotter; **calendar,** desk calendar, appointment calendar, appointment book, agenda; pad; scrapbook, **album; diary, journal; log; account book, ledger;** catalogue; annual; register

10 monument, memorial; obituary, **memento,** remembrance, testimonial; cup, trophy, prize, ribbon, plaque; inscription; **tablet,** stone, memorial stone; **pillar,** column; cross; war memorial; memorial statue; bust; **pyramid; tomb,** grave; **gravestone, tombstone;** headstone; mausoleum; cenotaph; **shrine**

11 registration, register, registry; recording, record keeping; enrolment, matriculation, enlistment; **listing, cataloguing,** indexing; chronicling; **entry,** insertion, posting; **inscription; booking,** logging

verbs

12 record, inscribe, register, enrol, matriculate, check in; **file,** index, catalogue, **list; chronicle;** minute; archive; **write; write up,** chalk up; **write down, set down, take down; note,** note down; **enter,** insert, write in; **book, log;** cut, carve, engrave; tape; record; videotape

adjectives

13 recorded, registered; inscribed, written down; **filed,** enrolled, **entered,** logged, booked, posted; documented; **on record,** on file; official, legal

14 documentary, archival; obituary; testimonial

531 RECORDER

nouns

1 recorder, registrar, register; archivist; librarian; **clerk,** filing clerk; bookkeeper, accountant; **scribe; secretary;** notary; scorekeeper, scorer, timekeeper

2 annalist, genealogist, chronicler; historian

532 INFORMATION

nouns

1 information, info (*nonformal*), gen (*nonformal*), **facts, data, knowledge;** public knowledge, open secret, common knowledge; general information; factual information, hard information; **evidence, proof; enlightenment; acquaintance,** briefing; **instruction; intelligence;** transmission, **communication;** re-

port, word, message, presentation, account, **statement;** dispatch, bulletin, handout (*nonformal*), fact sheet; release; publicity; **notice,** notification; notice board, bulletin board; announcement, publication; directory, guidebook

2 **inside information;** insider; privileged information, classified information

3 **clue; advice;** whisper; warning, caution

4 **hint,** gentle hint, **intimation, indication, suggestion, suspicion, inkling,** whisper, glimmer; **clue,** index, **symptom, sign,** track, scent, sniff, whiff, tip-off (*nonformal*); **implication, innuendo;** broad hint, gesture, signal, nod, wink, look, nudge, prompt

5 **informant, informer, source, adviser,** monitor; **reporter, announcer;** spokesperson, spokeswoman, spokesman, press secretary, press officer, information officer, mouthpiece; **publisher; authority,** witness, expert witness; **tout** (*nonformal*); **mass media,** print media, electronic media, the press, radio, television; channel, the grapevine; information network, network; information centre

6 **informer, telltale;** spy

7 signal, noise; bit; channel

verbs

8 **inform, tell, advise, advertise, give word,** mention to, **acquaint, enlighten,** familiarize, brief, verse; **instruct; let know,** notify, serve notice; **communicate; report; disclose**

9 **hint, intimate, suggest, insinuate, imply, indicate, hint at; leak;** allude to, glance at (*old*); **prompt,** put onto

10 **alert; confide,** confide to, whisper, buzz, breathe

11 **betray;** turn informer; testify against

12 tell on, squeal, sell out, sing, rat, stool, finger, shop

13 **learn,** awaken to, tumble to (*nonformal*)

14 **know;** be told, **hear, overhear, know well**

15 **keep informed,** keep posted (*nonformal*), stay briefed

adjectives

16 **informed, informed of, in the know**

17 **informative,** informing; **instructive, enlightening;** educational; advisory; **communicative**

18 telltale

533 NEWS

nouns

1 **news,** tidings, intelligence, **information, word; journalism,** cov
•erage; **the press,** broadcast news, radio journalism, television journalism; newspaper, newsletter, radio, television, press association, news service, press agency; press box, press gallery; quality press, tabloid press

2 **good news,** good word, glad tidings; bad news

3 **news item, article, story,** piece, copy; **exclusive, breaking story**

4 **message, dispatch, word,** com-

munication, press release, release; **letter, telegram**

5 **bulletin,** news report, **flash**

6 **report, rumour,** hearsay, unconfirmed report; **talk, whisper**

7 **gossip,** gossiping; **talk,** idle talk; groundless rumour, tale, story

8 **scandal, dirt** (*nonformal*), **malicious gossip,** titbit; gossip column; character assassination, **slander;** whispering campaign

9 **gossip, busybody,** telltale; gossip columnist

10 (*secret news channel*) **grapevine,** pipeline

verbs

11 **report,** tell, relate, bring word; put around, spread; **inform, announce**

12 **gossip, tattle**

adjectives

13 **gossiping,** taletelling

14 **reported, rumoured,** whispered; in circulation, going around, **current, rife**

adverbs

15 **reportedly, allegedly**

534 CORRESPONDENCE

nouns

1 **correspondence, letter writing,** written communication; personal correspondence, business correspondence

2 **letter, message,** communication, dispatch; **note, line; reply, answer**

3 **card, postcard,** postal card, picture postcard

4 **mail, post, postal services,** letter bag; mailing list; junk mail (*nonformal*); direct mail, mail-order selling; fan mail

5 **postage;** stamp, postage stamp; frank, postmark

6 **postbox, pillar box, mailbox;** mailbag

7 **postal service; postman**

8 **correspondent, letter writer,** writer; pen pal (*nonformal*)

9 **address, destination,** postcode

verbs

10 **correspond, communicate with, write, write to**

11 **reply, answer, acknowledge**

12 **mail, post,** dispatch; send; airmail

13 **address, direct**

adjectives

14 **postal,** post; mail-order, direct-mail

535 BOOK

nouns

1 **book, volume, tome;** publication, writing, **work,** production, title; trade book; **textbook, reference book;** notebook; **novel; best seller;** children's book; picture book; colouring book; prayer book; **classic, the bible, great work**

2 **publisher, publishing house, press,** vanity press; **editor,** trade editor, reference editor, dictionary editor; executive editor, managing editor; picture editor, copy editor, production editor; **printer**

3 **book, paperback, hardback**

4 **volume, tome,** folio

5 **edition, issue, copy; volume, number; printing,** impression, print run; series, set, boxed set, collection; back number

6 **manuscript, first edition**

7 **compilation, collection; collected works, selected works, complete works,** canon; **anthology;** album, scrapbook

8 **handbook, manual;** cookery book; nature book, field guide; travel guide, **guidebook**

9 **reference book, encyclopedia;** catalogue; calendar; index; directory; telephone directory, telephone book, phone book (*nonformal*); atlas; record book; dictionary, lexicon, glossary, thesaurus

10 **textbook, text, manual; exercise book;** grammar; reader, primer

11 **booklet, pamphlet,** brochure, leaflet

12 **design;** front matter, preliminaries, text, back matter; page, leaf, signature; title page, imprint; dedication, inscription; preface, foreword, introduction; contents, bibliography, index

13 **part, section,** book, volume; article; serial, instalment; **passage,** phrase, clause, **verse, paragraph, chapter, column**

14 **binding, cover, jacket,** dust jacket, wrapper

15 **bookshop,** bookstall, book club

16 **book end, bookcase, bookshelf;** folder, portfolio

17 **book collector, bookworm,** bibliophile

18 book printing, book manufacturing

536 PERIODICAL

1 **periodical,** serial, **journal; magazine, review;** organ, trade journal, daily, weekly, quarterly, **annual**

2 **newspaper,** news, **paper,** national newspaper, local newspaper **tabloid, broadsheet;** extra, special, extra edition, special edition

3 **the press,** journalism, Fleet Street; **communications, mass media**

4 **journalist, reporter;** investigative reporter; cub reporter; foreign correspondent, war correspondent; **editor,** managing editor, city editor, news editor, sports editor, leader writer, **columnist; photographer**

adjectives

5 **journalistic;** periodical; **editorial**

537 TREATISE

nouns

1 **piece,** treatment, handling, tract; contribution; examination, survey, **discourse,** exposition; dissertation, thesis, essay, paper, sketch, outline; paragraph, note; **article,** feature

2 **commentary; comment,** remark; criticism, critique, analysis; **review, report,** notice, write-up (*nonformal*); **editorial**

3 **essayist, writer, author**

4 **commentator, critic; editor, leader writer**

verbs

5 **write upon**, touch upon, **discuss**, **treat**, go into, inquire into, survey; discourse; **comment upon**, remark upon; **criticize, review**

adjectives

6 expository, critical

538 ABRIDGMENT

nouns

1 condensation, condensed version, abbreviation, brief, digest, **abstract**, epitome, sketch; **survey, review, overview; outline**, skeleton, draft

2 **summary**, rundown; sum, substance; pith, meat, **gist, core, essence, main point**

3 excerpt, extract, selection, passage; **clip** (*nonformal*); film clip, sound bite (*nonformal*)

4 **excerpts, extracts**, cuttings, clippings, snippets, fragments; **collection, anthology**

verbs

5 **shorten**, condense, cut; **summarize; outline, sketch**, encapsulate

adjectives

6 **abridged**, condensed, shortened

adverbs

7 in brief, in summary, in sum, in a nutshell

539 LIBRARY

1 **library, reading room**, book depository, learning centre

2 **librarianship**, library science, information science

3 **librarian, chief librarian**

4 **bibliography, index**, library catalogue, backlist

540 RELATIONSHIP BY BLOOD

nouns

1 **blood relationship**, blood, **kinship**, kindred, **relation, relationship**; alliance, connection; motherhood, maternity; fatherhood, paternity; brotherhood, fraternity; sisterhood; ancestry

2 **kindred, kin, family, relatives, relations**, people, folks (*nonformal*); flesh, blood; sibling; near relation, distant relation

3 **brother, sister,** halfbrother, halfsister, stepbrother, stepsister; **aunt**, auntie (*nonformal*), **uncle, nephew, niece; cousin,** first cousin, second cousin; **father, mother; son, daughter**

4 **race, people,** folk, family, house, clan, tribe, nation; line, blood, strain, **stock**, breed, brood, kind

5 **family,** brood, nuclear family, extended family; house, **people,** folk; **children,** descendants, progeny, **offspring, kids** (*nonformal*)

adjectives

6 **related, kindred; biological,** genetic; **natural,** by birth; sibling; foster

7 **racial, ethnic, tribal, national**

541 ANCESTRY

nouns

1 **ancestry**; parentage, **parenthood**

2 **fatherhood, paternity**

3 **motherhood, maternity**

4 **lineage, line, bloodline,** descent, birth, **blood,** breed, **family,** house, **strain, stock,** race, seed; father's side, mother's side

5 **genealogy,** pedigree, family tree

6 **heredity, inheritance, birth;** genetics, gene, chromosome, sex chromosome, X chromosome, Y chromosome; genetic code, DNA, RNA

7 **ancestors,** antecedents, predecessors, **fathers,** forefathers, forebears; **grandparents; elders, patriarchs**

8 **parent, ancestor, progenitor**

9 **father,** paternal ancestor, birth father; **stepfather, foster father**

10 (*nonformal terms*) **dad, daddy,** da, pappa, pater

11 **mother,** maternal ancestor, birth mother; **stepmother, foster mother**

12 (*nonformal terms*) **mum, mummy,** ma, mammy, mater

13 **grandfather**

14 (*nonformal terms*) **grandpa, granddad**

15 **grandmother**

16 (*nonformal terms*) **gran, grandma, granny**

adjectives

17 **ancestral; parental; paternal,** fatherly; **maternal,** motherly

18 **lineal, family**

19 **hereditary,** inherited, innate, genetic

542 POSTERITY

nouns

1 **posterity, issue, offspring, progeny,** fruit, seed, brood, blood, breed, family; **descent,** succession; **descendants,** heirs, inheritors, sons, **children, kids** (*nonformal*)

2 (*of animals*) young, brood, spawn, fry; litter, clutch, hatch

3 **descendant; offspring, child; son,** heir, **daughter,** heiress; grandchild, grandson, granddaughter, stepchild, stepson, stepdaughter; foster child

4 (*derived descendant*) offset, **branch,** sprout, shoot

5 **bastard,** illegitimate, love child (*nonformal*)

adjectives

6 **filial**

543 LOVEMAKING, ENDEARMENT

nouns

1 fondling, caressing, hugging, kissing, cuddling; **lovemaking, sexual intercourse**

2 (*nonformal terms*) **necking, petting,** snogging

3 **embrace, hug,** squeeze, bear hug (*nonformal*)

4 **kiss,** smack, French kiss

5 **endearment, sweet talk, sweet nothings**

6 (*terms of endearment*) **darling, dear,** sweetheart, sweet, **honey,**

sugar, love, lover, precious, babe, **baby,** doll, angel, lamb

7 **courtship, wooing,** gallantry

8 **proposal, popping the question**

9 **flirtation,** dalliance; **sheep's eyes, bedroom eyes** (*nonformal*)

10 **philandering, lechery**

11 **flirt, coquette,** gold digger, vamp; strumpet, **whore,** slag, tart (*both nonformal*)

12 **philanderer, ladykiller, ladies' man;** lecher, seducer, Casanova, Don Juan

13 **love letter,** billet-doux; **valentine**

verbs

14 **make love,** bill and coo; **go steady, see, date;** copulate

15 (*nonformal terms*) **snog, neck,** pet

16 **caress, pet, fondle**

17 **cuddle, snuggle, nestle,** nuzzle

18 **embrace, hug,** clasp, press, squeeze

19 **kiss,** smooch

20 **flirt,** coquet; philander, sow one's wild oats

21 **court, woo, chat up** (*nonformal*); serenade

22 **propose, pop the question**

adjectives

23 **flirtatious,** flirty, coquettish

544 MARRIAGE

nouns

1 **marriage, matrimony,** holy matrimony, match, union, alliance, wedding knot, wedded bliss

2 **wedding, marriage,** marriage ceremony; church wedding, civil ceremony, **white wedding; bridal suite; honeymoon;** forced marriage, shotgun wedding

3 **wedding party;** wedding attendant, usher; **best man; bridesmaid,** matron of honour

4 **newlywed; bridegroom, groom; bride,** blushing bride

5 **spouse, mate,** partner, consort, **better half** (*nonformal*)

6 **husband, married man,** man, old man (*nonformal*)

7 **wife, married woman,** wedded wife, woman, lady, matron

8 **married couple,** wedded pair, happy couple

9 **harem,** seraglio

10 **monogamist; bigamist, polygamist,** Bluebeard

11 **matchmaker,** Cupid (*nonformal*)

verbs

12 (*join in marriage*) **marry,** wed, join, unite, couple, match, join together; give away, marry off

13 (*get married*) **marry, wed,** mate, couple, pair off

14 **honeymoon**

15 **cohabit,** live together

adjectives

16 **matrimonial, marital, conjugal,** wedded, married

17 **monogamous; bigamous, polygamous**

18 **nubile,** ripe, of age,

19 **married, wedded,** mated, matched, coupled, paired, hitched (*nonformal*)

545 RELATIONSHIP BY MARRIAGE

nouns

1 **marriage relationship; connec-tion, family connection**

2 **in-laws** (*nonformal*); **brother-in-law, sister-in-law, father-in-law, mother-in-law, son-in-law, daughter-in-law**

3 **stepfather, stepmother; step-brother, stepsister; stepchild, stepson, stepdaughter**

adjectives

4 **by marriage**

546 CELIBACY

nouns

1 **celibacy, abstinence, virginity; bachelorhood, spinsterhood**

2 **celibate; monk, priest, nun**

3 **bachelor, confirmed bachelor, single man**

4 **spinster, old maid,** maiden, sin-gle woman; **virgin**

verbs

5 **be unmarried, be single, live alone**

adjectives

6 **celibate,** abstaining

7 **unmarried, single; virginal**

547 DIVORCE, WIDOWHOOD

nouns

1 **divorce, separation;** broken marriage, broken home

2 **divorcée, divorcé**

3 widowhood, widowerhood

4 **widow,** dowager; widower

verbs

5 **divorce, separate,** part, split up

6 **widow,** bereave

adjectives

7 **widowed; divorced, separated**

548 SCHOOL

nouns

1 **school, institute, academy**

2 **infant school, nursery school;** nursery, kindergarten

3 **primary school,** junior school, elementary school (*old*)

4 **secondary school,** middle school, academy, **high school; preparatory school,** prep school (*nonformal*); **public school, pri-vate school, grammar school** (*old*)

5 **college, university,** polytechnic (*old*); the campus

6 **military academy, naval acad-emy**

7 **art school,** music school, con-servatory, dance school

8 **church school, religious school;** Sunday school

9 **reform school,** correctional insti-tution; **youth custody centre,** borstal (*old*)

10 **school building, schoolhouse;** campus

11 **schoolroom, classroom; lecture hall**

12 **school board,** board of gover-nors; senate

adjectives

13 **scholastic, academic,** institutional, **school,** classroom; **university, collegiate**

549 TEACHING

nouns

1 **teaching,** instruction, **education,** schooling, tuition; enlightenment, illumination; tutoring, coaching, private teaching; direction, guidance

2 **indoctrination,** dictation; conditioning, brainwashing

3 **training,** preparation, grooming, cultivation, **development, improvement; discipline;** breaking; **upbringing,** rearing, raising, breeding, nurturing, fostering; **practice,** rehearsal, exercise, drill; **apprenticeship,** work experience; military training, basic training; vocational training

4 cramming, swotting (*nonformal*)

5 elementary education; initiation, **introduction; rudiments,** grounding, basics, ABC; **reading, writing, and arithmetic, three Rs**

6 instructions, directions, orders, briefing

7 **lesson, teaching, instruction, lecture,** discourse, exposition, **talk,** sermon; **assignment, exercise,** task, **homework**

8 **study;** discipline, **field,** speciality, area; **course, curriculum,** subject

9 physical education, games, gymnastics

verbs

10 **teach, instruct, educate, school; enlighten,** civilize; **direct, guide;** get across, **inform; show,** demonstrate

11 **tutor, coach;** cram, swot (*nonformal*)

12 **inculcate, indoctrinate,** instil, imbue; beat into, drill into; condition, brainwash, indoctrinate

13 **train; drill, exercise;** practice, rehearse; **prepare,** condition, groom, form; **rear, bring up,** breed; cultivate, develop, improve; **nurture,** foster; **discipline,** break in

14 **initiate, introduce**

15 **give instructions, brief**

16 **expound, exposit, explain; lecture,** discourse, hold forth; **preach, moralize**

17 **assign, give homework**

adjectives

18 **educational,** educating, teaching, **instructive;** cultural, edifying, enlightening, illuminating, **informative; didactic, lecturing,** preaching

19 **scholastic, academic, scholarly;** pedantic, pedagogic; **graduate,** postgraduate

20 **extracurricular**

550 MISTEACHING

nouns

1 **misleading, misinstruction;** perversion, corruption; mystification, obfuscation; **misinformation**

2 **propaganda;** indoctrination,

brainwashing; propagandist, agitprop

verbs

3 **misinform; mislead, misguide;** pervert, corrupt; mystify, obscure, obfuscate

4 **indoctrinate,** brainwash

adjectives

5 **misinformed; misguided, misled**

6 **misinforming; misleading;** obscuring, mystifying

551 LEARNING

nouns

1 **learning,** mental cultivation; **knowledge, erudition;** self-instruction, self-education

2 **absorption,** assimilation

3 **study, studying, application; reading, perusal;** brushing up; genning up; contemplation; practice, drill; **cramming, swotting** (*nonformal*)

4 **studiousness, scholarship;** bookishness, diligence

5 **aptitude, readiness;** willingness, motivation; **brightness, intelligence,** cleverness

verbs

6 **learn,** get (*nonformal*); **find out,** ascertain, discover

7 **absorb, acquire, take in,** assimilate, digest, soak up

8 **memorize,** fix in the mind

9 **master,** become adept in, become conversant with; get the hang of, learn the ins and outs

10 **learn by experience, live and learn,** learn by doing

11 be taught, receive instruction, **attend classes, take lessons; matriculate, enrol, register; train,** serve an apprenticeship

12 **study,** apply oneself; **read, peruse,** go over; examine, **pore over**

13 **browse, scan, skim,** dip into

14 **read up on,** gen up on, **swot,** cram

15 **study for, read,** specialize in; major in

adjectives

16 **educated, learned;** self-taught

17 **studious, scholarly, academic,** scholastic, donnish; pedantic, pedagogic

18 **apt, quick, ready;** receptive, willing, motivated; docile, pliable, impressionable; **bright, clever, intelligent**

552 TEACHER

nouns

1 **teacher,** instructor; schoolteacher, schoolmaster, master, dominie (*Scots*); **professor, academic,** don, fellow; mentor, guru

2 (*woman teachers*) **mistress;** schoolmistress; governess

3 (*academic ranks*) **professor,** reader, associate, don, fellow; lecturer, tutor; visiting professor; professor emeritus, Regius professor

4 **monitor, prefect**

5 **tutor,** crammer

6 **trainer, instructor, coach**

7 **principal, headmaster,** headmistress; president, chancellor, vice-chancellor, rector, master, dean

8 faculty, staff

9 chair, professorship, lectureship, readership, fellowship

adjectives

10 pedagogic, tutorial; professorial, **academic**

553 STUDENT

nouns

1 student, pupil, scholar, learner, **trainee**

2 disciple, follower, apostle, convert

3 schoolchild, schoolboy, schoolgirl; day boy, day girl; infant; fellow student, classmate

4 gifted student, dux (*Scots*); slow learner, underachiever

5 college student, university student

6 undergraduate; fresher, freshman

7 graduate, alumnus, alumna; postgraduate

8 novice, beginner, tyro, fledgling, new boy; **recruit,** rookie; **apprentice**

9 swot, bookworm

10 class, form, grade, year

adjectives

11 undergraduate, graduate, postgraduate; collegiate; **studious,** learned; bookish; **exceptional,** gifted, special

12 probationary, on probation; in detention

554 DIRECTION, MANAGEMENT

nouns

1 direction, management, managing, handling, **running,** conduct; **command, control, government; authority; regulation,** ordering; guidance, leading; steering, navigation

2 supervision, superintendence, heading, running; **charge,** care, auspices; **jurisdiction; responsibility,** accountability

3 administration, dispensation, decision-making

4 leadership, directorship, **presidency; dictatorship, sovereignty;** custody, stewardship

5 helm, rudder, tiller, wheel; **reins**

6 domestic management, housekeeping; domestic economy, **home economics**

7 scientific management, management consulting; time and motion study

verbs

8 direct, manage, regulate, conduct, handle, run; control, **command, head, govern; lead,** captain, skipper (*nonformal*)

9 guide, steer; herd, shepherd; pilot

10 supervise, boss, oversee, stand over

11 administer, administrate; preside over, chair

adjectives

12 directing, directive, directory; **managing, managerial; commanding, controlling,** governing; regulating; **head, chief;** leading, guiding

13 supervising, overseeing, superintendent

14 administrative, administrating; ministerial, **executive; presiding, officiating**

adverbs

15 in the charge of; under the auspices of, under the aegis of

555 DIRECTOR

nouns

1 director, director general, **governor,** rector, **manager, administrator;** impresario, producer

2 superintendent; supervisor, foreman, monitor, **head, boss,** chief; floor manager; controller, auditor

3 executive, officer, official; **president, chief executive, managing director;** prefect, warden; secretary, treasurer; chancellor, vicechancellor, dean

4 steward, bailiff, factor (*Scots*); butler, housekeeper; guardian, custodian; curator, librarian

5 chairman, chairwoman, **chair,** chairperson, convenor

6 leader, born leader, charismatic leader; führer, duce; **messiah**

7 guide, shepherd, herd, drover; tour guide, courier; **pilot, navigator,** helmsman

8 guiding star, polestar, North Star

9 compass, direction finder

10 directory, guidebook, handbook; telephone directory, phone book (*nonformal*); **bibliography;** catalogue, index; itinerary, road map

11 directorate, management, the administration, the executive; middle management; board, steering committee; executive committee

556 MASTER

nouns

1 master, lord, overlord; **chief, boss,** employer; elder, patriarch; teacher, rabbi, guru

2 mistress, governess; abbess, mother superior; first lady; matriarch, dowager

3 chief, principal; high priest (*nonformal*); superior, senior

4 (*nonformal terms*) top dog, big cheese, numero uno, kingpin

5 figurehead, nominal head, titular head; puppet, creature, stooge

6 governor, ruler; captain, master, commander, commandant, commanding officer; **director, manager, executive**

7 head of state, president; **premier, prime minister, chancellor**

8 sovereign, monarch, ruler; prince, crowned head, **emperor, king;** chief, chieftain

9 (*rulers*) caesar, kaiser, czar; pharaoh; Inca

10 (*Muslim rulers*) **sultan,** Grand Turk, caliph, imam, emir, naba, Mogul

11 queen, princess, empress

12 regent, protector

13 (*regional governors*) **governor, viceroy,** governor general; gauleiter

14 tyrant, despot, warlord; **dictator,** führer, duce, commissar, pharaoh, caesar, czar; martinet, disciplinarian, stickler

15 the authorities, **the Establishment, the ruling classes,** the powers that be; top brass (*nonformal*), the inner circle; **bureaucracy, officialdom**

16 **official,** officer, functionary; **civil servant, bureaucrat,** mandarin, apparatchik

17 (*public officials*) **secretary of state, minister,** junior minister; magistrate, justice of the peace; **mayor, lord mayor, provost** (*Scots*); **councillor,** elder, alderman, convenor

18 (*Air Force ranks*) Marshal of the RAF, Air Chief Marshal, Air Marshal, Air Vice-Marshal, Air Commodore, Group Captain, Wing Commander, Squadron Leader, Flight Lieutenant, Flying Officer, Pilot Officer; Warrant Officer, Flight Sergeant, Chief Technician, Sergeant, Corporal, Aircraftsman

19 (*Army ranks*) Field Marshal, General, Lieutenant-General, Major-General, Brigadier, Colonel, Lieutenant-Colonel, Major, Captain, Lieutenant, Second Lieutenant; Warrant Officer, Sergeant, Lance Corporal, Corporal, Private

20 (*Naval ranks*) Admiral of the Fleet, Admiral, Vice-Admiral, Rear-Admiral, Commodore, Captain, Commander, Lieutenant Commander, Lieutenant, Sub-Lieutenant, Acting Sub-Lieutenant; Warrant Officer, Chief Petty Officer, Petty Officer, Midshipman, Able Rating, Ordinary Rating

557 DEPUTY, AGENT

nouns

1 **deputy, proxy, representative,** surrogate, understudy; exponent, advocate, attorney, champion

2 **delegate; messenger,** herald, **emissary, envoy**

3 **agent,** instrument; steward; **official, clerk, secretary;** puppet, figurehead

4 **go-between, middleman,** intermediary, broker; connection (*nonformal*), **contact;** negotiator, mediator

5 **spokesman; spokeswoman, spokesperson;** press officer, mouthpiece (*nonformal*)

6 **ambassador, diplomat, consul, chargé d'affaires, attaché,** emissary, envoy

7 **foreign office,** diplomatic service; **embassy,** legation, **mission**

8 vice-president, vice-chancellor, vice-chairman, vice-regent, etc

9 **secret agent,** operative, undercover man, **spy, double agent,** spymaster, spycatcher

10 **detective, investigator,** operative; **police detective, CID;** house detective, store detective

11 (*nonformal terms*) private eye, gumshoe, tec

12 **secret service, intelligence,** counterintelligence

13 (*group of delegates*) **delegation,** deputation, commission, mission

verbs

14 **represent,** act for, speak for, **understudy, deputize**

adjectives

15 **deputy, acting**

16 **diplomatic, consular,** ministerial, plenipotentiary

adverbs

17 by proxy, on behalf of

558 SERVANT, EMPLOYEE

nouns

1 **retainer,** dependent; follower; vassal, liege; underling, **subordinate, minion, lackey,** flunky, stooge; slave

2 **servant,** help; domestic servant, house servant; day help, cleaning lady; menial, drudge; scullion

3 **employee, worker; hired hand, assistant; right-hand man**

4 **man, manservant,** gillie (*Scots*); **butler, valet;** driver, chauffeur; gardener; equerry

5 **attendant,** usher; page; cabin boy, purser; errand boy, office boy; orderly, batman; caddie; **steward, stewardess, hostess**

6 lackey, flunky, footman

7 **waiter, waitress, hostess; waiter,** head waiter, maitre d'; bartender, **barman, barmaid**

8 **maid,** servant girl, wench (*old*); scullery maid, **cook, chambermaid,** housemaid

9 major-domo, steward, **butler, housekeeper**

10 **staff, personnel, employees;** crew, gang, men, force

11 **service,** servitude; **employment, employ;** ministry; attendance; slavery, serfdom

verbs

12 **serve, work for;** administer to, minister to; **care for, look after; wait on,** attend on

adjectives

13 **serving,** ministering, waiting, **attending,** attendant; **menial, servile**

559 FASHION

nouns

1 **fashion, style, vogue, trend;** custom, convention; high fashion, haute couture (*French*)

2 **fashionableness;** popularity, prevalence, currency

3 **chic, elegance;** neatness, smartness

4 **the rage,** the latest thing

5 **fad, craze, rage;** novelty

6 **society, high society,** high life; right people, **smart set,** elite, jet set, beautiful people, A list, **incrowd, glitterati**

7 **trendsetter, clotheshorse;** fop, dandy, Beau Brummel

verbs

8 **catch on,** become popular, become the rage

9 **set the fashion** *or* **the tone**

10 go with the flow, swim with the tide, **jump on the bandwagon;** keep up with the Joneses, keep up appearances

adjectives

11 **fashionable, in fashion, in vogue;** popular, prevalent, current, up-to-date, **trendy** (*nonformal*), modern, new

12 **stylish,** modish, voguish

13 chic, smart, elegant; style-conscious; well-dressed, well-groomed; spruce, neat, dapper; swanky, posh (both *nonformal*); cosmopolitan, sophisticated

14 foppish, dandyish

15 trendy (*nonformal*), faddish

16 high-society, elite, jet-set

adverbs

17 fashionably, stylishly

18 smartly, elegantly, exquisitely

560 SOCIAL CONVENTION

nouns

1 social convention, convention, custom; propriety, **decorum,** decency, civility, good form, **etiquette**

2 the done thing, civilized behaviour

3 conformist, conventionalist, traditionalist

verbs

4 conform, fall into line

adjectives

5 conventional, orthodox, **correct,** right, **proper,** decent, meet; **accepted, recognized,** acknowledged, received, approved; **traditional, customary**

adverbs

6 conventionally, correctly; customarily, traditionally; properly

561 FORMALITY

nouns

1 formality, form; ceremony, ritual; stiffness, dignity, gravity, gravitas, weight, **solemnity; pomposity**

2 formalism, ritualism; **pedantry**

3 etiquette, manners, politeness, civility, social graces, decorum, good form; **protocol**

4 (*ceremonial function*) **ceremony, rite, ritual;** initiation, graduation; liturgy

verbs

5 formalize, ritualize, solemnize; **celebrate, observe**

6 stand on ceremony, follow protocol

adjectives

7 formal, formalistic; pedantic; stylized

8 ceremonial, ritual; grave, solemn; pompous; stately

9 stiff, stilted, prim, prissy, rigid

10 punctilious, scrupulous; precise, exact, meticulous; by the book; orderly, **methodical**

adverbs

11 formally; ritually; solemnly

12 stiffly, stiltedly, primly, rigidly

562 INFORMALITY

nouns

1 informality; casualness, ease; **sociability; affability; familiarity;** naturalness, simplicity, common touch

verbs

2 let one's hair down, not stand on ceremony, be oneself; relax, chill out (*nonformal*)

adjectives

3 informal, casual, easy; relaxed, affable, cordial, **sociable;** Bohemian, unconventional; **familiar; natural,** simple, plain, homely; unaffected, unassuming

adverbs

4 informally, unceremoniously, without ceremony, casually; **naturally,** simply, plainly

563 SOCIABILITY

nouns

1 sociability, affability, gregariousness, geniality; **hospitality;** intimacy, familiarity; **friendliness,** amiability; social grace, civility, **courtesy,** urbanity

2 camaraderie, comradeship, fellowship

3 conviviality, gaiety, cheer, festivity, **merriment,** revelry

4 social life, social intercourse; fellowship, community; commerce, congress, conversation, social relations

5 social circle, set, clique, **crowd**

6 association, fellowship, companionship, **company, society;** membership, participation, sharing, cooperation

7 visit, social call; formal visit; flying visit, look-in

8 appointment, engagement; date, blind date

9 rendezvous, tryst, assignation, **meeting**

10 social gathering, **get-together; dinner party,** reception, salon, soiree; reunion; wake

11 party, entertainment, festivity

12 (*nonformal terms*) bash, blast, bean-feast, rave-up, knees-up

13 tea, afternoon tea, high tea, cream tea

14 debut, coming out

15 (*sociable person*) mixer, life and soul, bon vivant, party animal (*nonformal*)

verbs

16 associate with, consort with, mingle with, mix with, hobnob with, keep company with

17 (*nonformal terms*) hang out *or* about with, go around with

18 visit, pay a visit, call on, **drop in on,** see

19 have a party, entertain

20 party, have fun, **live it up,** have a ball, paint the town red

adjectives

21 sociable, social, gregarious, affable; compatible, genial, congenial; hospitable; communicative; amiable, **friendly;** civil, urbane, courteous

22 convivial, jovial, jolly, festive

23 intimate, familiar, cosy, chatty; man-to-man, woman-to-woman

adverbs

24 sociably, socially, gregariously, affably

564 UNSOCIABILITY

nouns

1 unfriendliness; incompatibility; moroseness; self-sufficiency

2 aloofness, remoteness, detachment; coolness, coldness

3 seclusion, exclusiveness

verbs

4 keep oneself to oneself, prefer one's own company, **stand aloof**

adjectives

5 **unsociable, unsocial;** incompatible; **unfriendly;** uncommunicative; sullen, **morose;** self-sufficient, self-contained

6 **aloof, standoffish,** distant, remote, withdrawn, detached; **cool,** cold, frigid; inaccessible, **unapproachable**

565 SECLUSION

nouns

1 **seclusion,** retirement, withdrawal, retreat; separation, detachment; segregation, apartheid; **isolation,** ivory tower; **privacy, secrecy**

2 **monasticism**

3 **solitude, loneliness**

4 **desolation;** homelessness; helplessness; **abandonment, desertion**

5 **recluse, loner;** monk, nun; **hermit;** outcast, pariah

6 **retreat, hideaway,** cell, ivory tower, lair, sanctum

verbs

7 **retire,** live alone, live apart, lead a quiet life

adjectives

8 **secluded, withdrawn;** isolated, shut off, insular, **separate,** separated, **apart,** detached, removed; segregated; **remote,** out-of-the-way, off the beaten track

9 **private, reclusive**

10 **cloistered, hermitic; housebound**

11 **solitary, alone; in solitude,** by oneself, all alone; **lonely, lonesome, lone**

12 **forlorn,** abandoned, forsaken, deserted, friendless; **helpless, defenceless**

adverbs

13 in seclusion, in retirement, in retreat, in solitude; in privacy, in secrecy

566 HOSPITALITY, WELCOME

nouns

1 **hospitality; friendliness,** geniality, bonhomie, **generosity,** warmth

2 **welcome,** welcoming, **reception; open arms;** embrace, hug

3 **greetings, regards,** best wishes, salutations

4 **greeting, salutation,** salute; hail, **hello,** accost, address; nod, bow, curtsy; wave; handshake, embrace, hug, kiss; smile

5 **host,** mine host, hostess, landlord

6 **guest, visitor,** caller, company; uninvited guest

verbs

7 **receive, admit,** accept, take in, let in

8 **entertain; host,** preside; throw a party

9 **welcome,** make one feel at home; embrace, hug

10 **greet,** hail, accost, address; sa-

lute; **shake hands,** nod to, bow
to; curtsy, kiss

adjectives

11 **hospitable,** receptive, welcoming; **cordial,** amiable, gracious,
friendly, neighbourly, genial,
open, warm; generous, liberal

12 **welcome,** wanted, desired;
agreeable, desirable, acceptable;
grateful, gratifying, pleasing

adverbs

13 **hospitably, with open arms**

567 INHOSPITALITY

nouns

1 **unfriendliness, inhospitality**

2 **ostracism,** thumbs down; **banishment;** proscription, **ban;** boycott, blacklist, blackball; **rejection**

3 **outcast,** castaway; **pariah,** un-
touchable, leper; **outlaw; exile,**
expatriate; undesirable; persona
non grata

verbs

4 **spurn,** turn one's back on, have
no truck with, steer clear of

5 **ostracize, reject; exile,** banish;
ban, outlaw; boycott, blacklist,
blackball

adjectives

6 **inhospitable;** unreceptive,
closed; **unfriendly**

7 **uninhabitable,** unfit to live in

8 **unwelcome, unwanted;** undesirable, unacceptable; uninvited

9 **outcast, castaway;** outlawed; **rejected,** disowned; abandoned,
forsaken

568 FRIENDSHIP

nouns

1 **friendship, friendliness;** sociability; amiableness, congeniality;
affection, love, kindness

2 **fellowship,** companionship,
comradeship; **camaraderie, es-
prit de corps;** brotherhood, fraternity; sisterhood, sorority

3 **good terms,** friendly relations;
harmony, sympathy, fellow feeling, **rapport;** favour, goodwill,
regard, respect

4 **acquaintance;** introduction,
presentation

5 **familiarity, intimacy, closeness;**
affinity

6 **geniality,** cordiality, bonhomie,
warmth; hospitality

7 **devotion;** dedication, **commitment;** firmness, constancy

verbs

8 **be friends, know;** get on well
with, be inseparable

9 **befriend,** get acquainted, get to
know one another

10 (*nonformal terms*) click, hit it off,
get on like a house on fire

11 cultivate, court, make advances,
approach; suck up to (*nonformal*)

12 get in with, get on the good side
of, get in the good books of (*all
nonformal*)

13 **introduce, present,** acquaint

adjectives

14 **friendly, amicable,** harmonious;
amiable, congenial, pleasant,
agreeable, sociable; well-
intentioned, well-meaning

brotherly, fraternal; sisterly; neighbourly

15 **cordial**, genial, **warm**, affable; hospitable

16 **friends with**, friendly with; acquainted

17 **on speaking terms**, in favour

18 **familiar**, intimate, **close**, inseparable; thick as thieves (*nonformal*)

19 **matey**, chummy (*both nonformal*)

20 **devoted**, dedicated, committed, **fast**, steadfast, constant, **faithful**, staunch; tried, true, tested

adverbs

21 **amicably**, amiably, congenially, **pleasantly**; agreeably, **favourably**; cordially, genially, **warmly**; familiarly, intimately

569 FRIEND

nouns

1 **friend**, acquaintance; confidant, confidante; intimate, familiar; brother, fellow, neighbour; sympathizer, well-wisher, advocate, backer, supporter; **lover**, **partner**, significant other

2 **good friend**, best friend, bosom friend, devoted friend, faithful friend, fast friend, friend indeed

3 **companion**, fellow, comrade; associate, **colleague**, **partner**; roommate, flatmate; classmate, schoolmate; **team-mate**

4 (*nonformal terms*) **pal**, **chum**, **mate**, mucker, main man, home boy

570 ENMITY

nouns

1 **enmity**, unfriendliness; strain, **tension**; coolness, coldness, chill

2 **disaccord**, strained relations, alienation, **disaffection**, estrangement

3 **hostility**, antagonism, antipathy, **spite**, **malice**, malevolence, **hatred**, hate; **conflict**, contention, friction; belligerence

4 **animosity**, ill will, hard feelings, bad blood; **feud**, **vendetta**; **bitterness**, rancour, **acrimony**

5 **grudge**, grievance

6 **enemy**, foe, **adversary**, antagonist; bitter enemy, sworn enemy, archenemy; bane, bete noire

verbs

7 **antagonize**, set at odds; aggravate, exacerbate, **provoke**, embitter, infuriate, madden; alienate, estrange

8 **bear ill will**, harbour a grudge, have a bone to pick with; **hate**

adjectives

9 **unfriendly**, inimical; incompatible; **strained**, **tense**; **cool**, cold, chilly, frosty; inhospitable

10 **hostile**, **antagonistic**, snide, spiteful, malicious, malevolent, malignant, hateful, virulent, **bitter**, sore, acrid, caustic, venomous; conflicting, clashing, colliding; provocative, quarrelsome, belligerent

11 **alienated**, **estranged**, disaffected, separated, divided, torn; irreconcilable

12 at odds, at variance, at loggerheads, at cross-purposes, at sixes
and sevens, at each other's
throats

adverbs

13 coolly, coldly, frostily; antagonis-
tically

571 MISANTHROPY

nouns

1 **misanthropy,** cynicism, egoism,
hatred of mankind; man-hating,
misandry; woman-hating, **misogyny; sexism,** sex discrimination, chauvinism

2 **misanthrope, misanthropist,**
cynic; man-hater, misandrist;
woman-hater, **misogynist; chauvinist**

adjectives

3 **misanthropic,** cynical, **anti-
social;** man-hating, misandrist,
woman-hating, **misogynous; sexist,** chauvinistic

572 PUBLIC SPIRIT

nouns

1 **public spirit, civic virtue,** social
responsibility, good citizenship

2 **patriotism, nationalism;** chauvinism, jingoism, flag-waving;
sabre-rattling

3 **patriot, nationalist;** chauvinist,
jingoist, flag waver; hawk

adjectives

4 **public-spirited, civic; patriotic,**
nationalistic; chauvinist, jingoistic, hawkish

573 BENEFACTOR

nouns

1 **benefactor,** patron, backer, philanthropist; **good Samaritan**

2 **saviour,** redeemer, rescuer, lib-
erator

verbs

3 **benefit, aid,** assist, back, support

adjectives

4 aiding, befriending, assisting;
backing, supporting; saving, redeeming; liberating, freeing,
emancipating

adverbs

5 by one's good offices, on one's
shoulders

574 EVILDOER

nouns

1 **evildoer,** wrongdoer, malefactor,
public enemy, **villain,** delinquent, **criminal,** outlaw, felon,
crook (*nonformal*), thief

2 **troublemaker,** agitator

3 **ruffian,** thug, desperado, cut-
throat; gunman, killer

4 **hooligan,** tough, bruiser, ned
(*Scots*); **hood,** goon, hatchet
man, heavy

5 **savage,** barbarian, brute, beast,
animal; **vandal**

6 **monster,** fiend, demon, devil,
vampire, harpy, ghoul, **werewolf,**
ogre

7 **witch,** hag, she-devil, virago, siren, fury

575 JURISDICTION

nouns

1 **jurisdiction,** legal authority

2 **judiciary,** legal system, the courts; **justice,** judicial process

3 **bureau, office, department;** secretariat, ministry

verbs

4 **administer justice,** preside, sit in judgment, **judge**

adjectives

5 **judicatory,** judicative; juridic *or* juridical; **judicial,** judiciary

576 TRIBUNAL

nouns

1 **tribunal,** forum, board; **judiciary;** council; inquisition

2 **court, court of law, legal tribunal**

3 (*ecclesiastical courts*) Papal Court; Court of Arches, Court of Peculiars

4 **military court, court-martial,** naval court, captain's mast

5 **bench, woolsack,** seat of justice

6 **courthouse, court; courtroom;** jury box; witness stand, dock

adjectives

7 **tribunal,** judicial, judiciary, court

8 (*courts*) Judicial Committee of the Privy Council, House of Lords, Supreme Court of Judicature, High Court of Justice, High Court, Crown Court; Court of Session *and* High Court of Justiciary *and* Sheriff Court (*all Scots*)

577 JUDGE, JURY

nouns

1 **judge, magistrate, justice,** beak (*nonformal*); arbiter, adjudicator; umpire, referee

2 Lord High Chancellor, Master of the Rolls, Lord Chief Justice, Lord Justice; Lord Advocate (*Scots*)

3 **jury,** panel

4 **juror, foreman**

578 LAWYER

nouns

1 **lawyer,** attorney (*US*), **barrister, advocate** (*Scots*), counsel, legal adviser, legal practitioner

2 **jurist,** jurisprudent

3 (*nonformal terms*) shyster, legal eagle

4 **bar,** legal profession; representation, counsel, pleading; **practice,** law firm, partnership

verbs

5 **practice law;** be admitted to the bar; take silk

adjectives

6 lawyerlike; of counsel

579 LEGAL ACTION

nouns

1 **lawsuit, suit, litigation,** action, legal action, legal proceedings, prosecution; **case,** court case, cause

2 **summons, writ, subpoena, warrant**

3 **indictment, impeachment**

4 **jury selection,** empanelment; jury duty

5 **trial, hearing, inquiry,** inquest, assize (Scots); court-martial; examination, cross-examination

6 **pleading, plea,** argument; defence; refutation

7 **declaration, statement,** allegation; deposition, **affadavit;** claim; complaint; libel

8 **testimony; evidence;** argument; summing up

9 **judgment, decision; verdict, sentence;** acquittal

10 **appeal; retrial**

11 **party,** litigant, plaintiff, **defendant, accused;** witness; accessory

verbs

12 **sue, prosecute,** litigate, take to court

13 **summons, subpoena**

14 **indict, impeach,** arraign; prefer charges

15 **select** *or* **impanel a jury**

16 **call to witness; testify,** take the stand

17 **try,** give a hearing to, hear; **judge,** sit in judgment

18 **plead,** enter a plea; present one's case, rest one's case

19 **bring in a verdict,** pronounce sentence; **acquit; convict;** penalize

adjectives

20 litigious; actionable; sub judice

580 ACCUSATION

nouns

1 **accusation, charge, complaint;** accusing, denunciation; **indict**ment; **impeachment; allegation;** insinuation, implication, innuendo; **prosecution, suit, lawsuit**

2 **incrimination,** citation, involvement

3 **recrimination,** retort, countercharge

4 **trumped-up charge,** false witness, frame-up (*nonformal*)

5 **accuser, accusant;** informer; **plaintiff, claimant, petitioner,** suitor, **party;** prosecutor, the prosecution

6 **accused, defendant,** suspect, prisoner

verbs

7 **accuse;** charge, press charges; **indict, impeach;** denounce, **inform on; allege,** insinuate, imply

8 **blame,** lay the blame on

9 **accuse of, charge with**

10 **incriminate,** implicate, involve

11 **bear false witness; frame** (*nonformal*), trump up a charge

adjectives

12 **accusing, accusatory**

13 **incriminating,** incriminatory

14 **accused, charged,** blamed, denounced, **impeached, indicted, incriminated,** implicated; under a cloud

581 JUSTIFICATION

nouns

1 **justification, vindication;** clearing one's name; rehabilitation

2 **defence, plea,** pleading; argument, answer, reply, response; **refutation, denial, objection;** special pleading

3 excuse, alibi

4 extenuation, mitigation, palliation; saving grace; qualification, allowance; diminished responsibility

5 reason, cause, right, basis, grounds, foundation, substance

6 reasonableness, legitimacy

7 advocate, champion, proponent, defender; apologist

verbs

8 justify, vindicate; rehabilitate; clear one's name

9 defend, support; uphold, sustain; **advocate, champion,** espouse

10 excuse, explain, apologize for, have an alibi

11 extenuate, mitigate, palliate; make allowances for

adjectives

12 justifying, justificatory; **extenuating,** palliative

13 justifiable, defensible; forgivable, allowable; reasonable, **legitimate;** innocuous, inoffensive

582 ACQUITTAL

nouns

1 acquittal, verdict of not guilty, not proven verdict (*Scots*); **vindication,** clearing; **pardon,** Royal pardon; discharge, release

2 exemption, immunity; amnesty; stay

3 reprieve, respite, grace

verbs

4 acquit, clear, exonerate, absolve; **vindicate,** justify; **pardon,** excuse, forgive; discharge, **release,** dismiss, free, set free, let off

(*nonformal*); **exempt,** grant immunity

5 reprieve, grant a stay of execution

583 CONDEMNATION

nouns

1 condemnation, damnation, **guilty verdict;** denunciation, censure; conviction; **sentence, judgment;** capital punishment, death penalty

verbs

2 condemn, damn, doom; denounce; censure; convict, find guilty; pronounce judgment, **sentence**

3 stand condemned, be convicted, **be found guilty**

adjectives

4 condemnatory; censorious

584 PENALTY

nouns

1 penalty, penance; **sanctions,** punitive measures; **punishment;** reprisal, retaliation

2 handicap, disability, **disadvantage**

3 fine, damages; forfeit, forfeiture

verbs

4 penalize; impose sanctions; retaliate

5 fine, award damages

adverbs

6 on pain of, under penalty of

585 PUNISHMENT

nouns

1 **punishment**, chastening, correction, discipline; **retribution**; just deserts

2 (*forms of punishment*) **imprisonment**, penal servitude, incarceration, confinement; hard labour; torture, martyrdom; the rack, keelhauling, tar-and-feathering

3 **slap**, smack, whack, cuff, belt

4 **corporal punishment**, **beating**, thrashing, spanking; flogging, flailing, lashing; strapping, belting, **caning**

5 (*nonformal terms*) hiding, leathering, walloping

6 **capital punishment**, **execution**; **hanging**, the gallows; crucifixion; **electric chair** (*nonformal*); gassing; lethal injection; beheading, the guillotine; shooting, **firing squad**; burning at the stake; poisoning; stoning

7 **executioner**, hangman

8 jailer, turnkey

verbs

9 **punish**, chastise, chasten, **discipline**, correct, castigate, penalize; bring to book, deal with, make an example of

10 (*nonformal terms*) come down hard on, throw the book at

11 **slap**, smack, whack, cuff; box the ears, give a rap on the knuckles

12 **beat**, thrash, spank; **whip**, **flog**, flail, lash; thump, pummel; strap, **belt**, **cane**, birch; club, truncheon,

13 **thrash soundly**, batter

14 (*nonformal terms*) beat up, rough up, clobber; give a kicking *or* good hiding to, sort out

15 **torture**; put on the rack, break on the wheel; dismember, draw and quarter; impale, keelhaul

16 **execute**; **electrocute**; **behead**, **decapitate**, **guillotine**; **crucify**; **shoot**; **stone**; **poison**; **gas**; **garrote**

17 **hang**, lynch; hang, draw, and quarter

18 **catch it**, **get one's just deserts**, get one's fingers burned *or* one's knuckles rapped

19 **deserve punishment**, have it coming (*nonformal*), be heading for a fall

adjectives

20 **punishing**, chastising, chastening, corrective, **disciplinary**; **penal**, punitive

586 INSTRUMENTS OF PUNISHMENT

nouns

1 **whip**, **lash**, strap, thong, belt, birch, crop, cat

2 **rod**, **stick**, ruler, cane; **birch**; club

3 (*devices*) pillory, stocks; ducking stool; treadmill

4 (*instruments of torture*) **rack**, **wheel**, **Iron Maiden**; **thumbscrew**

5 (*instruments of execution*) **scaffold**, **gallows**, gibbet; block, guillotine; stake; cross; **noose**, rope; **electric chair**, hot seat (*nonformal*); gas chamber; **firing squad**

587 THE PEOPLE

nouns

1 **the people,** the populace, the public, **the general public,** everyone, everybody; **the population, the community, society,** the nation; common people, ordinary people, folk

2 **the masses,** the many, **the multitude,** the crowd, **the mob,** the majority, the herd, the great unwashed, the hoi polloi

3 **rabble; riffraff, dregs,** trash, scum, vermin

4 **the underprivileged,** the disadvantaged, **the poor,** the homeless, the dispossessed, **the underclass,** the unemployable, the lumpenproletariat

5 **common man,** little man, Everyman, **the man in the street;** proletarian, prole, plebian, pleb

6 **peasant,** son of the soil, **farmer;** yokel, country bumpkin, hick, hillbilly

7 **upstart,** parvenu; **nouveau riche; social climber,** name-dropper

adjectives

8 **demographic; national; popular, public, mass;** common, plebian, plain, ordinary, lowly, low, mean, base; **humble, homely;** earthy, vulgar, rude, coarse; upstart, nouveau riche

588 SOCIAL CLASS AND STATUS

nouns

1 **class, social class, socioeconomic class,** status group, social cat-

egory, order, grade, caste, estate, rank; **status,** standing, footing, prestige, rank, ranking, place, station, position, level, degree, stratum; **social structure, stratification, class structure,** power structure, hierarchy, ranking, ordering, social scale, gradation, division; **inequality, class conflict, class struggle; social mobility,** upward mobility, downward mobility

2 **upper class, aristocracy,** second estate, **ruling class,** elite, elect, the privileged, upper crust (*nonformal*); **nobility, gentry**

3 **aristocracy, high rank, quality;** birth, blue blood

4 **aristocrat, patrician; gentleman, lady**

5 **middle class,** bourgeoisie, educated class, professional class, white-collar workers, salaried workers; suburbia

6 **bourgeois,** white-collar worker, salaried worker, pillar of society

7 **lower class,** workers, working class, **proletariat,** proles (*nonformal*), blue-collar workers

8 **the underclass, the underprivileged**

9 **worker,** working man, working woman, proletarian, blue-collar worker, labourer, industrial worker, factory worker

adjectives

10 **upper-class, aristocratic,** patrician; genteel, gentlemanly, ladylike; **well-bred,** blue-blooded, of noble birth; posh (*nonformal*); **middle-class, bourgeois,** suburban, petty-bourgeois; **working**

class, blue collar, proletarian, lower-class; mobile, **upwardly mobile**; downwardly mobile, déclassé; **underprivileged, disadvantaged**

589 ARISTOCRACY, NOBILITY, GENTRY

(noble rank or birth)

nouns

1 **aristocracy, nobility,** landed gentry, titled aristocracy; elite, **upper class,** elect, upper crust *(nonformal)*; old nobility, **peerage;** royalty

2 **nobility, aristocracy;** quality, rank, distinction; noble birth, ancestry; blue blood; **royalty**

3 **gentry,** lesser nobility, landed gentry

4 **nobleman,** noble, gentleman; **peer; aristocrat,** patrician; **lord,** laird *(Scots),* **duke,** archduke, marquis, **earl, count,** viscount, **baron,** baronet; squire, esquire

5 **knight,** cavalier, chevalier; knight-errant

6 **noblewoman, lady; dame,** duchess, countess, **baroness**

7 **prince, heir apparent,** crown prince, prince regent, prince consort; **king; sheikh, khan, emir**

8 **princess,** infanta *(Spanish),* crown princess; **queen**

9 *(rank or office)* lordship, ladyship; dukedom, earldom, barony; knighthood; kingship, queenship

adjectives

10 **noble,** of noble birth, of high rank, exalted; **aristocratic, patrician;** gentle, genteel; gentlemanly, ladylike; chivalrous, knightly; **titled; regal**

11 **blue-blooded,** well-bred

590 POLITICS

nouns

1 **politics,** polity, the art of the possible, Realpolitik

2 **political science, politics,** government; **political philosophy,** political theory; comparative government; international relations, Geopolitik

3 **statesmanship,** statecraft, leadership

4 **policy;** line, **party line,** doctrine, philosophy, position; free enterprise, laissez-faire; planned economy, command economy; free trade; protectionism; autarky, economic self-sufficiency

5 **foreign policy,** foreign affairs; **diplomacy,** shuttle diplomacy; gunboat diplomacy; nationalism, **imperialism, colonialism,** expansionism; deterrence, containment, balance of power; isolationism, autarky; **internationalism,** peaceful coexistence, compromise, appeasement, détente

6 **platform,** programme; plank, issue

7 **party conference,** assembly, political convention

8 **candidacy,** candidature; standing *or* running for office

9 **nomination; acceptance**

10 **electioneering, campaigning,** pressing the flesh (*nonformal*); **rally**

11 **smear campaign,** whispering campaign, character assassination, dirty tricks, **mudslinging**

12 **election, general election, by-election;** presidential election; **referendum**

13 **constituency,** district, county, ward; European constituency

14 **suffrage, franchise, the vote;** universal suffrage

15 **voting, going to the polls; first past the post;** proportional representation *or* PR; single transferable vote *or* STV

16 **polls,** polling station; voting booth; ballot box

17 **returns,** election returns, **poll,** count; **recount;** landslide

18 **electorate,** electors; **constituency,** constituents; electoral college

19 **voter, elector;** proxy

20 **political party, party**

21 **party member,** stalwart, party hack; party faithful, rank and file

22 **neutral, independent,** floating voter

23 political influence, public opinion; lobbying

24 **power broker,** fixer, wire-puller

25 **pressure group, lobby,** interest group, single-issue group; vested interest

26 **front, movement, coalition;** popular front; people's front; grass-roots movement, ground swell

27 (*political corruption*) **graft,** jobbery; patronage; cronyism

verbs

28 **stand for office, run for office,** throw one's hat into the ring

29 **electioneer, campaign;** take to the hustings, hit the campaign trail; **canvass;** press the flesh (*nonformal*)

30 **support, back, endorse; nominate, elect,** vote

31 **hold office,** be incumbent

adjectives

32 **political;** governmental, civic; diplomatic; statesmanlike

33 **partisan,** loyal

34 **independent,** neutral

35 (*political parties*), Conservative Party, Labour Party, Liberal Democrats, Green Party, Scottish National Party, Plaid Cymru, SDLP, Sinn Féin

591 POLITICIAN

nouns

1 **politician,** politico; party leader; grandee; party hack

2 **statesman,** national leader; elder statesman

3 **legislator,** lawgiver; **Member of Parliament** *or* **MP;** Member of the European Parliament *or* MEP; whip, chief whip; councillor, mayor, provost (*Scots*)

4 (*political intriguer*) wheeler-dealer; **éminence grise, power behind the throne,** kingmaker, power broker

5 **candidate,** aspirant, hopeful; running mate; dark horse; stalking horse

6 **campaigner, electioneer**

7 **office bearer, incumbent;** lame duck; new broom (*nonformal*)

verbs

8 **go into politics;** run, campaign

adjectives

9 **statesmanlike**

592 POLITICO-ECONOMIC PRINCIPLES

nouns

1 **conservatism, reaction**

2 **middle of the road, centre**

3 **leftism, social democracy**

4 **radicalism, extremism;** anarchism, nihilism

5 **communism, Marxism,** Marxism-Leninism, Leninism, democratic centralism, dictatorship of the proletariat, Stalinism, Maoism; revisionism

6 **socialism,** collectivization, public ownership, nationalization, state socialism; guild socialism, utopian socialism, Fabian socialism

7 **welfarism;** welfare, relief, social security, unemployment benefit, old-age pensions; welfare state

8 **capitalism, laissez-faire,** private enterprise, private ownership, free trade; Thatcherism, New Right

9 **fascism,** national socialism, ultra-nationalism, authoritarianism

10 **conservative,** right-winger, dry, **Tory;** reactionary; royalist, monarchist, imperialist

11 **moderate;** wet, one-nation Tory; social democrat, liberal, progressive

12 **radical, extremist, revolutionary;** subversive; anarchist, nihilist

13 **communist, Marxist,** Marxist-Leninist, Stalinist, Maoist; fellow traveller

14 **socialist,** Fabian, collectivist

15 **Thatcherite**

16 **fascist, Nazi** *or* **national socialist,** ultra-nationalist, authoritarian

verbs

17 **politicize;** nationalize; privatize

adjectives

18 **conservative, right-wing,** dry; reactionary

19 **moderate, middle-of-the-road;** wet, one-nation; social democratic, liberal, progressive

20 **radical, extremist, revolutionary;** subversive; anarchic, nihilistic

21 **communist, Marxist,** Marxist-Leninist, Stalinist, Maoist

22 **socialist, left-wing;** Fabian, collectivist

23 **Thatcherite**

24 **fascist, Nazi** *or* **national socialist,** ultra-nationalist, authoritarian

593 GOVERNMENT

nouns

1 **government,** regulation; management, administration, supervision; **regime,** regimen; **rule, sovereignty,** reign

2 **control,** mastery, **command, power, jurisdiction,** dominion

3 **the government,** the authorities, central government; the establishment; Whitehall, **Downing Street;** His *or* Her Majesty's Government, the Crown

4 (*kinds of government*) federal government, federation; republic, commonwealth; **democracy, representative government;** socialism, social democracy, welfare state; **aristocracy,** oligarchy, feudal system; **monarchy,** absolute monarchy, constitutional monarchy; dictatorship, tyranny; police state, totalitarianism; **fascism, national socialism; communism,** Marxism; **military rule,** martial law; autonomy, self-government, home rule; **imperialism, colonialism;** provisional government; coalition government

5 (*supranational government*) **United Nations,** League of Nations (*old*); **European Union** *or* **EU**

6 (*principles of government*) democracy, power-sharing, pluralism, constitutionalism, rule of law; monarchism; feudalism; imperialism, colonialism; fascism, national socialism; communism, socialism; federalism, centralism

7 **absolutism, dictatorship,** despotism, tyranny, autocracy; **monarchy,** absolute monarchy; totalitarianism, authoritarianism; **one-party rule,** Leninism; benevolent despotism, paternalism

8 **despotism, tyranny,** oppression; iron heel, reign of terror; thought control

9 **bureaucracy,** red tape (*nonformal*)

verbs

10 **govern,** regulate; command, head, **lead;** preside over, chair; direct, manage, supervise, administer

11 **control;** hold the reins, be in the driver's seat, pull the strings (*all nonformal*)

12 **rule, sway, reign**

13 **dominate,** prevail; master; dictate, lay down the law

14 **domineer,** lord it over; browbeat, order around, intimidate, bully, walk all over, tyrannize, push around; grind down, break, **oppress,** suppress, repress, keep down; enslave, **subjugate;** compel, coerce

adjectives

15 **governmental, political, civil,** civic; **official, bureaucratic; democratic,** federal, constitutional, parliamentary; fascist *or* fascistic; monarchic, autocratic, absolute; **authoritarian,** totalitarian; despotic, **dictatorial;** self-governing, autonomous

16 **governing,** controlling, regulating, regulatory; **ruling, reigning, sovereign;** master, chief, boss, head; **dominant,** predominant, leading, paramount, supreme

17 **executive, administrative,** ministerial; official, bureaucratic

adverbs

18 **under control,** in hand

594 LEGISLATURE, GOVERNMENT ORGANIZATION

nouns

1 **legislature, parliament,** congress, assembly, diet, chamber

2 **cabinet,** kitchen cabinet, Star Chamber; shadow cabinet

3 **legislation, lawmaking;** enactment, passage

4 (*legislative procedure*) introduction, first reading, committee consideration, tabling, second reading, **debate,** filibustering, third reading, **vote,** division; closure, guillotine

5 **veto,** presidential veto

6 **referendum;** mandate; plebiscite

7 **bill,** clause, proviso, amendment

verbs

8 **legislate, enact, pass,** constitute; table, debate, veto, filibuster, kill; decree

adjectives

9 **legislative, parliamentary**

595 COMMISSION

nouns

1 **commission,** commissioning, **delegation,** devolution, investing, investment; commitment, entrusting, **assignment;** errand, task, office; care, responsibility, jurisdiction; mission, embassy; **authority, authorization;** warrant, licence, mandate, charge, trust

2 **appointment,** assignment, nomination, naming, selection; ordination; posting

3 **installation,** instalment, placement, **inauguration, investiture;** coronation

4 **engagement, employment,** hiring, appointment, taking on, recruitment, recruiting

5 **rental,** rent, lease, let; hire, hiring; **charter**

6 **enlistment,** enrolment; **conscription,** drafting, induction; call, draft, **call-up,** summons; **recruitment,** recruiting, mustering; mobilization

7 **nominee, candidate,** appointee

verbs

8 **commission, authorize,** empower; **delegate,** devolve, vest; assign, consign, commit, **charge, entrust;** licence, charter, warrant; detail, detach, post, transfer, send out

9 **appoint, assign,** designate, **nominate,** name, select, tab (*nonformal*); **ordain**

10 **install, induct, inaugurate,** invest; crown, enthrone

11 **be instated, take office,** accede; attain to

12 **employ, hire,** take on, recruit, headhunt (*nonformal*), engage, sign up

13 **rent, lease, let;** hire, charter

14 **rent out, lease out; hire out,** charter; **sublease, sublet,** farm, farm out

15 **enlist, enrol,** sign up; **conscript, draft, recruit,** induct, summon, call up; **mobilize,** muster

adjectives

16 **commissioned, authorized,** accredited; delegated, deputized, appointed

17 **employed, hired, paid,** mercenary; rented, leased, let; chartered

adverbs

18 **for hire,** for rent, to let, to lease

596 ASSOCIATE

nouns

1 **associate, colleague, companion,** collaborator, fellow, crony, consort, compatriot, brother, **ally, comrade**

2 **partner;** business partner, sleeping partner

3 **accomplice, cohort;** accessory

4 **co-worker,** fellow worker, workmate; **team-mate**

5 **assistant, helper,** auxiliary, aide; deputy, agent; attendant, second, acolyte; **servant, employee;** lieutenant, aide-de-camp

6 **right-hand man,** alter ego, confidant

7 **follower, disciple,** adherent; yes-man, sycophant, lackey

8 **supporter, backer,** promoter, patron, **champion,** defender, **advocate,** exponent, protagonist; well-wisher, sympathizer, fan, admirer, lover

597 ASSOCIATION

nouns

1 **association, society,** body; **alliance,** coalition, league, union; **bloc,** axis; **partnership;** federa-tion, confederation; unholy alliance, gang, ring, mob; **economic community,** common market, customs union, free trade area; credit union, cooperative

2 **community, society; clan,** caste; **family,** extended family, nuclear family; order, **class,** social class, economic class; colony, settlement; commune

3 **fellowship; society,** guild, order; **brotherhood,** fraternity; **sisterhood,** sorority; secret society, cabal

4 **party, interest, camp, side;** interest group, pressure group; minority group, vocal minority; silent majority; **faction,** division, sect, **wing,** splinter, breakaway group, offshoot

5 **school, sect,** class, order; **denomination,** communion, faith, church; disciples, followers, adherents

6 **clique,** coterie, set, circle, ring; crew, crowd, mob, outfit *(all nonformal)*; cell; inner circle, elite; old-boy network

7 **team, outfit, squad,** crew; eleven, fifteen, thirteen; etc; first team; bench, reserves, second team; platoon; complement; **cast,** company

8 **organization, establishment,** foundation, **institution, institute**

9 **company, firm,** concern, house, **business, industry,** enterprise; venture; trust, syndicate, consortium; chamber of commerce

10 **branch, division,** wing, arm, offshoot; chapter, lodge, chapel

11 **member,** affiliate, insider, initiate, card-carrying member; asso-

ciate, fellow; brother, sister,
comrade; honorary member, life
member

12 **membership, members,** associ-
ates, constituency, affiliates

13 **partisanship, factionalism;** sectarianism; party spirit, espirit de
corps

verbs

14 **join,** join up, **enter,** go into; **enlist, enrol,** sign up, take out
membership; combine, associate

15 **belong,** hold membership, subscribe, be in

adjectives

16 **associated, corporate,** incorporated; **combined**

17 **social, communal;** organizational; **sociable**

18 **cliquish,** clannish; **exclusive**

19 **partisan, factional;** sectarian

adverbs

20 **in association**

598 WEALTH

nouns

1 **wealth,** riches, **opulence; richness, wealthiness; prosperity,
affluence; money,** gold, lucre,
mammon; substance, **property,**
possessions, material wealth, assets; **fortune,** treasure

2 **large sum,** good sum, king's ransom

3 (*nonformal terms*) bundle, mega-
bucks, big money, serious money, heaps, mint, pile, wad, packet

4 (*rich source*) **mine, gold mine,**
bonanza, Eldorado; gravy train

(*nonformal*); cash cow (*nonformal*)

5 **the rich, the wealthy,** the well-
to-do, the haves (*nonformal*)

6 **rich man** *or* **woman;** fat cat,
moneybags; **plutocrat, capitalist;
millionaire,** billionaire

verbs

7 **get rich, feather one's nest,
strike it rich, coin it in** (*nonformal*)

adjectives

8 **wealthy, rich, affluent,** well-to-
do, well-off, prosperous, comfortable, flush

9 (*nonformal terms*) loaded, filthy
rich, rolling in it, made of money

599 POVERTY

nouns

1 **poverty; straits,** difficulties,
hardship, straitened circumstances

2 **indigence,** penury; impoverishment; **homelessness, destitution,** privation, **deprivation;
want,** need; hand-to-mouth existence

3 **the poor, the needy,** the have-
nots, **the disadvantaged, the
underprivileged;** the homeless;
the underclass

4 **beggar, pauper,** bag lady; bankrupt

verbs

5 **be poor,** be hard up, be destitute, be on one's uppers; want,
need; **starve,** live from hand to
mouth; not have two pennies to
rub together

6 **impoverish**, beggar; **bankrupt**

adjectives

7 **poor, badly off,** hard up; strapped, feeling the pinch, unable to make ends meet

8 **indigent, poverty-stricken, needy,** in need, in want, **disadvantaged, deprived, underprivileged, impoverished;** on one's uppers, down at heel

9 **destitute,** down-and-out; penniless, **bankrupt,** in the red, insolvent; **homeless,** landless

10 (*nonformal terms*) **broke,** flat broke, stony broke, strapped, skint

600 LENDING

nouns

1 **lending,** loaning, **moneylending;** usury, loan-sharking; **interest,** interest rate, lending rate, base rate

2 **loan,** advance

3 **lender, moneylender; banker;** money broker; pawnbroker; loan shark, usurer

4 **bank, building society,** friendly society; credit union; pawnbroker

verbs

5 **lend, loan, advance;** loan-shark

adjectives

6 **loaned, lent**

adverbs

7 **on loan,** on security; in advance

601 BORROWING

nouns

1 **borrowing; financing, mortgaging**

2 **adoption,** appropriation, **taking,** deriving; imitation, simulation, copying, **plagiarism,** pirating

verbs

3 **borrow,** raise money; pawn

4 **adopt,** appropriate, **take,** derive; imitate, simulate, copy, **plagiarize,** pirate

602 FINANCIAL CREDIT

nouns

1 **credit, trust,** tick (*nonformal*); tax credit, investment credit; credit standing, credit rating

2 **account,** credit account; **bank account,** savings account, current account; bank balance; expense account

3 **credit card,** plastic (*nonformal*), charge card, cash card, smart card

4 **creditor, investor,** shareholder

verbs

5 **credit,** credit to one's account; buy on credit, charge to one's account

adjectives

6 **credited,** of good credit

adverbs

7 **on credit,** on account, on trust; in instalments

603 DEBT

nouns

1 **debt, indebtedness,** obligation, **liability,** financial commitment, due, **dues, outstanding debt;** bills, charges; accounts payable; borrowing; bad debts; **national debt,** public debt

2 **arrears,** back payments; **deficit,** default, deferred payments; **overdraft**

3 **interest,** premium, price, **rate; interest rate,** bank rate, lending rate, borrowing rate; simple interest, compound interest; net interest, gross interest

4 **debtor,** borrower

verbs

5 owe, be indebted

6 **run into debt;** show a deficit, operate at a loss

adjectives

7 **indebted,** in debt, in the red

8 **due, payable,** outstanding, in arrears

604 PAYMENT

nouns

1 **payment,** paying off, paying up (*nonformal*), payoff; discharge, settlement, clearance, liquidation; debt service, interest payment; **down payment, deposit; cash,** payment in kind

2 **refund,** repayment, reimbursement

3 **recompense,** remuneration, **compensation, damages,** indemnity; retribution, redress, **reparation,** satisfaction, atonement;

amends, return; price, consideration

4 **pay, payment,** remuneration, compensation; **salary, wage, wages,** income, **earnings;** real wages, purchasing power; **pay packet, take-home pay,** net earnings; gross pay, taxable income; living wage, minimum wage; guaranteed income, fixed income; overtime, danger money, bonus

5 **fee,** stipend, **allowance,** emolument; reckoning, account, bill; hush money, blackmail, blood money

6 (*extra pay or allowance*) **bonus, premium, fringe benefit,** bounty, perks (*nonformal*); tip; **overtime**

7 **dividend; royalty;** commission, cut; mark-up

8 **maintenance, support, subsidy**

9 **paymaster,** purser, bursar, **cashier, treasurer; taxpayer,** ratepayer (*old*)

verbs

10 **pay,** render, tender; **recompense, compensate,** reward, satisfy, remit

11 **repay,** pay back, restitute, **refund, reimburse,** recoup; atone, redress, **make amends,** make good

12 **settle with,** reckon with, get quits with (*nonformal*)

13 **pay in full, pay off,** pay up (*nonformal*), discharge, settle, square, clear, satisfy, meet one's obligations

14 **pay out,** shell out

15 **pay over,** hand over, lay one's money down, show the colour of one's money

16 (*nonformal terms*) cough up, stump up, grease the palm with

17 **pay for,** bear the expense, foot the bill; **finance, fund;** chip in (*nonformal*), pay one's way, go Dutch (*nonformal*)

18 **earn,** be paid, draw wages, be salaried

adjectives

19 **paying,** remunerative; compensating, compensatory; **lucrative, profitable, moneymaking**

20 **paid, paid-up,** settled; spent, expended; **salaried, waged, hired**

21 **solvent,** out of debt, above water, in the black

adverbs

22 **in exchange for,** in compensation, in recompense, for services rendered

605 NONPAYMENT

nouns

1 **nonpayment, default,** failure to pay; dishonouring; bad debt

2 **moratorium; write-off,** cancellation

3 **insolvency, bankruptcy, receivership,** failure, queer terrain (*nonformal*); crash, collapse; insufficient funds, overdraft

4 **bankrupt,** failure, insolvent

5 **defaulter,** nonpayer, tax dodger

verbs

6 **not pay, dishonour, default**

7 **go bankrupt, go into receiver-**ship, fail, crash, collapse, **fold, go out of business**

8 **bankrupt, ruin,** break, drive to the wall, put out of business, sink

9 **write off,** declare a moratorium, forgive, cancel, nullify, wipe the slate clean

adjectives

10 **defaulting,** nonpaying, in arrears

11 **insolvent, bankrupt,** in receivership, out of business; **broke, ruined**

606 EXPENDITURE

nouns

1 **expenditure, spending,** expense; debit, debiting; budgeting; scheduling, costing; payment; consumption

2 **payments,** outgoings, outlay

3 **expenses, costs,** charges, liabilities, **overheads**

verbs

4 **spend, pay out;** shell out, fork out (*both nonformal*), put one's hands in one's pockets; **squander,** go on a spending spree, throw money around (*nonformal*); **invest,** lay out; budget, schedule, cost; **consume**

5 **afford,** spare the price, bear, stand, support, meet the expense of

607 RECEIPTS

nouns

1 **receipts, income, revenue,** profits, earnings, returns, proceeds; **takings,** gate receipts,

gate; **dividends,** payout; royalties, commissions

2 (*written acknowledgment*) **receipt,** acknowledgment, voucher

verbs

3 **receive,** pocket, acquire

608 ACCOUNTS

nouns

1 **accounts;** outstanding *or* unpaid accounts; receipts; assets; **accounts payable,** expenditures, liabilities; **budget,** budgeting

2 **account,** reckoning, tally, score, balance

3 **statement, bill,** itemized bill, account, reckoning, **invoice**

4 **account book, ledger,** journal, daybook; **register,** registry, **record book;** books; inventory, catalogue; **log,** logbook; bankbook, passbook; balance sheet

5 **entry,** item, minute, note, notation; **credit, debit**

6 **accounting, accountancy, bookkeeping; cost accounting, costing; audit, auditing;** stocktaking

7 **accountant, bookkeeper, clerk,** chartered accountant; actuary; **auditor**

verbs

8 **keep accounts, keep books;** log, note, minute; **credit, debit;** balance the books

9 **take account of, take stock,** overhaul; **audit**

10 **falsify accounts,** cook the books (*nonformal*)

11 **bill, invoice**

adjectives

12 accounting, bookkeeping; budgetary

609 TRANSFER OF PROPERTY OR RIGHT

nouns

1 **transfer, transference;** conveyance, conveyancing; delivery, assignment, consignment, sale, surrender, transmission, disposal; **exchange,** barter, trading

2 devolution, succession

verbs

3 **transfer,** convey, deliver; hand over, pass over; assign, consign; cede, surrender; **bequeath; sell, sell off;** sign over, sign away; transmit, hand down, pass on, devolve upon; **exchange,** barter, trade

4 **change hands,** change ownership

adjectives

5 **transferable,** conveyable, negotiable; bequeathable; **heritable**

610 PRICE, FEE

nouns

1 **price, cost, expense,** expenditure, **charge,** damage *and* score; rate, figure, amount; **quotation,** quoted price

2 **worth, value,** rate; face value; market value; street value; net worth

3 **valuation, evaluation,** pricing, price determination, assessment, appraisal, estimation, rating

4 price index, retail price index, cost of living index, misery index; rising prices, **inflation**, inflationary spiral

5 price controls, valorization; managed trade, price supports, price freeze; fair trade, free trade

6 fee, dues, **toll**, charge, **charges**, surcharge, exactment; licence fee, entry fee, admission

7 freight, haulage, carriage; tonnage

8 rent, rental

9 tax, taxation, duty, tribute, taxes, levy, toll, imposition; tithe; indirect taxation, direct taxation; progressive taxation, graduated taxation; regressive taxation, poll tax; tax deduction, write-off; tax relief, tax exemption, tax holiday

10 tax collector, taxman; customs officer, exciseman (old); Inland Revenue

verbs

11 price, value, evaluate, appraise, assess, rate; valorize; mark up, mark down, discount

12 charge, demand, require; overcharge, surcharge; exact, levy, impose, tax

13 cost, sell for, fetch, bring; come to, amount to

adjectives

14 priced, valued, evaluated, assessed, appraised, rated, prized; worth, valued at

15 taxable, declarable

16 tax-free, tax-exempt, tax-deductible; duty-free

adverbs

17 at a price, for a consideration

611 DISCOUNT

nouns

1 discount, cut, deduction, reduction; rebate, refund; allowance, concession; premium, percentage

verbs

2 discount, cut, deduct; rebate, refund

adverbs

3 at a discount, at a reduced rate

612 EXPENSIVENESS

nouns

1 expensiveness, costliness; richness, luxuriousness

2 value, worth

3 high price, fancy price, extortionate price, an arm and a leg (nonformal); sellers' market; inflation, overheating, inflationary spiral, stagflation

4 exorbitance, extravagance, excess

5 hidden cost, surcharge; extortion, daylight robbery

verbs

6 be overpriced, price out of the market, cost an arm and a leg (nonformal)

7 overprice; overcharge, surcharge; extort, swindle, exploit, fleece; profiteer

8 overpay, pay through the nose (nonformal)

9 inflate, heat up the economy; reflate

adjectives

10 **precious, dear, valuable;** priceless, **invaluable**

11 **expensive, dear,** costly; **fancy,** upmarket, sumptuous, **luxurious,** posh

12 **overpriced, exorbitant,** excessive, extravagant, unreasonable, **fancy,** outrageous, prohibitive; **extortionate; inflationary,** spiralling

adverbs

13 **dear, dearly;** at a premium, at great expense

14 **expensively,** richly, sumptuously, luxuriously

15 **exorbitantly,** excessively, grossly, **extravagantly, extortionately**

613 CHEAPNESS

nouns

1 **cheapness,** affordability, reasonableness

2 **low price,** nominal price, reasonable price; bargain prices; budget prices; buyers' market; reduced price, cut price, sale price

3 **bargain,** good buy, giveaway, **steal** *and* snip (*nonformal*)

4 **cheapening, depreciation, devaluation,** reduction, lowering; decline, slump, free fall

verbs

5 **be cheap,** cost little; get one's money's worth

6 **cheapen, depreciate, devaluate,** lower, reduce, **mark down,** cut prices, slash, shave, trim; fall, decline, slump

adjectives

7 **cheap, inexpensive,** low, frugal, **reasonable,** moderate, **budget, economy, economical**

8 dirt cheap, bargain-basement

9 **reduced,** cut-price, slashed, marked down, half-price

adverbs

10 **cheaply,** cheap, on the cheap (*nonformal*) reasonably, moderately; at a bargain, for a song (*nonformal*)

614 COSTLESSNESS

nouns

1 **gratuity,** no charge; gift, freebie (*nonformal*)

2 **freeloader,** sponger, scrounger

verbs

3 **give, present;** freeload, sponge, scrounge

adjectives

4 **gratuitous, free,** for free, for nothing, without charge, **complimentary,** on the house

adverbs

5 **gratuitously, gratis, free,** for nothing, without charge

615 THRIFT

nouns

1 **thrift, economy,** frugality, parsimony; **prudence,** carefulness, canniness; austerity, belt-tightening

2 **economizing, cost-effectiveness;** saving, skimping (*nonformal*), scraping

verbs

3 **economize, save;** scrimp, skimp (*nonformal*), scrape; make do, make ends meet; **save up,** save for a rainy day

4 **cut back,** cut down on one's expenses, tighten one's belt

adjectives

5 **economical, thrifty, frugal,** economizing; prudent, prudential; **careful,** canny, pennywise, parsimonious; **cost-effective, efficient**

adverbs

6 **economically, frugally;** prudently, carefully; sparingly; cost-effectively, efficiently

616 ETHICS

nouns

1 **ethics, principles, morals,** standards, norms; **ethic,** moral *or* ethical code, value system

2 **moral philosophy;** hedonism, Stoicism, nihilism, Christian morality, humanism

3 **morality, morals;** virtue

4 **amorality; immorality**

5 **conscience,** sense of right and wrong, superego

adjectives

6 **ethical, moral,** moralistic

617 RIGHT

nouns

1 **right, rightness,** the right thing

2 **propriety, decorum,** decency; righteousness

adjectives

3 **right,** rightful; fit, suitable; proper, correct, decorous, good, decent, appropriate, fitting, right and proper; right-minded, right-thinking

adverbs

4 **rightly,** rightfully; right; **by rights,** by right; properly, correctly

618 WRONG

nouns

1 **wrong,** wrongness, **impropriety,** unseemliness; delinquency, criminality, illegality, unlawfulness; abnormality, deviance, aberrance; sinfulness, wickedness; dysfunction, malfunction; malpractice

2 **abomination,** horror; scandal, disgrace, shame, atrocity, desecration, violation, sacrilege, infamy, ignominy

adjectives

3 **wrong,** wrongful; improper, incorrect, unseemly; unfit, inappropriate, unsuitable; delinquent, criminal, illegal, unlawful, fraudulent; abnormal, deviant, aberrant; dysfunctional; **evil, sinful, wicked;** not done, not cricket; abominable, terrible, scandalous, disgraceful, shameful, shameless, atrocious, sacrilegious, infamous, ignominious

adverbs

4 **wrongly, wrongfully;** wrong; improperly, incorrectly

619 DUENESS

nouns

1 **entitlement, deservedness;** expectations, prospects

2 **due,** one's due, what one has coming, recognition, credit

3 **deserts,** just deserts, dues, comeuppance (*nonformal*)

verbs

4 **be due,** be entitled to, have a rightful claim to, **have coming**

5 **deserve, merit,** earn, **richly deserve,** be worthy of

6 **get one's just deserts,** get one's comeuppance, **get what is coming to one, serve one right**

adjectives

7 **due, owed, owing,** payable

8 **rightful,** appropriate, proper; fit, becoming; **fair, just**

9 **justified,** warranted, entitled, qualified, worthy; **deserved, merited,** richly deserved, **well-earned**

10 **due, entitled to; deserving,** meriting, meritorious, worthy of

adverbs

11 **duly,** rightfully

620 UNDUENESS

nouns

1 **undeservedness,** unentitledness

2 **presumption,** assumption, imposition; **licence,** liberties, familiarity, presumptuousness; lawlessness; injustice

3 **seizure,** unlawful seizure, arrogation, appropriation, **infringe-ment,** encroachment, invasion, trespassing

4 **usurper,** pretender

verbs

5 **have no right to,** have no claim upon, not have a leg to stand on (*nonformal*)

6 **presume, assume,** venture, hazard, dare, **take the liberty,** go so far as to

7 **take liberties,** overstep, abuse a privilege; **inconvenience,** bother, trouble

8 **usurp, seize, arrogate, appropriate,** assume, adopt, take over, infringe, encroach, invade, trespass

adjectives

9 **undue,** unearned, **undeserved;** unwarranted, unjustified; unworthy, **undeserving**

10 **inappropriate,** improper; excessive

11 **presumptuous,** licentious

621 DUTY

nouns

1 **duty, obligation,** charge, **burden,** mission, imperative; deference, respect, allegiance, loyalty, homage; devotion, dedication, **commitment; business;** province, function, place; line of duty, call of duty; duties and responsibilities

2 **responsibility,** incumbency; liability, **accountability;** dutifulness, **devotion to duty,** sense of duty *or* obligation

verbs

3 **should, ought to**

4 **behave, become, befit,** be bound, be obliged, be under an obligation

5 **be responsible for,** answer for, be accountable for

6 **be one's responsibility, rest with,** devolve on, fall to one

7 **take upon oneself; answer for;** take the blame, be in the hot seat

8 **do one's duty,** discharge one's duty, do the right thing, do what is expected, answer the call of duty

9 **meet an obligation,** acquit oneself, redeem one's pledge

10 **obligate, oblige,** require, tie, **bind,** pledge, commit, saddle with, hold accountable *or* responsible

adjectives

11 **dutiful;** moral, ethical; conscientious, scrupulous, observant; **obedient;** deferential, respectful

12 **incumbent on,** behoving

13 **obligatory, binding,** imperative, peremptory, mandatory, necessary, **required**

14 **obliged,** obligated, **under obligation; bound, duty-bound,** tied, pledged, committed, saddled; **obliged to,** indebted to

15 **responsible, answerable; liable, accountable;** on one's head, to blame

adverbs

16 **dutifully,** in the line of duty, beyond the call of duty

622 PREROGATIVE

nouns

1 **prerogative, right,** due; power, authority; **claim,** demand, interest, title; natural right, divine right, birthright, property right

2 **privilege, license,** liberty, freedom, immunity; franchise, patent, copyright; blank cheque, **carte blanche;** favour, indulgence, dispensation

3 **human rights, rights of man; civil rights, civil liberties;** minority rights; gay rights, gay liberation

4 **women's rights, feminism,** women's liberation, women's lib (*nonformal*), women's movement

5 **feminist; suffragette**

verbs

6 **exercise a right,** claim a right, defend a right

623 IMPOSITION

nouns

1 **imposition,** infliction, charging, taxing; burdening; exaction, demand; obtrusiveness; inconvenience, trouble, bother

2 administration, giving; applying, application, dosing, dosage, meting out, prescribing; **forcing,** forcing upon, enforcing

3 **charge, duty, tax, task; burden,** weight, freight, cargo, load

verbs

4 **impose, impose on, inflict on, put on;** put, place, set, lay; **levy, exact,** demand; **tax,** task, charge, saddle with; subject to

5 **inflict, wreak,** do to, bring upon, visit upon

6 **administer, give,** bestow; apply, dish out (*nonformal*), mete out, prescribe; **force, force upon**

7 **take advantage of, impose on;** fob off on, foist on, shift the blame, pass the buck (*nonformal*)

adjectives

8 **imposed, inflicted;** burdened with, stuck with (*nonformal*); exacted, demanded

624 PROBITY

nouns

1 **probity, honesty, integrity,** rectitude, **virtue,** righteousness, **goodness, decency;** honour, reputability, nobility; respectability; principles, high ideals; **character,** moral fibre; **fairness,** justice

2 **conscientiousness,** scrupulousness, punctiliousness, meticulousness

3 **honesty,** veracity, truthfulness; credibility

4 **candour, frankness; sincerity,** authenticity; **openness,** directness, forthrightness; outspokenness, plain speaking; **bluntness,** bluffness

5 **trustworthiness, reliability,** dependability; responsibility

6 **fidelity, faithfulness, loyalty,** faith; **constancy,** firmness; **allegiance,** homage; bond, tie; attachment, adherence, devotion

verbs

7 **show good faith, keep one's word,** make good, play by the rules

8 **be frank, speak plainly,** speak out, speak one's mind, call a spade a spade

adjectives

9 **honest,** upright, upstanding, righteous, virtuous, **good,** clean, **decent; honourable, reputable,** creditable, worthy, noble, sterling; unimpeachable, blameless, irreproachable, unblemished, untarnished, unsullied; **respectable; ethical, moral; principled,** high-minded; **law-abiding, fair, just**

10 **straight,** above-board, on the level (*nonformal*); bona fide; authentic, veritable, genuine

11 **conscientious; scrupulous,** careful; punctual, punctilious, strict, meticulous, fastidious

12 **honest, truthful,** veracious

13 **candid, frank, sincere,** genuine, ingenuous, **open;** straightforward, direct, **forthright,** outspoken, blunt, bluff, brusque; unreserved, unconstrained

14 **unassuming; unaffected,** undisguised

15 **trustworthy, reliable, dependable,** responsible; tried, true, tested, proven; incorruptible, inviolable

16 **faithful, loyal,** devoted; true, constant, **steadfast, unswerving,** steady, consistent, stable, unfailing, staunch, firm, solid

adverbs

17 honestly, honourably, decently,
virtuously, nobly; high-mindedly,
morally, ethically; **conscientiously, scrupulously,** meticulously,
fastidiously

18 truthfully, truly, veraciously; in
truth

19 candidly, frankly, sincerely,
genuinely; in plain English, not
to mince words; **openly,**
outspokenly, directly, **plainly,
bluntly,** brusquely

**20 reliably, dependably, respon-
sibly**

21 faithfully, loyally; constantly,
steadfastly, responsibly, consist-
ently, **unfailingly,** unswervingly

625 IMPROBITY

nouns

1 improbity, dishonesty, dishonour; **corruption,** corruptness;
crookedness, criminality, fraudulence; underhandedness, shadi-
ness (*nonformal*), deviousness,
evasiveness

2 villainy, knavery (*old*), chicanery;
baseness, vileness, moral turpitude

3 deceitfulness, falseness, perjury;
insincerity; sharp practice; fraud;
artfulness, craftiness

4 untrustworthiness, irresponsibility, unreliability

5 infidelity, unfaithfulness, fickle-
ness, inconstancy; **disloyalty**

6 treachery, perfidy; duplicity,
double-dealing, foul play

7 treason, high treason; lese-

majesty, sedition; collaboration,
fraternization

**8 betrayal, double cross, stab in
the back**

9 corruptibility, venality

10 criminal, scoundrel, traitor, de-
ceiver

verbs

11 (*be dishonest*), live by one's wits;
evade; deceive, cheat; falsify, lie;
sail under false colours

**12 be unfaithful, go back on one's
word,** fail, break one's promise,
renege, perjure; forsake, desert;
pass the buck (*nonformal*), shift
the blame

**13 play one false; stab one in the
back;** bite the hand that feeds
one

14 betray, double-cross, two-time,
sell out *and* sell down the river;
mislead, lead one down the garden path; inform on

15 turn against, sell oneself, **sell
out** (*nonformal*); collaborate

adjectives

16 dishonest, dishonourable,
shameless, without remorse; **unscrupulous, unprincipled,** unethical, immoral, amoral; **corrupt,** corrupted, rotten; **crooked,
criminal,** fraudulent, underhand;
shady (*nonformal*), unsavoury,
dark, sinister, insidious, slippery,
devious, tricky, shifty, evasive;
fishy (*nonformal*), questionable,
suspicious, doubtful, dubious

17 villainous, knavish (*old*), reprobate, base, vile, degraded; **infamous, notorious**

18 deceitful; perjured, untruthful;
insincere, disingenuous; artful,

crafty, **calculating, scheming;** tricky, slippery as an eel (*nonformal*)

19 **untrustworthy, unreliable, undependable,** fly-by-night, **irresponsible,** not to be trusted

20 **unfaithful,** of bad faith; inconstant, fickle; **disloyal;** false, untrue

21 **treacherous, perfidious; shifty,** slippery, tricky; **double-dealing, two-faced**

22 **traitorous,** double-crossing *and* two-timing, betraying

23 **corruptible,** venal, **mercenary**

adverbs

24 **dishonestly, dishonourably;** criminally, crookedly, **fraudulently,** underhandedly; evasively, insidiously, deviously, shiftily, dubiously, deceitfully; notoriously, infamously

25 **unfaithfully;** treacherously, treasonably

626 HONOUR

nouns

1 **honour,** distinction, glory, credit

2 **award, reward, prize;** blue ribbon; fairy prize, consolation prize, booby prize; jackpot

3 **trophy,** laurels, crown, wreath, garland; **cup**

4 **citation,** eulogy, mention, kudos **accolade,** tribute, praise

5 **decoration,** order; ribbon, blue ribbon, cordon; garter; star, gold star

6 **medal, military honour,** order, medallion; service medal; war medal

7 scholarship, fellowship

verbs

8 **honour, do honour;** recognize, cite; decorate, pin a medal on

adjectives

9 **distinguished, honoured;** laureate

10 **honorary, honourable, honorific**

adverbs

11 **with honour,** with distinction

627 INSIGNIA

nouns

1 **insignia, regalia, emblem, badge, symbol,** logo, marking, attribute; chain, collar; staff, baton; uniform, dress; tartan, tie, regimental tie; figurehead, eagle; cross, skull and crossbones, swastika, hammer and sickle, rose, thistle, shamrock, fleur-de-lis; medal, decoration; heraldry

2 (*royal insignia*) regalia; sceptre, rod, orb; crown, royal crown, coronet; triple plume; seal, great seal, privy seal

3 (*ecclesiastical insignia*) tiara, triple crown; ring, keys; mitre, crook, pastoral staff; red hat

4 (*military insignia*) stripe, chevron, bar, pip, oak leaf

5 **flag, banner, standard,** pennant, jack, ensign; tricolour

628 TITLE

nouns

1 **title, honour**

2 (*honorifics*) Excellency, Eminence, Grace, Honour, Worship, His *or* Her Excellency; Lord, My

Lord, His Lordship; Lady, My Lady, Her Ladyship; Highness, Royal Highness; Majesty, Royal Majesty

3 Sir, sire; Esquire; Master, Mister; emir, khan, sahib

4 Mistress, madame

5 (*ecclesiastical titles*) Reverend, Very Reverend, His Grace; Monsignor, Holiness; Brother, Father, Mother; Rabbi

6 **degree, honours degree,** bachelor's degree, master's degree, doctorate

adjectives

7 **honourary;** titular; honorific

629 JUSTICE

nouns

1 **justice,** justness; equity; level playing field (*nonformal*); give-and-take, evenhandedness; balance, equality; **right,** rightness, propriety; summary, poetic justice, rough justice; **legality,** lawfulness

2 **fairness,** the right thing; level playing field; **fair play,** sportsmanship

3 **impartiality,** detachment, dispassion, **disinterest;** neutrality

verbs

4 **be just, be fair,** do the right thing; do justice to, see justice done

5 **play fair,** play the game, be a good sport

adjectives

6 **just, fair,** fair and square; equitable, balanced, even-handed;

right, rightful; justifiable, justified, warranted, defensible; due, deserved, merited; fit, proper, good; **lawful, legal**

7 **sporting,** sportsmanlike

8 **impartial, impersonal,** even-handed, equitable, **dispassionate, disinterested,** detached, objective; lofty, Olympian; **neutral,** unbiased; selfless, unselfish

adverbs

9 **justly, fairly;** rightly, duly, deservedly, properly; equally, evenly, equitably; **impartially, dispassionately, disinterestedly**

10 **in justice,** in reason, in all fairness, to be fair

630 INJUSTICE

nouns

1 **injustice;** iniquity; inequality; **wrong,** wrongness, impropriety; **unlawfulness, illegality**

2 **unfairness,** foul play, a hit below the belt

3 **partiality, bias,** leaning, inclination; interest, involvement, partisanship; favouritism, preference, nepotism; **discrimination, inequality**

4 **injustice, wrong, injury,** grievance; raw deal; **miscarriage of justice, gross;** atrocity, outrage

verbs

5 **hit below the belt,** give a raw deal

6 **do one an injustice,** wrong

7 **favour,** prefer, show preference, discriminate

adjectives

8 **unjust,** inequitable, iniquitous, **unbalanced,** uneven, unequal, discriminatory; **wrong,** wrongful, **unlawful, illegal**

9 **unfair,** not fair; not done, not cricket (*nonformal*); **dirty** (*nonformal*), foul, below the belt

10 **partial, interested,** involved, **partisan, one-sided,** influenced, swayed

11 **unjustifiable,** unreasonable, indefensible; **inexcusable, unforgivable,** unpardonable

adverbs

12 **unjustly, unfairly;** wrongfully, wrongly; unequally, unevenly; partially, one-sidedly; unjustifiably, unreasonably

631 SELFISHNESS

nouns

1 **selfishness, self-seeking, self-serving;** self-indulgence, hedonism; **careerism,** personal ambition; narcissism, egotism, self-love; self-sufficiency, self-absorption; remoteness, autism, catatonia; avarice, greed, possessiveness; individualism

2 **meanness,** smallness, pettiness, stinginess

3 **egotist, narcissist,** self-server, **careerist;** individualist, loner (*nonformal*)

verbs

4 **please oneself,** look out for number one; have one's cake and eat it

adjectives

5 **selfish, self-seeking, self-serving;** self-indulgent, hedonistic; **careerist;** narcissistic, egotistical; self-sufficient, self-absorbed; remote, autistic, catatonic; avaricious, greedy, possessive, grasping; individualistic

6 **mean,** small, petty, stingy

adverbs

7 **selfishly,** for oneself, in one's own interest

632 UNSELFISHNESS

nouns

1 **selflessness, humility;** modesty; **self-sacrifice,** self-denial; devotion, dedication, commitment, disinterest; **altruism**

2 **magnanimity, generosity,** liberality; idealism; **benevolence;** nobility, greatness, chivalry; heroism

verbs

3 **put oneself out,** bend over backwards, be generous to a fault

adjectives

4 **unselfish, selfless; altruistic;** humble; **modest;** self-sacrificing, devoted, dedicated, committed, disinterested

5 **magnanimous, generous, benevolent,** liberal; big-hearted; **high-minded,** idealistic; noble, great; chivalrous; heroic

adverbs

6 **unselfishly, altruistically**

7 **magnanimously, generously,** liberally; nobly; chivalrously

633 VIRTUE

nouns

1 **virtue, goodness,** rectitude, righteousness; the straight and narrow; **morality,** moral fibre

2 **purity;** chastity; innocence

3 prudence, justice, temperance, fortitude; faith, hope

verbs

4 **be good,** do the right thing, follow the straight and narrow

adjectives

5 **virtuous, good, moral;** upright, **honest;** righteous, just

6 **chaste,** immaculate, **pure,** innocent

634 VICE

nouns

1 **vice;** criminality; wrongdoing; immorality, **evil;** amorality; waywardness, wantonness; delinquency; backsliding

2 **vice, weakness,** flaw, frailty, failing; foible, **bad habit,** fault, imperfection

3 **iniquity, evil,** bad, wrong, error, villainy; **atrocity,** abomination, infamy, shame, disgrace, scandal, **sin**

4 **wickedness,** badness, sinfulness

5 moral turpitude; **corruption, degradation, decadence;** depravity, degeneracy; dissoluteness, profligacy

6 **hardness, callousness,** obduracy

7 **sewer, gutter;** den of iniquity, fleshpots, **brothel;** Sodom, Gomorrah, Babylon

verbs

8 **do wrong, sin;** misbehave

9 **go wrong,** stray, go astray, **err,** deviate; **fall, lapse,** slip; relapse, backslide

10 **corrupt,** sully, soil, defile

adjectives

11 **immoral, unethical;** amoral

12 **unclean, impure,** blemished, unchaste; **carnal,** wayward, wanton, prodigal; erring, **fallen, lapsed;** frail, weak; backsliding

13 **diabolical,** devilish, demonic, **satanic,** fiendish, hellish **infernal**

14 **corrupt,** corrupted, polluted, rotten, tainted, contaminated; warped, perverted; **decadent,** debased, degraded, **depraved, degenerate,** abandoned

15 **wicked, evil,** vicious, bad, naughty, **wrong, sinful;** dark, black, **base, low,** vile, foul, rank, flagrant, **heinous,** villainous, criminal; abominable, atrocious, monstrous, unspeakable; shameful, disgraceful, scandalous, **infamous,** unforgivable; **improper,** reprehensible, unworthy

16 **hardened, hard,** hard-hearted, obdurate, **callous, heartless, shameless, brazen**

17 **irredeemable,** unregenerate, incorrigible

adverbs

18 **wickedly, sinfully;** flagrantly; viciously

635 WRONGDOING

nouns

1 **wickedness, wrongdoing;** misbehaviour, misconduct, malprac-

tice; sin; vice; crime, law-breaking

2 misdeed, **misdemeanour, offence, injustice,** injury, wrong, iniquity, **error, fault,** breach, impropriety; **indiscretion, peccadillo,** lapse; transgression, trespass; **evil, sin, cardinal sin, mortal sin; crime, felony;** white-collar crime; computer crime; war crime; genocide; **outrage, atrocity**

3 **original sin, fall from grace**

verbs

4 **do wrong,** misbehave, **err,** offend; **sin;** transgress

adjectives

5 **wrong,** iniquitous, **sinful, wicked;** criminal

636 GUILT

nouns

1 **guilt,** guiltiness; **culpability,** blameworthiness; **implication,** involvement, **complicity;** remorse, guilty conscience

verbs

2 **be guilty; get caught in the act or** red-handed

adjectives

3 **guilty, criminal,** to blame, at fault; **culpable,** reprehensible, implicated, involved; red-handed; caught in the act **or** red-handed

adverbs

4 **in the act,** in flagrante delicto

5 **guilty,** sheepishly, with a guilty conscience

637 INNOCENCE

nouns

1 **innocence,** blamelessness, guiltlessness; clean hands, clear conscience, nothing to hide

2 **innocent,** babe, infant, child, lamb, dove, angel

verbs

3 **have a clear conscience,** have clean hands

adjectives

4 **innocent, not guilty;** faultless, blameless; sinless, with clean hands; uncorrupted, undefiled

5 **spotless,** stainless, unblemished, untainted, undefiled; pure, clean, immaculate, impeccable, white as the driven snow

6 **inculpable,** irreproachable; above suspicion

adverbs

7 **innocently,** with a clear conscience

638 ATONEMENT

nouns

1 **atonement,** reparation, making amends, **redress,** compensation, redemption, recompense

2 **apology, excuse,** regrets; acknowledgement, penitence, contrition, confession

3 **penance, penitence, repentance;** mortification, flagellation, **fasting;** purgatory; **hair shirt, sackcloth and ashes;** Lent

verbs

4 **atone, atone for,** compensate, redress, redeem, repair, satisfy,

give satisfaction, **make amends**, set right, make up for, pay one's dues; put one's house in order

5 **apologize, beg pardon**, ask forgiveness, get down on one's knees; take back

6 **do penance**, mortify oneself, purge oneself, flagellate oneself; wear a hair shirt *or* sackcloth and ashes

adjectives

7 **atoning**, redressing, compensatory, righting, **redeeming; apologetic**, repenting; cleansing, purifying

639 GOOD PERSON

nouns

1 good person, fine person, worthy, **good sort, gentleman**, perfect gentleman; **lady**, perfect lady; gem, jewel, pearl, diamond; rough diamond; honest man

2 (*nonformal terms*) **good bloke**, brick, good egg, Mr Nice Guy

3 good citizen, good neighbour, **pillar of society, salt of the earth**

4 **paragon**, ideal, shining example, **role model;** exemplar, epitome

5 **hero**, god; **heroine**, goddess; idol

6 holy man, guru; saint, angel

640 BAD PERSON

nouns

1 bad person, **undesirable, persona non grata;** bad example

2 **wretch;** beggar, tramp, down-and-out, dosser, drifter, drunkard, vagrant, vagabond; good-

for-nothing, ne'er-do-well, wastrel

3 **rascal**, rogue, knave, **scoundrel;** blackguard, bounder, cad

4 **reprobate, miscreant;** bad sort, wrong 'un (*nonformal*), black sheep; fallen angel, lost soul; degenerate, pervert; lecher, trollop, whore, pimp

5 (*nonformal terms*) bastard, shit, jerk; twerp, berk, twit

6 beast, animal; dog, mongrel; reptile, viper, serpent; snake; vermin; pig; insect, worm

7 **wrongdoer, sinner,** delinquent; culprit, offender

8 **criminal, felon, crook;** public enemy, **gangster,** racketeer, swindler; thief, thug; **outlaw,** fugitive, **convict,** jailbird (*nonformal*)

9 **the underworld,** gangland, **organized crime,** the mob, **the Mafia,** Cosa Nostra, Black Hand

641 DISREPUTE

nouns

1 **disrepute,** ill fame, bad report, bad character; **dishonour,** discredit, disapprobation

2 **notoriety,** disreputableness

3 **baseness, lowness, meanness,** shabbiness, shoddiness, **squalor, vulgarity, tastlessness,** tackiness; vileness, grossness, monstrousness, enormity; degradation, debasement, depravity

4 **infamy; ignominy;** degradation, demotion

5 **disgrace, scandal, humiliation;** shame, crying shame

6 **stigma; slur,** reproach, censure, reprimand, **aspersion;** black mark, stain, blemish

verbs

7 **lose face, disgrace oneself,** lose one's good name, sully one's reputation

8 **disgrace, dishonour,** discredit; **shame,** put to shame; hold up to public ridicule, **humiliate,** degrade, debase

9 **stigmatize,** brand, stain, besmirch, taint, blot, **blacken, smear,** soil, defile, slur; **disparage,** defame; **censure, reprimand;** pillory, crucify

adjectives

10 **disreputable, dishonourable, discreditable,** unsavoury, shady, seamy, sordid; ignoble, ignominious, **infamous, notorious**

11 **disgraceful, shameful,** pitiful, deplorable, sad, sorry, too bad; degrading, debasing, demeaning, unbecoming, beneath one; cheap, gutter; **humiliating; scandalous,** shocking, outrageous

12 **base, low, mean, poor, petty, paltry, small, little, shabby, shoddy, squalid,** scruffy, mangy (*nonformal*), **wretched, miserable,** abject, **despicable, contemptible,** abominable, obnoxious, **vulgar,** tasteless, crude, **disgusting,** odious, vile, foul, **dirty,** rank, gross, flagrant, grave, heinous, **atrocious,** monstrous, unspeakable, unmentionable; degraded, debased, depraved

13 **in disrepute,** in disfavour, in disgrace; disgraced, discredited, dis-

honoured, shamed; in the doghouse *and* under a cloud

14 **unnotable,** inglorious, unnoticed, **undistinguished,** unpopular; **unknown,** little known, obscure

adverbs

15 disreputably, dishonourably, discreditably, ignobly, **infamously,** ignominiously

16 **disgracefully, scandalously,** outrageously; **shamefully**

17 poorly, **miserably,** despicably, odiously, grossly, **atrociously**

642 REPUTE

nouns

1 **repute, reputation, name,** character, **fame, renown,** report, glory; celebrity, popularity, recognition; vogue; acclaim, **publicity, notoriety,** exposure

2 **reputability,** good reputation, good name, good report

3 **esteem,** estimation, honour, regard, respect, approval, approbation, account, favour, consideration, **credit,** Brownie points (*nonformal*)

4 **prestige, honour;** dignity; **rank, standing,** stature, position, station, face, **status**

5 **distinction,** mark, note; **importance, consequence,** significance; prominence, **eminence, greatness,** stardom; nobility, grandeur

6 **lustre,** radiance, brilliance, splendour, **glory;** halo, aura; **charisma,** mystique, glamour, magic; personality cult

7 (*posthumous fame*) **memory,** remembrance, legend, myth; **immortality,** undying fame, a place in history

8 **celebrity,** notable, luminary, worthy, big name, public figure; important person, **VIP; idol, hero, heroine,** folk hero; **star;** cult figure

verbs

9 **be somebody,** be something, **impress,** cut a dash, shine

10 **gain recognition,** be recognized, make a name for oneself

11 **honour;** dignify, adorn, grace

12 **glorify,** glamourize, **lionize;** exalt, elevate, ennoble; canonize, deify

adjectives

13 **reputable,** estimable, honourable, honoured; **meritorious,** noble, worthy, creditable; **respected,** respectable, **revered,** venerable; well-thought-of, held in esteem

14 **distinguished, noted,** notable, of note; **famous,** famed, renowned, honoured, **celebrated, popular,** acclaimed, **notorious,** well-known; legendary, mythical

15 **prominent,** conspicuous, outstanding, **important,** significant

16 **eminent, high,** exalted; **immortal;** great, grand, mighty; glorified, ennobled; **immortalized,** sanctified, canonized; **idolized,** deified, godlike

17 **illustrious,** glorious, brilliant, radiant, splendid, resplendent, bright, shining; **charismatic,** glamorous, magic, magical

adverbs

18 **honourably,** nobly

19 **famously,** notably, notoriously, popularly; **prominently, eminently,** conspicuously, outstandingly

643 SENSUALITY

nouns

1 **sensuality;** voluptuousness, luxury; **self-indulgence, hedonism;** epicureanism; pleasure principle, instant gratification; sensuousness

2 **carnality,** fleshliness; brutishness, brutality; coarseness, grossness; materialism

3 **sensualist,** voluptuary, pleasure-seeker, **hedonist;** epicure, gourmet

verbs

4 **live for the moment,** seize the day

adjectives

5 **sensual;** voluptuous, luxurious; **hedonistic, pleasure-seeking;** epicurean; sensuous

6 **carnal,** fleshly, **bodily, physical;** fallen, lapsed; animal, brutish, brutal; bestial, beastly; coarse, gross; earthy; material, materialistic

644 CHASTITY

nouns

1 **chastity,** virtue, **honour;** purity, innocence

2 **decency, propriety, decorum,** elegance, delicacy; **modesty**

3 continence, abstinence, **celibacy;**
virginity; Platonic love

adjectives

4 **chaste, virtuous, pure;** unsoiled,
unsullied, undefiled; **innocent**

5 **decent, modest,** decorous, delicate, elegant, **proper, becoming**

6 continent, abstinent, **celibate;**
virginal, **virgin,** intact; Platonic

645 UNCHASTITY

nouns

1 **impurity,** taintedness; indecency

2 incontinence, unrestraint

3 **debauchery,** dissipation; wom-
anizing, whoring

4 wantonness, waywardness; loose
morals, easy virtue, **promiscuity,**
sleeping around (*nonformal*)

5 **lasciviousness, lechery,** lewd-
ness, bawdiness; carnality, **sexu-**
ality; lust, sexiness; **obscenity;**
prurience, concupiscence; **sensu-**
ality, eroticism; erotomania,
nymphomania

6 **seduction;** betrayal, violation,
abuse; **rape,** sexual assault, date
rape

7 (*illicit sexual intercourse*) **adul-**
tery, cohabitation, extramarital
or premarital sex; **fornication;**
free love; incest

8 **prostitution,** street-walking; so-
liciting; pimping

9 **brothel, whorehouse,** house of
ill repute, bordello, cathouse,
den of iniquity, massage parlour,
disorderly house; **red-light dis-**
trict

10 **rake,** libertine, swinger, **woman-**

izer, philanderer, lady killer, Lo-
thario, **Casanova,** Don Juan

11 **lecher,** satyr, goat, dirty old man;
whoremaster; seducer; **rapist**

12 **adulterer,** fornicator

13 **tart,** strumpet, trollop, hussy,
slut, slag (*nonformal*), jade,
bitch, whore, loose woman

14 **courtesan;** seductress, **femme fa-**
tale, vamp, temptress

15 **prostitute, whore,** harlot, **call**
girl, hooker, streetwalker, scarlet woman, fallen woman; **white**
slave

16 **mistress, kept woman,** other
woman; live-in lover; concubine

17 **pimp,** ponce, madam; fancy
man, gigolo

verbs

18 **be promiscuous, sleep around,**
swing; debauch, **womanize,**
whore, philander, sow one's wild
oats; **fornicate,** cheat, commit
adultery

19 **seduce, betray, deceive,** mislead,
lead astray; **ravish, ravage, de-**
file, soil; violate, abuse; **rape**

20 **prostitute oneself,** streetwalk;
pimp, procure

adjectives

21 **unchaste, impure,** unclean; indecent; soiled, **defiled**

22 **uninhibited,** free; dissipated, dis-
solute, **debauched**

23 **wanton, wayward, loose,** lax,
slack, easy (*nonformal*), of easy
virtue, of loose morals, **promis-**
cuous

24 **illicit, adulterous,** extramarital,
premarital; incestuous

25 **scarlet, fallen;** whorish

26 lascivious, **lecherous**, **sexy**, **carnal**, **sexual**, lustful; concupiscent, libidinous, randy *and* horny (*both nonformal*); **bawdy**, lewd, adult, X-rated, pornographic, dirty, **obscene**; **erotic**, **sensual**

646 INDECENCY

nouns

1 indecency, indelicacy, impropriety, **indiscretion**

2 immodesty, **exhibitionism**; shamelessness; boldness

3 vulgarity, **coarseness**, crudeness, grossness, earthiness, raunchiness, frankness

4 obscenity; raunch, ribaldry, **pornography**, adult films, X-rated films; **smut**, **filth**

adjectives

5 indecent, **indelicate**, improper, inappropriate, **unseemly**, indiscreet

6 immodest, **shameless**, unashamed, **brazen**, **forward**, bold, pert

7 risqué, racy, spicy, suggestive

8 vulgar, uncouth, **coarse**, raw, broad, low, foul, gutter; **earthy**, frank

9 obscene, lewd, adult, bawdy, **pornographic**, lurid, **smutty**, blue, raunchy

647 ASCETICISM

nouns

1 asceticism, austerity, self-denial, monasticism; abstinence; mortification, flagellation; fasting

2 ascetic, **puritan**, hermit

verbs

3 deny oneself, abstain; wear a hair shirt, flagellate oneself

adjectives

4 ascetic, austere, **self-denying**, puritanical

648 TEMPERANCE

nouns

1 temperance, moderation, **sobriety**, frugality; self-denial, self-restraint, **self-control**, **self-discipline**

2 abstinence, abstention, abstemiousness; **celibacy**, chastity; Stoicism, plain living; vegan, **vegetarian**

3 teetotaller, nondrinker; nonsmoker; vegetarian, vegan; **ascetic**

verbs

4 restrain oneself, curb oneself, hold back, control oneself, **contain oneself**; **live plainly** *or* simply

5 abstain, refrain, forgo, spare, withhold, hold back, **avoid**, **shun**, pass up (*nonformal*) **deny oneself**, do without, go without

6 renounce, forswear, **give up**, abandon, stop; dry out, kick the habit, go on the wagon

adjectives

7 temperate, **moderate**, sober, frugal, restrained, **sparing**, measured

8 abstinent, abstemious; **teetotal**, on the wagon (*nonformal*); **celibate**, chaste; vegetarian, vegan; non-smoking; Stoic, plain-living; **ascetic**

adverbs

9 **moderately, sparingly,** frugally, in moderation

649 INTEMPERANCE

nouns

1 **self-indulgence,** over-indulgence; **excess, extravagance;** greed, gluttony; drunkenness

2 riotous living, high living, **debauchery,** carousing

3 **playboy,** night owl, party animal (*nonformal*)

verbs

4 **indulge,** indulge oneself; luxuriate in, wallow in; live off the fat of the land

5 **overdo,** overindulge, carry to excess, not know when to stop

6 **party** (*nonformal*), eat, drink, and be merry, carouse, burn the candle at both ends

adjectives

7 **indulgent,** self-indulgent; **excessive, extravagant,** extreme; uncontrolled, uninhibited

adverbs

8 **to excess,** to extremes, without restraint

650 MODERATION

nouns

1 **moderation, restraint;** prudence; balance, equilibrium, **stability;** temperance, sobriety; self-restraint, **self-control;** abstinence; calmness, serenity, tranquillity, repose, calm, cool (*non-*

formal); nonviolence, pacifism; impartiality, neutrality

2 **abatement, remission,** mitigation, defusing, **reduction,** lessening; **relaxation,** relaxing, slackening, **easing, loosening; alleviation;** tempering, softening; **deadening, dulling,** damping, blunting; drugging, sedating, sedation; **quieting,** quieting, lulling, **soothing, calming,** hushing

3 **mediator,** peacemaker; drug, **tranquillizer, sedative;** balm, salve; cushion, shock absorber

4 **moderate,** neutral, centrist

verbs

5 **moderate, restrain,** constrain, control; mitigate, defuse, abate, weaken, **diminish, reduce,** slacken, lessen, slow down; **alleviate,** allay, **temper; soften, subdue,** tame; **drug,** sedate, tranquilize; deaden, dull, blunt; smother, suppress, stifle; **damp, dampen**

6 **calm,** calm down, stabilize, tranquillize, **pacify,** mollify, appease; **quiet,** hush, rest, compose, **lull,** soothe; cool, **subdue,** quell; ease, steady, smooth

7 **cushion,** soften the blow, absorb the shock, break the fall; deaden, dampen, soften, suppress

8 **relax,** ease up, abate; slacken

adjectives

9 **moderate,** temperate, sober; **mild,** soft, bland, **gentle,** tame; peaceful; **judicious, prudent**

10 **restrained,** constrained, limited, controlled, **stable,** in control, in hand; tempered, **softened,** hushed, **subdued,** quelled, chastened

11 **level-headed**, dispassionate, even-tempered; tranquil, serene, calm, cool

12 **mitigating**, abating, **diminishing, reducing**, lessening, allaying, alleviating, **relaxing, easing**; tempering, **softening**, chastening, **subduing**; deadening, dulling, blunting, damping, dampening, cushioning

13 **tranquillizing**, pacifying, mollifying, appeasing; **calming**, hushing, quietening, **soothing**, restful

14 **narcotic, sedative,** anodyne

adverbs

15 **moderately, in moderation**, within bounds; soberly, prudently, judiciously, dispassionately; calmly, coolly, evenly

651 VIOLENCE

nouns

1 **violence**, venom, force, roughness, harshness, **severity, intensity**; savagery, destructiveness, **destruction**, vandalism; terrorism, barbarity, brutality, inhumanity, bloodlust; **rage, anger**

2 **turbulence, turmoil**, chaos, **rage**, frenzy, passion, fanaticism, zeal; **tumult, uproar**, racket, cacophony, pandemonium, **commotion**, disturbance, row

3 **rioting**, looting, plundering; laying waste, sacking; scorched earth; **attack, assault**, onslaught; killing, butchery, massacre, slaughter

4 **storm**, tempest, squall, **tornado**, cyclone, **hurricane, typhoon**; rainstorm, thunderstorm, snowstorm

5 **upheaval**, convulsion, cataclysm, catastrophe, disaster; earthquake, tidal wave

6 **outburst**, eruption, torrent, cascade

7 **explosion**, discharge, detonation, **blast**

8 (nonformal terms) devil, demon, fiend, brute, savage, monster, beast; rapist, mugger, killer; witch, fury, she-wolf, virago

9 **tough**, bruiser, **thug**, hoodlum

verbs

10 **rage, storm**, rant, rave; rampage, **destroy**, wreck, wreak havoc, ruin; **terrorize**, vandalize, brutalize; **riot**, loot, burn, sack, lay waste; **slaughter**, butcher; **attack**, assault, savage, mug

11 **seethe, boil**, fume, foam

12 **erupt**, break out, belch, **vomit**, spout, spew, discharge, eject

13 **explode, blow up**, go off; detonate, trigger, set off, let off; discharge, fire, shoot

14 **run amok**, go berserk, run riot, go on a rampage

adjectives

15 **violent**, venomous, severe, rigorous, furious, **fierce, intense**, sharp, keen, cutting; **destructive;** rough, bruising

16 **turbulent, raging, chaotic**, hellish, **tempestuous, frenzied, wild, frantic, furious, mad**, demented, insane

17 **unruly, disorderly, riotous**, wild, rampant; anarchic, revolutionary

18 **boisterous**, wild, **rowdy**, rough, rollicking

19 savage, fierce, ferocious, vicious, murderous, cruel, mindless, brutal, monstrous, inhuman, pitiless, ruthless, bloody; malign; wild, barbarous, barbaric, uncivilized

20 fiery, heated, inflamed; ardent, hot-headed, passionate, zealous

21 convulsive, cataclysmic, disastrous

22 explosive, volcanic

adverbs

23 violently, vehemently, virulently, rigorously, severely, fiercely, drastically; furiously, wildly, madly, like mad

24 frantically, furiously, madly; angrily

25 savagely, fiercely, ferociously, viciously, ruthlessly

652 GLUTTONY

nouns

1 gluttony, greed; overeating, overindulgence; eating disorder

2 glutton, trencherman, big eater; pig, greedyguts (*nonformal*); gourmand

verbs

3 gorge, stuff, guzzle, devour, bolt, gobble, gulp, wolf

4 stuff oneself, pig out (*nonformal*)

adjectives

5 gluttonous, greedy, voracious, ravenous, rapacious, insatiable

adverbs

6 greedily, voraciously

653 LEGALITY

nouns

1 legality, legitimacy, lawfulness, validity; jurisdiction; justice

2 legalization, decriminalization; authorization, sanction

3 law, statute, canon; act, enactment, measure, legislation; rule, ruling, regulation; dictate, edict, decree

4 law, legal system

5 legal code, body of law; civil code, penal code; statute book

6 constitution, written constitution, unwritten constitution; Bill of Rights

7 jurisprudence, law; forensic science; criminology, penology

verbs

8 legalize, legitimate, make legal, declare lawful, decriminalize; validate; authorize, sanction; constitute, ordain, establish; prescribe, formulate; regulate; decree; legislate, enact; enforce

9 codify, digest; compile, publish

adjectives

10 legal, legitimate, lawful, rightful, within the law; legally binding, enforceable; judicial, juridical; authorized, sanctioned, valid, applicable; constitutional; statutory; legislative; just

11 jurisprudent, legalistic; forensic; penological

adverbs

12 legally, legitimately, lawfully, by law, *de jure*

654 ILLEGALITY

nouns

1 **illegality, unlawfulness, lawlessness;** anarchy

2 **lawbreaking, violation,** infringement, transgression, contravention; delinquency, criminality

3 **offence, wrong,** illegality; violation; **crime, felony;** misdemeanour

verbs

4 **break the law,** infringe, contravene, violate, transgress; flout the law, take the law into one's own hands

adjectives

5 **illegal, unlawful, illegitimate, illicit,** lawless, wrongful, fraudulent, against the law; unauthorized, unofficial, **unconstitutional; punishable,** litigable, chargeable, actionable; **criminal,** felonious; outlaw, **outlawed;** contraband, black-market; under-the-counter; unregulated; anarchic

6 **illegitimate,** spurious, false

adverbs

7 **illegally, unlawfully, illegitimately, illicitly;** criminally, feloniously

655 RELIGIONS, CULTS, SECTS

nouns

1 **religion, belief, faith,** teaching, doctrine, creed, theology, orthodoxy; tradition

2 **sect, religious order, denomination, persuasion,** faction, **church,** communion, community, fellowship, order, school; offshoot, **schism,** division

3 **sectarianism, denominationalism**

4 **theism,** polytheism, pantheism, deism

5 **animism;** voodoo; shamanism; fetishism, totemism; nature worship

6 **Christianity,** Protestantism, Catholicism, Orthodox Christianity; Judeo-Christian belief; Christian fundamentalism

7 **Catholicism, Roman Catholicism;** popery, papism; ultramontanism; Catholic Church, Church of Rome

8 **Orthodoxy,** Eastern Orthodox Church, Greek Orthodox Church, Russian Orthodox Church

9 **Protestantism,** Reform; Evangelicalism; new theology

10 **Anglicanism; Church of England,** Established Church; Anglo-Catholicism; Broad Church

11 **Judaism;** Orthodox Judaism, Conservative Judaism, Reform Judaism

12 **Islam;** Sunnism, Shiism; Muslim fundamentalism

13 **theist,** polytheist, pantheist, **deist**

14 **Christian,** Nazarene

15 **sectarian,** denominationalist, schismatic

16 **Catholic, Roman Catholic,** papist; ultramontane

17 **Protestant,** dissenter; Evangelical; apostate

18 **Jew, Hebrew,** Israelite

19 Muslim, Sunni, Shiite; Muslim fundamentalist

adjectives

20 religious, theistic; polytheistic, pantheistic, deistic

21 sectarian, denominational, schismatic

22 nondenominational, nonsectarian, ecumenical

23 Protestant, Reformed, Evangelical; Lutheran, Calvinist; apostate

24 Catholic, Roman Catholic, RC, papist; ultramontane

25 Jewish, Hebrew; Orthodox, Conservative, Reform

26 Muslim, Islamic; Shiite, Sunni

27 (*Oriental*) Buddhist; Confucian; Taoist; Shintoist; Zoroastrian

656 THEOLOGY

nouns

1 **theology, religion, divinity**

2 **doctrine, dogma, creed**

3 **theologian,** theologist; scholastic, schoolman

adjectives

4 **theological, religious; divine;** doctrinal, canonical

657 DEITY

nouns

1 **deity, divinity,** godhead

2 **God,** Jehovah, **Allah**

3 (*Hinduism*) **Siva, Brahma,** Vishnu

4 (*Buddhism*) **Buddha,** the Blessed One

5 **Nature, Mother Nature**

6 **Christ, Jesus Christ,** the Nazarene

7 **The Holy Ghost** or **Spirit,** the Dove

adjectives

8 **divine,** heavenly, celestial; **transcendant,** supernatural; messianic

9 **almighty, omnipotent,** all-powerful; **omniscient,** all-seeing, all-knowing; **infinite,** omnipresent; eternal, everlasting, timeless, perpetual, immortal, permanent; one; immutable, unchanging; supreme, sovereign, highest; holy, hallowed, sacred; glorious, radiant, luminous; majestic; good, just, loving, merciful

658 MYTHICAL AND POLYTHEISTIC GODS AND SPIRITS

nouns

1 **the gods,** the immortals, the deities; **spirits**

2 **god, goddess, deity, divinity,** immortal; **idol,** false god

3 **demigod;** hero, heroine; cult figure

4 **spirit,** intelligence, supernatural being; demon; spectre; **evil spirits**

5 **water spirit** or **sprite,** spirit of the air, spirit of the earth

6 **fairyfolk,** elfenfolk, the little people; **fairyland**

7 **fairy, sprite;** elf, brownie, pixie, gremlin; imp, goblin, gnome, dwarf, leprechaun; banshee

8 **nymph,** dryad

9 **water god,** water sprite *or* spirit; Oceanid, **mermaid,** siren; Neptune, Poseidon, Triton

10 **forest god,** sylvan deity, faun, satyr; **Pan**

11 **guardian angel,** angel, **fairy godmother**

12 **Santa Claus,** Santa, Saint Nicholas, Father Christmas

13 **mythology,** legend, lore, **folklore**

adjectives

14 **mythical, mythological;** fabulous, legendary

659 ANGEL, SAINT

nouns

1 **angel,** seraph, cherub, archangel; **saint,** patron saint; martyr

2 **heavenly host,** choir invisible, angelic host

adjectives

3 **angelic,** seraphic, cherubic; **heavenly, celestial;** saintly; martyred

660 EVIL SPIRITS

nouns

1 **evil spirits, demons,** hellspawn, powers of darkness, lost souls, the damned

2 **The Devil, Satan,** Lucifer, Old Nick, the Prince of Darkness, Beelzebub

3 **demon,** fiend, **evil spirit, devil;** incubus, succubus, lamia, Lilith; ghoul, **vampire,** the undead

4 **imp,** pixie, sprite, elf, puck; **bad fairy, gremlin,** Hobgoblin; bogeyman

5 **Fury,** avenging spirit

6 **werewolf,** lycanthrope

7 **Satanism, devil-worship;** Black Mass; black magic, sorcery

8 **Satanist, devil-worshipper;** sorcerer

verbs

9 **bewitch,** bedevil, possess

adjectives

10 **demonic, devilish; satanic, diabolical; hellish; fiendish;** foul, damned; inhuman, ghoulish

11 **impish, puckish,** mischievous

661 HEAVEN

nouns

1 **Heaven,** Paradise, the kingdom of God; a better place

2 **the hereafter,** the afterworld, the afterlife, life after death

3 **Holy City, New Jerusalem,** Celestial City, City of God, God's Throne

4 (*mythological*) Mount Olympus; Elysium, Elysian Fields; Avalon; Islands of the Blessed, Garden of Hesperides; Valhalla

5 (*removal to heaven*) **resurrection,** apotheosis, ascension, assumption

adjectives

6 **heavenly,** paradisiacal; **celestial,** ethereal; unearthly, unworldly; otherworldly; **transcendental;** Elysian, Olympian; blessed, beatified, beatific, glorified, in glory

adverbs

7 **celestially,** ethereally; in heaven, on high, in glory, among the blest

662 HELL

nouns

1 **hell,** the underworld, inferno; **purgatory,** limbo

2 (*mythological*) **Hades,** Tartarus; River Styx, Lethe, River of Fire

verbs

3 **damn,** doom, cast into hell, doom to perdition

adjectives

4 **hellish, infernal;** fire-and-brimstone, sulphurous; devilish; Stygian; purgatorial, hellborn

adverbs

5 **infernally,** in hell, below, in torment

663 SCRIPTURE

nouns

1 **scripture, scriptures,** sacred texts, **bible;** sacred canon

2 **Bible, Holy Bible, the Scriptures, Holy Scripture,** Holy Writ, the Book, the Good Book, the Word

3 **Old Testament; New Testament,** Gospels, Good News; **Talmud, Torah;** Koran

4 **revelation, divine revelation; inspiration,** divine inspiration; **mysticism,** mystical experience, mystical intuition, contemplation, ecstasy; **prophecy,** prophetic revelation

adjectives

5 **scriptural, Biblical,** Old-Testament, New-Testament, Gospel; **revealed,** revelational; prophetic, apocalyptic; evangelical, gospel

6 **mystic, mystical**

664 SANCTITY

nouns

1 **sanctity, holiness; divinity,** heavenliness; sacrosanctity; godliness

2 **the sacred,** the holy, the holy of holies, the transcendant

3 **sanctification,** hallowing; purification; beatitude, blessing; **consecration,** dedication, devotion; **sainthood, beatification;** blessedness, grace, state of grace

4 **redemption, salvation,** conversion, new life, adoption; rebirth, second birth

verbs

5 **sanctify,** hallow; purify, cleanse; **bless; consecrate,** dedicate, devote; glorify, exalt; **beatify, canonize**

6 **redeem,** convert, save, give salvation

adjectives

7 **sacred, holy,** sacrosanct, **religious, spiritual,** heavenly, divine

8 **sanctified, hallowed; blessed,** consecrated, devoted, dedicated; **glorified, exalted, saintly,** beatified, canonized

9 **redeemed, saved,** converted, reborn, born-again

665 UNSANCTITY

nouns

1 **unholiness, profanity;** secularism, worldliness; humanism

2 **the profane,** the unholy; the secular, the temporal, **the worldly,** the mundane

adjectives

3 **unholy;** profane, **secular, temporal, worldly,** mundane

666 ORTHODOXY

nouns

1 **orthodoxy,** authenticity; traditionalism; gospel truth, **true faith**

2 **true believer,** orthodox Christian; Orthodox Jew; Sunni Muslim; fundamentalist

3 **strictness,** strict interpretation; **dogmatism,** hard line (*nonformal*); bigotry; **fundamentalism,** literalism

4 **bigot, dogmatist, fundamentalist**

adjectives

5 **orthodox; traditional,** standard, customary, conventional; literal, textual; **authoritative,** authentic, accepted, received, approved

6 **strict, bigoted, dogmatic, fundamentalist**

667 UNORTHODOXY

nouns

1 **unorthodoxy,** heterodoxy; **nonconformity**

2 **heresy,** false doctrine, misbelief; fallacy, error

3 **infidelity, atheism,** agnosticism

4 **paganism,** heathenism; animism; idolatry

5 **heretic; nonconformist**

6 **pagan, heathen;** animist; idolater

verbs

7 **err,** stray, deviate, wander, go astray

adjectives

8 **unorthodox,** heterodox; **heretical;** unsound, **fallacious,** erroneous

9 **atheistic,** agnostic, **unbelieving**

10 **pagan, heathen;** animistic; idolatrous

668 OCCULTISM

nouns

1 **occultism, esoterics;** hocus-pocus, mumbo jumbo; mysticism

2 **the supernatural,** the paranormal

3 **spiritualism,** necromancy

4 **psychic phenomenon;** poltergeist; telekinesis, psychokinesis; Ouija board

5 **clairvoyance, extrasensory perception *or* ESP;** second sight, sixth sense, intuition; premonition; divination

6 **telepathy, mind reading,** thought transference

7 **occultist,** esoteric, mystic

8 **psychic,** spiritualist, medium; necromancer

9 **clairvoyant**

10 **mind reader,** telepathist

verbs

11 **read someone's mind;** hold a séance, call up spirits

adjectives

12 **occult, esoteric,** mysterious,

mystic, mystical; **supernatural, paranormal**

13 **psychic,** spiritual; **telepathic, clairvoyant; extrasensory;** telekinetic, psychokinetic

669 SORCERY

nouns

1 **sorcery, magic, witchcraft,** wizardry; voodoo; spell, charm

2 **black magic,** the black art

3 **sorcerer, magician,** conjurer, **witch, wizard,** warlock

4 **magician,** illusionist

5 **shaman,** witch doctor, medicine man

verbs

6 **conjure, conjure up,** evoke, invoke, raise, summon, call up

7 bewitch, cast a spell

adjectives

8 **magic, magical,** sorcerous

670 SPELL, CHARM

nouns

1 **spell,** magic spell, charm; evil eye, **hex, jinx, curse;** exorcism

2 **bewitchment;** enchantment, entrancement, captivation; illusion; possession

3 **trance, ecstasy,** transport; meditation, contemplation; **rapture;** hypnosis

4 **incantation,** magic words; hocus-pocus, abracadabra, mumbo jumbo; open sesame

5 **charm, talisman,** amulet; good-luck charm, lucky white heather,

four-leaf clover, rabbit's foot; mascot

6 **wand, magic wand;** Aladdin's lamp; magic carpet; wishing well; wishbone

verbs

7 **cast a spell;** entrance, hypnotize, mesmerize

8 **charm, enchant,** fascinate, captivate

9 **bewitch, hex, jinx;** possess

10 **put a curse on,** put a hex on, give the evil eye

adjectives

11 **bewitching,** charming, **enchanting,** entrancing, fascinating, spellbinding

12 charmed, **enchanted; spellbound;** fascinated, captivated; **hypnotized, mesmerized**

13 **bewitched, possessed,** taken over

671 PIETY

nouns

1 **piety, piousness;** religion, faith; religiousness, religiosity; love of God, adoration; **devoutness,** devotion, worship; observance, conformity, dutifulness; **reverence,** veneration

2 **godliness;** fear of God; sanctity; **righteousness, holiness,** goodness; **spirituality**

3 **zeal,** zealotry; **evangelism,** revivalism; **fundamentalism,** fanaticism; sanctimoniousness

4 **believer,** God-fearing person; **devotee; zealot,** fundamentalist, militant; churchgoer; **convert,**

proselyte; **disciple,** follower, servant; **fanatic**

5 **the believing, the faithful, the** righteous, the good; the elect, the chosen, the saved; Christendom, the Church

verbs

6 **be pious, be religious; have faith,** love God, fear God; witness, bear witness, affirm, **believe;** keep the faith, fight the good fight

7 **be converted,** be born again, see the light

adjectives

8 **pious, religious, devout,** devoted; **reverent,** adoring, solemn; faithful, dutiful; affirming, witnessing, believing

9 **God-fearing, righteous, holy,** good; **spiritual,** pure, saintly; heavenly; **unworldly,** unearthly

10 converted, **redeemed, saved, born-again;** sanctified

11 **zealous,** fanatical, **sanctimonious,** fundamentalist

672 SANCTIMONY

nouns

1 **sanctimony, sanctimoniousness,** piety, pietism; **self-righteousness;** insincerity, hypocrisy; cant

2 **hypocrite,** pietist, humbug, **pharisee; Holy Willie** and the unco guid (*Robert Burns*)

verbs

3 be hypocritical, be sanctimonious; cant

adjectives

4 **sanctimonious, pious,** self-righteous, **holier-than-thou;** false, insincere, hypocritical; canting

673 IMPIETY

nouns

1 **impiety, apostasy; atheism,** agnosticism, irreligion; fall from grace

2 **sacrilege, blasphemy;** desecration; profanity

3 **blasphemer,** sacrilegist; **apostate,** renegade; **atheist,** agnostic, unbeliever

verbs

4 **desecrate,** commit sacrilege

5 **blaspheme;** vilify, abuse; curse, swear; take in vain

adjectives

6 **impious,** undutiful; **profane, sacrilegious,** blasphemous; apostate, lapsed, fallen; **atheistic,** agnostic, unbelieving

674 NONRELIGIOUSNESS

nouns

1 **nonreligiousness;** nonobservance; indifference; **secularization**

2 **secularism, wordliness,** mundaneness; materialism, Philistinism

3 **irreligion, ungodliness; impiety;** wickedness, sinfulness

4 **unbelief,** disbelief; infidelity; **atheism**

5 **scepticism, agnosticism,** doubt

6 **freethinking, humanism**

7 **unbeliever,** nonbeliever; **atheist;** infidel, pagan, heathen

8 **sceptic, agnostic,** doubter

9 **freethinker, humanist**

verbs

10 **disbelieve,** doubt

adjectives

11 **nonreligious;** unobservant, **non-practising;** indifferent; **secularized**

12 **worldly, earthly,** mundane, **temporal; profane,** carnal, **secular; materialistic,** material

13 **irreligious, unholy,** ungodly; impious; wicked, sinful

14 **godless,** unredeemed, lost, damned; **lapsed, fallen**

15 **unbelieving, disbelieving, faithless;** infidel, pagan, heathen; **atheist**

16 **sceptic, sceptical, agnostic,** doubtful, dubious, incredulous

17 **freethinking, secular**

675 WORSHIP

nouns

1 **worship, worshipping, adoration, devotion,** homage, **veneration,** reverence

2 **glorification,** glory, **praise,** exaltation

3 **paean;** hallelujah, hosanna; **hymn, psalm, anthem,** motet, canticle, chorale, **chant**

4 **prayer, supplication, litany,** invocation, entreaty, orison, **devotions;** meditation, contemplation, communion; **grace,** thanks, **thanksgiving**

5 **benediction, blessing;** sign of the cross; laying on of hands

6 **atonement,** appeasement, propitiation

7 **offering,** sacrifice, immolation; libation

8 **service, worship,** litany, **devotions; prayers,** prayer meeting; vigils, vespers, evensong; Mass

9 **worshipper, churchgoer,** celebrant

verbs

10 **worship, venerate,** adore, revere, honour, pay homage to

11 **glorify, praise,** laud, exalt, extol, bless, celebrate

12 **pray, supplicate,** invoke, implore, **beseech; say grace; give thanks**

13 **bless, give benediction;** cross, make the sign of the cross; lay hands on

14 **atone,** appease, propitiate; offer sacrifice, sacrifice, immolate before

adjectives

15 **worshipping,** worshipful; adoring, **devout,** devotional; **reverent,** reverential; supplicatory, supplicant, imploring, on bended knee, prostrate before; benedictory

676 IDOLATRY

nouns

1 **idolatry,** idol worship, fetishism; heathenism, paganism; animal worship, nature worship, Druidism; fire worship, sun worship; hero worship; Satanism, devil worship

2 idolization, fetishization; deification

3 idol; fetish, totem; **graven image, golden calf;** Baal, Juggernaut; sacred cow

4 idolater, fetishist, totemist; **heathen, pagan;** Druid; Satanist, devil worshipper

verbs

5 idolatrize, idolize; fetishize; **deify**

adjectives

6 idolatrous, idol worshipping; fetishistic, totemistic; heathen, pagan

677 THE MINISTRY

nouns

1 the ministry, the Church, the cloth, the pulpit; **priesthood,** call, vocation, sacred calling, holy orders; monasticism; celibacy

2 papacy, pontificate, **the Vatican,** Apostolic See, See of Rome

3 diocese, see, archdiocese, bishopric, archbishopric; province; synod, conference; **parish**

4 benefice, living, incumbency; rectory, vicarage, manse (Scots)

5 holy orders; calling, election, nomination, appointment, institution, installation, investiture; **ordination,** consecration, canonization

verbs

6 be ordained, take holy orders, take vows; take the veil, wear the cloth

7 ordain, frock, canonize, **consecrate;** saint

adjectives

8 ecclesiastical, ecclesiastic; ministerial, clerical, pastoral; **priestly; monastic**

9 papal, pontifical; popish *or* papish

10 ordained; in holy orders, of the cloth

678 THE CLERGY

nouns

1 clergy, ministry, the cloth; clerical order, clericals; **priesthood;** presbytery

2 clergyman, clergywoman, man *or* woman of the cloth, ecclesiastic, churchman, cleric, clerical; **minister,** parson, **pastor, rector, curate,** shepherd; chaplain; **preacher**

3 priest, father, padre, confessor, spiritual leader

4 evangelist, revivalist; missionary; TV evangelist, televangelist (*nonformal*)

5 (*Jewish*) **rabbi,** rabbinist, chief rabbi, scribe

6 (*Muslim*) imam, sheikh, mufti, fakir, mullah

7 (*Hindu*) Brahman, pundit, guru; yogi

8 (*Buddhist*) Lama, Dalai Lama

9 monk, monastic, cenobite, **mendicant, friar;** brother, prior, abbot; hermit, ascetic, celibate

10 nun; novice, **sister,** mother superior; abbess, prioress

679 THE LAITY

nouns

1 **the laity, lay persons,** laymen; laywomen; brothers, sisters, brethren; people; elders; flock, fold, sheep; **congregation,** parishioners, assembly; **parish**

2 **layman, laywoman; layperson;** parishioner, church member; brother, sister; elder

adjectives

3 **lay, nonordained; secular;** temporal, popular, civil

680 RELIGIOUS RITES

nouns

1 **rite, ritual,** holy rite, liturgy; **ceremony, service;** sacrament, mystery

2 (*Protestant sacraments*) baptism, Lord's Supper

3 (*Roman Catholic and Eastern sacraments*) baptism, confirmation, the Eucharist, penance, holy orders, matrimony, annointing of the sick *or* extreme unction

4 **baptism, christening,** immersion; **confirmation, bar mitzvah**

5 **Eucharist, Lord's Supper,** Last Supper, **Communion, the Sacrament;** body and blood of Christ, bread and wine

6 **Mass; the Liturgy**

7 **Bible,** Book of Psalms, prayer book, Book of Common Prayer

8 **holy day;** feast, fast; Sabbath; Sunday, lord's day; saint's day

verbs

9 **celebrate, observe, keep;** celebrate Mass, attend Communion, receive the Sacrament

10 **minister,** officiate, administer

11 **baptize, christen,** immerse; circumcise, confirm

12 **confess,** recieve absolution; absolve

adjectives

13 **ritual, ceremonial;** liturgical; sacramental

681 RELIGIOUS BUILDINGS

nouns

1 **church,** kirk (*Scots*), church house, house of God, place of worship; **chapel; mission;** cathedral

2 **temple; tabernacle; synagogue; mosque**

3 **shrine,** holy place; **sanctuary, sanctum**

4 **monastery, abbey,** friary, priory; **convent, nunnery**

5 **church house;** rectory, vicarage, parsonage, manse (*Scots*)

6 **bishop's palace; Vatican; Lambeth Palace**

7 (*church interior*) vestry, apse, choir, cloisters, crypt, nave, porch, organ loft

8 **altar,** Communion table, font, pulpit, lectern; cruet, chalice; pew, stall

adjectives

9 **ecclesiastical; cloistered**

682 SHOW BUSINESS, THEATRE

nouns

1 **show business,** showbiz (*nonformal*) **the theatre, the stage,** the boards

2 **stage show, show; play,** piece, vehicle, work; **hit,** success, critical success, audience success; failure, turkey, **flop**

3 **drama, tragedy; comedy,** burlesque, music hall, variety, pantomime, stand-up comedy

4 **act, scene;** turn, routine, sketch; introduction, prologue, epilogue, **finale;** intermission, interlude; **curtain call, encore**

5 **acting, playing,** performing, **performance; portrayal, characterization; impersonation,** miming, mimicking, mimicry; overacting, ham acting

6 **repertoire, repertory**

7 **role, part; cast;** lead, leading man, leading lady, hero, heroine; title role; bit, bit part, minor role, walk-on

8 **engagement, booking;** run, stand, circuit, tour

9 **performance, show,** presentation, production, entertainment, benefit performance, benefit; personal appearance; showcase; premiere, debut; farewell performance, swan song (*nonformal*)

10 **production,** mounting, staging, putting on; **rehearsal,** dress rehearsal, run-through

11 **theatre, house, auditorium;** opera house, concert hall; cabaret, nightclub, club, night spot

12 **stage,** the boards; orchestra pit, bandstand; stage right, stage left, backstage, **wings;** dressing room; curtain; stage door

13 **props,** costumes, makeup, greasepaint

14 **lights,** floodlights, footlights, limelight, arc light

15 **scenery,** decor, curtain, backdrop

16 **script,** text, score, libretto; prompt book, lines, cue

17 **dramatist;** playwright, scriptwriter, screenwriter; librettist, composer; choreographer

18 **producer,** showman, **impresario; director,** auteur; **stage manager;** set designer, costume designer; hairdresser; ticket collector, usher

19 **stagehand,** sceneshifter

verbs

20 **dramatize;** present, **stage, produce, mount,** put on, preview; **star,** feature, bill, headline; succeed, be a hit; fail, **flop,** bomb

21 **act, perform, play,** tread the boards; **star,** play the lead, get top billing; steal the show, upstage

22 **enact, act out;** represent, depict, **portray;** impersonate, mimic; play opposite, support

23 **overact,** ham, ham it up

24 **rehearse, practise,** go through, go over; read one's lines

adjectives

25 **dramatic; theatrical,** histrionic, thespian; **melodramatic;** milked (*nonformal*), overacted, hammy, operatic, balletic; stagestruck

26 **tragic,** heavy; **comic,** light; farcical, slapstick

adverbs

27 **on the stage,** before an audience; backstage, off stage; **in the
limelight**

683 DANCE

nouns

1 **dancing,** terpsichore, **dance;
choreography;** hoofing (*nonformal*)

2 **dance; ball,** masked ball, masquerade; barn dance, tea dance;
ceilidh

3 **dancer,** terpsichorean, hoofer
(*nonformal*); tap dancer; ballet
dancer, **ballerina;** modern dancer; chorus girl, Tiller girl, chorus
line; choreographer

4 **ballroom, dance hall;** casino

verbs

5 **dance,** trip, skip, hop, prance
(*nonformal*); shake, shuffle;
waltz, foxtrot

684 MOTION PICTURES

nouns

1 **motion pictures, movies, the
movies, the pictures,** moving
pictures, films, the film, the cinema, the screen, the silver screen,
the flicks (*nonformal*); **motion
picture, movie, picture, film,**
picture show; silent film; documentary film; **feature,** feature
film, main attraction; **short;** preview, sneak preview; training
film; **cartoon,** animation, computer graphics

2 **script,** screenplay, scenario; **dialogue, book; role,** lead, romantic
lead, stock character, cameo, bit

3 **movie studio,** film studio, animation studio, lot, back lot,
sound stage, location; **set, film
set,** props; **film company,** production company; **producer, director, actor, actress, film actor,
film actress,** player, star, character actor, supporting actor *or* actress, bit player, extra; **crew,** film
crew

4 **photography,** camera work, camera angle, camera position,
shot, take; screen test; **special effects; colour photography,** colour; cameraman *or* camera-
woman

5 **film editing, editing,** cutting;
fade, dissolve, mix

6 **movie theatre,** film theatre, **cinema; screen,** silver screen

verbs

7 **film, shoot**

685 ENTERTAINER

nouns

1 **entertainer,** public entertainer,
performer; artist, artiste; dancer;
song and dance man; chorus girl,
show girl; stripper; dancing girl,
belly dancer; **magician,** conjurer;
singer, musician; performance
artist

2 **actor, actress, player;** child actor; mime, mimic; strolling player; character; **villain,** bad guy *or*
heavy (*both nonformal*); foil,
stooge (*nonformal*), straight
man; romantic lead

3 circus artist; trapeze artist; tight-rope walker; acrobat, tumbler; bareback rider; juggler; lion tamer; snake charmer; clown

4 movie actor; movie star; **film star**

5 **lead,** leading man or lady, leading actor or actress, principal, **star,** superstar; **hero, heroine,** protagonist; **prima donna,** singer; prima ballerina

6 **supporting actor** or **actress; support,** supporting cast; **extra;** bit player; **understudy, stand-in,** standby, substitute

7 **comedian, comic;** funny-man; stand-up comic or comedian

8 **buffoon, clown, fool**

9 **cast,** characters; supporting cast; **company,** troupe; repertory company; chorus

686 MUSIC

nouns

1 **melody; tune, tone,** musical sound, musical quality; sweetness

2 **harmony, concord,** concert, accord, symphony; tune; unison

3 **air, tune, melody,** line, refrain, note, **song,** solo, strain, measure

4 **piece, composition,** production, work; **score; arrangement,** adaptation, setting

5 **classical music;** serious music

6 **popular music,** pop music, light music, poular song, **ballad;** pop

7 **dance music;** ragtime or rag

8 **jazz;** traditional jazz; **swing,** jive; mainstream jazz; avant-garde jazz

9 **rock'n'roll, rock music,** rock, hard rock, folk rock, country rock

10 **folk music,** folk songs, world music; folk ballads; country music; the blues

11 **march;** quick march; funeral or dead march; wedding march

12 **vocal music, song, singing,** warbling; choral singing; folk singing; crooning; yodelling; humming

13 **song,** lay, carol, ditty; **ballad**

14 **solo; aria**

15 **sacred music, church music; hymn;** psalm; anthem

16 part song, part singing; **duet; trio; quartet; chorus, choir;** choral singing

17 **round,** catch; canon

18 **part, line;** soprano, tenor, treble, alto, contralto, baritone, bass; drone; **accompaniment**

19 **passage, phrase,** musical phrase, part, motive, motif, theme, figure; **movement;** introductory phrase; exposition, development, variation; section; **verse; chorus, refrain;** cadence; interlude; bridge, bridge passage

20 **overture, prelude, introduction**

21 **impromptu, improvisation;** flourish, grace note; **run;** lick, hot lick

22 **score, music,** notation, musical notation, written music, transcript, version, edition, text, arrangement; **libretto; sheet music;** songbook; hymnbook

23 **staff,** stave; line, ledger line; bar, bar line

24 **execution, performance; render-**

ing, touch, expression; fingering; intonation; staccato, slur

25 musicianship; musical ear; musical sense; sense of rhythm; perfect pitch

26 sing (nonformal), singing, community singing; music festival; folk festival, jazz festival, rock festival; jam session (nonformal)

27 performance, musical performance, **programme**, musical programme; **concert**, symphony concert, chamber concert; promenade concert, prom (nonformal); **recital**; swan song, farewell performance

28 musical theatre; opera, grand opera, light opera; comic opera; musical comedy; musical; **ballet**

verbs

29 harmonize, be harmonious, accord, synchronize, **chime, blend,** blend in; tune, sound together

30 strike up, pipe up, burst into song

31 sing; **warble; chirp; twitter;** pipe; whistle; **chant; intone; croon; hum;** chorus

32 play, perform, render, do; interpret; make music; accompany

33 strum, pluck, pick, twang

34 sound, blow, toot, pipe; whistle

35 beat time, keep time, tap; count; **drum beat,** thump, pound

36 conduct, direct, lead

37 compose, write, arrange, set; harmonize; orchestrate; adapt; transcribe

adjectives

38 musical; music-loving

39 melodic; tuneful; pleasant, appealing, agreeable, catchy; lyrical; **sweet;** rich

40 harmonious, harmonizing, chiming, blending; consonant, **in accord,** in concert; synchronized, **in tune,** tuned; in unison, in chorus

41 vocal, singing; **choral;** operatic; treble, soprano, tenor, alto; baritone; bass

42 instrumental, orchestral

687 HARMONICS, MUSICAL ELEMENTS

nouns

1 harmony; music

2 arrangement, setting, adaptation; phrasing, intonation

3 pitch, tuning, tune, **tone, key, note,** register

4 voice; soprano; boy soprano; alto, contralto; tenor; baritone; bass; treble

5 scale, register, range; major scale, minor scale

6 notation, character, mark, symbol, signature, sign; dot; bar; key signature; slur, tie; expression mark

7 clef; bass clef, treble clef

8 note, musical note; tone; sharp, flat, natural; semibreve; minim; crotchet; quaver

9 key, key signature; major *or* minor key

10 ornament, embellishment; **flourish,** run; grace note; cadence

11 **interval**, note, tone; second, third, fourth, fifth, sixth, seventh, octave

12 **rest**, pause

13 **rhythm, beat, lilt, swing**

14 **tempo, time, beat**; time signature

15 **accent**, emphasis

16 **beat**, throb, pulse

adjectives

17 **rhythmic**; in rhythm; beating, throbbing, pulsing, pulsating

adverbs

18 **in time**, in tempo

688 MUSICIAN

nouns

1 **musician, music maker**; performer, interpreter, artiste, artist, **virtuoso; soloist;** street musician, busker

2 **player**, instrumentalist; accompanist

3 **wind player**, horn player, piper; trumpeter, trumpet major

4 **string musician;** guitarist, classical guitarist; violinist; bass player

5 **pianist**, piano player

6 **organist**, organ player

7 **drummer, percussionist**

8 **orchestra, band,** group; strings, woodwind *or* woodwinds, brass *or* brasses, string *or* woodwind *or* brass section

9 **singer, vocalist,** voice, lead singer; opera singer, prima donna; rap singer; blues singer; rock'n'roll singer; country singer

10 **minstrel**, ballad singer, bard; troubadour; street singer; **folk singer**

11 **choral singer**, choir member, chorister; **choirboy; chorus girl**

12 **chorus, choir,** choral group, choral society; glee club

13 **conductor**, leader, **music director; orchestra leader, band leader**, band major, drum major

14 **composer**, arranger; song writer, songsmith; lyricist

15 **music lover**, music fan *and* music buff (*both nonformal*)

16 **songbird**, singing bird, warbler; nightingale; canary, cuckoo, lark, thrush

689 MUSICAL INSTRUMENTS

nouns

1 **musical instrument;** string *or* stringed instrument; wind instrument; brass instrument; woodwind instrument; keyboard instrument

2 **harp**, lyre

3 **horn**; pipe; bagpipes, pipes; mouth organ, harmonica

4 **piano;** harpsichord; organ

5 **music box, musical box**

6 **percussion, drum**

690 VISUAL ARTS

nouns

1 **visual arts; art,** the arts; **fine arts; design,** designing; art form; abstract art; commercial art; sculpture; ceramics; photography; etching, engraving; decoration; artist

2 **craft, manual art,** industrial art; industrial design; woodwork

3 **painting,** colouring

4 (*art of drawing*) **drawing, draughtsmanship, sketching**

5 **artistry, art, talent,** artistic skill, flair, artistic flair, artistic invention; artistic temperament

6 **style; genre; school,** movement

7 **treatment; technique; composition, design,** arrangement; grouping, balance; **colour;** atmosphere, tone; shadow, shading; **line;** perspective

8 **work of art, art** object, art work, piece, **work, study, design, composition;** creation, brainchild; **masterpiece,** old master, classic; museum piece; grotesque; statue; mobile; nude, still life; bric-a-brac

9 **picture, image, likeness, representation; photograph; illustration,** illumination; miniature; copy, reproduction; print, colour print; engraving, stencil; abstraction, abstract; mural, fresco, wall painting; panorama; collage; still life; tapestry, mosaic; stained glass, icon

10 **scene, view; landscape;** pastoral; exterior, interior

11 **drawing;** line drawing; **sketch, draft;** pencil drawing, charcoal drawing, pastel, pastel painting; silhouette; doodle; rough outline, cartoon, **study,** design; diagram; graph; tracing

12 **painting, canvas, oil painting,** oil; **watercolour,** wash; finger painting

13 **portrait, portrayal;** head; profile; silhouette, shadow figure; miniature

14 **cartoon, caricature; comic strip;** comic section, comics; comic book; animated cartoon

15 **studio; gallery**

16 **easel;** drawing paper; canvas; brush, paintbrush; air brush; spray gun; pencil, drawing pencil; crayon, charcoal, chalk, pastel; pigments; varnish; **paint**

verbs

17 **portray, picture,** depict; **paint;** brush, brush in; colour, tint; daub (*nonformal*); **draw, sketch; draft;** pencil, chalk, crayon, charcoal; draw in, pencil in; dash off, scratch (*nonformal*); doodle; design; diagram; cartoon; copy, trace; stencil; hatch, shade

adjectives

18 **artistic; arty; aesthetic; tasteful; beautiful;** decorative, ornamental

19 **pictorial,** graphic, picturesque; photographic

691 GRAPHIC ARTS

nouns

1 **graphic arts, graphics; painting; drawing; photography; printing;** graphic artist

2 **engraving,** chiselling, incision, scratching, slashing, scoring; **inscription; marking,** line, scratch, slash, score; hatching; etch, etching; tint

3 **print,** imprint, impression; negative; colour print; **etching;** block, wood engraving, **woodcut**

4 **plate;** printing plate

5 **engraving tool,** point, etching point, needle, etching needle; punch, stamp, seal

verbs

6 **engrave, tool, sculpture, inscribe, mark,** line, crease, score, scratch, scrape, cut, carve, chisel; furrow; hatch; print

7 **etch,** corrode

adjectives

8 **engraved;** inscribed, marked, lined, creased, cut, carved, **sculptured,** grooved, furrowed; **printed,** imprinted, impressed, stamped

692 PHOTOGRAPHY

nouns

1 **photography;** colour photography; radiography, X-ray photography

2 **photographer,** press photographer

3 **photograph, photo** (*nonformal*), **picture, shot** (*nonformal*), **snapshot,** snap (*nonformal*); black-and-white photograph; colour photograph, colour print; slide, transparency; still, still photograph; aerial photograph; **portrait; mug shot** (*nonformal*)

4 **print,** positive; glossy; **enlargement; blueprint; slide,** transparency

5 **X ray,** X-ray photograph

6 (*motion pictures*) **shot; take;** close-up, long shot, medium shot, full shot, group shot

7 **exposure,** time exposure; shutter

speed; film speed; exposure meter, light meter

8 **film; negative;** printing paper, photographic paper; plate; black-and-white film, colour film; roll, cartridge; pack; frame

9 **projector; slide projector**

verbs

10 **photograph, shoot** (*nonformal*); snap; **film;** X-ray

11 **process; develop; print; blow up, enlarge**

693 SCULPTURE

nouns

1 **sculpture;** plastic art, **modelling;** masonry; **carving, woodcarving; engraving,** casting, moulding, plaster casting; sculptor

2 (*sculptured piece*) **sculpture; statue;** marble, bronze; mobile; cast

3 **relief; medallion; medal; cameo;** cut glass

4 (*tools, materials*) chisel, point, mallet, modelling tool; cutting torch; welding torch; modelling clay; plaster

verbs

5 **sculpture, sculpt; carve,** chisel, cut, engrave; weld; **model, mould;** cast, found

adjectives

6 **statuesque; monumental**

7 **sculptured; modelled; carved,** chiselled; in relief; embossed

694 ARTIST

nouns

1 **artist,** creator, maker; **master, old master; craftsman**

2 **illustrator;** commercial artist

3 **draughtsman;** drawer; **cartoonist**

4 **painter; oil painter;** portrait painter; pavement artist; scene painter

5 **photographer, cameraman**

6 **sculptor;** mason

7 graphic artist; engraver

8 **designer;** costume designer, dress designer

9 **architect,** civil architect; landscape architect, landscape gardener

10 **decorator;** interior decorator; window dresser

695 ARCHITECTURE, DESIGN

nouns

1 **architecture,** architectural design, building design, landscape gardening

2 **architect;** landscape architect, landscape gardener

3 **design, styling,** planning, shaping

696 LITERATURE

nouns

1 **literature; work,** literary work, text, literary text; works, complete works, canon, literary canon, author's canon; classics

2 **writing, composition; creative writing,** literary art, literary composition; journalism, newspaper writing, rewriting; magazine writing; artistry, literary power, literary artistry

3 **author, writer,** composer; **creative writer,** man of letters; prose writer; fiction writer; story writer; **novelist; poet; dramatist;** magazine writer; **essayist;** critic, literary critic, music critic, art critic, drama critic, dance critic; columnist

4 **hack writer,** hack, literary hack

verbs

5 **write,** author, pen, **compose,** formulate, produce, prepare; dash off, knock out, churn out (*nonformal*)

697 HISTORY

nouns

1 **history;** historical research; **chronicles;** chronicle, record; **oral history,** oral record; **biography,** memorial, **life,** story, **life story,** adventures, fortunes, experiences; legend; **autobiography, memoirs, journal, diary,** confessions; **profile, biographical sketch;** obituary; case history; **the past**

2 **story, tale, yarn, account,** narrative, narration, chronicle; **anecdote;** epic, saga

3 **historian; biographer**

verbs

4 **chronicle,** write history; **record**

5 **narrate, tell, relate, recount,** report, **recite**

adjectives

6 **historical, historic,** historically accurate; **chronicled;** chronological; **traditional, legendary;** biographical, autobiographical

7 **narrative; fictional**

adverbs

8 **historically;** by all accounts

698 POETRY

nouns

1 **poetry, verse, song, rhyme**

2 **poetic language; poetic licence, poetic justice**

3 **bad poetry,** doggerel; nonsense verse

4 **poem, verse, rhyme**

5 **collection, anthology;** poetic works

6 metre, free verse

7 **metre,** measure; rhythm, cadence; accent, stress, emphasis, **beat; foot**

8 **rhyme;** rhyme scheme; blank verse

9 (*poetic divisions*) measure, strain; syllable; **line;** verse; refrain, chorus

10 Muse; poetic genius, **inspiration**

11 **poet;** ballad maker; **lyric poet;** epic poet; pastoral poet; **beat poet**

verbs

12 rhyme; scan

adjectives

13 **poetic; metric; rhythmic,** scanning; rhyming

699 PROSE

nouns

1 **prose,** prose fiction; prose rhythm; prose style

adjectives

2 **prose,** in prose

3 **prosaic; plain, common, commonplace, ordinary,** mundane; **matter-of-fact;** pedestrian, **unimaginative;** insipid, flat; humdrum, tiresome, **dull**

700 FICTION

nouns

1 **fiction,** narrative, narrative literature, prose fiction; **narration,** relation, recital, telling, recounting, review, portrayal, description, presentation; **storytelling**

2 **narration, narrative, relation, recital,** rehearsal, telling, recounting, review

3 **story, short story,** tale, narrative, yarn, account, narration, chronicle, relation, version; **novel**

4 (*story elements*) **plot,** fable, argument, story, story line; **structure,** plan, design; **subject, topic, theme,** motif; **action;** incident, episode; **complication;** climax; device, contrivance; **gimmick** (*nonformal*); **character;** dialogue; **tone, atmosphere,** mood; **setting,** world, milieu, background, local colour

5 **narrator; author, writer, novelist**

verbs

6 **narrate, tell, relate, recount,** report, **recite,** rehearse

adjectives

7 **fictional**; mythical, mythological, **legendary**, **fabulous**; **romantic**; romanticized; historical

8 **narrative**; anecdotal

701 OCCUPATION

nouns

1 **occupation, work, job, employment**, business, employ, **activity, function**, enterprise, undertaking, **work, affairs**, labour; affair, matter, concern, interest; **commerce**

2 **task, work, stint, job**, labour, chore, odd job; **assignment, charge**, project, errand, **mission**, commission, **duty**, service, exercise; homework

3 **function, office, duty, job**, province, place, **role**, part; **capacity**, character, **position**

4 **sphere**, profession, province, turf (*nonformal*), department, area, discipline, orbit, realm, arena, domain, walk; **speciality; beat**, round

5 **position, job**, employment, situation, **office, post, place**, station, **appointment**, engagement; tenure; opening, vacancy; second job, moonlighting (*nonformal*)

6 **vocation, occupation, business, work, line**, walk, **calling**, mission, **profession, practice, pursuit, speciality**, specialization, **trade**; **career**, life's work; **craft**

7 **hobby**, sideline, side interest, pastime; amateur pursuit; unpaid work, volunteer work

verbs

8 **occupy, engage**, devote, spend, **employ**, occupy oneself, **busy oneself**, devote oneself

9 **do**; engage in, take up; be doing; practice

10 **work**, work at, work for, be employed; **moonlight** (*nonformal*); labour, toil

11 **function, serve**; perform as, act as, do duty

adjectives

12 **occupied, busy**, working; practical, realistic; utilitarian; materialistic; prosaic; **commercial**

13 **occupational, vocational**, functional; **professional**, pro (*nonformal*); official; technical, industrial

702 EXERTION

nouns

1 **exertion, effort, energy**, elbow grease; **endeavour**; **trouble, pains**; might and main, muscle

2 **strain**, straining, **stress**, tension, stretch; tug, pull, haul, heave

3 **struggle, fight**, battle, **tussle**, scuffle, hassle (*nonformal*)

4 **work, labour, employment**, industry, toil; **drudgery, sweat**, slavery, rat race (*nonformal*); unskilled labour; dirty work, donkey work; **grind** (*nonformal*), fag; **manual labour**, handiwork, stroke; **workload**, work schedule; task

5 **hard work**, hard grind (*nonformal*)

6 **exercise**; **practice**, **drill**, **workout**; yoga; constitutional

(*nonformal*), stretch; physical education

7 parallel bars, horse, rings; trapeze; trampoline; medicine ball; punching bag; rowing machine; weight

verbs

8 exert, exercise, ply, employ, use, put forth; practise

9 exert oneself, spread oneself; endeavour; apply oneself

10 strain, tense, stress, stretch, tax, press, rack; pull, tug, haul, heave; sweat blood

11 struggle, strive, contend, fight, battle, buffet, scuffle, tussle, wrestle, hassle (*nonformal*), agonize, sweat it

12 work, labour; busy oneself

13 work hard; slave, slave away, toil away; work overtime, work late; overwork

14 drudge, fag, grub, toil, plod, slog, hammer away, pound away, struggle along, struggle on, work away; wade through

15 get rolling, get busy, get down to business *or* work; set about; get cracking (*nonformal*); attack, tackle (*nonformal*); plunge into, dive into; take on, undertake

16 work, busy, keep busy, drive, tax; overwork; burden, oppress

adjectives

17 labouring, working, struggling, striving, straining; toiling, slaving, plodding, slogging

18 laborious, arduous, strenuous, painful, troublesome, onerous, oppressive; heavy, hefty (*nonformal*), tough (*nonformal*), uphill, gruelling, punishing, crushing, killing; laboured, forced, strained; straining, intensive

adverbs

19 laboriously, strenuously; with effort, hard; manfully

703 WORKER, DOER

nouns

1 agent, actor, performer, worker, practitioner, perpetrator; producer, maker, creator, author; architect; agent, medium; operator, operative

2 worker, labourer; workman; factory worker, industrial worker; construction worker; office worker, white-collar worker; career woman; wage earner, salaried worker; breadwinner; wage slave; employee, servant; hand; labourer, common labourer, unskilled labourer, day labourer; casual, casual labourer; agricultural worker; full-time worker, part-time worker; temporary employee, temporary, office temporary, temp (*nonformal*); self-employed person; labour force, work force, shop floor; labour market

3 drudge, hack, slave, galley slave; slave labour

4 professional; seasoned professional; doctor, lawyer, teacher, accountant; social worker

5 amateur, layman

6 skilled worker, skilled labourer, mechanic; craftsman; technician; apprentice; master craftsman

7 **engineer,** professional engineer; **technician,** technical worker; engineering, technology

704 UNIONISM

nouns

1 **unionism,** trade unionism; trades unionism; **collective bargaining; arbitration;** industrial relations; labour relations

2 trade union, trades union; organized labour; collective bargaining

3 **unionist, trade unionist, union member,** trades unionist; shop steward; negotiator; union officer

4 **strike,** walkout (*nonformal*), industrial action; work stoppage; work-to-rule; general strike; **boycott;** revolt

verbs

5 **strike,** go out, walk out; slow down; sit down; **boycott;** picket; **lock out;** revolt

705 MONEY

nouns

1 **money, currency, legal tender,** sterling, **cash,** hard cash; coinage; gold; silver; **hard currency**

2 (*nonformal terms*) **dough, bread,** change, coin, brass, tin, loot

3 coin, piece; **gold piece;** guinea, sovereign

4 paper money; note; bank note

5 penny; pence; new pence; shilling, bob (*nonformal*); half crown; crown; pound, quid (*nonformal*); guinea; fiver

6 foreign money, foreign denominations; **foreign exchange;** exchange rate

7 **counterfeit,** counterfeit money; **forgery,** bad cheque

8 cheque; blank cheque; traveller's cheque; postal order; IOU; chequebook

9 **token, counter, coupon; ticket**

10 **sum;** lump sum

11 **funds, finances,** purse, budget, pocket; treasury; treasure, **assets,** resources, total assets, worth, net worth, **means,** cash flow; balance; pool, **fund, kitty** (*nonformal*); bank account; reserves, cash reserves; savings, nest egg (*nonformal*); life savings

12 **capital, fund;** circulating capital, floating capital; fixed capital, working capital; risk *or* venture capital

13 **money market; borrowing; lending**

14 **cash,** ready money *or* cash, cash in hand, **cash flow;** treasury

15 **petty cash, pocket money, pin money,** spending money, **change,** small change

16 precious metals; **gold; silver; bullion**

17 **coining,** coinage; **counterfeiting, forgery**

verbs

18 **issue, circulate**

19 **borrow, lend**

20 **coin, mint; counterfeit, forge**

21 **cash,** cash in (*nonformal*)

adjectives

22 **monetary, financial;** fiscal

23 convertible, liquid; negotiable

706 FINANCE, INVESTMENT

nouns

1 **finance, finances, money matters;** financial world, financial industry, **high finance,** investment banking, international banking; economics

2 **financing, funding, backing,** financial backing, **sponsorship,** support, financial support; subsidy; **capitalizing**

3 **investment, venture, risk,** speculation

4 **banking,** money dealing, money changing; investment banking; banking industry

5 **financial condition; credit rating**

6 **crisis,** financial crisis

7 **financier, capitalist,** finance capitalist; investor; financial expert; economist; international banker

8 **backer, sponsor, patron, supporter,** angel (*nonformal*); fundraiser

9 **banker;** investment banker; bank manager; bank clerk, cashier

10 **treasurer,** financial officer, purser; **cashier;** accountant, auditor; curator, steward, trustee; receiver

11 **treasury;** repository; **safe,** money chest, **locker, chest;** piggy bank, bank; **vault,** strong room; cash register, **till; public treasury,** public funds

12 **bank,** banking house, lending institution; cash machine; **central bank,** Bank of England; World Bank; clearing house

13 **purse, wallet, pocketbook, bag, handbag,** money belt, money clip, **pocket;** purse strings

verbs

14 **finance, back, fund, sponsor, patronize, support,** provide for, pay for; subsidize; set up

15 **invest,** place, put, sink; **risk, venture; invest in;** speculate

adjectives

16 **solvent, sound,** substantial, solid, good; good for

17 **insolvent,** unsound, indebted

707 BUSINESSMAN, MERCHANT

nouns

1 **businessman,** businesswoman; entrepreneur; big businessman, magnate, tycoon (*nonformal*), top executive, business leader; director, manager; **industrialist;** banker, financier

2 **merchant, trader, dealer; tradesman; shopkeeper; wholesaler;** middleman; importer, exporter; **distributor; retailer;** franchise

3 **salesman, seller; clerk,** shop assistant; **agent;** sales manager; sales force, sales personnel

4 **travelling salesman, commercial traveller;** door-to-door salesman

5 **vendor,** pedlar

6 **auctioneer,** auction agent

7 **broker,** insurance broker, mortgage broker; stockbroker; pawnbroker; estate agent

8 **rag-and-bone man; junk dealer**

adjectives

9 **business, commercial**

708 COMMERCE, ECONOMICS

nouns

1 **commerce, trade, traffic,** truck, **dealing, dealings; business; market,** marketing; **industry;** big business, small business; free trade

2 **trade, trading, doing business, trafficking;** barter, bartering, **exchange,** interchange, swapping (*nonformal*); give-and-take, horse trading (*nonformal*), **dealing**

3 **negotiation, bargaining, haggling,** haggle; coming to terms; collective bargaining

4 **transaction, deal,** business deal, negotiation, operation; package deal

5 **bargain, deal** (*nonformal*); **trade, swap** (*nonformal*); horse trade (*nonformal*); hard bargain

6 **custom,** patronage, trade; **goodwill,** good name

7 **economy, economic system,** market economy; public sector, private sector

8 **standard of living; cost of living**

9 **business cycle, economic cycle;** peak, peaking; low, bottoming out (*nonformal*); **prosperity,** boom (*nonformal*); crisis, **recession, depression, downturn;** upturn, expanding economy, recovery; **growth,** economic growth, business growth, expansion, market expansion, **economic expansion; trade cycle;** trade deficit, trade gap; **monetary cycle; inflation,** deflation

10 **economics;** political economy

11 **economist;** political economist

12 **commercialism;** industrialism; mass marketing

13 **commercialization;** industrialization

verbs

14 **trade, deal, traffic, do business; barter; exchange,** change, interchange, **swap** (*nonformal*), switch; trade off; trade in; **ply one's trade**

15 **deal in, trade in, traffic in, handle,** carry, be in; market, merchandise, **sell,** retail, wholesale

16 **trade with, deal with, traffic with;** shop at, **patronize**

17 **bargain, negotiate, haggle, deal; bid,** bid for, beat down

18 **strike a bargain, make a deal;** shake hands; bargain for, agree to; be on (*nonformal*)

adjectives

19 **commercial, business, trade, trading;** industrial; wholesale, retail; economic

709 ILLICIT BUSINESS

nouns

1 **illicit business, illegitimate business, illegal operations, shady dealings; racket** (*nonformal*); **organized crime; black market; drug traffic; prostitution; white slavery; protection racket;** gambling

2 **smuggling,** contraband

3 contraband, smuggled goods; narcotics, drugs, dope (*nonformal*), jewels

4 pusher *and* **dealer** (*both nonformal*); **smuggler**

5 fence, receiver, **receiver of stolen goods**

verbs

6 smuggle, run, sneak

710 PURCHASE

nouns

1 purchase, buying, purchasing, shopping, marketing; shopping around; impulse buying; shopping spree; mail-order buying, catalogue buying; instalment buying; hire purchase; consumer society, consumer power

2 option, first refusal

3 market, public, purchasing public; youth market; **clientele, customers,** patronage, **custom,** trade

4 customer, client; patron, regular

5 buyer, consumer; shopper

verbs

6 purchase, buy, procure; buy up, corner the market, monopolize; buy out; buy in, buy into; buy back

7 shop, go shopping; shop around; browse

8 bid, offer

adjectives

9 purchasing, buying

10 bought, purchased

711 SALE

nouns

1 sale; wholesale; retail; market, demand, outlet; mass market; turnover; cash sale

2 selling, marketing; mail-order selling, catalogue selling; **vending, peddling, hawking;** market research; consumer survey; sales campaign, promotion, sales promotion; hard sell (*nonformal*), soft sell (*nonformal*)

3 sale; bazaar, car boot sale, garage sale, flea market

4 auction, auction sale; Dutch auction

5 sales talk, sales pitch, patter

verbs

6 sell, merchandise, market, move, turn over, sell off; **sell out;** sell up; **retail; wholesale;** dump, unload; undercut

7 dispense, peddle, hawk

8 auction, auction off; knock down

9 be sold, sell, bring, realize, sell for

adjectives

10 sales, market, **marketing, retail,** wholesale

11 commercial; in demand

adverbs

12 for sale, up for sale, on the market; marked down

13 at auction, under the hammer

712 MERCHANDISE

nouns

1 **merchandise, commodities, wares, goods,** effects; **items,** oddments; **consumer goods,** consumer items, retail goods; **stock; staples; inventory; line;** sideline; job lot; mail-order goods, catalogue goods; **luxury goods**

2 **commodity, ware, product, article, item; staple,** staple item; special, loss leader; seconds

3 **textiles; men's wear, children's wear; leather goods**

4 fixtures, white goods, **appliances; hardware;** home furnishings

5 **furniture,** furnishings, home furnishings

6 toiletries; cosmetics

7 **groceries,** food items, baked goods, packaged goods, canned goods, tinned goods; **produce**

713 MARKET

nouns

1 **market, store, shop,** salon, boutique, emporium, house, establishment; retail store; wholesale house; discount store, discount house; warehouse; mail-order house; **general store; department store; co-op;** chain store; trading post; **supermarket**

2 **market, open market; shopping centre,** shopping mall; **bazaar, fair,** trade fair, show, exposition; flea market; street market

3 **booth, stall, stand;** kiosk, news kiosk

4 **vending machine,** coin machine, slot machine

5 **showroom;** auction room

6 **counter;** showcase

714 STOCK MARKET

nouns

1 **stock market, the market**

2 **bear market; slump; crash**

3 **rigged market; insider trading**

4 **stock exchange, exchange,** the City, **stock market;** pit

5 **financial district,** the City, Wall Street

6 **stockbroker, broker,** dealer

7 **speculator,** operator; smart operator; **bear; bull;** inside trader

8 **trust,** investment company; investment trust, holding company; unit trust; trust fund

9 **trading; speculation; venture,** flutter; liquidation, profit taking; **takeover,** hostile takeover, takeover bid

10 **manipulation, rigging;** monopoly

verbs

11 **trade, speculate,** venture, operate; make a killing (*nonformal*)

12 **sell,** convert, liquidate; dump, unload

13 **corner;** monopolize; buy up

715 SECURITIES

nouns

1 **stock, shares;** holdings, portfolio, investment portfolio

2 **dividend; interest; return, yield**

3 **price, quotation;** opening price, closing price; high, low; market price; issue price; face value; market value; swings, fluctuations; rally, decline

verbs

4 **issue, float;** go public (*nonformal*)

716 WORKPLACE

nouns

1 **workplace, workshop;** shop floor, working space; **bench;** counter; **work station; desk;** studio; **establishment, facility,** installation; **company,** institution, house, firm, concern, agency, organization; **corporation; financial institution, stock exchange, bank; shop, market, store; restaurant, eating place**

2 **plant, factory, works,** manufacturing plant; assembly plant; assembly *or* production line; **power station; mill;** yard, shipyard; mint; refinery; brewery; dairy; pottery; industrial park, industrial estate; enterprise zone

3 **foundry;** steelworks, steel mill; forge, furnace

4 **repair shop; garage;** hangar

5 **laboratory, lab** (*nonformal*); research laboratory

6 **office,** shop (*nonformal*); headquarters, executive office, corporate headquarters; office suite, executive suite; chambers; **study; embassy,** consulate; box office, booking office, ticket office; branch, branch office, local office

717 WEAVING

nouns

1 **weaving, weave, texture, tissue; fabric, web;** lacing; twining, entwining; knitting; **braiding,** plaiting

2 **braid, plait, wreath**

3 **loom,** weaver; hand loom; knitting machine; shuttle

verbs

4 **weave; twine,** entwine; **braid,** plait, **knit,** twist; loop

adjectives

5 **woven,** textile; **interwoven;** laced; **knit;** twined, entwined; **braided,** plaited

718 SEWING

nouns

1 **sewing, needlework,** stitching; garment making

2 **sewer, seamstress; tailor**

verbs

3 **sew, stitch;** stitch up, sew up; **tailor**

719 CERAMICS

nouns

1 **ceramics, pottery**

2 **ceramic ware, ceramics; pottery, crockery; china, porcelain;** cement; pot, vase, urn, jug, bowl; tile; brick; glass

3 **wheel; kiln,** oven, stove, furnace

verbs

4 **pot,** shape; mould; **fire,** bake; glaze

adjectives

5 **ceramic,** earthen, clay, enamel, china, porcelain; fired, baked, glazed

720 AMUSEMENT

nouns

1 **amusement, entertainment, diversion,** solace, **recreation, relaxation;** pastime; **mirth; pleasure, enjoyment**

2 **fun,** action (*nonformal*); **play, sport;** game; **good time,** lovely time, pleasant time; picnic *and* ball (*both nonformal*), great fun; wild oats

3 **festivity, merriment, gaiety,** conviviality; cavorting; **revelry,** revelling, revels; nightlife

4 **festival, festivity,** festive occasion, gala, do (*nonformal*); **feast, banquet;** picnic; party; carnival; harvest festival; **field day;** gala day

5 **frolic, play,** romp

6 **revel, lark,** ploy; **celebration; party;** spree, bout, fling; **drinking bout**

7 **sport; athletics**

8 **game;** card game; board game; parlour game; **play; contest; race;** event; bout; match; **gambling**

9 **tournament,** gymkhana, **field day;** rally

10 **playground;** field, playing field; football pitch; cricket ground, croquet lawn, bowling green; bowling alley; links, golf links, golf course; putting green; **gymnasium, gym** (*nonformal*); **court,**

badminton court, basketball court, tennis court, squash court; pool hall; racecourse, track; ice rink, skating rink; **playroom**

11 **swimming pool, pool,** swimming bath

12 **entertainment; entertainment industry, show business; theatre;** cabaret; **nightclub,** night spot; discotheque *or* disco (*nonformal*); dance hall, ballroom, dance floor; casino; **resort**

13 **park,** public park, pleasure garden *or* ground, common; **amusement park,** fun fair, carnival; fairground; **theme park,** safari park

14 **merry-go-round,** roundabout, ride; slide; swing; roller coaster

15 **toy, plaything, sport;** trinket; **doll,** paper doll, rag doll, teddy bear, puppet, glove puppet, toy soldier, tin soldier; rocking horse; **hoop; top, spinning top; jack-in-the-box; chessboard; marble;** air gun

16 **man; piece; bishop, knight, king, queen, pawn, rook** *or* **castle**

17 **player; playboy** (*nonformal*); contestant

18 **athlete, player,** amateur athlete, professional athlete, competitor, sportsman

19 **master of ceremonies; marshal;** host

verbs

20 **amuse, entertain, divert,** regale, refresh, enliven, exhilarate; **relax,** loosen up; **delight,** tickle, titillate, convulse

21 amuse oneself; **relax**, loosen up; have fun; kill time

22 play, sport; **frolic, frisk, romp**, lark about (*nonformal*), cavort, flounce, trip, skip; dance; horse around (*nonformal*), fool around, carry on (*nonformal*)

23 make merry, **revel**, lark (*nonformal*), skylark, **let off steam**; cut loose; **celebrate**

24 feast, banquet

adjectives

25 amused, entertained; diverted, delighted, tickled, tickled pink, titillated

26 amusing, entertaining, diverting, beguiling; **fun**; recreational; delightful, titillating; humorous

27 festive; **merry, gay, jolly, jovial**, joyful, convivial, hilarious

28 playful, sportive

29 sporting, sports; athletic; gymnastic; acrobatic

adverbs

30 in fun, for fun; for kicks *and* for laughs (*both nonformal*)

721 SPORTS

nouns

1 sport, sports, athletics, athletic competition, game, sports activity, play, contest; **ball game**; gymnastics; outdoor sport; **winter sport**; **combat sport**, martial art; cycling, cross-country cycling, road racing, track racing; **motor sport**, jet skiing, water skiing; roller skating; **target sport**, archery, darts, trap shooting; **throwing sport**; **weightlifting**, weight training

verbs

2 play, compete; practise, train, work out

722 GAMBLING

nouns

1 gambling, betting, hazarding, risking, staking, laying odds; speculation, play; drawing lots, tossing a coin

2 gamble, chance, risk, risky thing, hazard; bet, sporting chance, luck of the draw, roll *or* throw of the dice, toss-up, toss; pot luck; speculation, venture; calculated risk; uncertainty; fortune, luck

3 bet, wager, stake, hazard, shot (*nonformal*); sure thing; long shot

4 pot, jackpot, pool, stakes, kitty; bank

5 gambling odds, odds; price; even break; short odds, long odds, long shot; even chance, good chance, small chance, no chance

6 gambling game, game of chance, game; card game

7 dice; crooked *or* loaded dice

8 (*throw of dice*) throw, cast, roll

9 poker, draw poker, stud poker, bet, raise

10 roulette; wheel

11 cheating, con *and* racket *and* scam (*all nonformal*); deception

12 lottery, sweepstake *or* sweep; raffle; tombola, lucky dip

13 bingo; bingo card, counter

14 roulette wheel; pinball machine;

slot machine, one-armed bandit (*nonformal*)

15 **casino, gambling house,** gambling den

16 **bookmaker,** turf accountant; tout

17 **gambler, player; speculator,** adventurer; punter; high roller; professional gambler; sharp, sharper; compulsive gambler

18 **cheat,** hustler (*nonformal*); **dupe, victim,** sucker (*nonformal*)

verbs

19 **gamble, play; speculate;** draw lots, cast lots; toss; raffle off

20 **chance, risk, hazard, venture,** wager; **gamble on; take a chance, chance it; take chances,** tempt fate

21 **bet, wager, gamble, hazard, stake,** punt, lay odds; **bet on, back;** bet against; **cover, call,** see

22 **cheat;** load the dice, mark the cards

adjectives

23 speculative, **uncertain; hazardous, risky; lucky,** winning, hot *and* on a roll (*both nonformal*); **unlucky,** losing

723 EXISTENCE

nouns

1 **existence, being;** subsistence, entity, essence; **occurrence,** presence; life

2 **reality; truth; authenticity**

3 **fact,** the case; **simple fact,** sober truth; hard fact, actual fact; axiom, premise; **accepted fact,** well-known fact, established fact, inescapable fact; given fact, giv-

en, **circumstance; salient fact,** significant fact

4 **the facts,** the particulars, the details, the specifics, **the data;** the picture (*nonformal*); essentials, brass tacks (*nonformal*)

verbs

5 **exist, be,** be in existence; breathe, **live; subsist, stand,** obtain, hold, prevail; **occur,** be present, be there, be found

6 **live on,** persist, last, endure

7 **vegetate,** merely exist

8 **exist in, consist in,** subsist in, lie in, rest in, repose in, reside in, abide in, inhabit, dwell in

9 **become,** go, get; turn into; grow; be changed

adjectives

10 **existing,** in existence; **being,** in being; **living; present, extant, prevalent, current,** afoot, on foot

11 **real, actual,** factual, veritable, for real (*nonformal*), simple, sober, **hard; absolute, positive; self-evident;** accepted, conceded, stipulated, given; admitted, well-known, **established, inescapable, indisputable, undeniable; demonstrable,** provable; empirical, **objective,** historical; **true;** genuine, **authentic; substantial**

adverbs

12 **really, actually; genuinely, truly; in reality,** in effect, in fact; positively, absolutely; obviously, manifestly

724 NONEXISTENCE

nouns

1 vacancy, deprivation, emptiness; vacuum, void; absence

2 **nothing, nil,** naught; zero, cipher; nothing whatever, nothing at all

3 **none,** not any, none at all

verbs

4 **not exist,** be absent or lacking or wanting

5 **be annihilated,** be destroyed, be eradicated; **go; vanish, disappear,** evaporate, fade, fade away, fly, flee, dissolve, melt away, pass, pass away (*nonformal*); **perish, expire,** pass away, **die**

6 **annihilate, exterminate,** eradicate, **eliminate,** liquidate, **wipe out, stamp out**

adjectives

7 without being; **minus, missing,** lacking, wanting; **void,** devoid, empty, inane; **negative**

8 **unreal,** unrealistic, not real; **immaterial; imaginary, imagined, fantastic, fanciful;** illusory

9 **no more, extinct, defunct, dead,** expired, passed away; vanished; perished, annihilated; gone, all gone; finished (*nonformal*), done for (*nonformal*)

725 SUBSTANTIALITY

nouns

1 **substance, body,** mass; **solidity,** density; **stability,** firmness, **strength,** durability

2 **substance, stuff, fabric, material, matter; elements,** constituents, ingredients, components, atoms, building blocks, parts

3 **something, thing; being, entity,** unit, individual; **person,** personality, **body, soul; creature; organism,** life form, living thing, life; **object**

4 **embodiment, incarnation**

verbs

5 **embody, materialize**

adjectives

6 **substantial; solid, concrete; tangible,** sensible, appreciable, palpable; **material; real; created,** contingent

7 **sturdy, stable, solid,** sound, firm, steady, tough, stout, **strong, rugged; durable,** lasting, enduring; **hard,** dense, steely; **well-made,** well-built; **massive,** bulky, heavy, chunky

adverbs

8 **substantially,** essentially, materially

726 UNSUBSTANTIALITY

nouns

1 **fragility; transience**

2 zero; **nonentity,** cipher, puppet, dummy; **trifle;** nothing

3 **spirit,** air, thin air, breath, smoke, vapour, mist, **shadow;** illusion; phantom

adjectives

4 **insubstantial; intangible; immaterial;** weightless; **transient,** ephemeral, fleeting, fugitive

5 **thin, tenuous,** subtle, fine, refined; airy, windy, gaseous; gossamer, shadowy; **illusory, unreal;** fatuous, inane; **imaginary,** fanciful

6 **fragile, frail; flimsy,** shaky, weak, **unsound,** infirm

7 **groundless, without foundation,** unfounded

727 STATE

nouns

1 **state,** mode; **status, situation,** position, standing, footing, location, bearings, spot; **rank,** estate, station, place, **standing; condition,** circumstance; **case, lot; predicament, plight,** pass, fix *and* jam *and* spot (*all nonformal*)

2 **good condition, bad condition;** form, order, repair, **shape** (*nonformal*)

3 **mode, manner, way,** tenor, vein, fashion, style; **form,** shape, guise, complexion, make-up; **role,** capacity, character, part

verbs

4 **fare; get on** *or* **along, manage** (*nonformal*), **contrive, make out** (*nonformal*), come through, get by; **turn out,** come out, shape up (*nonformal*)

728 CIRCUMSTANCE

nouns

1 **circumstance, occurrence, occasion, event, incident;** juncture, contingency, eventuality; **condition**

2 **circumstances, environment,** context, frame, setting, surround, parameters

3 **particular, instance, item, detail,** point, case, fact, matter, article, element, part, ingredient, factor, facet, aspect, thing; **respect, regard,** angle; trifle; incidental, minor detail

4 thoroughness; accuracy

5 specification, analysis

verbs

6 **specify, spell out, detail; analyse; cite,** document; **substantiate**

adjectives

7 **circumstantial,** conditional, provisional; **incidental,** occasional, contingent, **accidental, chance,** fortuitous, casual, inessential

8 environmental, surrounding, attending, attendant, limiting, determining

9 **detailed, minute, full, particular,** meticulous, fussy, precise, exact, specific, special

adverbs

10 **thus,** this way, **so,** just so; similarly, precisely

11 **accordingly, therefore**

12 conditionally, provisionally; provided

13 **fully, in full, in detail,** minutely, specifically, particularly, in particular, wholly, completely, **at length**

729 INTRINSICALITY

nouns

1 **essence, substance,** stuff, very stuff; **epitome, embodiment,** incarnation, model, pattern, flower; **essential,** principle, fundamental, axiom; **gist,** nucleus, centre, focus, kernel, **core, pith,** meat; **heart,** soul, spirit, sap, marrow

2 **nature, character, quality, constitution,** composition, **characteristics,** constituents; physique; **build,** frame, constitution, system; **temperament,** temper, fibre, **disposition,** spirit, ethos, genius; **way, habit,** tenor, cast, hue, tone, grain, vein, streak, mould, brand, stamp; **kind, sort, type, property, characteristic; tendency**

3 inside, insides (*nonformal*), nerve centre; **spirit, soul, heart;** the quick

adjectives

4 **intrinsic,** internal, **inner,** inward; **inherent,** resident, implicit; **ingrained;** deep-seated; **subjective,** esoteric, private, secret

5 **innate, inborn,** congenital; **native, natural,** natural to, native to, indigenous; **constitutional,** bodily, physical, temperamental, organic; **genetic, hereditary,** inherited, radical, rooted; **instinctive**

6 **essential; fundamental;** primary, primitive, elementary, elemental, simple, original, **basic, underlying;** substantial, material; constituent

adverbs

7 **intrinsically, inherently,** innately; internally, **inwardly;** originally; **naturally**

8 **essentially, fundamentally, primarily, basically; at bottom;** in essence, in substance; substantially, materially

730 EXTRINSICALITY

nouns

1 **accessory, extra;** auxiliary, **supplement,** addition, adjunct; **subsidiary,** subordinate, secondary; **contingency,** accident

adjectives

2 **external,** outward, outside, outlying; **extraneous,** foreign; **objective,** impersonal

3 unnecessary, superfluous; **accessory, extra,** auxiliary; **additional, supplementary, secondary,** subsidiary, subordinate; **incidental,** circumstantial, contingent; **accidental, chance,** fortuitous, casual; **indeterminate, unpredictable,** capricious

731 ACCOMPANIMENT

nouns

1 **company, association, society,** community; **companionship, fellowship,** partnership

2 **attendant,** accessory

3 **accompanist; attendant,** companion, fellow, mate, consort, **partner**

4 **escort, conductor, usher,** shepherd; **guide; bodyguard,** guard, **convoy;** companion, travel companion

5 attendance, following, entourage, suite, followers, train; **court;** parasite

verbs

6 accompany, attend, associate with, consort with, couple with; **combine, associate,** confederate

7 escort, conduct, usher, shepherd, **guide, lead;** guard; **attend**

adjectives

8 accompanying, attending, attendant, concomitant; combined, associated, coupled, paired; fellow, twin, joint, joined, mutual; **simultaneous, concurrent,** synchronized; parallel

adverbs

9 together, collectively, mutually, jointly, in conjunction, communally; **simultaneously,** coincidentally, concurrently, at once

732 ASSEMBLAGE

nouns

1 assembly, collection, gathering, congregation; convergence; junction; combination; muster; roundup; **comparison;** census, survey, inventory

2 assembly, gathering, congregation, congress, conference, **meeting;** convention, council; mass meeting, **rally,** sit-in, demonstration; **session,** sitting; **panel,** forum; committee, commission; **party, festivity,** reception, **dance,** ball; rendezvous, date, assignation

3 company, group, grouping, network, **party, band, knot, gang, crew,** complement, cast, outfit, pack, troop, troupe, corps; squad, platoon, battalion, regiment, brigade, division, fleet; **team,** squad, string; bevy; detachment, contingent, **party, faction,** movement, wing; peer group, age group; salon, clique, **set**

4 throng, multitude, horde, host, army, legion; flock, cluster, galaxy; **crowd,** press, crush, flood, spate, deluge, mass; **mob,** rabble, rout, jam

5 (*animals*) **flock, bunch, pack,** colony, host, army, **herd, drove,** litter

6 (*birds, insects*) **flock, swarm;** hive

7 bunch, group, grouping, crop, **cluster, clump,** knot; grove, copse, thicket; **batch, lot**

8 bundle, pack, package, packet, **parcel,** sack, bag; sheaf; bouquet, posy

9 accumulation, gathering; conglomeration; aggregate; **mass, lump;** stockpile

10 pile, heap, stack; mound, hill; molehill; bank, embankment, dune; haystack; snowdrift; pyramid

11 collection, fund; corpus, **body,** compilation; anthology, treasury; **museum, library,** zoo, aquarium

12 set, suite, series

13 assortment, variety, mixture; conglomeration, oddments

14 assembly line, production line

15 collector, connoisseur, enthusiast

verbs

16 come together, assemble, congregate, collect; ally; **unite;** muster, **meet, gather,** gang up (*nonformal*), mass; **merge,** converge, flow together, fuse; flock together; herd together; **throng, crowd,** swarm, teem, surge, seethe, mill, stream; **be crowded,** be mobbed; **cluster,** bunch; gather around; rally, rally around; **huddle,** close ranks; rendezvous; **couple, link,** link up

17 convene, meet, sit; summon, call together

18 gather; drum up, muster, rally, **mobilize; collect,** raise, take up; **accumulate, amass;** conglomerate; **combine, join, bring together,** get together, **gather together,** pack, pack in, cram; **bunch,** bunch up; **cluster; group; gather in;** round up; **put together,** make up, compile; pair, match, partner; **compare**

19 pile, pile on, heap, stack; drift

20 package, parcel up, **pack;** wrap, **wrap up**

adjectives

21 assembled, collected, gathered; congregated; meeting, in session; **combined; joined;** joint; **accumulated,** massed, **amassed,** heaped, stacked, piled; **clustered,** bunched, lumped, knotted; bundled, packaged, wrapped up

22 crowded, packed, crammed; compact, firm, solid, dense; **teeming, swarming, crawling,** bristling, **full**

23 cumulative, total, overall

733 DISPERSION

nouns

1 dispersion, scattering; distribution, spreading, strewing, sowing, **spread,** publication, **dissemination;** divergence; expansion, splay; **diffusion,** thinning, watering, weakening; **evaporation;** fragmentation, shattering; sprinkling, spattering; peppering

2 dispersal, separation, parting; release, detachment; dismissal; dissolution, disintegration

verbs

3 disperse, scatter, distribute, broadcast, sow, disseminate, propagate, publish; **diffuse,** spread, strew; radiate, diverge; expand, splay, **issue,** retail, dispense

4 dissipate, dispel, dissolve, dilute, thin out, water down, weaken; **evaporate;** drive away, clear away

5 sprinkle, spatter, splatter, splash; **dot; pepper**

6 disband, disperse, scatter, separate, part, break up, split up; part company; **release,** detach, discharge, let go; dismiss; **dissolve,** disintegrate

adjectives

7 dispersed, scattered, distributed, dissipated, disseminated, strewn, broadcast, **spread, widespread,** diffuse, discrete, sparse; **diluted,** thinned, watered, weakened; **sporadic**

8 sprinkled, spattered, splattered, splashed, **peppered,** spotted, dotted, speckled, **studded**

9 **scattering, spreading**

adverbs

10 sparsely, **sporadically,** in places; at large, everywhere, throughout

734 INCLUSION

nouns

1 **inclusion,** coverage, incorporation, assimilation, reception; **membership,** participation, admission, eligibility

2 **involvement, implication;** assumption, presumption

verbs

3 **include, comprise, contain,** hold, **take in; cover,** occupy, take up, fill; **embrace,** encompass, enclose, encircle, incorporate, assimilate, admit, receive; count in

4 **involve, implicate,** imply, assume, presume, presuppose, **call for,** require

adjectives

5 **included,** embraced, covered, subsumed; built-in; **involved**

6 **inclusive, including, containing, comprising, covering, embracing,** encompassing, enclosing, encircling, assimilating, incorporating; counting, numbering

7 **comprehensive, sweeping, complete;** whole; **overall,** universal, global, **total,** blanket

735 EXCLUSION

nouns

1 **exclusion,** exception, omission; **restriction,** narrowing, demarcation; **rejection,** repudiation; **ban,** bar, taboo, injunction; prohibition, embargo, blockade; boycott

2 **elimination,** culling, eviction; withdrawal, **removal,** detachment; discard, eradication, clearance, expulsion, suspension; **deportation, exile;** disposal, disposition; **liquidation, purge**

3 xenophobia; **segregation, separation,** division; **isolation,** insulation, seclusion; quarantine; racial segregation, apartheid; **outsider,** stranger; **foreigner, alien,** outcast, outlaw

verbs

4 **exclude, bar,** lock out, **shut out, keep out,** preclude; **reject, repudiate,** ostracize, **ignore; ban,** prohibit, **leave out,** omit, pass over, ignore; relegate; **blockade**

5 **eliminate, dispose of, remove,** eject, expel, **deport, exile,** outlaw; clear out; **weed out; cut out;** eradicate, **purge, liquidate**

6 **segregate, separate,** divide, cordon off; **isolate; set apart,** keep apart; **set aside,** put aside; sift, screen, sieve

adjectives

7 **excluded, barred,** precluded; not included; **ignored;** relegated; **banned,** prohibited; **expelled,** ejected; deported, exiled; **blockaded**

8 **segregated, separated, divided; isolated,** insulated, secluded; **set apart**

9 **exclusive, excluding;** exceptional, prohibitive, preventive, restrictive; **select,** selective; narrow, insular, parochial, snobbish

10 excluding, barring, bar, exclusive of, precluding, omitting, without, **leaving out; except, except for, save,** saving; **besides,** beside, **aside from**

736 EXTRANEOUSNESS

nouns

1 **intruder, foreign body; impurity,** blemish; speck, spot, blot; **misfit; black sheep**

2 **alien, stranger, foreigner, outsider,** barbarian; **exile,** outcast, outlaw, refugee

3 **newcomer;** settler, immigrant; **intruder,** stowaway

adjectives

4 **extraneous, foreign, alien,** strange, exotic; **external;** ulterior, outside; intrusive

adverbs

5 **abroad,** overseas

737 RELATION

nouns

1 **relation, relationship, connection; association,** bond, union, alliance, **tie,** link, liaison, junction, **combination; affinity, rapport,** sympathy, accord; **closeness, proximity,** approximation, intimacy; **relations, dealings,** affairs, business, transactions; **similarity**

2 **dependence,** contingency; uncertainty, variability, variance; **correlation**

3 **kinship,** blood relationship; family relationship, affinity

4 **relevance; connection,** reference, **bearing,** concern, interest, respect, regard

verbs

5 **relate to,** refer to, **apply to,** regard, **concern, involve,** touch, affect, interest; **pertain to,** belong to; **agree with,** answer to, correspond to, chime with; connect, deal with, touch upon

6 **relate, associate, connect,** link, link up, marry up, bind, tie, couple, bracket, equate, identify; **parallel; correlate**

adjectives

7 **relative;** indeterminate, uncertain, variable; pertaining, pertinent, referring

8 **approximate; near, close; comparable,** proportionate; **like,** similar

9 **related, connected; linked,** tied, coupled, joined; **associated, allied;** interlocked, **interrelated,** involved, implicated, overlapping; parallel; **congenial,** sympathetic, compatible

10 **kindred, akin,** related

11 **relevant, pertinent,** cogent, material, applicable, pertaining, appropriate

adverbs

12 **relatively,** comparatively, proportionately

738 UNRELATEDNESS

nouns

1 **irrelevance;** disconnection, independence

verbs

2 not concern, not involve, not entail

3 foist, drag in; impose on

adjectives

4 unrelated, unconnected; disconnected, dissociated, detached, discrete, removed, **separated,** segregated, apart, independent; **isolated,** insular; **foreign, alien,** strange, exotic; incomparable; extraneous

5 irrelevant, immaterial, inappropriate; extraneous; incidental

6 far-fetched, remote, distant, strained, forced, dragged in; **imaginary;** improbable

739 CORRELATION

nouns

1 correlation; equilibrium, balance, symmetry; **correspondence, equivalence**

2 interaction, interplay; alternation; meshing; **interchange, cooperation**

3 correspondent, counterpart; each other, one another

verbs

4 correlate, interrelate, interconnect, interlock

5 interact, interplay; mesh, fit; **interchange; cooperate**

6 reciprocate, correspond, correspond to, respond to, answer, answer to; **complement**

adjectives

7 correlated; interrelated, interconnected, interlocked, interdependent

8 interacting, interactive

9 reciprocal; corresponding, answering, analogous, equivalent; **complementary**

10 mutual, common, joint, communal, shared, very same, none other, respective, two-way

adverbs

11 mutually, commonly, communally, **jointly;** respectively

740 SAMENESS

nouns

1 sameness, identity, coincidence, correspondence, agreement; **equivalence, equality, unity,** homogeneity

2 identification, likening, unification, combination, union, fusion, merger, blending, synthesis

3 the same, very same, none other, **equivalent; duplicate,** double, twin, copy, replica, facsimile, carbon copy

verbs

4 coincide, correspond, agree, chime with, match, tally

5 identify, make one, unify, unite, join, combine, coalesce, synthesize, merge, blend, fuse

6 reproduce, copy, **duplicate,** clone

adjectives

7 identical; same, one; indistinguishable; alike, all alike, like; **duplicate,** twin; **homogeneous**

8 coinciding, coincidental; **corresponding; synonymous, equivalent; equal**

adverbs

9 **identically, alike;** coincidentally, correspondingly; **equally; like-wise**

741 CONTRARIETY

nouns

1 **opposition; antithesis, contrast,** contradiction; **antagonism, hostility,** perversity, **antipathy, confrontation,** showdown, clashing, collision, cross-purposes, conflict; discrepancy, inconsistency, **disagreement**

2 **the opposite, the contrary, the antithesis, the reverse;** opposite number (*nonformal*); opposite

3 **paradox, irony, ambiguity**

verbs

4 counter, **contradict,** contravene, go against; **oppose;** conflict, clash; contrast with, **offset,** counteract

adjectives

5 **contrary;** perverse, **opposite, contradictory; converse, reverse,** inverse; **adverse, opposing, opposed;** dead against; **antagonistic,** repugnant, negative, hostile, belligerent, inimical, discordant; inconsistent, conflicting, clashing, at cross-purposes, at loggerheads; balancing, counterbalancing, compensating

6 **paradoxical,** ambivalent, **ironic;** equivocal, **ambiguous**

adverbs

7 counter, **vice versa,** upside down, on the contrary, at loggerheads; rather, otherwise; perversely

742 DIFFERENCE

nouns

1 **difference, distinction; variation,** variance, variety, **mixture, diversity; deviation,** departure; **disparity,** gap, inequality; **discrepancy,** inconsistency, incongruity; disagreement, dissent; **contrast,** opposition

2 distinction; **nicety, subtlety,** fine point; **nuance**

3 **differentiation, discrimination, distinction;** demarcation; **separation,** division, analysis, segregation; **modification, alteration, change,** variation, diversification; specialization

verbs

4 **differ, vary,** diverge, **deviate from,** depart from; **disagree with,** conflict with, contrast with, clash with

5 **differentiate; distinguish, discriminate; separate,** sever, segregate, divide; set apart; **modify,** vary, diversify, **change;** specialize; analyse; split hairs

adjectives

6 **different,** differing, unlike, not like, **dissimilar; distinct,** differentiated, discrete, separate; **various,** variant, varying, varied, heterogeneous, motley, assorted, diverse; **several,** many; **divergent; disparate,** unequal; inconsistent, incongruous, incompatible, irreconcilable; **disagreeing,** in disagreement; **at odds,** at variance, clashing, discordant; **contrasting,** poles apart, worlds apart; **contrary**

7 other, another, else, otherwise; **unique,** rare, **special,** peculiar

8 distinguishing, characterizing; diagnostic; **distinctive,** characteristic, peculiar, idiosyncratic

adverbs

9 differently, variously

10 otherwise; else

743 UNIFORMITY

nouns

1 uniformity; stability, firmness, constancy, persistence, perseverance, continuity, **consistency;** correspondence, accordance; unity, **homogeneity; equanimity,** equilibrium, serenity, tranquility, calm, calmness, cool (*nonformal*)

2 regularity, constancy, smoothness; **sameness, monotony;** monotone, drone

verbs

3 persist, prevail, persevere; drag on

4 make uniform, regulate, stabilize; harmonize, balance; **level,** smooth out, even out, flatten; **assimilate,** standardize, stereotype; clone (*nonformal*)

adjectives

5 uniform, equable, equal, **even; level,** flat, smooth; **regular, constant,** steadfast, persistent, continuous; unruffled, unbroken, unchanged; invariable, immutable; unchanging, steady, stable; **ordered,** balanced, measured; **orderly,** methodical, systematic, mechanical, faceless, automatic;

consistent, homogeneous, **alike,** all alike, monolithic

6 same; monotonous, humdrum, repetitive, drab, grey, usual; tedious, boring

adverbs

7 uniformly, equably, **evenly;** dully, routinely

8 regularly; constantly, steadily, continually; **invariably,** without exception; methodically, systematically; **always;** like clockwork

744 NONUNIFORMITY

nouns

1 irregularity, disorder; difference; inequality; **inconsistency,** variability, wavering, **instability;** **variation, deviation,** divergence, differentiation; **diversity,** diversification; variety

verbs

2 diversify, vary, waver; **differentiate,** diverge; **differ;** dissent; break up, break down, fragment, partition

adjectives

3 uneven, irregular, ragged, choppy, jerky, jagged, rough, disorderly; **different,** unequal; **inconsistent, variable,** varying, **changeable,** capricious, impulsive, erratic, spasmodic, sporadic, wavering, **unstable, unsteady,** deviating, divergent; **diversified; nonconformist,** unorthodox; various, motley

adverbs

4 irregularly, unsteadily, erratically, spasmodically, impulsively, sporadically

745 MULTIFORMITY

nouns

1 variety, diversity, diversification, variation, variability, multiplicity

verbs

2 diversify, vary, ring changes

adjectives

3 variable, versatile; **manifold,** multiple

4 varied, assorted, heterogeneous; **various,** diverse, sundry, **several, many**

746 SIMILARITY

nouns

1 similarity, likeness, sameness; **resemblance;** analogy, correspondence, conformity, accordance, agreement, comparability, comparison, **parity; approximation,** approach, closeness; likening, **simile, metaphor; simulation, imitation,** copying, aping, mimicking, takeoff; identity

2 kinship, affinity, family resemblance

3 likeness, like; parallel; counterpart, complement; **approximation,** rough idea, sketch; equivalent; **fellow; companion, twin,** brother, sister; alter ego

4 set, group, matching pair, couple, pair, twins

verbs

5 resemble, be like; suggest, evoke, call up; **look like,** mirror; **take after,** follow, sound like; **approximate,** approach, come close; **compare with;** correspond, match, parallel; imitate,

simulate, copy, ape, mimic, take off, counterfeit

adjectives

6 similar, like, alike, not unlike; **resembling,** following, suggestive of; **simulated, imitated,** imitation, copied, counterfeit, **mock,** synthetic; homogeneous, identical

7 analogous, comparable; corresponding, equivalent; **parallel; matching;** duplicate, twin

8 suchlike, so

9 approximating, approximate; **near, close**

10 very like, uncommonly like, remarkably like

11 lifelike, faithful, **realistic,** natural

adverbs

12 similarly, correspondingly, **like, likewise; thus;** so; identically

747 COPY

nouns

1 copy, representation, facsimile, **image, likeness, resemblance,** picture, portrait, fair copy; **imitation, counterfeit,** forgery, fake (*nonformal*)

2 reproduction, duplication

3 duplicate, duplication, double, clone; representation, **reproduction, replica,** facsimile, model

4 transcript; carbon copy; microfiche; recording

5 print; reprint; second edition; **facsimile; photograph,** negative, print, enlargement, photocopy

6 cast, casting; **mould,** moulding

7 reflection; shadow, silhouette, outline; **echo**

verbs

8 copy, reproduce, duplicate; clone; **transcribe;** trace

748 MODEL

nouns

1 model, pattern, standard, criterion; original, type, prototype, archetype; precedent

2 example, representative, type, symbol, emblem, exponent; illustration, demonstration; **instance,** case, object lesson

3 sample, specimen; piece, taste; instance

4 ideal, idol; shining example, hero; model, role model, paragon, epitome

5 artist's model; dummy

6 mould, form, cast, negative; stamp, seal

verbs

7 exemplify, epitomize; **emulate,** follow

adjectives

8 model, exemplary, typical, representative, standard, classic; ideal; archetypal

749 DISSIMILARITY

nouns

1 disparity, diversity, divergence, gap, **contrast, difference; disguise,** camouflage, masking

verbs

2 not resemble; differ

3 disguise, camouflage

adjectives

4 dissimilar; unlike; disparate, diverse, divergent, **contrasting, different;** odd

5 nothing like; way off, way out

750 AGREEMENT

nouns

1 agreement, accord, accordance; **concord; harmony, cooperation,** peace, rapport, **unison,** union, chorus; **correspondence,** coincidence, overlap, symmetry, equivalence; compatibility, affinity; **conformity,** uniformity; **consistency,** coherence; **assent**

2 understanding; compact

3 (*general agreement*) consensus, unanimity, meeting of minds

4 adjustment, adaptation, compromise, arbitration; **regulation,** accommodation, squaring, integration, assimilation; reconciliation

5 fitness, suitability, propriety; aptitude, qualification; **relevance**

verbs

6 agree, accord, harmonize, concur, cooperate, **correspond, conform,** coincide, parallel, intersect, overlap, **match,** tally, register, square, jibe (*nonformal*); **be consistent,** fit together, chime, chime with; **assent, go together,** go with, conform with, square with

7 (*make agree*) **harmonize,** coordinate, accord, assimilate; **adjust, set,** regulate, **accommodate, reconcile,** synchronize; adapt, fit, tailor, measure, adjust to, trim to, cut to, gear to, key to; fix, **rectify**, right, set right; **tune**

8 **suit**, fit, **qualify, do**, serve, be OK (*nonformal*)

adjectives

9 **agreeing, in agreement; in accord, concurring**, positive, affirmative, **in harmony**, in accordance, **at one, like-minded, unanimous; harmonious**, consonant; **consistent;** uniform, coherent, equivalent, **coinciding**, answerable; commensurate, proportionate; **agreeable**, congenial, compatible, cooperative; **synchronized**

10 **apt, appropriate, suitable;** applicable, relevant, likely, opportune; **fitting**, becoming; **fit**, fitted, qualified, **suited**, adapted, geared, tailored; **right**, just right, happy

adverbs

11 **in step**, in concert, **in unison**, in chorus, **in line, in keeping**, just right; with it (*nonformal*); **unanimously, as one, harmoniously**

751 DISAGREEMENT

nouns

1 **disagreement, discord, jarring**, clashing; **difference, variance**, divergence, diversity; **disparity**, discrepancy, inequality; antagonism, **opposition, conflict**, controversy, dissension; **dissent**, contradiction

2 **inconsistency, incongruity**, heresy; paradox, **ambiguity**

3 **irrelevance**; abnormality, anomaly

4 **misfit, nonconformist**, individualist; **freak**

verbs

5 **disagree, differ**, vary, **conflict**, clash, **jar**, jangle, collide, cross swords, break off; **dissent**, object, **negate, contradict**, counter

adjectives

6 **disagreeing, differing, discordant**; dissident; disproportionate; divergent, variant; **at variance, at odds**, at war, at loggerheads, at cross-purposes; **hostile**, antagonistic, repugnant; **jarring**, clashing, grating, jangling; **contradictory, contrary; disagreeable**, negative, incompatible

7 **inappropriate**, misplaced, **irrelevant; unsuited; unfit**, inept, unqualified; **unsuitable**, improper, unseemly

8 **inconsistent, incongruous**, incoherent, **incompatible**, irreconcilable; disproportionate, paradoxical, **absurd; abnormal**, anomalous

9 **nonconformist**, individualistic, perverse; **unorthodox**, heretical

752 EQUALITY

nouns

1 **equality, parity**, par, **identity;** equivalence, **correspondence; likeness; balance**, poise, **equilibrium;** symmetry, proportion; justice

2 **equating;** evening up; integration, accommodation, adjustment; equal opportunity

3 **the same; tie, draw**, dead heat (*nonformal*), stalemate, deadlock,

impasse, photo finish, even money

4 **equal, match,** twin, fellow, **like, equivalent,** opposite number, counterpart, parallel; **peer,** colleague, peer group

verbs

5 **equal, match, rival, correspond; amount to,** come to, run to, reach, touch; **balance,** parallel; break even (*nonformal*); **tie, draw**

6 **equate; even,** even up, square, level; **balance,** balance out; **compensate;** counterbalance, cancel; coordinate, integrate; fit, accommodate, adjust

adjectives

7 **equal,** like, **alike, even,** level, par, at parity, commensurate, proportionate; **square,** quits; half-and-half, **fifty-fifty; drawn, tied**

8 **equivalent, tantamount; identical;** corresponding

9 **balanced, poised**

adverbs

10 **equally, correspondingly, proportionately, evenly; identically;** without distinction, indifferently; as, **so;** as well

753 INEQUALITY

nouns

1 **inequality, disparity, difference; irregularity;** imbalance; **inadequacy,** shortcoming; handicap; **injustice**

verbs

2 overbalance, upset

adjectives

3 **unequal,** disparate, **uneven; irregular;** disproportionate, asymmetric; ill-matched; **inadequate,** insufficient

4 **unbalanced,** off-balance, leaning; **lopsided; unstable,** unsteady

adverbs

5 **unequally,** disproportionately, unevenly

754 WHOLE

nouns

1 **whole, totality, entirety;** unity, integrity, wholeness

2 **total, sum,** sum total, grand total

3 **all, everything; package,** set, complement, package deal; **the lot;** A to Z

4 (*nonformal terms*) whole hog, the works

5 **wholeness,** totality, **unity, fullness**

6 **major part, best part,** better part, **most; majority,** generality; **bulk, mass,** body, main body; **lion's share; substance,** gist, meat, essence, thrust

verbs

7 **integrate,** unite

8 **total, amount to, come to;** number, comprise, contain, encompass

adjectives

9 (*not partial*) **whole, total, entire,** aggregate, gross, all; integral, integrated; **one; inclusive, exhaustive,** comprehensive; universal

10 intact, untouched, virgin, unspoiled

11 undivided; complete

adverbs

12 (*not partially*) **wholly, entirely,** all; **totally,** from A to Z; **altogether;** en masse, en bloc; **collectively,** bodily

13 on the whole, on balance, **mainly, mostly, chiefly,** substantially, essentially, almost entirely, **virtually;** approximately, nearly, all but

755 PART

nouns

1 part, portion, fraction; percentage; **division; share,** quota, piece; cut (*nonformal*); **section,** sector, **segment;** quarter; **item,** detail, particular; instalment; **subdivision;** detachment, contingent; **cross section,** sample, random sample; **component,** module, constituent, ingredient; **adjunct; remainder**

2 (*part of writing*) section, prologue, epilogue, foreword, preface, introduction, text, chapter, verse, article; sentence, clause, phrase, paragraph, passage; number, book; sheet, page

3 piece, particle, bit, scrap, bite, **fragment, morsel, crumb,** snatch, snack; **cut,** cutting, clip, clipping, shaving, rasher, snip, snippet, chip, slice, dollop, scoop; **shred,** stitch; **splinter, sliver; lump, hunk, chunk;** stump, butt, end; modicum

4 member, organ; limb; branch, bough, twig; runner, tendril; spur; **arm, leg;** tail; hand; **wing**

5 dose, portion; slug *and* shot *and* dram (*all nonformal*)

verbs

6 separate, share, share out, distribute, cut, cut up, slice, slice up, divide; analyse

adjectives

7 partial, part; **fragmentary;** incomplete, open-ended

adverbs

8 partly, partially, part, **in part**

9 piecemeal; by degrees, by inches; by instalments

756 COMPLETENESS

nouns

1 totality; wholeness, entirety; unity, integrity; solidity, solidarity; **thoroughness; universe,** cosmos

2 fullness, saturation, saturation point, congestion

3 full measure, fill, full house; **load, capacity**

4 completion, fulfilment, consummation, culmination, perfection, realization, **accomplishment,** closure

5 limit, end, extremity, extreme, climax, maximum, ceiling, **peak,** summit, **pinnacle,** crown, top; **utmost,** highest degree; **all, the whole**

verbs

6 (*make whole*) **complete,** mature; **fill in, fill out,** eke out; **make up,** make good, replenish, refill; **accomplish,** fulfil

7 **fill, charge, load; stuff, wad,** pad, **pack,** crowd, **cram,** jam; **fill up,** top up; saturate, congest

adjectives

8 **complete, whole, total,** global, **entire,** intact, solid; **full, full-scale;** mature, ripe, developed

9 **thorough,** exhaustive, intensive, comprehensive, radical, sweeping; **pervasive,** ubiquitous, **universal; unmitigated, unqualified, unconditional,** unrestricted, **all-out,** wholesale; **out-and-out,** outright, downright, straight; congenital, born, **consummate,** perfect, veritable; **utter, absolute, total; sheer,** clear, clean, **pure,** plumb (*nonformal*), **plain,** regular (*nonformal*)

10 **full,** filled, flush, round; brimming; **overcrowded;** stuffed, **packed, crammed,** swollen, bulging, bursting; **saturated,** soaked; congested

11 **fraught, laden, loaded, charged,** burdened

12 **completing, fulfilling,** filling; **complementary**

adverbs

13 **completely, totally, entirely, wholly, fully,** roundly, **altogether,** exhaustively, comprehensively; **unconditionally;** outright; **thoroughly,** inside out (*nonformal*); in full

14 **absolutely, perfectly, quite,** right, stark, clean, sheer, plumb (*nonformal*), **plain;** irretrievably, irrevocably

15 **utterly, all out,** flat out

16 **throughout, all over,** overall; every inch, every bit

757 INCOMPLETENESS

nouns

1 **deficiency,** imperfection, **inadequacy; immaturity; short measure**

2 (*part lacking*) **deficiency,** want, **lack, need, deficit,** defect, **shortage,** shortfall; **omission,** gap, hiatus, hole, vacuum, break, interval

verbs

3 **lack,** want, want for; **fall short**

adjectives

4 **incomplete, deficient,** defective, unfinished, **imperfect, inadequate; undeveloped,** underdeveloped, stunted, **immature,** infant, embryonic, **wanting, lacking,** needing, missing, **partial,** part, failing; in arrears; **scanty; short,** scant; **sketchy,** patchy

5 **mutilated,** garbled, **mangled, butchered,** docked, hacked, lopped, cut short

adverbs

6 **partially,** by halves, in instalments, imperfectly, inadequately

758 COMPOSITION

nouns

1 **composition, constitution, construction, formation,** fabrication, fashioning, shaping, organization; **embodiment,** incorporation, incarnation; **make; building,** structure, structuring; **assembly;** synthesis; **combination; compound; junction; mixture**

2 **component, constituent, ingredient, element, factor, part,**

module; **feature,** aspect, speciality, circumstance, detail, item

verbs

3 **compose, constitute,** construct, fabricate; **incorporate,** embody; **form, organize,** shape; **enter into,** go into; **make, make up, build,** build up, assemble, put together; **consist of;** contain; **combine; join; mix**

adjectives

4 **composed of, made of,** consisting of; composing, comprising, constituting, including, containing

5 **component,** constituent, integral

759 MIXTURE

nouns

1 **mixture,** mixing, blending; composition, **mingling; fusion;** amalgamation, **integration; merger, combination**

2 infiltration, penetration; saturation, soaking

3 **corruption,** contamination, pollution, **doctoring** (*nonformal*); lacing; watering down

4 **compound, mixture, composite, blend,** composition, concoction, **combination,** marriage

5 **conglomeration, assortment,** mixed bag, jumble, **mix, mess, patchwork, oddments,** all sorts

6 (*slight admixture*) **tinge, touch, dash, smack,** taint, tint, **trace,** vestige, hint, inkling, intimation, suspicion, suggestion, whiff, thought, shade; sprinkling, seasoning

7 **hybrid,** cross, half-caste; **mongrel**

8 **mixer, blender;** cement mixer, churn; melting pot

verbs

9 **mix, mingle,** intermingle; **blend,** stir in; **amalgamate, integrate,** coalesce, **fuse, merge,** compound, compose, concoct; **combine;** mix up, stir up, **scramble,** shuffle, **jumble;** knead, work

10 **imbue,** breathe, instil, infiltrate, **impregnate, permeate,** pervade, penetrate; **tinge,** temper, colour, dye, flavour, season; **saturate,** steep, brew

11 **adulterate, corrupt,** contaminate, **debase,** pollute, **tamper with, doctor** (*nonformal*); spike (*nonformal*), lace; **dilute,** water, water down (*nonformal*)

adjectives

12 **mixed, mingled,** blended, compounded, amalgamated; **combined; composite,** compound, **complex,** intricate; multinational, heterogeneous, varied, **miscellaneous,** motley, dappled, patchy; indiscriminate, **scrambled, jumbled;** equivocal, **ambiguous,** ambivalent, ironic; eclectic

13 **hybrid, mongrel,** crossed

760 SIMPLICITY

nouns

1 **simplicity, purity;** unity, integrity, homogeneity, uniformity

2 **simplification,** streamlining, refinement, distillation; stripping,

narrowing, confining; oversimplifying

verbs

3 **simplify**, streamline, **reduce**; purify, refine, distil; strip, strip down; narrow, confine, zero in (*nonformal*); oversimplify; **analyse**

4 **disentangle**, untangle, unwind, **unravel**; clarify, clear up, sort out

adjectives

5 **simple**, **plain**, bare, no-frills (*nonformal*), mere; **single**, uniform, homogeneous; **pure**; **essential**, elementary, indivisible, **primary**, primitive, prime, **fundamental**, basic; **austere**, chaste, spare, stark, severe; homely

6 **unadulterated**, unspoiled, untouched, intact, virgin, unsophisticated; **clear**, purified, refined, distilled; **neat**, **straight**, absolute, sheer, naked, bare

7 **uncomplicated**, straightforward

8 **simplified**, streamlined, stripped down

9 **oversimplified; simplistic**

adverbs

10 **simply**, **plainly**, **purely**; merely, barely; **singly**, **solely**, only, **alone**, exclusively, just

761 COMPLEXITY

nouns

1 **complexity**, complication, entanglement, perplexity, **intricacy**, ramification, technicality, subtlety

2 **complex**, **tangle**, mess; knot;

maze, **labyrinth**; **wilderness**, **jungle**, morass

verbs

3 **complicate**, **involve**, **confound**, **confuse**, muddle, **mix up**, implicate; tangle, snarl up

adjectives

4 **complex**, **complicated**, perplexed, **confused**, confounded, **involved**, implicated, **intricate**, elaborate, convoluted; **mixed up**; **tangled**, **entangled**, **snarled**, knotted, matted, twisted; meandering; **devious**, roundabout, subtle

762 JOINING

nouns

1 **joining**, junction, connection, **union**, unification, bond, bonding, conjunction, liaison, marriage, tie; merger, merging; **combination**; conglomeration; **coupling**, **bracketing**, pairing, wedding; **linking**; **meeting**, convergence, gathering, massing, clustering; communication, intercourse

2 **fastening**, attachment; **binding**, bonding, gluing, sticking, tying, linking, hooking, clasping; knot; adhesive; bond

3 **joint**, join, juncture, union, connection, link, coupling; clinch, embrace; **pivot**, **hinge**; **knee**; **elbow**; **wrist**; **ankle**; **knuckle**; **hip**; **shoulder**; **neck**; seam, stitch; boundary

verbs

4 **put together**, **join**, **unite**, unify, bond, **connect**, associate, band,

merge, **assemble**, accumulate; **join up; gather,** mobilize, marshal, mass, amass, **collect; combine; couple,** pair, marry, wed, **link,** link up, yoke, tie, chain, bracket; glue, tape, cement, weld; **put together,** piece together, stick together; span; **include,** encompass, take in, cover, embrace, comprise

5 **interconnect,** interlock

6 **fasten, fix, attach;** graft; **secure,** anchor, moor; cement, knit, set, **make fast;** clinch, clamp; tighten

7 **hook,** hitch; **clasp,** clip, snap; **button,** buckle, zip; lock; **pin,** skewer, peg, nail, tack, staple, screw, bolt, rivet; **sew,** stitch; **wedge,** jam

8 **bind, tie, lash,** strap, lace, wire, chain; **tie up,** bind up; **wrap,** wrap up; **bandage,** bandage up, swathe

9 **yoke, hitch up;** harness; saddle; tether, fetter

10 (be joined) **join, connect, unite, meet,** meet up, link up, merge, converge, **come together;** communicate; grow together; adhere, clinch, embrace

adjectives

11 **joint, combined,** joined, corporate; concurrent; inclusive, comprehensive

12 **joined, united, connected, coupled,** linked, knit, bracketed, associated, incorporated, integrated, **merged,** gathered, assembled, accumulated, **collected; associated; allied;** intimate; undivided; **wedded,** matched, married, paired, mated; **tied, bound,** knotted, lashed

13 **fast, fastened, fixed,** secure, firm, close, tight, set; **bonded,** glued, cemented, taped; **jammed,** wedged, stuck, frozen, seized up

14 **inseparable, indivisible**

15 **joining, connecting,** meeting; **communicating;** linking, binding

adverbs

16 **jointly, together; in common,** in partnership, mutually, in concord; **all together,** as one, in unison, in agreement, in harmony; concurrently, at once

17 **securely, firmly, fast,** tight

763 ANALYSIS

nouns

1 **analysis, breakdown;** dissection; separation, **division, subdivision**

2 detailing; outlining

3 **classification, categorization, sorting,** sorting out, sifting, grouping; **weighing, evaluation,** gauging, assessment, appraisal, **judgment**

4 **outline, plan,** scheme, chart, flow chart, graph; table, index; **diagram,** blueprint; catalogue

5 **analyst, examiner**

verbs

6 **analyse, break down,** dissect; **divide,** subdivide; separate, isolate

7 **enumerate,** number, detail; **outline,** chart

8 **classify,** class, categorize, catalogue, **sort,** sort out, sift, group; weigh, weigh up, **evaluate, judge,** gauge, assess, appraise

adjectives

9 **analytical,** analytic

764 SEPARATION

nouns

1 **separation,** segregation; **parting, removal,** withdrawal, isolation, detachment; **subtraction;** divorce; **division,** subdivision, partition

2 fission, cleavage, dichotomy; **cutting, slitting,** slashing, **splitting,** slicing; **tearing,** ripping, hacking, chopping, butchering, mutilation

3 **disruption, dissolution;** revolution; **disintegration,** shattering, splintering, fragmentation; **bursting; scattering**

4 **break,** breakage, **breach,** burst, **rupture, fracture, crack,** cleft, **fissure, cut, split,** slit; slash, slice; **gap, rift,** rip, tear; chip, splinter

5 **dissection, analysis,** breakdown

6 taking apart; undoing; **stripping**

verbs

7 **separate, divide,** draw apart, dissociate, disassociate, grow apart, disengage, **disconnect; part, divorce; alienate, segregate,** separate off, isolate, shut off, set apart, cut off; **withdraw, leave, depart;** subtract; delete; **expel,** eject, throw out, cast off

8 **come apart,** come unstuck, **disintegrate,** fall apart, break up, unravel; give way

9 **detach, remove,** disengage, take off; **unfasten, undo, free, release,** liberate, loose, unleash; loosen; cast off, weigh anchor; unbutton, unscrew; **untie,** unzip

10 **sever,** cut off, axe, amputate; **split;** halve, bisect; **cut,** carve, **slice,** prune, trim; slit, snip; **chop,** hack, **slash;** butcher; saw; **tear**

11 **break, burst,** bust (*nonformal*), breach; **fracture, rupture; crack,** split; snap; chip

12 **shatter, splinter; smash,** crush, crunch, squash; demolish, break up, smash up; **scatter,** disperse, diffuse; **fragment; pulverize,** grind, mince

13 **tear apart, shred; dismember; mangle,** mutilate, maim; skin, flay, strip, peel

14 take apart, tear down; **dismantle, demolish**

15 **dissect, analyse,** break down

16 **partition; divide,** divide up, **split,** split up, cut up, subdivide

17 **part company, part, separate,** split up, disband, scatter, **disperse,** break up, diverge

adjectives

18 **separate, distinct, discrete;** un**connected, unattached,** unaccompanied, unattended; divergent; **isolated,** insular, detached, detachable, autonomous; **independent,** self-contained; **subdivided,** partitioned

19 **separated,** disjointed, **disconnected,** disengaged, detached, **divided,** removed, divorced, **alienated,** estranged, **segregated,** isolated, cloistered, shut off; **scattered,** dispersed; dislocated

20 **unfastened, undone, loose, free,** loosened, clear; **untied,** un

leashed, unfettered; unstuck; un-
buttoned, unzipped; unscrewed;
adrift, afloat, floating, free

21 **severed, cut; splintered,** cracked,
split, slit; rent, torn; tattered,
shredded, **in shreds; dismem-
bered,** in pieces

22 **broken, burst, ruptured; shattered,** fragmentary, fragmented

23 **separating, dividing,** parting

adverbs

24 **separately,** piecemeal; **apart,**
adrift, **in two;** apart from, away
from, aside from; objectively

25 sporadically, spasmodically

26 **to pieces, to bits,** to shreds

765 COHESION

nouns

1 **cohesion, coherence, adherence,
sticking,** sticking together, clinging, binding, clotting; **conglomeration; clustering,** massing,
bunching

2 **consistency,** connection; **junction;** continuity, sequence, orderliness

3 **tenacity,** retention; consistency;
persistence, **obstinacy**

4 **sticker; glue, cement,** paste,
plaster

5 **conglomeration, conglomerate,**
cluster, bunch, mass, clot

verbs

6 **adhere, stick, cling,** hold; **persist,** stay, stay put *(nonformal)*;
cling to; hang on, hold on; clasp,
grasp, hug, embrace, clinch;
stick together; grow together;
solidify, set, conglomerate; con-

geal, coagulate, **clot; cluster,**
mass, bunch

7 **be consistent,** connect with, follow; **join,** link up

8 **stick together, cement, bind,
paste, glue,** gum; weld, fuse

adjectives

9 **cohesive, coherent;** adhering,
sticking, clinging, inseparable;
cemented, stuck; **concrete, solidified, set, congealed,** clotted,
coagulated; **consolidated;** clustered, massed, bunched

10 **consistent, connected;** continuous, **serial,** uninterrupted. **consecutive;** orderly; **joined**

11 **adhesive;** tenacious; sticky,
tacky; **persistent, stubborn, obstinate**

766 NONCOHESION

nouns

1 inconsistency; unravelling; **dissolution, chaos,** anarchy, **disorder,**
confusion; **scattering**

verbs

2 **loosen, slacken, relax;** slack off;
ease off, let up; **loose, free,** let
go, unleash; unravel; **scatter,** disperse

adjectives

3 **incoherent, inconsistent,** tenuous; disconnected, unconnected,
unravelled, open; **disordered,**
chaotic, anarchic, confused; broken, detached, discrete

4 **loose, slack, lax, relaxed,** easy,
sloppy, shaky, rickety; flapping,
streaming; hanging, drooping,
dangling; baggy

767 COMBINATION

nouns

1 **combination,** composition; **union, unification,** marriage, wedding, coupling, linking; **incorporation,** conglomeration; amalgamation, consolidation, assimilation, **integration,** inclusion; **junction;** conjunction; **alliance, association, merger,** league; takeover; **federation, confederation;** centralization; **fusion,** blend, blending; coalition; **synthesis;** package, package deal; **agreement; addition**

2 **mixture, compound**

verbs

3 **combine, unite, unify,** marry, wed, couple, link, yoke together; **incorporate,** amalgamate, consolidate, assimilate, **integrate,** solidify, coalesce, put together; **connect, join; mix; add; merge, blend,** stir in, **fuse; encompass,** include, comprise

4 **league, ally, associate;** confederate, **join forces,** stand together, close ranks; **marry, wed, couple,** link; **band together,** club together, gang up (*nonformal*); pair off, partner; **conspire**

adjectives

5 **combined, united,** amalgamated, incorporated, consolidated, integrated, assimilated, one, **joined,** joint; **merged,** blended, fused; **mixed;** eclectic

6 **allied, associated,** associate, corporate; in league; conspiratorial; in partnership; teamed, coupled, paired, married, wed, wedded, coupled, linked

7 **combining, uniting,** incorporating; federal

768 DISINTEGRATION

nouns

1 **disintegration, decomposition, dissolution, decay,** breakdown, fragmentation; **destruction;** erosion, corrosion, crumbling, wear, wasting, wasting away

verbs

2 **disintegrate, decompose, decay,** dissolve, come apart, **break up,** crack up, split, fall to pieces; **erode,** corrode, crumble

adjectives

3 decomposing, disintegrating; **destructive, ruinous;** corrosive; **dilapidated,** disintegrated, worn-out, worn, wrecked

769 ORDER

nouns

1 **order, arrangement; organization;** deployment; **formation, structure, configuration,** array, layout; **system;** routine; **peace,** quiet, **tranquillity; regularity,** uniformity; symmetry, proportion, concord, **harmony**

2 **continuity,** logical order; degree; hierarchy, gradation, rank, place; **sequence**

3 **orderliness, tidiness, neatness,** good condition; **discipline,** method, system

verbs

4 **order, arrange, organize, regulate;** deploy, marshal; **form,** line up, set up, lay out; **pacify,** tran-

quillize; harmonize; standardize; grade, rank

5 **form, take shape,** crystallize, **shape up;** come together, gather around, rally round

adjectives

6 **orderly,** ordered, **regular, methodical, formal,** uniform, **systematic,** symmetrical, **harmonious;** businesslike, routine, steady, normal, habitual, usual; **arranged**

7 **in order; in shape;** fixed

8 **tidy, trim, neat,** spruce, sleek, smart, snug, tight; well-groomed

adverbs

9 **methodically, systematically, regularly,** uniformly, harmoniously, like clockwork

10 **in order, in turn,** in sequence, in succession

770 ARRANGEMENT

nouns

1 **arrangement, ordering,** structuring, shaping, forming, constitution; **deployment,** placement, marshalling; **distribution,** allocation, allotment; **formation,** formulation, **configuration,** form, array; syntax; **order**

2 **organization,** ordering, planning, regulation, rationalization; **adjustment,** tuning, tinkering

3 **grouping, classification,** categorization; **gradation, ranking,** placement; **sorting,** sifting, screening, culling, selection

4 **table,** code, digest, **index, inventory,** census

5 **rearrangement, reorganization, restructuring,** shake-up (*nonformal*)

verbs

6 **arrange,** order, right; sort out

7 **distribute, fix, place,** set out, allocate, **compose, marshal,** array; align, **line up; allot,** parcel out, deal out

8 **organize,** rationalize; **harmonize,** synchronize, tune up; standardize; **regulate,** adjust, coordinate, fix, settle; **plan,** chart

9 **classify, group,** categorize; **grade, rank; sort; separate,** divide; collate; **sift,** sieve

10 tidy, **tidy up,** trim, **straighten up, clean up,** groom, spruce up (*nonformal*), **clear up**

11 **rearrange, reorganize, restructure,** tinker with, tune up; **shake up;** redistribute

adjectives

12 **arranged, ordered,** composed, constituted, fixed, placed, aligned, marshalled, grouped, ranked, **graded;** organized, standardized; regulated, harmonized, synchronized; **classified,** categorized, **sorted,** assorted; **orderly**

13 **organizational,** structural

771 CLASSIFICATION

nouns

1 **classification, categorization,** placement, **sorting, grouping; grading,** ranking, rating, classing; division, subdivision; cataloguing, filing; analysis, **arrangement**

2 **class, category, head, order, division,** branch, set, **group,** grouping, bracket; **section; grade,** rank, rating, status, stratum, level, station, position; **caste,** clan, race, blood, kin; **subdivision**

3 **kind, sort, type, variety,** species, genus, genre, denomination, designation, description, style, manner, **nature, character,** persuasion; **stamp, brand,** colour; **make,** mark, label, shape, form, mould

4 **hierarchy,** establishment, pecking order; domain, realm, **kingdom**

verbs

5 **classify,** class, assign, designate; **categorize,** class, assign, designate; **range;** order, rank, rate, **grade; sort; divide, analyse,** subdivide, break down; catalogue, list, file, index

adjectives

6 **typical, special,** specific, characteristic, particular, peculiar, distinctive, defining

7 **classified,** sorted, assorted, **graded, grouped,** ranked, rated; placed; filed, on file

adverbs

8 **at all,** whatever, whatsoever

772 DISORDER

nouns

1 **disorder; disarray,** disturbance, **irregularity,** turbulence; **disruption;** disintegration

2 **confusion, chaos,** anarchy; **muddle,** morass

3 **jumble, scramble, mess,** turmoil, hash; **clutter, litter**

4 **commotion, tumult,** turmoil, uproar, racket, riot, **disturbance, rumpus** (*nonformal*), **fracas, hassle,** rampage; trouble, bother, **fuss**

5 **pandemonium, hell, bedlam; cacophony,** din, noise, racket

6 carelessness, negligence

verbs

7 **come apart, disintegrate,** degenerate

8 **disorder; confuse,** sow confusion, **muddle,** jumble, jumble up; **upset, disturb**

9 **riot; make trouble, cut loose, run wild, run riot,** go berserk

adjectives

10 **disordered, random; incoherent;** formless, amorphous, shapeless; disproportionate, misshapen; **irregular, haphazard,** desultory, **erratic,** sporadic, spasmodic, fitful, indiscriminate, casual, frivolous, capricious, vague, dispersed, wandering, **aimless,** straggling, straggly; senseless, meaningless, gratuitous

11 **disorderly, in disorder,** disordered, **disorganized; upset, disturbed,** perturbed, unsettled, disconcerted; **turbulent;** misplaced; awry, amiss, askew

12 **dishevelled, rumpled,** ruffled, **tousled;** shaggy, matted

13 **slovenly, careless, loose, slack,** negligent; **untidy,** unsightly, unkempt; messy, sloppy (*nonformal*), **shabby,** shoddy, grubby (*nonformal*), tacky (*nonformal*); bedraggled; in rags, ragged, tat-

tered; **squalid**, sordid; dilapidated, ruinous

14 **confused, chaotic,** anarchic, **muddled, jumbled,** scattered; mixed up

adverbs

15 **in disorder, in disarray, in confusion;** willy-nilly (*nonformal*)

16 **haphazardly,** irregularly, **erratically,** indiscriminately, **carelessly;** sporadically, spasmodically; **at random, by chance**

17 vaguely, **aimlessly**

773 DISARRANGEMENT

nouns

1 convulsion; disturbance; disorder; insanity

verbs

2 **disorder,** disarray; rumple, ruffle; **litter, clutter,** scatter

3 **confuse, muddle, jumble,** confound, scramble; **shuffle; mix up**

4 **upset, disturb,** trip up, trouble, distract, throw (*nonformal*), agitate, convulse, embroil

adjectives

5 **confused, disordered**

774 CONTINUITY

nouns

1 **continuity,** monotony, **uniformity;** smoothness; **constancy;** equilibrium, stability

2 **series, succession,** run, **sequence,** progression, course, gradation; **continuum;** descent; **connection, chain;** chain reaction; **line, string,** thread, queue, **row,** bank, tier; array; **round,** cycle, rotation, routine, recurrence; gamut, spectrum, scale; drone, monotone, hum, buzz

3 **procession, train, column, line, string;** stream

verbs

4 **continue,** be continuous, **connect, join,** link, run on

5 **align, line up,** array

6 **line up,** queue

7 **file; parade,** march past

adjectives

8 **continuous,** continued, **continual,** continuing; **uninterrupted,** monotonous; **connected, linked, unbroken, uniform,** homogeneous; unremitting; **incessant, constant,** steady, stable, **ceaseless,** unceasing, **endless,** unending, never-ending, **interminable,** perennial; **cyclical,** repetitive, **recurrent,** periodic

9 **consecutive, successive;** serial

adverbs

10 **continuously, continually;** without stopping, on end; **endlessly,** repeatedly

11 progressively, **in succession, in turn**

775 DISCONTINUITY

nouns

1 **interruption, suspension, break,** gap, hiatus; **interval, pause,** interim, lull, cessation, **intermission**

verbs

2 **discontinue, interrupt, break,** break off

adjectives

3 incoherent, discontinued, disconnected, unconnected, broken; irregular; fragmentary, interrupted, suspended; discrete; intermittent, fitful; patchy; jerky, spasmodic

adverbs

4 at intervals; haphazardly, occasionally, infrequently, intermittently, spasmodically; willy-nilly, sporadically

776 PRECEDENCE

nouns

1 the lead, front seat, pole position; priority, preference, urgency; superiority

verbs

2 precede, come first, head, front, lead, take precedence, have priority; lead off, kick off

3 prefix, preface, introduce

adjectives

4 preceding, prior, antecedent, leading; preliminary, preparatory, inaugural; first, foremost, chief

5 former, foregoing; aforementioned, said, named, same

adverbs

6 before; above

777 SEQUENCE

nouns

1 sequence, succession; descent, line; series; order; priority; progression, procession, rotation; continuity; continuation, extension

verbs

2 succeed, follow, ensue, come next; inherit, take over

adjectives

3 succeeding, successive, following, ensuing, subsequent, consequent; next

778 PRECURSOR

nouns

1 precursor, forerunner; pioneer; scout, explorer, guide; leader; herald, announcer, messenger; predecessor, precedent, ancestor; vanguard, avant-garde, innovator

2 countdown, warm-up; prelude, preamble, preface, foreword, introduction; prefix; preliminary; overture; premise; innovation, breakthrough

verbs

3 go before, pioneer; guide; lead; precede; herald, count down, lead in, usher in, introduce

adjectives

4 preceding; preliminary, exploratory, pioneering, inaugural; advanced, avant-garde, original

779 SEQUEL

nouns

1 sequel, consequence; continuation, continuance; supplement, appendix, back matter; suffix; postscript or PS; epilogue, conclusion; refrain, chorus; afterthought, second thoughts; last words, swan song

2 wake, trail, train; tail

3 **aftermath**, side effect, by-product, spin-off

4 **successor**, **replacement**, substitute, stand-in; **descendant**, posterity, **heir**, inheritor

verbs

5 **succeed**, follow, come next, come after

780 BEGINNING

nouns

1 **beginning**, **commencement**, **start**, starting point, square one (*nonformal*); **outset**, outbreak, onset; dawn; **creation**, **foundation**, **establishment**, **institution**, origin; **launching**, launch; **opening**; fresh start, new departure

2 **beginner**; newcomer, new arrival; entrant, **novice**; **recruit**; **apprentice**, trainee, learner; baby, infant

3 **initiation**, first move, opening move, gambit, **first step**; first glance, first sight, first impression

4 **origin**, inception; birth; infancy, childhood, youth; beginnings, cradle

5 **inauguration**, **introduction**, initiation; **launching**, floating, unveiling; debut, coming out

6 **basics**, **essentials**, **rudiments**, **elements**; **principles**, first principles, first steps; introduction

verbs

7 **begin**, **commence**, **start**; set out, set sail, dive in (*nonformal*), **go ahead**

8 **start up**, set forth, set out

9 enter, take up, go into

10 **initiate**, **originate**, **create**, invent; pioneer; **lead**, lead off

11 **inaugurate**, institute, **found**, **establish**, set up; **install**, initiate; **introduce**, broach, bring up, raise; **launch**, float; christen (*nonformal*); **usher in**, ring in (*nonformal*); turn on, start up

12 **originate**, be born, **become**, **arise**, **come forth**, **issue**, issue forth, come out; burst forth, break out, erupt

adjectives

13 **beginning**, **initial**, **incipient**, **introductory**, **prime**, **primary**, primitive, primeval; **original**, **first**; aboriginal; **elementary**, **fundamental**; rudimentary, **formative**; **creative**, **inventive**; embryonic, in embryo, budding; infant

14 **first**, **foremost**, front, **head**, **chief**, **principal**, premier, **leading**, main

adverbs

15 **first**, firstly, **at first**, first off, for starters (*nonformal*), up front (*nonformal*); **principally**, mainly, chiefly; **primarily**, initially; **originally**, **in the beginning**; from scratch (*nonformal*)

781 MIDDLE

nouns

1 **middle**, **midst**; thick; centre; **heart**, **core**, nucleus, kernel; interior; **waist**, waistline, girth; equator; diameter

2 middle distance; **half**; **middle ground**, midway, halfway house

adjectives

3 **middle**, mediocre, average, **medium, mean**, mid; **central**, core; interior; **intermediate**; equidistant, halfway, midway, equatorial; moderate, middle-of-the-road

adverbs

4 **midway, halfway**

782 END

nouns

1 **end**, end point, ending, **termination, terminus, terminal**, expiry, **cessation**, ceasing, consummation, culmination, **conclusion, finish, finale**, the end, finishing, stoppage, curtain, curtains (*nonformal*); **death; last**, last legs; **goal**, destination, resting place, finish line, wire (*nonformal*); catastrophe, resolution; last words, swan song, dying words, epilogue; **fate, destiny, doom; happy ending**

2 **extremity, extreme; limit, boundary, pole; tip**, point, nib; tail, **tail end**, fag end; bitter end; stub, stump, butt

3 **close**, closing, cessation; decline, lapse; last lap

verbs

4 **end, terminate**, determine, close, **finish, conclude**, resolve, wind up (*nonformal*); end up; wrap up (*nonformal*), sew up (*nonformal*); call off (*nonformal*); **dispose of**, polish off (*nonformal*); **stop, cease;** abort; **kill**, extinguish, knock out (*nonformal*), wipe out (*nonformal*); **cancel, delete**, censor, erase

5 **expire, die**, end up, land up; lapse, become extinct, run out, **pass away**, die away, go out, blow over

6 **complete**, perfect, finish, finish off, finalize

adjectives

7 **ended, terminated, concluded, finished, complete**, perfected, settled, decided; **over; done**, done with, over with, through (*nonformal*); **dead, defunct**, extinct; defeated; cancelled, deleted, censored

8 (*nonformal terms*) **dead meat**, done for, wiped out, washed up

9 **ending, closing, concluding, finishing, ultimate**, definitive, crowning, capping

10 **final, terminal**, definitive, **conclusive; last**, eventual, farthest, extreme, **ultimate**

adverbs

11 **finally; ultimately, eventually; lastly**, last, **at last**, at length; **in conclusion;** conclusively

783 TIME

nouns

1 **time, duration**, continuity, term, while, tide, space; real time; tense; **period**, time frame; the past, the present, the future

2 Time, **Father Time**

verbs

3 **elapse, lapse, pass, expire**, run out; **flow**, run, proceed, advance, fly, slip, slide, glide; **continue**, last, **endure**

4 **spend time, pass time**, kill time (*nonformal*), take time; buy time;

weekend, winter, summer; keep
time, measure time

adjectives

5 **chronological;** lasting, continuous

adverbs

6 **when, upon which, whereupon,**
at which, whenever

7 **then,** concurrently, simultaneously

8 in the meantime, meanwhile

9 **then,** thereupon; **again,** anon

10 **whenever;** if ever, once

784 TIMELESSNESS

nouns

1 **timelessness,** eternity

adjectives

2 **timeless,** dateless

adverbs

3 **never, not ever,** at no time, on
no occasion; **nevermore**

785 INFINITY

nouns

1 **infinity; endlessness;** immensity;
eternity, forever

adjectives

2 **infinite, boundless, endless,
limitless; unlimited; interminable; immeasurable,** incalculable, innumerable; countless;
immense, untold; inexhaustible;
universal; perpetual, eternal

adverbs

3 **infinitely; immeasurably,** immensely; **endlessly; forever,**
eternally

786 PERIOD

nouns

1 **period, point, juncture,** stage;
interval, time frame, space,
span, stretch; **time,** while, **moment,** minute, instant, hour, day,
season; spell

2 (*periods*) **moment, second; minute;** hour; **day; weekday; week;**
fortnight; **month,** moon; calendar month, lunar month; **quarter;** term, session, academic
year; **year,** annum; **decade; century; millennium**

3 **term,** time, duration, **tenure;**
spell

4 **age, generation,** time, day, date,
cycle

5 **era, epoch, age;** Golden Age, Silver Age; Ice Age, glacial epoch;
Stone Age, Bronze Age, Iron Age,
Steel Age; Middle Ages, Dark
Ages

6 (*modern age*) Technological Age,
Atomic Age, Computer Age,
Space Age

787 SPELL

(*period of duty, etc*)

nouns

1 **spell,** stretch, go (*nonformal*)

2 **turn, bout, round,** innings, **time,**
place, say; opportunity, chance;
relief, spell

3 **shift, tour,** stint, bit, **watch,**
time, **turn; day shift, night shift,**
back shift; **part-time, full-time;**
overtime

4 **term,** time; **tenure;** tour; prison
term, stretch (*nonformal*)

verbs

5 **take turns**, alternate; **time off**, **relieve**, cover; hold office; **enlist**, sign up

788 INTERIM
(intermediate period)

nouns

1 **interim, interval, interlude, intermission,** pause, break, recess, coffee break, interruption; **lull,** quiet spell, relief, vacation, holiday, time off; **respite; intermission,** interval

2 **meantime, meanwhile,** while, the while

verbs

3 **intervene;** pause, break, **recess**

adjectives

4 **interim, temporary,** tentative, provisional

adverbs

5 **meanwhile, meantime,** in the interim

789 DURATION

nouns

1 **durability, endurance,** duration; **continuance,** maintenance, constancy, **stability, persistence, permanence,** standing, **long standing;** longevity; antiquity, **age; survival,** viability; useful life, shelf life

2 continuation, extension, lengthening, lingering

3 **long time,** long while; **century, eternity,** years

4 **lifetime, life,** life expectancy, lifespan; **generation, age**

verbs

5 **endure,** bide, **abide,** dwell, **continue,** run, extend, **go on,** carry on, hold on, stay on; live, **live on,** subsist, exist; **persist;** maintain, sustain, **remain, stay,** hold, stand, prevail, hold out; **survive,** live on, live through; wear, wear well

6 **linger on,** go on, **wear on,** crawl, creep, drag, **drag on**

7 **outlast, outlive,** survive

8 **prolong,** continue, **extend, lengthen, draw out,** spin out; linger on, dwell on; dawdle

adjectives

9 **durable, lasting, enduring, abiding, continuing,** remaining, **stable, persistent,** perennial; **steadfast, constant,** immutable, evergreen, **permanent, long-lasting,** long-standing; long-term; tough, hardy, vital; **ancient,** aged, antique; **perpetual**

10 **protracted, prolonged,** extended, lengthened; **long,** interminable, marathon, lasting, **lingering,** languishing; long-winded

11 **lifelong,** lifetime, for life

adverbs

12 **long, for long,** persistently; morning, noon, and night; long ago, long since, time immemorial

790 TRANSIENCE
(short duration)

nouns

1 **transience, impermanence, mutability, instability;** short duration; **mortality,** death

2 **brevity; swiftness**

3 **short time, little while,** little, **instant, moment,** small space, spurt, **short spell;** no time

4 **vagabond,** wanderer, drifter, derelict, homeless person, tramp, hobo

5 bubble, smoke, flash in the pan

verbs

6 (*be transient*) **flit, fly,** fleet; pass, vanish, evaporate, dissolve, disappear, fade, melt, sink

adjectives

7 **transient, transitory,** transitive; temporary; **frail, brittle, fragile,** insubstantial; changeable, unstable; capricious, fickle, impulsive, **impetuous; short-lived, ephemeral,** volatile, **momentary;** deciduous; **passing,** fleeting, flying, fading, dying; perishable, mortal

8 **brief, short,** quick, brisk, swift, fleet, speedy, meteoric, flashing; short-term

adverbs

9 **temporarily,** awhile

10 fleetingly, **briefly, shortly,** swiftly, quickly; **momentarily**

791 PERPETUITY

(endless duration)

nouns

1 **perpetuity; eternity; permanence, duration, indestructibility; constancy,** stability, continuance; infinity

2 **forever, an eternity,** endless time

3 **immortality,** eternal life, eternal youth

4 **perpetuation,** preservation; immortalization

verbs

5 **perpetuate, preserve, immortalize; freeze, embalm**

adjectives

6 **perpetual, everlasting,** permanent, indestructible; **eternal, infinite;** timeless, immemorial; **endless,** unending, never-ending; **interminable; continual,** continuous, steady, **constant, ceaseless,** unceasing, **incessant,** unremitting, uninterrupted

7 **perennial, evergreen**

8 **immortal,** everlasting, incorruptible; frozen, embalmed

adverbs

9 **perpetually, everlastingly, eternally, permanently, constantly,** continually, steadily, **ceaselessly, incessantly, endlessly, infinitely**

10 **always, all along;** invariably, without exception

11 **forever; ever; for good,** for keeps (*nonformal*)

12 **for life, till death**

792 INSTANTANEOUS-NESS

(imperceptible duration)

nouns

1 **instantaneousness,** momentariness, **immediacy**

2 **suddenness, abruptness;** unexpectedness

3 **instant, moment, second,** split second, minute, twinkle, **twin-**

kling, wink, flash, tick, stroke, breath, twitch

adjectives

4 **instantaneous**, instant, momentary, **immediate**; **simultaneous**

5 **sudden**, **abrupt**, **precipitate**, **precipitous**; **hasty**, headlong, impulsive, impetuous; speedy, swift, quick; **unexpected**, unforeseen; **surprising**, startling, electrifying, shocking

adverbs

6 **instantly**, momentarily, **instantaneously**; **immediately**; **quickly**

7 **at once**, now, **right now**, **right away**, straightaway, forthwith, this minute, **without delay**; **simultaneously**; all together

8 **suddenly**, sudden, sharp; impulsively, hastily; **unexpectedly**; unawares, **surprisingly**

793 EVENT

nouns

1 **event**, **eventuality**, effect, issue, outcome, result, aftermath, consequence; **realization**, incidence; contingency, contingent; accident

2 **event**, **occurrence**, **incident**, **episode**, **experience**, **adventure**, **happening**, **phenomenon**, fact, reality, particular, circumstance, **occasion**

3 **affair**, **concern**, **matter**, thing, interest, **business**, job (*nonformal*), **transaction**, proceeding, doing

4 **affairs**, **concerns**, **matters**, circumstances, relations, **dealings**, **proceedings**, doings, goings-on

(*nonformal*); the world, life, the time; **conditions**

verbs

5 **occur**, **happen**, **take place**, go on, **transpire**, be realized, come, **come off** (*nonformal*), come about, come true, pass, pass off, go off, **befall**

6 **turn up**, **show up** (*nonformal*), **come along**, chance, **crop up**, **arise**, **come**, appear, approach, materialize, present itself

7 **turn out**, **result**

8 **experience**, **have**, **know**, **feel**, taste; **encounter**, **meet**, meet with; **undergo**, **go through**, labour under, **endure**, **suffer**, sustain, pay, spend

adjectives

9 **happening**, **occurring**, **current**, **actual**, passing, taking place, on, **going on**, **ongoing** (*nonformal*), **prevalent**, **prevailing**, that is, afloat, afoot, under way, in hand, doing; incidental, circumstantial, accompanying; accidental; occasional; resultant

10 **eventful**, **momentous**, **stirring**, bustling; phenomenal

11 **eventual**, **coming**, **final**, last, ultimate; **contingent**, collateral, secondary, indirect

adverbs

12 **eventually**, **ultimately**, **finally**

794 MEASUREMENT OF TIME

nouns

1 **chronology**, timekeeping, timing, clocking; **dating**

2 time, the time; hour, minute; time signal, bell

3 date, time, day; datemark; date line

4 timepiece, ship's watch; **clock,** Big Ben, **watch;** hourglass, sundial

5 calendar; almanac; Chinese calendar, Gregorian calendar, Hindu calendar, Muslim calendar, Roman calendar

6 chronicle, register, record; journal, diary; time sheet, time book, **log;** clock card; date slip; **timetable,** schedule, time chart; time scale

7 chronologer; watchmaker; diarist; calendar maker

verbs

8 time, keep time, mark time, measure time; **clock** (*nonformal*)

9 ring in, ring out; clock in, clock out; check in, check out

10 date, date from, date back; **predate,** backdate; **postdate;** update

adjectives

11 chronologic(al), temporal; **chronometric(al);** dated

adverbs

12 o'clock; half past; quarter to, quarter past

795 ANACHRONISM

nouns

1 anachronism, mistiming, misdating; anticipation; earliness, lateness

verbs

2 mistime, misdate; lag

adjectives

3 anachronistic; mistimed, misdated; **early;** behindhand, **late; overdue; dated,** out-of-date

796 PREVIOUSNESS

nouns

1 previousness, earliness, priority, precedence; previous state; **anticipation;** past time

2 antecedent, precedent, premise; forerunner, **precursor,** ancestor

verbs

3 be prior, precede; herald, proclaim, announce; **anticipate**

adjectives

4 previous, prior, early, earlier, former, prime, first, **preceding,** foregoing, above, antecedent; older, elder, senior

adverbs

5 previously, hitherto; before, early, earlier; already, yet; **formerly**

797 SUBSEQUENCE

(later time)

nouns

1 succession, following, sequence; next life; remainder, hangover (*nonformal*); future time

2 sequel, follow-up, aftermath; consequence, effect; **posterity,** offspring, descendant, heir, inheritor; **successor;** replacement, line, dynasty, family

verbs

3 **follow, succeed,** replace, displace, overtake; **ensue,** issue, emanate, attend; **result;** follow up, trail, track

adjectives

4 **subsequent, after, later, following, succeeding,** successive, consecutive, ensuing, attendant; **junior,** younger

adverbs

5 **subsequently, after, afterwards,** later, next; since; **thereafter,** thereupon, **then**

6 **after which, whereupon,** on, upon

798 SIMULTANEITY

nouns

1 **simultaneity,** coincidence, co-occurrence; **coexistence;** unison; accompaniment

2 **contemporary,** concomitant

3 **tie,** dead heat, draw

verbs

4 **coincide,** concur; **coexist; synchronize,** keep time; **accompany, agree,** match

adjectives

5 **simultaneous, concurrent,** concomitant; **coexisting;** contemporary; accompanying, collateral

6 **synchronized; in time,** in step

adverbs

7 **simultaneously,   concurrently; together,** all together, as one, in chorus, in unison

799 THE PAST

nouns

1 **the past,** former times, past times, times past, **yesterday;** recent past; **history,** past history

2 **olden times,** early times, **olden days**

3 **antiquity, ancient times,** time immemorial, ancient history

4 **memory, remembrance, recollection, reminiscence,** looking back; revival

verbs

5 **pass,** be past, elapse, lapse, be gone, fade away; **disappear; die**

adjectives

6 **past, gone,** by, **bygone,** ago, **over,** departed, passed, passed away, elapsed, lapsed, vanished, faded, no more; **dead,** expired, extinct, defunct, deceased; run out, blown over, finished, forgotten, wound up; **obsolete,** hasbeen, dated, antique, **antiquated**

7 **reminiscent, retrospective, remembered, recollected; relived; restored, revived**

8 **former,** past, fore, **previous,** late, recent, **once, onetime,** sometime, then; **prior; ancient, immemorial,** early, primitive, primeval, prehistoric; **old**

9 **foregoing, preceding;** last, latter

10 **back,** backward; early; retrospective

adverbs

11 **formerly, previously; earlier, before,** before now, **hitherto; then; yesterday,** recently; **historically**

12 **once,** one day, time was

13 **ago, since,** gone by; back, back when; backward

14 **long ago,** long since, ages ago, **years ago; of old,** early

15 **since,** ever since, until now; **long since,** ages ago

800 THE PRESENT

nouns

1 **the present,** present time; **now; today,** this day; **this point,** this stage, nowadays; **the times,** these days; **newness,** modernity

adjectives

2 **present, immediate,** latest, current, running, **existing,** actual, topical, that is, as is, that be; **present-day, modern; contemporary;** up-to-date, fresh, **new**

adverbs

3 **now, at present, today,** this day, **nowadays;** this night, **tonight;** here, **just now**

4 **until now, hitherto,** till now, **so far, as yet,** to date, yet, already, still

801 THE FUTURE

nouns

1 **the future,** future, eventuality; **tomorrow; near future,** offing; **distant future; prospect,** outlook, anticipation, expectation, probability, prediction, forward look, foresight, prophecy, clairvoyance, crystal ball

2 **destiny, fate,** doom; Paradise, Heaven; Hell; the unknown, **the grave;** afterlife

3 **doomsday,** day of reckoning, Judgment Day

4 **eventuality,** finality

5 **advent, coming**

verbs

6 **come,** come on, **approach,** near; **loom,** threaten, await, be imminent; **predict,** foresee, envisage, foretell, prophesy; **anticipate, expect,** hope for, look for, **project,** plot, plan, scheme, think ahead

adjectives

7 **future, later; coming, forthcoming, imminent,** approaching, nearing, **prospective; eventual,** ultimate, **to come; projected,** plotted, planned, desired, **predicted,** prophesied, foreseen, anticipated, envisaged, probable; determined, fatal, fated, destined, doomed

adverbs

8 **later,** anon; **tomorrow; soon, before long;** probably, predictably, hopefully

9 **in future,** thereafter, **henceforth,** from here on in

10 **in time, eventually,** ultimately

11 **sometime, someday,** sooner or later

802 IMMINENCE

nouns

1 **imminence;** coming, **approach**

verbs

2 **be imminent, loom,** hover, **threaten, menace,** lower; **brew;** gather; **approach, near,** await, face, confront

adjectives

3 **imminent, impending,** waiting, lurking, **threatening, looming,** lowering, **menacing, brewing,** gathering; **coming, forthcoming, to come, approaching, nearing,** looming; **near, close,** immediate, instant, **at hand; in prospect,** in view, in store; future

adverbs

4 **any time,** any moment, any second, any minute, any hour, any day

803 NEWNESS

nouns

1 **newness,** freshness, mint condition, immaturity, callowness; **novelty;** originality; strangeness

2 **novelty, innovation;** vanguard, **avant-garde**

3 **modernity;** modernization, updating; space age

4 **modern,** modern man; new generation; fledgling, new man, upstart

verbs

5 **innovate, invent,** coin, mint, inaugurate; **renew,** renovate

6 **modernize,** streamline; update

adjectives

7 **new, young, fresh; unused, original;** untouched; virginal, intact, maiden; green; **immature,** undeveloped, raw, fledgling

8 **fresh, additional, further,** other, another; renewed

9 **mint;** newborn; like new

10 (*nonformal terms*) **brand-new, spanking new; just out; hot**

11 **novel, original, unique, different;** strange, unusual, uncommon; unfamiliar; **first ever**

12 **recent, late; latter, later**

13 **modern,   contemporary, present-day,** latter-day, now (*nonformal*), fashionable, **up-to-date;** in; **advanced,** progressive, modernizing, **avant-garde;** far out, way out, modernized, streamlined

14 **newest, latest,** last, most recent

adverbs

15 **newly,** freshly, new, **anew,** once more, from scratch (*nonformal*), **afresh,** again

16 **now,** recently, lately, latterly, **of late;** just now, right now (*nonformal*)

804 OLDNESS

nouns

1 **age;** seniority, senior citizenship, senility, **old age; antiquity;** old order, old style

2 **tradition, custom;** ancient wisdom; mythology, legend, folklore; racial memory

3 staleness,   disuse;   **old-fashionedness,** unfashionableness

4 **antiquarian; archaeologist;** classicist, medievalist; antique dealer, antique collector

5 **antiquity, antique, relic; remains,** survival, vestige; **fossil;** petrified wood; **artefact;** cave painting; ancient manuscript

6 **ancient, prehistoric mankind;** primate, fossil man; **primitive,**

aboriginal; cave dweller; bog man

7 (*antiquated person*) has-been; old fogy, granny (*nonformal*), **old woman; old man,** elder, old-timer (*nonformal*)

verbs

8 **age,** grow old; date; rust, fade, perish

adjectives

9 **old, age-old;** ancient, **antique,** venerable, hoary; of old; timeless; **immemorial; elderly**

10 **primitive, primeval;** aboriginal; ancestral; **prehistoric**

11 **traditional;** mythological, heroic; **legendary,** unwritten, oral, handed down; **customary,** conventional, understood, recognized, acknowledged, received; **longstanding,** established, fixed, rooted; folk

12 **antiquated, antique, old;** Victorian; classical, medieval; **fossil,** fossilized, petrified

13 **stale, musty,** rusty, dusty, mouldy; **worn; moth-eaten,** crumbling, dilapidated, ruined

14 **obsolete, extinct,** dead, past, run out, **outworn**

15 **old-fashioned, dated,** out, out-of-date, **outdated, outmoded,** disused, **unfashionable**

16 **stuffy, stodgy; aged,** senile

17 **secondhand, used,** worn, hand-me-down (*nonformal*)

18 **older,** senior, major, elder; **oldest,** eldest

805 TIMELINESS

nouns

1 **timeliness,** convenience; **expediency,** fitness, propriety, suitability; pregnancy, expectancy

2 **opportunity, chance, time, occasion; opening,** room, scope, space, place, liberty, fair; **opportunism;** equal opportunity, positive discrimination; **trump card;** stepping-stone

3 **good opportunity, good chance,** favourable opportunity, golden opportunity, suitable occasion, **good time,** high time, due season

4 **crisis, critical point,** crunch, crucial period, climax; **turning point,** hinge; critical juncture, crossroads; pass, strait, extremity; spot (*nonformal*); **emergency,** red alert

5 **crucial moment,** critical moment, decisive moment, turning point, climax; **right moment;** eleventh hour; **zero hour,** target date, deadline

verbs

6 **seize the opportunity,** take the chance; **make one's move; commit oneself**

7 **take advantage of,** profit by, **cash in on**

adjectives

8 **timely, opportune,** convenient; **expedient,** meet, fit, fitting, suitable, appropriate; **favourable,** ripe, lucky, heaven-sent, fortunate, happy

9 **critical, crucial,** decisive; pregnant, loaded, charged; emergent

10 **incidental, occasional, casual,** accidental

adverbs

11 **in good time;** in the nick of time, just in time

12 **incidentally, by the way; while on the subject;** speaking of; **in passing;** for example

806 UNTIMELINESS

nouns

1 **untimeliness,** inconvenience; **awkwardness; intrusion,** interruption; **prematurity; lateness,** afterthought

2 **wrong time, bad time,** unfortunate time; evil hour

verbs

3 **mistime;** be engaged, be preoccupied

4 **talk out of turn,** interrupt, intrude, butt in (*nonformal*); blow it (*nonformal*)

5 **miss out, miss the boat,** oversleep

adjectives

6 **inconvenient; inappropriate,** irrelevant, improper, unfit, wrong, unsuitable, untoward, intrusive; **unfavourable,** unfortunate, unhappy, unlucky; **premature; late**

807 EARLINESS

nouns

1 **early hour; head start,** running start, beginnings, very beginning, preliminaries; **anticipation, foresight;** advance notice, lead time, readiness, preparation

2 **haste, rush, impulse**

3 **promptness,** readiness; **alacrity,** swiftness, rapidity, expedition, dispatch

4 **early bird** (*nonformal*), early riser; **precursor**

verbs

5 **be early;** gain time

6 **anticipate, foresee,** foretaste; **forestall,** go before

adjectives

7 **early; forehand**

8 **premature, too early, too soon;** precipitate, hasty; **unprepared,** impulsive, rushed; not firm; **precocious, forward, advanced,** far ahead

9 **prompt, punctual, immediate, instant,** instantaneous, **quick,** speedy, swift, decisive, alert, **ready**

10 **earlier,** previous

adverbs

11 **early, beforehand,** early on, in advance, in anticipation, ahead, before

12 **in time, in good time, soon enough,** early enough; **just in time,** in the nick of time

13 **prematurely, too soon,** too early; impulsively, hastily

14 **punctually, precisely,** exactly, sharp; **on time**

15 **promptly, without delay,** directly, **immediately, instantly, at once, right away,** straightaway, **forthwith, quickly,** swiftly, speedily, decisively, smartly

16 **soon, presently, directly, shortly,** before long

808 LATENESS

nouns

1 **lateness, tardiness;** late hour, small hours; eleventh hour, last minute, high time

2 **delay,** stoppage, obstruction, **block,** blockage; delayed reaction, afterthought; slowness, lag, time lag, dragging; **detention,** suspension, **obstruction, hindrance;** delaying action; **wait, halt, stay, stop,** break, pause, interim, respite; reprieve; **red tape**

3 **waiting; lingering,** dawdling

4 **postponement, deferral,** carrying over; **adjournment**

5 **procrastination, hesitation;** slowness

6 **latecomer,** late arrival; slow starter

verbs

7 **be late,** be overdue; **stay late;** oversleep

8 **delay, detain,** make late, slacken, lag, slow down, **hold up** (*nonformal*), check, **stay, stop,** arrest, impede, **block,** hinder, obstruct

9 **postpone, delay, defer,** put off, reserve, waive, **suspend,** stay, hang fire; **prolong, extend,** continue, adjourn, recess; **hold over, put aside, shelve;** sleep on

10 hesitate, hang, hang back, hang fire; hold off (*nonformal*); **stall**

11 **wait, delay, stay,** bide, abide; take time; **linger, loiter,** dawdle; stick around (*nonformal*); **hold on** (*nonformal*), sit tight (*nonformal*); wait up; sit up; **await**

adjectives

12 **late, belated,** slow, backward, back, **overdue;** delayed, detained, **held up** (*nonformal*), retarded, **arrested,** blocked, obstructed, stopped, jammed, congested; **postponed,** held up, put off

13 **delaying;** go-slow; **obstructive; lingering,** loitering, lagging, **slow,** sluggish, shuffling, backward; **lazy;** slack, work-shy, lax

14 later; last-minute, deathbed

adverbs

15 **late, behind, belatedly,** backward, slow, **behind time; far on, deep into**

16 **slow, slowly,** deliberately, leisurely

809 FREQUENCY

nouns

1 **frequency;** prevalence, **common occurrence, incidence,** relative incidence

2 **constancy, regularity,** continuity; repetition; **rapidity, staccato,** chattering, stuttering, **vibration,** shuddering

verbs

3 be frequent, occur often, continue, recur; shudder, vibrate, oscillate

adjectives

4 **frequent,** many, **recurrent; common, prevalent,** usual, routine, habitual, ordinary, everyday

5 **constant, continual, perennial;** steady, sustained, **regular; incessant, ceaseless, unceasing,** unremitting, relentless, unrelenting,

unchanging, uninterrupted, unbroken; **perpetual;** repeated; **rapid, staccato,** stuttering, chattering, machine gun; pulsating, vibrating, **oscillating**

adverbs

6 **frequently, commonly,** usually, ordinarily, routinely, habitually; **often; repeatedly; many times;** often enough, not infrequently, not seldom

7 **constantly, continually, steadily,** regularly, **incessantly, ceaselessly,** ever, without stopping; **perpetually, always; rapidly;** daily, hourly

810 INFREQUENCY

nouns

1 **infrequency;** rarity, scarcity, uniqueness; **slowness**

adjectives

2 **infrequent, rare,** scarce, **uncommon,** unique, unusual, seldom seen; **sparse; one-time**

3 **occasional, casual, incidental; odd,** sometime, extra, side, out-of-the-way, spare, **part-time**

adverbs

4 **infrequently, seldom, rarely, uncommonly,** scarcely, hardly; **sparsely**

5 **occasionally,** on occasion, **sometimes, at times;** irregularly, sporadically

6 **once, one-time**

811 REPETITION

nouns

1 **repetition, reproduction,** duplication, doubling, redoubling; **recurrence,** return, reincarnation, rebirth, reappearance, renewal, resumption; echo, parroting, rehearsal; **quotation; imitation**

2 **recounting, recital, rehearsal;** reprint; review, summary; practised; elaboration, dwelling upon; copy

3 **redundancy;** stammering, stuttering; padding, filling

4 **monotony,** monotone, drone; **tedium; humdrum,** chime, jingle; rhyme

5 **repeat,** ditto *(nonformal),* echo; **refrain,** burden, chant, chorus

6 **encore,** repeat performance, repeat; replay, return match

verbs

7 **repeat,** do again, **reproduce, duplicate,** double, redouble, ditto *(nonformal),* **echo, parrot; rattle off,** reel off, regurgitate; renew, revive; say again, repeat oneself, **quote; copy,** imitate

8 **reiterate, rehearse, recount, recite,** review, run over, sum up, summarize, resume, encapsulate; reprint; practice, say over, quote oneself, pad, fill; **reaffirm,** reassert

9 insist upon, **harp on,** labour

10 drum, beat, hammer, pound; drum into

11 (*be repeated*) **repeat, recur, come again, return, reappear, resume;** resound, reverberate, echo; revert; keep coming

adjectives

12 repeated, reproduced, doubled, redoubled; **duplicated;** regurgitated; **echoed; quoted; reiterated,** reiterate

13 recurrent, recurring, **returning,** reappearing, cyclical, periodic, yearly, monthly, weekly, daily, frequent, incessant, continuous; haunting

14 repetitious, repetitive, repeating; **imitative;** echoing

15 monotonous; tedious; humdrum, chiming, chanting; **rhyming**

adverbs

16 repeatedly, often, frequently, many times, several times

17 again, over, over again, **once more,** encore, two times, twice over, ditto; **anew,** afresh

812 REGULARITY OF RECURRENCE

nouns

1 regularity, predictability, smoothness; **repetition; uniformity; constancy**

2 cyclical motion, piston motion, pendulum motion; alternation; rhythm, metre, beat; **recurrence,** reappearance, return

3 round, revolution, rotation, cycle, circle, wheel, **circuit; beat, pulse;** course, series, **bout,** turn, spell

4 anniversary; bank holiday; jubilee, silver jubilee, golden jubilee, diamond jubilee; centenary; **wedding anniversary; birthday;** name day; leap year; **religious holiday,** holy day

verbs

5 (*occur periodically*) **recur, return, repeat,** reappear, **come again; rotate, revolve,** turn, circle, wheel, cycle, **roll around,** go round; alternate; undulate; **oscillate, pulse, pulsate**

adjectives

6 regular, methodical, ordered, orderly; **uniform; constant**

7 seasonal, serial; measured, steady, even, **rhythmic; recurrent,** recurring; **intermittent,** reciprocal, alternate, every other; circling, wheeling, rotary, pulsing, beating

8 momentary; hourly; daily; weekly; fortnightly; **monthly; quarterly; yearly, annual;** centenary

adverbs

9 regularly, systematically, methodically, like clockwork, punctually, steadily; **intermittently; uniformly; constantly**

10 periodically; rhythmically, in time, **hourly, daily,** etc; every hour, every day, etc

11 alternately, by turns, in turns, in rotation, turn about, every other

813 IRREGULARITY OF RECURRENCE

nouns

1 irregularity; uncertainty; **variability,** eccentricity; stagger, wobble, weaving

verbs

2 **fluctuate**, vary, lack regularity

adjectives

3 **irregular; unsteady, uneven,** rough, unequal, uncertain, unsettled; **variable; capricious, erratic,** eccentric, wobbly, wobbling, weaving, staggering; **fitful, jerky,** halting; **sporadic,** patchy, spotty, choppy, **broken, disconnected; intermittent, desultory, fluctuating, wavering,** wandering, rambling, veering; flickering

adverbs

4 **irregularly; unsteadily,** roughly, uncertainly; **erratically; intermittently; sporadically, spasmodically;** at random

814 CHANGE

nouns

1 **change, alteration, modification; variation,** variety, difference, diversity, diversification; **deviation,** diversion, **divergence; switch, turn, reversal; shift,** transition; **conversion, renewal,** revival; remaking, restructuring; **adaptation, adjustment,** accommodation, fitting; **reform, improvement; degeneration, deterioration,** worsening, disorder

2 **revolution, break,** sudden change, **upheaval,** overthrow, sea change

3 **transformation; translation; metamorphosis; permutation; displacement;** reincarnation; metabolism

4 **innovation, introduction,** discovery, invention, coinage; **breakthrough, leap; novelty**

5 **transformer, innovator;** precursor; **agent,** catalyst; yeast, ferment; **modifier**

verbs

6 **be changed, change,** turn into; **alter, mutate; vary,** diversify; **deviate, diverge,** turn, **shift,** veer, swerve, warp; change sides; **revive; improve,** mitigate; **degenerate, deteriorate, worsen**

7 **change, alter; mutate; modify;** adapt; accommodate, adjust, fit, **qualify; vary, diversify; convert, renew,** change over, exchange, **revive;** remake, **rebuild,** reconstruct, restructure; **reform, improve,** better, mitigate; **revolutionize,** subvert, overthrow, break up; worsen, deform

8 **transform, transfigure; translate**

9 **innovate,** invent, discover, **pioneer, revolutionize, introduce;** coin

adjectives

10 **changed, altered, modified,** qualified, **transformed;** translated; deviant; divergent; **converted, renewed,** revived, rebuilt; **reformed,** improved, **better; degenerate, worse,** unmitigated; subversive, **revolutionary;** changeable

815 PERMANENCE

nouns

1 **permanence, constancy,** firmness, solidity, **endurance,** duration, long standing; durability; **stability; immobility,** hardening, **rigidity**

2 **maintenance, preservation, conservation**

3 **conservative;** diehard; **right-winger,** old school

verbs

4 **remain, endure,** last, stay, persist, bide, abide, stand, hold

5 **be conservative,** save, preserve; let be, do nothing

adjectives

6 **permanent, unchanging, immutable; unchanged, unaltered,** intact; **constant, persistent,** sustained, fixed, firm, solid, steadfast, faithful; unchecked, unfailing; **lasting, enduring,** abiding, remaining, continuing; **durable; perpetual;** stable; **immobile, static,** stationary, frozen, **rigid**

7 **conservative, preservative;** backward, old-fashioned; **right-wing**

adverbs

8 **permanently,** steadfastly; **perpetually,** invariably, **forever, always;** rigidly

9 **as is, as usual**

816 CHANGEABLENESS

nouns

1 **changeableness, mutability, transience;** mobility; fluidity; **resilience, adaptability, flexibility**

2 **instability; uncertainty,** inconsistency; **variability,** restlessness; irregularity; **eccentricity**

3 **changing, variation;** alternation; **mood swings; wavering,** shifting; **exchange,** trading, musical chairs

4 (*comparisons*) kaleidoscope, chameleon, shifting sands, rolling stone; water; the weather

verbs

5 **change, fluctuate, vary; shift;** alternate, vacillate, oscillate; waver, swing, sway, wobble, flounder, stagger; **turn; exchange,** trade

adjectives

6 **changeable;** transient, **transitory; variable,** chequered; **movable,** mobile; **plastic,** rubbery, fluid; **resilient, adaptable,** adjustable, **flexible**

7 **changeable, changing, shifting,** uncertain, inconsistent; **shifty,** unreliable; **unstable,** infirm, restless, **unsettled, unsteady,** spineless, shapeless, indecisive, irresolute; **variable;** unpredictable; whimsical, **capricious, fickle; erratic, eccentric;** volatile, giddy, dizzy, moody, impulsive, impetuous; **fluctuating,** alternating, **vacillating, wavering,** wavy, flickering, fitful, shifting; irregular, spasmodic; irresponsible, uncontrolled

adverbs

8 uncertainly, **unsteadily,** erratically; **impulsively**

817 STABILITY

nouns

1 **stability, firmness, solidity; security;** reliability; **constancy;** nerve, stoicism, **cool** (*nonformal*); **equilibrium, balance; steady state; uniformity**

2 **fixture; establishment,** confirmation

3 **immobility; firmness,** solidity, rigidity; inertia

4 unchangeability, immutability; permanence

5 indestructibility, immortality; invulnerability

6 (*comparisons*) rock, bedrock, foundation

verbs

7 stabilize; firm, firm up; steady, balance; immobilize, freeze, keep, retain; transfix, stick or hold down

8 secure, tie, chain, tether; wedge, jam; fasten; anchor, moor; confirm, ratify

9 fix, define, set, settle; establish, found, ground, lodge, seat; root; set in, plant, implant, bed; print, imprint, stamp, inscribe, etch, engrave; stereotype

10 (*become firmly fixed*) root, take root; stick; seize up, freeze; lodge

11 stand fast, stay put (*nonformal*); hold out; weather

adjectives

12 stable, substantial, firm, solid, sound; rock-like; fast, secure, steady, steadfast; balanced, in equilibrium; well-balanced; unshakable, cool (*nonformal*), impassive, stolid, stoic; reliable, predictable

13 established, stabilized, entrenched, vested; confirmed; settled, set; in place; deep-rooted, deep-seated; ingrained, implanted, embedded; imprinted; engraved, etched, embossed

14 fixed, fastened, anchored, riveted; set, settled

15 immovable, immobile, stationary, frozen; firm, adamant, rigid, inflexible

16 stuck, fast, fixed, transfixed, caught, fastened, tied, chained, tethered, anchored, moored, held; jammed, congested, packed, wedged; seized up, frozen; grounded, stranded

17 unchanging, unalterable, immutable; constant, invariable; lasting, unremitting, permanent; irrevocable, irreversible; irretrievable

18 indestructible, incorruptible; immortal; invulnerable, invincible, impregnable; indelible

818 CONTINUANCE

nouns

1 continuance, continuation; extension, lengthening; survival, holding out; maintenance, sustenance; run; progress; persistence, perseverance; endurance, stamina, staying power; continuity; repetition

2 resumption, revival, renewal, reappearance; fresh start, new beginning

verbs

3 continue, carry on; remain, bide, abide, stay, linger; go on, keep on, keep going, carry on, hold on, soldier on, plug away (*nonformal*); never cease; endure

4 sustain, prolong, extend, perpetuate, lengthen; maintain, keep, hold, retain, preserve; keep up, keep going, keep alive, survive

5 persist, persevere; survive, manage, get along; go on, press on; reiterate

6 **resume, renew; revive,** resuscitate; reopen, **return to,** begin again

adjectives

7 **continuing, abiding;** staying, remaining; **continuous, ceaseless, unceasing,** unending, endless, incessant, unremitting, steady, sustained, protracted, **persistent; repetitive; resumed,** renewed, reopened

819 CESSATION

nouns

1 **cessation,** discontinuation; cease, ending, termination; **close,** shutdown; renunciation, abandonment

2 **stop,** stoppage, **halt, arrest,** check; stand, **standstill;** full stop, dead stop; **strike, walkout; end,** ending, final whistle, checkmate; **tie,** stalemate, deadlock; **terminal,** terminus

3 **pause, rest, break, recess, intermission,** interim, interval, interlude; **respite; interruption, suspension; postponement; remission;** drop, lull, lapse; truce; **holiday,** time off, day off, recess, playtime, leisure

verbs

4 **cease, discontinue, end, stop, halt,** terminate, abort, cancel, **quit; desist, refrain,** leave off; relinquish, renounce, abandon

5 **stop, halt,** stop dead, **stall; pull up; stop short; stick,** jam, hang fire, seize up, freeze; **cease fire,** stand down

6 (*stop work*) **lay off, knock off** (*nonformal*); shut down, close down; **strike,** walk out

7 **pause, rest, relax; recess,** break

8 **interrupt, suspend, break off,** cut off

9 **stop, stay, halt, arrest, check,** flag down, wave down; **block, brake, dam, stem; pull up,** draw rein; freeze, stop short, cut short; checkmate, stalemate, deadlock

10 **turn off, shut off,** shut, shut down, close; **phase out,** phase down; **kill, cut,** switch off

820 CONVERSION

nouns

1 **conversion; change,** sea change, **transformation; transition,** passage, **shift; reversal; relapse,** lapse, descent; **breakthrough; growth,** progress, development; **resolution; reduction, simplification;** assimilation, adoption, assumption

2 **new start, new beginning,** fresh start, clean slate, square one (*nonformal*); **reform, revival,** redemption, amendment, improvement, renewal, **rebirth**

3 **renunciation, desertion,** treason, abandonment; degeneration

4 **rehabilitation,** recovery, readjustment, restoration

5 **indoctrination; brainwashing;** subversion, alienation, corruption

6 **conversion,** persuasion

7 **convert,** disciple

8 traitor, deserter, **renegade**

9 **missionary,** evangelist

10 melting pot, test tube, cauldron; anvil, lathe; transformer, engine, motor, machine

verbs

11 **convert; change over, shift;** make over; **change, transform; change into, turn into, become,** bring to, reduce to; **make,** render; **reverse;** turn back

12 regroup, rearrange; renew; reclaim, redeem, amend; set straight; **reform, rehabilitate**

13 defect; desert, turn against; lapse, relapse; degenerate

14 **rehabilitate,** reclaim, recover, restore, readjust

15 **indoctrinate, brainwash;** subvert, alienate, corrupt

16 **convince, persuade, win over**

17 **turn into, become, change into, grow into,** lapse into, open into

adjectives

18 **convertible,** changeable, **transitional**

19 **converted, changed, transformed;** naturalized, assimilated; **reformed,** renewed, redeemed

20 degenerate, **renegade**

821 REVERSION

nouns

1 **reversion, relapse, regression,** lapse, slipping back; **reverse, reversal, turn; return;** disenchantment; **rehabilitation,** redemption; restoration

2 **returnee;** prodigal son

verbs

3 **revert, regress, reverse, return;** slip back, lapse, relapse

4 **turn back, change back,** go back, hark back, turn around

5 **revert to,** return to

adjectives

6 **regressive, retrograde;** reactionary

822 REVOLUTION

nouns

1 **revolution, violent change,** sweeping change, clean slate; **overthrow,** overturn, upset, convulsion, spasm, subversion; breakdown; **cataclysm, catastrophe, debacle; revolution; revolt**

2 anarchism, terrorism

3 **revolutionary; rebel;** anarchist, terrorist; subversive; Marxist, Communist, Red

verbs

4 **revolutionize; overthrow, overturn,** upset; **revolt**

adjectives

5 **revolutionary;** cataclysmic, catastrophic; **radical,** sweeping

6 **revolutionary;** Marxist, Communist

823 EVOLUTION

nouns

1 **evolution;** gradual change; **development, growth,** rise; flowering, blossoming; ripening; accomplishment; **advance,** advancement; **progress,** progression; **elaboration,** enlargement, amplification, **expansion**

2 **unfolding,** unrolling, unwinding; revelation

3 genesis; biological evolution;
natural selection, adaptation

verbs

**4 evolve; develop, grow; progress,
advance;** accomplish; ripen, mellow, mature; flower, bloom, blossom, bear fruit

5 elaborate, develop, work out,
enlarge, amplify; **expand,** detail, flesh out, spell out (*nonformal*); complete

6 unfold, unroll, unwind, reveal

adjectives

7 evolutionary; evolving, developing, unfolding; maturing; progressing, advancing

824 SUBSTITUTION

nouns

**1 substitution, exchange, change,
switch; representation,** deputation, **delegation; agency; replacement;** provision

2 substitute, substitution, replacement; change, exchange;
counterfeit, imitation, copy; surrogate; reserves, bench (*nonformal*), spares; **alternate,** alternative; **successor; proxy,** dummy, ghost; vicar, agent, representative; **deputy; vice, vice-president, etc; relief, stand-in, understudy;** double; **equivalent,** equal; analogy, comparison; **metaphor; symbol, sign,** token, icon

3 scapegoat, whipping boy

verbs

**4 substitute, exchange, change,
switch; pass off**

5 substitute for; act for; relieve,
cover for; ghost; **represent; supplant, supersede,** succeed, **replace,** displace, crowd out

6 delegate, deputize, commission

adjectives

7 substitute, alternate, alternative, other, equivalent, token, dummy, utility, secondary; ad hoc, provisional; mock, counterfeit, imitation; **proxy;** makeshift, reserve, **spare,** stopgap, temporary, provisional

adverbs

8 instead, rather; by proxy

825 INTERCHANGE

nouns

1 interchange, exchange; cooperation; permutation; alternation; **interplay, compromise; give-and-take, retaliation;** cross fire

2 trading, trade, swap (*nonformal*), **switch;** barter

verbs

3 interchange, exchange, change; alternate; convert, commute; **trade, swap** (*nonformal*), **switch; reciprocate, trade off,** compromise, settle, respond; pay back, compensate, return; **retaliate; cooperate**

adjectives

4 interchangeable, changeable, standard; equivalent; **even,** equal; **convertible;** retaliatory; **reciprocal; mutual,** give-and-take

adverbs

5 **interchangeably; in exchange, in return;** evenly; mutually; **in turn,** by turns, turn about

826 GENERALITY

nouns

1 **generality; generalization; labelling,** stereotyping

2 **prevalence, currency,** occurrence; **normality**

3 **all, everyone, everybody, whole, totality; everything**

4 **any, anything,** any one, either; **anybody, anyone**

5 **whatever, whatsoever, what, whichever**

6 **whoever, whomever,** anyone

7 (*idea or expression*) **generalization,** general idea, **abstraction,** sweeping statement; **platitude, conventional wisdom,** commonplace

verbs

8 **generalize; broaden, widen,** expand, extend, spread; **label,** stereotype

9 **prevail, predominate,** dominate, reign, rule; be in (*nonformal*)

adjectives

10 **general, generalized,** generic, **indefinite,** indeterminate, vague, abstract, nebulous, unspecified, bland, neutral

11 **prevalent, prevailing, common,** popular, **current;** reigning, **ruling, predominant, dominant;** rife, rampant, epidemic; **ordinary, normal, average, usual,** routine, standard, stereotyped

12 **extensive, broad, wide,** liberal, diffuse, large-scale, **sweeping;** widespread, **far-reaching; wholesale, indiscriminate**

13 **universal,** galactic, planetary, world-wide, **global; total;** cosmopolitan, international; **national**

14 **every, all,** any, whichever; **each,** each one; every one

15 **trite, commonplace,** hackneyed, overworked, stereotyped

adverbs

16 **generally, in general;** generally speaking, **broadly, roughly; usually, ordinarily, commonly, normally;** at large, altogether, overall; **predominantly, mostly,** chiefly, mainly

17 **universally; everywhere, all over,** internationally; without exception, **invariably, always**

827 PARTICULARITY

nouns

1 **particularity, individuality, differentiation,** uniqueness; identity; **personality,** soul; wholeness, integrity; **individualism**

2 **speciality,** specialness, **specificness,** definiteness

3 **the specific,** the special, **the particular,** the concrete, the individual, the unique; original

4 **characteristic, peculiarity,** speciality, individualism, **character,** nature, **trait,** quirk, mannerism, **feature; mark,** marking, hallmark, index; badge, token; **brand,** cast, stamp, seal, mould, cut, figure, shape; impression; **idiosyncrasy; quality, property,**

attribute; savour, flavour, taste, aroma, odour, smack, tang, taint

5 **self, ego; oneself, I,** myself, me, myself, number one (*nonformal*), yours truly (*nonformal*); yourself, himself, herself, itself, ourselves, yourselves; themselves; you; he, she; him, her; they, them; it; inner self, inner man; other self, alter ego

6 **specification, designation,** denomination; **allocation,** attribution, selection, assignment

7 **specialization;** individualization, personalization

8 **characterization,** distinction, **differentiation;** definition, description

verbs

9 **specialize; individualize,** personalize; itemize, detail, spell out

10 **characterize, distinguish, differentiate, define, describe; mark,** mark out, **set apart;** be characteristic

11 **specify, designate, stipulate,** determine, single out, feature, highlight, focus on, mention, select, pick out, **fix,** set, assign, pin down; **name,** state, mark, **indicate, signify,** point out

adjectives

12 **particular, special, specific, express,** precise, **concrete; singular, individual; personal,** private, intimate, inner; **fixed, definite, defined,** distinct, different, certain, absolute; **distinguished,** noteworthy, **exceptional, extraordinary;** minute, detailed

13 **characteristic, peculiar, singular,** single, intrinsic, unique, dis-

tinctive, marked, distinguished, notable; appropriate, proper; idiosyncratic, **in character**

14 **this,** this one; **these; that,** that one; those

adverbs

15 **particularly, specially, especially, specifically,** expressly, exactly, precisely, **in particular; definitely, distinctly;** in detail, singly, separately

16 **personally,** privately, **individually; in person**

17 **characteristically, peculiarly,** singularly, intrinsically, **uniquely,** markedly, **distinctively**

18 **namely,** nominally

19 **each, apiece;** respectively

828 SPECIALITY

nouns

1 **speciality, line, pursuit, pet subject, business, field,** area, main interest; **vocation; forte, strong point; specialization;** way, manner, **style,** type; **lifestyle,** preferences

2 **special, feature,** main feature; **leader,** lead item

3 **specialist, expert, authority,** scholar, connoisseur; technician; pundit, critic; amateur; fan, buff

verbs

4 **specialize, feature; narrow, restrict,** limit, confine; specialize in, **be into** (*nonformal*), follow, pursue

adjectives

5 **specialized,** specialist; technical; **restricted, limited,** confined;

featured; expert, authoritative, knowledgeable

829 CONFORMITY

nouns

1 **conformity; compliance,** acquiescence, obedience, observance, **orthodoxy;** strictness; **accordance, correspondence,** harmony, agreement; **uniformity; consistency; accommodation,** adaptation, flexibility, adjustment; reconciliation

2 **conformist,** sheep, parrot, yesman; **conventionalist**

verbs

3 **conform, comply, correspond,** accord, harmonize; **adapt,** adjust, **accommodate,** bend, meet, suit, fit, shape; agree with, go by, observe, follow, yield; reconcile, settle, compose; shape, mould; rectify, correct, **discipline**

4 **toe the line; fit in;** pass muster

adjectives

5 **adaptable,** adjustable; flexible, submissive, obedient

6 **conformist, conventional; orthodox;** kosher; in accord, in keeping, in line, in step; **corresponding,** harmonious

adverbs

7 in conformity, **obediently,** submissively; **conventionally,** traditionally

830 NONCONFORMITY

nouns

1 **nonconformity, inconsistency,** incongruity; originality; **dissent, protest, disagreement; deviation**

2 heresy, originality

3 **nonconformist, original,** eccentric, deviant, maverick (*nonformal*), dropout, Bohemian, hippie, freak (*nonformal*); **misfit,** ugly duckling; **dissenter; heretic**

verbs

4 break step; drop out, opt out; **dissent, protest**

adjectives

5 contrary; **deviant,** unusual; **dissenting, dissident**

6 **unconventional, unorthodox, eccentric,** heretical; unfashionable, not done; breakaway; original, maverick

7 **out of line,** out of step

831 NORMALITY

nouns

1 **normality, naturalness;** health, propriety, **regularity;** realism; **order**

2 mediocrity; **generality, prevalence,** currency

3 **the normal, the usual, the ordinary, the common,** the commonplace, the day-to-day

4 **rule, law, principle, standard,** criterion, canon, code, maxim, prescription, guideline, regulation; **norm, model,** ideal; **form, formula**

verbs

5 **normalize, standardize, regularize;** codify, formalize

adjectives

6 **normal, natural; general;** typical; prescribed, model, ideal, desired; realistic; **orderly**

7 **usual, regular; customary,** habitual, accustomed, standard, regulation, conventional; **common, commonplace, ordinary,** average, **everyday,** mediocre, familiar, household, vernacular, stock; **prevailing, predominating,** current, popular; **universal**

adverbs

8 **normally, naturally; regularly; typically,** usually, commonly, ordinarily, customarily, habitually, generally; mostly, chiefly, mainly; **as usual**

832 ABNORMALITY

nouns

1 **abnormality;** strangeness; **anomaly; aberration; irregularity, deviation,** divergence, **difference; eccentricity; monstrosity**

2 **rarity,** uniqueness; impossibility

3 **oddity, peculiarity, absurdity; strangeness;** monstrosity, deformity

4 (odd person) oddity, **oddball** and **weirdo** (both nonformal); **eccentric; fanatic, crank,** zealot; **outsider,** foreigner; **alien;** loner, hermit; tramp; maverick; **outcast,** outlaw, scapegoat; **nonconformist**

5 (odd thing) **oddity, curiosity, anomaly; rarity,** exception; conversation piece

6 **monstrosity, monster,** abortion, **freak**

7 **the supernatural, the occult,** mystery, strangeness

8 **miracle, sign, wonder;** fantasy

adjectives

9 **abnormal, unnatural; anomalous, irregular,** eccentric, erratic, divergent, **different;** stray, wandering; formless, shapeless; **subnormal**

10 **unusual, uncommon, unfamiliar, rare, unique,** breakaway; unexpected

11 **odd, queer, peculiar, absurd,** singular, curious, quaint, eccentric, funny, rum; **strange,** surreal, **weird,** unearthly

12 **fantastic,** fanciful, **unbelievable, impossible, incredible,** incomprehensible, unimaginable, unexpected, inconceivable

13 **monstrous, deformed,** misshapen, **grotesque, bizarre**

14 **extraordinary, exceptional, remarkable,** noteworthy, **wonderful, marvellous,** fabulous, mythical, legendary; **stupendous,** prodigious, phenomenal; unprecedented; indescribable, unspeakable

15 **supernatural, superhuman, unearthly,** unworldly, eerie; **spiritual; mysterious**

16 **miraculous, prodigious; magical,** enchanted, bewitched

adverbs

17 **unusually, uncommonly, incredibly, unnaturally,** abnormally, unexpectedly; **rarely, seldom,** hardly ever

18 **extraordinarily, exceptionally, remarkably, wonderfully, marvellously,** fabulously

19 **oddly, peculiarly,** singularly, curiously, **strangely, fantastically,** grotesquely; eerily, mysteriously

833 LIST

nouns

1 **list, items, schedule, register; inventory,** repertory; tally sheet; waiting list; short list

2 **table,** contents

3 **catalogue; bibliography; file**

4 **dictionary,** word list, **glossary, thesaurus, vocabulary,** terminology

5 **bill,** statement, account, ledger, books; **menu,** invoice

6 **roll, roster,** scroll, rota; **roll call,** muster, **census, poll,** questionnaire, returns; **calendar, agenda, program**

7 **index, listing, cataloguing,** filing, card file, thumb index; **registration,** registry

verbs

8 **list, enumerate, catalogue,** tally; **register,** post, enrol, enrol; **file, index;** calendar; **schedule**

adjectives

9 **listed, enumerated, entered, catalogued,** tallied; filed; **scheduled,** programmed

834 ONENESS

(state of being one)

nouns

1 **unity, individuality,** identity; **uniqueness;** purity, simplicity, **integrity, unification,** integration, fusion, combination; solidity, solidarity, **wholeness; uniformity**

2 **loneliness, privacy, solitude;** aloofness, detachment, seclusion, **withdrawal, alienation, isolation;** celibacy

3 **one, I, unit,** ace, atom; none else, no other, nothing else

4 **individual, entity, item,** article, point; person, soul, body; **individuality**

verbs

5 **unify,** make one; **integrate, unite**

6 **stand alone,** withdraw

adjectives

7 **one, single, singular, individual, sole, unique, solitary, lone;** exclusive; **integral,** indivisible, atomic, undivided, solid, uniform, simple, whole; an, any, either

8 **alone, solitary, solo, isolated,** insular, apart, separate, alienated, withdrawn, aloof, detached, removed; **lone, lonely, private,** reserved, reticent, shy; **friendless, unaccompanied,** unattended; **unaided, single-handed,** solo

9 **sole, unique,** singular, absolute, **alone,** lone, **only;** odd

10 **integrated,** integral; **unified,** united, composite

11 **unilateral, one-sided**

12 **unifying, uniting, combining;** connecting

adverbs

13 **singly, individually,** particularly; **singularly, alone, solo, unaided;** separately, apart; **once**

14 **solely, exclusively, only,** merely, **purely,** simply; **entirely, wholly,** totally

835 DOUBLENESS

nouns

1 **pairing, coupling; doubling,** duplication; **dichotomy,** halving; **duplicity,** hypocrisy; **irony,** ambiguity

2 **two, couple, pair, twosome,** duet; match, mates; **the two, both**

3 **twins,** identical twins; Siamese twins

verbs

4 **double,** duplicate, twin; **halve,** bisect; **mate, match,** couple; **pair,** pair off, pair up

adjectives

5 **two, dual, double,** doubled, duplicated; bisected; twin, identical, matched, duplicated; hypocritical

6 **both,** the two, the pair

7 **coupled, paired,** matched, matted

836 DUPLICATION

nouns

1 **duplication,** reproduction, doubling; **repetition,** echoing; **imitation,** parroting; **copying; duplicate**

2 **repeat,** encore; echo

verbs

3 **duplicate,** ditto (*nonformal*); **double,** double up; **twin; reproduce,** redouble; **repeat; copy**

adjectives

4 **double, doubled, duplicate,** duplicated, reproduced, cloned

adverbs

5 **doubly;** twice, two times

6 **secondly,** second

7 **again,** another time, **once more,** once again, over again, **anew,** afresh, freshly, newly

837 BISECTION

nouns

1 halving; **dichotomy, halving, division;** subdivision; forking, branching

2 **half;** hemisphere, semicircle, **fifty percent**

3 **diameter,** equator, halfway mark, partition, boundary

verbs

4 **bisect, halve, divide,** subdivide; fission, fork, branch

adjectives

5 **half, part, partly, partial,** halfway

6 **halved, bisected, divided;** branched, branching; **split,** cleft

adverbs

7 **in half, in two,** by two; apart

838 PLURALITY

(more than one)

nouns

1 **several,** some, a few, more; plural number, the plural; variety

2 **majority, most, bulk, mass;** lion's share

3 multiplication, multiplying, proliferation, **increase; duplication;**
multiple

verbs

4 multiply, proliferate, **increase,
duplicate; pluralize**

adjectives

5 plural, more, several; **some;** various; many, numerous

6 multiple, multiplied, **manifold;**
increased

7 majority, most

adverbs

8 and others, et cetera

839 NUMEROUSNESS

nouns

1 multiplicity, profusion; **plenty,**
abundance

2 (*indefinite number*) **a number, a
few,** several, umpteen (*nonformal*)

3 (*large number*) **multitude,
throng;** numbers, quantities,
lots, **scores, host, army,** legion,
mob; **swarm, flock,** bevy, pack,
bunch

4 (*immense number*) **a myriad,** a
thousand, a million, a billion, etc

verbs

5 teem with, abound with, swarm
with, crawl with; clutter, crowd,
jam, pack, overwhelm, overflow;
multiply; outnumber

adjectives

6 numerous, many, manifold;
multiple, **myriad,** thousand, million, billion

7 several, sundry, various

8 abundant, copious, ample, **plentiful**

9 teeming, swarming, thronging,
overcrowded, **crawling,** proliferating, crowded, packed, jammed,
rife, lavish, prodigal, **profuse,**
thick

10 innumerable, countless, untold,
incalculable, immeasurable, inexhaustible, endless, infinite

adverbs

11 profusely, thickly, copiously,
abundantly; infinitely, immeasurably; **no end** (*nonformal*)

840 FEWNESS

nouns

1 scarcity, rarity; smallness

2 a few, handful, scattering, sprinkling, trickle

3 minority, least; the minority, the
few

adjectives

4 few, not many

5 sparse, scant, **infrequent,** scarce,
poor, thin, slim, meagre; miserly,
tight; **scattered,** sprinkled; rare

6 fewer, less, smaller

7 minority, least

adverbs

8 sparsely, thinly; **scarcely,** rarely,
infrequently; in places

841 CAUSE

nouns

1 cause, occasion, grounds, background, stimulus, base, **basis,** element, principle, factor; **causa-**
tion

2 reason, rationale, underlying reason, **explanation; pretext, pretence, excuse**

3 immediate cause, trigger, spark; **domino effect,** ripple effect; provocation, **last straw**

4 author, agent, **originator,** generator, producer, maker, beginner, **creator, parent, mother, father;** instigator, catalyst

5 source, origin, derivation, **rise, beginning,** conception, inception, commencement, **head; background; root,** grass roots; stem, stock

6 well, spring, fountain, font; mine, quarry

7 egg, germ, nucleus, **seed; embryo;** bud; **loins; womb,** matrix, uterus

8 birthplace, breeding ground; incubator; **nest, cradle,** nursery

9 principle, interest, issue, burning issue, commitment, faith; **movement,** activity; **drive, campaign, crusade;** zeal, passion, fanaticism

verbs

10 cause, bring about, effect, realize; **impact,** influence; **occasion, make, create, engender,** generate, **produce,** breed; **originate,** spark, set off, trigger; bear, bring forth, author, **father, conceive;** set up, found, establish, inaugurate, institute

11 induce, lead, procure, get, obtain, contrive; **effect, bring on, call forth, elicit, evoke, provoke,** inspire, influence, instigate, egg on, **motivate**

12 determine, decide; **necessitate,** entail, require; contribute to, lead to, **advance, forward,** influence

adjectives

13 causal; formative, decisive

14 original, primary, primitive, primeval, **elementary,** elemental, **basic, rudimentary,** crucial, central, radical, **fundamental;** embryonic, pregnant

842 EFFECT

nouns

1 effect, result, consequence, sequel; eventuality, **upshot, outcome;** spin-off, offshoot, offspring, issue, aftermath, legacy; **product, fruit,** first fruits, crop, harvest; **development, corollary;** derivative, by-product

2 impact, force, reaction; backlash, reflex, response; **mark, imprint,** impression

3 aftermath; wake, trail

verbs

4 result, ensue, issue, follow, attend, accompany; **turn out,** fare; prove; **become of,** come of, come about; **develop,** unfold; terminate, end; **end up,** come out

5 result from, come from, emerge from, **spring from, stem from; depend on,** hang on

adjectives

6 resultant, following, ensuing; consequent, entailed, required; **final;** derivative

adverbs

7 in consequence, naturally, necessarily, inevitably, of course, and so; **therefore; accordingly; finally**

843 ATTRIBUTION

nouns

1 **attribution, assignment,** assignation, placement, application, attachment, **charge, blame; indictment; responsibility, credit, honour**

2 citation, tribute; confession; **reference;** trademark, signature

verbs

3 **attribute, assign, ascribe,** give, place, put, apply, attach, refer

4 **attribute to, ascribe to,** assign to, refer to, point to; **pin on,** attach to, connect with, fasten upon, saddle with; blame, indict, **charge to;** acknowledge, confess

5 trace to, derive from; father

adjectives

6 accountable, explicable; owing, **due,** derivative; **charged,** alleged; **credited, attributed**

adverbs

7 **hence, therefore,** whence, then, thence, **accordingly;** for that; thus

8 **why,** how come (*nonformal*), **what for,** for which

844 OPERATION

nouns

1 **operation, functioning, action, performance, working, work,** exercise, practice; agency; management, direction, conduct, running, execution, oversight; **handling,** manipulation; responsibility; **occupation**

2 **process, procedure,** course; **act,** step, measure, initiative, move, manoeuvre

3 **feasibility,** viability

4 **operator; handler; manager, executive;** agent; driver

verbs

5 **operate, function, run, work; manage, direct, conduct;** perform; **handle,** manipulate, manoeuvre; deal with, see to; be responsible

6 operate on, **work on, affect, influence,** bear on

7 (*be operative*) **operate, function, work, act, perform, go, run**

8 **function as,** work as, **act as**

adjectives

9 **operative, operational, functional,** practical; effective, efficient

10 **workable,** manageable, negotiable; **practicable, feasible,** practical, viable

11 **operating, operational, working, functioning,** functional, active, running, **going; in operation, in practice, in force,** at work; in hand

12 operational, functional; **managerial**

845 PRODUCTIVENESS

nouns

1 **productivity; fertility, pregnancy;** richness, **abundance**

2 proliferation, multiplication; **reproduction, production**

3 **fertilization,** enrichment

4 **fertilizer,** dressing; manure, dung, compost; phosphate, ammonia, nitrogen, nitrate

verbs

5 **produce, be productive, proliferate,** be fruitful, **multiply,** engender; **reproduce**

6 **fertilize, enrich,** fatten, feed; impregnate; dress, manure

adjectives

7 **productive, fruitful, fertile, pregnant, rich,** flourishing, thriving, blooming; **prolific, teeming,** swarming, bursting, **plentiful,** copious, generous, **abundant, luxuriant, lush**

8 **bearing,** yielding, producing

9 **fertilizing, enriching,** fattening

846 UNPRODUCTIVE-NESS

nouns

1 **unfruitfulness, barrenness,** dryness, aridity, famine; **sterility, infertility; birth control, contraception,** family planning; abortion; impotence, incapacity

2 **wasteland,** desolation, barren land; **desert, dust bowl;** .desert island; **wilderness,** wilds; bush, outback (*Australia*)

verbs

3 be unproductive, **lie fallow**

adjectives

4 **unproductive, infertile, sterile,** impotent, ineffectual; **barren, desert, arid,** dry, dried-up, exhausted, drained, **waste, desolate; childless;** fallow; celibate; virgin

5 unoriginal, derivative

847 PRODUCTION

nouns

1 **production, creation, invention, conception,** originating, beginning; **devising,** fabrication, **concoction,** coinage, contrivance; **generation**

2 **production, making,** design, fashioning, formation, formulation; engineering, processing, conversion; casting, **shaping,** moulding; **assembly,** composition; **workmanship, craftsmanship, skill; construction, building,** erection, architecture; **fabrication; mining,** extraction, **refining; growing,** cultivation, **raising,** harvesting

3 **industry, mass production,** production line, assembly line; industrialization; **cottage industry**

4 **establishment, foundation,** constitution, institution, installation, formation, **organization,** inauguration, **inception**

5 **performance, execution, accomplishment, achievement,** realization, operation

6 **bearing, yielding; fruition**

7 **producer, maker,** craftsman; **manufacturer,** industrialist; **creator, author;** mother, father; ancestors; **precursor; originator,** instigator; **founder,** organizer, founding father; **inventor,** discoverer; engineer; **builder, architect,** planner, designer

verbs

8 **produce, create, make,** manufacture, **form,** formulate, evolve, fashion, **fabricate,** cast, shape, carve out, mould, frame; **construct, build,** erect, put up, raise, rear; make up, prepare, compose, write, devise, design, concoct, **put together, assemble**

9 **process,** convert; carve, chisel; **mine,** extract, pump, **refine; raise,** rear, **grow,** cultivate, harvest

10 **establish, found,** institute, install, form, **set up, organize,** inaugurate, realize, materialize

11 **perform, do,** work, act, execute, **accomplish, achieve,** re-alize, engineer, **bring about,** cause; mass-produce, industrialize

12 **originate, invent, conceive,** discover, **make up, devise,** contrive, concoct, fabricate, coin, mint, frame, hatch; think up, **design,** plan; **generate, develop,** mature, **evolve;** breed, engender, spawn, hatch

13 **bear, yield, produce;** bring forth; bear fruit

adjectives

14 **manufacturing, industrial**

15 **structural,** building; housing; **architectural**

16 **creative, productive, constructive,** formative; inventive

17 **produced, made;** executed, performed, done; grown, raised

18 **made,** man-made; **manufactured,** created, formed, shaped, cast, forged, fashioned, **built, constructed,** fabricated; **mass-**produced; homemade, hand-made, **processed; assembled; custom-made,** purpose-built; **ready-made;** prefabricated; **mined,** extracted, **refined; grown, raised,** harvested, gathered

19 **invented,** originated, **conceived,** discovered; fabricated, coined, minted

adverbs

20 **in production;** in hand; under construction

848 PRODUCT

nouns

1 **product,** end product; **work, handiwork, artefact; creation;** creature; **offspring,** child, fruit; **result, effect,** issue, outcome; **invention,** coinage, brainchild; **concoction,** composition

2 **production,** produce, proceeds, net, **yield, output, crop,** harvest, return

3 **extract, distillation,** essence; **by-product,** spin-off, offshoot; **residue,** waste, dregs, ash

849 INFLUENCE

nouns

1 **influence, power,** force, clout (*nonformal*), potency, pressure, say; prestige, favour, credit, esteem, **personality, leadership, charisma, magnetism, charm; weight,** consequence, importance, eminence; **authority,** control, **domination; hold; sway, reign, rule; mastery,** supremacy, dominance, predominance; lev-

erage, purchase; **persuasion, suggestion**

2 favour, interest; **connections**

3 intrigues, deals, schemes, **games**, ploys; lobbying

4 orbit; vantage, footing, **territory**, turf, constituency, **power base**

5 openness; weakness

6 heavyweight, hidden hand, manipulator, **pressure group**, lobby; the Establishment, powers that be

verbs

7 **influence, affect, sway**, bias, incline, predispose, **move**, prompt, lead; colour, slant; **induce, persuade**, work; wear down, soften up; ingratiate oneself

8 (*exercise influence over*) **govern, rule, control**, order, **regulate**, direct, guide; **determine**, decide

9 lean on (*nonformal*), **work on**, bear upon; **approach**; lobby

10 **have influence, be influential, weigh, tell, count**, cut ice, be persuasive

11 hypnotize, mesmerize, **dominate**

12 gain influence; take hold, move in

adjectives

13 **influential, powerful, potent, strong**; **effective**, telling; **weighty**, momentous, important, substantial, **prestigious**, authoritative, reputable; **persuasive, winning**, magnetic, charming, enchanting, charismatic

14 **dominant, predominant**, ruling, swaying, prevailing; **ascendant**

15 open-minded, accessible, receptive, responsive, amenable; vul-

nerable; pliable; **susceptible, impressionable**, weak

850 ABSENCE OF INFLUENCE

nouns

1 powerlessness, impotence; **weakness**

2 invulnerability; **obstinacy**

adjectives

3 **powerless**, impotent; **weak, ineffective**, ineffectual; lightweight

4 inflexible; **unpersuadable**, unresponsive; impervious, closed to; invulnerable; **obstinate**

851 TENDENCY

nouns

1 **tendency, inclination, leaning**, weakness; liability; readiness, willingness, eagerness, aptitude, **disposition, propensity**, affinity, prejudice, **liking**, delight, soft spot; hunger; thirst; **bent, turn, bias**, slant; probability

2 trend, drift, course, current, flow, stream, movement, motion, run, **tenor**, tone, **set**, swing, bearing, line, direction

verbs

3 **tend, incline**, be disposed, **lean, trend**, set, **go**, turn, tilt, bias, bend to, swing toward, point to, look to

adjectives

4 **tending**; leaning, inclining

852 LIABILITY

nouns

1 **liability; probability,** contingency, chance, eventuality; possibility; responsibility; indebtedness

2 **liability,** openness, exposure; vulnerability

verbs

3 **be liable;** gamble; owe

4 **incur,** invite, welcome, **bring on;** fall into; get, gain, acquire

adjectives

5 **liable, likely, prone;** probable; responsible, answerable; **in debt,** indebted; **exposed, susceptible,** at risk, open, **vulnerable**

6 **liable to, subject to,** dependent on; **capable of,** ready for; **likely to,** apt to; obliged to

853 INVOLVEMENT

nouns

1 **involvement, implication, entanglement,** engagement; **inclusion; absorption**

verbs

2 **involve, implicate,** tangle, engage, **draw in,** interest, concern; absorb

3 **be involved, be into** (*nonformal*), participate

adjectives

4 **involved, implicated;** interested, concerned; **included**

5 **involved in,** implicated in, enmeshed in, **absorbed in**

854 CONCURRENCE

nouns

1 **collaboration; cooperation; agreement; coincidence;** accompaniment; **union, conjunction,** combination, association, alliance; conspiracy, collusion; **accordance,** correspondence

verbs

2 **concur, collaborate, cooperate;** conspire, collude, connive; **combine, unite, associate,** join; harmonize; **coincide,** synchronize; **accord,** correspond, **agree**

adjectives

3 **concurrent; collaborative,** collective; conspiratorial; **united, joint, combined, concerted,** associated; concomitant, accompanying; **agreeing,** harmonious

adverbs

4 **concurrently, jointly,** in concert, **together;** as one

855 COUNTERACTION

nouns

1 **opposition, contradiction;** antagonism, antipathy, **conflict, friction,** interference, clashing, collision; reaction, **backlash, recoil,** backfire; resistance, dissent, revolt

2 cancellation, frustration, undoing; **offsetting,** counterbalancing, balancing

3 **antidote,** remedy, offset; buffer

4 **counterbalance;** undercurrent; cross wind

5 **retort,** comeback (*nonformal*); defence

verbs

6 **counteract**, counter; **oppose**, antagonize; **resist**, fight back, defend oneself; **dissent**; **cross**, **contradict**, contravene, **conflict**, **clash**, collide

7 **neutralize**, annul, cancel, negate, invalidate, void, frustrate, thwart, undo; **offset**, **counterbalance**

adjectives

8 **counteracting**, **opposing**; contradictory; **antagonistic**, hostile, inimical, repugnant, **conflicting**, **clashing**; reactionary; resistant, dissident, revolutionary, breakaway, nonconformist, perverse

9 **neutralizing**, stultifying; **balanced**, poised, offset; **offsetting**, counterbalancing

adverbs

10 **in opposition to**, counter to

856 SUPPORT

nouns

1 **support**, **backing**, **aid**; **upkeep**, maintenance, **sustaining**, sustenance; **reinforcement**; subsidy; **power base**, **constituency**, **party**; **approval**; assent

2 **supporter**, **support**; bearer, carrier; staff, walking stick, crutch; **advocate**; **stay**, **prop**; **mainstay**, backbone, spine, neck; athletic supporter; brassiere, bra (*nonformal*), corset, girdle; **reinforcement**; **backing**

3 **buttress**; **embankment**, bank; **breakwater**, jetty; pier; beam

4 **footing**, **foothold**, hold, perch; stand

5 **foundation**, **base**, basis, footing, basement, pavement, **ground**, groundwork, seat; **fundamental**, **principle**; premise; root, radical

6 **foundation stone**, **cornerstone**, headstone

7 **base**, **pedestal**; **stand**, standard; **shaft**, **upright**, **column**, **pillar**, **post**, jack, pole, staff, pier, banister, balustrade; **trunk**, stem, stalk

verbs

8 **support**, bear, carry, **hold**, **sustain**, **maintain**, **bolster**, **reinforce**, back, back up, shoulder, **hold up**, **bear up**, bolster up, keep up, buoy up; **uphold**, upkeep; shore; stay, mainstay; **underlie**; cradle; cushion, pillow; **subsidize**; assent; concur; **approve**

9 **rest on**, **stand on**, **lie on**, recline on, **lean on**, **sit on**, perch, ride; rely on

adjectives

10 **supporting**, **supportive**, **bearing**, carrying, burdened; **holding**, upholding, maintaining, sustaining

11 **supported**, **borne**, **upheld**, **sustained**, maintained; bolstered

adverbs

12 **on**, **across**, astride

857 IMPULSE, IMPACT

nouns

1 **impulse**; **drive**, **power**; **force**; **clout** (*nonformal*); **impetus**; **momentum**; incitement, incentive, compulsion

2 **thrust, push, shove,** boost (*nonformal*); **pressure; stress;** press; **prod, poke, punch,** jab, dig, nudge; **bump,** jolt; **jostle, hustle; butt**

3 **impact, collision,** clash, **encounter,** meeting, **bump, crash; shock,** brunt; concussion, percussion; hammering; **onslaught**

4 **hit, blow,** stroke, knock, rap, pound, buffet, slam, bang, crack, **whack, smack,** smash, dash, swipe, swing, **punch; beating**

5 **punch,** blow; box, cuff

6 **tap, rap, pat,** dab, touch, tip; **flick,** brush; **peck**

7 **slap,** smack, **spank;** whip, **lash**

8 **kick,** boot; punt, kicking

9 **stamp,** stomp (*nonformal*), clump

verbs

10 **impel; drive, move,** animate; **thrust,** power; goad; **propel;** motivate, incite; compel

11 **thrust, push, shove,** boost (*nonformal*); press, stress, bear upon; **ram;** bulldoze, muscle, steamroller; **drive, force,** run; **prod, poke, punch,** jab, dig, nudge; **bump,** jog, jolt, shake, rattle; **jostle,** hustle; elbow, shoulder; **butt;** assault

12 **collide, clash,** meet, encounter; **bump, hit,** strike, knock, bang; run into, bump into, **crash into,** impact; **crash,** smash

13 **hit, strike, knock; poke,** punch, jab, **smack,** clap, crack, swipe, **whack; thump,** snap

14 **pound, beat,** hammer, maul, knock, rap, bang, thump, buffet, batter, pulverize, paste (*nonfor-*

mal), pummel, pelt; thrash; spank; whip

15 (*nonformal terms*) **clobber,** rough up, deck, wallop

16 **tap, rap, pat,** dab, touch, tip; **flick,** tickle, graze, brush; **peck**

17 **slap, smack; box, cuff;** buffet; **spank;** whip

18 **kick,** boot; knee

19 **stamp,** stomp (*nonformal*), trample, tread

adjectives

impelling

20 **impelling; moving,** motive, **driving;** thrusting

21 crashing, smashing

858 REACTION

nouns

1 **reaction, response,** feedback; reply, answer; **reflex,** reflection; echo, bounce back, resonance; return; revulsion

2 **recoil,** resilience, **bounce,** bound, spring, **rebuff; backlash, backfire,** boomerang; ricochet

3 recoil; evasion, avoidance; **flinch,** wince, cringe; **side step,** shy; **dodge, duck** (*nonformal*)

verbs

4 **react, respond,** reply, answer

5 **recoil, bounce, bound, spring;** kick back; **backfire, boomerang;** backlash, lash back; ricochet

6 retreat, recoil, fade, **fall back,** reel back; **shrink, flinch,** wince, **cringe;** shy, evade, avoid, sidestep, cop out (*nonformal*); **dodge, duck** (*nonformal*); swerve

adjectives

7 **responsive; reactionary; reflex,**
reflexive

8 **recoiling, resilient; bouncing,**
bouncy, springy

859 PUSHING, THROWING

nouns

1 **pushing,** propelling; shoving;
drive, thrust, motive power,
driving force; **push, shove;** butt;
shunt

2 **throwing, projection,** flinging,
slinging; **pitching, tossing,** casting, hurling, lobbing, chucking,
heaving, bowling, rolling; **shooting,** firing, gunning; archery

3 **throw,** toss, fling, sling, hurl, lob,
heave, shy; pitch, toss; flip; put;
(*football*) pass; (*tennis*) serve;
service; bowl

4 **shot,** discharge; gunfire; gun,
cannon; bullet; **volley,** spray;
gunshot

5 **missile;** ball; discus

6 **propeller;** propellant, driver;
wheel; piston

7 **pitcher,** bowler

8 shot; **gunner, gunman;** hunter;
archer; **marksman**

verbs

9 **push, propel,** impel, **shove,**
thrust; **drive, move,** forward, advance; project; butt; shunt; pedal; **roll,** bowl, trundle

10 **throw, fling, sling, pitch, toss,**
cast, hurl, heave, chuck, lob,
shy, launch, dash, let fly, let rip;
flip; bowl; pass; serve; put

11 **shoot, fire,** let off, let fly, **discharge,** eject; detonate; shoot at,
gun for (*nonformal*); strike, hit,
plug (*nonformal*); shoot down,
fell, drop; **riddle, pepper,** pelt;
torpedo; **load, prime, charge;**
cock

12 **start,** start up, crank up; **launch,**
float; send; bundle off

adjectives

13 propelling; **motive; driving,
pushing, shoving**

14 **ballistic, missile**

860 PULLING

nouns

1 **pulling, drawing, draft,** dragging,
heaving, tugging, towing; **pull;
hauling;** attraction; extraction

2 **pull, draw,** heave, haul, **tug,**
strain, drag

3 **jerk, yank** (*nonformal*), **twitch,**
pluck, hitch, wrench

verbs

4 **pull, draw,** heave, haul, lug, **tug,
tow;** trail, train; **drag**

5 **jerk, yank** (*nonformal*); **twitch,**
pluck, snatch, hitch, wrench

adjectives

6 **pulling, drawing,** hauling, tugging, towing

861 LEVERAGE, PURCHASE

nouns

1 **leverage, purchase, hold,** advantage; **foothold,** footing

2 **fulcrum,** axis, pivot, bearing, rest

3 **lever; bar, crowbar;** pedal, crank; limb

4 **arm;** forearm; wrist; elbow; upper arm, biceps

5 **winch;** reel

verbs

6 **prise, lever, wedge;** crowbar

7 **reel in,** wind in, bring in, draw in, tighten, draw taut; winch, reel

862 ATTRACTION

nouns

1 **attraction,** attractiveness; **pull,** drag, draw, tug; magnetism; gravity, gravitation; **affinity, sympathy**

2 focus, centre; **lure**

3 **magnet,** magnetic needle; magnetic pole, magnetic north

verbs

4 **attract, pull, draw,** drag, tug; lure

adjectives

5 attracting, drawing, pulling; **attractive, magnetic;** charismatic; sympathetic; **alluring**

adverbs

6 attractively; magnetically, charismatically

863 REPULSION

nouns

1 **repulsion,** repellence; polarization

2 **rebuff; dismissal,** cold shoulder, snub, cut; turn-off (*nonformal*); refusal; discharge

verbs

3 **repel, rebuff, turn back,** beat back; drive away, chase; **send packing,** dismiss; snub, cut, brush off, drop; spurn, refuse; **ward off,** hold off, keep off, fend off; eject, discharge

adjectives

4 **repulsive,** repellent, **repelling**

adverbs

5 repulsively, repellently

864 EJECTION

nouns

1 throwing out, **expulsion, discharge, ousting,** removal; **rejection**

2 **eviction,** ousting

3 **depopulation;** devastation, desolation

4 **banishment,** exclusion; **expatriation, exile; deportation,** transportation, **extradition**

5 **dismissal, discharge; layoff,** removal, displacing; suspension; **retirement; the sack,** the boot

6 **evacuation, elimination,** removal; **clearance;** exhaustion, venting, emptying, depletion; **unloading; draining, drainage**

7 **expulsion, discharge,** emission; **eruption, outburst;** jet, spout, squirt, spurt

8 **vomiting, retching,** heaving, gagging; nausea; **vomit,** spew

9 **belch, burp** (*nonformal*), wind, gas; **hiccup; flatulence**

10 **ejector; evictor; bouncer** (*nonformal*)

verbs

11 **eject, expel, discharge,** exclude, **reject,** remove; **oust, put out,** turn out; **throw out;** throw overboard, discard, throw away

12 **drive out, run out,** chase away; drum out; **freeze out** (*nonformal*), force out, send packing

13 **evict, oust,** dislodge, dispossess, put out, turn out

14 devastate, desolate

15 **banish, expel, cast out,** thrust out, relegate, **ostracize,** exclude, spurn, snub, cut; **exile, expatriate, deport,** transport, send away; **extradite; deport**

16 dismiss, hustle out, **send packing;** bow out

17 **dismiss, discharge, expel, cashier,** drum out, **lay off,** suspend, make redundant, turn out, release, let go, remove, displace, replace; demote; depose; **retire**

18 (*nonformal terms*) **fire, sack,** kick, boot

19 **exterminate, annihilate;** purge, liquidate; **throw off,** cast off; **eliminate, get rid of;** throw away

20 **evacuate; eliminate,** remove; **empty,** deplete, **exhaust,** vent, drain; **clear, purge,** flush out; defecate

21 **unload,** unpack, **discharge, dump**

22 **let out, emit, exhaust,** evacuate; **exhale,** expire, breathe out, blow, puff; fume, steam, smoke, reek

23 **discharge, exhaust, expel;** erupt; pour, decant; **spew,** jet, spout, squirt, **spurt**

24 **vomit,** spew, **regurgitate, throw up,** be sick, retch, heave, gag

25 **belch, burp** (*nonformal*); **hiccup**

26 **fart** (*nonformal*), break wind

865 OVERRUNNING

nouns

1 **overrunning;** seizure, taking; **overflowing; exaggeration;** surplus, excess; superiority

2 **invasion,** swarming, swarm, ravage, plague; **overrunning**

3 **trespass,** incursion, intrusion, **encroachment, infringement**

verbs

4 **overrun,** go beyond; **overstep; overshoot;** exaggerate; exceed, **overdo**

5 **beset,** invade, swarm, ravage, plague; **overrun, crawl with,** swarm with; spread over; run riot, cover; seize

6 **overrun;** override; **trample, step on; inundate, overwhelm;** overflow; shout down

7 **pass;** bypass; **pass over, cross,** ford; step over, straddle

8 **overstep, trespass,** intrude, **encroach, infringe,** invade; usurp

adjectives

9 **overrun;** overgrown; **inundated,** overwhelmed; buried

10 **infested,** beset, ravaged; **lousy**

866 SHORTCOMING

nouns

1 **shortcoming, shortfall; shortage,** deficit; **inadequacy; default, arrears;** decline; slump; **imperfection; inferiority; failure**

verbs

2 **fall short,** stop short, not reach;
want, lack; decline, lag, lose
ground, slump, collapse, fall
away, **lose out, fail**

3 **fall through,** fall down, fall flat,
collapse, break down

4 **miss,** miscarry, go amiss, go
astray; misfire; **miss out**

adjectives

5 **short of, deficient,** inadequate;
insufficient; inferior; lacking,
wanting, minus

adverbs

6 **behind, behindhand,** in arrears

7 **amiss, astray,** in vain, vainly

867 ELEVATION

nouns

1 **elevation, raising, lifting, rearing,** escalation, **erection;**
uplifting; upheaval; assumption;
height; ascent; increase

2 **crane; jack, hoist,** lift; lever;
tackle

3 **lift, elevator;** escalator

verbs

4 **elevate, raise, rear,** escalate,
erect, heighten, lift, boost, **hoist,**
heave; raise up, lift up; buoy up;
uphold; lob, loft

5 **exalt, elevate;** deify

6 **help up,** put on; mount

7 **pick up,** take up, **gather up;**
draw up, haul up; dredge up

adjectives

8 **raised, lifted, elevated;** rearing,
rampant; **exalted, lofty; erect,
upright; high**

9 **elevating,** lifting; **uplifting**

868 DEPRESSION

nouns

1 **depression, lowering; sinking;**
reduction; degradation; descent;
decrease

2 **overthrow,** overturn; fall, downfall; downpour

3 **crouch, stoop,** bend, squat; **bow,**
kneeling, **curtsy;** bob, duck, nod;
crawling, grovelling

verbs

4 **depress, lower,** debase, **sink,** reduce; bear down

5 **fell, drop, bring down,** lay low;
raze, level; pull down; **cut down,**
chop down, mow down; **knock
down, floor,** ground; trip up,
topple, tumble; **prostrate;** throw
down

6 **overthrow,** overturn; depose; demote

7 **drop,** let go of

8 **crouch, duck, cower;** stoop,
bend, squat down, get down;
hunch down

9 **bow,** bend, kneel, **curtsy,** bob,
duck; prostrate oneself; crawl,
grovel

10 **sit down,** be seated

11 **lie down,** couch, **recline;** prostrate

adjectives

12 **depressed, lowered,** debased, reduced, **fallen; sunken,** submerged; downcast; prostrated;
prostrate; low

869 CIRCUITOUSNESS

nouns

1 **deviation; digression, excursion,** circling, wheeling, circulation, rounding, orbit; spiral; **turn**

2 **circuit, round, revolution, circle, cycle,** orbit; round trip, beat, rounds, tour, turn, lap, loop

3 **detour, bypass, roundabout way,** roundabout, circuit, digression, deviation, excursion

verbs

4 **go roundabout,** meander, deviate, **detour, go around, bypass;** deviate; digress

5 **circle, circuit, circulate;** go about; **wheel,** orbit, round; cycle; spiral; revolve; encompass, encircle; surround; skirt, flank; lap; girdle

6 **turn,** go around, round

adjectives

7 **circuitous, roundabout, out-of-the-way, oblique, indirect,** meandering; **deviating,** discursive; evasive; **circular, round;** spiral; orbital; rotary

adverbs

8 **circuitously,** indirectly, round about

870 ROTATION

nouns

1 **rotation, revolution,** roll, **spin,** circulation; **turning, whirling,** swirling, **spinning,** wheeling; spiralling; swivelling, pivoting; **roll-ing,** trundling, bowling

2 **whirl,** wheel, reel, **spin, turn,**

round; spiral; pirouette; **swirl,** twirl; **whirlpool; whirlwind**

3 revolutions, revs (*nonformal*)

4 **rotor; roller, top,** roundabout; **wheel,** disk; rolling stone

5 **axle, axis; pivot, swivel;** fulcrum; pin; **hub; hinge**

6 **bearing,** ball bearing

verbs

7 **rotate, revolve, spin, turn,** round, **spiral;** circle; circulate; **swivel, pivot, wheel;** pirouette; wind, twist, screw

8 **roll,** trundle, bowl; tumble

9 **whirl,** twirl, **wheel,** reel, spin, swirl

adjectives

10 **rotating, revolving, turning, whirling,** swirling, twirling, **spinning,** wheeling, **reeling; rolling**

11 **rotary;** spiral

adverbs

12 **round, around,** round about, in circles; clockwise, anticlockwise

871 OSCILLATION

nouns

1 **vibration,** wavering; **frequency;** resonance

2 **waving,** wave motion, **brandishing, flourishing,** flaunting, shaking; wave

3 **pulse, beat, throb;** beating, throbbing; staccato, drumming; **rhythm, tempo;** flutter; **heartbeat**

4 **wave, ray;** electromagnetic wave; **light; radio wave;** mechanical wave; acoustic wave, **sound wave; shock wave; tidal wave;**

wavelength; frequency; resonance; period

5 **alternation; coming and going,** ebb and flow; teetering, tottering

6 **swing, sway, rock, lurch, roll, reel;** wag; wave, waver

7 **pendulum; swing;** rocking chair; shuttle; shuttlecock

verbs

8 **oscillate, vibrate, fluctuate,** vacillate, waver, wave; **swing, sway, reel, rock, lurch;** wag, waggle; **wobble, bob;** shake, flutter

9 **wave, undulate; brandish, flourish,** flaunt, shake, swing; **flap, flutter;** wag

10 **pulsate, pulse, beat, throb;** beat time, tick; drum

11 **alternate,** reciprocate, swing, teeter, shuttle; zigzag

adjectives

12 **oscillating, vibrating,** periodic, **fluctuating;** wavering; vacillating; resonant

13 **waving,** undulating

14 **swinging, swaying,** reeling, rocking, lurching, rolling

15 **pulsating, pulsing, beating, throbbing,** staccato; rhythmic

16 **alternate, reciprocal,** to-and-fro

adverbs

17 to and fro, back and forth, in and out, up and down

872 AGITATION

nouns

1 **agitation,** frenzy, excitement; **trepidation,** nervousness, upset; **unrest,** malaise, unease, restlessness; fever; **disquiet; disturb-**ance, commotion, **turmoil, turbulence,** swirl, tumult, rout, fuss, row, bluster, fluster, flurry, bustle; **disorder**

2 **shaking,** quaking, **quivering,** shivering, trembling, shuddering, vibration; spasms; chattering

3 **shake, quake, quiver,** falter, **tremor,** tremble, shiver, shudder; **wobble;** bob, **shock,** jolt, jostle; **bounce,** bump; **jerk, twitch,** tic

4 **flutter,** flit, **flicker, waver,** dance; **sputter, splutter, flap,** flop (non-*formal*); **beat,** beating; throb

5 **twitching,** jerking, fidgets

6 **spasm, convulsion, paroxysm,** throes; **orgasm,** sexual climax; **seizure,** grip, attack, **fit,** epilepsy; stroke

verbs

7 **agitate, shake, disturb,** shake up, **disquiet, upset, trouble, stir,** flutter, fret, ruffle, rumple, ripple, convulse; **churn,** whip, whisk, beat; **excite; stir up;** work up

8 **shake,** quake, vibrate, **tremble,** quiver, shudder, shiver; **wobble;** jog, **jolt,** jostle, hustle, **bounce,** jump, bump

9 **flutter,** flick, **flicker,** gutter, wave, **waver,** dance; **sputter, splutter, flap,** flip, beat; pulse; throb

10 **twitch, jerk;** itch; **fidget**

11 **wiggle, wriggle;** wag, waggle; writhe, squirm

12 **flounder,** flounce, **stagger,** totter, stumble, falter; roll, rock, reel, lurch, career, **swing, sway;** toss, **tumble,** thrash about

adjectives

13 agitated, disturbed, perturbed, **troubled, upset, ruffled,** flustered, unsettled; stirred up, shaken; feverish, jumpy, **nervous,** restless, **uneasy, turbulent;** excited

14 **shaking, vibrating,** chattering, **quivering, quavering, quaking, shivering, shuddering, trembling, tremulous, shaky;** wobbly

15 **fluttering, flickering, wavering,** dancing; sputtering, spluttering; unsteady

16 **jerky, twitching,** fidgety, jumpy, **spastic,** spasmodic, convulsive; fitful

17 **jolting, bouncy, bumpy,** choppy, rough; **jarring**

18 wriggling; wiggling; squirming; writhing

adverbs

19 **restlessly,** uneasily, nervously, feverishly; **excitedly**

20 **shakily;** unsteadily; spasmodically

873 SPECTATOR

nouns

1 **spectator, observer;** onlooker, **viewer,** beholder; **witness;** bystander; **viewer,** couch potato (*nonformal*)

2 **audience;** house, crowd, gate, fans

3 **sightseer, tourist**

4 **tour,** walking tour, bus tour

verbs

5 witness, see, look on, eye, gape; take in, **look at, watch;** attend

874 INTELLECT

nouns

1 **intellect, mind, reason, rationality, intelligence,** mentality, mental capacity, **understanding,** reasoning, conception; **brain, brains, thought;** head

2 **wits, senses,** faculties; consciousness

3 **mind's core;** inner man; subconscious

4 **psyche, spirit, soul, heart, mind;** inner man, **ego,** the self

5 **brain;** grey matter, head

adjectives

6 **mental, intellectual, rational, reasoning, thinking,** conceptual; intelligent; psychic, psychological, spiritual; cerebral; subjective, internal

875 INTELLIGENCE, WISDOM

nouns

1 **intelligence, understanding, comprehension,** apprehension, conception; rationality, **sense, wit, intellect;** capacity, mental capacity, mentality, mental age; sanity; knowledge

2 **brightness, brilliance,** aptitude, gift, **talent, flair, genius;** dexterity; ready wit, quick wit

3 **cunning,** craft; subtlety

4 **acumen, foresight,** providence; **insight,** penetration; **perception, sensibility**

5 **wisdom;** depth; conventional wisdom, received wisdom

6 **reasonableness,** reason, rationality, sanity; **practicality; sense;** level head, cool head, balance, coolness

7 **judgment; prudence,** providence; consideration, reflection, **thoughtfulness;** discretion, discrimination

8 **genius,** spirit, soul; **inspiration, creativity;** talent

verbs

9 scintillate, sparkle

adjectives

10 **intelligent,** intellectual; conceptual, discursive; **knowing,** understanding, reasonable, rational, sensible, bright; sane

11 no-nonsense; awake, **wide-awake,** alive, **alert**

12 **smart, brainy** (*nonformal*), bright, brilliant, clever, **gifted,** talented; **sharp,** keen; **quick,** nimble, adroit, dexterous

13 **shrewd,** artful, cunning, knowing, crafty, wily, sly, **subtle;** insinuating, insidious, devious, calculating

14 **astute, understanding, discerning,** penetrating, incisive, acute, cogent, piercing; **perceptive**

15 **wise,** sage, **knowing; learned; profound,** deep

16 **sensible, reasonable,** rational, logical; **practical,** pragmatic, philosophical; balanced, cool, **sound, sane,** sober, well-balanced

17 **judicious, prudent,** careful, **considerate,** circumspect, **thoughtful; discreet;** discriminating; enlightened

adverbs

18 **intelligently,** knowingly; **reasonably,** rationally, sensibly; **smartly, cleverly; shrewdly,** artfully; **wisely, judiciously, prudently,** discreetly, thoughtfully

876 WISE PERSON

nouns

1 **wise man, wise woman, sage,** master, mistress, authority; **philosopher,** thinker; rabbi; doctor; guru; elder, elder statesman; illuminate; mentor; **intellect; intellectual; scholar**

2 wise guy, smartarse (*nonformal*)

877 UNINTELLIGENCE

nouns

1 **irrationality; ignorance; foolishness;** incapacity, ineptitude; low IQ

2 **incomprehension, blindness,** unconsciousness

3 **stupidity, density, dullness,** slowness, lethargy

4 **empty-headedness;** vacuity, inanity

5 vacancy, vacuum, emptiness, mental void

6 **superficiality, shallowness;** frivolousness, lightness

7 **feeblemindedness,** infirmity, weakness, softness

8 **mental deficiency,** mental handicap; **arrested development,** simplicity; **idiocy;** insanity

9 **senility,** decline; **second childhood,** dotage

10 **puerility,** childishness, immaturity

verbs

11 be stupid; drool, slobber, dither, dote

adjectives

12 unthinking, irrational, unwise, inept; **senseless, mindless,** brainless, **foolish; ignorant**

13 uncomprehending; myopic; **blind**

14 stupid, dumb, dense, thick (*non-formal*)

15 dull, dim, wooden, heavy, sluggish, slow

16 mixed-up, muddled; dizzy (*nonformal*), foggy

17 vacant, empty, hollow, inane, blank

18 superficial, shallow; frivolous, light

19 weak, feeble, infirm, soft

20 mentally deficient, mentally defective, mentally handicapped, retarded, backward, arrested, subnormal, simple; **idiotic, moronic, imbecile;** spastic (*nonformal*); cracked, crazy; babbling, drooling, dithering

21 senile, decrepit; **childish,** doting

22 immature, childish; infantile, babyish

adverbs

23 stupidly; foolishly

878 FOOLISHNESS

nouns

1 foolishness, folly, stupidity; ineptitude; frivolity, giddiness; triviality; **nonsense, idiocy; madness,** lunacy, **insanity; eccentricity,** clowning

2 indiscretion, irrationality; immaturity

3 absurdity, nonsense

4 (*foolish act*) **folly, stupidity,** absurdity; **indiscretion;** blunder

verbs

5 be foolish; be stupid; **fool,** trifle, clown, clown around

6 gull, dupe, **make a fool of**

adjectives

7 foolish, stupid, dumb (*nonformal*); **silly,** dizzy (*nonformal*); **fatuous,** inept, **inane; futile; senseless, thoughtless,** brainless; **idiotic,** moronic, imbecile; **crazy, mad,** daft; **insane;** infatuated, credulous, fond, doting; sentimental; dazed

8 unwise, imprudent, indiscreet; inconsiderate, thoughtless, mindless, unthinking; **unreasonable, unsound,** senseless, **irrational,** reckless, inadvisable; **ill-advised;** misguided; myopic; **suicidal**

9 absurd, nonsensical, ridiculous, ludicrous; **foolish, crazy;** preposterous, fantastic, grotesque, monstrous, wild, weird, **outrageous,** incredible, beyond belief, extravagant, **bizarre**

10 gullible; naive, inexperienced, impressionable

adverbs

11 foolishly, stupidly; blindly, thoughtlessly; absurdly, ridiculously

879 FOOL

nouns

1 **fool; clown; lunatic**

2 **stupid person,** dolt, dunce, clod, donkey, **dope,** nitwit, halfwit; **scatterbrain**

3 (*nonformal terms*) **chump,** sap, basket case, ninny, silly Billy (*nonformal*); **airhead,** dummy, bonehead, thickhead, headbanger, dunderhead

4 **oaf, lout,** boor, yokel, hick, clod

5 **idiot, imbecile, moron,** halfwit, mental defective; cretin; **simpleton**

880 SANITY

nouns

1 **sanity,** sound mind, healthy mind, right mind (*nonformal*), senses, reason, **rationality,** reasonableness, lucidity, balance; normality; **mental health**

adjectives

2 **sane, rational,** reasonable, sensible, **lucid,** normal, balanced, **sound,** right

881 INSANITY, MANIA

nouns

1 **insanity, lunacy, madness; mental illness, mental disease;** brain damage; **mania;** alienation, mental disturbance, **derangement;** distraction, disorientation, mental instability, **sick mind,** irrationality; possession; mental deficiency

2 (*nonformal terms*) craziness; a screw loose; lame brains

3 **psychosis,** psychopathy, neurosis

4 **schizophrenia,** catatonia; **paranoia**

5 **depression, melancholia;** mood swings

6 **frenzy,** fury, fever, **rage; seizure, fit,** paroxysm, spasm, **convulsion**

7 **delirium,** brainstorm; incoherence, wandering, raving, ranting

8 (*nonformal terms*) the DT's, the shakes; the heebie-jeebies; pink elephants

9 **fanaticism,** zealousness, bigotry; extremism

10 **mania, craze, infatuation, enthusiasm,** passion, fascination, bug (*nonformal*), rage

11 **obsession,** preoccupation, **hang-up** (*nonformal*), **fixation,** complex, fascination; **compulsion;** ruling passion, fixed idea, **possession**

12 **asylum,** lunatic asylum, **madhouse,** mental institution, mental home, bedlam; mental hospital; padded cell

13 **lunatic, madman, maniac,** raving lunatic

14 (*nonformal terms*) **nut,** nutter, nutcase, loony, headcase, psycho, crackpot

15 **psychotic,** mental case, **psychopath;** paranoiac; schizophrenic; manic depressive

16 **fanatic, buff** and **fan** (*both nonformal*), freak (*nonformal*), devotee, **zealot, enthusiast,** crank (*nonformal*)

verbs

17 **be insane;** have a screw loose (*nonformal*); **wander, ramble;**

rave, rage, **rant;** dote, babble; go berserk

18 go mad, crack up

19 (*nonformal terms*) **go crazy,** go nuts, go bananas, freak out, flip out

20 madden, craze, drive mad, unbalance, distract, derange

21 obsess, possess, infatuate, **preoccupy;** grip, hold; **drive,** compel, impel

adjectives

22 insane, mad, sick, crazed, **lunatic, daft, unsound, demented, deranged,** deluded, disoriented, unhinged, **unbalanced,** not right, **touched,** irrational, senseless; manic; odd, strange, off; abnormal, mentally deficient

23 (*nonformal terms*) **crazy,** nutty, dotty, potty, bats, nuts, bananas, cuckoo, flipped, mental, cracked

24 psychotic, mentally ill, mentally sick; disturbed, neurotic; schizophrenic; manic; **paranoid**

25 possessed, demonic

26 rabid, raving mad, frenzied, frantic, frenetic; **mad, wild, furious, violent;** desperate; **beside oneself,** uncontrollable; **raving, raging,** ranting; berserk

27 delirious, off; giddy, dizzy; **wandering, rambling,** raving, ranting, babbling, incoherent

28 fanatic, fanatical, rabid; bigoted; **extreme,** extremist; unreasonable, irrational

29 obsessed, possessed, infatuated, preoccupied, **hung up** (*nonformal*), gripped, held

30 obsessive, obsessional; obsessing, possessing, preoccupying;

driving, impelling, **compulsive,** compelling

adverbs

31 madly, insanely, crazily; fanatically, etc

882 ECCENTRICITY

nouns

1 eccentricity, idiosyncrasy, **oddity, peculiarity,** strangeness; anomaly, irregularity, deviation, divergence, aberration; **nonconformity,** unconventionality

2 quirk, twist, mannerism, conceit, whim

3 eccentric, character; **nonconformist,** recluse

4 freak, character, crackpot, nut, wierdo, oddball, crank

adjectives

5 eccentric, erratic, idiosyncratic, **queer, odd, peculiar,** strange, singular, anomalous, funny; unnatural, abnormal, irregular, divergent, deviant, different, exceptional; unconventional; quirky, dotty, whimsical; solitary, reclusive

6 funny, loopy, nutty, weird

883 KNOWLEDGE

nouns

1 knowledge, knowing; **command,** reach; **acquaintance, familiarity,** intimacy; **information,** data, items, facts; **certainty;** protocol; **intelligence; experience, knowhow, expertise;** technique

2 recognition, realization; perception, insight, illumination; consciousness, awareness, note, notice; sense, sensibility; appreciation

3 understanding, comprehension; conception; grasp, grip, command, mastery; intelligence; wisdom

4 learning, enlightenment, education, schooling, instruction, illumination; attainments, accomplishments, skills; sophistication

5 scholarship, erudition, reading, letters; literacy; numeracy; culture; book learning; classical scholarship, humanism

6 profound knowledge, expertise, proficiency; specialism; general knowledge

7 lore, corpus; canon; literature, publications, materials; bibliography; encyclopedia

8 science, art, study, discipline; field, province, domain, area, arena, sphere, speciality; technology; social science

9 scientist; scholar; authority, expert; intellectual

verbs

10 know, perceive, recognize, discern, see, make out; conceive; realize, appreciate, understand, comprehend, fathom; grasp, seize

11 know well, command, know by heart, know backwards

adjectives

12 knowing, knowledgeable, informed; conscious, aware, mindful; intelligent; understanding, comprehending; perceptive; shrewd, wise

13 aware of, conscious of, mindful of, appreciative of; privy to; alive to, awake to; wise to (*nonformal*); informed of

14 informed, enlightened, instructed, versed, educated, taught; posted, briefed, trained; up on, up-to-date, abreast of

15 versed in, informed in, up on, strong in, master of, proficient in, familiar with, conversant with, acquainted with

16 well-informed, well-educated, well-read, widely read

17 learned, erudite, educated, cultured, cultivated, literate, civilized, scholarly, studious; wise; profound, deep

18 literary, bookish; pedantic, donnish

19 intellectual; highbrow; elitist

20 understandable, comprehensible, discernible, conceivable, appreciable, perceptible

21 known, recognized, ascertained, conceived, grasped, seized, perceived, discerned, appreciated, understood, comprehended, realized

22 well-known, widely known, commonly known, universally recognized, familiar, household, common, current; proverbial; public, notorious; commonplace, trite, hackneyed

23 scientific; technical; technological

adverbs

24 knowingly, consciously, intelligently, studiously

884 INTELLECTUAL

nouns

1 **intellectual, intellect;** thinker; pundit; **highbrow** (*nonformal*); wise man

2 **scholar;** student; **learned man,** genius; literary man; philosopher; classicist, humanist

3 **bookworm;** bibliophile

4 **dilettante, dabbler,** amateur

885 IGNORANCE

nouns

1 **ignorance, inexperience;** innocence, simplicity

2 **unconsciousness;** incomprehension; blindness, deafness

3 dark, darkness; savagery, barbarism; dark age

4 **unlearnedness; illiteracy;** unintellectuality; bold ignorance

5 **slight knowledge,** vague notion, smattering; superficiality, shallowness

6 **the unknown;** sealed book, riddle, enigma, mystery, puzzle; **unknown quantity,** dark horse

7 **ignoramus,** dunce, fool; **illiterate;** lowbrow (*nonformal*)

verbs

8 **be ignorant,** know nothing, be blind

9 **not know;** wonder; scratch the surface, dabble, toy with; pass, give up

adjectives

10 **ignorant,** uncomprehending, simple, **dumb** (*nonformal*), empty, inane, uninitiated, **unfamil-**

iar; inexperienced; green, innocent, ingenuous, gauche, awkward, naive, raw; groping, tentative, unsure

11 **unaware, unconscious;** mindless; unwitting, unsuspecting; **blind to, deaf to,** dead to; asleep, napping

12 **uneducated;** misinformed; hoodwinked, deceived; **illiterate, unread;** barbarous, pagan, heathen

13 half-baked (*nonformal*), **shallow, superficial;** immature; dabbling, amateur, amateurish

14 **unknown,** unsuspected; unexplored; unidentified, virgin, untouched; undiscovered, sealed; **unfamiliar,** strange; incalculable; enigmatic, mysterious, puzzling

adverbs

15 unwittingly, **unawares;** unconsciously

886 THOUGHT

nouns

1 **thought,** thinking, **reasoning**

2 **consideration, contemplation,** reflection, speculation, meditation, **musing, deliberation,** brooding, study, pondering; counsel

3 **thoughtfulness,** melancholy; preoccupation, absorption, abstraction, **concentration,** study; **introspection**

4 **thoughts;** train of thoughts; stream of consciousness

5 **afterthought,** second thoughts; **reconsideration,** reappraisal, rethinking, re-examination, review

verbs

6 **think,** conceive, form ideas; **reason**

7 **think hard,** rack one's brains; **puzzle over**

8 **concentrate,** brood on; **think about,** give thought to; think through, puzzle out, sort out, reason out

9 **consider, contemplate,** speculate, reflect, study, ponder, weigh, deliberate, debate, meditate, muse, brood; **toy with,** play with; think over, mull over, turn over

10 **consider,** entertain, inquire into; **sleep upon**

11 **reconsider,** re-examine, review; rethink

12 **think of,** seize on; **contemplate, consider**

13 (*look upon mentally*) **contemplate, look upon, view, regard,** see, **envisage, visualize,** imagine

14 **occur to,** strike one, grab one (*nonformal*), **suggest itself,** present itself

15 **impress, strike,** grab (*nonformal*), hit; **sink in** (*nonformal*)

16 **preoccupy,** occupy, **absorb, engross;** obsess

adjectives

17 **cognitive,** conceptual, **mental; rational,** logical; **thoughtful, contemplative,** reflective, speculative, meditative, **pensive,** wistful; introspective; **sober, serious**

18 **absorbed, engrossed,** introspective, rapt, abstracted, **preoccupied**

adverbs

19 **thoughtfully,** reflectively; **pensively,** wistfully; **on second thoughts**

887 IDEA

nouns

1 **idea; thought, notion,** concept, conception, conceit, fancy; **perception,** sense, impression, **mental image,** mental picture; reflection, observation; **opinion;** supposition, **theory**

2 **archetype,** prototype, model, ideal

3 **abstract idea, abstraction,** general idea, generality

4 **main idea,** guiding principle, crowning principle, **big idea** (*nonformal*)

5 **good idea,** great idea, bright idea, **insight; brainchild** (*nonformal*), inspiration

6 **ideology,** body of ideas; world view; philosophy; **ethos**

adjectives

7 ideal, **conceptual,** fanciful; **intellectual; theoretical; ideological**

888 ABSENCE OF THOUGHT

nouns

1 **thoughtlessness; vacuity,** vacancy; foolishness; tranquillity; **oblivion,** forgetfulness, amnesia

adjectives

2 **thoughtless, unthinking,** vacuous, vacant, blank, relaxed, empty, fatuous, inane; unoccupied; calm, tranquil; oblivious; passive

889 INTUITION, INSTINCT

nouns

1 **intuition, sixth sense;** understanding, tact; **revelation, insight,** inspiration; second sight

2 **instinct, impulse;** collective unconscious; race memory; **reflex,** spontaneous reaction

3 **hunch** (*nonformal*), sense, **premonition,** foreboding; suspicion, **impression, feeling**

verbs

4 **sense, feel,** get the impression, know instinctively

adjectives

5 **intuitive,** sensing, feeling

6 **instinctive,** natural, **inherent, innate;** unconscious, subliminal; **involuntary, automatic,** spontaneous, impulsive

adverbs

7 **intuitively; instinctively,** automatically, spontaneously

890 REASONING

nouns

1 **reasoning, reason,** logical thought, rationalization; **rationality;** demonstration, proof; philosophy

2 **logic;** dialectics

3 (*methods*) **deduction, inference; generalization;** synthesis, analysis

4 **argument,** controversy, dispute, debate, **contention;** defence, apology; polemics; examination, cross-examination

5 **argument, case, plea; reason, consideration;** refutation; pros, cons; **dialogue,** dialectic

6 **premise, proposition, position, assumption,** presupposition, hypothesis, thesis, theorem, statement, assertion, basis, ground, foundation; **axiom,** postulation

7 **reasonableness, sense,** common sense, **logic, reason**

8 **good reasoning, right thinking,** sound reasoning, irrefutable logic; cogent argument, strong argument; good case, good reason, sound evidence, strong point

9 **thinker;** rationalist; logician; philosopher

10 disputant, debater; polemicist

verbs

11 **reason;** rationalize; **deduce,** infer; analyse; theorize

12 **argue, dispute,** plead, cross swords, lock horns, **contend,** contest, bicker, wrangle; thrash out; **quibble**

13 **be reasonable, be logical, make sense,** figure (*nonformal*); hold good, hold water (*nonformal*)

adjectives

14 **reasoning, rational;** analytic, analytical

15 **argumentative, controversial, contentious,** quarrelsome

16 **logical, reasonable, rational,** cogent, **sensible, sane, sound,** legitimate, justifiable; credible; plausible

17 **reasoned, advised, considered, calculated,** meditated, contemplated, deliberated, studied

18 analytical, discursive; categorical, hypothetical, conditional

adverbs

19 **reasonably**, logically, rationally, **sensibly;** in reason, within reason

891 SOPHISTRY

nouns

1 **sophistry**, subtlety; **false reasoning; fallacy; speciousness; insincerity; equivocation;** perversion, distortion; obfuscation

2 **irrationality**, invalidity; **inconsistency**, incongruity

3 empty words; bad case, weak point; **fallacy, circular argument**

4 subterfuge; **evasion, hedging, sidestepping,** dodging, shifting, fencing, parrying

verbs

5 pervert, distort, misapply; explain away, rationalize

6 quibble, bicker, split hairs, pick nits; obscure, prevaricate, fence, parry, shift, **dodge, evade,** sidestep, hedge, skate around (*nonformal*)

adjectives

7 **fallacious, specious,** hollow; deceptive, empty; **insincere**

8 **illogical, unreasonable, irrational, senseless, invalid,** faulty, flawed; inconclusive, inconsequential; **inconsistent,** incongruous, loose, unconnected; contradictory

9 **unsound,** insubstantial, weak, feeble, poor, flimsy

10 **groundless, unfounded,** untenable, unwarranted, idle, empty, vain

11 **equivocatory;** petty, trivial, trifling; shuffling, hedging, **evasive**

adverbs

12 **illogically, unreasonably, irrationally;** baselessly, groundlessly

892 TOPIC

nouns

1 **topic, subject, matter, subject matter, concern,** category; **theme, text,** motif, **case, question, problem, issue; point,** gist; substance, essence, basis

2 **caption, title, heading, head, headline;** legend, motto; title page

verbs

3 focus on, distinguish, set forth, specify; caption, title, head; **headline**

893 INQUIRY

nouns

1 **inquiry,** inquiring, probing, **inquest;** inquiring mind; analysis

2 **examination, exam** (*nonformal*), **test, quiz;** oral examination, viva (*nonformal*); **audition, hearing;** multiple-choice test; written examination; test paper; final examination, final (*nonformal*)

3 **examination,** inspection, scrutiny; survey, review, **study,** scan, run-through

4 **investigation, research,** inquiry into; **probe;** criminal investiga-

tion, detection; legislative investigation, hearing; witch-hunt

5 **checkup, check;** spot check; physical examination, **physical;** testing, drug testing, alcohol testing

6 **re-examination, review,** reappraisal

7 **reconnaissance;** exploration, **scouting**

8 **surveillance,** following, trailing, tailing (*nonformal*), observation; **spying,** espionage, **intelligence;** bugging (*nonformal*), electronic surveillance

9 **question, query, inquiry, interrogation, problem, issue, topic;** question mark, burning question; leading question; rhetorical question

10 **interview,** press conference

11 **questioning,** interrogation, querying; **quiz, examination;** challenge, dispute

12 **grilling;** police interrogation; **cross-examination**

13 **survey,** inquiry, questionnaire; exit poll; **poll;** consumer research, market research

14 **search, quest,** hunt; **rummage,** ransacking, **forage;** exploration, probe; **body search**

15 interrogator; examiner; **detective**

16 **examiner; inspector, monitor,** observer; **investigator**

17 seeker; hunter; researcher, fact finder, research worker

verbs

18 **inquire, ask, question, query;** ask after, inquire after, ask about, ask questions

19 **interrogate,** question, query, quiz, test, examine; **pump;** interview

20 **grill;** roast (*nonformal*), **cross-examine**

21 **investigate,** sift, explore, **look into,** go into, delve into, poke into, pry into; **probe,** sound, plumb, fathom; check on, nose into; poke about

22 **examine, inspect,** scrutinize, survey, **look at,** peer at, **observe,** scan, peruse, study; look over; go over, run over, pore over; **monitor, review,** check

23 **scrutinize,** examine thoroughly, vet

24 **scan, skim,** glance at, dip into, touch upon; thumb through

25 **re-examine, reconsider,** rethink, review

26 scout, spy; **watch,** stake out (*nonformal*); bug (*nonformal*); check up

27 **canvass,** survey, **poll,** sample

28 **seek, hunt,** quest, pursue, follow; **look up; look for,** search out, search for, hunt for, fish for, angle for, dig for; **ask for,** inquire for; **gun for**

29 **search, hunt,** explore; research; **search through,** look through, go through; dig, delve, burrow, root, poke, pry; poke around, nose around; forage; frisk (*nonformal*)

30 grope for, **feel for,** fumble, scrabble, poke around

31 ransack, rummage, rake, scour, comb; rifle; **look everywhere**

32 **search out,** hunt out, ferret out, fish out, dig out, root out

33 **trace**, **stalk**, track, trail; follow, follow up, tail (*nonformal*); nose out, **trace down**, hunt down, track down

adjectives

34 **inquiring**, **questioning**, **querying**, **quizzical**, curious; interrogative

35 **examining**, testing, trying, tentative; groping, feeling; **investigative**, **exploratory**

36 **searching**, probing, prying, **nosy** (*nonformal*)

adverbs

37 **in question, at issue, under consideration**, under examination, under investigation, under surveillance

894 ANSWER

nouns

1 **answer**, reply, response; retort, rejoinder, reaction, return; **acknowledgement**; receipt; echo

2 **rebuttal**; **rejoinder**, defence; refutation

verbs

3 **answer**, offer, proffer, **reply**, **respond**, say; **retort**, return, throw back; **react**; **acknowledge**; echo, reverberate

4 **rejoin**; refute

adjectives

5 **answering**, **replying**, **responsive**, responding; returning; echoing

adverbs

6 **in answer**, in reply, in response, in return

895 SOLUTION

nouns

1 **solution**, resolution, **answer**, **reason**, **explanation**; **finding**, conclusion, determination, verdict, judgment; **outcome**, **upshot**, **result**, issue, end; accomplishment; **solving**, resolving, cracking; unravelling, untangling; **deciphering**, **decoding**; interpretation; **scenario**

verbs

2 **solve**, **resolve**, **clear up**, get right, **work out**, find out, figure out, **straighten out**, iron out, sort out, puzzle out; undo, untangle, disentangle, **unravel**, **decipher**, decode, crack; **make out**, interpret; **answer**, explain; **fathom**; guess, divine

adjectives

3 **solvable**, **resolvable**, workable, answerable; explicable; **decipherable**

896 DISCOVERY

nouns

1 **discovery**, **finding**, **detection**, spotting, sighting; recognition, determination; **location**; **disclosure**, **exposure**, revelation, uncovering, unearthing, excavation; **find**, **strike**; **invention**

verbs

2 **discover**, **find**, get; strike, hit; **locate**; **hunt down**, search out, track down, trace; **learn**, find out, determine; invent

3 **come across**, meet with, **encounter**, run into, bump into

(*nonformal*), strike on, fall on, trip over, stumble upon

4 uncover, unearth, dig up, exhume, excavate; **disclose, expose, reveal,** bring to light

5 detect, spot, (*nonformal*), **see,** spy, sense, pick up, notice, discern, **perceive,** make out, recognize, distinguish, identify

6 sniff, smell, nose out

7 catch, catch out; catch napping, catch at

8 see through, penetrate; catch on to, wise up to (*nonformal*)

9 turn up, show up, be found; materialize, **come to light,** come out

897 EXPERIMENT

nouns

1 experiment, experimentation; testing, **trial;** controlled experiment

2 test, trial, try; essay; determination; **proof,** verification; standard, criterion; acid test; probation; **feeling out, sounding out;** test case

3 workout, rehearsal, practice; dry run, dummy run; **trial run;** bench test; audition, hearing

4 probe, sounder; straw poll; sample, random sample

5 laboratory, lab (*nonformal*), research laboratory; field station; **proving ground;** think tank (*nonformal*)

6 bench scientist, researcher, research worker; experimental engineer; test driver, test pilot

7 subject, patient, sample; laboratory animal, **guinea pig**

verbs

8 experiment, research, test, try, essay, **prove, verify,** validate, substantiate, confirm; sample, taste; try on

9 sound out, feel out, probe, read; test out

10 stand up, hold up, pass, **pass muster,** get by (*nonformal*)

adjectives

11 experimental, test, trial; pilot; **tentative,** provisional; empirical

12 tried, tested, proved, verified, confirmed

adverbs

13 experimentally, by trial and error

14 on trial, under examination, on probation, under suspicion

898 COMPARISON

nouns

1 comparison, matching, **likening,** comparing, **analogy;** weighing, balancing, opposition; **contrast;** distinction; confrontation; **relation;** correlation; simile, metaphor, allegory

2 verification,   confirmation, checking; check

3 comparability; equivalence; ratio, proportion, balance; **similarity**

verbs

4 compare, liken, assimilate, liken to, compare with; **relate;** parallel; **match,** match up; view together; **contrast, oppose, weigh,** balance

5 collate; verify, confirm, check

6 be comparable, compare, measure up to; **match, parallel;** vie, vie with, rival; **resemble**

adjectives

7 comparative, relative, **comparable,** commensurate, parallel, **analogous; similar**

8 incomparable, **unlike,** dissimilar

adverbs

9 comparatively, relatively; comparably

899 DISCRIMINATION

nouns

1 discrimination; finesse, refinement, delicacy; nicety, subtlety; **tact,** feel, feeling, sense, **sensitivity, sensibility;** intuition, instinct; appreciation; taste; palate; ear, educated ear; eye, good eye

2 penetration, **perception, insight, flair; judgment,** acumen; analysis

3 distinction, differentiation, separation, division, segregation, demarcation; **nuance**

verbs

4 discriminate, distinguish, separate, separate out, divide, analyse, subdivide, **segregate,** sever, **differentiate, set apart,** sift out, sieve, screen out, sort, classify, sort out; **pick out, select; split hairs**

5 be discriminating, discriminate; **be tactful;** be tasteful; shop around

6 distinguish between, tell apart

adjectives

7 discriminating, selective; **tactful, sensitive;** appreciative; **critical; distinguishing;** precise, accurate, exact; fine, delicate, subtle, refined; fastidious; distinctive

8 discerning, perceptive, astute, judicious

adverbs

9 discriminately; **tactfully; tastefully**

900 INDISCRIMINATION

nouns

1 casualness, promiscuity; indiscretion, insensitivity; **generality**

2 indistinction, vagueness; indefiniteness; uniformity; facelessness

verbs

3 confound, confuse, mix, muddle, **blur**

adjectives

4 indiscriminate; wholesale, **general, blanket;** uncritical, undemanding; **casual, promiscuous; indiscreet, imprudent;** tactless, insensitive

5 indistinguishable, undistinguished, **indistinct, alike, infinite;** faceless, impersonal; standard, interchangeable, stereotyped, uniform

901 JUDGMENT

nouns

1 judgment, judging, deeming; arbitration; **resolution; choice; discrimination**

2 criticism; censure; approval; cri-

tique, review, notice, report, comment

3 **estimate,** estimation; view, opinion; **assessment, appraisal,** appreciation, reckoning, **stocktaking,** valuation, **evaluation,** value judgment, analysing, weighing, gauging, ranking, **rating;** measurement; comparison

4 **conclusion, deduction, inference,** consequence, corollary; derivation

5 **verdict, decision,** determination, finding; diagnosis, prognosis; **decree, ruling,** order, **pronouncement, award,** action, **sentence; condemnation,** doom; precedent

6 **judge;** justice; arbiter; referee, umpire

7 **critic;** connoisseur; **censor;** reviewer, **commentator**

verbs

8 **judge;** adjudicate; **consider,** regard, hold, **deem,** esteem, count, account, think of; **suppose, presume**

9 **estimate, reckon,** guess, figure (*nonformal*); **assess,** appraise, gauge, rate, rank, class, mark, **value, evaluate,** weigh, prize, appreciate; **measure**

10 **conclude;** find, hold; deduce, derive, extract, **gather,** collect, glean, fetch; **infer;** induce; **reason,** reason that

11 **decide, determine; find,** ascertain; **resolve, settle,** fix

12 **hold court; hear, try; referee,** umpire; arbitrate

13 **pass judgment; find;** pronounce, report, **rule,** decree, order; **sen-**

tence, pass sentence, doom, condemn

14 **criticize;** censure; **approve; review;** comment upon

15 **rank, rate,** count, be regarded

adjectives

16 **judicial,** judicious; evaluative; critical

adverbs

17 on balance, considering, after all; therefore

902 PREJUDGMENT

nouns

1 **preconception, presumption, supposition;** ulterior motive, hidden agenda, **prejudice**

verbs

2 **presuppose, presume,** be predisposed

adjectives

3 **preconceived, presumed,** presupposed; predetermined, **predisposed**

903 MISJUDGMENT

nouns

1 **misjudgment, miscalculation,** wrong impression; misreading, misinterpretation; **inaccuracy, error**

verbs

2 **misjudge, miscalculate,** misread, misinterpret; err

904 OVERESTIMATION

nouns

1 **overestimatation,** overrating, overvaluation; **overstatement, exaggeration**

verbs

2 **overestimate,** overrate, overvalue, idealize; **overstate, exaggerate**

adjectives

3 **overestimated,** overrated, overvalued; **exaggerated**

905 UNDERESTIMATION

nouns

1 **underestimation,** underrating, undervaluation; belittlement, **depreciation,** deprecation, disparagement

verbs

2 **underestimate, underrate,** undervalue; **depreciate, deprecate,** minimize, belittle; disparage

adjectives

3 **underestimated, underrated,** undervalued

906 THEORY, SUPPOSITION

nouns

1 **theory, hypothesis,** speculation; analysis, **explanation,** abstraction

2 **theory, explanation,** proposal, proposition; **hypothesis**

3 **supposition;** assumption, presumption, conjecture, inference, surmise, guesswork; **proposition,** thesis, premise; **axiom**

4 **guess, conjecture,** perhaps, speculation, guesswork, surmise, educated guess

5 (*vague supposition*) **suggestion, suspicion,** inkling, hint, sense, feeling, intuition, intimation, impression, notion, **idea**

verbs

6 **theorize,** hypothesize speculate

7 **suppose, assume, presume,** surmise, expect, **suspect, infer, understand,** gather, conclude, deduce, consider, reckon, divine, imagine, **fancy,** dream, conceive, **believe, deem,** feel, **think,** say; take it

8 **conjecture, guess,** hazard a guess

9 **postulate;** lay down, assert; advance, **propose, propound**

adjectives

10 **theoretical, hypothetical, speculative;** intuitive; generalized, abstract, ideal; academic; impractical, armchair

11 **supposed, assumed, presumed, inferred,** understood, **reputed,** alleged; given, granted, agreed, stipulated

adverbs

12 **theoretically,** ideally; **in theory,** on paper

13 **supposedly, presumably,** reputedly; **seemingly**

907 PHILOSOPHY

nouns

1 **philosophy,** philosophical speculation; school of philosophy, school of thought

2 **materialism; idealism**

3 **monism; pantheism**

4 **pluralism; dualism**

5 **philosopher, thinker,** speculator

verbs

6 **philosophize,** reason, probe

adjectives

7 **philosophical,** philosophic

908 BELIEF

nouns

1 **belief,** credence, credit, faith, trust; hope; **confidence, assurance; certainty; reliance, dependence;** reception, acquiescence; **credulity**

2 **a belief,** tenet, dogma, precept, **principle,** canon, maxim, axiom; **doctrine,** teaching

3 **religion, faith;** school, cult, ideology, world view; **creed;** gospel

4 **manifesto;** solemn declaration; sworn statement

5 **conviction, persuasion, certainty; firm belief,** moral certainty, fixed opinion

6 **opinion, sentiment, feeling, sense, impression,** reaction, **notion, idea, thought,** mind, thinking, **attitude,** stance, posture, position, **view,** eye, sight, observation, **conception,** concept, **estimation,** consideration, **theory,**
assumption, presumption, **conclusion, judgment; public opinion,** popular belief, conventional wisdom; ethos

7 **profession, confession,** declaration

8 **believability,** persuasiveness, credibility, acceptability; **reliability**

9 **believer; true believer;** the faithful; ideologist

verbs

10 **believe, trust, accept,** receive, buy (*nonformal*); **swallow;** be certain

11 **think,** be persuaded, be convinced; **suppose,** assume, presume, judge, **guess,** surmise, suspect, expect (*nonformal*), conceive, **imagine, fancy;** deem, hold, regard, consider, maintain, reckon, estimate; view as, take, take it

12 **state, assert,** swear, declare, **affirm,** vow, warrant, confess, profess

13 **be confident,** have confidence, **be satisfied,** be convinced, be certain, feel sure, rest assured

14 **believe in,** confide in, **trust in**

15 lean on, **count on,** reckon on, **swear by**

16 **trust,** confide in, rely on, depend on, **trust in**

17 **convince; convert,** win over, bring round, talk round, **persuade;** satisfy, assure; be convincing, carry conviction

18 **convince oneself, persuade oneself**

19 **find credence, be believed,** be accepted, be received

adjectives

20 **believing,** undoubting; faithful, pious, observant, **devout; convinced, confident,** positive, dogmatic, secure, **persuaded, satisfied,** assured; sure, certain

21 **trusting,** confiding, unsuspecting; childlike, innocent, naive; **credulous;** reliant, dependent

22 **believed,** credited, held, trusted, accepted; received; **undoubted,** unsuspected, **unquestioned,** undisputed

23 **believable, credible;** conceivable, **plausible;** trustworthy; reliable; **unquestionable**

24 **convincing,** well-founded, **persuasive,** impressive, satisfying, satisfactory, decisive, absolute, conclusive; authoritative

25 **doctrinal,** dogmatic, mandatory, of faith

adverbs

26 **undoubtingly,** unquestioningly, trustfully; piously, devoutly; with faith; **with confidence,** on faith

909 CREDULITY

nouns

1 **credulity, blind faith,** unquestioning belief; trustingness, unsuspiciousness; infatuation, fondness

2 **gullibility,** persuadability; softness, weakness; simplicity, naivety

3 **superstition;** popular belief, tradition, lore, folklore; charm, spell

4 **trusting soul; dupe;** sucker *and* pushover (*both nonformal*)

adjectives

5 **credulous, trusting; unsuspecting;** unthinking, uncritical; fond, infatuated, doting; **superstitious**

6 **gullible;** soft, **simple;** ingenuous, unsophisticated, green, naive

910 UNBELIEF

nouns

1 **disbelief,** discredit; **incredulity;** denial, rejection; heresy; infidelity, atheism

2 **doubt, reservation, question,** scepticism; suspicion, distrust, mistrust, **misgiving,** diffidence; apprehension; **uncertainty**

3 **unbelievability, incredibility, implausibility,** inconceivability; doubtfulness, questionableness

4 **doubter,** doubting Thomas; scoffer, sceptic, cynic, unbeliever

verbs

5 **disbelieve, discredit;** negate, **deny;** scoff at; **reject**

6 **doubt,** half believe, have reservations, **distrust,** mistrust, be uncertain; **suspect, question,** query, **challenge,** contest, dispute

7 **be unbelievable,** be incredible, defy belief; stagger

adjectives

8 **disbelieving;** faithless; unconvinced; **incredulous; heretical; irreligious**

9 **doubting,** doubtful, in doubt, dubious; questioning; sceptical; **distrustful,** mistrusting; **suspicious,** suspecting, wary; **agnostic;** uncertain

10 **unbelievable, incredible,** unthinkable, **implausible,** unimagi-

nable, inconceivable, beyond belief; preposterous, absurd, ridiculous; **doubtful,** dubious, **questionable, unconvincing, suspicious,** suspect, funny

11 **doubted, questioned,** disputed, contested; **distrusted,** mistrusted; **suspect, under suspicion,** discredited, exploded, rejected

adverbs

12 **doubtfully, dubiously,** suspiciously; with reservations, with caution

13 **unbelievably, incredibly,** unthinkably

911 INCREDULITY

nouns

1 **incredulity, inconvincibility,** suspicion, wariness, caution; scepticism

verbs

2 **disbelieve; be sceptical;** not swallow, not accept, **reject**

adjectives

3 **incredulous, suspicious, suspecting,** wary, cautious, guarded; sceptical

4 **sophisticated, wise,** hardheaded, practical, realistic

912 EVIDENCE, PROOF

nouns

1 **evidence, proof; grounds, facts, data,** premises; **fact; indication, manifestation, sign, symptom,** mark, token, mute witness; documentation; **clue;** exhibit

2 **testimony, witness;** testimonial; **statement, declaration, asser**tion, avowal, allegation, admission, **disclosure,** profession, word; sworn statement

3 **proof, demonstration, determination,** establishment, settlement; conclusive evidence

4 **confirmation,** proof, bearing out, ratification, **verification; corroboration, support,** supporting evidence, backing, reinforcement, strengthening; **documentation**

5 **citation, reference,** quotation, instance, example, case, particular, item, illustration, demonstration

6 **witness,** spectator; **bystander; informant,** informer; character witness

verbs

7 **evidence, show,** witness to, testify to; **demonstrate, illustrate,** exhibit, manifest, display, express; **attest, indicate, signify,** mark, **denote, point to,** bear on; touch on; **imply, suggest,** involve; argue, breathe, tell

8 **testify, attest, give evidence,** witness; **disclose; vouch,** warrant, swear, acknowledge, **affirm,** allege, **certify**

9 **prove, demonstrate, show; establish,** fix, **determine,** ascertain, make out; **settle;** hold good, hold water; follow, follow from

10 **confirm, affirm, attest,** warrant, uphold (*nonformal*), **substantiate,** authenticate, validate, certify, ratify, **verify; corroborate,** bear out, support, **sustain,** fortify, back up, reinforce, strengthen; **document;** prove

11 produce, **advance, present, offer,** proffer, invoke, allege, plead, **bring forward; rally,** marshal, deploy, array

12 cite, name, instance, **exemplify, illustrate,** demonstrate; **document;** quote

13 refer to, appeal to, invoke

adjectives

14 **evidential, factual,** symptomatic, **significant, indicative;** founded on, grounded on, based on; implicit, suggestive; material, telling, convincing, weighty; overwhelming, damning; **conclusive, decisive,** final, indisputable, irrefutable, sure, certain, absolute; documented, documentary; **valid;** authentic, reliable, eyewitness; hearsay, circumstantial

15 **confirming;** substantiating, verifying, corroborating, **supporting;** demonstrative

16 provable, **demonstrable,** sustainable, verifiable

17 **proved, proven, demonstrated,** shown; **established,** fixed, settled, determined, ascertained; **confirmed, substantiated,** attested, **authenticated,** certified, validated, verified; **corroborated,** borne out

18 **unrefuted,** unanswered, undenied

adverbs

19 on the evidence, judging by; **in confirmation,** in support of

20 to illustrate, for example, for instance; thus

913 DISPROOF

nouns

1 disproving, **invalidation,** explosion, negation; exposure

2 **refutation,** confounding, **answer,** complete answer; discrediting **overthrow,** upset, upsetting, subversion, undermining, demolition; **contradiction, denial; conclusive argument**

verbs

3 **disprove, invalidate,** discredit, belie; **negate; expose, show up,** blow up, **puncture,** deflate; undercut

4 **refute, confound,** parry, answer, dismiss, dispose of; **overthrow,** overturn, overwhelm, upset, subvert, defeat, demolish, undermine; crush; silence, shut up; **contradict,** counter, run counter, deny

adjectives

5 **refuting,** confounding; contradictory, contrary

6 **disproved, invalidated,** negated, discredited, belied; **exposed,** shown up; **punctured,** deflated, **exploded; refuted,** confounded; **upset, overthrown,** overturned, **contradicted,** disputed, denied; dismissed, discarded, rejected

7 not proved, not shown; **unsettled; unconfirmed, unsubstantiated; groundless, unfounded; inconclusive,** indecisive

914 QUALIFICATION

nouns

1 **qualification, limitation, limiting, restriction, modification,** hedge, hedging; **specification; allowance, concession,** grant; **reservation, exception,** exemption; **exclusion,** ruling out; special case

2 **condition, provision, proviso; specification,** parameter, given, **limitation; contingency, circumstance; requisite, prerequisite,** obligation; escape clause; **terms,** provisions; grounds; ultimatum

verbs

3 **qualify, limit,** hedge, hedge about, **modify, restrict,** restrain, circumscribe, box in (*nonformal*), narrow; adjust to; regulate by; alter; **temper, season,** soften, moderate, **mitigate,** abate, reduce, diminish

4 **make conditional, make contingent, stipulate;** insist upon

5 **allow for,** provide for, **consider;** allow; **grant, concede,** admit, admit exceptions; **relax, waive, set aside,** ease; disregard, discount

6 **depend,** hang, rest, hinge; rest with

adjectives

7 **qualifying, modifying,** altering; **limiting, restricting,** restrictive, bounding; circumstantial, contingent; **mitigating,** softening

8 **conditional, provisional, specified, stipulated,** fixed, stated, given; **temporary,** expedient

9 **contingent, dependent, depending;** contingent on, based on, turning on; circumscribed by; boxed in (*nonformal*); **subject to,** incidental to, incident to

10 **qualified, modified, conditioned, limited, restricted,** hedged, hedged about; **tempered, seasoned,** softened, **mitigated**

adverbs

11 **conditionally, provisionally, with qualifications; temporarily**

915 NO QUALIFICATIONS

adjectives

1 **unqualified, unconditional, unrestricted, unlimited,** unmitigated, **categorical,** straight; unaltered, unadulterated, intact; **implicit,** unquestioning; **explicit, express, unequivocal,** clear, unmistakable; **peremptory,** indisputable; **without exception, positive, absolute, flat,** definite, definitive, decided, decisive, fixed, final, conclusive; **complete, entire, whole, total,** global; **utter,** perfect, downright, outright, out-and-out, all-out

916 FORESIGHT

nouns

1 **foresight,** looking ahead, forecast; **prediction;** preview; **prospect, anticipation,** contemplation; providence, discretion, preparation, provision, readiness, prudence

2 **forethought;** caution; lead time, advance notice; run-up; foreboding; **foretaste**

verbs

3 **foresee, anticipate,** contemplate, envisage, look ahead, look beyond; **predict;** know beforehand

adjectives

4 **foreseeing;** prepared, ready, prudent; intuitive

5 **foreseeable; foreseen**

917 PREDICTION

nouns

1 **prediction, foretelling,** forecasting, **prognosis, prophecy,** prophesying; **forecast, promise;** prospectus; foresight; foreboding; omen; **guesswork,** speculation; **probability**

2 **divination;** crystal gazing; crystal ball; astrology

3 **prophet;** psychic; astrologer; **oracle**

verbs

4 **predict, foretell, forecast, prophesy,** see ahead, **foresee; divine;** tell fortunes; read palms, guess, speculate; **bet, bet on, gamble**

adjectives

5 forewarning; **prophetic, foreseeing**

6 **ominous,** foreboding

7 **predictable, foreseeable, probable; improbable**

8 **predicted,** prophesied, **foretold, forecast;** foreseen

918 NECESSITY

nouns

1 **necessity, obligation, compulsion, duress**

2 **requirement, requisite; necessity, need, want,** occasion; need for, **call for, demand; prerequisite; must; essential,** indispensable; **necessities, essentials, bare necessities**

3 **urgent need, dire necessity; urgency,** imperative, immediacy, pressure; **predicament**

4 **reflex action,** conditioning; **instinct,** impulse

5 **no choice, no alternative, only choice**

6 **inevitability,** necessity; **certainty;** fate

verbs

7 **necessitate, oblige,** dictate, constrain; insist upon, **compel**

8 **require, need, want, call for; demand,** ask, claim, exact

9 **be necessary;** be obliged, **must, have to,** should, need, **need to**

adjectives

10 **necessary, obligatory, compulsory,** entailed, mandatory; **urgent, imperative,** without choice

11 **requisite, required, needed,** necessary, **wanted, called for,** indicated; **essential, vital, indispensable,** irreplaceable; prerequisite

12 **involuntary, instinctive, automatic, mechanical,** reflex, reflexive, conditioned; **unconscious,** unthinking, blind; **unwitting,** un-

intentional, unwilling; **compulsive**; forced; **impulsive**

13 **inevitable, unavoidable,** necessary, **inescapable,** irrevocable; uncontrollable; **relentless,** inexorable, inflexible; irresistible; **certain,** fateful, **sure;** destined, **fated**

adverbs

14 **necessarily, of necessity,** from necessity; without choice; **willynilly;** if necessary, if need be

15 **involuntarily, instinctively, automatically, mechanically;** blindly, **unconsciously, unwittingly,** unintentionally, **compulsively; unwillingly**

16 **inevitably,** necessarily; irrevocably; uncontrollably; relentlessly, inexorably; **certainly, surely**

919 PREDETERMINATION

nouns

1 decree; foregone conclusion; **necessity**

2 **fate,** fatality, **fortune, lot,** cup, **portion,** future; **destiny,** destination, end; **doom, God's will; inevitability;** stars, planets, astrology; **Providence, Heaven**

3 **determinism, fatalism**

verbs

4 necessitate, **ordain,** fate, mark, appoint; **doom**

adjectives

5 **determined, predetermined, predestined;** foregone

6 **destined, fated,** fateful, ordained, written, marked, in store; **doomed; inevitable**

920 PREARRANGEMENT

nouns

1 plotting, planning, scheming; **reservation,** booking

2 **schedule, programme, bill, calendar, roster,** rota; blueprint, budget; **prospectus; agenda; menu**

verbs

3 **prearrange;** plot, plan, scheme; **reserve, book**

4 (nonformal terms) **fix, rig,** pack; sew up; frame, set up; throw

5 **schedule, line up** (nonformal), **slate, book,** bill, programme, budget

adjectives

6 cut out; premeditated, plotted, planned, schemed; cut-and-dried

7 (nonformal terms) **fixed, rigged,** packed; sewn up; set-up

8 **scheduled,** booked, billed, to come

921 POSSIBILITY

nouns

1 **possibility, probability, likelihood;** the possible, the feasible; **potential,** potentiality, contingency, eventuality; **chance, prospect;** off chance; hope; even chance;

2 **practicality,** feasibility; viability; access, **availability**

verbs

3 **be possible,** could be, might be

4 make possible, **enable,** permit

adjectives

5 possible; probable, likely; conceivable, imaginable; plausible; potential; contingent

6 practicable, practical, feasible, workable, negotiable; viable

7 accessible, within reach; open; obtainable, available

adverbs

8 possibly, conceivably, perhaps, maybe

9 at all, ever; if possible, God willing

922 IMPOSSIBILITY

nouns

1 impossibility, hopelessness, no chance; absurdity, paradox; impossible, the impossible

verbs

2 be impossible, contradict itself

3 make impossible, rule out, disqualify, bar, prohibit

adjectives

4 impossible, not possible, inconceivable, unimaginable, unthinkable, out of the question; hopeless; absurd, ridiculous, preposterous; paradoxical; excluded, barred, prohibited

5 impracticable, impractical; unworkable; insurmountable, insuperable, beyond one

6 inaccessible, beyond reach; impenetrable, impervious; closed to, denied to, lost to; unavailable

adverbs

7 impossibly, inconceivably

923 PROBABILITY

nouns

1 probability, likelihood; chance, odds; expectation, prospect; good chance; presumption; tendency; possibility

verbs

2 be probable, seem likely, could be, promise, be promising, think likely, daresay, presume, suppose

adjectives

3 probable, likely, liable, apt, promising, hopeful; foreseeable, predictable; statistical

4 plausible; reasonable; credible, conceivable

adverbs

5 probably, likely, most likely, very likely; doubtless, no doubt, presumably

924 IMPROBABILITY

nouns

1 poor prospect, poor outlook, fat chance (*nonformal*); small chance, little chance, no chance

verbs

2 be improbable, not be likely, be far-fetched

adjectives

3 improbable, unlikely, far-fetched, hardly possible, doubtful, dubious, questionable, implausible, incredible, unbelievable; unexpected, unpredictable

925 CERTAINTY

nouns

1 **certainty, assurance,** certain knowledge; **necessity, inevitability; truth; fact**

2 (*nonformal terms*) **sure thing,** dead certainty, dead cert, sure thing

3 **reliability, validity;** predictability; **stability, firmness, solidity, security; authenticity**

4 **confidence,** conviction, belief, assurance, security; **faith; trust; self-confidence, self-reliance**

5 **assurance;** reassurance; **determination; verification, corroboration,** check, double-check, checking; **confirmation**

verbs

6 **be certain, be confident,** feel sure, rest assured, **have no doubt,** not doubt; **know, just know**

7 **make sure, make certain, assure, ensure, certify; ascertain, find out; determine,** decide, **establish,** settle, fix, clear up, sort out; **reassure**

8 **verify, confirm,** test, prove, validate, **check,** double-check

adjectives

9 **certain, sure;** bound; **positive, absolute, definite;** decisive, conclusive; clear, unequivocal, unmistakable, unambiguous; **necessary,** predetermined, predestined, **inevitable; true**

10 **obvious, patent, unquestionable, undeniable, self-evident;** indisputable, **irrefutable,** absolute; **demonstrable, provable;**

well-founded, well-established; factual, **real,** actual

11 **undoubted, unquestioned, undisputed,** unchallenged; **doubtless,** beyond question

12 **reliable, dependable, sure, trustworthy;** predictable; **secure, solid, sound, firm,** fast, **stable, substantial,** staunch, steady, **steadfast, faithful, unfailing**

13 **authoritative, authentic, official;** standard, approved, accepted, received

14 **assured,** made sure; **determined, decided,** ascertained; settled, established, fixed, set, stated, secure; **certified,** attested, guaranteed, warranted, tested, tried

15 **confident, sure,** secure, **assured,** reassured, decided, determined; **convinced,** persuaded, positive, **self-confident, self-assured**

16 **dogmatic,** didactic, **positive,** peremptory; **opinionated;** doctrinaire

adverbs

17 **certainly, surely, assuredly, positively, absolutely, definitely,** decidedly, decisively, distinctly, clearly, unequivocally, unmistakably; **for certain,** in truth; **indeed;** truly; of course

18 **surely, sure,** sure enough, for sure (*nonformal*)

19 **unquestionably, without question, undoubtedly, admittedly, undeniably;** doubtless, **no doubt, without doubt**

926 UNCERTAINTY

nouns

1 uncertainty; chance, luck; indecision, hesitation, hesitancy; suspense; doubt; disbelief

2 bewilderment, embarrassment, confusion, perplexity, puzzlement, predicament, plight, quandary, dilemma, puzzle, problem; ambiguity

3 insecurity, infirmity, instability, hazard, danger, risk, peril

4 (an uncertainty) gamble, guess, estimate, chance; contingency; question, open question; undecided issue, loose end; grey area, borderline case

verbs

5 be uncertain, feel unsure; depend; doubt, question, puzzle over, agonize over; wonder; flounder, grope

6 think twice; falter, dither, hesitate, vacillate

7 baffle, confound, daze, muddle, mystify, puzzle

8 (nonformal terms) stump, floor, throw, get, beat

9 make uncertain, obscure, muddle, muddy, confuse

adjectives

10 uncertain, unsure; doubting, agnostic, sceptical, unconvinced; unpredictable, incalculable, unaccountable; equivocal, imprecise, ambiguous; fickle, capricious, whimsical, erratic, variable, wavering, changeable; hesitant, hesitating, indecisive, irresolute

11 doubtful, in doubt, dubious, questionable, problematic, problematical, speculative, debatable, arguable, controversial, suspicious, suspect; in question, in dispute, at issue

12 undecided, unsettled; untold; dependent, pending, depending, contingent, conditional, conditioned; open, in question, at issue, in suspense

13 vague, indefinite, indecisive, indeterminate, random, chance; indefinable, unclear, indistinct, fuzzy, obscure, confused, hazy, shadowy, misty, foggy, murky, blurred, veiled; loose, lax, inaccurate, imprecise; unspecified; broad, general, sweeping; amorphous, shapeless; disordered, chaotic, incoherent

14 unreliable, treacherous, unsure, insecure, unsound, infirm, unstable, insubstantial, unsteady, desultory, shaky; precarious, hazardous, dangerous, perilous, risky, ticklish; shifty, shifting, slippery; provisional, tentative, temporary

15 bewildered, disconcerted, embarrassed, disturbed, upset, perturbed, bothered, confused; guessing; lost, astray, adrift, at sea, disoriented; insecure

16 perplexed, confounded, mystified, puzzled, nonplussed, baffled, muddled, dazed; in suspense

17 (nonformal terms) beat, licked, stuck, floored, stumped, thrown, boggled

18 bewildering, confusing, distracting, disconcerting, embarrass-

ing, disturbing, **upsetting**; perplexing, **baffling**, mystifying, mysterious, puzzling, funny; **enigmatic**

adverbs

19 uncertainly; doubtfully, dubiously; in suspense, at sea

20 vaguely, **indefinitely**; broadly, generally

927 CHANCE

nouns

1 **chance, luck; fortune**, fate, destiny, lot; uncertainty; break (*nonformal*), the breaks (*nonformal*); **probability**; **risk, gamble; opportunity**

2 Chance, Fortune, Luck, Lady Luck

3 (*chance event*) **happening, accident**, adventure, hazard; contingency; **fluke**, freak; lucky shot, long shot

4 **good chance**, sporting chance, even chance, good possibility; **likelihood, possibility**, probability, favourable prospect; **sure bet, best bet**, main chance

5 **small chance**, little chance, dark horse, poor lookout (*nonformal*), little opportunity, **off chance, outside chance** (*nonformal*), remote possibility, slim chance, fighting chance; poor bet, long shot (*nonformal*)

6 **no chance, impossibility**, hopelessness

verbs

7 **chance**, hazard, **happen**, come, **turn up**, pop up (*nonformal*), befall

8 **risk, gamble, bet; predict**

adjectives

9 **chance; risky** (*nonformal*); **fortuitous, accidental, lucky**, fortunate; **casual**, incidental, contingent; indeterminate; **unexpected, unpredictable, unforeseen**

10 **aimless**, mindless; **haphazard, random**, stray, inexplicable, unaccountable, promiscuous, indiscriminate, casual

11 **unintentional**, unintended, **unwitting, unthinking**, unconscious, involuntary

adverbs

12 **by chance, by accident, accidentally, casually**, incidentally, by coincidence, by hazard; somehow

13 **aimlessly; haphazardly**, inexplicably, unaccountably, indiscriminately, casually, **at random**

14 **unintentionally, unwittingly**, unexpectedly, unconsciously, involuntarily

928 TRUTH

nouns

1 **truth**, very truth; historical truth, **objective truth, fact, reality**; truthfulness

2 **a truth, an axiom;** a premise, a given

3 **the truth**, the case; gospel, gospel truth, Bible truth, revealed truth

4 (*nonformal terms*) **what's what**, God's truth, it, the goods, the gospel, the lowdown

5 **accuracy, correctness, exactness; precision; perfection**; fidel-

ity; the letter; strictness, severity, rigidity; nicety, delicacy

6 validity, solidity, authority, weight, force

7 authenticity, legitimacy; realism, naturalness; absolute likeness; **honesty, sincerity**

verbs

8 be true, prove true, hold true, hold good, hold water (*nonformal*), **hold up, stand up, hold,** remain valid; **be truthful**

9 seem true, ring true, sound true, **carry conviction,** convince, persuade, win over

10 be right, be correct; be OK (*nonformal*), add up

11 be accurate, be precise; make precise

12 come true, come about, turn out

adjectives

13 true, truthful; so, gospel; **real, veritable,** objective, **factual, actual, historical,** documentary; objectively true; **certain,** undoubted, unquestionable; **ascertained, proved, proven, verified,** validated, **certified,** demonstrated, confirmed, determined, established, attested, substantiated, **authenticated,** corroborated

14 valid, sound, well-founded, hard, solid, substantial; consistent, logical; **good, just; cogent, weighty, authoritative; legal, lawful, legitimate, binding**

15 genuine, authentic, real, natural, realistic, **lifelike,** literal; verbatim, **legitimate,** rightful, lawful; **bona fide, good, sincere, honest;** candid; undisguised, un-

affected; unassuming, simple, **original;** unqualified; **unadulterated; pure,** sterling, twenty-four carat

16 accurate, correct, right, proper, just; dead right, bang on (*nonformal*), straight; **faultless,** flawless, impeccable; **absolute, perfect**

17 exact, precise, express; even, square; **faithful;** direct; constant; **infallible, strict,** close, severe, **rigorous,** rigid; **nice,** delicate, subtle, **fine,** refined; pinpoint, microscopic

adverbs

18 truly, really, in truth, actually, historically, objectively, rigorously, strictly, strictly speaking, unquestionably, without question, **in reality, in fact,** technically, with truth; **indeed, certainly; undoubtedly**

19 genuinely, really, naturally, **honestly**

20 accurately, correctly, rightly, properly, straight; **perfectly,** impeccably; **just right,** just so; **so**

21 exactly, precisely, to a T, expressly; **just, dead,** right, straight, even, square, **plumb,** directly, squarely, point-blank; verbatim, **literally, faithfully, strictly,** rigorously, rigidly; **definitely, positively, absolutely**

929 WISE SAYING

nouns

1 maxim, proverb, saw, saying, witticism, phrase, word, byword, motto, moral; **precept,** teaching, text, verse; golden saying, proverbial saying; pithy saying, conventional wisdom; proverbs, wisdom

2 axiom, truth, self-evident truth, home truth, obvious truth; theorem; proposition; principle; formula; rule, law, dictate, golden rule

3 platitude, saw, old saw, commonplace, banality, chestnut (*nonformal*),

4 motto, slogan; epithet; inscription

adjectives

5 proverbial; pithy, pungent, succinct, terse, crisp, pointed; banal, tired, trite

930 ERROR

nouns

1 error; untruth; wrong; fallacy; fault, sin, flaw; aberration; heresy; perversion, distortion; mistaking, delusion, illusion; misinterpretation

2 inaccuracy; tolerance, allowance; negligence; approximation; deviation, uncertainty

3 mistake, fault; misconception, misapprehension, misunderstanding; misprint, typist's error; clerical error; miscalculation; misuse; failure, miss, miscarriage

4 slip, lapse, oversight, omission; stumble; false note

5 blunder, gaffe; stupidity, indiscretion; botch, bungle

6 (*nonformal terms*) boob, bloomer, howler, clanger

verbs

7 not square, not figure (*nonformal*)

8 err, go wrong, go amiss, go astray, go awry, stray, deviate, wander; lapse, slip, slip up, trip, stumble; miscalculate; boob (*nonformal*)

9 be wrong, be mistaken; take wrong, be misled, be misguided; deceive oneself, be deceived, delude oneself

10 do amiss; misuse; mismanage; misprint, misread

11 mistake; misunderstand, misinterpret; confuse, mix up, not distinguish

12 blunder, blot one's copy book; embarrass oneself; botch, bungle

13 fluff, blow; put one's foot in it; trip up

adjectives

14 erroneous, untrue, not true, not right; wrong; false, illogical; faulty, flawed, defective, at fault; out, off; wide of the mark; awry, askew; erring, straying, astray, adrift; heretical, unorthodox; perverted, distorted; deceptive, illusory

15 inaccurate, incorrect, imprecise; negligent; vague; approximate, inexact

16 mistaken, in error, erring, wrong

17 unreliable; garbled; unfounded

adverbs

18 erroneously, falsely, by mistake; wrongly; mistakenly; amiss, astray

19 incorrectly

931 ILLUSION

nouns

1 **illusion, delusion,** deluded belief; **misconception,** false belief, wrong impression; **dream, daydream**

2 semblance, **appearance; show,** false light

3 **fancy, imagination**

4 **phantom, spectre; shadow, shade; fantasy,** wildest dream; **figment of the imagination, apparition,** appearance; **vision; shape, form, figure, presence**

5 **optical illusion**

6 **mirage, will o' the wisp**

7 **hallucination;** dream

verbs

8 **hallucinate**

adjectives

9 **illusory; dream-like; visionary; imaginary; erroneous; fantastic; unreal; unfounded; false,** misleading; **seeming,** apparent, ostensible; phantom; surreal

932 DISILLUSIONMENT

nouns

1 **disillusionment, disillusion, disenchantment,** enlightenment; awakening, rude awakening; disappointment

verbs

2 **disillusion; disabuse,** correct, put straight, enlighten; open one's eyes, wake up; disappoint, disenchant; bring one back to earth; burst the bubble; debunk (*nonformal*); expose, show up

3 be disillusioned, be disenchanted, have one's eyes opened

adjectives

4 **disillusioning,** disenchanting, enlightening

5 **disillusioned, disenchanted,** enlightened, set right, put straight; disappointed

933 MENTAL ATTITUDE

nouns

1 **attitude,** mental attitude; psychology; **position, posture,** stance; **feeling, sentiment;** opinion

2 **outlook,** mental outlook; **point of view, viewpoint, standpoint,** perspective, position, stand; side; footing, basis; **view,** sight, light, eye; respect, regard; angle, slant, way of looking at things

3 **disposition, character, nature, temper, temperament,** constitution, stamp, type, stripe, make, mould; **inclination,** mind, **tendency,** grain, vein, set, **leaning,** propensity, preference; **bent, turn, bias,** slant, cast, warp, twist; idiosyncrasy, eccentricity, individualism; aptitude; strain, streak

4 **mood, humour, feeling, feelings, state of mind, frame of mind, temper, morale,** tone, note, **vein; mind,** heart

5 (*pervading attitudes*) **climate,** spiritual climate, moral climate, mores, norms, **ethos,** ideology, world view, Zeitgeist

verbs

6 **view; be disposed to,** prefer, lean toward

adjectives

7 **temperamental,** constitutional; emotional; mental, intellectual, ideological; spiritual; characteristic; innate

8 **disposed, predisposed, prone, inclined, given,** bent, bent on, apt, likely, **minded**

adverbs

9 **temperamentally,** constitutionally; emotionally; mentally, intellectually; morally, spiritually

934 BROAD-MINDEDNESS

nouns

1 **breadth,** latitude; broad mind, spacious mind

2 liberalism, libertarianism; free thought

3 **openness,** open-mindedness, receptiveness; open mind

4 **tolerance,** toleration; **indulgence, forbearance, patience,** long-suffering; **permissiveness;** charity, **magnanimity; compassion** , sympathy; sensitivity

5 **impartiality,** even-handedness, **justice, fairness, objectivity, detachment, disinterestedness;** indifference, neutrality

6 liberal; bleeding heart

verbs

7 **keep an open mind,** not write off, suspend judgment, keep an open mind, judge on its merits; **tolerate; accept, condone,** brook, abide with; **live with** (*nonformal*); shut one's eyes to, look the other way, **overlook, disregard, ignore**

adjectives

8 **broad-minded, broad, wide,** catholic, wide-ranging; cosmopolitan; ecumenical

9 **liberal;** libertarian

10 **open-minded, open, receptive,** undogmatic, unfanatical

11 **tolerant; indulgent, lenient; forbearing, patient, long-suffering; charitable, generous, magnanimous;** compassionate, sympathetic, sensitive

12 **unprejudiced, unbiased; impartial, fair, just,** equitable, objective, dispassionate, impersonal, detached, disinterested; indifferent, neutral

13 **liberalizing, liberating, broadening,** enlightening

935 NARROW-MINDEDNESS

nouns

1 **narrow-mindedness,** narrowness; **small-mindedness, meanness, pettiness; bigotry,** fanaticism; blind spot, tunnel vision; closed mind; narrow views

2 **intolerance;** insensitivity

3 **prejudice,** preconception; **bias,** bent, leaning, inclination; jaundiced eye; partisanship, favouritism

4 **discrimination; xenophobia, chauvinism,** jingoism; fascism; neo-Nazism; class prejudice, class distinction, class hatred,

class war; anti-Semitism; **racism,** racialism, racial discrimination; colour bar (*old*), **segregation,** apartheid; sex discrimination, sexism, male chauvinism, misogyny; ageism, age discrimination; social prejudice

5 **bigot; racist, racialist; chauvinist,** xenophobe; **sexist,** male chauvinist, man-hater, misogynist; fanatic

verbs

6 blind oneself

7 judge beforehand

8 **discriminate against;** bait, **bash**

9 **prejudice,** prejudice against, **jaundice, influence, sway, bias;** warp, twist, bend, distort

adjectives

10 **narrow-minded,** narrow, closed, mean-spirited; **small, little, mean, petty; bigoted,** fanatical; provincial, insular, parochial; hidebound, straitlaced, stuffy (*nonformal*); authoritarian; **shortsighted,** unimaginative

11 intolerant

12 **prejudiced, biased, jaundiced, coloured; partial,** one-sided, partisan; influenced, swayed, warped, twisted; **chauvinistic,** xenophobic; **racist; sexist;** dogmatic, doctrinaire, **opinionated**

936 CURIOSITY

nouns

1 **curiosity, inquisitiveness; interest;** thirst for knowledge, inquiring *or* enquiring mind; **attention; alertness,** vigilance; nosiness

(*nonformal*), prying; **morbid curiosity**

2 inquisitive person; **busybody,** nosy parker (*nonformal*)

verbs

3 **be curious, take an interest;** be alert, be watchful, be vigilant; prick up one's ears, pay attention; interrogate, quiz, question, inquire, query; stare, gape, peer; seek, dig up, nose out

4 **pry, snoop,** stick *or* poke one's nose into; meddle, interfere

adjectives

5 **curious, inquisitive,** inquiring, interested, quizzical; **alert,** tuned in (*nonformal*), **attentive; morbid;** itchy

6 **prying,** snooping

937 INCURIOSITY

nouns

1 disinterest, **indifference, apathy,** carelessness, **lack of interest;** aloofness, detachment, withdrawal

verbs

2 **take no interest in, not care;** be indifferent

adjectives

3 **uninquisitive,** bored; **inattentive; uninterested,** unconcerned, disinterested, **indifferent, apathetic,** passive, impassive, stolid; phlegmatic, listless; careless, heedless, regardless, mindless; aloof, detached, distant, withdrawn

938 ATTENTION

nouns

1 **attention, attention span; heed;** consideration, thought, mind; **awareness, consciousness, alertness; notice;** concentration; **curiosity**

2 **interest, concern, curiosity; enthusiasm,** passion, ardour, zeal; special interest

3 **absorption, concentration, application, study, preoccupation,** engagement, **involvement;** obsession; rapt attention; contemplation, meditation

4 **close attention,** close study, scrutiny, fixed regard, strict attention

verbs

5 **attend to,** look to, **see to;** not forget, **turn to**

6 **heed, attend,** tend, mind, watch, observe, regard, look, see, view, mark, remark, note, notice

7 hark, listen, hear

8 **pay attention, take heed, look out, watch out** (nonformal), **take care; look sharp;** miss nothing; **concentrate on, study,** scrutinize

9 **take note of, take into consideration** or **account, bear in mind**

10 **mention,** touch on; **single out,** pick out, focus on, **feature,** highlight; **direct to,** address to; **mention,** specify, touch on, cite, **refer to,** allude to; **point out, point to**

11 **strike one, impress one, excite notice,** arouse notice

12 **interest, concern, titillate,** tantalize, **attract,** invite, **fascinate, provoke, stimulate, arouse, excite,** excite interest

13 **absorb, immerse, occupy, preoccupy, engage,** involve; **obsess, grip, fascinate, enthral, hold spellbound,** grab (nonformal), charm, mesmerize, hypnotize

adjectives

14 **attentive, heedful, mindful;** intent, diligent, assiduous, intense, earnest, concentrated; **careful;** observant; watchful, aware, alert; **curious;** meticulous, niggling, pernickety

15 **interested,** concerned; **alert to, sensitive to; curious;** tantalized, titillated, fascinated, excited; enthusiastic, passionate

16 **engrossed, absorbed,** single-minded, **occupied, preoccupied, engaged, intent, obsessed,** swept up, involved, **engrossed in, lost in, immersed in,** submerged in, buried in; contemplating, contemplative, studying, studious, meditative, meditating

17 **gripped, fascinated, enthralled, rapt, spellbound,** charmed, enchanted, mesmerized, **hypnotized,** fixed, caught, riveted

18 **interesting, stimulating, provocative,** provoking; **titillating, tantalizing, inviting, exciting;** lively, racy, juicy, spicy; readable

19 **absorbing,** consuming, **gripping,** riveting, **arresting,** engaging, attractive, **fascinating, enthralling,** enchanting, magnetic, hypnotic, mesmerizing

adverbs

20 **attentively,** with attention; with interest; **intently,** without distraction

939 INATTENTION

nouns

1 indifference; disregard; **carelessness,** negligence; distraction, **daydreaming**

verbs

2 **be inattentive,** not attend, not notice, miss, not heed; **disregard, overlook, ignore**

3 **wander, stray,** ramble; **daydream**

4 **dismiss,** think no more of, forget; **shrug off,** laugh off (*nonformal*)

5 **escape one,** get by, be missed, not register

adjectives

6 **inattentive, distracted;** careless, **scatter-brained,** scatty (*nonformal*)

7 **oblivious, unconscious, preoccupied**

8 **unwary, unprepared, asleep,** sleeping, nodding, napping; daydreaming, in a world of one's own

940 DISTRACTION, CONFUSION

nouns

1 **distraction, diversion**

2 **abstraction, preoccupation, absorption,** musing; **dreaming, daydreaming, brown study,** trance; dream, **daydream,** fantasy

3 **confusion, fluster, flutter,** flurry; disorientation, **muddle,** daze; **disorder,** chaos, jumble, **bewilderment, embarrassment, disturbance, upset,** frenzy, bother; haze, fog, mist, cloud; **perplexity**

4 **dizziness, vertigo,** spinning head, **lightheadedness, giddiness,** wooziness (*nonformal*)

5 **flightiness, giddiness,** frivolity, scattiness (*nonformal*), foolishness

verbs

6 **distract, divert,** take one's mind off, cause one's mind to wander; trip up

7 **confuse, mix up, fluster; flummox, ruffle, muddle, befuddle, daze; disconcert, embarrass, put out, disturb, bother,** bug (*nonformal*); fog, mist, cloud

8 **dizzy,** make one's head reel *or* swim

9 **muse, moon** (*nonformal*), **dream, daydream,** fantasize; be lost in thought, be away in a world of one's own, be not with it (*nonformal*)

adjectives

10 **distracted, distraught,** wandering, rambling; **wild, frantic, beside oneself**

11 **bemused, musing, preoccupied, absorbed, engrossed,** taken up; **absent,** faraway, elsewhere, somewhere else, not there; pensive, meditative; lost; rapt, transported, ecstatic; **unconscious, oblivious; dreaming, dreamy,**

drowsing, dozing, nodding, napping; **daydreaming**

12 **confused, mixed-up; flustered**, ruffled, rattled; **upset**, unsettled, **disorganized, disordered**, disoriented, disorientated, chaotic, jumbled; shaken, **disconcerted**, **embarrassed, disturbed**, perturbed, bothered; **perplexed**

13 **muddled, befuddled**; adrift, at sea, foggy, hazy, misted, misty, cloudy

14 **dazed, dazzled, silly**, knocked silly; **groggy** (*nonformal*); **dizzy, giddy**, spinning, swimming, turned around; **drunk, drunken**

15 **harebrained, giddy**, frivolous; **thoughtless, brainless**

941 IMAGINATION

nouns

1 **imagination**, imagining, **fancy, fantasy**; mind's eye

2 **creative thought**, conception; lateral thinking; poetic imagination, artistic imagination; inspiration, muse; genius

3 **invention, inventiveness, originality, creativity**, fabrication, ingenuity; **fertility; fiction**

4 whim, figment, imagination, invention; brainchild; **imagining**, fancy, imagery; **fantasy, make-believe**; phantom, vision, apparition, **fiction**, myth, romance; wildest dreams; **bubble, illusion**; hallucination, delirium

5 **picture, vision, image**, mental image, mental picture, concept, **conception, imagery**

6 **idealism; ideal**; wishful thinking, wish fulfilment

7 **dream; daydream**, pipe dream (*nonformal*); **vision; nightmare**, bad dream

8 **inventor; creative artist**, poet; **visionary, idealist**; prophet; **dreamer**, wishful thinker; **romantic**; utopian; escapist; enthusiast

verbs

9 **imagine, fancy, conceive**; invent, create, originate, make, think up, dream up, shape, mould, coin, hatch, concoct, fabricate, produce; **suppose; fantasize**

10 **visualize, envisage, picture**, represent, **see; call up**, summon up, conjure up, realize

11 **idealize, romanticize; dream**; dream of, dream on; **daydream**

adjectives

12 **imaginative**, conceptual; **inventive, original**, shaping, **creative, ingenious; productive**, fertile, prolific, teeming, pregnant; **inspired**

13 **imaginary, imagined, fancied**; unreal, unrealistic; **illusory**

14 **fanciful**, whimsical; **fantastic**, extravagant, preposterous, wild, baroque, florid; bizarre, grotesque

15 **fictitious, make-believe**, fictional, fabricated; **fabulous, mythical**, mythological, legendary

16 **aerial, ethereal;** gossamer

17 **ideal, idealized;** utopian; heavenly, celestial

18 **visionary, idealistic; romantic, romanticized**, romanticizing; **impractical, unrealistic;** starry-eyed

19 dreamy; dreaming, daydreaming, entranced, enchanted, spellbound, spelled, charmed

20 imaginable, conceivable

942 UNIMAGINATIVE-NESS

nouns

1 unimaginativeness; prosaicness; dullness, dryness; aridity, infertility; **unoriginality**

2 (*practical attitude*) **realism, practicality,** hardheadedness; earthliness, wordliness; **pragmatism; reasonableness, rationality**

3 realist, pragmatist

adjectives

4 unimaginative; prosaic, unpoetic; **literal; mundane; staid, stuffy** (*nonformal*); stolid; **dull, dry;** arid, barren, infertile; **unoriginal, uninspired; uninventive**

5 realistic, practical; pragmatic, scientific; unromantic, unsentimental, **hardheaded, matter-of-fact, down-to-earth;** worldly, earthy, secular; sensible, reasonable, rational; **simplistic**

943 SPECTRE

nouns

1 spectre, ghost, phantom, shadow, **apparition,** presence, shape, form; **spirit;** zombie; vision; banshee; poltergeist

2 double, fetch

3 eeriness, ghostliness, weirdness, spookiness (*nonformal*)

verbs

4 haunt, possess, control

adjectives

5 spectral; ghostly, spiritual, psychic; phantom, shadowy; **occult, supernatural**

6 disembodied, bodiless, immaterial

7 weird, eerie, uncanny, unearthly, macabre; spooky (*nonformal*)

8 haunted, possessed

944 MEMORY

nouns

1 memory, remembrance, recollection, mind; **mind's eye; short-term memory, long-term memory; group memory,** collective memory, race memory

2 retention, retentiveness, memory span; good memory; total memory, photographic memory, total recall

3 remembering, remembrance, recollection, recall; reflection, reconsideration; **retrospect,** hindsight, looking back; flashback, **reminiscence,** review; **memorization,** rote learning

4 recognition, identification; realization

5 reminder, remembrance; prompt; cue, hint; **memorandum**

6 memento, remembrance, token, trophy, souvenir, keepsake, relic, favour; commemoration, memorial; **memorabilia**

7 mnemonics, memory training

verbs

8 remember, recall, recollect; reflect; **think of,** call *or* bring to mind, evoke, revive, recapture, bring back; **think back,** look back; review; **reminisce**

9 recognize, know, tell, distinguish, make out; **identify, place;** realize

10 bear in mind, retain, keep; **treasure, cherish**

11 sink in, penetrate, make an impression; stick in the mind; obsess; plague one

12 recur, come back, re-enter

13 memorize, study; learn by heart, learn verbatim; recite, repeat, parrot

14 instil, impress, imprint, stamp, inscribe, etch; get across

15 review, brush up; cram (*nonformal*), swot up (*nonformal*)

16 remind, bring back; **recall,** suggest, carry back; **prompt;** nudge

adjectives

17 recollective; mnemonic; **retrospective,** in retrospect; **reminiscent,** mindful, suggestive, evocative

18 remembered, recollected, recalled; enduring, lasting; vivid, fresh, alive

19 remembering, mindful; haunted, plagued, obsessed

20 memorable; notable

21 unforgettable, indelible; haunting, persistent, recurrent, nagging; obsessive

945 FORGETFULNESS

nouns

1 forgetfulness, absent-mindedness; short memory; **oblivion, forgetting;** forgiveness

2 memory loss, amnesia; failure; **memory gap,** blackout (*nonformal*); false memory

3 block, mental block; repression, suppression, defence mechanism

verbs

4 forget; not remember, fail to remember; lose sight of

5 unlearn, obliterate; **forgive**

6 be forgotten, escape one, slip one's mind

adjectives

7 forgotten, unremembered, lost, erased, effaced, obliterated

8 forgetful, unmindful, absent-minded, **oblivious;** amnesic; blocked, repressed, suppressed, sublimated; heedless

9 forgettable, unmemorable

adverbs

10 forgetfully, absent-mindedly

946 SUFFICIENCY

nouns

1 sufficiency, adequacy, enough; exact measure, right amount; bare minimum, just enough

2 plenty, plenitude; myriad, numerousness; **amplitude; substantiality; abundance, copiousness;** exuberance; **liberality, generosity; extravagance; wealth, opulence,** richness, affluence; maximum; **fullness**, repletion; **preva-lence, profusion**, riot; much, lots

verbs

3 **suffice, do**, just do, serve; work, **avail**; serve the purpose, **suit**; qualify, meet, fulfil, **satisfy**, meet requirements; **pass muster, pass**; hold, stand, stand up, take it, bear; stretch (*nonformal*), reach, go around

4 **abound**, teem, crawl with, swarm with; proliferate; **over-flow**, flood

adjectives

5 **sufficient; enough, ample**, sub-stantial, **plenty, satisfactory, ad-equate**, decent, due; competent; commensurate, proportionate; suitable, fit; **good enough**, up to, equal to; minimal, minimum

6 **plentiful**, in plenty; numerous, much, many; **ample**; wholesale; abundant, **copious**, exuberant, riotous; flush; **lavish, generous, liberal, extravagant, prodigal; luxuriant, rich, fat, wealthy, opulent, affluent, full**, overflow-ing; inexhaustible; **profuse**; prevalent, rife

adverbs

7 **sufficiently, amply,** substantially, **satisfactorily, enough;** compe-tently, **adequately**

8 **plentifully, in plenty, abundant-ly,** in abundance, copiously, no end (*nonformal*); **lavishly, gener-ously, liberally, extravagantly; fully,** to the full; richly, opulent-ly; **profusely**

947 INSUFFICIENCY

nouns

1 **insufficiency, inadequacy;** short supply; **incompetence,** unsuit-ability

2 **meagreness;** meanness, narrow-ness (*nonformal*), stinginess, par-simony; smallness, paltriness; austerity

3 **scarcity**, sparsity; **dearth, pau-city,** poverty; **rarity,** uncommon-ness

4 **want, lack, need, deficiency, deficit, shortage, shortfall,** in-completeness, shortcoming, im-perfection; **destitution,** impover-ishment, deprivation; starvation, famine, drought

5 **pittance,** dole

6 **undernourishment, malnutri-tion**

verbs

7 **want, lack, need, require;** miss

8 **be insufficient**, not qualify, **fall short;** want, want for, lack, fail

adjectives

9 **insufficient, inadequate;** defec-tive, incomplete, imperfect, defi-cient, lacking, failing, wanting; **unsatisfactory; incompetent,** unequal to, unqualified

10 **meagre, slight,** skimpy; scanty; spare; miserly, stingy, mean; aus-tere, ascetic; frugal, sparing; poor, impoverished; small, puny, paltry; thin, lean, skinny, slim, slender, scrawny; dwarfed, stunt-ed; limited; watered, watery; sub-sistence, starvation

11 **scarce, sparse, scanty; in short supply, rare,** uncommon

12 ill-equipped, ill off; underfed, undernourished; shorthanded, shortstaffed; **empty-handed, poor,** impoverished; starved, half-starved, starving, famished

13 wanting, lacking, needing, missing; **short, short of; out of,** destitute of, bare of, void of, empty of, devoid of, forlorn of, bereft of, deprived of, bankrupt in

adverbs

14 insufficiently; inadequately

15 slightly, poorly, frugally, sparingly

16 scarcely, sparsely, scantily, skimpily; rarely, uncommonly

948 EXCESS

nouns

1 excess, extravagance, overindulgence, **intemperance;** abandon; gluttony; extremity, **extremes; outrageousness, unreasonableness;** hyperbole, **exaggeration**

2 superabundance, overabundance, **plethora, oversupply; overdose;** spate, avalanche, landslide, deluge, flood

3 surfeit, glut

4 fat; duplication, overlap; **luxury,** extravagance, **embellishment; padding, filling**

5 surplus, leftovers, plus; margin; **remainder, balance, leftover, extra, spare;** bonus, dividend; gratuity, tip

6 overdoing; overkill; **overwork,** tax, strain

7 stretching, straining, stretch, strain, tension; inflation, swelling

verbs

8 swarm, run riot, teem; overflow, flood, spill over, overrun, overgrow, fill

9 exceed, surpass, pass, top, transcend, go beyond; overstep, overrun, **overreach**

10 overdo, go too far, go overboard; **overreact; overtax,** overexert, overuse; **overwork; exaggerate**

11 overstretch, stretch, strain; **overexpand,** inflate, swell

12 overdose; **flood, deluge,** inundate, engulf, swamp, overwhelm; lavish with

13 overload, overburden, overcharge; stuff, crowd, cram, jam, pack, choke; **gorge, satiate; saturate,** soak, drench

adjectives

14 excessive, inordinate, extravagant; unrestrained, abandoned; extreme; monstrous, enormous, jumbo, gigantic; too much, a bit much; **exorbitant, undue, outrageous, unreasonable; boundless; fabulous; exaggerated**

15 superfluous, redundant; excess, in excess; unnecessary, expendable, dispensable, **needless,** gratuitous, uncalled-for; spare, to spare

16 surplus, remaining, unused, leftover; over, **over and above; extra,** spare

17 lavish, prodigal, overgenerous; **swarming, teeming,** overpopulated; plentiful

18 overloaded, saturated, drenched, soaked; gorged, overfed, bloated, swollen, **stuffed, crowded, overcrowded,**

crammed, jammed, packed, jam-packed; choked, **congested,** stuffed up; overflowing, running over; **bursting,** distended, **swollen,** bloated

adverbs

19 excessively, inordinately, overly, over, too much; **too; unduly, outrageously**

20 **in** or **to excess, to extremes,** flat out (*nonformal*), too far

21 lavishly, extravagantly

22 unnecessarily, needlessly

949 SATIETY

nouns

1 satisfaction, fullness, surfeit, glut; contentment; **saturation**

2 overdose

verbs

3 satisfy, allay; **surfeit, glut, gorge;** fill, fill up; saturate; **stuff, cram; overfill,** overdose, overfeed

4 **have enough, have one's fill; be fed up** (*nonformal*), have had it

adjectives

5 satiated, sated, satisfied; gorged, replete; **full,** full of, saturated; **stuffed,** crammed; **fed up** (*nonformal*); disgusted, **sick of,** tired of, sick and tired of

6 satisfying, filling

950 EXPEDIENCE

nouns

1 **expedience** or **expediency, desirability; fitness,** propriety, decency, **suitability,** feasibility, **convenience; usefulness; advantage, profit;** wisdom, prudence

2 **expedient, means, provision, measure, step, action,** effort, **move, manoeuvre,** course of action; tactic, **device,** contrivance, stratagem, **shift; resort;** answer, solution; **last resort**

verbs

3 come in handy; **forward, advance, promote, profit, benefit; work, serve,** do the trick (*nonformal*); **be fitting,** fit, be right

4 **make do,** cope, manage, manage with, do with

adjectives

5 **expedient, desirable, advisable; appropriate, fit, fitting, right, proper,** good, **becoming,** likely, **suitable,** feasible, **convenient,** happy; timely, opportune; **useful, advantageous, favourable; profitable,** worthwhile; **wise**

6 **practical,** practicable; feasible, workable; **efficient,** effective

7 **makeshift, stopgap,** improvised; **ad hoc;** temporary, provisional

adverbs

8 **appropriately, suitably,** rightly, properly, conveniently; practically; desirably, advantageously

951 INEXPEDIENCE

nouns

1 **inexpedience; unsuitability,** incongruity; **inconvenience,** awkwardness; worthlessness, futility, uselessness

2 **disadvantage, drawback, liability; detriment,** prejudice, loss, damage, hurt, harm, injury; **handicap,** disability; drag

3 **inconvenience, trouble, bother;** awkwardness, clumsiness

verbs

4 **inconvenience, put out, burden, embarrass; trouble, bother,** impose upon; harm

adjectives

5 **undesirable, inadvisable; impractical,** unworkable; **ill-advised, unwise; unfit, inappropriate, unsuitable,** inept, **improper, wrong,** bad; unfortunate, unhappy; unprofitable; futile

6 **disadvantageous, unfavourable;** unprofitable, unrewarding, worthless, useless; **detrimental,** harmful

7 **inconvenient; awkward,** clumsy, unwieldy, troublesome

adverbs

8 **inappropriately, unsuitably;** unfortunately, unhappily

9 uselessly; **inconveniently, with** difficulty

952 IMPORTANCE

nouns

1 **importance, significance, consequence,** consideration, note, mark, **moment, weight, gravity;** concern, interest; **priority,** precedence, superiority, **supremacy;** value, worth, merit, excellence; self-importance

2 **prominence, eminence, greatness,** distinction; prestige, esteem, reputation, honour, glory, renown, dignity, **fame; stardom,** celebrity

3 **gravity, seriousness,** solemnity

4 **urgency;** pressure, **stress,** tension; **crisis, emergency;** moment of truth, turning point, climax

5 **important thing,** chief thing, **the point, main point,** main thing, issue; **essential,** fundamental; **gist, core; crux,** crucial point; turning point, **climax, crisis;** cornerstone; landmark, milestone, bench mark

6 **feature, highlight,** high spot, main attraction

7 **personage, important person, somebody, notable,** figure; **celebrity,** famous person, personality; name, big name, very important person; **worthy; dignitary; magnate;** tycoon, baron; power; Establishment; brass, top brass

8 (*nonformal terms*) **big shot,** big cheese, big noise, something, VIP; queen bee

9 **chief, principal,** chief executive, **king; leading light, star,** superstar, prima donna, lead

10 (*nonformal terms*) **boss,** top dog, Mr Big, his nibs

verbs

11 **matter,** signify, **count, tell, carry weight,** be prominent, stand out, mean much; be something, be somebody; be featured, star

12 **value,** esteem, **treasure, prize,** appreciate, **rate highly,** think highly of, think well of

13 **emphasize, stress,** feature, highlight, **accent, accentuate, highlight,** spotlight; **star,** underline; rub in; harp on; dwell on

14 **feature,** headline (*nonformal*); **star**

15 **dramatize,** play up

adjectives

16 important, major, momentous, significant, considerable, substantial, material, **great,** grand, big; superior

17 of importance, of significance, of consequence, of note; of concern, of interest; viable

18 notable, noteworthy, celebrated, remarkable, marked; memorable, unforgettable; striking, telling; **eminent, prominent,** conspicuous, noble, **outstanding, distinguished;** prestigious, esteemed, reputable; **extraordinary, exceptional, special,** rare

19 weighty, grave, sober, sobering, solemn, serious, earnest; fateful, fatal; formidable, awe-inspiring, imposing

20 emphatic, decided, positive, forceful, forcible; **emphasized, stressed,** accented, accentuated, pointed

21 urgent, imperative, compelling, pressing, insistent, instant; crucial, critical

22 vital, all-important, crucial; **essential,** fundamental, indispensable, basic, material; **central,** focal

23 paramount, principal, leading, foremost, main, chief, number one (nonformal), premier, **prime, primary, supreme,** cardinal; highest, uppermost, topmost, ranking, **dominant,** predominant, master, controlling, **overruling,** overriding

adverbs

24 importantly, significantly, materially, greatly, grandly; eminently, prominently, conspicuously, **outstandingly,** notably, markedly, remarkably

953 UNIMPORTANCE

nouns

1 unimportance, insignificance, indifference; inferiority; **smallness; pettiness;** irrelevance

2 meanness, sadness, worthlessness

3 triviality; superficiality, shallowness; **frivolity; foolishness,** silliness; emptiness; vanity, idleness, futility

4 trivia, trifles; rubbish, trash; details, minor details

5 trifle, triviality, oddment, trinket, bauble, toy; joke, farce, child's play

6 a nobody, nonentity, a nothing, cipher; lightweight, mediocrity

7 dalliance, flirtation; toying, fiddling, playing, fooling, tinkering, pottering; dabbling, smattering; loitering, idling

8 (nonformal terms) fiddling around, horsing around, fooling around, messing around, playing around, mucking around

9 dabbler; amateur, dilettante; **flirt**

verbs

10 be unimportant, be of no importance, **not matter,** not count, matter little, **not make any difference**

11 make little of, underplay, play down, **minimize, make light of**

12 trifle; flirt; toy, play, fool, play at, potter, tinker; **dabble;** toy with, fiddle with, play with; idle, loiter

13 (*nonformal terms*) **monkey around,** horse around, fool around, **play around, mess around,** muck around, muck about, mess around

adjectives

14 unimportant, of no importance, of no concern, of no matter, of little *or* no consequence; inferior, secondary

15 insignificant, inconsequential, immaterial; unessential, inessential, **not vital,** dispensable; unimpressive; **inconsiderable,** negligible; **small, little,** minute, minor, inferior; irrelevant

16 trivial, trifling, slight, slender, flimsy; **superficial, shallow; frivolous, light,** airy, frothy; idle, futile, vain; **foolish,** fatuous, **silly; inane,** empty; trite

17 petty, puny, niggling

18 paltry, poor, common, **mean, sorry, sad, pitiful,** pitiable, pathetic, **despicable, contemptible,** beneath contempt, **miserable, wretched,** vile, **shabby,** scruffy, shoddy, **crummy** (*nonformal*), rubbishy; **cheap, worthless,** valueless

19 unworthy, worthless

adverbs

20 unimportantly, insignificantly; pettily; trivially; superficially; frivolously, lightly, idly

954 GOODNESS

nouns

1 goodness, excellence, quality, class (*nonformal*); **virtue, grace; merit; value, worth;** fairness; **superiority, skilfulness;** wholeness, healthiness; **kindness, benevolence; helpfulness; usefulness;** pleasantness

2 preeminence, supremacy; magnificence

3 acceptability; sufficiency

4 good, welfare, well-being, benefit; interest, advantage; behalf; blessing, boon; profit, gain

5 good thing; treasure, gem, jewel, diamond, pearl; pride, **pride and joy,** prize, trophy; catch, find (*nonformal*); godsend, windfall

6 wonder, prodigy, genius, virtuoso, **star, superstar**

7 (*nonformal terms*) **humdinger, peach,** dream, ace, corker, knockout, something else

8 the best, the very best, the tops (*nonformal*); **choice, pick, elite,** chosen; **cream, flower,** prize, champion, queen; paragon

9 harmlessness; innocence

verbs

10 do good, profit; benefit, help, serve, advance, favour

11 excel, surpass, outdo, pass; equal, emulate, rival, vie, vie with; **make the most of**

adjectives

12 good, excellent, fine, nice, fair; **splendid, capital, grand,** noble; royal, regal; very good; commendable; skilful; **sound,**

healthy; virtuous; kind, benevolent; beneficial, helpful; profitable; favourable; useful; pleasant; valid

13 (nonformal terms) **great,** swell, neat, cool, super, **dynamite,** ripping, delicious, stunning, smashing, solid; OK, okay, A-OK

14 **superior,** above par; **high-class,** high-quality, **world-class**

15 **superb, super** (nonformal), **exquisite; magnificent,** splendid, tremendous, **marvellous, wonderful,** glorious, divine, heavenly, terrific, sensational; sterling, golden

16 **best,** very best, **prime,** optimum; **choice, select,** elite; **prize, champion; supreme,** paramount, **unsurpassed, peerless**

17 **first-rate, first-class;** matchless; champion

18 (nonformal terms) tip-top, topnotch, tops

19 **tolerable, fair,** moderate, **decent,** respectable, presentable, good enough, **pretty good, not bad,** adequate, satisfactory, **all right, OK** or **okay** (nonformal); **acceptable, passable;** sufficient

20 **harmless;** well-meaning, wellmeant; **innocuous,** innocent; inoffensive; **benign**

adverbs

21 **excellently,** nicely, finely, **splendidly,** famously; **well,** very well, **fine** (nonformal), right

22 **superbly,** exquisitely, **magnificently,** tremendously, marvellously, wonderfully, gloriously, divinely

23 **tolerably, fairly,** moderately, **adequately, satisfactorily, acceptably,** presentably, decently; fairly well, well enough, pretty well; **rather, pretty**

955 BADNESS

nouns

1 **badness, evil,** viciousness; iniquity, sinfulness, wickedness; inferiority; unkindness, malevolence; unpleasantness

2 squalor, filth, **nastiness;** brutality; **worthlessness**

3 **evil, bad, wrong, ill; harm, hurt,** injury, damage, detriment; **destruction;** mischief, havoc; outrage, atrocity; grievance, woe; poison; blight, venom, **bane; corruption,** pollution, infection

4 **bad influence, ill wind;** curse; spell; **evil eye**

5 **viciousness;** disease

verbs

6 **harm, hurt; injure,** wound, **damage; destroy; wrong,** do wrong; **abuse,** bash (nonformal), batter, outrage, violate, maltreat; torment, **harass,** hassle (nonformal), persecute, savage, crucify, torture; **corrupt,** taint, pollute, infect, defile; poison; blight; **curse;** jinx; threaten, menace; doom; condemn

adjectives

7 **bad, evil, ill,** untoward, sinister; **wicked, wrong, vicious;** sinful; criminal; unhealthy; **inferior;** unkind, malevolent; unfavourable; unpleasant; inaccurate; improper

8 (*nonformal terms*) **lousy, shitty, crappy, crummy,** god-awful

9 **terrible, dreadful,** awful (*nonformal*), dire, horrible, horrid; atrocious, outrageous, heinous, villainous; **deplorable,** lamentable, regrettable, pitiful, pitiable, woeful, grievous, sad; flagrant, **scandalous,** shameful, **shocking,** infamous, **notorious;** shoddy, shabby, **base;** odious, **obnoxious,** offensive, **disgusting,** repulsive, loathsome, **abominable, detestable, despicable,** contemptible, hateful; **reprehensible;** rank, fetid, foul, filthy, vile, **nasty,** squalid, sordid, **wretched;** beastly, brutal; worst; too bad; below par; **worthless**

10 damned, cursed; hellish, devilish, fiendish, satanic, demonic, diabolical, unholy

11 **harmful, hurtful,** distressing, **damaging, detrimental, pernicious,** mischievous; venomous, poisonous, toxic, virulent; **malignant,** malign, malevolent, vicious; disadvantageous; deadly, lethal; ominous

adverbs

12 **badly,** bad (*nonformal*), **ill,** evil, wrong, wrongly, amiss

13 **terribly, dreadfully, horribly, awfully** (*nonformal*), **atrociously, outrageously;** scandalously, shamefully, notoriously, offensively, **disgustingly;** nastily; brutally, savagely, viciously

956 BANE

nouns

1 **bane, curse, affliction, plague,** pest, calamity, scourge, **torment,** grievance, woe, **burden;** disease; death; evil, harm; destruction

2 **blight;** cancer; mould, fungus, mildew, rust; rot

3 **poison, venom; pesticide; insecticide;** antiseptic, disinfectant, antibiotic

957 PERFECTION

nouns

1 **perfection, flawlessness; purity; chastity**

2 height, top, ultimate, summit, pinnacle, peak, climax

3 archetype, prototype, **epitome; classic,** masterpiece, **ideal;** role model; **paragon**

verbs

4 **perfect,** develop, ripen, mature; improve; complete

adjectives

5 **perfect, ideal, faultless, flawless, impeccable,** absolute; **just right;** spotless, stainless, immaculate, **pure,** unadulterated; chaste; infallible; **matchless, peerless**

6 **sound, intact, whole, entire, complete; full;** total, utter, unqualified

7 **unharmed, unhurt, uninjured,** unscathed, **unspoiled,** virgin; harmless; unmarked; **unbroken;** bright, fresh, untouched

8 **perfected, finished,** polished, refined; **classic, classical,** expert, proficient; ripened, ripe, matured, mature, developed; **consummate**, exemplary, model

adverbs

9 **perfectly**, ideally; **impeccably; just right; wholly, entirely, completely, fully,** thoroughly, totally, absolutely

958 IMPERFECTION

nouns

1 **imperfection; shortcoming, deficiency,** lack, want, shortage, **inadequacy;** inaccuracy; **mediocrity;** immaturity; impurity

2 **fault, defect, deficiency, inadequacy, imperfection; flaw;** problem, snag, drawback; **crack,** rift; **weakness,** frailty, infirmity, failure, **failing, foible, shortcoming; blemish; malfunction**

verbs

3 **fall short,** miss, miss out, not qualify

adjectives

4 **imperfect,** not perfect; **defective, faulty, inadequate, deficient,** short, lacking, wanting; erroneous, **fallible;** inaccurate, imprecise; **unsound, incomplete,** unfinished, **partial,** patchy, sketchy, uneven; makeshift; **damaged, impaired;** mediocre; **blemished;** immature, undeveloped

adverbs

5 **imperfectly, inadequately; incompletely,** partially

959 BLEMISH

nouns

1 **blemish, disfigurement,** scar; scratch; scab; blister; **birthmark,** mole; freckle; pimple, sty; wart; **deformity; flaw, defect, fault**

2 **bruise**

3 **stain, taint, tarnish;** mark, brand, **stigma; spot, blot, blotch,** patch, speck, fleck; dab; **smudge, smear;** splash, splatter, spatter

verbs

4 **blemish, disfigure,** deface, **flaw, mar;** scar; **deform, distort**

5 **spot, blot;** spatter, **splatter,** splash

6 **stain, discolour, taint, tarnish; mark,** brand; smear, daub; **darken, blacken;** scorch, singe; **dirty, soil**

adjectives

7 **blemished, disfigured,** defaced, scarred; deformed, distorted; **faulty, flawed, defective**

8 **spotted, spotty, blotchy;** speckled; freckly; spattered, splattered, splashed

9 **stained, discoloured, tainted, tarnished;** darkened, blackened, murky, smoky, inky; soiled

10 **bloodstained, bloody, gory**

960 MEDIOCRITY

nouns

1 **mediocrity,** modesty, **indifference;** respectability; **dullness**

2 **normality**

3 **inferiority,** coarseness

4 low grade, low class, low quality, poor quality; second best

5 mediocrity, nothing or nobody special; **nobody, nonentity; middle class, bourgeoisie; suburbia**

6 irregular

adjectives

7 mediocre, indifferent, fair, moderate, modest, medium; respectable, passable, **tolerable; so-so;** dull, tedious; insipid, wishy-washy

8 ordinary, average, normal, **common, commonplace; unremarkable; conventional; middle-class, bourgeois; suburban;** usual, regular

9 inferior, poor, common, coarse; shabby, seedy; cheap, paltry; irregular; second-best; **second-rate,** third-rate; **second-class**

10 below par, below standard, substandard

adverbs

11 fairly, moderately, modestly, **indifferently, so-so; tolerably**

961 DANGER

nouns

1 danger, peril, jeopardy, hazard, risk, menace, threat; crisis, emergency, plight, predicament

2 dangerousness, riskiness; insecurity, instability, unsteadiness; **unreliability;** unpredictability, **uncertainty**

3 exposure, liability, susceptibility; nakedness, helplessness

4 vulnerability; weakness

5 (*hidden danger*) rocks, reefs; shallows, shoals; sands; quick-

sands; undercurrent; **pitfall;** trap, booby trap, snare

verbs

6 endanger, imperil; risk, gamble, gamble with; jeopardize, compromise, **put in jeopardy; expose**

7 take chances, chance, risk, gamble, hazard; **tempt Providence** or **fate, defy danger,** play with fire; **dare, brave**

8 be in danger, have one's back to the wall

adjectives

9 dangerous, perilous, bad, ugly, serious, critical, beset or fraught with danger; alarming, **menacing, threatening**

10 hazardous, risky, chancy; adventurous

11 unsafe, unhealthy (*nonformal*); **unreliable,** treacherous, **insecure, unsound,** unstable, unsteady, shaky, rocky; **unsure, uncertain,** unpredictable, doubtful, dubious

12 precarious, touch-and-go, **critical, delicate**

13 in danger, in jeopardy, in peril, at risk; endangered, jeopardized, threatened

14 unprotected, unsheltered, uncovered, **unguarded, undefended,** unattended, unwatched; **unarmed,** bare-handed; **defenceless, helpless;** unsuspecting

15 exposed, open, naked; liable, susceptible

16 vulnerable; weak

adverbs

17 **dangerously, perilously,** critically; **precariously**

962 SAFETY

nouns

1 **safety, security; protection,** safeguard; **invulnerability**

verbs

2 **be safe; keep safe, come through;** weather, ride out; tide over

3 **play safe** (*nonformal*), watch oneself, watch out; assure oneself, make sure, keep an eye out; **save, protect**

adjectives

4 **safe, secure;** immune, immunized; insured; **protected;** unhurt, unharmed, unscathed, intact, untouched

5 **trouble-free; guaranteed;** dependable, reliable, trustworthy, sound, stable, steady, firm; harmless; **invulnerable**

6 **in safety, out of danger**

7 **snug, cosy**

adverbs

8 **safely, securely,** reliably

963 PROTECTION

nouns

1 **protection, guard, safekeeping,** policing, law enforcement; **patrol;** vigilance, watchful eye; **safeguarding, security, safety;** shelter, cover, shade; **refuge;** preservation; **defence**

2 **care, charge,** keeping, nurture, nurturing, custody, fostering;

auspices, patronage, guidance; jurisdiction, **management, ministry, administration, government**

3 **safeguard, guard; shield, screen;** umbrella; patent, copyright; mudguard, **bumper, buffer, cushion,** pad, padding; goggles, mask; helmet, hard hat (*nonformal*), crash helmet; lifeline, safety rail; handrail; **anchor; parachute; safety net;** contraceptive

4 **insurance,** assurance; **social security; insurance company, insurance policy**

5 **protector, keeper;** patron; **champion, defender**

6 **guardian, warden,** governor; **custodian,** steward, **keeper, caretaker,** warder, attendant; **curator;** janitor; **shepherd;** game warden, gamekeeper; **ranger,** forest ranger; lifeguard

7 **chaperon; governess;** escort

8 **nurse,** nanny; **baby-sitter**

9 **guard; advance guard, vanguard; rear guard;** coast guard; armed guard, security guard; jailer; **garrison;** cordon

10 **watchman, watch; lookout,** lookout man; **sentinel, sentry; scout; patrol, patrolman;** nightwatchman

11 **watchdog,** guard dog; sheep dog

12 **warden, porter, janitor,** commissionaire, usher; receptionist

13 **picket,** demonstrator, picket line

14 **bodyguard; convoy; escort;** guards

15 **policeman, constable, officer, police officer;** military policeman *or* MP; detective; police-

woman; police constable; mounted policeman; **sheriff, marshal;** deputy sheriff, deputy, bound bailiff; sergeant, police sergeant; inspector, police inspector; superintendent; commissioner, police commissioner

16 (*nonformal terms*) cop, copper, pig, bizzy, bobby; the cops, the law, the fuzz

17 **police, police force; constabulary; posse;** vigilantes

verbs

18 **protect, guard, safeguard, secure, keep,** bless, make safe, **police; insure;** ensure, guarantee; **cushion;** champion; defend; **shelter, shield, screen, cover; harbour; arm**

19 **care for; take care of;** preserve; provide for, support; **look after,** attend to, minister to, watch over, **watch, mind, tend; foster,** nurture, cherish, nurse; **mother**

20 **watch, keep watch, keep guard;** stand guard; be on the lookout; **police,** patrol

adjectives

21 **protected, guarded,** safeguarded, defended; **safe; sheltered, shielded,** screened, covered; policed; armed; invulnerable

22 **protective,** guardian; vigilant, watchful; protecting, guarding, safeguarding, sheltering, **shielding,** screening, covering; fostering, parental; defensive

964 REFUGE

nouns

1 **refuge, sanctuary, asylum, haven, port, harbour;** safe haven; bird sanctuary, preserve, game preserve; **stronghold; political asylum**

2 **recourse, resource, resort;** last resort; **hope; expedient**

3 **shelter, cover;** concealment; cave, earth; **bunker;** trench; storm cellar; air-raid shelter, fallout shelter

4 **asylum, home,** retreat; poorhouse, workhouse; **orphanage; hospice;** old folks' home, rest home, nursing home; foster home; halfway house

5 **retreat,** recess, hiding place, **hideaway,** hideout; **sanctum, holy ground; den,** lair, mew; safe house; **cloister,** cell; **ivory tower;** study, library

6 **harbour, haven, port, seaport; anchorage,** moorings; road, roads; berth, slip; **dock,** marina, basin; dry dock; shipyard, dockyard; **wharf, pier,** quay; landing, jetty; breakwater; seawall; embankment

verbs

7 **take refuge, take shelter,** seek refuge, **claim sanctuary;** take cover

8 **make port, reach safety**

965 PROSPERITY

nouns

1 **prosperity; success; welfare, well-being,** happiness; **comfort, ease,** security; **luxury;** upward

mobility; high standard of living; **affluence, wealth**

2 **good fortune** or **luck, fortune, luck,** the breaks (*nonformal*); luckiness, blessing

3 **stroke of luck;** blessing; **fluke,** break, lucky break (*all nonformal*)

4 **good times;** heyday; prosperity; golden era, **golden age; utopia; heaven**

5 **roaring trade; boom,** booming economy, expanding economy

6 **lucky dog** (*nonformal*)

verbs

7 **prosper,** get on well, do well; **turn out well, go well; succeed;** get on (*nonformal*); **advance,** progress, make progress, make headway, get ahead (*nonformal*)

8 **thrive, flourish, boom;** blossom, bloom, flower

9 **be prosperous, make good,** grow rich

10 **live well,** live high

11 **be fortunate, be lucky,** be in luck; strike it lucky (*nonformal*)

adjectives

12 **prosperous; successful; well-paid;** affluent, **wealthy; comfortable**

13 **thriving, flourishing, prospering, booming** (*nonformal*); vigorous, exuberant; going strong (*nonformal*); **blooming,** blossoming, flowering

14 **fortunate, lucky; in luck;** blessed, favoured; **auspicious**

adverbs

15 fortunately, luckily

966 ADVERSITY

nouns

1 **adversity,** adverse circumstances, difficulties, **hardship, trouble,** troubles, care, stress, pressure; **hard life,** dog's life; annoyance, irritation, aggravation; **difficulty; trial,** tribulation, cross, curse, blight, **affliction;** plight, predicament

2 **misfortune, mishap, misadventure,** grief; **disaster, calamity, catastrophe,** cataclysm, **tragedy; shock, blow; accident,** casualty, collision, crash; **wreck,** shipwreck

3 **reverse, reversal, setback; comedown,** descent

4 **unluckiness**

5 **bad luck,** ill luck, **hard luck,** hard lines, **tough luck,** raw deal (*nonformal*); **ill fortune,** bad fortune, ill wind

6 **hard times,** bad times; rainy day; **depression,** recession, **slump**

7 **unfortunate,** poor unfortunate; **loser;** victim

verbs

8 **oppress,** weigh down, **burden,** load, overload

9 **have trouble; have a hard time of it;** be unlucky, have bad or rotten luck

10 **come to grief,** have a mishap, fall; sink, drown; **founder**

11 **come down in the world,** go downhill, slip, come down; **deteriorate,** degenerate, decline; **go**

to pot (*nonformal*), hit rock bottom

12 bring bad luck; jinx

adjectives

13 adverse, untoward, detrimental, unfavourable; sinister; hostile, antagonistic; contrary, counter, conflicting, opposing, opposed, opposite, in opposition; **difficult, troublesome, hard,** trying, rigorous, stressful; wretched, miserable; **not easy;** harmful

14 unfortunate, unlucky, sad, unhappy, hapless; **out of luck;** underprivileged, depressed; fatal, dire, **ominous, inauspicious**

15 disastrous, calamitous, catastrophic, cataclysmic, tragic, fatal, dire, grievous; destructive; **life-threatening, terminal**

adverbs

16 adversely, unfavourably

17 unfortunately, unluckily, sadly, unhappily

18 disastrously, grievously, tragically

967 HINDRANCE

nouns

1 hindrance, hindering, **hampering; impediment; resistance, opposition;** suppression, repression, restriction, restraint; **obstruction,** blocking, blockage, clogging; traffic jam; **interruption,** interference; **detention, delay,** holdup, setback; **inhibition;** constriction, squeeze, cramp, stranglehold; **closure**

2 prevention, stop, stoppage, stopping; stay, staying, halt, halting; **prohibition; discouragement**

3 frustration, thwarting, balking, foiling; confounding; **defeat,** upset; check, checkmate

4 obstacle, obstruction; block, blockade, cordon, curtain; **difficulty;** hurdle, hazard; **deterrent; drawback,** objection; **stumbling block; hitch, catch**

5 barrier, bar; gate; fence, wall; rampart; **defence,** buffer, parapet, mound; bank, embankment; ditch, moat; dam, weir; boom, jam; roadblock

6 impediment, embarrassment; encumbrance; **trouble, difficulty; handicap,** disadvantage, inconvenience, penalty; **burden,** imposition, cross, weight; **load,** pack, cargo, freight; lumber

7 curb, check, damper; **brake;** shackle, chain, fetter

8 spoilsport, wet blanket, **killjoy,** grouch

verbs

9 hinder, impede, inhibit, arrest, check, curb, snub; **resist, oppose;** stonewall (*nonformal*), stall; **suppress, repress; interrupt;** intervene, interfere, meddle; damp, dampen; **delay,** detain; **hold back, keep back,** set back, hold up (*nonformal*); **restrain**

10 hamper, impede, cramp, embarrass; involve, tangle, snarl; fetter, shackle; **handcuff; encumber, burden,** lumber, **saddle with,** press down; **handicap;** cripple

11 obstruct, get in the way; dog, **block,** blockade, block up; **jam,**

crowd, pack; **bar**, barricade, bolt, lock; shut out; shut off, **close**, close tight, shut tight; constrict, squeeze; **strangle**, **stifle**, suffocate, **choke**; stop up

12 stop, stay, halt; **brake**, slow down; **block**, **stall**, deadlock

13 prevent, prohibit, forbid; **bar**; save, help, **keep from**; deter, discourage; avert, **keep off**, ward off, fend off, repel, deflect; forestall, forestall, preclude, exclude, anticipate; rule out

14 thwart, frustrate, foil, cross, **balk**; spike, scotch, checkmate; **counter**, contravene, counteract; confront, brave, defy, challenge; **defeat**; upset, disrupt, confound, disconcert, **baffle**, perplex, stump (*nonformal*); elude; sabotage, **spoil**, **ruin**, dash, blast; **destroy**

15 (*nonformal terms*) **queer**, foul up, louse up

adjectives

16 **hindering**, troublesome; inhibiting, repressive; strangling, stifling, choking; restrictive; **obstructive**, obstructing; contrary

17 **hampering**, impeding; onerous, oppressive, cumbersome

18 **preventive**, preventative; **prohibitive**, forbidding; deterrent, discouraging

19 **frustrating**, disconcerting, baffling

968 DIFFICULTY

nouns

1 **difficulty**, hardness, toughness (*nonformal*); complication, intricacy, **complexity**

2 **hard job**, chore; **handful** (*nonformal*)

3 **trouble**, **the matter**; problem, **inconvenience**, disadvantage; **ado**; can of worms (*nonformal*); **evil**; bother, annoyance, anxiety, worry

4 **predicament**, **plight**, **strait**, straits; **pinch**, **bind**, situation, emergency; morass, swamp, quicksand; **embarrassment**; complication

5 (*nonformal terms*) **pickle**, crunch, hobble; **spot**, tight spot; scrape, jam, hot water; mess

6 **impasse**, cleft stick; **cul-de-sac**, blind alley, dead end; **extremity**, wit's end; **stalemate**, deadlock; stand, standstill, halt, stop

7 **dilemma**, no-win situation, **quandary**; vexed question, thorny problem, knot, crux, poser, teaser, perplexity, puzzle, enigma; paradox

8 **crux**, hitch, pinch, rub, snag, catch

9 inconvenience; **awkwardness**, **clumsiness**

verbs

10 **be difficult**, present difficulties

11 **have difficulty**, have trouble, be hard put; struggle, flounder

12 **get into trouble**, put one's foot in it (*nonformal*); **get in a mess** (*nonformal*)

13 **trouble**, beset; **bother**, get one down (*nonformal*), disturb, perturb, irk, plague, **torment**, drive one up the wall (*nonformal*); **harass**, vex, **distress**; inconvenience, **put out**; concern, worry;

puzzle, perplex; be too much for; be the matter

14 **cause trouble,** bring trouble; ask for trouble, ask for it (*nonformal*)

15 **embarrass; involve**

16 **corner**

adjectives

17 **difficult; not easy,** no picnic; **hard, tough** (*nonformal*), rigorous, brutal, severe; **wicked** (*nonformal*), **formidable; arduous, strenuous, laborious;** steep, uphill; delicate, tricky, sticky (*nonformal*); critical; exacting, demanding; intricate, complex

18 **troublesome;** irksome, painful, annoying; oppressive, onerous; **trying, gruelling**

19 **unwieldy, unmanageable;** inconvenient, impractical; **awkward, clumsy, cumbersome;** contrary, perverse; ponderous, bulky

20 **troubled,** beset; **bothered, vexed,** irked, annoyed; **plagued, harassed;** distressed, perturbed; inconvenienced, embarrassed; **worried, anxious;** puzzled

21 **in trouble,** out of one's depth

22 (*nonformal terms*) in a jam, in a pickle, in fix; in a mess, in hot water

23 **in a dilemma, in a quandary**

24 **at one's wit's end, at a loss; nonplussed, baffled, perplexed, bewildered,** mystified

25 **cornered,** in a corner

26 **hard-pressed, hard up** (*nonformal*); **desperate, at the end of one's tether**

27 **stranded, grounded,** aground, high and dry; **stuck;** castaway, marooned, wrecked, shipwrecked

adverbs

28 **with difficulty;** painfully; **strenuously, laboriously**

29 **awkwardly, clumsily;** ponderously

969 FACILITY

nouns

1 **facility, ease, easiness; smoothness,** freedom; easy going, plain sailing; clarity; **simplicity**

2 **convenience,** practicality; **flexibility;** adaptability, feasibility

3 **easy thing,** simple matter; easy target, sitting duck (*nonformal*)

4 (*nonformal terms*) **cinch,** pushover, breeze, waltz, picnic, piece of cake

5 **facilitating, easing,** smoothing, smoothing out; **speeding,** quickening, hastening; streamlining; lubricating, greasing, oiling

6 **freeing, clearing;** simplification

verbs

7 **facilitate, ease; smooth, pave the way; open up, unclog,** unblock, loose; **lubricate,** grease, oil; **speed,** quicken, hasten; **help along, aid; explain,** make clear; simplify

8 **do easily,** make short work of

9 **unload,** relieve; **disentangle,** unscramble; **extricate,** disengage, **free,** free up, clear; liberate

10 **go easily, run smoothly,** work well, go like clockwork; give no trouble, be painless, be effortless

11 **have it easy,** have it all one's own way; win easily; win hands down (*nonformal*)

12 **take it easy** (*nonformal*); take it in one's stride, make light of, think nothing of

adjectives

13 **easy, facile, effortless,** smooth, painless; cushy (*nonformal*); plain, uncomplicated, straightforward, **simple,** easy as pie (*nonformal*); **clear;** glib; **light;** nothing to it; casual

14 **smooth-running**

15 **handy;** flexible, pliant, yielding, pliable, **manageable; convenient,** foolproof, practical, user-friendly; adaptable, feasible

adverbs

16 **easily, effortlessly, readily, simply,** lightly, without difficulty; no sweat (*nonformal*); hands down (*nonformal*); **smoothly,** like clockwork

970 UGLINESS

nouns

1 **ugliness, unattractiveness;** plainness; gracelessness, clumsiness, ungainliness; **disfigurement, defacement**

2 **hideousness; repulsiveness; deformity**

3 **eyesore,** blot, blemish, **sight** (*nonformal*), **fright, horror, mess,** no beauty, ugly duckling; monster, **monstrosity;** witch, **hag**

verbs

4 **offend, look bad;** look a sight (*nonformal*); **disfigure,** deface, blot, blemish, mar, spoil

adjectives

5 **ugly, unsightly, unattractive, unlovely, inelegant; homely, plain; disfigured,** defaced, blemished, marred, spoiled

6 **unprepossessing;** grim, grim-faced,

7 shapeless; **deformed,** misshapen; grotesque; monstrous

8 graceless; clumsy, **ungainly**

9 **hideous, horrid, horrible, frightful, dreadful, terrible, awful** (*nonformal*); **repulsive,** repellent, repelling, **repugnant,** offensive, foul, loathsome, revolting; **ghastly,** gruesome, grisly

adverbs

10 **hideously, horribly, frightfully, dreadfully, terribly, awfully** (*nonformal*); **repulsively,** offensively

971 BEAUTY

nouns

1 **beauty, prettiness, handsomeness, attractiveness, loveliness, charm,** grace, elegance; bloom, glow

2 **fairness**

3 **good looks; shapeliness,** good figure, good shape, nice body; **gracefulness; beauties, charms, delights**

4 **daintiness, delicacy**

5 **splendour; brilliance,** brightness, radiance, lustre; **glamour**

6 **vision, picture** (*nonformal*), sight for sore eyes (*nonformal*)

7 **beauty, charmer,** beauty queen; glamour girl, cover girl, model; sex goddess

8 (*nonformal terms*) **doll, dish,** angel, honey, dream, stunner, peach, raving beauty

9 adornment; decoration; **beauty care,** beauty treatment

10 makeup, cosmetics, **beauty products; powder, talcum, talcum powder; rouge; lipstick; nail polish;** eyeliner, mascara, eye shadow, kohl; cold cream, hand cream, vanishing cream; foundation; **eyebrow pencil; puff, powder puff; compact, vanity case**

11 **beautician;** hairdresser; barber; manicurist

verbs

12 **beautify, prettify, doll up** (*nonformal*), grace, **adorn; decorate;** set off; **make up,** titivate

13 **look good;** beggar description; shine, **bloom, glow**

adjectives

14 **beautiful; pretty, handsome, attractive, lovely, graceful;** elegant; cute

15 **fair, good-looking, nice-looking,** presentable, agreeable, becoming, pleasing, bonny; **shapely,** well-built, curvaceous, buxom; slender

16 **fine, exquisite, dainty, delicate**

17 **gorgeous, ravishing; glorious,** heavenly, divine, sublime; **resplendent, splendid; brilliant,** bright, radiant, shining, beaming, glowing, blooming, sparkling, **dazzling; glamorous**

18 (*nonformal terms*) dishy; **raving,** devastating, **stunning**

19 decorative; beautified, made-up, titivated

adverbs

20 **beautifully, handsomely, attractively;** elegantly, exquisitely; charmingly

21 **daintily, delicately; cutely**

22 **gorgeously, gloriously,** divinely; splendidly; **brilliantly,** brightly, radiantly

972 HEAT

nouns

1 **heat, hotness; warmth, warmness; fever; heating, burning**

2 (*metaphors*) ardour, fervour; eagerness; excitement; **anger; sexual desire;** love

3 **temperature;** boiling point; melting point, freezing point; zero, absolute zero

4 **extreme heat, intense heat, red heat, white heat, tropical heat,** sweltering heat

5 **sultriness, stuffiness, closeness,** humidity, mugginess

6 **hot weather,** sunny weather; summer, midsummer, high summer; Indian Summer, **dog days; heat wave; midday sun; warm weather, fair weather**

7 **hot day,** summer day; scorcher (*nonformal*), roaster (*nonformal*)

8 **hot air;** thermal

9 **hot water,** boiling water; **steam,** vapour; geyser

10 (*hot place*) **oven, furnace,** inferno, hell; steam bath; **tropics;** equator

11 **glow; flush, blush, bloom,** redness

12 **fire; blaze, flame; combustion, ignition; conflagration;** flicker;

bonfire, beacon; wildfire, forest fire; open fire; campfire; pyre, funeral pyre

13 **flare, flash,** flash fire, **blaze,** burst, outburst

14 **spark,** sparkle

15 **coal,** live coal, brand, firebrand, **ember,** burning ember; **cinder**

16 **fireworks, pyrotechnics**

17 **thermal unit;** centigrade *or* Celsius scale, Fahrenheit scale; **calorie;** therm

18 **thermometer;** mercury; thermostat

verbs

19 (*be hot*) **burn, scorch,** scald, **swelter, roast,** toast, cook, bake, fry, boil, simmer, stew; **blaze,** spark, **catch fire, flame, flare,** flare up; **flicker; glow;** smoulder; steam; sweat; gasp, pant; **suffocate, stifle,** smother, choke

20 **smoke, fume,** reek

adjectives

21 **warm, thermal; sunny;** fair, mild; **summery; temperate,** warmish; **tropical,** equatorial, subtropical; **tepid, lukewarm**

22 **hot, heated; sweltering; burning,** scorching, searing, scalding, blistering, baking, roasting, grilling, simmering; **boiling,** seething; **piping hot,** burning hot, roasting hot, scorching hot, sizzling hot; **red-hot,** white-hot; ardent; flushed, sweating, sweaty; overheated; feverish

23 **fiery,** firelike

24 **burning, ignited,** kindled, **blazing,** ablaze, ardent, flaring, flaming, inflamed, alight, **on fire,** in

flames; **live, living; glowing;** sparking; **flickering, guttering; smouldering; smoking,** fuming

25 **sultry, stifling, suffocating, stuffy, close,** oppressive; **humid, sticky** (*nonformal*), **muggy**

26 **warm-blooded,** hot-blooded

27 **centigrade, Fahrenheit**

973 HEATING

nouns

1 **heating, warming, heating system;** cooking

2 **boiling, stewing, simmering;** boil; simmer

3 **melting, fusion,** liquefying; **thawing,** thaw

4 **ignition, lighting,** lighting up, **kindling,** firing

5 **burning, combustion,** blazing, flaming; **scorching,** singeing; **searing,** branding; **blistering; cauterization; cremation; distilling, distillation; refining, smelting; spontaneous combustion**

6 **burn,** scald, scorch, singe; brand; sunburn; windburn; **first-** *or* **second-** *or* **third-degree burn**

7 **arson,** fire-raising; **pyromania**

8 **incendiary, arsonist;** pyromaniac, firebug (*nonformal*)

9 **flammability, inflammability**

10 **heater, warmer; stove, furnace; cooker;** burner, jet, element, heating element

11 **fireplace, hearth, fireside;** hob; fireguard, fire screen; fender; chimney, chimney piece, chimney-pot, chimney-stack; flue

12 **fire iron, andiron;** tongs, fire

tongs; poker; spit; grate, grating; grid, griddle, grill; damper

13 **incinerator,** burner; crematorium

14 **blowtorch,** blowlamp, torch; **burner**

15 hot iron, **branding iron,** brand

16 (*products of combustion*) slag; **ashes,** ash; **cinder,** clinker; coal; coke, charcoal, lava, carbon; **soot; smoke**

verbs

17 **heat,** raise the temperature, hot *or* hot up, **warm,** warm up, fire up, stoke up; overheat; preheat; **reheat,** warm over; mull; steam; cook

18 (*metaphors*) **excite, inflame;** incite, **kindle, arouse;** anger, **enrage**

19 **sun,** bask, sun oneself, sunbathe

20 **boil, stew, simmer; distil**

21 **melt,** liquefy; **run;** refine, smelt; **thaw,** thaw out; defrost, de-ice

22 **ignite, set fire to, set alight, kindle, light,** torch (*nonformal*), touch off; **burn; feed, stoke;** bank

23 **catch fire,** catch, take; **burn,** blaze, **blaze up,** burst into flames

24 **burn, scorch; singe, blister;** cauterize; char

25 **burn up, incinerate, cremate,** consume; **burn down,** burn to the ground, go up in smoke

adjectives

26 **heating, warming;** fiery, burning,

27 **incendiary**

28 **flammable, inflammable, combustible**

29 **heated, warmed,** warmed up, centrally heated; overheated; reheated, warmed-over; hot

30 **burned, burnt,** gutted, burned-out; **scorched, blistered,** parched, singed, charred, reduced *or* burnt to ashes, burnt to a cinder, incinerated, cremated, consumed; sunburned

31 **molten, melted,** fused, liquefied

974 FUEL

nouns

1 **fuel,** energy source; fossil fuel, alternative energy, renewable energy, solar power, nuclear power, wind power

2 **coal dust, slack, dross** (*Scots*)

3 **firewood,** wood; **kindling,** kindling wood; logs

4 **lighter,** light; pocket lighter, **torch,** taper, spill; **brand, flint**

5 **match,** safety match

6 **tinder,** touchwood

verbs

7 **fuel;** stoke, feed; detonate, explode

8 **fuels;** anthracite, briquettes, brown coal, butane, charcoal, coal, coke, diesel fuel *or* diesel oil *or* derv, gasoline, jet fuel, kerosene, lignite, natural gas, North Sea gas, paraffin, peat, petrol, propane, rocket fuel, unleaded petrol, uranium

975 INCOMBUSTIBILITY

nouns

1 fire resistance

2 **extinguishing,** extinction, **quenching,** dousing (*nonformal*), putting out; **choking, damping, stifling, smothering;** controlling; fire fighting; going out, dying, burning out

3 **extinguisher, fire extinguisher;** fire engine; sprinkler, sprinkler system; hydrant, fire hydrant; fire hose

4 **fire fighter, fireman; fire brigade**

5 fire resistance; fire retardant; asbestos; fire door; fire break

verbs

6 **extinguish, put out, quench,** douse (*nonformal*), **snuff,** snuff out, blow out, stamp out; stub out; **choke, damp, smother, stifle;** bring under control, contain

7 **burn out, go out,** die out *or* down *or* away, fizzle out

adjectives

8 noncombustible, nonflammable

9 **fireproof, flameproof,** fire-resistant, fire-retardant

10 **extinguished,** quenched, **out;** contained, under control

976 COLD

nouns

1 **cold, coldness; coolness,** freshness; low temperature, arctic temperature; chilliness, bite; **chill, nip;** iciness; bleakness, bitterness, severity; freezing point; absolute zero

2 (*sensation of cold*) chill, chilliness; **shivering, shivers; goose pimples,** goose bumps, gooseflesh; **frostbite;** chilblains

3 **cold weather,** bleak weather, raw weather, bitter weather, wintry weather, arctic weather, **freezing weather;** cold snap, cold spell; **freeze,** frost, hard frost; winter, hard winter

4 **ice,** frozen water; **icicle; ice sheet, ice field, ice barrier; floe, ice floe;** pack ice; **iceberg,** growler; calf; **glacier; black ice;** ice cubes; crushed ice

5 **hail,** hailstone; **hailstorm**

6 **frost,** Jack Frost; hoarfrost, rime, ground frost, air frost

7 **snow;** powder snow, wet snow; flurry, blizzard; **snowflake,** flake; **snowdrift;** snow line; snowscape; snowball, snowman; avalanche; **slush; snow fence; igloo**

8 **sleet**

verbs

9 **freeze,** be cold, grow cold, lose heat; **shiver, quiver,** quake, shake, tremble, shudder; **chatter;** chill

10 (*make cold*) **freeze, chill,** nip, bite, cut, **pierce,** penetrate; numb

11 **hail, sleet, snow;** snow in; snow under; frost up, ice up, ice over

adjectives

12 **cool,** temperate, chill, **chilly,** parky (*nonformal*), **fresh,** brisk, crisp, bracing, **invigorating,** stimulating

13 **cold, freezing,** freezing cold, **crisp, brisk,** nippy, **raw, keen, sharp,** bitter, biting, **piercing,**

penetrating, snell (*Scots*); severe, rigorous; slushy; **icy, ice-cold,** glacial; **frigid; subzero,** below zero; numbing; **wintry, arctic;** stone-cold

14 (*feeling cold*) **cold, freezing; shivering,** shivery; **frozen**

15 **frosty**

16 **snowy;** snow-covered; snow-capped

17 **snowed up,** snowbound, snowed in

977 REFRIGERATION

nouns

1 **refrigeration, cooling, chilling; freezing; air conditioning**

2 **cooler,** chiller; fan; ice bucket *or* pail, wine cooler; ice bag, ice pack

3 **refrigerator, fridge,** icebox

4 **freezer, deep freeze**

5 **cold storage**

6 **coolant,** refrigerant

verbs

7 **refrigerate;** cool, chill

8 **freeze; deep-freeze**

adjectives

9 **cooling, chilling, freezing**

10 **cooled, chilled; air-conditioned;** iced

11 **frozen,** frozen solid; **icy,** ice-cold; deep-frozen

978 LIGHT

nouns

1 **light,** radiant energy, visible energy; visible radiation, **illumination,** radiation, radiance; light

source; infrared light, ultraviolet light

2 **shine, lustre, sheen, gloss,** glint; **glow, gleam,** flush; **incandescence**

3 **lightness,** luminosity

4 **brightness, brilliance, splendour,** radiance, glory: **glare,** blaze

5 **ray,** radiation, **beam, stream, streak, pencil, patch,** laser beam

6 **flash, blaze, flare, flame, gleam,** glint

7 **glitter, glimmer, shimmer, twinkle, glisten, sparkle, scintillation;** glittering, glimmering, shimmering, twinkling, glistening, sparkling

8 **firefly,** glowworm

9 **flicker, flutter, dance, quiver;** flickering, fluttering, guttering, dancing, quivering; **play**

10 **reflection;** iceblink, whiteout

11 **daylight,** day, daytime; **natural light; sunlight, sunshine;** midday sun, noonday sun, full sun; **dusk, sunset,** twilight, gloaming (*Scots*); **dawn, sunrise,** break of day; sunbeam, ray of sun *or* sunlight *or* sunshine

12 **moonlight,** moonshine, moonbeams

13 **starlight,** starshine

14 **luminescence;** will-o'-the-wisp, jack-o'-lantern; St Elmo's fire

15 **halo,** aura, aureole, circle, ring; **rainbow,** solar halo, lunar halo; mock sun, sun dog

16 **polar lights, aurora;** northern lights, aurora borealis, merry

dancers; southern lights, aurora australis

17 **lightning**, flash of lightning, bolt of lightning, **thunderbolt**, forked or chain lightning, sheet lightning, ball lightning

18 iridescence, opalescence; mother-of-pearl

19 **lighting, illumination;** arc light, candlelight, electric light, fluorescent light, neon light, torchlight, floodlight, spotlight; contrast, chiaroscuro, highlights

20 electricity gas, oil, paraffin; light source

21 luminous intensity, luminous power, luminous flux; photon; **exposure meter**, light meter

verbs

22 **shine**, shine forth, **burn, give light; glow, beam, gleam; flash, flare, blaze, flame;** be bright, shine brightly; **glare;** daze, blind, dazzle

23 **glitter, glimmer, shimmer, twinkle, blink; sparkle, spark; glisten**

24 **flicker**, gutter, **flutter, waver, dance,** play, quiver

25 luminesce, phosporesce, fluoresce

26 **grow light**, grow bright, **lighten,** brighten; dawn, break

27 **illuminate, light, light up, lighten,** enlighten, brighten, brighten up; shed light on, throw or cast light on; spotlight, highlight; floodlight

28 light, strike a light, turn or switch on the light

adjectives

29 **luminous; incandescent; radiant: shining,** shiny, burning, streaming; **gleaming,** glinting; **glowing,** aglow; blushing, flushing; **sunny; starry**

30 **light, lucid;** translucent, transparent; **clear,** serene; **cloudless**

31 **bright, brilliant, vivid, splendid, resplendent,** refulgent, **flamboyant,** flaming; **glaring,** garish; **dazzling,** bedazzling, blinding, pitiless

32 **shiny,** shining, **glossy, polished,** burnished

33 **flashing, blazing, flaming, flaring, burning;** aflame, ablaze

34 **glittering, glimmering, shimmering, twinkling, blinking,** glistening, **sparkling**

35 **flickering,** wavering, dancing, flickery, quivering; blinking, flashing

36 pearly, iridescent

37 luminescent

38 **illuminated,** lit, **lit up,** floodlit; **alight, glowing;** ablaze, blazing, fiery; sunlit, moonlit, starlit; star-spangled, star-studded

39 **illuminating, lighting, lightening,** brightening

40 **photosensitive, light-sensitive**

979 LIGHT SOURCE

nouns

1 **light source, light, lamp,** light bulb, lantern, candle, taper, torch, flame; match; **fluorescent light,** fluorescent tube; fire; sun, moon, stars

2 **candle,** taper; dip; wax candle; rush candle

3 **torch,** flaming torch, flambeau, link (*old*); **flare,** signal flare; beacon

4 **traffic light;** red *or* stop light, green light

5 firefly, glowworm

6 chandelier, light fixture, candlestick

7 **wick,** taper, mantle

980 DARKNESS, DIMNESS

nouns

1 **darkness, dark; obscurity; night,** dead of night; pitch-darkness, total darkness; **blackness,** swarthiness

2 **murkiness, murk; dimness; semidarkness,** bad light, halflight; dusk, twilight, gloaming (*Scots*)

3 **shadow, shade;** gloom

4 **gloom, gloominess, sombreness;** lowering

5 **dullness, flatness,** lifelessness, drabness, lack of sparkle

6 **darkening, dimming;** eclipsing; **shading,** overshadowing, **clouding,** clouding over; blackening

7 blackout

8 **eclipse;** total eclipse, partial eclipse; solar eclipse, lunar eclipse

verbs

9 **darken, obscure, eclipse; black out;** become overcast, cloud over; cast a shadow over; over-shadow; **cloud,** cloud over; **dim; blacken**

10 **dull, deaden; tone down**

11 turn *or* switch off, extinguish

12 **get** *or* **grow dark, darken, dim, grow dim**

adjectives

13 **dark, black,** shrouded in darkness, pitch-black; ebony: sunless, starless, moonless

14 **gloomy, sombre;** lowering; stormy, cloudy, clouded, overcast

15 **dusky; murky, dim,** dimmed

16 **shadowy, shady, shaded;** overshadowed

17 **lacklustre; dull, dead, lifeless, sombre, drab,** wan, **flat**

18 obscuring

adverbs

19 in darkness, at *or* by night; dimly, wanly

981 SHADE

nouns

1 **shade, screen, curtain,** drape, blind, veil; **sunshade,** parasol, umbrella; **cover**

2 **eyeshade,** visor, goggles, dark glasses, **sunglasses,** shades (*nonformal*)

3 **lamp shade**

4 **filter;** smoked glass, frosted glass, stained glass

verbs

5 **shade, screen,** veil, curtain

adjectives

6 **screening, veiling**

7 **shaded, screened,** veiled; shady

982 TRANSPARENCY

nouns

1 **transparency, lucidity, clarity**

adjectives

2 **transparent;** see-through, revealing; **lucid,** pellucid, **clear,** limpid; crystal-clear; **diaphanous,** sheer, thin; **gossamer,** gauzy

3 **glass, glassy**

983 ELECTRICITY, MAGNETISM

nouns

1 **electricity; electrical science**

2 **current, electric current, power,** juice (*both nonformal*)

3 **magnetic field, electromagnetic field**

4 **circuit, electrical circuit,** path

5 **charge,** positive charge, negative charge; live wire

6 **discharge, arc; shock**

7 **magnetism,** magnetic attraction; diamagnetism, electromagnetism, ferromagnetism

8 **pole,** magnetic pole; positive pole, negative pole; anode, cathode; north pole, south pole

9 **magnetic field, electromagnetic field**

10 attraction; repulsion

11 **voltage,** potential difference; tension, high tension, low tension

12 **resistance**

13 **conductor, semiconductor, superconductor, nonconductor, insulator**

14 **induction,** electromagnetic induction

15 capacitance

16 **power, wattage**

17 **power station, power plant;** power grid, **national grid**

18 **blackout, power failure,** power cut

19 **battery,** accumulator; electricity meter, meter; wire, cable, flex

20 **electrician;** linesman; power worker

21 **electrical engineer**

22 electrification

23 **electrolysis;** electroplating; ion, anion, cation; electrolyte

verbs

24 **electrify,** energize, **charge;** wire, wire up; shock, electrocute; switch on *or* off, turn on *or* off; short-circuit, short

25 **magnetize;** demagnetize, degauss

26 electrolyze; electroplate

27 **insulate,** isolate; **earth**

adjectives

28 **electric, electrical;** electrified, electric, battery-powered, cordless

29 **magnetic,** diamagnetic, ferromagnetic, **electromagnetic**

30 **charged, electrified, live,** hot; high-tension, low-tension

31 **positive, negative, neutral**

32 insulating, nonconducting, nonconductive

984 RADIO

nouns

1 **radio, wireless; communications, telecommunication**

2 radio, radio receiver, receiver, transistor radio, transistor, tuner, wireless

3 radio transmitter, transmitter

4 aerial, antenna

5 radio station, transmitting station, **studio; relay station; pirate station, offshore station**

6 network

7 radio signal, signal, beam

8 radio wave, electromagnetic wave; **long wave, medium wave, short wave, microwave;** carrier, carrier wave; **wavelength**

9 frequency; very high frequency *or* VHF, ultra high frequency *or* UHF; kilohertz *or* kHz, megahertz *or* MHz

10 station, channel, wavelength, frequency

11 amplitude modulation *or* **AM,** frequency modulation *or* FM

12 radio broadcasting, broadcasting, the airwaves; commercial radio, local radio, community radio, pirate radio, ham radio

13 broadcast, programme, show; discussion programme, phone-in, panel game, soap, magazine programme, serial, series; outside broadcast, live relay

14 station identification; jingle; signature tune, theme song

15 commercial, advertisement; trailer

16 reception; fading, **interference,** static, atmospherics; **jamming**

17 audience, listener

18 broadcaster; newscaster, news-reader; commentator; presenter,

host; disc jockey *or* DJ (*nonformal*); announcer

19 radio technician, radio engineer; radio operator; radio ham

verbs

20 broadcast, radio, transmit, send; sign on; sign off, go off the air, close down

21 monitor, check

22 listen in, tune in; tune up, tune down

adjectives

23 radio, wireless

985 TELEVISION

nouns

1 television, TV, telly, the box (*both nonformal*); **cable, cable television, cable TV, satellite, satellite television, satellite TV; pay television, pay TV, subscription television, subscription TV**

2 programme, show; studio show, outside broadcast; prime time; television series, serial, drama, miniseries, TV movie, situation comedy *or* sitcom, game show, quiz show, chat show, current affairs programme, documentary, docudrama, children's programme; news reader, anchor man, anchor woman; ratings

3 channel, frequency, station

4 (*reception*) **picture, image; colour television, black-and-white** *or* monochrome **television;** definition; interference, snow, ghost; **HDTV** *or* **high definition television, NICAM, Teletext** (*trademark*)

5 television studio, TV station

6 **outside broadcast unit**

7 **transmitter,** television mast

8 **relay station, booster station;** communication satellite, satellite relay

9 **television camera, videocamera,** camcorder

10 **television, television** *or* **TV set, TV,** telly, the box (*both nonformal*)

11 **video,** videorecorder, VCR

12 **viewer**

13 TV repairman; cameraman, camera operator, film crew

verbs

14 **televise, broadcast**

15 video, record, tape

adjectives

16 televisual, video; telegenic

986 NUCLEAR PHYSICS

nouns

1 **nuclear physics,** particle physics; quantum mechanics, wave mechanics; molecular physics; radiology

2 **atomic scientist, nuclear physicist,** particle physicist

3 **atom,** nuclide; ion; shell; atomic mass, atomic number

4 **isotope**

5 **elementary particle,** subatomic particle; nucleus

6 **fission, nuclear fission,** fission reaction, **splitting the atom;** chain reaction

7 **fusion, nuclear fusion,** fusion reaction

8 nuclear fuel; fissionable material, fissile material; **critical mass;** parent element, daughter element; end product

9 **accelerator, particle accelerator**

10 **reactor, nuclear reactor,** atomic pile

11 **atomic energy, nuclear energy, nuclear power**

12 **atomic explosion,** thermonuclear explosion; ground zero; blast wave; mushroom cloud; fallout; **atom** *or* **atomic bomb, hydrogen bomb** *or* **H-bomb,** neutron bomb, nuke (*nonformal*); fallout shelter

verbs

13 bombard; split the atom

adjectives

14 **nuclear,** thermonuclear

15 **fissionable,** fissile

987 TOOLS, MACHINERY

nouns

1 **tool, instrument, implement, utensil; apparatus, device,** mechanical device, contrivance, contraption (*nonformal*), gadget, gizmo (*nonformal*), means; **power tool;** machine tool

2 **cutlery; knife, axe, dagger,** sword, blade; steel, cold steel

3 **machinery, machine, mechanism,** mechanical device; heavy machinery; farm machinery; mill; pump; **engine,** motor; power plant, **power source,** drive, motive power; **appliance,** facility, domestic appliance; fixture; labour-saving device

4 mechanism, machinery, **movement, action, motion, works,** workings, inner workings; drive train, power train; wheels, gear;

5 gear, gearing, gear train; rack; first, second, third, fourth, fifth, low, high, overdrive, neutral, reverse; **transmission,** gearbox; automatic transmission; manual transmission

6 mechanic, grease monkey (*nonformal*)

verbs

7 tool, tool up; **machine,** mill; **mechanize,** automate, motorize

adjectives

8 mechanical; power, powered, motorized; **mechanized**

988 AUTOMATION

nouns

1 automation, automatic control; computerization

2 system engineering, systems analysis; systems planning, systems design; circuit analysis; information technology

3 remote control; radio control

4 automatic device; robot, automation, mechanical man

5 control panel, console; graphic panel; set-up board

6 computer, computer science, computer unit, hardware, computer hardware

7 system engineer, systems analyst; computer engineer, computer technician, **computer programmer, programmer, information scientist**

verbs

8 automate; program; computerize

adjectives

9 automated, automatic; computerized, computer-controlled

989 COMPUTER SCIENCE

nouns

1 computer science, computers, computing; **computerization, data processing, information science,** information processing, information science; computer security; hacking

2 computer, machine, **hardware,** computer hardware; **processor,** microprocessor; **mainframe,** work station, home computer, micro, personal computer or PC, desktop, laptop

3 circuit, circuitry, integrated circuit, **chip,** silicon chip, microchip; **peripheral,** input device, output device; **port,** serial port

4 input device, keyboard, reader, tape reader, scanner, optical scanner, joystick, light pen, mouse, trackball or trackerball

5 drive, disk drive, tape drive

6 disk, floppy disk or floppy (*nonformal*) or diskette, hard disk, Winchester disk; tape

7 memory, storage, core, bubble memory, RAM, ROM

8 retrieval, access, random access, direct access

9 output device, terminal, workstation, visual display unit or VDU, **monitor, printer,** dot-matrix printer, laser printer; **modem**

10 **software, program,** computer program, software package, routine

11 **word processor,** text editor, editor, **computer application,** applications program

12 **language,** programming language, machine language, computer language, high-level language, assembly language, query language; virus, **computer virus,** logic bomb

13 **bit, binary digit; byte,** kilobyte, megabyte

14 **data, information; file,** record, data bank, database, directory

15 **network, computer network,** communications network; system, computer system; Internet

16 **programmer,** systems programmer, application programmer, systems analyst, systems engineer, operator, technician; hacker (*nonformal*)

verbs

17 **program,** boot, boot up, log in, log out, run, load, **compute; keyboard,** key in, input

adjectives

18 **computerized;** computer-aided, computer-controlled

990 FRICTION

nouns

1 **friction, rubbing; drag**

2 **abrasion, erosion,** wearing away, wear; **erasure,** rubbing away *or* off *or* out; grinding, filing, rasping; chafing; scraping;

grazing, scratching, scuffing; **scrape,** scratch; scrubbing, scrub; scouring, **polishing,** sanding, smoothing, buffing, dressing, shining

3 **massage,** massaging, stroking, kneading; **rubdown;** whirlpool bath, Jacuzzi (*trademark*); facial massage, facial

verbs

4 **rub, massage,** knead, rub down; caress, pet, stroke

5 **abrade,** gnaw, gnaw away; **erode,** erode away, wear, wear away; erase, rub away *or* off *or* out; **grind, rasp, file,** grate; **chafe,** fret, gall; **scrape, graze, scuff,** bark, skin; **fray, scrub,** scour

6 **buff, burnish, polish,** rub up, sandpaper, **sand,** smooth, dress, shine

adjectives

7 **frictional,** friction; **rubbing**

8 **abrasive,** gnawing; scraping; **grinding, rasping;** chafing

991 DENSITY

nouns

1 **density, solidity,** firmness, **compactness, closeness, congestion,** crowdedness; **impenetrability,** impermeability; hardness; **consistency,** thickness; **viscousness**

2 **indivisibility, inseparability;** cohesion, coherence; unity; insolubility

3 **condensation, compression, concentration,** consolidation; hardening, **solidification; clumping, clustering**

4 **thickening,** coagulation, clotting, **setting,** gelling; **curdling**

5 **precipitation,** deposit, sediment

6 **solid,** body, mass; lump, clump, cluster; **block,** cake; concrete; conglomeration

7 **clot,** coagulate; blood clot; **coagulant,** clotting factor; **curd**

verbs

8 **densify; condense, compress,** compact, **consolidate, concentrate;** congest, squeeze, press, crowd, cram, jam; **solidify**

9 **thicken; congeal, coagulate, clot,** set; gel; **curdle;** cake, lump, clump, cluster, knot

10 **precipitate,** deposit, sediment

adjectives

11 **dense, compact, close;** close-knit; **thick, heavy; condensed, compressed,** compacted, concrete, consolidated, concentrated; **crowded, jammed,** packed, congested, crammed; **solid,** firm, substantial; impenetrable, impermeable; **hard;** viscous

12 **indivisible, inseparable;** cohesive, coherent; unified; insoluble

13 **thickened; congealed,** coagulated, clotted; **curdled; jellied;** lumpy; caked

adverbs

14 **densely, close,** closely, **thick,** thickly, heavily; solidly, firmly

992 HARDNESS, RIGIDITY

nouns

1 **hardness, callousness, strength,** toughness; solidity, impenetrability; resistance; obduracy

2 **rigidity, firmness, tension,** tautness, tightness

3 **stiffness, inflexibility; stubbornness**

4 **hardening, toughening,** firming; **strengthening; stiffening,** starching; solidification; **setting**

5 (*comparisons*) stone, rock, marble, diamond; steel, iron, nails; concrete, cement; brick; bone

verbs

6 **harden, firm, toughen;** steel

7 **solidify, set,** cake; condense, thicken; **crystallize**

8 **stiffen,** starch; **strengthen, toughen;** brace, reinforce; **tense,** tighten

adjectives

9 **hard, solid, tough;** resistant, steely; **stony,** rock-hard; obdurate; hard-hearted

10 **rigid,** stiff, firm, **tense,** taut, tight; starched

11 **inflexible, intractable,** unbending, unyielding, **stubborn,** unalterable, immutable; **immovable;** adamant

12 **hardened, toughened,** steeled; **callous; solidified,** set; crystallized, granulated; crusty; **stiffened, strengthened;** reinforced

13 **hardening, toughening**

993 SOFTNESS, PLIANCY

nouns

1 **softness, give; gentleness,** delicacy, tenderness; leniency; fluffiness; silkiness

2 pliancy, plasticity, flexibility, adaptability; give; suppleness, litheness, impressionability, susceptibility, receptiveness, sensibility, sensitiveness; submissiveness

3 flaccidity, flabbiness, limpness, floppiness; looseness, laxness, relaxation

4 (*comparisons*) putty, clay, dough, butter; velvet, satin, silk; wool; pillow, cushion; baby's bottom; down, feathers

5 softening, easing, padding, cushioning; **relaxation;** mellowing

verbs

6 soften, soften up; **ease,** cushion; mollify; **subdue;** mellow; **relax,** loosen; limber up; massage, knead, plump up, fluff, shake up; **mash, smash,** squash, pulp

7 yield, give, relent, relax, bend, give way; submit

adjectives

8 soft; mild, gentle, easy, delicate, tender; mellow; softened, mollified

9 pliable, flexible, plastic, elastic, yielding, giving, bending; adaptable; submissive; **impressionable,** susceptible, responsive, receptive, sensitive

10 flaccid, flabby, limp, floppy; **loose,** lax, relaxed

11 spongy, pulpy, pithy

12 squashy, squelchy

13 fluffy, downy, feathery; woolly; furry

14 velvety; plush; satiny; **silky**

15 softening, easing; subduing, mollifying; **relaxing,** loosening

adverbs

16 softly, gently, easily, delicately, tenderly; submissively

994 ELASTICITY

nouns

1 elasticity, give; bounce; stretch; spring; **flexibility; adaptability**

2 stretching; extension; **stretch,** tension, strain

3 elastic; rubber; stretch fabric, spandex; gum; rubber band; spring; springboard; trampoline

verbs

4 stretch; extend

5 give, yield; bounce, spring

adjectives

6 elastic, resilient, springy, bouncy; stretchy; **flexible;** rubbery

995 TOUGHNESS

nouns

1 toughness, resistance; strength, hardiness, vitality, stamina; stubbornness, **stiffness, tenacity; durability; hardness**

verbs

2 toughen, harden, stiffen, strengthen; **endure**

adjectives

3 tough, resistant; stubborn, stiff; **heavy-duty; strong, hardy,** vigorous; **tenacious, durable,** lasting; **hard**

4 unbreakable, shatterproof

5 toughened, hardened

996 BRITTLENESS, FRAGILITY

nouns

1 **brittleness, crispness; fragility, frailty,** delicacy, flimsiness; **vulnerability**

verbs

2 **break, shatter,** fragment, **disintegrate**

adjectives

3 **brittle, crisp, fragile, frail,** delicate, flimsy, **breakable;** crumbly; **vulnerable**

997 POWDERINESS, CRUMBLINESS

nouns

1 **powderiness, dustiness;** chalkiness; flourines

2 **graininess,** grittiness

3 crispness, crumbliness; brittleness

4 **pulverization;** fragmentation; powdering, crumbling; abrasion; grinding, milling, grating, shredding; **beating, pounding, shattering,** mashing, smashing, crushing; disintegration

5 **powder, dust; crumb,** crumble; **meal,** bran, flour; grits; filings, sawdust; soot; **particle**

6 **grain,** granule; **grit, sand; gravel,** shingle

7 **crusher; mill; grinder; grater;** shredder; masher; roller, steamroller

verbs

8 **pulverize, powder,** disintegrate; **fragment,** shatter; **crumble; grind, grate, shred; mill; beat, pound,** mash, smash, crush, crunch, squash

9 **powder, crumble, disintegrate,** break up

adjectives

10 **powdery, dusty; pulverized,** powdered, disintegrated; ground, grated, milled; **crushed; fragmented; shredded;** fine, **chalky;** floury; scaly; flaky

11 **grainy, granulated;** sandy, gritty, gravelly

12 crisp, **crumbly**

998 MATERIALITY

nouns

1 **materiality;** corporeality, embodiment; substantiality, concreteness; physicality

2 **matter, material, substance, stuff; element;** earth, air, fire, water; elementary particle, fundamental particle; elementary unit, building block; constituent, component; **atom; molecule**

3 **body,** physical body, material body, person, **figure, form,** frame, **physique,** bones, flesh; **torso, trunk**

4 **object, article, thing,** something; artefact

5 (*nonformal terms*) **gadget;** thingumabob, thingumajig, **gimmick,** gizmo

6 **materialism; naturalism;** realism; worldliness, earthliness

7 **materialization**; substantiation; **embodiment**, personification, **incarnation; reincarnation**

verbs

8 **materialize**; substantiate; **embody**, personify, incarnate; **reincarnate**

adjectives

9 **material, substantial**; corporeal, **bodily; physical; fleshly**; worldly, earthly, **secular**

10 **embodied, incorporated**, incarnate

999 IMMATERIALITY

nouns

1 **immateriality**; incorporeality, **bodilessness; unsubstantiality**; intangibility; **unearthliness, unworldliness**; supernaturalism; **spirituality**, ghostliness

2 **immaterialism, idealism**; spiritualism

3 **idealist**; spiritualist; occultist; medium

4 **dematerialization; disembodiment**; spiritualization

verbs

5 dematerialize, **disembody**; **spiritualize**

adjectives

6 **immaterial**; insubstantial, **intangible**; incorporeal; bodiless; disembodied; unphysical; unfleshly; airy, ghostly; **spiritual**, psychic; **unearthly**, unworldly; supernatural; **occult**

7 **idealistic**, immaterialistic; spiritualist

1000 MATERIALS

nouns

1 **materials**, substances, stuff; **raw material, staple, stock; store, supply**

2 **bricks and mortar; roofing**, tiles; **flooring**, paving stone; masonry, stonework, flagstone; stone; mortar, plasters; **cement, concrete**; brick; tiling

3 **wood lumber, timber**; pole, post, beam, **board**, plank; slab; boarding; panelling; plywood; log; driftwood; firewood

4 cane, bamboo

5 **paper**; sheet, leaf, page; stationery; cardboard

6 **plastic**; thermoplastic; adhesive; synthetic rubber

verbs

7 **store, stock**, stock up, restock; **process**, utilize

1001 INORGANIC MATTER

nouns

1 **inorganic matter**, nonorganic matter; inanimate *or* lifeless *or* nonliving matter, inert matter, dead matter

2 **inanimateness, lifelessness**, inertness; **insensibility**, unconsciousness

adjectives

3 **inorganic**, nonorganic; **mineral**, nonbiological; material

4 **inanimate**, dead, **lifeless**; inert; unconscious, **insensible**, unfeeling; dumb, mute

1002 OILS, LUBRICANTS

nouns

1 **oil, fat, grease;** vegetable oil, animal oil; **ester;** essential oil; saturated fat, unsaturated fat

2 **lubricant,** lubricating oil, lubricating agent; graphite; glycerin; wax; mucus; petroleum jelly

3 **ointment, balm, salve, lotion, cream; soothing syrup;** cold cream, hand lotion, face cream, lanolin; sun block, suntan lotion

4 **petroleum,** rock oil, fossil oil; **fuel;** fuel oil; crude oil; motor oil

5 **oiliness, greasiness;** fattiness; richness; **soapiness;** smoothness, **slickness,** slipperiness

6 **lubrication, oiling, greasing;** anointment

verbs

7 **oil,** grease; **lubricate;** anoint; smear, daub; wax

adjectives

8 **oily, greasy,** unctuous; **fatty;** rich; soapy; smooth, slick, **slippery**

9 lubricating; emollient, soothing

1003 MINERALS, METALS

nouns

1 **mineral; inorganic substance**

2 **ore,** mineral

3 **metal,** elementary metal; precious metals, base metals, rare metals; gold dust; leaf metal, metal foil; metalwork, metalware

4 **alloy,** fusion, compound

5 **cast; ingot, bullion;** sheet metal

6 **mine, pit; quarry; workings;** opencast; shaft; coal mine, colliery; strip mine; gold mine, silver mine, etc

7 **deposit,** mineral deposit; **vein,** seam, dike

8 **mining;** coal mining, gold mining, etc; strip mining; prospecting; gold rush

9 **miner,** mineworker, coal miner, collier; gold miner

10 **mineralogy; geology;** mining engineering; **metallurgy**

11 **mineralogist; metallurgist; geologist;** mining engineer

verbs

12 **mine;** quarry; pan; prospect

adjectives

13 **mineral;** inorganic; mineralized, petrified

14 **metal, metallic**

15 brass, brassy; bronze; copper; gold, golden; gilt; nickel; silver; iron, ferric, ferrous; steel; tin; lead, leaden; pewter; mercurial; gold-plated, silver-plated, etc

1004 ROCK

nouns

1 **rock, stone; igneous rock;** volcanic rock; granite, basalt, **lava; sedimentary rock;** limestone, sandstone; crag; bedrock

2 **sand;** sand dune, sand hill

3 **gravel; shingle; pebble,** gravelstone; **boulder**

4 **precious stone, gem, gemstone;** crystal; semiprecious stone; birthstone

verbs

5 petrify, crystallize; harden

adjectives

6 **stone, rock;** petrified; flinty; marblelike; slatelike

7 **stony, rocky;** sandy, gritty; gravelly, shingled; pebbled; crystal; craggy

1005 CHEMISTRY, CHEMICALS

nouns

1 **chemistry,** chemical science

2 **element,** chemical element; table of elements, periodic table; free radical; **ion; atom; molecule,** macromolecule; trace element, minor element; **chemical, chemical compound;** organic chemical, biochemical, inorganic chemical; agent, **reagent**

3 **acid;** acidity; **base, alkali,** nonacid; pH; neutralizer, antacid; alkalinity

4 **valency,** valence

5 **atomic weight,** atomic mass, mass number; **molecular weight;** atomic number

6 chemical process, chemical action; **chemical apparatus,** beaker, Bunsen burner, test tube

verbs

7 **chemicalize;** alkalize; acidify; oxidize, reduce; catalyze

adjectives

8 **chemical;** biochemical; elemental, elementary; acid; alkaline, nonacid, basic

1006 LIQUIDITY

nouns

1 **liquidity, fluidity; moisture; fluency,** flow, flux

2 **fluid, liquid;** liquor, drink, beverage; **juice, sap;** milk; water; **body fluid,** blood

adjectives

3 **fluid, flowing,** runny; **liquid;** watery; **juicy,** succulent; **wet**

4 **milky,** lactic

1007 SEMILIQUIDITY

nouns

1 **semiliquidity;** creaminess

2 **viscosity;** thickness; **stickiness, tackiness**

3 **mucosity;** sliminess

4 **muddiness,** muckiness, slushiness, sloppiness, squashiness

5 **semiliquid,** semifluid; **paste,** putty, cream; **pulp; jelly,** gel; **glue;** size; mucus; **dough,** batter

6 **gum,** chewing gum, bubble gum

7 **mud,** muck, slush, sludge, slime; clay, slip

8 **puddle,** slop

verbs

9 **emulsify;** cream; churn, whip, beat up; **thicken,** curdle, clot, coagulate; jell

adjectives

10 **semiliquid,** semifluid; creamy

11 **viscous, viscid; thick,** stodgy; curdled, clotted, coagulated; **sticky, tacky,** adhesive; clammy, slimy

12 **mucous,** snotty (*nonformal*)

13 **slimy; muddy,** slushy, sloppy, squashy

1008 MOISTURE

nouns

1 **moisture, damp, wet; dampness, moistness, wetness;** rainfall

2 **humidity, mugginess,** stickiness

3 **water;** steam, water vapour

4 **dew, dewdrops**

5 **sprinkle, spray, shower;** froth, foam; **splash,** slosh; **splatter,** spatter

6 **wetting, moistening, dampening, damping; watering, irrigation;** hosing; **sprinkling, spraying; splashing,** splattering, spattering; bath, bathing, rinsing; **flooding,** drowning, deluge; **immersion**

7 **soaking, drenching;** ducking, dunking (nonformal); soak; **saturation**

8 **sprinkler,** spray, spray can, aerosol; nozzle; **shower;** syringe

verbs

9 be damp; **drip, weep; seep, ooze;** exude; sweat; secrete

10 **moisten, dampen, wet,** damp; **water, irrigate; sprinkle, spray; splash,** slosh, splatter, spatter; dabble, paddle; slop; hose; syringe; sponge

11 **soak, drench, souse; saturate,** permeate; **bathe,** wash, rinse, flush; **steep,** brew

12 **flood, float, inundate, deluge,** swamp, drown; duck, dip, dunk (nonformal); **submerge;** rain

adjectives

13 **moist; damp; wet;** tacky; **humid, dank, muggy, sticky;** rainy; marshy, boggy

14 **watery, aquatic;** liquid; sloppy

15 **soaked, drenched,** soused, bathed, steeped; **saturated,** permeated; **waterlogged; soaking; wringing wet; sodden, soggy;** dripping; dribbling, seeping, weeping, oozing; flooded, overflowed, inundated, deluged, drowned, submerged, immersed, dipped, dunked (nonformal)

16 **wetting, dampening, moistening,** watering; **drenching, soaking**

1009 DRYNESS

nouns

1 **dryness, aridity; drought; thirst**

2 **drying, desiccation; dehydration;** drainage; withering

verbs

3 thirst; drink up, soak up, sponge up

4 **dry, desiccate, dehydrate;** smoke; cure; burn, fire, bake, parch, scorch; **wither, shrivel;** soak up; **wipe,** rub, swab, brush; towel; drain

adjectives

5 **dry, arid; thirsty;** sandy, dusty; desert

6 fine, fair, pleasant

7 **dried, dehydrated, desiccated; parched, baked,** burnt, scorched; **withered, shrivelled,** wizened

8 **drying, dehydrating**

9 **watertight, waterproof**

INDEX

a
  adj quantitative 230.5

A list
  n society 559.6

abandon
  n zeal 92.2
  ecstasy 96.8
  carelessness 325.2
  exuberance 415.3
  excess 948.1
  v quit 179.9
  leave undone 325.7
  desert 355.5
  break the habit 359.3
  discard 375.7
  surrender 418.7
  disregard 420.3
  relinquish 460.2
  renounce 648.6
  cease 819.4

abandoned
  adj zealous 92.9
  available 211.13
  neglected 325.14
  forsaken 355.8
  disused 375.8
  uninhibited 415.22
  relinquished 460.4
  forlorn 565.12
  outcast 567.9
  corrupt 634.14
  excessive 948.14

abbey
  n monastery 681.4

ability
  n capability 18.2
  means 369.2
  readiness 390.4
  skill 398.1
  talent 398.4

able
  adj capable 18.9
  fitted 390.14
  competent 398.22

aboard
  adv here 150.23
  on board 173.28

abortion
  n miscarriage 395.5
  monstrosity 832.6
  unfruitfulness 846.1

about
  adv around 200.11
  near 212.20
  approximately 230.6

about to
  adj prepared 390.13

above
  adj superior 235.12
  higher 258.14
  previous 796.4
  adv additionally 239.10
  on high 258.15
  before 776.6

above all
  adv chiefly 235.17

abroad
  adj away from home
    211.11
  adv outdoors 197.10
  wide 247.16
  wide 247.18
  overseas 736.5

absence
  n want 211.1
  leaving 211.4
  vacancy 724.1

absolute
  adj omnipotent 18.8
  downright 233.12
  affirmative 319.7
  authoritative 402.14
  mandatory 405.10
  unrestricted 415.25
  governmental 593.15
  real 723.11
  thorough 756.9
  unadulterated 760.6

particular 827.12
  sole 834.9
  convincing 908.24
  evidential 912.14
  unqualified 915.1
  certain 925.9
  obvious 925.10
  accurate 928.16
  perfect 957.5

absolutely
  adv utterly 233.21
  positively 319.9
  really 723.12
  perfectly 756.14
  certainly 925.17
  exactly 928.21
  perfectly 957.9

abuse
  n misuse 374.1
  molesting 374.2
  berating 495.6
  vilification 498.2
  seduction 645.6
  v exploit 372.14
  misuse 374.1
  maltreat 374.5
  berate 495.17
  vilify 498.7
  seduce 645.19
  blaspheme 673.5
  harm 955.6

academic
  adj scholastic 548.13
  scholastic 549.19
  studious 551.17
  pedagogic 552.10
  theoretical 906.10
  n teacher 552.1

academy
  n school 548.1
  secondary school 548.4

accent
  n regional accent
    509.8

emphasis 509.9
emphasis 687.15
metre 698.7
v emphasize 952.13

accept
v take for granted
114.2
condone 125.6
assent 317.7
acknowledge 317.10
ratify 317.11
adopt 356.14
undertake 389.3
submit 418.5
consent 426.2
receive 464.6
approve 494.7
receive 566.7
believe 908.10
keep an open mind
934.7

acceptable
adj desirable 91.29
agreeable 98.12
eligible 356.23
welcome 566.12
tolerable 954.19

acceptance
n composure 97.2
contentment 98.1
patience 125.1
admission 178.2
assent 317.1
acknowledgment 317.3
ratification 317.4
adoption 356.4
leniency 412.1
submission 418.1
consent 426.1
receiving 464.1
approval 494.1
nomination 590.10

accepted
adj approved 317.13
chosen 356.25
customary 358.12
undertaken 389.4

approved 494.17
conventional 560.5
orthodox 666.5
real 723.11
believed 908.22
authoritative 925.13

access
n openness 158.2
in 178.3
entrance 180.1
entrance 180.5
passageway 368.3
practicality 921.2
retrieval 988.5
v arrive 177.6
enter 180.7

accident
n accessory 730.1
event 793.1
happening 927.3
misfortune 966.2

accommodation
n orientation 152.3
capacity 243.2
accustoming 358.6
facilities 370.3
facility 434.9
adjustment 450.4
compromise 453.1
giving 463.1
adjustment 750.4
equating 752.2
change 814.1
conformity 829.1

accord
n unanimity 317.5
compact 422.1
accordance 440.1
peace 449.1
harmony 686.2
relation 737.1
agreement 750.1
v concur 317.8
permit 428.9
get along 440.2
give 463.12
harmonize 686.29

agree 750.6
harmonize 750.7
conform 829.3
concur 854.2

account
n recounting 334.3
record 530.1
report 530.7
information 532.1
credit account 602.2
fee 604.5
reckoning 608.2
statement 608.3
esteem 642.3
story 697.2
story 700.3
bill 833.5
v judge 901.8

accounts
n outstanding or
unpaid accounts
608.1

accurate
adj meticulous 324.12
discriminating 899.7
correct 928.16

accused
adj charged 580.14
n party 579.11
defendant 580.6

achieve
v arrive 177.6
do 313.6
accomplish 392.4
succeed with 394.8
perform 847.11

achieved
adj accomplished
392.9

achievement
n arrival 177.1
performance 313.2
act 313.3
accomplishment 392.1
exploit 477.5
performance 847.5

acid

adj acrimonious 17.13
acid 58.6
pungent 59.6
caustic 135.21
chemical 14.8
n vinegar 58.2
acidity 14.3

acknowledged
adj accepted 317.13
conventional 560.5
traditional 804.11

across
adj traverse 161.9
diagonal 195.18
adv cross 161.13
diagonally 195.22
on 856.12

act
n action 313.1
action 313.3
law 653.3
scene 682.4
process 844.2
v behave 306.3
serve 313.4
impersonate 334.11
sham 339.14
perform 682.21
operate 844.7
perform 847.11

acting
adj performing 313.10
deputy 557.15
n action 313.1
impersonation 334.4
sham 339.2
playing 682.5

action
n behaviour 306.1
activity 313.1
act 313.3
activity 315.1
undertaking 389.1
fight 442.4
operation 443.4
lawsuit 579.1
plot 700.4

fun 720.2
operation 844.1
verdict 901.5
expedient 950.2
mechanism 986.4

actions
n behaviour 306.1

active
adj energetic 17.12
moving 163.6
lively 315.13
effective 372.19
observant 419.4
operating 844.11

activity
n animation 17.4
motion 163.1
behaviour 306.1
action 313.1
action 315.1
occupation 701.1
principle 841.9

actor
n fake and fraud 485.6
movie studio 684.3
actress 685.2
agent 703.1

actress
n movie studio 684.3
actor 685.2

acts
n behaviour 306.1

actual
adj real 723.11
happening 793.9
present 800.2
obvious 925.10
true 928.13

actually
adv decidedly 233.18
really 723.12
truly 928.18

ad
n advertisement 337.6

add
v attach 239.4
combine 767.3

added
adj attached 239.8

adding
n computation 239.3

addition
n increase 237.1
attachment 239.1
adjunct 240.1
wing 240.3
expansion 245.1
acquisition 457.1
accessory 730.1
combination 767.1

additional
adj additive 239.7
supplementary 239.9
unnecessary 730.3
fresh 803.8

address
n abode 217.1
request 425.1
remark 509.3
speech 524.2
destination 534.9
greeting 566.4
v speak to 509.20
make a speech 524.7
direct 534.13
greet 566.10

adequate
adj able 18.9
satisfactory 98.11
sufficient 946.5
tolerable 954.19

administration
n performance 313.2
governance 402.5
distribution 462.2
government 593.1
giving 623.2
care 963.2
n dispensation 554.3

admission
n admittance 178.2
entrance 180.1
acknowledgment 317.3
confession 336.3

permission 428.1
receiving 464.1
fee 610.6
inclusion 734.1
testimony 912.2

admit
v receive 178.9
enter 180.7
adopt 215.3
acknowledge 317.10
confess 336.7
permit 428.9
receive 464.6
receive 566.7
include 734.3
allow for 914.5

admitted
adj accepted 317.13
revealed 336.9
permitted 428.15
approved 494.17
real 723.11

adopt
v admit 215.3
approve 356.14
use 369.5
appropriate 465.19
appropriate 601.4
usurp 620.8

adopted
adj naturalized 215.5
chosen 356.25

adult
adj grown 14.3
mature 289.9
lascivious 645.26
obscene 646.9
n man 290.1

advance
n progression 153.1
approach 158.1
course 163.2
offer 424.1
promotion 431.1
loan 600.2
evolution 823.1
v progress 153.2

further 153.5
approach 158.3
move 163.4
be instrumental 369.6
improve 377.7
improve 377.9
make good 394.7
propose 424.5
promote 431.2
be useful 434.17
lend 600.5
elapse 783.3
evolve 823.4
determine 841.12
push 859.9
postulate 906.9
produce 912.11
come in handy 950.3
do good 954.10
prosper 965.7

advanced
adj front 207.9
improved 377.13
preceding 778.4
modern 803.13
premature 807.8

advantage
n upper hand 235.2
benefit 372.4
facility 434.9
leverage 861.1
expedience or
expediency 950.1
good 954.4

advertising
n promotion 337.5

advice
n counsel 407.1
clue 532.3

advised
adj reasoned 890.17

adviser
n counsel 407.3
informant 532.5

affair
n love affair 95.5
undertaking 389.1

occupation 701.1
concern 793.3

affairs
n action 313.1
occupation 701.1
relation 737.1
concerns 793.4

affect
v wear 5.33
touch 84.12
impress 84.13
move 136.5
sham 339.14
assume 485.8
relate to 737.5
operate on 844.6
influence 849.7

affected
adj moved 84.21
spurious 339.17
pretentious 485.10
elaborate 515.7
grandiloquent 526.6

afford
v provide 370.7
give 463.12
furnish 463.15
spare the price 606.5

afraid
adj scared 118.21
weak 347.12
cowardly 476.6

Africa
n Northern
Hemisphere 220.6

after
adj subsequent 797.4
adv behind 157.6
subsequently 797.5

after all
adv on balance 901.17

afternoon
adj afternoon 300.7
n PM 300.1

afterwards
adv subsequently
797.5

again
  adv additionally 239.10
  then 783.9
  newly 803.15
  over 811.17
  another time 836.7

against
  adj disapproving 495.19

age
  n years 289.1
  generation 786.4
  era 786.5
  durability 789.1
  lifetime 789.4
  seniority 804.1
  v grow old 289.8
  grow old 804.8

aged
  adj mature 289.10
  elderly 289.11
  mature 290.6
  durable 789.9
  stuffy 804.16

agency
  n machinery 369.3
  workplace 716.1
  substitution 824.1
  operation 844.1

agenda
  n notebook 530.9
  roll 833.6
  schedule 920.2

agent
  n intermediary 204.3
  instrument 369.4
  mediator 451.3
  instrument 557.3
  assistant 596.5
  actor 703.1
  agent 703.1
  salesman 707.3
  transformer 814.5
  substitute 824.2
  author 841.4
  operator 844.4
  element 14.2

aggression
  n enterprise 315.6
  ferocity 443.10
  attack 444.1

aggressive
  adj energetic 17.12
  enterprising 315.19
  partisan 441.15
  warlike 443.17
  offensive 444.24
  gruff 490.7

ago
  adj past 799.6
  adv since 799.13

agree
  v be willing 309.3
  assent 317.7
  concur 317.8
  come to an agreement
    317.9
  contract 422.5
  coincide 740.4
  accord 750.6
  coincide 798.4
  concur 854.2

agree with
  v be good for 72.3
  concur 317.8
  get along 440.2
  relate to 737.5
  conform 829.3

agreed
  adj assenting 317.12
  contracted 422.11
  supposed 906.11

agreement
  n assent 317.1
  unanimity 317.5
  obligation 421.2
  compact 422.1
  consent 426.1
  accord 440.1
  sameness 740.1
  similarity 746.1
  accord 750.1
  combination 767.1
  conformity 829.1

n collaboration 854.1

agricultural
  adj rustic 224.4
  agrarian 112.19

agriculture
  n farming 112.1

ahead
  adj front 207.9
  superior 235.12
  adv forward 153.8
  before 207.11
  early 807.11

aid
  n remedy 77.1
  help 434.1
  subsidy 463.8
  support 856.1
  v advance 153.5
  help 434.11
  subsidize 463.19
  benefit 573.3
  facilitate 969.7

aim
  n direction 152.1
  motive 360.1
  intention 365.1
  objective 365.2
  intent 503.2
  v direct 152.4
  head 152.6
  intend 365.4
  endeavour 388.4

aimed
  adj directed 152.12

air
  n looks 32.4
  ambience 200.3
  feather 284.2
  ozone 302.1
  breeze 303.3
  behaviour 306.1
  tune 686.3
  spirit 726.3
  matter 997.2
  gas 111.2
  the heavens 114.2
  v air out 302.9

divulge 336.5
publish 337.10
make public 337.11
show off 486.13
discuss 523.10

Air Force
n branch 446.17

air force
n squadron 446.24

aircraft
n vehicle 170.1
aeroplane 172.1

airport
n airfield 175.8
destination 177.5

alarm
n fear 118.1
warning 384.1
alert 385.1
signal 502.15
call 502.16
v frighten 118.15
alert 385.2

album
n record 41.11
notebook 530.9
compilation 535.7

alcohol
n beverage 10.44
sedative 77.11
antiseptic 77.13

alert
adj awake 23.8
on the alert 324.14
prepared 390.13
prompt 807.9
no-nonsense 875.11
curious 936.5
attentive 938.14
n warning sign 384.7
alarm 385.1
v warn 384.4
alarm 385.2
confide 532.10

alive
adj living 292.9
active 315.13

alert 324.14
no-nonsense 875.11
remembered 944.18

all
adj whole 754.9
every 826.14
adv wholly 754.12
n everything 754.3
limit 756.5
everyone 826.3
universe 114.1

all about
adv all round 200.12

all but
adv nearly 212.22
on the whole 754.13

all over
adv everywhere 149.10
throughout 756.16
universally 826.17

all right
adj well 74.10
tolerable 954.19

all sorts
n conglomeration
759.5

all the way
adv through thick and
thin 345.10

alleged
adj affirmed 319.8
pretended 361.5
accountable 843.6
supposed 906.11

allegedly
adv ostensibly 361.6
reportedly 533.15

alliance
n treaty 422.2
affiliation 435.2
blood relationship
540.1
marriage 544.1
association 587.1
relation 737.1
combination 767.1
n collaboration 854.1

allied
adj related 737.9
joined 762.12
associated 767.6

allow
v acknowledge 317.10
permit 428.9
give 463.12
allow for 914.5

allowed
adj accepted 317.13
permitted 428.15
given 463.24

allowing
adj permissive 428.13

almost
adv nearly 212.22

alone
adj solitary 565.11
solitary 834.8
sole 834.9
adv independently
415.30
simply 760.10
singly 834.13

along
adv forward 153.8
extensively 253.9

alongside
adj side 209.4
adv in parallel 194.6
aside 209.7

already
adv previously 796.5
until now 800.4

also
adv additionally 239.10

alternative
adj voluntary 356.21
substitute 824.7
n option 356.2
substitute 824.2

altogether
adv additionally 239.10
wholly 754.12
completely 756.13
generally 826.16

always
adv regularly 743.8
all along 791.10
constantly 809.7
permanently 815.8
universally 826.17

AM
n morning 299.1

amateur
adj half-baked 885.13
n connoisseur 481.4
layman 703.5
specialist 828.3
dilettante 884.4
dabbler 953.9

amazing
adj astonishing 113.8

ambassador
n diplomat 557.6

ambition
n social climbing 91.10
motive 360.1
intention 365.1

ambitious
adj aspiring 91.27
enterprising 315.19
ostentatious 486.14

America
n Northern
Hemisphere 220.6

amnesty
n pardon 139.2
exemption 582.2

amount
n quantity 230.1
quantity 230.2
degree 231.1
price 610.1

amp
n amplifier 41.9

an
adj quantitative 230.5
one 834.7

analysis
n psychoanalysis 83.2
discussion 523.6
commentary 537.2

specification 728.5
differentiation 742.3
breakdown 763.1
dissection 764.5
classification 771.1
deduction 890.3
inquiry 893.1
penetration 899.2
theory 906.1

ancient
adj aged 289.11
durable 789.9
former 799.8
old 804.9
n prehistoric mankind
804.6

and others
adv et cetera 838.8

and so
adv in consequence
842.7

anger
n darkness 37.2
ill humour 101.1
wrath 143.5
violence 651.1
ardour 971.24
v make angry 143.22
excite 972.18

angle
n viewpoint 27.7
aspect 32.3
station 150.2
point 264.1
particular 728.3
outlook 933.2
v go sideways 209.3
crook 264.2
fish 367.10

angry
adj sore 26.11
dark 37.8
annoyed 87.21
angered 143.27
stormy 303.17

animal
adj cruel 135.24

carnal 643.6
n beast 135.13
barbarian 482.7
savage 574.5
beast 640.6

anniversary
n bank holiday 812.4

announce
v herald 124.13
affirm 319.5
enunciate 337.12
state 509.17
report 533.11
be prior 796.3

announced
adj affirmed 319.8
published 337.17

announcement
n affirmation 319.1
informing 328.2
proclamation 337.2
information 532.1

annual
adj momentary 812.8
n plant 296.3
notebook 530.9
periodical 536.1

another
adj additional 239.9
other 742.7
fresh 803.8

answer
n communication
328.1
remark 509.3
letter 534.2
defence 581.2
reaction 858.1
reply 894.1
solution 895.1
refutation 913.2
expedient 950.2
v communicate with
328.7
avail 372.15
reply 534.11
reciprocate 739.6

react 858.4
offer 894.3
solve 895.2
refute 913.4

answer to
v relate to 737.5
reciprocate 739.6

anxiety
n lack of pleasure 87.1
eagerness 92.1
apprehension 117.1
apprehension 118.4
suspense 121.3
impatience 126.1
trouble 968.3

anxious
adj joyless 87.20
eager 92.8
concerned 117.6
apprehensive 118.23
in suspense 121.11
impatient 126.5
troubled 968.20

any
adj quantitative 230.5
every 826.14
one 834.7
n some 230.3
anything 826.4

any time
adv any moment 802.4

anybody
n any 826.4

anyone
n any 826.4
whoever 826.6

anything
n some 230.3
any 826.4

anyway
adv anyhow 369.9

anywhere
adv wherever 150.22

apart
adj secluded 565.8
unrelated 738.4
alone 834.8

adv away 247.17
privately 330.19
separately 764.24
singly 834.13
in half 837.7

apart from
adv separately 764.24

apartheid
n seclusion 565.1
xenophobia 735.3
discrimination 935.4

apartment
n flat 217.12

appalling
adj horrid 89.19
terrible 118.29

apparent
adj visible 30.6
appearing 32.11
exterior 197.6
manifest 333.8
gilded 339.18
illusory 931.9

apparently
adv visibly 30.8
seemingly 32.12
externally 197.9
manifestly 333.14
falsely 339.23

appeal
n loveliness charm 88.2
desirability 91.12
sweetness 95.6
allure 362.1
plea 425.2
retrial 579.10
v attract 362.6
implore 425.11

appeal to
v implore 425.11
address 509.20
refer to 912.13

appear
v show 30.4
become visible 32.8
seem 32.10

attend 210.8
come out 333.6
be revealed 336.8
come out 337.16
turn up 793.6

appearance
n apparition 32.1
exterior 32.2
arrival 177.1
outward appearance 197.1
features 248.3
manifestation 333.1
sham 339.2
semblance 887.1
phantom 931.4

appearing
adj apparent 32.11
manifesting 333.9

application
n dressing 77.17
industry 315.5
perseverance 345.1
use 372.1
request 425.1
study 551.3
administration 623.2
attribution 843.1
absorption 938.3

applied
adj used 372.22

apply
v carry out 372.9
administer 623.6
attribute 843.3

appointed
adj chosen 356.25
commissioned 595.16

appointment
n election 356.9
accession 402.11
allotment 462.3
engagement 563.8
assignment 595.2
engagement 595.4
holy orders 677.5
position 701.5

appreciate
v savour 54.4
enjoy 86.12
be grateful 141.3
respect 146.4
measure 286.7
understand 506.7
know 883.10
estimate 901.9
value 952.12

approach
n coming or going
toward 158.1
arrival 177.1
entrance 180.5
closeness 212.1
plan 366.1
manner 369.1
attempt 388.2
offer 424.1
similarity 746.1
imminence 802.1
v near 158.3
converge 160.2
arrive 177.6
near 212.7
approximate 212.8
communicate with
328.7
use 369.5
attempt 388.5
make advances 424.7
address 509.20
cultivate 568.11
resemble 746.5
turn up 793.6
come 801.6
be imminent 802.2
lean on 849.9

approaches
n waterway 173.6

approaching
adj nearing 158.1
converging 160.3
arriving 177.8
near 212.14
future 801.7

imminent 802.3

appropriate
adj useful 372.16
decorous 481.7
fitting 515.5
right 617.3
rightful 619.8
relevant 737.11
apt 750.10
timely 805.8
characteristic 827.13
expedient 950.5
v take possession
457.10
adopt 465.19
steal 467.12
adopt 601.4
usurp 620.8

approval
n respect 146.1
ratification 317.4
consent 426.1
sanction 494.1
esteem 642.3
support 856.1
criticism 901.2

approved
adj accepted 317.13
chosen 356.25
favoured 494.17
conventional 560.5
orthodox 666.5
authoritative 925.13

area
n space 149.1
location 150.1
region 220.1
size 243.1
study 549.8
sphere 701.4
speciality 828.1
science 883.8

arena
n space 149.1
hall 188.4
setting 200.2
enclosure 203.3

sphere 220.2
site 448.1
sphere 701.4
science 883.8

argue
v affirm 319.5
signify 502.17
mean 503.5
dispute 890.12
evidence 912.7

argument
n quarrel 441.5
contention 442.1
pleading 579.6
testimony 579.8
defence 581.2
plot 700.4
controversy 890.4
case 890.5

arm
n member 2.4
inlet 228.1
branch 597.10
member 755.4
forearm 861.4
v empower 18.5
fortify 445.9
protect 963.18

armed
adj provided 370.13
prepared 390.13
embattled 443.19
under arms 445.13
protected 963.21

armed forces
n defence forces
446.16

arms
n military science
443.5
weapons 447.1

army
n unit 446.18
forces 446.19
throng 732.4
flock 732.5
multitude 839.3

around
adv everywhere 152.20
round 200.11
near 212.20
round 870.12

arrange
v plan 366.7
prepare 390.6
settle 422.8
settle 451.7
compose 686.37
order 769.4
order 770.6
classify 771.5

arranged
adj planned 366.11
contracted 422.11
orderly 769.6
ordered 770.12

arrangement
n form 248.1
structure 252.1
structure 252.1
plan 366.1
preparation 390.1
compact 422.1
adjustment 450.4
compromise 453.1
ornament 483.1
piece 686.4
score 686.22
setting 687.2
treatment 690.7
order 769.1
ordering 770.1
classification 771.1

arrest
n seizure 76.6
restraint 413.1
capture 414.6
seizure 465.2
stop 819.2
v slow 166.8
restrain 413.6
pick up 414.15
capture 465.18
delay 808.8

stop 819.9
hinder 967.9

arrested
adj retarded 166.11
undeveloped 391.10
restrained 413.12
late 808.12
mentally deficient 877.20

arrival
n landing 175.6
coming 177.1
entrant 180.4

arrive
v appear 32.8
arrive at 177.6
make good 394.7

arriving
adj approaching 177.8
adv on arrival or arriving 177.9

arsenal
n armoury 447.2

art
n representation 334.1
knack 398.6
science 398.7
visual arts 690.1
artistry 690.5
science 883.8

article
n writing 528.8
news item 533.3
part 535.13
piece 537.1
commodity 712.2
particular 728.3
section 755.2
individual 834.4
object 997.4

artist
n expert 398.11
entertainer 685.1
musician 688.1
visual arts 690.1
creator 694.1

artistic

adj skilful 398.20
tasteful 481.5
arty 690.18

as
adv how 369.8
equally 752.10

as one
adv unanimously 317.15
cooperatively 435.6
in step 750.11
jointly 762.16
simultaneously 798.7
concurrently 854.4

as well
adv additionally 239.10
equally 752.10

Asia
n Northern Hemisphere 220.6

aside
adv in an undertone 43.20
sideways 209.6
sidelong 209.7
privately 330.19
in reserve 371.15
n interjection 204.2

ask
v demand 406.5
request 425.9
invite 425.13
inquire 893.18
require 918.8

ask for
v encourage 360.20
demand 406.5
request 425.9
seek 893.28

asking
n request 425.1

asleep
adj sleeping 22.19
unconscious 25.8
unaware 885.11
unwary 939.8

aspect

n look 32.3
particular 728.3
component 758.2
astrology 114.17

assault
n attack 444.1
berating 495.6
rioting 651.3
v attack 444.12
rage 651.10
thrust 857.11

assembly
n council 408.1
council 408.1
party conference 590.8
legislature 594.1
the laity 679.1
collection 732.1
gathering 732.2
composition 758.1
production 847.2

assessment
n measurement 286.1
valuation 610.3
classification 763.3
estimate 901.3

assets
n supply 371.2
means 456.6
wealth 598.1
accounts 608.1
funds 705.11

assistance
n remedy 77.1
aid 434.1
subsidy 463.8

assistant
adj helping 434.20
n subordinate 417.4
helper 434.7
employee 558.3
helper 596.5

associated
adj communal 461.8
corporate 597.16
accompanying 731.8
related 737.9

association
n free association
83.20
council 408.1
affiliation 435.2
participation 461.1
fellowship 563.6
society 597.1
company 731.1
relation 737.1
combination 767.1
n collaboration 854.1

assume
v sham 339.14
undertake 389.3
receive 464.6
appropriate 465.19
affect 485.8
imply 504.4
presume 620.6
usurp 620.8
involve 734.4
suppose 906.7
think 908.11

assumed
adj spurious 339.17
undertaken 389.4
pretended 485.11
implied 504.7
supposed 906.11

assured
adj composed 97.13
hopeful 115.10
insolent 133.7
promised 421.7
secured 423.9
believing 908.20
made sure 925.14
confident 925.15

asylum
n hiding place 331.4
lunatic asylum 881.12
refuge 964.1

home 964.4

at all
adv anyhow 369.9
whatever 771.8
ever 921.9

at first
adv first 780.15

at last
adv finally 782.11

at least
adv moderately 234.10

at once
adv hastily 386.8
together 731.9
jointly 762.16
now 792.7
promptly 807.15

at one
adj in accord 440.3
agreeing 750.9

at present
adv now 800.3

at risk
adj liable 852.5
in danger 961.13

at times
adv occasionally 810.5

at which
adv when 783.6

at work
adj busy 315.17
operating 844.11

athletics
n sport 720.7
sport 721.1

atmosphere
n ambience 200.3
treatment 690.7
plot 700.4
gas 111.2

attached
adj added 239.8

attached to
adj fond of 95.29

attack
n seizure 76.6
war 443.1

assault 444.1
berating 495.6
articulation 509.5
rioting 651.3
spasm 872.6
v undertake 389.3
jump 442.11
declare war 443.13
assault 444.12
assail 495.18
rage 651.10
get rolling 702.15

attacking

adj assailing 444.23

attempt

n trial 388.2
undertaking 389.1
v try 388.5
undertake 389.3

attempted

adj undertaken 389.4

attend

v listen 39.9
be at 210.8
serve 434.18
accompany 731.6
escort 731.7
follow 797.3
result 842.4
witness 873.5
heed 938.6

attending

adj serving 558.13
environmental 728.8
accompanying 731.8

attention

n hearing 39.1
carefulness 324.1
alertness 324.5
curiosity 936.1
attention span 938.1

attitude

n opinion 908.6
mental attitude 933.1

attract

v endear 95.22
interest 362.6

pull 862.4
interest 938.12

attraction

n desirability 91.12
allure 362.1
lure 362.3
pulling 860.1
attractiveness 862.1
repulsion 982.10

attractive

adj delightful 88.6
desirable 91.29
alluring 362.8
attracting 862.5
absorbing 938.19
beautiful 971.14

audience

n audition 39.2
house 39.6
visitor 210.5
recipient 464.3
conference 523.5
house 873.2
listener 983.17

aunt

n brother 540.3

author

n writer 528.12
essayist 537.3
writer 696.3
narrator 700.5
agent 703.1
agent 841.4
producer 847.7
v write 696.5
cause 841.10

authority

n power 18.1
supremacy 235.3
expert 398.11
prerogative 402.1
power 402.2
prestige 402.4
governance 402.5
command 405.1
authorization 428.3
connoisseur 481.4

certificate 530.6
informant 532.5
commission 595.1
prerogative 622.1
specialist 828.3
influence 849.1
wise man 876.1
scientist 883.9
validity 928.6
n direction 554.1

automatic

adj spontaneous 350.10
uniform 743.5
instinctive 889.6
involuntary 918.12
automated 987.9
n gun 447.10

automatically

adv intuitively 889.7
involuntarily 918.15

autumn

adj seasonal 298.8
n fall 298.4

available

adj present 210.12
open 211.13
idle 316.16
handy 372.18
prepared 390.13
obtainable 457.14
accessible 921.7

avenue

n outlet 181.7
passageway 368.3

average

adj medium 232.3
middle 781.3
prevalent 826.11
usual 831.7
ordinary 960.8
n mean 232.1
v average out 232.2

avoid

v shun 148.7
evade 155.6
shun 353.6

abstain 648.5
retreat 858.6
award
 n giving 463.1
 gift 463.4
 reward 626.2
 verdict 901.5
 v give 463.12
aware
 adj sensible 24.11
 knowing 883.12
 attentive 938.14
aware of
 adj conscious of
  883.13
awareness
 n sensation 24.1
 recognition 883.2
 attention 938.1
away
 adj gone 33.4
 absent 211.10
 adv backwards 154.11
 hence 179.17
 elsewhere 211.15
 off 247.14
 apart 247.17
away from
 adv separately 764.24
awful
 adj horrid 89.19
 awesome 113.7
 terrible 118.29
 terrible 955.9
 hideous 970.9
baby
 adj miniature 244.10
 infant 287.11
 n honey 95.10
 doll 95.14
 miniature 244.5
 youngster 288.1
 infant 288.8
 ingenue 401.3
 coward 476.3
 darling 543.6
 beginner 780.2

back
 adj rear 208.9
 backward 799.10
 late 808.12
 adv backwards 154.11
 in compensation 323.6
 in reserve 371.15
 ago 799.13
 n setting 200.2
 rear 208.1
 ridge 208.3
 v reverse 154.6
 move 163.4
 come last 208.8
 secure 423.7
 back up 434.13
 commend 494.9
 benefit 573.3
 support 590.31
 finance 706.14
 bet 722.21
 support 856.8
backed
 adj approved 494.17
background
 n setting 200.2
 the distance 247.3
 experience 398.9
 arena 448.1
 motif 483.6
 plot 700.4
 cause 841.1
 source 841.5
backing
 adj approving 494.15
 aiding 573.4
 n means 369.2
 consent 426.1
 patronage 434.4
 patronage 434.4
 financing 706.2
 support 856.1
 supporter 856.2
 confirmation 912.4
bad
 adj nasty 55.6
 ominous 124.16

 misbehaving 307.5
 crippled 378.26
 decayed 378.33
 wicked 634.15
 undesirable 951.5
 evil 955.7
 dangerous 961.9
 adv badly 955.12
 n iniquity 634.3
 evil 955.3
badly
 adv poorly 236.9
 bad 955.12
bag
 n sack 186.2
 hang 193.2
 quantity 233.3
 breast 269.4
 purse 706.13
 bundle 732.8
 v load 150.15
 hang 193.6
 bulge 269.8
 grab 457.9
 catch 465.17
baker
 n cook 11.2
balance
 n equanimity 97.3
 mean 232.1
 difference 241.7
 remainder 242.1
 symmetry 250.1
 counterbalance 323.2
 supply 371.2
 harmony 515.2
 account 608.2
 justice 629.1
 moderation 650.1
 treatment 690.7
 funds 705.11
 correlation 739.1
 equality 752.1
 stability 817.1
 reasonableness 875.6
 sanity 880.1
 comparability 898.3

surplus 948.5
v compensate 250.3
weigh 283.8
offset 323.4
make uniform 743.4
equal 752.5
equate 752.6
stabilize 817.7
compare 898.4

balanced
adj composed 97.13
symmetrical 250.4
harmonious 515.6
just 629.6
uniform 743.5
poised 752.9
stable 817.12
neutralizing 855.9
sensible 875.16
sane 880.2

ball
n sphere 268.1
dance 683.2
assembly 732.2
missile 859.5
v snowball 268.4

ballet
n musical theatre
686.28

ballot
n vote 356.6
v vote 356.17

balls
n guts 477.2
bull 505.3

ban
n prohibition 429.1
disapproval 495.1
ostracism 567.2
exclusion 735.1
v excise 241.9
prohibit 429.3
disapprove 495.9
ostracize 567.5
exclude 735.4

band
n stripe 38.5

strip 257.4
belt 266.2
layer 282.1
line 502.6
orchestra 688.8
company 732.3
v encircle 200.6
put together 762.4

bank
n incline 195.4
border 202.4
side 209.1
shore 223.2
shoal 262.2
store 371.6
preserve 382.6
building society 600.4
treasury 706.11
banking house 706.12
workplace 716.1
pot 722.4
pile 732.10
series 774.2
buttress 856.3
barrier 965.7
v store 371.9
fortify 445.9
ignite 1020.22

Bank of England
n bank 706.12

banking
n money dealing 706.4

banned
adj prohibited 429.7
excluded 735.7

bar
adj excluding 735.10
n stripe 38.5
line 253.3
shaft 259.1
shoal 262.2
obstruction 279.2
lock 413.5
line 502.6
legal profession 578.4
stripe 627.4
staff 686.23

notation 687.6
exclusion 735.1
lever 861.3
barrier 967.5
v cross 161.6
fence 203.7
excise 241.9
close 279.5
stop 279.6
prohibit 429.3
exclude 735.4
make impossible 922.3
obstruct 967.11
prevent 967.13

bare
adj naked 6.14
vacant 211.12
mere 234.8
open 333.10
worn 378.27
unadorned 484.8
plain-speaking 517.3
simple 760.5
unadulterated 760.6
v divest 6.5
disclose 336.4

barely
adv hardly 234.9
narrowly 256.17
simply 760.10

base
adj offensive 89.18
servile 129.11
• inadequate 236.7
low 482.13
demographic 587.8
villainous 625.17
wicked 634.15
low 641.12
terrible 955.9
n station 150.2
point of departure
179.5
basement 190.2
headquarters or HQ
199.4
bottom 260.4

cause 841.1
foundation 856.5
pedestal 856.7
acid 14.3
v establish 150.16

based on
adj evidential 912.14
contingent 914.9

basic
adj underlying 190.8
essential 729.6
simple 760.5
original 841.14
vital 952.22
chemical 14.8

basically
adv essentially 729.8

basis
n motive 360.1
reason 581.5
cause 841.1
foundation 856.5
premise 890.6
topic 892.1
outlook 933.2

bass
adj deep 45.9
vocal 686.41
n part 686.18
voice 687.4

bath
n shower 70.8
dip 70.9
washbasin 70.12
wetting 19.6
v wash 70.19

bathroom
n toilet 12.10
baths 70.10
lavatory 188.22

battle
n fight 442.4
war 443.1
operation 443.4
struggle 702.3
v contend against 436.4

quarrel 441.10
contend 442.10
war 443.12
struggle 702.11

bay
n nook 188.3
shore 223.2
ocean 226.2
inlet 228.1
recess 270.6
v blare 44.10
cry 51.2

be
v exist 723.5

be able
v be up to 18.6

be at
v attend 210.8

be called
v be known as 512.12

be found
v lie 150.10
exist 723.5
turn up 896.9

be in
v belong 597.15
deal in 708.15
prevail 826.9

be on
v use 78.5
strike a bargain 708.18

be seen
v show 30.4

be there
v have place 150.9
be present 210.6
exist 723.5

be used to
v get used to 358.10

beach
n shore 223.2
v shipwreck 173.16

beans
n vegetables 10.32

bear
n speculator 714.7
v give birth 1.3

endure 125.4
transport 167.8
submit 418.5
suffer 428.10
support 434.12
hold 459.7
afford 606.5
cause 841.1
yield 847.13
support 856.8
suffice 946.3

bearing
adj born 1.4
yielding 845.8
supporting 856.10
adv transportation 167.2
n looks 32.4
direction 152.1
behaviour 306.1
gesture 502.14
meaning 503.1
relevance 737.4
yielding 847.6
trend 851.2
fulcrum 861.2
ball bearing 870.6

beat
adj licked 926.17
n staccato 46.1
sphere 220.2
routine 358.5
route 368.1
accent 509.9
rhythm 687.13
tempo 687.14
throb 687.16
metre 698.7
sphere 701.4
cyclical motion 812.2
round 812.3
circuit 869.2
pulse 871.3
flutter 872.4
v drum 46.4
defeat 235.7
foam 305.5

injure 378.12
defeat 396.5
clobber 397.8
thrash 585.12
drum 811.10
pound 857.14
pulsate 871.10
agitate 872.7
flutter 872.9
stump 926.8
pulverize 996.8
beaten
adj bubbly 305.6
defeated 397.13
beating
adj staccato 46.7
rhythmic 687.17
seasonal 812.7
pulsating 871.15
n staccato 46.1
defeat 397.1
corporal punishment
585.4
hit 857.4
pulse 871.3
flutter 872.4
pulverization 996.4
beautiful
adj artistic 690.18
pretty 971.14
beautifully
adv handsomely
971.20
beauty
n harmony 515.2
prettiness 971.1
charmer 971.7
become
v behove 621.4
go 723.9
originate 780.12
convert 820.11
turn into 820.17
becoming
adj decorous 481.7
rightful 619.8
decent 644.5

apt 750.10
expedient 950.5
fair 971.15
bed
n bottom 190.1
bottom 190.4
furniture 218.1
waterway 225.2
layer 282.1
accommodation 370.3
garden 112.9
v fix 817.9
plant 112.17
tend 113.6
bedroom
n chamber 188.7
beef
n roast beef 10.13
muscularity 15.2
gripe 106.5
v moan 99.6
bitch 106.16
before
adv in front 156.4
ahead 207.11
preferably 356.27
above 776.6
previously 796.5
formerly 799.11
early 807.11
begin
v commence 780.7
beginning
adj initial 780.13
n commencement
780.1
source 841.5
production 847.1
behalf
n benefit 372.4
good 954.4
behaviour
n conduct 306.1
action 313.1
behind
adj retarded 166.11
adv after 157.6

in the rear 208.10
late 808.15
behindhand 866.6
n rear 208.1
arse 208.5
being
adj existing 723.10
n heart 84.3
organism 291.2
person 297.3
existence 723.1
something 725.3
belief
n religion 655.1
credence 908.1
confidence 925.4
believe
v be pious 671.6
suppose 906.7
trust 908.10
believe in
v confide in 908.14
believed
adj credited 908.22
bell
n gong 45.4
time 794.2
belong
v have place 150.9
hold membership
597.15
below
adv down 185.13
low 260.9
infernally 662.5
belt
n waistband 5.15
region 220.1
strip 257.4
band 266.2
layer 282.1
try 388.3
slap 585.3
whip 586.1
v beat 585.12
bench
n fitness 75.1

saddle 402.10
council 408.1
woolsack 576.5
team 597.7
workplace 716.1
substitute 824.2

benefit
n kindness 134.7
use 372.4
aid 434.1
estate 456.4
benevolence 463.5
performance 682.9
good 954.4
v do a favour 134.12
avail 372.15
aid 434.11
aid 573.3
come in handy 950.3
do good 954.10

bent
adj distorted 251.9
angular 264.3
curved 265.7
disposed 933.8
n direction 152.1
bias 195.3
aptitude 398.5
tendency 851.1
disposition 933.3
prejudice 935.3

beside
adj side 209.4
excluding 735.10
adv in conjunction
212.21

besides
adj excluding 735.10
adv additionally 239.10

best
adj superlative 235.13
very best 954.16
v defeat 396.5

bet
n gamble 722.2
wager 722.3
poker 722.9

v wager 722.21
predict 917.4
risk 927.8

better
adj superior 235.12
preferable 356.24
better off 377.14
changed 814.10
v excel 235.6
improve 377.9
change 814.7

bid
n attempt 388.2
offer 424.1
appeal 425.2
v command 405.7
bid for 424.6
bargain 708.17
offer 710.8

big
adj large 243.15
adult 289.9
important 952.16

bike
n cycle 170.6
cycle 170.6

bill
n point 269.6
poster 337.7
advertising matter
337.8
clause 594.7
fee 604.5
statement 608.3
statement 833.5
schedule 920.2
v invoice 608.11
dramatize 682.20
schedule 920.5

billion
adj numerous 839.6

bills
n debt 603.1

bird
n poultry 10.21
dame 68.6

birth

n childbirth 1.1
generation 69.6
life 292.1
lineage 541.4
heredity 541.6
aristocracy 588.3
origin 780.4

birthday
n anniversary 812.4

bishop
n man 720.16

bit
n modicum 234.2
point 271.2
portion 462.5
signal 532.7
role 682.7
script 684.2
piece 755.3
shift 787.3
binary digit 988.13

bitter
adj acrimonious 17.13
flavoured 53.8
sharp 55.5
pungent 68.8
unpleasant 89.17
sour 101.23
caustic 135.21
resentful 143.25
hostile 570.10
cold 975.13

bizarre
adj awesome 113.7
humorous 473.2
monstrous 832.13
absurd 878.9
fanciful 941.14

black
adj pitch-black 37.7
dark-skinned 37.9
sullen 101.24
ominous 124.16
wicked 634.15
dark 979.13
n blackness 37.1
mourning 106.7

blame
n censure 495.3
attribution 843.1
v censure 495.11
lay the blame on 580.8
attribute to 843.4

blamed
adj accused 580.14

blind
adj visually impaired 28.10
sightless 29.7
closed 279.8
uncomprehending 877.13
involuntary 918.12
n trick 341.6
pretext 361.1
shade 980.1
v deprive of sight 29.5
hoodwink 341.17
shine 977.22

block
n suppression 83.14
boundary 202.3
plot 220.4
lump 243.10
obstruction 279.2
scaffold 586.5
print 691.3
delay 808.2
mental block 945.3
obstacle 967.4
solid 990.6
v stop 279.6
cover 281.18
fend off 445.10
delay 808.8
stop 819.9
obstruct 967.11
stop 967.12

blocked
adj stopped 279.9
late 808.12
forgetful 945.8

blood
n gore 2.18

life force 292.2
killing 294.1
blood relationship 540.1
kindred 540.2
race 540.4
lineage 541.4
posterity 542.1
class 771.2
fluid 15.2

bloody
adj bleeding 12.22
cruel 135.24
murderous 294.21
warlike 443.17
cursed 498.9
savage 651.19
bloodstained 959.10
v bleed 12.17

blow
n pain 87.5
surprise 122.1
disappointment 123.1
gust 303.4
strong or stiff or high or howling wind 303.9
act 313.3
hit 857.4
punch 857.5
misfortune 966.2
v waft 303.14
ripen 392.7
squander 471.3
mouth off 487.5
sound 686.34
let out 864.22
fluff 930.13

blown
adj tainted 378.34

blue
adj melancholy 103.23
obscene 646.9

blues
n sulks 101.10
dumps 103.6

board

n food 10.1
rations 10.6
accommodation 370.3
council 408.1
directorate 555.11
tribunal 576.1
wood lumber 999.3
v feed 8.17
dine 8.20
mount 184.11
face 281.22
provision 370.9
accommodate 370.10
raid 444.18

boat
n ship 171.1
v navigate 173.9

bob
n float 171.9
weight 283.4
penny 705.5
crouch 868.3
shake 872.3
v cut or style the hair 3.13
shorten 254.4
cavort 351.6
bow 868.9
oscillate 871.8

bobby
n cop 963.16

body
n the person 2.1
guy 67.5
population 216.1
figure 248.4
thickness 269.2
corpse 293.12
person 297.3
association 597.1
substance 725.1
something 725.3
collection 732.11
major part 754.6
individual 834.4
solid 990.6
physical body 997.3

bomb
  n atomic bomb or
    atom bomb 447.19
  v fall flat 108.4
  blow up 380.18
  dramatize 682.20
bombing
  n mission 175.5
  bombardment 444.6
bond
  n compact 422.1
  security 423.1
  pledge 423.2
  fidelity 624.6
  relation 737.1
  joining 762.1
  fastening 762.2
  v pledge 423.8
  put together 762.4
bone
  adj skeleton 2.19
  n stone 991.5
bones
  n heart 84.3
  corpse 293.12
  refuse 376.3
  body 997.3
bonus
  n extra 240.4
  find 457.6
  gratuity 463.5
  pay 604.4
  premium 604.6
  surplus 948.5
book
  n publication 337.1
  volume 535.1
  paperback 535.3
  part 535.13
  script 684.2
  section 755.2
  v record 530.12
  list 833.3
  prearrange 920.3
  schedule 920.5
books
  n account book 608.4

bill 833.5
boom
  n noise 44.3
  reverberation 45.2
  peal 47.4
  heightening 237.2
  business cycle 708.9
  roaring trade 965.5
  barrier 967.5
  v din 44.7
  reverberate 45.6
  thunder 47.9
  grow 237.6
  murmur 509.19
  thrive 965.8
boost
  n promotion 431.1
  thrust 857.2
  v cheer 100.7
  be useful 434.17
  commend 494.9
  thrust 857.11
  elevate 867.4
boot
  n kick 857.8
  v cloak 5.29
  kick 857.18
  fire 864.18
  program 988.17
boots
  n footwear 5.21
border
  n exterior 197.2
  edge 202.4
  frontier 202.5
  partition 204.4
  side 209.1
  sphere 220.2
  garden 112.9
  v edge 202.9
  side 209.2
  adjoin 212.9
borders
  n environment 200.1
bored
  adj joyless 87.20
  uninterested 109.12

languid 316.18
  uninquisitive 937.3
boring
  adj wearying 109.10
  same 743.6
  n hole 278.3
born
  adj given birth 1.4
  thorough 756.9
boss
  adj governing 593.16
  n superior 235.4
  bulge 269.2
  superintendent 555.2
  master 556.1
  top dog 952.10
  v rough 274.4
  supervise 554.10
both
  adj the two 835.6
  n two 835.2
bother
  n annoyance 87.2
  dither 96.6
  bustle 315.4
  imposition 623.1
  commotion 772.4
  confusion 940.3
  inconvenience 951.3
  trouble 968.3
  v annoy 87.13
  distress 87.16
  vex 89.15
  concern 117.3
  take liberties 620.7
  confuse 940.7
  inconvenience 951.4
  trouble 968.13
bottle
  n container 186.1
  v preserve 382.8
bottom
  adj deepest 190.7
  n ship 171.1
  underside 190.1
  bed 190.4
  buttocks 208.4

base 260.4
valley 270.7
fortitude 477.4
bought
adj purchased 710.10
bound
adj limited 201.7
enclosed 203.9
stopped 279.9
resolute 344.10
tied 413.15
promised 421.7
obliged 621.14
joined 762.12
certain 925.9
n boundary 202.3
leap 351.1
recoil 858.2
v speed 165.6
circumscribe 201.4
limit 201.5
circumscribe 202.7
border 202.9
enclose 203.5
leap 351.1
recoil 858.5
bow
n reverence 146.2
rostrum 207.3
curve 265.2
bend 265.3
bulge 269.2
longbow 447.7
greeting 566.4
crouch 868.3
v fawn 129.7
bow down 146.6
curve 265.6
bend 868.9
bowl
n silver 8.12
cavity 270.2
ceramic ware 719.2
throw 859.3
v hollow 270.10
push 859.9
throw 859.10

roll 870.8
box
n container 186.1
compartment 188.2
coffin 295.11
store 371.6
punch 857.5
v package 203.8
wrap 281.19
contend 442.10
slap 857.17
boxing
n packaging 203.2
fighting 442.6
boy
n lad 288.5
boycott
n objection 318.2
ostracism 567.2
strike 704.4
exclusion 735.1
v object 318.5
ostracize 567.5
strike 704.5
boyfriend
n swain 95.12
brain
adj skeleton 2.19
n nervous system 2.9
liver 10.19
intellect 874.1
grey matter 874.5
v strike dead 294.15
branch
n fork 171.4
stream 224.1
tributary 224.3
fork 296.17
corps 446.17
offset 542.4
division 597.10
office 716.6
member 755.4
class 771.2
v fork 162.6
angle 264.2
bisect 837.4

brand
n mark 502.5
label 502.13
nature 729.2
kind 771.3
characteristic 827.4
stain 959.3
coal 971.37
burn 972.6
hot iron 972.15
lighter 973.4
v mark 502.19
label 502.20
stigmatize 641.10
stain 959.6
brave
adj courageous 477.13
showy 486.15
n serviceman 446.5
hero 477.5
v confront 207.7
defy 439.3
face 477.9
take chances 961.7
thwart 967.14
bread
n food 10.1
the staff of life 10.26
dough 705.2
break
n respite 20.2
kindness 134.7
boundary 202.3
crack 213.2
escape 354.1
falling-out 441.4
deficiency 757.2
breakage 764.4
interruption 775.1
interim 788.1
delay 808.2
revolution 814.2
pause 819.3
chance 927.1
stroke of luck 965.3
v weaken 16.8
make laugh 107.9

break in – broadcast

set out 179.8
crack 213.4
come out 337.16
injure 378.12
break up 378.20
conquer 397.9
subdue 417.8
domesticate 417.9
violate 420.4
domineer 593.14
bankrupt 605.8
burst 764.11
discontinue 775.2
intervene 788.3
pause 819.7
grow light 977.26
shatter 995.2
tend 113.6

break in
v intrude 205.5
domesticate 417.9
train 549.13

break-in
n burglary 467.5

breakfast
n continental breakfast 8.6
v dine 8.20

breaking
n quelling 417.3
violation 420.2
training 549.3

breast
n leg 10.22
heart 84.3
bosom 269.4
v confront 207.7
contend against 436.4

breath
n breathing 2.14
murmur 43.3
odour 60.1
life 292.1
life force 292.2
puff 303.2
spirit 726.3
instant 792.3

vapour 111.1

breathing
adj respiratory 2.20
living 292.9
n respiration 2.14

breed
n race 540.4
lineage 541.4
posterity 542.1
v generate 69.8
be pregnant 69.12
grow 237.6
train 549.13
cause 841.10
originate 847.12
raise 113.5

breeding
n procreation 69.2
training 549.3
planting 112.13
stock raising 113.1

bridge
n observation point 27.8
railway 368.7
span 368.8
passage 686.19
v lie over 281.27

brief
adj short 254.6
taciturn 329.7
concise 519.5
short 790.8
n report 530.7
condensation 538.1
v advise 407.4
inform 532.8
give instructions 549.15

briefly
adv shortly 254.9
concisely 519.6
fleetingly 790.10

bright
adj colourful 34.17
clean 70.25
sunny 88.10

cheerful 100.11
optimistic 115.11
favourable 124.17
alert 324.14
apt 551.18
illustrious 642.17
intelligent 875.10
smart 875.12
unharmed 977.22
gorgeous 971.17
brilliant 977.31

brilliant
adj colourful 34.17
skilful 398.20
witty 474.9
illustrious 642.17
smart 875.12
gorgeous 971.17
bright 977.31

bring
v fetch 167.10
induce 360.21
cost 610.13
inflict 623.5
be sold 711.9

broad
adj spacious 149.8
voluminous 243.16
wide 255.6
humorous 473.2
burlesque 493.14
vulgar 646.8
extensive 826.12
vague 926.13
broad-minded 934.8
n dame 68.6

broadcast
adj published 337.17
dispersed 733.7
n publication 337.1
programme 983.13
planting 112.13
v communicate 328.6
publish 337.10
disperse 733.3
radio 983.20
televise 984.14

plant 112.17

broadcasting
  n disclosure 336.1
  publication 337.1
  radio broadcasting
    983.12
  planting 112.13

broke
  adj bereft 458.8
  flat broke 599.10
  insolvent 605.11

broken
  adj rough 274.6
  impaired 378.23
  ruined 380.25
  conquered 397.15
  subdued 417.12
  meek 418.13
  burst 764.22
  incoherent 766.3
  incoherent 775.3
  irregular 813.3

bronze
  adj brass 12.15
  n sculpture 693.2

brother
  n sister 540.3

Brother
  n Reverend 628.5

brothers
  n the laity 679.1

brown
  v cook 11.4

brush
  n touch 64.1
  tail 208.6
  contact 212.5
  hinterland 222.2
  scrub 296.14
  fight 442.4
  easel 690.16
  tap 857.6
  v kiss 64.7
  sweep 70.23
  contact 212.10
  portray 690.17
  tap 857.16

dry 110.4
tend 113.6

budget
  adj cheap 613.7
  n portion 462.5
  accounts 608.1
  funds 705.11
  schedule 920.2
  v ration 462.10
  spend 606.4
  schedule 920.5

build
  n muscularity 15.2
  form 248.1
  figure 248.4
  structure 252.1
  nature 729.2
  v establish 150.16
  construct 252.4
  compose 758.3
  produce 847.8

build up
  v increase 237.4
  enlarge 254.4
  publicize 337.15
  exaggerate 340.2
  compose 758.3

building
  adj structural 847.15
  n house 217.5
  structure 252.1
  structure 252.2
  composition 758.1
  production 847.2

built
  adj made 847.18

built-in
  adj included 734.5

bull
  n cock 67.8
  rubbish 505.3
  speculator 714.7

bunch
  n amount 230.2
  bulge 269.2
  flock 732.5
  group 732.7

conglomeration 765.5
multitude 883.3
v come together
  732.16
gather 732.18
adhere 765.6

burden
  n affliction 87.8
  load 187.2
  capacity 243.2
  pressure 283.5
  duty 621.1
  charge 623.3
  repeat 811.5
  bane 956.1
  impediment 967.6
  v distress 87.14
  oppress 89.16
  load 150.15
  load 283.10
  work 702.16
  inconvenience 951.4
  oppress 966.8
  hamper 967.10

buried
  adj underground
    261.11
  underwater 261.12
  concealed 331.11
  overrun 865.9

burn
  n scald 972.6
  v pain 26.7
  seethe 143.15
  cremate 295.19
  injure 378.12
  rage 651.10
  scorch 971.41
  ignite 972.22
  catch fire 972.23
  scorch 972.24
  shine 977.22
  dry 110.4

burning
  adj sore 26.11
  nippy 59.7
  in heat 66.26

feverish 76.23
fervent 84.16
heated 96.22
seething 143.28
vehement 525.12
hot 971.44
ignited 971.46
heating 972.26
luminous 977.29
flashing 977.33
n smarting 26.3
cremation 295.2
heat 917.7
combustion 972.5

burst
adj impaired 378.23
broken 764.22
n report 47.1
run 165.3
bustle 315.4
volley 444.8
break 764.4
flare 971.35
v blast 47.8
break 378.20
break 764.11

bus
n commercial vehicle
170.11
v drive 168.29

bush
n shrubbery 296.9
woodland 296.11
brush 296.14
wasteland 846.2

business
adj commercial 707.9
commercial 708.19
n action 313.1
activity 315.1
undertaking 389.1
company 597.9
duty 621.1
occupation 701.1
vocation 701.6
commerce 708.1
relation 737.1

affair 793.3
speciality 828.1

businessman
n businesswoman
707.1

busy
adj occupied 315.17
ornate 483.11
occupied 701.12
v work 702.16

butter
n putty 992.4
v coat 281.23

buy
v assent 317.7
purchase 710.6
believe 908.10

buying
adj purchasing 710.9
n purchase 710.1

by
adj past 799.6
adv in reserve 371.15

by two
adv in half 837.7

cabinet
n container 186.1
den 188.8
furniture 218.1
council 408.1
kitchen cabinet 594.2

cable
n cord 257.2
telegram 332.8
line 332.10
battery accumulator
982.19
television 984.1
v wire 332.12

cage
n close quarters 414.7
v enclose 203.5
confine 414.12
drive 113.7

cake
n ga|cil|teau 10.38
solid 990.6

v thicken 990.9
solidify 991.7

call
n cry 50.1
cry 51.1
telephone call 332.7
demand 406.1
appeal 425.2
invitation 425.4
summons 502.16
enlistment 595.6
the ministry 677.1
v cry 50.4
cry 51.2
warble 51.5
telephone 332.11
summon 405.9
invite 425.13
name 512.10
bet 722.21

call for
n requirement 918.2
v fetch 167.10
summon 405.9
demand 406.5
oblige 409.5
request 425.9
involve 734.4
require 918.8

called
adj named 512.13

called for
adj requisite 918.11

calling
n motive 360.1
naming 512.2
holy orders 677.5
vocation 701.6

calm
adj placid 97.12
unmoved 114.3
nerveless 120.2
quiet 164.10
peaceful 449.7
level-headed 650.11
thoughtless 888.2
n composure 97.2

calmness 114.1
lull 164.5
moderation 650.1
uniformity 743.1
v not turn a hair 97.6
quiet 164.7
pacify 450.7
calm down 650.6

camp
n camping 214.4
detention camp 727.26
encampment 448.3
party 597.4
v settle 150.17
pitch 214.10

campaign
n journey 168.4
war 443.3
principle 841.9
v journey 168.17
electioneer 590.30
go into politics 591.8

can
n nick 414.9
v be able 18.6
preserve 382.8
may 428.12

canal
n duct 2.16
channel 225.1
waterway 225.2
inlet 228.1
narrow 256.3
trench 276.2
v furrow 276.3

cancer
n blight 956.2

candidate
n fancier 454.5
applicant 425.7
aspirant 591.5
nominee 595.7

cannot
v not be able 19.8

cap
n headdress 5.20
summit 189.2

head 189.4
cover 281.5
fuse 447.14
v cloak 5.29
top 189.7
excel 235.6
top 281.20

capable
adj able 18.9
fitted 390.14
competent 398.22

capable of
adj liable to 852.6

capacity
n ability 18.2
extent 149.5
volume 243.2
means 369.2
skill 398.1
talent 398.4
function 701.3
mode 727.3
full measure 756.3
intelligence 875.1

cape
n point 269.6

capital
adj top 189.8
literal 527.8
good 954.12
n metropolis 199.5
capital city 219.3
means 369.2
supply 371.2
type 529.6
fund 705.12

capitalism
n nonintervention
415.9
laissez-faire 592.8

capitalist
n rich man or woman
598.6
financier 706.7

Captain
n Field Marshal 556.19
Admiral of the Fleet

556.20

caption
n title 892.2
v focus on 892.3

car
n automobile 170.7
railway car 170.13

carbon
n slag 972.16

card
n identification 502.11
notice board 530.8
postcard 534.3
v comb 70.21

care
n medicine 81.1
affliction 87.8
sorrow 103.10
anxiety 117.1
carefulness 324.1
usage 372.2
custody 414.5
observance 419.1
support 434.3
patronage 434.4
caution 479.1
commission 595.1
charge 963.2
adversity 966.1
n supervision 554.2
v mind 324.6

career
adj skilled 398.24
n progression 153.1
course 163.2
vocation 701.6
v flounder 872.12

careful
adj mindful 324.10
cautious 479.7
economical 635.1
conscientious 624.11
judicious 875.17
attentive 938.14

carefully
adv thoughtfully
324.15

cautiously 479.10
economically 615.6

caring
adj careful 324.10
helping 434.20
n sympathy 84.5
carefulness 324.1
support 434.3

carp
v find fault 495.13

carpet
n ground covering 190.3
rug 281.9
v floor 281.21

carried
adj chosen 356.25

carry
v be pregnant 69.12
extend 149.6
transport 167.8
adopt 356.14
triumph 396.3
deal in 708.15
support 856.8

carry on
v be patient 125.3
keep going 315.12
persevere 345.2
play 720.22
endure 789.5
continue 818.3
continue 818.3

carry out
v fulfil 313.7
apply 372.9
bring about 392.5
execute 422.9

carrying
adj supporting 856.10
adv transportation 167.2

cartoon
n motion pictures 684.1
drawing 690.11
caricature 690.14

v portray 690.17

case
n sufferer 76.12
container 186.1
frame 252.3
blanket 281.10
hull 281.15
casing 281.16
lawsuit 579.1
state 727.1
particular 865.1
example 748.2
argument 890.5
topic 892.1
citation 912.5
v package 203.8
wrap 281.19

cash
n payment 604.1
money 705.1
ready money or cash 705.14
v cash in 705.21

cast
adj formative 248.8
made 847.18
n looks 32.4
colour 34.1
dressing 77.17
form 248.1
team 597.7
role 682.7
characters 685.9
sculpture 693.2
throw 722.8
nature 729.2
company 732.3
casting 747.6
mould 748.6
characteristic 827.4
disposition 933.3
ingot 12.5
v shed 6.10
clap 150.13
form 248.6
sculpture 693.5
produce 847.8

throw 859.10

castle
n estate 217.6
stronghold 445.6

cat
n whip 586.1

catalogue
n description 334.2
record 133.1
notebook 530.9
reference book 535.9
directory 555.10
account book 608.4
outline 763.4
bibliography 833.3
v record 530.12
classify 763.8
classify 771.5
list 833.8

catch
n ambition 91.10
lover 95.11
trick 341.6
snag 406.3
lock 413.5
capture 465.10
round 686.17
good thing 954.5
obstacle 967.4
crux 968.8
v hear 39.10
take ill 76.15
trap 341.20
acquire 457.8
grab 457.9
take 465.17
catch out 896.7
catch fire 972.23

catching
adj poisonous 73.5
contagious 76.27
taking 465.25
n seizure 465.2

category
n class 771.2
topic 892.1

cathedral

n church 681.1

Catholic
adj Roman Catholic
655.24

catholic
adj broad-minded
934.8

Catholic
n Roman Catholic
655.16

caught
adj stuck 817.16
gripped 938.17

cause
n motive 360.1
lawsuit 579.1
reason 581.5
occasion 841.1
v prompt 360.12
compel 409.4
bring about 841.10
perform 847.11

cautious
adj slow 166.9
careful 324.10
hesitant 347.11
careful 479.7
incredulous 911.3

cave
n lair 217.23
cavern 270.4
shelter 964.3
v hollow 270.10

ceasefire
n truce 450.5

ceiling
n boundary 202.3
roof 281.6
limit 756.5

celebrate
v observe 472.2
praise 494.10
formalize 561.5
glorify 675.11
observe 680.9
make merry 720.23

celebrated

adj distinguished
642.14
notable 952.18

celebration
n spree 79.4
treat 86.3
rejoicing 107.1
celebrating 472.1
revel 720.6

cell
n compartment 188.2
plant cell 291.3
prison 414.8
retreat 565.6
clique 597.6
retreat 964.5

central
adj interior 198.6
middle 199.9
medium 232.3
chief 235.14
middle 781.3
original 841.14
vital 952.22

centre
n interior 198.2
middle 199.1
mean 232.1
middle ground 452.3
essence 729.1
middle 781.1
focus 862.2
v converge 160.2
centralize 199.7

century
n moment 786.2
long time 789.3

ceremony
n celebration 472.1
formality 561.1
rite 561.4
rite 680.1

certain
adj expectant 121.10
quantitative 230.5

secured 423.9
particular 827.12
believing 908.20
evidential 912.14
inevitable 918.13
sure 925.9
true 928.13

certainly
adv decidedly 233.18
inevitably 918.16
surely 925.17
truly 928.18

chain
n jewel 483.5
insignia 627.1
series 774.2
curb 967.7
v bind 413.9
put together 762.4
bind 762.8
secure 817.8

chair
n furniture 218.1
saddle 402.10
professorship 552.9
chairman 555.5
v administer 554.11
govern 593.10

chairman
n chairwoman 555.5

challenge
n objection 318.2
opposition 436.1
resistance 438.1
dare 439.2
declaration of war
443.6
questioning 893.11
v confront 207.7
object 318.5
demand 406.5
claim 406.6
contradict 436.6
offer resistance 438.3
defy 439.3
compete 442.14
attack 443.13

doubt 910.6
thwart 967.14
chamber
 n room 188.1
 compartment 188.2
 bedroom 188.7
 council 408.1
 legislature 594.1
champion
 adj matchless 235.15
 best 954.16
 first-rate 954.17
 n superior 235.4
 victor 396.2
 champ 398.15
 defender 445.7
 deputy 557.1
 advocate 581.7
 supporter 596.8
 the best 954.8
 protector 963.5
 v back 434.13
 defend 445.8
 defend 581.9
 protect 963.18
championship
 n supremacy 235.3
 victory 396.1
 patronage 434.4
chance
 adj circumstantial
  728.7
 unnecessary 730.3
 vague 926.13
 risky 927.9
 n gamble 722.2
 turn 787.2
 opportunity 805.2
 liability 852.1
 possibility 921.1
 probability 923.1
 uncertainty 926.1
 gamble 926.4
 luck 927.1
 v attempt 388.5
 risk 722.20
 turn up 793.6

hazard 927.7
take chances 961.7
chancellor
 n principal 552.7
 executive 555.3
 head of state 556.7
change
 n dough 705.2
 petty cash 705.15
 differentiation 742.3
 alteration 814.1
 conversion 820.1
 substitution 824.1
 substitute 824.2
 v don 5.32
 vacillate 347.8
 trade 708.14
 differentiate 742.5
 be changed 814.6
 alter 814.7
 fluctuate 816.5
 convert 820.11
 substitute 824.4
 interchange 825.3
changed
 adj altered 814.10
 converted 820.19
changing
 adj changeable 816.7
 n variation 816.3
channel
 n waterway 173.6
 outlet 181.7
 bed 190.4
 stream 224.1
 conduit 225.1
 narrow 256.3
 trench 276.2
 passageway 368.3
 informant 532.5
 signal 532.7
 station 983.10
 frequency 984.3
 v focus 199.8
 conduct 225.14
 furrow 276.3
chaos

 n confusion 249.1
 anarchy 403.2
 turbulence 651.2
 inconsistency 766.1
 confusion 772.2
 confusion 940.3
 space 114.3
chapter
 n conference 408.4
 part 535.13
 branch 597.10
 section 755.2
character
 n guy 67.5
 description 334.2
 letter 527.1
 phonetic symbol 527.2
 probity 624.1
 repute 642.1
 actor 685.2
 notation 687.6
 plot 700.4
 function 701.3
 mode 727.3
 nature 729.2
 kind 771.3
 characteristic 827.4
 eccentric 882.3
 freak 882.4
 disposition 933.3
characteristics
 n nature 729.2
characters
 n cast 685.9
charge
 n kick 96.3
 load 187.2
 burden 283.5
 precept 404.1
 injunction 405.2
 custody 414.5
 dependent 417.5
 attack 444.1
 load 447.15
 accusation 580.1
 commission 595.1
 price 610.1

fee 610.6
duty 621.1
duty 623.3
task 701.2
attribution 843.1
care 963.2
positive charge 982.5
n supervision 554.2
v animate 17.9
burden 283.10
prime 390.9
command 405.7
admonish 407.5
rush 444.16
accuse 580.7
commission 595.8
demand 610.12
impose 623.4
fill 756.7
shoot 859.11
electrify 982.24

charged
adj weighted 283.14
accused 580.14
fraught 756.11
critical 805.9
accountable 843.6
electrified 982.30

charges
n debt 603.1
expenses 606.3
fee 610.6

charity
n love 95.1
benevolence 134.4
benevolence 134.4
patronage 434.4
accord 440.1
philanthropy 463.3
donation 463.6
tolerance 934.4

charm
n sweetness 95.6
allure 362.1
lure 362.3
jewel 483.5
sorcery 669.1

spell 670.1
talisman 670.5
influence 849.1
superstition 909.3
beauty 971.1
v delight 86.9
endear 95.22
persuade 360.22
fascinate 362.7
enchant 670.8
absorb 938.13

charming
adj delightful 88.6
endearing 95.24
alluring 362.8
bewitching 670.11
influential 849.13

chart
n map 150.5
representation 334.1
diagram 366.3
diagram 366.3
outline 763.4
v locate 150.11
represent 334.8
plot 366.9
enumerate 763.7
organize 770.8

charter
n exemption 415.8
grant 428.5
rental 595.5
v commission 595.8
rent 595.13
rent out 595.14

chase
n furrow 276.1
woodland 296.11
pursuit 367.1
hunting 367.2
v follow 157.3
emboss 269.9
pursue 367.8
hunt 367.9
make haste 386.4
repel 863.3

chat

n chatter 522.2
heart-to-heart 523.3
v chatter 522.4
prattle 523.8

cheap
adj worthless 376.7
inexpensive 613.7
disgraceful 641.11
paltry 953.18
inferior 960.9
adv cheaply 613.10

check
n checks 38.4
slowing 166.4
measure 286.2
rout 397.2
restraint 413.1
confinement 414.1
stop 819.2
checkup 893.5
verification 898.2
assurance 953.18
frustration 967.3
curb 967.7
v variegate 38.6
slow 166.8
thwart 397.10
restrain 413.6
confine 414.12
fend off 445.10
delay 808.8
stop 819.9
examine 893.22
collate 898.5
verify 925.8
hinder 967.9
monitor 983.21

checked
adj tartan 38.11
retarded 166.11

cheese
n dairy products 10.43

chemical
adj biochemical 14.8
n element 14.2

cheque
n blank cheque 705.8

chest
n breast 269.4
store 371.6
treasury 706.11

chicken
adj cowardly 476.6
n coward 476.3

chief
adj leading 156.3
top 189.8
front 207.9
main 235.14
directing 554.12
governing 593.16
preceding 776.4
first 780.14
paramount 952.23
n superior 235.4
superintendent 555.2
master 556.1
principal 556.3
sovereign 556.8
principal 952.9

chief executive
n executive 555.3
chief 952.9

child
n little one 288.3
person 297.3
ingenue 401.3
descendant 542.3
innocent 637.2
product 848.1

childhood
n boyhood 287.2
origin 780.4

children
n young people 288.2
family 540.5
posterity 542.1

china
adj ceramic 719.5
n silver 8.12
ceramic ware 719.2

chocolate
n sweets 10.36

choice

adj tasteful 481.5
best 954.16
n will 308.1
selection 356.1
free will 415.6
elegance 515.1
judgment 901.1
the best 954.8

cholesterol
n fat 7.6

choose
v will 308.2
elect 356.12

choosing
adj selective 356.22
n choice 356.1

chopped
adj nicked 275.3

chosen
adj selected 356.25
n the best 954.8

Christ
n Jesus Christ 657.6

Christian
adj kind 134.13
n Nazarene 655.14

church
n school 597.5
sect 655.2
kirk 681.1

cigarette
n fag 80.4

cinema
n movie theatre 684.6

circle
n environment 200.1
circus 219.7
sphere 220.2
curve 265.2
circus 266.1
clique 597.6
round 812.3
circuit 869.2
halo 977.15
orbit 114.14
v move 163.4
encircle 200.6

round 266.4
recur 812.5
circuit 869.5
rotate 870.7

circuit
n journey 168.4
sphere 220.2
circle 266.1
route 368.1
engagement 682.8
round 812.3
round 869.2
detour 869.3
electrical circuit 982.4
circuitry 988.3
v circle 869.5

circumstances
n assets 456.6
environment 728.2
affairs 793.4

city
adj urban 219.8
n town 219.1
state 220.5

civil
adj public 297.9
decorous 481.7
courteous 489.11
sociable 563.21
governmental 593.15
lay 699.5

civilian
adj antiwar 449.8
n citizen 449.4

claim
n extortion 183.5
profession 361.2
demand 406.1
possession 454.1
estate 456.4
declaration 579.7
prerogative 622.1
v make a pretext of
361.3
demand 406.5
pretend to 406.6
possess 454.4

take 465.13
require 918.8

claimed
adj pretended 361.5
spoken for 406.10

claiming
n taking 465.1

clash
n report 47.1
rasp 58.1
jangle 52.2
discord 441.1
fight 442.4
impact 857.3
v conflict 34.13
jangle 49.9
jar 52.3
disagree 441.8
contend 442.10
counter 741.4
disagree 751.5
counteract 855.6
collide 857.12

class
n rank 231.2
nomenclature 512.1
form 553.10
social class 588.1
community 597.2
school 597.5
category 771.2
goodness 954.1
v classify 763.8
classify 771.5
estimate 901.9

classic
adj model 748.8
perfected 957.8
n book 535.1
work of art 690.8
archetype 957.3

classical
adj antiquated 804.12
perfected 957.8

clean
adj pure 70.25
shapely 250.5

honest 624.9
spotless 637.5
thorough 756.9
adv cleanly 70.29
absolutely 756.14
v cleanse 70.18

cleaning
adj cleansing 70.28
n cleansing 70.2

clear
adj distinct 30.7
audible 41.15
vacant 211.12
manifest 333.8
free 415.19
unimpeded 415.24
quit 415.28
plain 506.10
legible 506.11
elegant 515.4
thorough 756.9
unadulterated 760.6
unfastened 764.20
unqualified 915.1
certain 925.9
easy 969.13
light 977.30
transparent 981.2
adv wide 247.18
v refine 70.22
rise above 258.8
leap 351.5
manage 394.9
extricate 416.7
profit 457.12
acquit 582.4
pay in full 604.13
evacuate 864.20
unload 969.9

clearly
adv audibly 41.17
decidedly 233.18
manifestly 333.14
intelligibly 506.12
certainly 925.17

clever
adj skilful 398.20

cunning 398.28
cunning 400.12
witty 474.9
apt 551.18
smart 875.12

client
n customer 710.4

climate
n ambience 200.3
weather 302.2
spiritual climate 933.5

climb
n ascent 184.1
ascent 195.6
v move 163.4
ascend 175.15
climb up 184.10

clinic
n hospital 82.9
hospital room 188.21

clock
n furniture 218.1
timepiece 794.4
v time 794.8

close
adj stuffy 164.13
near 212.14
narrow 256.12
tight 279.10
meticulous 324.12
taciturn 329.7
secretive 330.15
concise 519.5
familiar 568.18
approximate 737.8
approximating 746.9
fast 762.13
imminent 802.3
exact 928.17
sultry 971.47
dense 990.11
adv near 212.20
nearly 212.22
densely 990.14
n plot 220.4
completion 392.2
closing 782.3

cessation 819.1
v shut 279.5
arrange 422.8
end 782.4
turn off 819.10
obstruct 967.11

closed
adj shut 279.8
secret 330.11
inhospitable 567.6
narrow-minded 935.10

closely
adv nearly 212.22
narrowly 256.17
densely 990.14

closer
adj nearer 212.18

closest
adj nearest 212.19

closing
adj ending 782.9
n closure 279.1
signing 422.3
close 782.3

closure
n closing 279.1
introduction 594.4
completion 756.4
hindrance 967.1

clothes
n clothing 5.1
blanket 281.10

clothing
adj dress 5.34
n clothes 5.1

cloud
n cloud bank 304.1
confusion 940.3
vapour 111.1
v cover 281.18
cloud over 304.3
conceal 331.6
confuse 940.7
darken 979.9

club
n resort 217.24
fist 447.4

rod 586.2
theatre 682.11
v beat 585.12

coach
n railway car 170.13
trainer 390.5
trainer 552.6
v advise 407.4
tutor 549.11

coal
n live coal 971.37
slag 972.16
v fuels 973.8

coalition
n affiliation 435.2
front 590.27
association 597.1
combination 761.1

coast
n border 202.4
side 209.1
shore 223.2
shore 223.2
v glide 168.31
navigate 173.9
do nothing 314.2
take it easy 316.13

coat
n hair 3.1
jacket 5.10
colour 34.8
cover 281.2
blanket 281.11
sheet 282.2
v cloak 5.29
colour 34.12
spread on 281.23

code
n cipher 330.6
telegraph 332.2
rule 404.2
table 770.4
rule 831.4

cold
adj colouring 34.14
sexless 66.27
unfeeling 85.9

indifferent 93.6
insolent 133.7
heartless 135.23
reticent 329.8
aloof 564.6
unfriendly 570.9
freezing 975.13
freezing 975.14
n coldness 975.1

collapse
n exhaustion 605.3
breakdown 76.8
descent 185.1
decline 238.2
deflation 246.4
damage 378.1
debacle 380.4
crash 395.3
defeat 397.1
insolvency 605.3
v weaken 16.8
burn out 21.5
take ill 76.15
descend 185.5
cave in 246.8
break down 378.21
fall 395.10
go bankrupt 605.7
fall short 866.2
fall through 866.3

colleague
n companion 569.3
associate 596.1
equal 754.2

collect
v store up 371.10
gather 457.11
come together 732.16
gather 732.18
put together 762.4
conclude 901.10

collected
adj composed 97.13
stored 371.12
assembled 732.21
joined 762.12

collection

n store 371.1
gathering 457.2
donation 463.6
edition 535.5
compilation 535.7
excerpts 538.4
anthology 698.5
assembly 732.1
fund 732.11

collective
adj cooperative 435.5
communal 461.8
concurrent 854.3

college
n university 548.5

Colonel
n Field Marshal 556.19

colour
n hue 34.1
bright colour 34.4
pigment 34.8
ambience 200.3
ornament 483.1
photography 684.4
treatment 690.7
kind 771.3
v tinge 34.12
blush 130.8
flush 143.14
pervert 251.6
misrepresent 335.3
ornament 483.7
portray 690.17
imbue 759.10
influence 849.7

coloured
adj in colour 34.15
prejudiced 935.12

colours
n battle flag 443.11

column
n tower 258.5
pillar 259.5
cylinder 268.2
monument 530.10
part 535.13
procession 774.3

base 856.7

combat
n contention 442.1
fight 442.4
war 443.1
v contend against 436.4
contend 442.10

combination
n concoction 390.3
affiliation 435.2
assembly 732.1
relation 737.1
identification 740.2
composition 758.1
mixture 759.1
compound 759.4
joining 762.1
composition 767.1
unity 834.1
n collaboration 854.1

combined
adj cooperative 435.5
associated 597.16
accompanying 731.8
assembled 732.21
mixed 759.12
joint 762.11
united 767.5
concurrent 854.3

come
v appear 32.8
climax 66.22
approach 158.3
arrive 177.6
emerge 181.8
occur 793.5
turn up 793.6
come on 801.6
chance 927.7

come back
v recur 944.12

come from
v result from 842.5

come in
v land 175.18
arrive 177.6

enter 180.7
be received 464.8

come into
v acquire 457.8
inherit 464.7

come on
v progress 153.2
improve 377.7
make good 394.7
come 801.6

come out
v emerge 181.8
come forth 333.6
be revealed 336.8
appear 337.16
come forth 354.10
fare 727.4
originate 780.12
result 842.4
turn up 896.9

come to
v quicken 292.6
recover 381.18
cost 610.13
equal 752.5
total 754.8

come up
v ascend 184.7

comedy
n wit 474.1
drama 682.3

comfort
n rest 20.1
pleasure 86.1
contentment 98.1
ease 112.1
condolence 138.1
aid 434.1
prosperity 965.1
v console 112.6
commiserate 138.2
aid 434.11

comfortable
adj holiday 20.10
content 98.7
contented 112.11
homely 217.29

wealthy 598.8
prosperous 965.12

comic
adj witty 474.9
tragic 682.26
n wit 474.6
comedian 685.7

coming
adj approaching 158.4
arriving 177.8
emerging 181.15
eventual 793.11
future 801.7
imminent 802.3
n appearance 32.1
approach 158.1
arrival 177.1
advent 801.5
imminence 802.1

command
n field of view 30.3
supremacy 235.3
will 308.1
skill 398.1
governance 402.5
precept 404.1
commandment 405.1
compulsion 409.1
control 593.2
knowledge 883.1
understanding 883.3
n direction 554.1
v rule 235.11
rise above 258.8
will 308.2
order 405.7
possess 454.4
direct 554.4
govern 593.10
know well 883.11

commander
n skipper 174.5
superior 235.4
governor 556.6

comment
n notation 326.5
commentary 537.2

criticism 901.2
v remark 509.18

commerce
n communication 328.1
social life 563.4
occupation 701.1
trade 708.1

commercial
adj occupied 701.12
business 707.9
business 708.19
in demand 711.11
n advertisement 337.6
advertisement 983.15

commission
n precept 404.1
injunction 405.2
portion 462.5
delegation 557.13
commissioning 595.1
dividend 604.7
task 701.2
assembly 732.2
v command 405.7
authorize 595.8
delegate 824.6

commissioner
n policeman 963.15

commitment
n zeal 92.2
resolution 344.1
undertaking 389.1
committal 414.4
obligation 421.2
dedication 462.4
consignment 463.2
devotion 568.7
commission 595.1
duty 621.1
selflessness 632.1
principle 841.9

committed
adj zealous 92.9
resolute 344.10
promised 421.7
devoted 568.20

obliged 621.14
unselfish 632.4

committee
n select committee
408.2
assembly 732.2

common
adj trite 108.9
medium 232.3
inferior 236.6
public 297.9
cooperative 435.5
communal 461.8
commonplace 482.12
simple 484.6
vernacular 508.12
plain-speaking 517.3
demographic 587.8
prosaic 699.3
mutual 739.10
frequent 809.4
prevalent 826.11
usual 831.7
well-known 883.22
paltry 953.18
ordinary 960.9
n green 296.7
park 720.13

commons
n dining room 188.9

commonwealth
n federal government
593.4

communication
adv transfer 167.1
n communion 328.1
communications 332.1
passageway 368.3
giving 463.1
speech 509.1
conversation 523.1
information 532.1
message 533.4
letter 534.2
joining 762.1

communications

n media 328.4
signalling 332.1
the press 536.3
radio 983.1

communism
n communion 461.2
Marxism 592.5
federal government
593.4
democracy 593.6

communist
adj Marxist 592.21

Communist
adj revolutionary 822.6

communist
n Marxist 592.13

Communist
n revolutionary 822.3

community
n population 216.1
mankind 297.1
cooperation 435.1
accord 440.1
communion 461.2
social life 563.4
society 597.2
sect 655.2
company 731.1

company
n unit 446.18
association 563.6
guest 566.6
team 597.7
firm 597.9
cast 685.9
workplace 716.1
association 731.1
group 732.3

compare
v gather 732.18
liken 898.4
be comparable 898.6

comparison
n assembly 732.1
similarity 746.1
substitute 824.2
matching 898.1

estimate 901.3

compensation
n balancing 250.2
repayment 323.1
repair 381.6
reparation 466.2
reprisal 491.2
recompense 604.3
pay 604.4
atonement 638.1

compete
v contend 442.14
play 721.2

competing
adj competitive 442.19

competition
n hostility 436.2
rivalry 442.2

competitive
adj opposing 436.7
competing 442.19

complain
v groan 106.15
object 318.5
offer resistance 438.3

complaint
n disease 76.1
grievance 106.4
objection 318.2
resistance 438.1
disapproval 495.1
declaration 579.7
accusation 580.1

complete
adj downright 233.12
perfect 392.11
comprehensive 734.7
undivided 754.11
whole 756.8
ended 782.7
unqualified 915.1
sound 957.6
v perform 313.9
perfect 392.6
execute 422.9
mature 756.6
perfect 782.6

elaborate 823.5
perfect 957.4

completed
adj done 392.10

completely
adv utterly 233.21
fully 728.13
totally 756.13
perfectly 957.9

complex
adj difficult 507.12
mixed 759.12
complicated 761.4
difficult 968.17
n inferiority complex
83.12
tangle 761.1
obsession 881.11

complicated
adj difficult 507.12
complex 761.4

comprehensive
adj great 233.6
voluminous 243.16
broad 255.6
sweeping 734.7
whole 754.9
thorough 766.9
joint 762.11

compromise
n adjustment 450.4
middle ground 452.3
composition 453.1
foreign policy 590.5
adjustment 750.4
v reconcile 450.8
compound 453.2
interchange 825.3
endanger 961.6

computer
n computer science
987.6
machine 988.2

computers
n computer science
988.1

concentrate
n extract 183.7
v converge 160.2
focus 199.8
intensify 237.5
contract 246.5
brood on 886.8
densify 990.8

concentrate on
v pay attention 938.8

concentrated
adj central 199.9
contracted 246.9
attentive 938.14
dense 990.11

concentration
n convergence 160.1
squeezing 183.6
centralization 199.6
heightening 237.2
contraction 246.1
industry 315.5
firmness 344.2
perseverance 345.1
thoughtfulness 886.3
attention 938.1
absorption 938.3
condensation 990.3

concept
n idea 887.1
opinion 908.6
picture 941.5

concern
n sensitivity 24.3
sympathy 84.5
anxiety 117.1
consideration 134.3
carefulness 324.1
undertaking 389.1
company 597.9
occupation 701.1
workplace 716.1
relevance 737.4
affair 793.3
topic 892.1
interest 938.2
importance 952.1

v give concern 117.3
relate to 737.5
involve 853.2
interest 938.12
trouble 968.13

concerned
adj anxious 117.6
involved 853.4
interested 938.15

concerns
n worry 117.2
affairs 793.4

concert
n unanimity 317.5
harmony 686.2
performance 686.27

concluded
adj completed 392.10
ended 782.7

conclusion
n affirmation 319.1
completion 392.2
signing 422.3
sequel 779.1
end 782.1
solution 895.1
deduction 901.4
opinion 908.6

concrete
adj substantial 725.6
cohesive 765.9
particular 827.12
dense 990.6
n ground covering 190.3
pavement 368.6
solid 990.6
stone 991.5
v cover 295.23
plaster 281.24

condition
n fitness 75.1
disease 76.1
rank 231.2
readiness 390.4
stipulation 406.2
state 727.1

circumstance 728.1
provision 914.2
v limit 201.5
accustom 358.8
fit 390.8
inculcate 549.12
train 549.13

conditions
n affairs 793.4

conduct
n behaviour 306.1
performance 313.2
operation 844.1
n direction 554.1
v transport 167.8
channel 225.14
practise 313.8
perform 313.9
direct 554.8
direct 686.36
escort 731.7
operate 844.5

conference
n audition 39.2
council 408.1
forum 408.3
chapter 408.4
congress 523.5
discussion 523.6
diocese 677.3
assembly 732.2

confidence
n equanimity 97.3
hope 115.1
expectation 121.1
secret 330.5
belief 908.1
conviction 925.4

confident
adj composed 97.13
hopeful 115.10
fearless 477.15
believing 908.20
sure 925.15

confined
adj laid up 76.24
limited 201.7

enclosed 203.9
local 220.8
narrow 256.12
restricted 413.14
in confinement 414.18
specialized 828.5

confirm
v strengthen 15.12
ratify 317.11
accustom 358.8
secure 423.7
baptize 680.11
secure 817.8
experiment 897.8
collate 898.5
affirm 912.10
verify 925.8

confirmed
adj accepted 317.13
chronic 358.17
established 817.13
tried 897.12
proved 912.17
true 928.13

conflict
n psychological stress 83.7
hostility 436.2
discord 441.1
contention 442.1
fight 442.4
hostility 570.3
opposition 741.1
disagreement 751.1
opposition 855.1
v clash 34.13
clash 52.3
disagree 441.8
counter 741.4
disagree 751.5
counteract 855.6

confrontation
n opposition 206.1
meeting 212.4
conference 523.5
opposition 741.1
comparison 898.1

confused
adj inconspicuous 31.6
shy 130.12
formless 249.4
complex 761.4
incoherent 766.3
chaotic 772.14
disordered 773.5
vague 926.13
bewildered 926.15
mixed-up 940.12

confusion
n chaos 249.1
rout 397.2
anarchy 403.2
inconsistency 766.1
chaos 772.2
bewilderment 926.2
fluster 940.3

congress
n convergence 160.1
communication 328.1
council 408.1
conference 523.5
social life 563.4
legislature 594.1
assembly 732.2

connected
adj clear 506.10
related 737.9
joined 762.12
consistent 765.10
continuous 774.8

connection
n intermediary 204.3
junction 212.3
communication 328.1
passageway 368.3
mediator 451.3
blood relationship 540.1
marriage relationship 545.1
go-between 557.4
relation 737.1
relevance 737.4
joining 762.1

joint 762.3
consistency 765.2
series 774.2

conscious
adj awake 23.8
sensible 24.11
living 292.9
intentional 365.8
knowing 883.12

consciousness
n wakefulness 23.1
sensation 24.1
wits 874.2
recognition 883.2
attention 938.1

conservation
n storage 371.5
preservation 382.1
maintenance 815.2

conservative
adj right-wing 592.18

Conservative
adj Jewish 655.25

conservative
adj preservative 815.7
n right-winger 592.10
diehard 815.3

Conservative Party
adj 590.36

consider
v be considerate 134.10
care 324.6
discuss 523.10
contemplate 886.9
entertain 886.10
think of 886.12
judge 901.8
suppose 906.7
think 908.11
allow for 914.5

considerable
adj great 233.6
large 243.15
important 952.16

considerably
adv greatly 233.14

consideration
n thoughtfulness 134.3
respect 146.1
carefulness 324.1
motive 360.1
gratuity 463.5
courtesy 489.1
discussion 523.6
recompense 604.3
esteem 642.3
judgment 875.7
contemplation 886.2
argument 890.5
opinion 908.6
attention 938.1
importance 952.1

considered
adj intentional 365.8
reasoned 890.17

considering
adv on balance 901.17

consistent
adj clear 506.10
faithful 624.16
uniform 743.5
agreeing 750.9
connected 765.10
valid 928.14

constable
n policeman 963.15

constant
adj firm 344.11
persevering 345.8
habitual 358.13
observant 419.4
devoted 568.20
faithful 624.16
uniform 743.5
continuous 774.8
durable 789.9
perpetual 791.6
continual 809.5
regular 812.6
permanent 815.6
unchanging 817.17
exact 928.17

constantly

adv faithfully 624.21
regularly 743.8
perpetually 791.9
continually 809.7
regularly 812.9

constitution
n structure 252.1
written constitution 653.6
nature 729.2
nature 729.2
composition 758.1
arrangement 770.1
establishment 847.4
disposition 933.3

constitutional
adj healthy 72.4
governmental 593.15
legal 653.10
innate 729.5
temperamental 933.7
n exercise 75.2
walk 168.8
exercise 702.6

construction
n structure 252.1
structure 252.2
interpretation 326.1
word form 511.4
composition 758.1
production 847.2

consultant
n expert 398.11
adviser 407.3

consumer
n eater 8.15
user 372.7
buyer 710.5

consumption
n eating 8.1
waste 238.3
shrinking 246.3
use 372.1
consuming 373.1
waste 378.4
waste 458.2
expenditure 606.1

contact
n touch 64.1
touch 212.5
communication 328.1
go-between 557.4
v touch 212.10
communicate with 328.7

contain
v put in 198.5
limit 201.5
enclose 203.5
close 279.5
restrain 413.6
include 734.3
total 754.8
compose 758.3
extinguish 974.6

contained
adj extinguished 974.10

containing
adj inclusive 734.6
composed of 758.4

contemporary
adj simultaneous 798.5
present 800.2
modern 803.13
n concomitant 798.2

content
adj contented 98.7
willing 309.5
assenting 317.12
consenting 426.4
n contentment 98.1
contents 187.1
capacity 243.2
v satisfy 98.4

contents
n content 187.1
design 535.12
table 832.2

contest
n contention 442.1
engagement 442.3
game 720.8
sport 721.1

v deny 320.4
contend against 436.4
contradict 436.6
contend 442.10
dispute 442.17
argue 890.12
doubt 910.6

context
n environment 200.1
circumstances 728.2

continent
adj abstinent 644.6

continue
v lengthen 253.6
persevere 345.2
be continuous 774.4
elapse 783.3
endure 789.5
prolong 789.8
postpone 808.9
be frequent 809.3
carry on 818.3

continued
adj continuous 774.8

continuing
adj persevering 345.8
continuous 774.8
durable 789.9
permanent 815.6
abiding 818.7

contract
n undertaking 389.1
obligation 421.2
compact 422.1
v take ill 76.15
compress 246.5
shorten 254.4
narrow 256.9
close 279.5
commit 421.5
be engaged 421.6
bargain 422.5
acquire 457.8
v make small 244.8

contrary
adj negative 320.5
perverse 346.10

opposing 436.7
perverse 741.5
different 742.6
disagreeing 751.6
deviant 830.5
refuting 913.5
adverse 966.13
hindering 967.16
unwieldy 968.19
adv opposite 206.6

contrast
n opposition 206.1
opposition 741.1
difference 742.1
disparity 749.1
comparison 898.1
lighting 977.19
v oppose 206.4
compare 898.4

contribute
v provide 370.7
participate 461.4
subscribe 463.14

contribution
n demand 406.1
participation 461.1
giving 463.1
donation 463.6
piece 537.1

control
n supremacy 235.3
self-control 344.5
skill 398.1
governance 402.5
governance 402.5
restraint 413.1
subjugation 417.1
mastery 593.2
influence 849.1
n direction 554.1
v pilot 175.13
have power 402.12
restrain 413.6
direct 554.8
hold the reins 593.11
moderate 650.5
govern 849.8

haunt 943.4

controlled
adj strong-willed
344.13
restrained 413.12
restrained 650.10

controversial
adj contentious 101.26
argumentative 890.19
doubtful 926.11

controversy
n quarrel 441.5
contention 442.1
disagreement 751.1
argument 890.4

convention
n custom 358.1
rule 404.2
chapter 408.4
compact 422.1
treaty 422.2
conference 523.5
fashion 559.1
social convention
560.1
assembly 732.2

conventional
adj customary 358.12
prescriptive 404.4
contractual 422.10
orthodox 560.5
orthodox 666.5
traditional 804.11
conformist 829.6
usual 831.7
ordinary 960.8

conversation
n communication
328.1
speech 509.1
exchange 523.1
social talk 563.4

converted
adj improved 377.13
redeemed 664.9
redeemed 671.10
changed 814.10

changed 820.19

conviction
n hope 115.1
condemnation 583.1
persuasion 908.5
confidence 925.4

convince
v persuade 360.22
persuade 820.16
convert 908.17
seem true 928.9

convinced
adj believing 908.20
confident 925.15

cook
n chef 11.2
maid 558.8
v prepare 11.4
burn 971.41
heat 972.17

cooked
adj stewed 11.6

cooking
adj culinary 11.5
n cookery 11.1
heating 972.1

cool
adj colouring 34.14
unfeeling 85.9
indifferent 93.6
calm 97.12
unmoved 114.3
aloof 132.11
insolent 133.7
quiet 164.10
reticent 329.8
cautious 479.7
aloof 564.6
unfriendly 570.9
level-headed 650.11
stable 817.12
sensible 875.16
great 954.13
temperate 975.12
n composure 97.2
calm 114.1
moderation 650.1

uniformity 743.1
stability 817.1
v deter 364.4
pacify 450.7
calm 650.6
refrigerate 976.7

cooperation
n collaboration 435.1
communion 461.2
association 563.6
interaction 739.2
agreement 750.1
interchange 825.1
n collaboration 854.1

cope
n the heavens 114.2
v support oneself
370.12
make do 950.4

cope with
v treat 306.5
perform 313.9
treat 372.10

copy
n reproduction 69.1
reproduction 321.3
image 334.5
writing 528.8
manuscript 529.4
news item 533.3
edition 535.5
picture 690.9
the same 740.3
representation 747.1
recounting 811.2
substitute 824.2
v reproduce 69.7
imitate 321.5
impersonate 334.11
write 528.14
adopt 601.4
portray 690.17
reproduce 740.6
resemble 746.5
reproduce 747.8
repeat 811.7
duplicate 836.3

core
adj middle 781.3
n substance 187.4
interior 198.2
centre 199.1
summary 538.2
essence 729.1
middle 781.1
important thing 952.5
memory 988.7

corner
n deviation 155.1
nook 188.3
angle 264.1
recess 270.6
hiding place 331.4
v monopolize 714.13
corner 968.16

corporate
adj associated 597.16
joint 762.11
allied 767.6

corporation
n tummy 2.13
workplace 716.1

corps
n branch 446.17
unit 446.18
company 732.3

correct
adj meticulous 324.12
well-mannered 489.13
appropriate 515.5
conventional 560.5
right 617.3
accurate 928.16
v revise 377.12
remedy 381.11
reprove 495.15
punish 585.9
conform 829.3
disillusion 932.2

correspondent
n letter writer 534.8
counterpart 739.3

corruption
n perversion 251.2

bribery 363.1
pollution 378.2
decay 378.6
mispronunciation
510.5
taboo word 511.6
misleading 550.1
improbity 625.1
moral turpitude 634.5
contamination 759.3
indoctrination 820.5
evil 955.3

cost
n loss 458.1
price 610.1
v spend 606.4
sell for 610.13

costs
n expenses 606.3

cottage
n bungalow 217.7

cotton
n dressing 77.17

could be
v be possible 921.3
be probable 923.2

council
adj advisory 408.5
n assembly 408.1
conference 523.5
tribunal 576.1
assembly 732.2

count
n amount 230.2
nobleman 589.4
returns 590.18
v enumerate 230.4
beat time 686.35
have influence 849.10
judge 901.8
rank 901.15
matter 952.11

counter
adj backward 154.10
opposing 436.7
adverse 966.13
adv opposite 206.6

vice versa 741.7
n stern 208.7
retaliation 491.1
token 705.9
showcase 713.6
workplace 716.1
bingo 722.13
v deny 320.4
oppose 436.3
contend against 436.4
fend off 445.10
retaliate 491.3
contradict 741.4
disagree 751.5
counteract 855.6
refute 913.4
thwart 967.14

country
adj rustic 222.4
outback 222.5
n region 220.1
land 221.1

countryside
n the country 222.1

county
n state 220.5
country 221.1
constituency 590.14

coup
n act 313.3
stratagem 400.3
accession 402.11
seizure 465.2

couple
n set 746.4
two 835.2
v copulate 66.20
marry 544.12
marry 544.13
come together 732.16
relate 737.6
put together 762.4
combine 763.3
league 764.7
double 835.4

courage
n pluck 344.3

nerve 477.1

course
n serving 8.10
dish 10.7
direction 152.1
progression 153.1
career 163.2
travel 168.1
journey 168.4
voyage 173.2
flow 224.4
channel 225.1
layer 282.1
policy 366.4
route 368.1
manner 369.1
arena 448.1
track 502.8
study 549.8
series 774.2
round 812.3
process 844.2
trend 851.2
v flow 224.15

court
adj tribunal 576.7
n enclosure 203.3
estate 217.6
council 408.1
court of law 576.2
courthouse 576.6
playground 720.10
attendance 731.5
v curry favour 129.9
solicit 425.14
woo 543.21
cultivate 568.11

cover
n ground covering
190.3
covering 281.2
lid 281.5
blanket 281.10
concealment 331.1
veil 331.2
veil 331.2
hiding place 331.4

disguise 341.11
pretext 361.1
pretext 361.1
binding 535.14
protection 963.1
shelter 964.3
shade 980.1
v extend 149.6
traverse 168.16
close 279.5
stop 279.6
cover up 281.18
compensate 323.3
conceal 331.6
hide behind or under
  361.4
bet 722.21
include 734.3
put together 762.4
take turns 787.5
beset 865.5
protect 963.18
coverage
n size 243.1
covering 281.1
cover 281.2
news 533.1
inclusion 734.1
covered
adj covert 281.28
concealed 331.11
secured 423.9
included 734.5
protected 963.21
covering
adj coating 281.30
concealing 331.15
inclusive 734.6
protective 963.22
n exterior 197.2
coverage 281.1
cover 281.2
sheet 282.2
concealment 331.1
covers
n blanket 281.10
crack

n report 47.1
snap 47.2
detonation 47.3
cleft 213.2
furrow 276.1
opening 278.1
try 388.3
break 764.4
hit 857.4
fault 958.2
v crash 47.6
snap 47.7
blast 47.8
crack up 119.8
cut 213.4
furrow 276.3
explain 326.8
injure 378.12
break 378.20
break 764.11
hit 857.13
solve 895.2
craft
n ship 171.1
deceit 341.3
skill 398.1
art 398.7
manual art 690.2
vocation 701.6
cunning 875.3
crash
n noise 44.3
report 47.1
crash landing 175.7
descent 185.1
decline 238.2
debacle 384.4
collapse 395.3
defeat 397.1
insolvency 605.3
bear market 714.2
impact 857.3
misfortune 966.2
v snooze 22.12
hit the hay 22.15
din 44.7
crack 47.6

penetrate 180.8
descend 185.5
inhabit 214.6
fall 395.10
go bankrupt 605.7
collide 857.12
crazy
adj distorted 251.9
mentally deficient
  877.20
foolish 878.7
absurd 878.9
nutty 881.23
cream
adj light 36.6
n cleanser 70.17
the best 954.8
ointment 11.3
semiliquid 16.5
v foam 305.5
emulsify 16.9
create
v form 248.6
originate 322.3
initiate 780.10
cause 841.10
produce 847.8
imagine 941.9
created
adj substantial 725.6
made 847.18
creation
n forming 248.5
structure 252.1
work of art 690.8
beginning 780.1
production 847.1
product 848.1
universe 114.1
creative
adj original 322.4
beginning 780.13
productive 847.16
imaginative 941.12
credibility
n honesty 624.3
believability 908.8

credit
n thanks 141.2
trust 602.1
entry 608.5
due 619.2
honour 626.1
esteem 642.3
attribution 843.1
influence 849.1
belief 908.1
v thank 141.4
credit to one's account 602.5
keep accounts 608.8

crew
n flight crew 176.3
staff 558.10
clique 597.6
team 597.7
movie studio 684.3
company 723.3

crime
n wickedness 635.1
misdeed 635.2
offence 654.3

criminal
adj wrong 618.3
dishonest 625.16
wicked 634.15
wrong 635.5
guilty 636.3
illegal 654.5
bad 955.7
n evildoer 574.1
scoundrel 625.10
felon 640.8

crisis
n financial crisis 706.6
business cycle 708.9
critical point 805.4
urgency 954.2
important thing 952.5
danger 961.1

critical
adj ill 76.21
meticulous 324.12
explanatory 326.11

fastidious 480.6
faultfinding 495.21
expository 537.6
crucial 805.9
discriminating 899.7
judicial 901.16
urgent 952.21
dangerous 961.9
precarious 961.12
difficult 968.17

criticism
n flak 495.4
commentary 537.2
censure 901.2

crop
n mouth 2.12
head of hair 3.3
growth 296.2
yield 457.5
whip 586.1
bunch 732.7
effect 842.1
production 848.2
harvest 112.14
v feed on or upon 8.27
excise 241.9
shorten 254.4
farm 112.15
harvest 112.18

cross
adj irritable 101.19
angry 143.27
crossed 161.8
traverse 161.9
cross-shaped 161.10
adv across 161.13
n crux 161.4
monument 530.10
scaffold 586.5
insignia 627.1
hybrid 759.3
adversity 966.1
impediment 967.6
v disappoint 123.2
converge 160.2
intersect 161.6

traverse 168.16
navigate 173.9
deny 320.4
oppose 436.3
contradict 436.6
bless 675.13
counteract 855.6
pass 865.7
thwart 967.14

crossed
adj disappointed 123.5
cross 161.8
cross-shaped 161.10
hybrid 759.13

crossing
adj converging 160.3
n convergence 160.1
intersection 161.1
intersection 161.2
travel 168.1
voyage 173.2
opposition 436.1

crowd
n audience 39.6
social circle 563.5
clique 597.6
throng 732.4
audience 873.2
v hasten 386.3
come together 732.16
fill 756.7
teem with 839.5
overload 948.13
obstruct 967.11
densify 990.8

crown
n summit 189.2
head 189.4
head 189.5
supremacy 235.3
circle 266.1
finishing touch 392.3
victory 396.1
jewel 483.5
trophy 626.3
regalia 627.2
penny 705.5

limit 756.5
v top 189.7
top 281.20
complete 392.6
install 595.10

crucial
adj critical 805.9
original 841.14
urgent 952.21
vital 952.22

cry
n call 50.1
call 51.1
lament 106.3
cheer 107.2
publicity 337.4
appeal 425.2
catchword 511.9
v call 50.4
call 51.2
weep 106.12
proclaim 337.13

crying
adj vociferous 50.7
howling 51.6
tearful 106.21
demanding 406.9
n weeping 106.12

crystal
adj stony 13.7
n precious stone 13.4

cue
n script 682.16
reminder 944.5

cultural
adj educational 549.18

culture
n mankind 297.1
society 358.2
cultivation 377.3
taste 481.1
good breeding 489.4
scholarship 883.5
agriculture 112.1
cultivation 112.12
v cultivate 112.16
raise 113.5

cup
n container 186.1
cavity 270.2
victory 396.1
monument 530.10
trophy 626.3
fate 919.2
v ladle 167.11
hollow 270.10

cure
n remedy 77.1
treatment 82.5
curing 381.7
v remedy 77.19
treat 82.11
break off 359.2
remedy 381.13
preserve 382.8
dry 110.4

curious
adj odd 832.11
inquiring 893.34
inquisitive 936.5
attentive 938.14
interested 938.15

currency
n publicity 337.4
fashionableness 559.2
money 705.1
prevalence 826.2
mediocrity 831.2

current
adj published 337.17
customary 358.12
reported 533.14
fashionable 559.11
existing 723.10
happening 793.9
present 800.2
prevalent 826.11
usual 831.7
well-known 883.22
n direction 152.1
course 163.2
flow 224.4
wind 303.1
trend 851.2

electric current 982.2

curriculum
n study 549.8

curtains
n death 293.1
end 782.1

custody
n vigilance 324.4
care 414.5
care 963.2
n leadership 554.4

customer
n guy 67.5
client 710.4

customers
n market 710.3

cut
adj pained 87.23
cleft 213.6
formative 248.8
furrowed 276.4
impaired 78.23
concise 519.5
engraved 691.8
severed 764.21
n crack 213.2
degree 231.1
curtailment 238.4
form 248.1
notch 275.1
furrow 276.1
trench 276.2
sheet 282.2
thrust 444.2
mark 502.5
dividend 604.7
discount 611.1
part 755.1
piece 755.3
break 764.4
characteristic 827.4
rebuff 863.2
v pain 26.7
offend 143.21
slash 195.10
crack 213.4
reduce 238.7

delete 241.10
form 248.6
shorten 254.4
prick 271.5
notch 275.2
furrow 276.3
injure 378.12
repulse 427.5
apportion 462.6
record 530.12
shorten 254.4
discount 611.2
engrave 691.6
sculpture 693.5
separate 755.6
sever 764.10
turn off 819.10
repel 863.3
banish 864.15
freeze 975.10
cultivate 112.16
harvest 112.18

cut in
v intrude 205.5
interrupt 205.6

cut off
adj bereft 458.8
v end 380.12
dispossess 465.23
separate 764.7
sever 764.10
interrupt 819.8

cutting
adj acrimonious 17.13
penetrating 96.31
caustic 135.21
sharp 271.7
vigorous 525.10
violent 651.15
n plant 296.3
apportionment 462.1
abbreviation 519.3
film editing 684.5
piece 755.3
fission 764.2
harvest 112.14

cycle

n bicycle 170.6
circle 266.1
series 774.2
age 786.4
round 812.3
circuit 869.2
v exercise 75.3
recur 812.5
circle 869.5

cycling
n riding 168.5
sport 721.1

dad
n daddy 541.10

daily
adj recurrent 811.13
momentary 812.8
adv constantly 809.7
periodically 812.10
n periodical 536.1

damage
n injury 378.1
loss 458.1
disadvantage 951.2
evil 955.3
v impair 378.9
harm 955.6

damaged
adj impaired 378.23
imperfect 958.4

damaging
adj impaired 378.23
corroded 378.35
harmful 955.11

damn
adj cursed 498.9
v destroy 395.10
censure 495.11
curse 498.5
vilify 498.7
condemn 583.2
doom 662.3

dance
n dancing 683.1
ball 683.2
assembly 732.2
flutter 872.4

flicker 977.9
v exude cheerfulness
   100.6
rejoice 107.5
trip 683.5
play 720.22
flutter 872.9
flicker 977.24

dancing
adj fluttering 872.15
flickering 977.35
n terpsichore 683.1
flicker 977.9

danger
n insecurity 926.3
peril 961.1

dangerous
adj unreliable 926.14
perilous 961.9

dark
adj inconspicuous 31.6
blackish 37.8
sullen 101.24
ominous 124.16
cloudy 304.4
secret 330.11
secretive 330.15
obscure 507.13
dishonest 625.16
wicked 634.15
black 979.13
n darkness 885.3
darkness 979.1

darkness
n low profile 31.2
blackness 37.1
swarthiness 37.2
gloom 103.7
night 300.4
obscurity 507.3
dark 885.3
dark 979.1

data
n information 532.1
knowledge 883.1
evidence 912.1
information 988.14

date
n lover 95.11
appointment 563.8
assembly 732.2
age 786.4
time 794.3
v make love 543.14
date from 794.10
age 804.8

daughter
n brother 540.3
descendant 542.3

David
n hero 477.6

dawn
adj morning 299.4
n the dawn of day 299.2
beginning 786.1
daylight 977.11
v grow light 977.26

day
n period 786.1
moment 786.2
age 786.4
date 794.3
daylight 977.11

dead
adj dull 108.6
inert 164.12
closed 279.8
lifeless 293.22
languid 316.18
no more 724.9
ended 782.7
past 799.6
obsolete 804.14
lacklustre 979.17
inanimate 1.4
adv directly 152.18
exactly 928.21

deadline
n boundary 202.3
crucial moment 805.5

deal
n amount 230.2
lot 233.4

act 313.3
compromise 453.1
transaction 708.4
bargain 708.5
v give 463.12
trade 708.14
bargain 708.17

deal with
v treat 306.5
perform 313.9
communicate 328.5
treat 372.10
accomplish 392.4
discuss 523.10
punish 585.9
trade with 708.16
relate to 737.5
operate 844.5

dealer
n merchant 707.2
stockbroker 714.6

dealing
n act 313.3
commerce 708.1
trade 708.2

deals
n intrigues 849.3

dean
n senior 290.4
principal 552.7
executive 555.3

dear
adj beloved 95.23
precious 612.10
expensive 612.11
adv dearly 612.13
n sweetheart 95.9
darling 543.6

death
n fatal illness 76.2

Death
n Grim Reaper 293.2

death
n end 380.2
end 782.1
transience 790.1
bane 956.1

debate
n contention 442.1
discussion 523.6
introduction 594.4
argument 890.4
v hesitate 347.7
discuss 523.10
orate 524.8
legislate 594.8
consider 886.9

debt
n indebtedness 603.1

debut
n coming out 563.14
performance 682.9
inauguration 780.5

decade
n moment 786.2

decent
adj kind 134.13
indulgent 412.7
decorous 481.7
conventional 560.5
right 617.3
honest 624.9
modest 644.5
sufficient 946.5
tolerable 954.19

decide
v will 308.2
resolve 344.6
induce 360.21
determine 841.12
govern 849.8
determine 901.11
make sure 925.7

decided
adj downright 233.12
affirmative 319.7
resolute 344.10
ended 782.7
unqualified 915.1
assured 925.14
confident 925.15
emphatic 952.20

decision
n will 308.1

resolution 344.1
choice 356.1
judgment 579.9
verdict 901.5

decisive
adj resolute 344.10
mandatory 405.10
critical 805.9
prompt 807.9
causal 841.13
convincing 908.24
evidential 912.14
unqualified 915.1
certain 925.9

deck
n ground covering
190.3
layer 282.1
v clothe 5.28
overcome 397.6
ornament 483.7
clobber 857.15

declaration
n acknowledgement
317.3
affirmation 319.1
announcement 337.2
decree 405.4
remark 509.3
statement 579.7
profession 908.7
testimony 912.2

declared
adj affirmed 319.8
published 337.17

decline
n lowering 185.2
descent 195.5
subsidence 238.2
deterioration 378.3
cheapening 613.4
price 715.3
close 782.3
shortcoming 866.1
senility 877.9
v weaken 16.8
fail 76.16

recede 159.2
sink 185.6
incline 195.9
decrease 238.6
age 289.8
reject 357.2
sink 378.15
refuse 427.3
cheapen 613.6
fall short 866.2
come down in the
world 966.11

declined
adj rejected 357.3

dedicated
adj zealous 92.9
resolute 344.10
devoted 568.20
unselfish 632.4
sanctified 664.8

deep
adj coloured 34.15
low 45.9
heartfelt 84.22
spacious 149.8
interior 196.6
great 233.6
broad 255.6
profound 261.9
abstract 507.14
wise 875.15
learned 883.17
adv out of one's depth
261.13
n pit 261.2

deeply
adv internally 198.8

defeat
n disappointment
123.1
failure 395.1
beating 397.1
frustration 967.3
v disappoint 123.2
beat 235.7
do for 380.11
triumph over 396.5

get the better of 397.5
refute 913.4
thwart 967.14

defeated
adj disappointed 123.5
worsted 397.13
ended 782.7

defence
n guard 445.1
pleading 579.6
plea 581.2
retort 855.5
argument 890.4
rebuttal 894.2
protection 963.1
barrier 967.5

defend
v guard 445.8
support 581.9
protect 963.18

defender
n champion 445.7
advocate 581.7
supporter 596.8
protector 963.5

defending
adj defensive 445.11

defensive
adj defending 445.11
protective 963.22

deficit
n difference 241.7
arrears 603.2
deficiency 757.2
shortcoming 866.1
want 947.4

defined
adj distinct 30.7
circumscribed 201.6
clear 506.10
particular 827.12

definitely
adv visibly 30.8
particularly 827.15
certainly 925.17
exactly 928.21

definition

n distinctness 30.2
limiting 201.1
interpretation 326.1
explanation 503.3
clarity 506.2
naming 512.2
characterization 827.8
picture 984.4
degree
n grade 231.1
measure 286.2
extent 286.3
class 588.1
honours degree 628.6
continuity 769.2
degrees
n points of the
compass 152.2
delay
n slowing 166.4
stoppage 808.2
hindrance 967.1
v dawdle 166.7
slow 166.8
do nothing 314.2
put away 375.6
detain 808.8
postpone 808.9
wait 808.11
hinder 967.9
delayed
adj retarded 166.11
late 808.12
delegation
n accession 402.11
commitment 463.2
deputation 557.13
commission 595.1
substitution 824.1
deliberately
adv slowly 166.12
intentionally 365.10
slow 808.16
delicate
adj frail 16.12
sensitive 24.12
soft 34.20

tasty 54.7
sensitive 84.18
considerate 134.16
dainty 234.7
thin 256.13
smooth 280.7
light 284.10
meticulous 324.12
nice 480.8
elegant 481.6
decent 644.5
discriminating 899.7
exact 928.17
precarious 961.12
difficult 968.17
fine 971.16
soft 992.8
brittle 995.3
delicious
adj edible 8.32
tasty 54.7
delectable 88.9
great 954.13
delight
n happiness 86.2
tendency 851.1
v tickle 86.9
be pleased 86.11
rejoice 107.5
exult 487.7
amuse 720.20
delighted
adj pleased 86.14
amused 720.25
deliver
v release 111.6
transfer 167.6
do 313.6
rescue 383.3
accomplish 392.4
succeed 394.6
liberate 416.4
hand 463.13
say 509.16
transfer 609.3
perform 847.11
delivered

adj liberated 416.10
delivery
adv transportation
167.2
n birth 1.1
rescue 383.1
liberation 416.1
giving 463.1
articulation 509.5
transfer 609.1
demand
n extortion 183.5
claim 406.1
request 425.1
prerogative 622.1
imposition 623.1
sale 711.1
requirement 918.2
v prescribe 405.8
summon 405.9
ask 406.5
oblige 469.5
request 425.9
charge 610.12
impose 623.4
require 918.8
demanded
adj imposed 623.8
demanding
adj meticulous 324.12
exacting 406.9
strict 410.5
teasing 425.18
difficult 968.17
democracy
n communion 461.2
federal government
593.4
power-sharing 593.6
democratic
adj governmental
593.15
demonstrate
v object 318.5
explain 326.8
manifest 333.5
mirror 334.10

show off 486.13
teach 549.10
evidence 912.7
prove 912.9
cite 912.12

demonstrated
adj manifested 333.13
proved 912.17
true 928.13

demonstration
n objection 318.2
explanation 326.4
display 333.2
representation 334.1
display 486.4
assembly 732.2
example 748.2
reasoning 890.1
proof 912.3
citation 912.5

denied
adj rejected 357.3
disproved 913.6

deny
v not admit 320.4
retract 348.8
reject 357.2
withhold 427.4
prohibit 429.3
contradict 436.6
disbelieve 910.5
refute 913.4

department
n sphere 220.2
bureau 575.3
sphere 701.4

departure
n disappearance 33.1
deviation 155.1
leaving 179.1
leave 179.4
exit 181.2
absence 211.4
death 293.1
digression 520.4
difference 742.1

depend

v hang 914.6
be uncertain 926.5

dependent
adj suspended 193.9
subject 417.10
trusting 908.21
contingent 914.9
undecided 926.12
n follower 157.2
charge 417.5
retainer 558.1

depending
adj contingent 914.9
undecided 926.12

depressed
adj joyless 87.20
dejected 103.22
low 260.7
dented 270.14
lowered 868.12
unfortunate 966.14

depression
n mental disorder 83.6
despair 87.6
distress 89.5
dejection 103.3
decrease 238.1
lowness 260.1
deepening 261.6
hollowness 270.1
cavity 270.2
notch 275.1
business cycle 708.9
lowering 868.1
melancholia 881.5
hard times 966.6

depth
n space 149.1
interiority 198.1
size 243.1
thickness 255.2
deepness 261.1
pit 261.2
wisdom 875.5

deputy
adj acting 557.15
n mediator 451.3

proxy 557.1
assistant 596.5
substitute 824.2
policeman 963.15

describe
v interpret 326.7
portray 334.9
characterize 827.10

description
n interpretation 326.1
portrayal 334.2
fiction 700.1
kind 771.3
characterization 827.8

desert
adj unproductive 846.4
dry 110.5
n open space 149.4
wasteland 846.2
v quit 179.9
go over 348.7
flee 353.10
abandon 355.5
be unfaithful 625.12
defect 820.13

design
n trick 341.6
intention 365.1
plan 381.1
diagram 366.3
stratagem 400.3
motif 483.6
intent 503.2
front matter 535.12
visual arts 690.1
treatment 690.7
work of art 690.8
drawing 690.11
styling 695.3
plot 700.4
production 847.2
v intend 365.4
plan 366.7
portray 690.17
produce 847.8
originate 847.12

designed

adj intentional 365.8
planned 366.11

designer
n planner 366.6
costume designer
694.8
producer 847.7

desire
n lust 66.5
wish 91.1
ambition 91.10
love 95.1
hope 115.1
will 308.1
intention 365.1
request 425.1
v lust 66.19
wish 91.13
hope 115.6
will 308.2
intend 365.4
request 425.9

desk
n furniture 218.1
workplace 716.1

despair
n bitterness 87.6
dejection 103.3
desperation 116.2
v lose heart 103.16
despair of 116.8

desperate
adj hopeless 116.10
reckless 478.7
rabid 881.26
hard-pressed 968.26

desperately
adv hopelessly 116.15
rashly 478.9

destroy
v excise 241.9
kill 294.10
spoil 378.10
ruin 380.10
defeat 397.5
rage 651.10
harm 955.6

thwart 967.14

destroyed
adj spoiled 378.24
ruined 380.25

destruction
n elimination 241.3
killing 294.1
damage 378.1
ruin 380.1
defeat 397.1
loss 458.1
violence 651.1
disintegration 768.1
evil 955.3
bane 956.1

detail
n exactness 324.3
unit 446.18
motif 483.6
particular 728.3
part 755.1
component 758.2
v allot 462.9
amplify 520.7
commission 595.8
specify 728.6
enumerate 763.7
elaborate 823.5
specialize 827.9

detailed
adj meticulous 324.12
minute 728.9
particular 827.12

details
n description 334.2
trivia 953.4

detained
adj retarded 166.11
confined 414.18
late 808.12

detective
n investigator 557.10
interrogator 893.15
policeman 963.15

determination
n limiting 201.1
measurement 286.1

will 308.1
resolution 344.1
obstinacy 346.1
intention 365.1
endeavour 388.1
solution 895.1
discovery 896.1
test 897.2
verdict 901.5
proof 912.3
assurance 925.2

determine
v direct 152.4
circumscribe 201.4
will 308.2
resolve 344.6
induce 360.21
intend 365.4
end 782.4
specify 827.11
decide 841.12
govern 849.8
discover 896.2
decide 901.11
prove 912.9
make sure 925.7

determined
adj circumscribed
201.6
resolute 344.10
trial 388.8
future 801.7
proved 912.17
predetermined 919.5
assured 925.14
confident 925.15
true 928.13

develop
v grow 14.2
enlarge 245.4
enlarge 245.5
grow 245.7
mature 289.7
manifest 333.5
improve 377.7
elaborate 377.10
amplify 520.7

train 549.13
process 692.11
evolve 823.4
elaborate 823.5
result 842.4
originate 847.12
perfect 957.4

developed
adj grown 14.3
grown 245.12
mature 289.10
improved 377.13
complete 956.8
perfected 957.8

developing
adj evolutionary 823.7

development
n physical
development 14.1
birth 69.6
increase 237.1
growth 245.3
growth 289.5
refinement 377.2
amplification 520.6
training 549.3
passage 686.19
conversion 820.1
evolution 823.1
effect 842.1

device
n trick 341.6
pretext 361.1
plan 366.1
agency 369.3
instrument 369.4
stratagem 403.3
figure of speech 518.1
letter 527.1
plot 700.4
expedient 950.2
tool 986.1

devoted
adj zealous 92.9
loving 95.26
obedient 311.3
resolute 344.10

observant 419.4
dedicated 568.20
faithful 624.16
unselfish 632.4
sanctified 664.8
pious 671.8

dialogue
n talk 523.2
script 684.2
plot 700.4
argument 890.5

diamond
n good person 639.1
good thing 954.5
stone 991.5

diary
n notebook 530.9
history 697.1
chronicle 794.6

die
v disappear 33.2
succumb 293.14
decline 378.15
perish 380.23
stall 395.14
be annihilated 724.5
expire 782.5
pass 799.5

diet
adj dieting 256.16
n dieting 7.9
legislature 594.1
v go on a diet 7.15
eat 8.19
reduce 256.11

difference
n remainder 241.7
dissent 318.1
disagreement 441.2
distinction 742.1
irregularity 744.1
disparity 749.1
disagreement 751.1
inequality 753.1
change 814.1
abnormality 832.1

different

adj differing 742.6
uneven 744.3
dissimilar 749.4
novel 803.11
particular 827.12
abnormal 832.9
eccentric 882.5

difficult
adj perverse 346.10
finicky 480.7
hard 507.12
adverse 966.13
not easy 968.17

difficulties
n worry 599.1
adversity 966.1

difficulty
n disagreement 441.2
complexity 507.2
adversity 966.1
obstacle 967.4
impediment 967.6
hardness 968.1

dining
adj eating 8.30
n eating 8.1

dinner
n breakfast 8.6

diplomatic
adj consular 557.16
political 590.33

direct
adj straight 152.11
straight 263.6
artless 40.1
outspoken 415.21
natural 484.7
clear 506.10
elegant 515.4
plain-speaking 517.3
candid 624.13
exact 928.17
adv directly 152.18
v point 152.4
pilot 170.10
focus 199.8
channel 225.14

command 405.7
v muck up 71.13
find 896.2

advise 407.4
stain 959.6
discovered

address 534.13
disabled
adj invented 847.19

teach 549.10
adj weakened 16.15
discovery

manage 554.8
incapacitated 19.16
n disclosure 336.1

govern 593.10
crippled 378.26
find 457.6

conduct 686.36
disappeared
innovation 814.4

operate 844.5
adj absent 211.10
finding 896.1

govern 849.8
disappointed
discrimination

directed
adj discontented 99.7
n fastidiousness 480.1

adj guided 152.12
let down 123.5
taste 481.1

direction
unfulfilled 393.3
elegance 515.1

n line 152.1
disapproving 495.19
partiality 630.3

motivation 360.2
disillusioned 932.5
differentiation 742.3

precept 404.1
disappointment
judgment 875.7

directive 405.3
n discontent 99.1
finesse 899.1

advice 407.1
blighted hope 116.3
judgment 901.1

pointer 502.4
forlorn hope 123.1
xenophobia 935.4

teaching 549.1
omission 393.1
discuss

operation 844.1
collapse 395.3
v confer 523.9

trend 851.2
disapproval 495.1
debate 523.10

n management 554.1
disillusionment 932.1
write upon 537.5

directly
disaster
discussion

adv direct 152.18
n fatality 294.7
n conference 523.5

straight 263.7
debacle 380.4
debate 523.6

naturally 484.11
upheaval 651.5
disease

plainly 517.4
misfortune 966.2
n illness 76.1

candidly 624.19
discipline
viciousness 955.5

promptly 807.15
n limitation 201.2
bane 956.1

soon 807.16
self-control 344.5
v infect 76.18

exactly 928.21
strictness 410.1
dish

director
training 549.3
n serving 8.10

n director general
study 549.8
silver 8.12

555.1
punishment 585.1
culinary concoction

governor 556.6
sphere 701.4
10.7

producer 682.18
orderliness 769.3
cooking 11.1

movie studio 684.3
science 883.8
doll 971.8

businessman 707.1
v limit 201.5
v hollow 270.10

dirty
regiment 410.4
dishes

adj dingy 37.10
train 549.13
n silver 8.12

grimy 71.19
punish 585.9
dismissed

stormy 303.17
conform 829.3
adj rejected 357.3

cloudy 304.4
discover
disproved 913.6

cursing 498.8
v see 27.11
display

unfair 630.9
learn 551.6
n appearance 32.2

base 641.12
innovate 814.9
spectacle 32.7

lascivious 645.26
originate 847.12
show 197.4

front 207.1
demonstration 333.2
publication 337.1
show 486.4
v bring out 195.5
manifest 333.5
make public 337.11
show off 486.13
signify 502.17
evidence 912.7

dispute
n resistance 438.1
quarrel 441.5
contention 442.1
argument 890.4
questioning 893.11
v object 318.5
deny 320.4
offer resistance 438.3
quarrel 441.10
contest 442.17
argue 890.12
doubt 910.6

distance
n station 150.2
setting 200.2
remoteness 247.1
length 253.1
extent 286.3
reticence 329.2
v pass 235.10

distant
adj faint 43.14
aloof 132.11
remote 247.8
reticent 329.4
aloof 564.6
far-fetched 738.6
uninquisitive 937.3

distinct
adj plain 30.7
audible 41.15
manifest 333.8
clear 506.10
different 742.6
separate 764.18
particular 827.12

distinction
n glory 233.2
elegance 515.1
nobility 589.2
honour 626.1
mark 642.5
difference 742.1
nicety 742.2
differentiation 742.3
characterization 827.8
comparison 898.1
differentiation 899.3
prominence 952.2

distinguished
adj eminent 233.9
superior 235.12
honoured 626.9
noted 642.14
particular 827.12
characteristic 827.13
notable 952.18

distribution
n disposal 462.2
dispersion 733.1
arrangement 770.1

district
n location 150.1
region 220.1
state 220.5
constituency 590.14

divide
v diverge 162.4
bound 202.7
partition 204.6
count 230.4
measure 286.7
fall out 441.9
sow dissension 441.12
apportion 462.6
segregate 735.6
differentiate 742.5
separate 755.6
analyse 763.6
separate 764.7
partition 764.16
classify 770.9
classify 771.5

bisect 837.4
discriminate 899.4

divided
adj discordant 441.13
alienated 570.11
segregated 735.8
separated 764.19
halved 837.6

dividend
n portion 462.5
royalty 604.7
interest 715.2
surplus 948.5

division
n aberration 162.1
partition 204.4
disagreement 441.2
falling-out 441.4
unit 446.18
navy 446.22
apportionment 462.1
class 588.1
introduction 594.4
party 597.4
branch 597.10
sect 655.2
company 732.3
xenophobia 735.3
differentiation 742.3
part 755.1
analysis 763.1
separation 764.1
classification 771.1
class 771.2
halving 837.1
distinction 899.3

divisions
n contents 187.1

divorce
n separation 547.1
separation 764.1
v separate 547.5
separate 764.7

do
n festival 720.4
v be satisfactory 98.6
go 168.15

average 232.2
behave 306.3
effect 313.6
practise 313.8
impersonate 334.11
clip 341.19
avail 372.15
accomplish 392.4
perform 419.3
play 686.32
engage in 701.9
suit 750.8
perform 847.11
suffice 946.3

do for
v kill 294.10
fix 380.11

do something
v take action 313.5

do to
v inflict 623.5

do with
v use 372.8
treat 372.10
make do 950.4

doctor
n physician 81.4
professional 703.4
wise man 876.1
v practise medicine 81.10
treat 82.11
aid 434.11
adulterate 759.11

document
n writing 528.8
official document 530.5
v specify 728.6
confirm 912.10
cite 912.12

dog
n cock 67.8
beast 640.6
v annoy 87.13
worry 117.4
follow 157.3

pursue 367.8
hunt 367.9
obstruct 967.11

doing
adj happening 793.9
n behaviour 306.1
action 313.1
act 313.3
affair 793.3

domestic
adj residential 217.28

dominant
adj chief 235.14
victorious 396.6
authoritative 402.14
governing 593.16
prevalent 826.11
predominant 849.14
paramount 952.23

don
n teacher 552.1
professor 552.3
v put on 5.32

done
adj well-done 11.7
used up 373.4
completed 392.10
ended 782.7
produced 847.17

door
n entrance 180.5
porch 180.6
outlet 181.7
doorway 278.5

double
adj false 339.21
two 835.5
doubled 836.4
n fold 277.1
image 334.5
the same 740.3
duplicate 747.3
substitute 824.2
fetch 943.2
v intensify 237.5
fold 277.5
repeat 811.7

duplicate 835.4
duplicate 836.3

doubt
n apprehension 118.4
suspicion 144.2
scepticism 674.5
reservation 910.2
uncertainty 926.1
v suspect 144.3
disbelieve 674.10
half believe 910.6
be uncertain 926.5

down
adj dejected 103.22
descending 185.11
lower 260.8
defeated 397.13
adv downward 185.13
n feather 3.11
smoothness 280.3
air 284.2
putty 992.4
v devour 8.21
take 125.7

down on
adj disapproving 495.19

draft
n displacement 261.5
diagram 366.3
recruit 446.14
writing 528.8
condensation 538.1
enlistment 595.6
drawing 690.11
pulling 860.1
v draw off 183.11
outline 366.10
write 528.14
enlist 595.15
portray 690.17

drama
n representation 334.1
tragedy 682.3
programme 984.2

dramatic
adj emotive 84.17

theatrical 486.20
theatrical 682.25
draw
n the same 752.3
tie 798.3
pull 860.2
attraction 862.1
v smoke 80.7
extract 183.9
draw off 183.11
lengthen 253.6
represent 334.8
describe 334.9
acquire 457.8
receive 464.6
hang 585.17
portray 690.17
equal 752.5
pull 860.4
attract 862.4
drawing
adj pulling 860.6
attracting 862.5
n drafting 183.3
representation 334.1
diagram 366.3
draughtsmanship 690.4
line drawing 691.11
graphic arts 691.1
pulling 860.1
drawn
adj haggard 21.8
lengthened 253.8
equal 752.7
dreadful
adj horrid 89.19
terrible 118.29
terrible 955.9
hideous 970.9
dream
n aspiration 91.9
pipe dream 115.4
illusion 931.1
hallucination 931.7
abstraction 940.2
daydream 941.7
humdinger 954.7

doll 971.8
v suppose 906.7
muse 940.9
idealize 941.11
dress
adj clothing 5.34
n clothing 5.1
suit 5.5
gown 5.12
insignia 627.1
v clothe 5.28
groom 70.20
smooth 273.5
equip 370.8
prepare 390.6
ornament 483.7
fertilize 845.6
buff 989.6
cultivate 112.16
dressed
adj clothing 5.34
prepared 390.13
dressing
n clothing 5.1
cooking 11.1
application 77.17
fertilizer 845.4
abrasion 989.2
cultivation 112.12
dried
adj dehydrated 110.7
drink
n potion 8.4
beverage 10.44
nip 79.5
cocktail 79.6
fluid 15.2
v wet one's whistle
8.28
eat 178.10
absorb 178.12
party 649.6
drinking
n lapping 8.3
social drinking 79.3
eating 178.4
drive

n vim 17.2
power 18.1
desire 91.1
acceleration 165.4
ride 168.6
enterprise 315.6
impulse 350.1
urge 360.6
haste 386.1
campaign 443.3
attack 444.1
vigour 525.3
principle 841.9
impulse 857.1
pushing 859.1
machinery 986.3
disk drive 988.5
v set in motion 163.5
go for a drive 168.29
drive 168.29
pilot 175.13
excavate 270.12
hustle 315.11
compel 409.4
push 444.15
work 702.16
impel 857.10
thrust 857.11
push 859.9
obsess 881.21
herd 113.7
driver
n motorist 169.8
man 558.4
operator 844.4
propeller 859.6
driving
adj moving 163.6
rainy 301.5
enterprising 315.19
motivating 360.24
motivating 360.24
compulsory 409.10
attacking 444.23
vigorous 525.10
impelling 857.20
propelling 859.13

obsessive 881.30
n **riding** 168.5

drop
n **drink** 79.5
leakage 181.4
descent 185.1
descent 195.5
trickle 224.7
modicum 234.2
decline 238.2
mite 244.6
sphere 268.1
plunge 352.1
deterioration 378.3
pause 819.3
v **take off** 6.6
weaken 16.8
leak 181.11
descend 185.5
trickle 224.17
decrease 238.6
gravitate 283.11
strike dead 294.15
plunge 352.5
give up 355.7
break the habit 359.3
abdicate 375.4
relinquish 460.2
shoot 859.11
repel 863.3
fell 868.5
let go of 868.7

drove
n **flock** 732.5
v **drive** 113.7

drug
n **anaesthetic** 25.3
medicine 77.4
narcotic drug 77.5
narcotic 78.2
mediator 650.3
v **put to sleep** 22.17
deaden 25.4
dope 82.12
moderate 650.5

drugs
n **contraband** 709.3

drunk
adj **fervent** 84.16
dazed 940.14
n **spree** 79.4

dry
adj **raucous** 49.15
sour 58.5
thirsty 91.25
dull 108.6
tedious 109.9
satirical 493.13
sober 501.3
plain-speaking 517.3
conservative 592.18
unproductive 846.4
unimaginative 942.4
arid 110.5
n **conservative** 592.10
v **preserve** 382.8
desiccate 110.4

duchess
n **noblewoman** 589.6

due
adj. **expected** 121.12
payable 603.8
owed 619.7
entitled to 619.10
just 629.6
accountable 843.6
sufficient 946.5
adv **directly** 152.18
n **debt** 603.1
one's due 619.2
prerogative 622.1

duke
n **nobleman** 589.4

dull
adj **colourless** 35.7
unfeeling 85.9
apathetic 85.13
dry 108.6
tedious 109.9
inert 164.12
blunt 272.3
languid 316.18
plain-speaking 517.3
prosaic 699.3

dim 877.15
unimaginative 942.4
mediocre 960.7
lacklustre 979.17
v **weaken** 16.9
deaden 25.4
discolour 35.5
muffle 42.8
blunt 85.7
relieve 111.5
blunt 272.2
moderate 650.5
deaden 979.10

dust
n **dirt** 71.6
land 223.1
air 284.2
corpse 293.12
refuse 376.3
refuse 376.3
powder 996.5
v **clean** 70.18

duty
n **respect** 146.1
function 372.5
demand 406.1
tax 610.9
obligation 621.1
charge 623.3
task 701.2
function 701.3

dying
adj **unhealthy** 76.19
impatient 126.5
receding 168.5
terminal 293.23
transient 790.7
n **decrease** 238.1
death 293.1
extinguishing 974.2

each
adj **every** 826.14
adv **apiece** 827.19

each other
n **correspondent** 739.3

eager
adj **desiring** 91.20

anxious 92.8
expectant 121.10
impatient 126.5
willing 309.5
active 315.13
enterprising 389.5
prepared 390.13
consenting 426.4

ear
adj skeleton 2.19
n lug 2.7
hearing 39.1
external ear 39.7
bulge 269.2
discrimination 899.1

earl
n nobleman 589.4

earlier
adj lower 260.8
previous 796.4
previous 807.10
adv previously 796.5
formerly 799.11

early
adj anachronistic
795.3
previous 796.4
former 799.8
back 799.10
forehand 807.7
adv previously 796.5
long ago 799.14
beforehand 807.11

earn
v acquire 457.8
be paid 604.18
deserve 619.5

earnings
n acquisition 457.1
gain 457.3
pay 604.4
receipts 607.1

earth
n ground covering
190.3
lair 217.23
land 223.1

corpse 293.12
shelter 964.3
matter 997.2

Earth
n the world 114.10

earth
v insulate 982.27

ease
n rest 20.1
pleasure 86.1
contentment 98.1
comfort 112.1
leisure 387.1
aid 434.1
elegance 515.1
fluency 525.2
informality 562.1
prosperity 965.1
facility 969.1
v relieve 111.5
abate 238.8
lighten 284.4
liberalize 415.12
aid 434.11
calm 650.6
allow for 914.5
facilitate 969.7
soften 992.6

easily
adv comfortably
112.14
slowly 166.12
effortlessly 969.16
softly 992.16

east
adj northern 152.13
adv eastward 152.16
n points of the
compass 152.2

eastern
adj northern 152.13

easy
adj comfortable 112.11
at ease 112.12
good-natured 134.14
slow 166.9
light 284.10

indolent 316.17
leisurely 331.8
elegant 515.4
fluent 525.8
informal 562.3
wanton 645.23
loose 766.4
facile 969.13
soft 992.8
adv cautiously 479.10

eat
v feed 8.19
take 125.7
put away 178.10
consume 373.2
corrode 378.18
party 649.6

eaten
adj corroded 378.35

eating
adj feeding 8.30
n feeding 8.1
drinking 178.4

economic
adj commercial 708.19

economics
n finance 706.1
political economy
708.10

economy
adj cheap 613.7
n parsimony 469.1
thrift 615.1
economic system
708.7

edge
n acrimony 17.5
summit 189.2
border 204.4
advantage 235.2
straight line 263.2
cutting edge 271.1
v border 202.9
side 209.2
go sideways 209.3
sharpen 271.6

edition

n rendering 326.2
   issue 535.5
   score 686.22

editor
n publisher 535.2
   journalist 536.4
   commentator 537.4
   word processor 988.11

editorial
adj journalistic 536.5
n commentary 537.2

educated
adj improved 377.13
   learned 551.16
   informed 883.14
   learned 883.17

education
n cultivation 377.3
   teaching 549.1
   learning 883.4

educational
adj informative 532.17
   educating 549.18

effect
n power 18.1
   aspect 32.3
   meaning 503.1
   event 793.1
   sequel 797.2
   result 842.1
   product 848.1
v do 313.6
   use 369.5
   accomplish 392.4
   execute 422.9
   cause 841.10
   induce 841.11

effective
adj powerful 18.7
   able 18.9
   active 372.19
   vigorous 525.10
   operative 844.9
   influential 849.13
   practical 950.6

effectively
adv powerfully 18.10

   ably 18.11
   usefully 372.24
   eloquently 525.14

effects
n property 456.1
   merchandise 712.1

efficiency
n ability 18.2
   utility 372.3
   skill 398.1

efficient
adj able 18.9
   effective 372.19
   competent 398.22
   economical 615.5
   operative 844.9
   practical 950.6

effort
n act 313.3
   endeavour 388.1
   attempt 388.2
   undertaking 389.1
   exertion 702.1
   expedient 950.2

egg
n ovum 291.8
   bird's egg 291.10
   germ 841.7

eggs
n fried eggs 10.25

either
adj one 834.7
n any 826.4

elderly
adj aged 289.11
   old 804.9

elected
adj chosen 356.25

election
n choice 356.1
   appointment 356.9
   accession 402.11
   general election 590.13
   holy orders 677.5

electoral
adj selective 356.22

electric

adj electrical 982.28
   electric 982.28

electricity
n electrical science
   982.1

elegant
adj graceful 481.6
   ornate 483.11
   grandiose 486.17
   tasteful 514.4
   fluent 525.8
   chic 559.13
   decent 644.5
   beautiful 971.14

element
n particular 728.3
   component 758.2
   cause 841.1
   heater 972.10
   matter 997.2
   chemical element 14.2

elements
n contents 187.1
   substance 725.2
   basics 780.6

eleven
n team 597.7

elite
adj exclusive 480.10
   high-society 559.16
   best 954.16
n nobility 235.5
   elect 356.11
   society 559.6
   upper class 588.2
   aristocracy 589.1
   clique 597.6
   the best 954.8

else
adj other 742.7
adv additionally 239.10
   otherwise 742.10

elsewhere
adj bemused 940.11
adv away 211.15

embarrassed
adj humiliated 128.12

blushing 130.13
bewildered 926.15
confused 940.12
troubled 968.20

embarrassment
n chagrin 87.4
humiliation 89.6
humiliation 128.2
shyness 130.4
bewilderment 926.2
confusion 940.3
impediment 967.6
predicament 968.4

embassy
n house 217.5
foreign office 557.7
commission 595.1
office 716.6

emerge
v show 30.4
appear 32.8
come out 181.8
come forth 354.10

emergency
n hospital room
188.21
crisis 805.4
urgency 952.4
danger 961.1
predicament 968.4

emerging
adj emergent 181.15

emotion
n feeling 84.1
excitement 96.1

emotional
adj emotive 84.15
excitable 96.28
temperamental 933.7

emphasis
n accent 509.9
accent 687.15
metre 698.7

empire
n country 221.1
governance 402.5
sovereignty 402.8

employed
adj busy 315.17
used 372.22
hired 595.17

employees
n staff 558.10

employment
n action 313.1
use 387.1
utilization 372.6
service 558.11
engagement 595.4
occupation 701.1
position 701.5
work 702.4

empty
adj hungry 91.24
vacant 211.12
concave 270.13
false 399.21
vain 376.9
meaningless 505.6
impassive 507.18
without being 724.7
vacant 877.17
ignorant 885.10
thoughtless 888.2
fallacious 891.7
groundless 891.10
trivial 953.26
v run out 181.10
draw off 183.11
evacuate 864.20

enable
v empower 18.5
fit 390.8
authorize 428.11
make possible 921.4

encounter
n meeting 212.4
contest 442.3
impact 857.3
v approach 158.3
confront 207.7
meet 212.11
confront 436.5
experience 793.8

collide 857.12
come across 896.3

encourage
v cheer 100.7
comfort 112.6
hearten 360.20
admonish 407.5
abet 434.14
be useful 434.17
hearten 477.12

encouraging
adj cheering 100.16
comforting 112.13
promising 115.12
provocative 360.26

end
n boundary 202.3
remainder 242.1
death 293.1
motive 360.1
objective 365.2
fate 380.2
completion 392.2
piece 755.3
limit 756.5
end point 782.1
stop 819.2
solution 895.1
fate 919.2
v finish 380.12
perish 380.23
complete 392.6
terminate 782.4
cease 819.4
result 842.4

end up
v arrive 177.6
end 782.4
expire 782.5
result 842.4

ended
adj completed 392.10
terminated 782.7

ending
adj closing 782.9
n completion 392.2
end 782.1

cessation 819.1
stop 819.2

endless
adj wordy 520.11
continuous 774.8
infinite 785.2
perpetual 791.6
continuing 818.7
innumerable 839.10

enemy
adj opposing 436.7
warlike 443.17
n opponent 437.1
foe 570.6

energy
n strength 15.1
vigour 17.1
power 18.1
animation 315.2
industry 315.5
exertion 702.1

engaged
adj busy 315.17
promised 421.7
contracted 422.11
embattled 443.19
participating 461.7
engrossed 938.16

engine
n melting pot 820.10
machinery 986.3

engineer
n planner 366.6
sapper 446.10
professional engineer
703.7
producer 847.7
v plot 366.8
manage 394.9
manoeuvre 400.10
perform 847.11

engineering
n engineer 703.7
production 847.2

enjoy
v savour 54.4
be pleased with 86.12

possess 454.4

enormous
adj large 233.7
huge 243.19
excessive 948.14

enough
adj satisfactory 98.11
sufficient 946.5
adv sufficiently 946.7
n sufficiency 946.1

ensure
v make sure 925.7
protect 963.18

enter
v appear 32.8
go in or into 180.7
insert 182.3
record 530.12
join 597.14
take up 780.9
list 833.8

entered
adj recorded 530.13
listed 833.9

entering
adj arriving 177.8
incoming 180.11

enterprise
n vim 17.2
act 313.3
dynamism 315.6
plan 366.1
endeavour 388.1
undertaking 389.1
daring 477.5
exploit 477.5
company 597.9
occupation 701.1

entertainment
n meal 8.5
pleasure 86.1
party 563.11
performance 682.9
amusement 720.1
entertainment industry
720.12

enthusiasm

n animation 17.4
eagerness 92.1
willingness 309.1
vehemence 525.5
mania 881.10
interest 938.2

enthusiastic
adj energetic 17.12
fervent 84.16
enthused 92.10
willing 309.5
vehement 525.12
interested 938.15

entire
adj whole 754.9
complete 756.8
unqualified 915.1
sound 957.6

entirely
adv wholly 754.12
completely 756.13
solely 834.14
perfectly 957.9

entitled
adj authorized 428.16
justified 619.9

entitled to
adj due 619.10

entrance
n in 178.3
entry 180.1
entry 180.5
introduction 182.1
portal 188.16
intrusion 205.1
channel 225.1
door 278.5
v put to sleep 22.17
fascinate 362.7
cast a spell 670.7

entry
n in 178.3
entrance 180.1
entrance 180.5
portal 188.16
door 278.5
memorandum 530.4

registration 530.11
item 608.5
environment
  n surroundings 200.1
  surrounding 200.4
  circumstances 728.2
environmental
  adj ecological 200.8
  surrounding 728.8
equal
  adj parallel 194.5
  symmetrical 250.4
  proportionate 462.13
  coinciding 740.8
  uniform 743.5
  like 752.7
  interchangeable 825.4
  n match 752.4
  substitute 824.2
  v parallel 194.3
  match 752.5
  excel 954.11
equality
  n symmetry 250.1
  justice 629.1
  sameness 740.1
  parity 752.1
equally
  adv justly 629.9
  identically 740.9
  correspondingly 752.10
equipment
  n provision 370.1
  munitions 370.4
  preparation 390.1
  fitting 390.2
  talent 398.4
equivalent
  adj reciprocal 739.9
  coinciding 740.8
  analogous 746.7
  agreeing 750.9
  tantamount 752.8
  substitute 824.7
  interchangeable 825.4
  n the same 740.3
  likeness 746.3

equal 752.4
substitute 824.2
era
  n epoch 786.5
error
  n misinterpretation
  327.1
  miss 395.4
  bungle 399.5
  iniquity 634.3
  misdeed 635.2
  heresy 667.2
  misjudgment 903.1
  untruth 930.1
escape
  n departure 179.1
  outlet 181.7
  absence 211.4
  avoidance 353.1
  getaway 369.1
  v absent oneself 211.7
  make or effect one's
  escape 354.6
  extricate oneself 416.8
escaped
  adj loose 354.11
especially
  adv chiefly 235.17
  particularly 827.15
essential
  adj basic 190.8
  fundamental 729.6
  simple 760.5
  requisite 918.11
  vital 952.22
  n essence 729.1
  requirement 918.2
  important thing 952.5
essentially
  adv substantially 725.8
  fundamentally 729.8
  on the whole 754.13
establish
  v fix 150.16
  accustom 358.8
  legalize 653.8
  inaugurate 780.11

fix 817.9
cause 841.10
found 847.10
prove 912.9
make sure 925.7
established
  adj located 150.18
  customary 358.12
  confirmed 358.17
  real 723.11
  traditional 804.11
  stabilized 817.13
  proved 912.17
  assured 925.14
  true 928.13
establishment
  n foundation 150.7
  nobility 235.5
  structure 252.2
  organization 597.8
  market 713.1
  workplace 716.1
  hierarchy 771.4
  beginning 780.1
  fixture 817.2
  foundation 847.4
  proof 912.3
estate
  n mansion 217.6
  rank 231.2
  interest 456.4
  class 588.1
  state 727.1
ethnic
  adj racial 540.7
Europe
  n Northern
  Hemisphere 220.6
eve
  n evening 300.2
even
  adj horizontal 192.7
  parallel 194.5
  symmetrical 250.4
  straight 263.6
  smooth 273.9
  neutral 452.6

uniform 743.5
equal 752.7
seasonal 812.7
interchangeable 825.4
exact 928.17
adv exactly 928.21
v level 192.6
balance 250.3
smooth 273.5
equate 752.6

even more
adv additionally 239.10

evening
adj twilight 300.8
n balancing 250.2
eve 300.2

event
n game 720.8
circumstance 728.1
eventuality 793.1
occurrence 793.2

eventually
adv finally 782.11
ultimately 793.12
in time 801.10

ever
adv forever 791.11
constantly 809.7
at all 921.9

ever since
adv since 799.15

every
adj all 826.14

every day
adv periodically 812.10

everybody
n the people 587.1
all 826.3

everyday
adj customary 358.12
simple 484.6
vernacular 508.12
frequent 809.4
usual 831.7

everyone
n the people 587.1
all 826.3

everything
n all 754.3
all 826.3

everywhere
adj omnipresent 210.13
adv here 149.10
around 152.20
universally 826.17
universally 114.21

evidence
n manifestation 333.1
clue 502.9
information 532.1
testimony 579.8
proof 912.1
v show 912.7

evident
adj visible 30.6
distinct 30.7
manifest 333.8

evil
adj ominous 124.16
wrong 618.3
wicked 634.15
bad 955.7
adv badly 955.12
n vice 634.1
iniquity 634.3
misdeed 635.2
badness 955.1
bad 955.3
bane 956.1
trouble 968.3

exact
adj meticulous 324.12
elegant 514.4
punctilious 561.10
detailed 728.9
discriminating 899.7
precise 928.17
v demand 406.5
oblige 409.5
wrest 465.22
charge 610.12
impose 623.4

require 918.8

exactly
adv meticulously 324.16
punctually 807.14
particularly 827.15
precisely 928.21

examination
n scrutiny 27.6
diagnosis 82.3
discussion 523.6
piece 537.1
trial 579.5
argument 890.4
exam 893.2
inspection 893.3
questioning 893.11

examine
v scrutinize 27.13
discuss 523.10
study 551.12
interrogate 893.19
inspect 893.22

example
n sample 53.4
representative 334.7
warning 384.1
representative 748.2
citation 912.5

excellent
adj superior 235.12
skilful 398.20
tasteful 481.5
good 954.12

except
adj excluding 735.10
v excise 241.9
reject 357.2
exempt 415.13

exception
n marvel 113.2
objection 318.2
rejection 357.1
stipulation 465.2
exemption 415.8
criticism 495.4
exclusion 735.1

oddity 832.5
qualification 914.1

excess
adj superfluous 948.15
n surplus 242.4
exaggeration 340.1
exorbitance 612.4
self-indulgence 649.1
overindulgence 865.1
extravagance 948.1

excessive
adj exaggerated 340.3
overpriced 612.12
inappropriate 788.7
indulgent 649.7
inordinate 948.14

exchange
n communication
328.1
telephone number
332.6
banter 475.1
retaliation 491.1
conversation 523.1
transfer 609.1
trade 708.2
stock exchange 714.4
changing 816.3
substitution 824.1
substitute 824.2
interchange 825.1
v transfer 609.3
trade 708.14
change 814.7
change 816.5
substitute 824.4
interchange 825.3

exchange rate
n foreign money 705.6

excited
adj fervent 84.16
affected 84.21
impassioned 96.20
impatient 126.5
agitated 872.13
interested 938.15

excitement

n passion 84.2
emotion 96.1
arousal 96.11
impatience 126.1
incitement 360.4
agitation 872.1
ardour 971.24

exciting
adj thrilling 96.30
provocative 360.26
alluring 362.8
vehement 525.12
interesting 938.18

exclusive
adj contemptuous
148.8
limiting 201.9
closed 279.8
selective 356.22
prohibitive 429.6
selective 480.10
cliquish 597.18
excluding 735.9
one 834.7
n news item 533.3

excuse
n pardon 139.2
pretext 361.1
alibi 581.3
apology 638.2
reason 841.2
v forgive 139.3
exempt 415.13
explain 581.10
acquit 582.4

executive
adj administrative
554.14
administrative 593.17
n officer 555.3
governor 556.6
operator 844.4

exercise
n motion 75.2
action 313.1
use 372.1
training 549.3

lesson 549.7
task 701.2
practice 702.6
operation 844.1
v work out 75.3
practise 313.8
use 372.8
train 549.13
exert 702.8

exhibition
n spectacle 32.7
display 333.2
display 486.4

exile
n homeless person
151.4
migrant 169.5
emigration 181.6
outcast 567.3
elimination 735.2
alien 736.2
banishment 864.4
v emigrate 181.13
ostracize 567.5
eliminate 735.5
banish 864.15

exist
v be present 210.6
live 292.5
be 723.5
endure 789.5

existence
n presence 210.1
life 292.1
being 723.1

existing
adj in existence 723.10
present 800.2

exotic
adj colourful 34.17
distant 247.8
alluring 362.8
extraneous 736.4
unrelated 738.4

expansion
n space 149.1
increase 237.1

extension 245.1
exaggeration 340.1
amplification 520.6
business cycle 708.9
dispersion 733.1
evolution 823.1

expect
v hope 115.6
be expectant 121.5
come 801.6
suppose 906.7
think 908.11

expect to
v plan on 121.9

expectations
n prospects 121.4
entitlement 619.1

expected
adj anticipated 121.12

expecting
adj pregnant 69.18
expectant 121.10

expenditure
n use 372.1
consumption 373.1
waste 458.2
spending 606.1
price 610.1

expense
n loss 458.1
expenditure 606.1
price 610.1

expensive
adj dear 612.11

experience
n sensation 24.1
practice 398.9
event 793.2
knowledge 883.1
v sense 24.6
feel 84.10
have 793.8

experienced
adj accustomed 358.14
practised 398.26

experiences
n history 697.1

experiment
n attempt 388.2
experimentation 897.1
v research 897.8

expert
adj skilful 398.20
specialized 828.5
perfected 957.8
n artist 398.11
adviser 407.3
connoisseur 481.4
specialist 828.3
scientist 883.9

explain
v expound 326.8
make clear 506.6
expound 549.16
excuse 581.10
solve 895.2
facilitate 969.7

explanation
n unfolding 326.4
definition 503.3
reason 841.2
solution 895.1
theory 906.1
theory 906.2

explosion
n detonation 47.3
outburst 96.9
outburst 143.9
heightening 237.2
discharge 651.7
disproving 913.1

export
adv transfer 167.1
v transfer 167.6
send 167.9
send abroad 181.14

exposed
adj uncovered 6.12
visible 30.6
airy 302.10
windblown 303.18
open 333.10
liable 852.5
disproved 913.6

open 961.15

exposure
n removal 6.1
visibility 30.1
distinctness 30.2
appearance 32.1
display 333.2
disclosure 336.1
publicity 337.4
repute 642.1
time exposure 692.7
liability 852.2
discovery 896.1
disproving 913.1
liability 961.3

express
adj fast 165.12
manifest 333.8
particular 827.12
unqualified 915.1
exact 928.17
n train 170.12
v affirm 319.5
manifest 333.5
describe 334.9
signify 502.17
say 509.16
phrase 514.3
evidence 912.7

expressed
adj phrased 514.4

expression
n manifestation 333.1
indication 502.3
remark 509.3
word 511.1
diction 514.1
execution 686.24

extend
v reach 149.6
increase 237.4
enlarge 245.4
enlarge 245.5
spread 245.6
reach out 247.5
be long 253.5
lengthen 253.6

broaden 255.4
straighten 263.5
offer 424.4
give 463.12
protract 520.8
endure 789.5
prolong 789.8
postpone 808.9
sustain 818.4
generalize 826.8
stretch 993.4

extended
adj spacious 149.8
increased 237.7
expanded 245.10
lengthened 253.8
wordy 520.11
protracted 789.10

extension
n space 149.1
increase 237.1
adjunct 240.1
wing 240.3
expansion 245.1
length 253.1
lengthening 253.4
meaning 503.1
sequence 777.1
continuation 789.2
continuance 818.1
stretching 993.2

extensive
adj spacious 149.8
large 233.7
voluminous 243.16
expansive 245.9
long 253.7
broad 255.6
broad 826.12

extent
n space 149.1
capacity 149.5
quantity 230.1
degree 231.1
size 243.1
distance 247.1
length 253.1

breadth 255.1
quantity 286.3

external
adj exterior 197.6
outward 730.2
extraneous 736.4

extra
adj additional 239.9
unused 375.10
unnecessary 730.3
occasional 810.3
surplus 948.16
adv additionally 239.10
n bonus 240.4
newspaper 536.2
movie studio 684.3
supporting actor or
actress 685.8
accessory 730.1
surplus 948.5

extraordinary
adj wonderful 113.6
unexpected 122.9
remarkable 233.10
particular 827.12
exceptional 832.14
notable 952.18

extreme
adj exquisite 24.13
bordering 202.10
farthest 247.12
rebellious 312.10
exaggerated 340.3
indulgent 649.7
final 782.10
fanatic 881.28
excessive 948.14
n exaggeration 340.1
limit 756.5
extremity 782.2

extremely
adv somewhat 231.7

eye
adj skeleton 2.19
visual 27.19
n visual organ 2.6
orb 27.9

discrimination 899.1
opinion 908.6
outlook 933.2
v look 27.12
scrutinize 27.13
gaze 27.14
witness 873.5

fabric
n material 4.1
substance 187.4
structure 252.1
structure 252.2
frame 252.3
weaving 717.1
substance 725.2

face
n looks 32.4
pride 127.1
cheek 133.3
precipice 191.3
exterior 197.2
front 207.1
countenance 207.4
sham 339.2
type 529.6
prestige 642.4
v expect 121.5
oppose 206.4
confront 207.7
veneer 281.22
plaster 281.24
confront 436.5
defy 439.3
brave 477.9
be imminent 802.2

faced
adj layered 282.5

facilities
n accommodation
370.3
equipment 370.4

facing
adj opposite 206.5
fronting 207.10
adv forward 207.12
n blanket 281.11

fact

n the case 723.3
particular 728.3
event 793.2
evidence 912.1
certainty 925.1
truth 928.1

factor
n steward 555.4
particular 728.3
component 758.2
cause 841.1

factory
n plant 716.2

facts
n information 532.1
knowledge 883.1
evidence 912.1

fail
v weaken 16.8
weaken 76.16
be inferior 236.4
neglect 325.6
decline 378.15
be unsuccessful 395.8
go bankrupt 605.7
be unfaithful 625.12
dramatize 682.20
fall short 866.2
be insufficient 947.8

failed
adj useless 376.5
unsuccessful 395.15

failing
adj languishing 16.18
unhealthy 76.19
deteriorating 378.36
unsuccessful 395.15
incomplete 757.4
insufficient 947.9
n vice 634.2
fault 958.2

failure
n ineffectiveness 19.3
disappointment 123.1
inadequacy 236.3
neglect 325.1
deterioration 378.3

omission 393.1
no go 395.1
bankrupt 395.7
defeat 397.1
indifference 420.1
insolvency 605.3
bankrupt 605.4
stage show 682.2
shortcoming 866.1
mistake 930.3
memory loss 945.2
fault 958.2

fair
adj light 35.9
light 36.6
bright 88.10
favourable 124.17
courteous 489.11
rightful 619.8
honest 624.9
just 629.6
unprejudiced 934.12
good 954.12
tolerable 954.19
mediocre 960.7
good-looking 971.15
warm 971.43
fine 110.6
n market 713.2
festival 720.4
opportunity 805.2

fairly
adv somewhat 231.7
moderately 234.10
justly 629.9
tolerably 954.23
moderately 960.11

faith
n zeal 92.2
hope 115.1
obedience 311.1
observance 419.1
school 597.5
fidelity 624.6
prudence 633.3
religion 655.1
piety 671.1

principle 841.9
belief 908.1
religion 908.3
confidence 925.4

fall
n false hair 3.9
descent 185.1
tumble 185.3
descent 195.5
waterfall 224.11
decline 238.2
autumn 298.4
plunge 352.1
deterioration 378.3
relapse 379.1
downfall 380.3
collapse 395.3
defeat 397.1
overthrow 868.2
v descend 185.5
tumble 185.8
hang 193.6
decrease 238.6
rain 301.4
plunge 352.5
decline 378.15
relapse 379.2
tumble 380.22
fall down 395.10
lose 397.11
cheapen 613.6
go wrong 634.9
come to grief 966.10

fall in
v collapse 246.8
obey 311.2

fallen
adj ruined 380.25
defeated 397.13
unclean 634.12
carnal 643.6
scarlet 645.25
impious 675.6
godless 674.14
depressed 868.12

falling
adj descending 185.11

suspended 193.9
downhill 195.15
deteriorating 378.36

falls
n waterfall 224.11

false
adj untrue 339.16
double 339.21
deceptive 341.21
deceitful 341.22
unfaithful 625.20
illegitimate 654.6
sanctimonious 672.4
erroneous 930.14
illusory 931.9

fame
n glory 233.2
publicity 337.4
repute 642.1
prominence 952.2

familiar
adj trite 108.9
insolent 133.7
customary 358.12
vernacular 508.12
informal 562.3
intimate 563.23
intimate 568.18
usual 831.7
well-known 883.22
n friend 569.1

family
adj lineal 541.18
n nomenclature 512.1
kindred 540.2
race 540.4
brood 540.5
lineage 541.4
posterity 542.1
community 597.2
sequel 797.2

famous
adj eminent 233.9
distinguished 642.14

fan
n buff 92.5
fork 162.3

ventilator 302.8
ventilator 303.13
supporter 596.8
specialist 828.3
cooler 976.2
v air 302.9
incite 360.16

fancy
adj edible 8.32
skilful 398.20
ornate 483.11
ostentatious 486.14
grandiose 486.17
ornate 526.8
expensive 612.11
overpriced 612.12
n inclination 91.3
love 95.1
will 308.1
whim 349.1
preference 356.5
idea 887.1
imagination 931.3
imagination 941.1
whim 941.4
v desire 91.13
love 95.18
suppose 906.7
think 908.11
imagine 941.9

fans
n audience 873.2

fantastic
adj wonderful 113.6
remarkable 233.10
fabricated 339.19
unreal 724.8
fanciful 832.12
absurd 878.9
illusory 931.9
fanciful 941.14

fantasy
n alienation 83.13
desire 91.1
whim 349.1
miracle 832.8
phantom 931.4

abstraction 940.2
imagination 941.1
whim 941.4

far
adj distant 247.8
adv by far 233.16
far off 247.15

farm
adj rustic 222.4
agricultural 112.19
n house 217.5
location 112.7
stock farm 113.4
v rent out 595.14
grow 112.15
raise 113.5

farmer
n peasant 587.6
peasant 112.4

farming
adj agricultural 112.19
n agriculture 112.1

fascinating
adj delightful 88.6
wonderful 113.6
alluring 362.8
bewitching 670.11
absorbing 938.19

fashion
n clothing 5.1
aspect 32.3
form 248.1
structure 252.1
custom 358.1
manner 369.1
style 514.2
style 559.1
mode 727.3
v form 248.6
produce 847.8

fashionable
adj in fashion 559.11
modern 803.13

fashioned
adj formative 248.8
made 847.18

fast

adj swift 165.12
close 279.10
devoted 568.20
fastened 762.13
stable 817.12
stuck 817.16
reliable 925.12
adv swiftly 165.13
securely 762.17
n starvation diet 500.2
holy day 680.8
v not eat 500.4

fat
adj stout 243.17
distended 245.13
stubby 254.8
thick 255.7
heavy 283.12
gainful 457.16
plentiful 946.6
n fatty acid 7.6
duplication 948.4
oil 11.1

fate
n end 380.2
portion 462.5
end 782.1
destiny 801.2
inevitability 918.6
fatality 919.2
chance 927.1
v allot 462.9
necessitate 919.4

father
n senior 290.4
brother 540.3
paternal ancestor
541.9
priest 678.3
author 841.4
producer 891.7
v generate 69.8
cause 841.10
trace to 843.5

fault
n crack 213.2
vice 634.2

misdeed 635.2
error 930.1
mistake 930.3
defect 958.2
blemish 959.1
v complain 106.15
deprecate 495.10

favour
n inclination 91.3
kindness 134.7
pity 136.1
respect 146.1
superiority 249.1
preference 356.5
patronage 434.4
approval 494.1
good terms 568.3
privilege 622.2
esteem 642.3
influence 849.1
interest 849.2
memento 944.6
v desire 91.13
be kind 134.9
respect 146.4
prefer 356.16
improve 377.9
indulge 412.5
aid 434.11
abet 434.14
be useful 434.17
oblige 434.19
approve 494.7
prefer 630.7
do good 954.10

favoured
adj preferable 356.24
exempt 415.27
approved 494.17
fortunate 965.14

favourite
adj approved 494.17
n darling 95.15

fax
n facsimile 332.9

fear
n anxiety 117.1

fright 118.1
nervousness 119.1
weak will 347.4
cowardice 476.1
v be afraid 118.10
hesitate 347.7

feature
n aspect 32.3
looks 32.4
piece 537.1
motion pictures 684.1
component 758.2
characteristic 827.4
special 828.2
highlight 952.6
v manifest 333.5
dramatize 682.20
specify 827.11
specialize 828.4
mention 938.10
emphasize 952.13
headline 952.14

featured
adj conspicuous
333.12
specialized 828.5

features
n looks 32.4
outline 202.2
face 207.4
appearance 248.3

federal
adj governmental
593.15
combining 767.7

federation
n affiliation 435.2
federal government
593.4
association 597.1
combination 767.1

fee
n stipend 604.5
dues 610.6

feed
n fodder 10.4
v nourish 7.13

dine 8.17
eat 8.19
gratify 86.7
encourage 360.20
provision 370.9
foster 434.16
fertilize 845.6
ignite 972.22
fuel 973.7
raise 113.5
tend 113.6
feeding
adj eating 8.30
n nutrition 7.1
eating 8.1
feel
n touch 64.1
ambience 200.3
texture 280.1
knack 398.6
discrimination 899.1
v sense 24.6
appear 32.10
touch 64.6
feel deeply 84.10
contact 212.10
experience 793.8
sense 889.4
suppose 906.7
feeling
adj emotional 84.15
intuitive 889.5
examining 893.35
n sensation 24.1
touch 64.1
touching 64.2
emotion 84.1
pity 136.1
ambience 200.3
hunch 889.3
discrimination 899.1
suggestion 906.5
opinion 908.6
attitude 933.1
mood 933.4
feelings
n feeling 84.1

mood 933.4
fell
adj terrible 118.29
n fur 4.2
skin 281.3
v level 192.6
strike dead 294.15
raze 380.19
conquer 397.9
shoot 859.11
drop 868.5
fellow
adj cooperative 435.5
accompanying 731.8
n guy 67.5
boy 288.5
person 297.3
image 334.5
teacher 552.1
professor 552.3
friend 569.1
companion 569.3
associate 596.1
member 597.11
accompanist 731.3
likeness 746.3
equal 752.4
felt
n material 4.1
female
adj feminine 68.11
n she 68.4
feminist
n suffragette 622.5
fence
n wall 203.4
fortification 445.4
receiver 709.5
barrier 967.5
v wall 203.7
contend 442.10
fortify 445.9
quibble 891.6
festival
n festivity 720.4
fever
n feverishness 76.7

anaemia 76.9
fever pitch 96.7
agitation 872.1
frenzy 881.6
heat 971.23
few
adj insignificant 234.6
least 236.8
not many 840.4
fewer
adj less 840.6
fibre
n nutrient 7.2
filament 257.1
organic matter 291.1
nature 729.2
fiction
n fabrication 339.7
lie 339.8
writing 528.8
narrative 700.1
invention 941.3
whim 941.4
field
n space 149.1
setting 200.2
enclosure 203.3
sphere 220.2
plot 220.4
arena 448.1
arena 448.1
study 549.8
playground 720.10
speciality 828.1
science 883.8
tract 112.8
fierce
adj acrimonious 17.13
frenzied 96.25
passionate 96.29
cruel 135.24
warlike 443.17
violent 651.15
savage 651.19
fifteen
n team 597.7
fifth

n interval 687.11
gear 986.5

fight
n quarrel 441.5
contest 442.3
battle 442.4
ferocity 443.10
struggle 702.3
v contend against
436.4
quarrel 441.10
contend 442.10
war 443.12
struggle 702.11

fighter
n military aircraft
172.6
combatant 461.1

fighting
adj contending 442.18
warlike 443.17
n contention 442.1
contention 442.1
boxing 442.6
war 443.1

figure
n aspect 32.3
apparition 32.5
outline 202.2
form 248.1
form 248.4
doll 334.6
diagram 366.3
motif 483.6
figure of speech 518.1
price 610.1
passage 686.19
characteristic 827.4
phantom 931.4
personage 952.7
body 997.3
v form 248.6
mirror 334.10
personify 518.2
be reasonable 890.13
estimate 901.9

file

n document 530.5
notice board 530.8
catalogue 833.3
data 988.14
v march 168.26
sharpen 271.6
grind 273.8
store 371.9
record 530.12
classify 771.5
parade 774.7
list 833.8
abrade 989.5

fill
n full measure 756.3
v load 150.15
pack 187.6
top 189.7
pervade 210.7
stop 279.6
provide 370.7
observe 419.2
possess 454.4
include 734.3
charge 756.7
reiterate 811.8
swarm 948.8
satisfy 949.3

filled
adj full 756.10

filled with
adj permeated 210.15

filling
adj completing 756.12
satisfying 949.6
n lining 187.3
extra 240.4
redundancy 811.3
fat 948.4

film
n blanket 281.11
sheet 282.2
fog 304.2
notice board 530.8
motion pictures 684.1
negative 692.8
v blur 31.4

cover 281.18
shoot 684.7
photograph 692.10

films
n motion pictures
684.1

final
adj departing 179.15
completing 392.8
mandatory 405.10
terminal 782.10
eventual 793.11
resultant 842.6
evidential 912.14
unqualified 915.1
n examination 893.2

finally
adv ultimately 782.11
eventually 793.12
in consequence 842.7

finance
n finances 706.1
v support 434.12
subsidize 463.19
pay for 604.17
back 706.14

financial
adj monetary 705.22

find
n finding 457.6
discovery 896.1
good thing 954.5
v arrive 177.6
provide 370.7
discover 896.2
conclude 901.10
decide 901.11
pass judgment 901.13

find out
v learn 551.6
solve 895.2
discover 896.2
make sure 925.7

finding
n find 457.6
solution 895.1
discovery 896.1

fine
verdict 901.5

fine
adj edible 8.32
healthy 74.8
pleasant 88.5
tiny 244.10
thin 256.13
sharp 271.7
smooth 280.7
rare 285.4
meticulous 324.12
nice 480.8
elegant 481.6
ornate 483.11
grandiose 486.17
thin 726.5
discriminating 899.7
exact 928.17
good 954.12
exquisite 971.16
powdery 996.10
fair 110.6
adv excellently 954.21
n damages 584.3
v award damages 584.5

finger
n digit 64.5
v touch 64.6
tell on 532.12

fingers
n clutches 459.4

finish
n boundary 202.3
symmetry 250.1
polish 273.2
texture 280.1
completion 392.2
accomplishment 398.8
good breeding 489.4
end 782.1
v polish 273.7
consume 373.2
perfect 377.11
end 380.12
complete 392.6
end 782.4

finished
adj symmetrical 250.4
sleek 273.10
used up 373.4
screwed up 378.25
done for 380.26
completed 392.10
skilled 398.24
elegant 515.4
no more 724.9
ended 782.7
past 799.6
perfected 957.8

finishing
adj completing 392.8
ending 782.9
n consumption 373.1
revision 377.4
completion 392.2
end 782.1

fire
n vim 17.2
passion 84.2
fever pitch 96.7
inspiration 360.9
gunfire 444.7
vehemence 525.5
blaze 971.34
light source 978.1
matter 997.2
v animate 17.9
excite 96.12
incite 360.16
kindle 360.17
inspire 360.19
explode 651.13
pot 719.4
shoot 859.11
sack 864.18
heat 972.17
dry 110.4

fired
adj inspired 360.30
ceramic 719.5

firm
adj stout 15.17

close 279.10
staunch 344.11
inflexible 346.8
rigorous 410.6
faithful 624.16
sturdy 725.7
crowded 732.22
fast 762.13
permanent 815.6
stable 817.12
immovable 817.15
reliable 925.12
trouble-free 962.5
dense 990.11
rigid 991.10
n company 597.9
workplace 716.1
v stabilize 817.7
harden 991.6

firmly
adv strongly 15.22
resolutely 344.15
stiffly 346.14
rigorously 410.8
securely 762.17
densely 990.14

first
adj leading 156.3
front 207.9
front 207.9
chief 235.14
preceding 776.4
beginning 818.15
foremost 780.14
previous 796.4
adv before 207.11
preferably 356.27
firstly 780.15
n gear 986.5

first place
n supremacy 235.3

first-class
adj superlative 235.13
first-rate 954.17

fish
n sole 10.23
v go fishing 367.10

fishing
adj pursuing 367.11
n fishery 367.3

fit
adj healthy 74.8
hearty 74.12
eligible 356.23
fitted 390.14
competent 398.22
right 617.3
rightful 619.8
just 629.6
apt 750.10
timely 805.8
sufficient 946.5
expedient 950.5
n seizure 76.6
outburst 96.9
bustle 315.4
fitting 390.2
spasm 872.6
frenzy 881.6
v outfit 5.30
have place 150.9
equip 370.8
condition 390.8
interact 739.5
harmonize 750.7
suit 750.8
equate 752.6
change 814.7
conform 829.3
come in handy 950.3

fitness
n hygiene 72.2
health 74.1
condition 75.1
eligibility 356.10
readiness 390.4
decorum 481.7
suitability 750.5
timeliness 805.1
expedience or
expediency 950.1

fitted
adj eligible 356.23
provided 370.13

adapted 390.14
competent 398.22
apt 750.10

fitting
adj useful 372.16
decorous 481.7
appropriate 515.5
right 617.3
apt 750.10
timely 805.8
expedient 950.5
n fit 390.2
change 814.1

fixed
adj located 150.18
motionless 164.11
circumscribed 201.6
firm 344.11
confirmed 358.17
clobbered 397.14
fast 762.13
in order 769.7
arranged 770.12
traditional 804.11
permanent 815.6
fastened 817.14
stuck 817.16
particular 827.12
proved 912.17
conditional 914.8
unqualified 915.1
rigged 920.7
assured 925.14
gripped 938.17

flag
n pavement 368.6
banner 627.5
v weaken 16.8
fatigue 21.4
burn out 21.5
fail 76.16
dawdle 166.7
floor 281.21
languish 378.16
signal 502.22

flash
n glance 27.4

lightning 165.5
bulletin 533.5
instant 792.3
flare 971.35
blaze 977.6
v burst forth 32.9
shine 977.22

flat
adj colourless 35.7
discordant 52.4
dull 108.6
spatial 149.7
inert 164.12
horizontal 192.7
prostrate 192.8
deflated 246.11
low 260.7
straight 263.6
smooth 273.9
vain 376.9
prosaic 699.3
uniform 743.5
unqualified 915.1
lacklustre 979.17
adv horizontally 192.9
n horizontal 192.7
apartment 217.12
smooth 273.3
note 687.8

flavour
n taste 53.1
characteristic 827.4
v season 54.6
imbue 759.10

fled
adj escaped 354.11

fleet
adj agile 398.21
brief 790.8
n ships 171.8
navy 446.22
company 732.3
v flit 790.6

flesh
n sexuality 66.2
skin 281.3
organic matter 291.1

mankind 297.1
kindred 540.2
body 997.3

flight
  n course 163.2
  velocity 165.1
  aviation 175.1
  trip 175.3
  departure 179.1
  exit 353.4
  escape 354.1
  air force 446.24
  arrow 447.6

float
  n raft 171.9
  v drift 173.21
  swim 173.23
  take off 184.9
  buoy 284.6
  rise 284.7
  issue 715.4
  inaugurate 780.11
  start 859.12
  flood 19.12

floor
  n ground covering 190.3
  bed 190.4
  horizontal 192.3
  boundary 202.3
  layer 282.1
  layer 282.1
  arena 448.1
  v carpet 281.21
  overcome 397.6
  fell 868.5
  stump 926.8

flour
  n cereal 10.31
  powder 996.5

flow
  n excretion 12.1
  course 163.2
  flux 224.4
  tide 224.13
  trend 851.2
  liquidity 15.1

  v move 163.4
  travel 168.14
  glide 168.31
  run out 181.10
  hang 193.6
  stream 224.15
  elapse 783.3

flower
  n posy 296.20
  essence 729.1
  the best 954.8
  v mature 289.7
  be in flower 296.27
  evolve 823.4
  thrive 965.8

flown
  adj escaped 354.11

fly
  n lap 281.4
  v disappear 33.2
  speed 165.6
  glide 168.31
  be airborne 175.12
  pilot 175.13
  run off or away 179.11
  take off 184.9
  flee 353.10
  be annihilated 724.5
  elapse 783.3
  flit 790.6

flying
  adj vanishing 33.3
  flowing 163.7
  fast 165.12
  airborne 175.21
  hasty 386.5
  transient 790.7
  n aviation 175.1

focus
  n convergence 160.1
  focal point 199.2
  centralization 199.6
  essence 729.1
  centre 862.2
  v concentrate 199.8

folk
  adj traditional 804.11

  n population 216.1
  race 540.4
  family 540.5
  the people 587.1

follow
  v look 27.12
  come after 157.3
  line up 194.4
  come last 208.8
  be inferior 236.4
  practise 313.8
  emulate 321.7
  pursue 367.8
  observe 419.2
  understand 506.7
  resemble 746.5
  exemplify 748.7
  be consistent 765.7
  succeed 777.2
  succeed 779.5
  succeed 797.3
  specialize 828.4
  conform 829.3
  result 842.4
  seek 893.28
  trace 893.33
  prove 912.9

following
  adj trailing 157.5
  pursuing 367.11
  similar 746.6
  succeeding 777.3
  subsequent 797.4
  resultant 842.6
  n trailing 157.1
  follower 157.2
  imitation 321.1
  pursuit 367.1
  attendance 731.5
  succession 797.1
  surveillance 893.8

food
  n nutrient 7.2
  foodstuff 10.1

fool
  n dupe 343.1
  laughing stock 493.7

buffoon 685.8
clown 879.1
ignoramus 885.7
v make a fool of
341.15
be foolish 878.5
trifle 953.12

foot
n member 2.4
base 190.2
extremity 190.5
metre 698.7
v stroll 168.24

for example
adv incidentally 805.12
to illustrate 912.20

for instance
adv to illustrate 912.20

for that
adv hence 843.7

for which
adv why 843.8

force
n strength 15.1
energy 17.1
power 18.1
quantity 230.1
enterprise 315.6
brute force 409.2
meaning 503.1
vigour 525.3
staff 558.10
violence 651.1
impact 842.2
influence 849.1
impulse 857.1
validity 928.6
v motivate 360.11
compel 409.4
administer 623.6
thrust 857.11
cultivate 112.16

forced
adj unwilling 310.5
stiff 516.3
laborious 702.18
far-fetched 738.6

involuntary 918.12

forces
n work force 18.4
army 446.19

ford
n shoal 262.2
passageway 368.3
v pass 865.7

forecast
adj predicted 917.8
n foresight 916.1
prediction 917.1
v predict 917.4

foreign
adj alien 197.8
external 730.2
extraneous 736.4
unrelated 738.4

foreign office
n diplomatic service
557.7

foreign policy
n foreign affairs 590.5

forest
adj woodland 296.30
n woodland 296.11
v plant 112.17

forever
adv for keeps 459.9
infinitely 785.3
ever 791.11
permanently 815.8
n infinity 785.1
an eternity 791.2

forget
v write off 139.5
dismiss 939.4
not remember 945.4

forgotten
adj forgiven 139.7
unrecognized 142.4
past 799.6
unremembered 945.7

form
n aspect 32.3
apparition 32.5
lair 217.23

shape 248.1
figure 248.4
structure 252.1
rule 358.4
manner 369.1
rule 404.2
motif 483.6
class 553.10
formality 561.1
good condition 727.2
mode 727.3
mould 748.6
arrangement 770.1
kind 771.3
rule 831.4
phantom 931.4
spectre 943.1
body 997.3
v formalize 248.6
take form 248.7
construct 252.4
train 549.13
compose 758.3
order 769.4
take shape 769.5
produce 847.8
establish 847.10

formal
adj formative 248.8
structural 252.5
pompous 486.18
gallant 489.12
stiff 516.3
formalistic 561.7
orderly 769.6

formation
n form 248.1
forming 248.5
structure 252.3
word form 511.4
composition 758.1
order 769.1
arrangement 770.1
production 847.2
establishment 847.4

formed
adj formative 248.8

structural 252.5
made 847.18

former
  adj foregoing 776.5
  previous 796.4
  past 799.8

formerly
  adv previously 796.5
  previously 799.11

formula
  n rule 404.2
  recipe 404.3
  rule 831.4
  axiom 929.2

forth
  adv forward 153.8
  hence 179.17
  out 181.18

forthcoming
  adj approaching 158.4
  emerging 181.15
  future 801.7
  imminent 802.3

fortnight
  n moment 786.2

fortunately
  adv favourably 124.20
  luckily 965.15

fortune
  n wealth 598.1
  gamble 722.2
  fate 919.2
  chance 927.1
  good fortune or luck
    965.2

forum
  n square 219.6
  conference 408.3
  arena 448.1
  discussion 523.6
  tribunal 576.1
  assembly 732.2

forward
  adj eager 92.8
  insolent 133.7
  progressive 153.6
  meddling 205.9

front 207.9
willing 309.5
strong-willed 344.13
foolhardy 478.8
immodest 646.6
premature 807.8
  adv forwards 153.8
forwards 207.12
  v advance 153.5
send 167.9
be instrumental 369.6
improve 377.9
hasten 386.3
be useful 434.17
deliver 463.13
determine 841.12
push 859.9
come in handy 950.3

foster
  adj related 540.6
  v nourish 8.18
advance 153.5
look after 324.9
motivate 360.11
encourage 360.20
improve 377.9
nurture 434.16
hold 459.7
train 549.13
care for 963.19

found
  v establish 150.16
form 248.6
sculpture 693.5
inaugurate 780.11
fix 817.9
cause 841.10
establish 847.10

foundation
  n establishment 150.7
  base 190.2
  preparation 390.1
  endowment 463.9
  reason 581.5
  organization 597.8
  beginning 780.1
  rock 817.6

establishment 847.4
base 856.5
premise 890.6
makeup 971.10

founded
  adj formative 248.8

founder
  n producer 847.7
  v capsize 173.18
  sink 185.6
  sink 352.7
  break down 378.21
  sink 395.9
  come to grief 966.10

fourth
  n interval 687.11
  gear 986.5

fox
  n charmer 400.6

frame
  n body 2.1
  base 190.2
  form 248.1
  figure 248.4
  structure 252.1
  framework 252.3
  film 692.8
  circumstances 728.2
  nature 729.2
  body 997.3
  v border 202.9
  plan 366.7
  phrase 514.3
  bear false witness
    580.11
  produce 847.8
  originate 847.12
  fix 920.4

framework
  n the skeleton 2.2
  outline 202.2
  frame 252.3

frank
  adj communicative
    328.9
  artless 401.4
  outspoken 415.21

plain-speaking 517.3
talkative 522.6
candid 624.13
vulgar 646.8
n postage 534.5

fraud

n sham 339.2
fake 339.9
fraudulence 341.8
impostor 342.4
theft 467.1
deceitfulness 625.3

free

adj available 211.13
voluntary 309.6
idle 316.16
communicative 328.9
escaped 354.11
leisure 387.3
at liberty 415.19
quit 415.28
liberated 416.10
liberal 470.3
gratuitous 614.4
uninhibited 645.22
unfastened 764.20
unfastened 764.20
adv freely 415.29
on one 463.27
gratuitously 614.5
v release 111.6
rescue 383.3
liberalize 415.12
exempt 415.13
liberate 416.4
extricate 416.7
acquit 582.4
detach 764.9
loosen 766.2
unload 969.9

freed

adj free 415.19
liberated 416.10

freedom

n leisure 387.1
liberty 415.1
liberality 470.1

privilege 622.2
facility 969.1

frequent

adj habitual 358.13
many 809.4
recurrent 811.13
v haunt 210.10

frequently

adv habitually 358.19
commonly 809.6
repeatedly 811.16

fresh

adj refreshing 9.3
clean 70.25
youthful 74.13
additional 239.9
windy 303.16
original 322.4
unused 375.10
present 800.2
new 803.7
additional 803.8
remembered 944.18
unharmed 957.7
cool 975.12

friend

n acquaintance 569.1

friendly

adj comfortable 112.11
homely 217.29
favourable 434.22
sociable 563.21
hospitable 566.11
amicable 568.14

friendship

n friendliness 568.1

frightened

adj alarmed 118.24
nervous 119.11
alarmed 385.3

front

adj frontal 207.9
first 780.14
n appearance 32.2
the lead 156.1
weather 175.10
appearance 197.1

exterior 197.2
fore 207.11
vanguard 207.2
weather map 302.3
sham 339.2
affectation 485.1
movement 590.27
v oppose 206.4
lead 207.6
confront 436.5
brave 477.9
precede 776.2

frozen

adj terrified 118.25
fast 762.13
immortal 791.8
permanent 815.6
immovable 817.15
stuck 817.16
cold 975.14
frozen solid 976.11

fruit

n produce 10.34
seed 296.24
yield 457.5
posterity 542.1
effect 842.1
product 848.1

fruits

n gain 457.3

frustration

n psychological stress 83.7
disappointment 123.1
rout 397.2
evasion 400.5
cancellation 855.2
thwarting 967.3

fuel

n energy source 973.1
petroleum 11.4
v provision 370.9
stoke 973.7

full

adj coloured 34.15
great 233.6
stout 243.17

broad 255.6
thick 255.7
stopped 279.9
unrestricted 415.25
detailed 728.9
crowded 732.22
complete 756.8
filled 756.10
plentiful 946.6
satiated 949.5
sound 957.6

full of
adj satiated 949.5

full-time
n shift 787.3

fully
adv in full 728.13
completely 756.13
plentifully 946.8
perfectly 957.9

fun
adj sexy 88.7
amusing 720.26
n pleasure 86.1
merriment 100.5
joke 474.3
action 720.2

function
n action 313.1
intention 365.1
use 372.5
duty 621.1
occupation 001.1
office 701.3
v act 313.4
serve 701.11
operate 844.5
operate 844.7

fund
n supply 371.2
funds 705.11
capital 705.12
collection 732.11
v provide 370.7
support 434.1
subsidize 463.19
pay for 604.17

finance 706.14

fundamental
adj basic 190.8
essential 729.6
simple 760.5
beginning 780.13
original 841.14
vital 952.22
n essence 729.1
foundation 856.5
important thing 952.5

funding
n financing 706.2

funds
n means 384.2
assets 456.6
finances 705.11

funeral
adj funereal 295.21
n burial 295.5

funny
adj humorous 473.2
witty 474.9
inexplicable 507.16
ambiguous 521.4
odd 832.11
eccentric 882.5
loopy 882.6
unbelievable 910.10
bewildering 926.18

furious
adj hectic 92.12
frenzied 96.25
passionate 96.29
infuriated 143.30
hasty 386.5
reckless 478.7
violent 651.15
turbulent 651.16
rabid 881.26

furniture
n furnishings 218.1
equipment 370.4
furnishings 712.5

further
adj additional 239.9
yonder 247.10

fresh 803.8
v advance 153.5
be useful 434.17

future
adj later 801.7
imminent 802.3
n betrothed 95.16
the future 801.1
fate 919.2

G
n gravity 283.3

gain
n increase 237.1
profit 457.3
good 954.4
v arrive 177.6
improve 377.7
triumph 396.3
acquire 457.8
receive 464.6
incur 852.4

gains
n winnings 237.3
gain 457.3

gallery
n observation point 27.8
audience 39.6
hall 184.4
corridor 188.15
porch 188.18
balcony 188.19
showroom 188.20
layer 282.1
passageway 368.3
museum 371.8
studio 690.15

game
adj willing 309.5
plucky 344.12
resolute 477.14
n meat 10.12
objective 365.2
intrigue 386.5
quarry 367.7
stratagem 400.3
contest 442.3

laughing stock 493.7
fun 720.2
card game 720.8
sport 721.1
gambling game 722.6

games
n contest 442.3
physical education
549.9
intrigues 849.3

gang
n staff 558.10
association 597.1
company 732.3

gap
n interval 213.1
crack 213.2
valley 270.7
opening 278.1
difference 742.1
disparity 749.1
deficiency 757.2
break 764.4
interruption 775.1

garage
n coach or carriage
house 188.23
repair shop 716.4

garden
n bed 112.9
v farm 112.15

gardening
n flower 296.20
horticulture 112.2

gas
n anaesthetic 77.12
bull 505.3
belch 864.9
fluid 111.2
v execute 585.16

gate
n entrance 180.5
porch 180.6
valve 225.9
head gate 225.10
receipts 607.1
audience 873.2

barrier 967.5

gathered
adj folded 277.7
stored 371.12
assembled 732.21
joined 762.12
made 847.18

gathering
adj imminent 802.3
n collection 457.2
assembly 732.1
assembly 732.2
accumulation 732.9
joining 762.1
harvest 112.14

gay
adj homosexual 66.28
happy 86.15
festive 720.27
n homosexual 66.14

gear
n clothing 5.1
rigging 171.10
tackle 257.3
equipment 370.4
luggage 456.3
mechanism 986.4
gearing 986.5

gene
n genetic material
291.5
heredity 541.6

general
adj generalized 826.10

General
n Field Marshal 556.19

general election
n election 590.13

generally
adv approximately
212.23
all in all 232.5
in general 826.16
normally 831.8
vaguely 926.20

generation
n procreation 69.2

birth 69.6
age 786.4
lifetime 789.4
production 847.1

generous
adj benevolent 134.15
forgiving 139.6
much 233.8
voluminous 243.16
indulgent 412.7
charitable 463.22
liberal 470.3
hospitable 566.11
magnanimous 632.5
productive 845.7
tolerant 934.11
plentiful 946.6

genius
n ability 18.2
superior 235.4
inspiration 360.9
talent 398.4
talented person 398.12
master 398.13
nature 729.2
brightness 875.2
spirit 875.8
scholar 884.2
creative thought 941.2
wonder 954.6

gentle
adj faint 43.14
good-natured 134.14
pitying 136.6
slow 166.9
light 284.10
lenient 412.6
meek 418.13
noble 589.10
moderate 650.9
soft 992.8
v tend 113.6

gentleman
n male 67.4
aristocrat 589.4
nobleman 589.4
good person 639.1

gently
adv faintly 43.19
slowly 166.12
meekly 418.16
softly 992.16

genuine
adj natural 401.5
straight 624.10
candid 624.13
real 723.11
authentic 928.15

gesture
n gesticulation 502.14
hint 532.4
v gesticulate 502.21

get
v hear 39.10
take ill 76.15
fetch 167.10
waste 294.11
acquire 457.8
receive 464.6
take 465.13
learn 551.6
become 723.9
induce 841.11
incur 852.4
discover 896.2
stump 926.8

get away
v set out 179.8
escape 354.6

get back
v recover 466.6

get in
v arrive 177.6
enter 180.7
mount 184.11
intrude 205.5

get into
v penetrate 180.8

get on
v depart 179.6
mount 184.11
make good 394.7
prosper 965.7

get out

v beat it 179.7
exit 181.9
extract 183.9
be revealed 336.8
escape 354.6
extricate 416.7

get to
v worry 117.4
extend to 247.6
communicate with 328.7

getting
n acquisition 457.1
receiving 464.1

giant
adj huge 243.19
gigantic 258.12
n strong man 15.6
colossus 243.12

gift
n talent 398.4
present 463.4
gratuity 614.1
brightness 875.2

girl
n woman 68.5
doll 95.14
maid 288.6

girlfriend
n doll 95.14

give
n softness 992.1
pliancy 992.2
elasticity 993.1
v provide 370.7
present 463.12
say 509.16
present 614.3
administer 623.6
attribute 843.3
yield 992.7
yield 993.5

give up
v despair 118.8
relinquish 355.7
break the habit 359.3
abdicate 375.4

surrender 418.7
resign 433.2
relinquish 460.2
not understand 507.9
renounce 648.6
not know 885.9

given
adj allowed 463.24
real 723.11
supposed 906.11
conditional 914.8
disposed 933.8
n fact 723.3
condition 914.2

giving
adj charitable 463.22
liberal 470.3
pliable 992.9
n benevolence 134.4
informing 328.2
donation 463.1
administration 623.2

glad
adj pleased 86.14
happy 86.15
cheerful 100.11
cheering 100.16

glass
adj glassy 981.3
n container 186.1
smooth 273.3
barometer 302.6
ceramic ware 719.2

glasses
n silver 8.12

global
adj round 268.5
comprehensive 734.7
complete 756.8
universal 826.13
unqualified 915.1

glory
n eminence 233.2
circle 266.1
grandeur 486.5
honour 626.1
repute 642.1

lustre 642.6
glorification 675.2
prominence 952.2
v exult 487.7

go
n act 313.3
enterprise 315.6
try 388.3
spell 787.1
v disappear 33.2
have pace 150.9
head 152.6
progress 153.2
move 163.4
travel 168.14
go at 168.15
depart 179.6
die 293.14
perish 380.23
become 723.9
be annihilated 724.5
operate 844.7
tend 851.3

go ahead
v progress 153.2
begin 780.7

go back
v retreat 154.5
come last 208.8
turn back 821.4

go down
v capsize 173.18
sink 185.6
sink 352.7
decline 378.15
sink 395.9

go for
v head for 152.8
fetch 167.10
intend 365.4
abet 434.14
pitch into 444.13

go in
v narrow 256.9

go into
v undertake 389.3
participate 461.4

discuss 523.10
write upon 537.5
join 597.14
compose 758.3
enter 780.9
investigate 893.21

go on
v progress 153.2
depart 179.6
behave 306.3
persevere 345.2
manage 394.9
chatter 522.4
endure 789.5
linger on 789.6
occur 793.5
continue 818.3
persist 818.5

go out
v exit 181.9
die 293.14
strike 704.5
expire 782.5
burn out 974.7

go through
v squander 471.3
rehearse 682.24
experience 793.8
search 893.29

go to
v repair to 168.21
extend to 247.6

go-ahead
adj progressive 153.6
n progression 153.1
enterprise 315.6

goal
n destination 177.5
motive 360.1
objective 365.2
score 394.4
end 782.1

god
n hero 639.5

God
n Jehovah 657.2

going

adj operating 844.11
n disappearance 33.1
progression 153.1
travel 168.1
departure 179.1
death 293.1

going on
adj happening 793.9

gold
adj brass 12.15
n wealth 598.1
money 705.1
precious metals 705.16

golden
adj favourable 124.17
superb 954.15
brass 12.15

gone
adj away 33.4
past hope 116.13
departed 179.16
absent 211.10
dead 293.22
used up 373.4
lost 458.7
no more 724.9
past 799.6

good
adj tasty 54.7
pleasant 88.5
favourable 124.17
kind 134.13
skilful 398.20
praiseworthy 494.18
right 617.3
honest 624.9
just 629.6
virtuous 633.5
almighty 657.9
God-fearing 671.9
solvent 706.16
valid 928.14
genuine 928.15
expedient 950.5
excellent 954.12
adv kindly 134.18
n utility 372.3

welfare 954.4
good at
  adj skilled in 398.25
good for
  adj healthy 72.4
  useful 372.16
  helpful 434.21
  solvent 706.16
goods
  adv freight 167.5
  n material 4.1
  property 456.1
  merchandise 712.1
governing
  adj authoritative
    402.14
  directing 554.12
  controlling 593.16
government
  n state 220.5
  governance 402.5
  political science 590.2
  regulation 593.1
  care 963.2
  n direction 554.1
governor
  n jailer 414.10
  director 555.1
  ruler 556.5
  viceroy 556.13
  guardian 963.6
grace
  n loveliness charm
    88.2
  benevolence 134.4
  pity 136.1
  pardon 139.2
  skill 398.1
  taste 481.1
  elegance 515.1
  fluency 525.2
  reprieve 582.3
  sanctification 664.3
  prayer 675.4
  goodness 954.1
  beauty 971.1
  v honour 642.11

beautify 971.12
grade
  n incline 195.4
  degree 231.1
  class 553.10
  class 588.1
  class 771.2
  v incline 195.9
  graduate 231.4
  size 243.14
  smooth 273.5
  order 769.4
  classify 770.9
  classify 771.5
gradually
  adv little by little
    166.13
  by degrees 231.6
grain
  n feed 10.4
  modicum 234.2
  drop 244.6
  texture 280.1
  grass 296.5
  seed 296.24
  nature 729.2
  disposition 933.3
  granule 996.6
  v coarsen 280.4
grand
  adj dignified 127.12
  great 233.6
  large 243.15
  grandiose 486.17
  lofty 525.13
  eminent 642.16
  important 952.16
  good 954.12
grandfather
  n old man 290.2
  grandfather 541.13
grandmother
  n old woman 290.3
  grandmother 541.15
grant
  n concession 428.5
  giving 463.1

subsidy 463.8
qualification 914.1
  v acknowledge 317.10
  confess 336.7
  permit 428.9
  give 463.12
  allow for 914.5
granted
  adj accepted 317.13
  given 463.24
  supposed 906.11
grass
  n cereal 296.5
  grassland 296.8
grateful
  adj thankful 141.5
  welcome 566.12
grave
  adj painful 26.10
  dark 37.8
  sedate 97.14
  solemn 102.3
  gloomy 103.24
  dignified 127.12
  great 233.6
  lofty 525.13
  ceremonial 561.8
  base 641.12
  weighty 952.19
  n death 293.1
  tomb 295.15
  monument 530.10
great
  adj grand 233.6
  chief 249.15
  large 243.15
  authoritative 402.14
  magnanimous 632.5
  eminent 642.16
  important 952.16
  swell 954.13
  n ace 398.14
greater
  adj superior 235.12
  higher 258.14
greatest
  adj furthest 233.13

superlative 235.13

greatly
  adv largely 233.14
  importantly 952.24

green
  adj immature 287.9
  immature 391.9
  inexperienced 399.14
  new 803.7
  ignorant 885.10
  gullible 909.6
  n lawn 296.7

grey
  adj colourless 35.7
  aged 289.11
  same 743.6

grip
  n skill 398.1
  governance 402.5
  hold 459.2
  spasm 872.6
  understanding 883.3
  v hold 459.6
  seize 465.14
  obsess 881.21
  absorb 938.13

gross
  adj thick 255.7
  base 641.12
  carnal 643.6
  whole 754.9
  n injustice 630.4
  v profit 457.12

ground
  adj bottom 190.7
  powdery 996.10
  n station 150.2
  ground covering 190.3
  bed 190.4
  setting 200.2
  region 220.1
  land 223.1
  motive 360.1
  arena 448.1
  foundation 856.5
  premise 890.6
  v establish 150.16

restrict 413.8
confine 414.12
fix 817.9
fell 868.5

grounds
  n closeness 212.1
  dregs 242.2
  green 296.7
  real estate 456.5
  reason 581.5
  cause 841.1
  evidence 912.1
  condition 914.2

group
  n amount 230.2
  orchestra 688.8
  company 732.3
  bunch 732.7
  set 746.4
  class 771.2
  v gather 732.18
  classify 763.8
  classify 770.9
  classify 771.5

grow
  v develop 14.2
  increase 237.6
  develop 245.7
  grow 245.7
  grow up 258.9
  mature 289.7
  vegetate 296.26
  become 723.9
  evolve 823.4
  process 847.9
  farm 112.15
  raise 113.5

growing
  adj increasing 237.8
  grown 245.12
  immature 287.9
  n production 847.2
  raising 112.11

grown
  adj grown-up 14.3
  grown-up 245.12
  adult 289.9

produced 847.17
made 847.18

growth
  n physical
    development 14.1
  anaemia 76.9
  increase 237.1
  development 245.3
  development 289.5
  crop 296.2
  vegetation 296.25
  business cycle 708.9
  conversion 820.1
  evolution 823.1

guarantee
  n oath 319.4
  promise 421.1
  security 423.1
  sponsor 423.5
  v testify 319.6
  promise 421.4
  secure 423.7
  protect 963.18

guaranteed
  adj promised 421.7
  secured 423.9
  assured 925.14
  trouble-free 962.5

guard
  n conductor 169.11
  vigilance 324.4
  jailer 414.10
  defence 445.1
  defender 445.7
  escort 731.4
  protection 963.1
  safeguard 963.3
  advance guard 963.9
  v preserve 382.7
  defend 445.8
  escort 731.7
  protect 963.18

guardian
  adj protective 963.22
  n jailer 414.10
  steward 555.4
  warden 963.6

guards
  n elite troops 446.11
  bodyguard 963.14

guerrilla
  n irregular 446.12

guess
  n conjecture 906.4
  gamble 926.4
  v solve 895.2
  estimate 901.9
  conjecture 906.8
  think 908.11
  predict 917.4

guest
  n visitor 566.6

guide
  n gutter 225.3
  interpreter 326.6
  adviser 407.3
  pointer 504.4
  shepherd 555.7
  escort 731.4
  precursor 778.1
  v lead 156.2
  pilot 173.10
  advise 407.4
  teach 549.10
  steer 554.9
  escort 731.7
  go before 778.3
  govern 849.8

guilt
  n guiltiness 636.1

guilty
  adj criminal 636.3
  adv sheepishly 636.5

gulf
  n crack 213.2
  eddy 224.12
  ocean 226.2
  inlet 228.1
  pit 261.2
  pit 270.3
  opening 278.1

gun
  n mercenary 446.13
  firearm 447.10

guy
  n fellow 67.5

habit
  n clothing 5.1
  suit 5.5
  substance abuse 78.1
  custom 358.3
  mannerism 485.2
  nature 729.2

hair
  n pile 3.1
  short distance 212.2
  narrowness 256.1
  filament 257.1
  skin 281.3

half
  adj proportionate 462.13
  part 837.5
  n portion 462.5
  middle distance 781.2
  hemisphere 837.2

hall
  n entrance 180.5
  assembly hall 188.4
  corridor 188.15
  house 217.5
  arena 448.1

halt
  n standstill 164.3
  delay 808.2
  stop 819.2
  prevention 967.2
  impasse 968.6
  v quiet 164.7
  dawdle 166.7
  stroll 168.24
  stammer 510.7
  cease 819.4
  stop 819.5
  stop 819.9
  stop 967.12

ham
  n member 2.4
  leg 168.11
  v overact 682.23

hand
  n member 2.4
  cabin boy 174.4
  side 209.1
  helping hand 434.2
  applause 494.2
  pointer 504.4
  signature 512.9
  handwriting 528.3
  worker 703.2
  member 755.4
  v deliver 463.13

handed
  adj sided 209.5

handful
  n modicum 234.2
  a few 840.2
  hard job 968.2

handle
  n bulge 269.2
  v touch 64.6
  pilot 173.10
  treat 306.5
  perform 313.9
  use 372.8
  treat 372.10
  discuss 523.10
  direct 554.8
  deal in 708.15
  operate 844.5
  tend 113.6

handling
  n touching 64.2
  performance 313.2
  usage 372.2
  utilization 372.6
  piece 537.1
  operation 844.1
  n direction 554.1

hands
  n work force 18.4
  governance 402.5
  clutches 459.4

handsome
  adj liberal 470.3
  beautiful 971.14

hang

n droop 193.2
knack 398.6
v take off 184.9
hang down 193.6
suspend 193.8
lynch 585.17
hang 585.17
hesitate 808.10
depend 914.6

hanging
adj downcast 185.12
suspended 193.9
loose 766.4
n pendency 193.1
pendant 193.4
cover 281.2
capital punishment 585.6

happen
v occur 793.5
chance 927.7

happening
adj occurring 793.9
n event 793.2
accident 927.3

happily
adv gladly 86.18
cheerfully 100.17
favourably 124.20

happiness
n delight 86.2
contentment 98.1
cheerfulness 100.1
prosperity 965.1

happy
adj glad 86.15
cheerful 100.11
favourable 124.17
apt 750.10
timely 805.8
expedient 950.5

harbour
n destination 177.5
inlet 228.1
refuge 964.1
haven 964.6
v house 214.9

hold 459.7
protect 963.18

hard
adj strong 15.14
callous 85.12
unrepentant 105.5
harsh 135.22
heartless 135.23
pitiless 135.23
industrious 315.18
inflexible 346.8
obdurate 346.9
firm 410.6
difficult 507.12
phonetic 509.23
hardened 634.16
real 723.11
sturdy 725.7
valid 928.14
adverse 966.13
difficult 968.17
dense 990.11
solid 991.9
tough 994.3
adv near 212.20
laboriously 702.19

hardly
adv barely 234.9
narrowly 256.17
infrequently 810.4

hardy
adj strong 15.14
hearty 74.12
perennial 296.33
courageous 477.13
durable 789.9
tough 994.3

harm
n damage 378.1
disadvantage 951.2
evil 955.3
bane 956.1
v impair 378.9
inconvenience 951.4
hurt 955.6

has-been
adj past 799.6

n old fogy 804.7

hat
n headdress 5.20
v cloak 5.29
top 281.20

hate
n hostility 90.2
hatred 94.1
aversion 94.3
hostility 570.3
v respond 84.11
dislike 90.3
detest 94.5
bear ill will 570.8

have
v give birth 1.3
compel 409.4
suffer 428.10
possess 454.4
hold 459.7
receive 464.6
experience 793.8

have to
v be compelled 409.9
be necessary 918.9

haven
n destination 177.5
refuge 964.1
harbour 964.6

having
adj possessing 454.9

he
n male 67.4
self 827.5

head
adj top 189.8
front 207.9
directing 554.12
governing 593.16
first 780.14
n member 2.4
head of hair 3.3
heading 189.4
pate 189.5
front 207.1
front 207.1
source 224.2

superior 235.4
point 269.6
foam 305.2
superintendent 555.2
portrait 690.13
class 771.2
source 841.5
intellect 874.1
brain 874.5
caption 892.2
v turn 152.6
lead 156.2
top 189.7
lead 207.6
gravitate 283.11
direct 554.8
govern 593.10
precede 776.2
focus on 892.3

headed
  adj topped 189.10

heading
  adj leading 156.3
  topping 189.9
  n head 189.4
  front 207.1
  caption 892.2
  n supervision 554.2

headline
  n caption 892.2
  v dramatize 682.20
  focus on 892.3
  feature 952.14

headquarters
  n office 716.6

heads
  n opposite side 206.3

healing
  adj remedial 77.20
  n therapy 82.1
  cure 381.7

health
  adj medical 81.11
  n well-being 74.1
  normality 831.1

healthy
  adj wholesome 72.4

fine 74.8
large 243.15
good 954.12

hear
  v sense 24.6
  listen 39.9
  catch 39.10
  know 532.14
  try 579.17
  hold court 901.12
  hark 39.1

hearing
  adj auditory 39.12
  n senses 24.5
  ear 39.1
  audition 39.2
  earshot 39.4
  trial 579.5
  examination 893.2
  investigation 893.4
  workout 897.3

heart
  n internal organs 2.10
  liver 10.19
  passion 84.2
  soul 84.3
  substance 187.4
  interior 198.2
  centre 199.1
  life force 292.9
  fortitude 477.4
  essence 729.1
  inside 729.3
  middle 781.1
  psyche 874.4
  mood 933.4

heat
  n lust 66.5
  fever 76.7
  passion 84.2
  fever pitch 96.7
  race 442.9
  hotness 971.23
  v raise the
     temperature 972.17

Heaven
  n Styx 293.3

Paradise 661.1
destiny 801.2
fate 919.2

heavily
  adv dully 108.10
  passively 164.15
  heavy 283.16
  densely 990.14

heavy
  adj dull 108.6
  inert 164.12
  great 233.6
  thick 255.7
  ponderous 283.12
  luxuriant 296.32
  cloudy 304.4
  languid 316.18
  tragic 682.26
  laborious 702.18
  sturdy 725.7
  dull 877.15
  dense 990.11
  adv heavily 283.16
  n hooligan 574.4

height
  n space 149.1
  degree 231.1
  supremacy 235.3
  size 243.1
  altitude 258.1
  elevation 258.2
  elevation 867.1
  top 957.2

held
  adj reserved 371.13
  possessed 454.8
  stuck 817.16
  obsessed 881.29
  believed 908.22

helicopter
  n rotor plane 172.5

Hell
  n Styx 293.3

hell
  n the underworld
     662.1

Hell

n destiny 801.2

hello
n greeting 566.4

help
n remedy 77.1
aid 434.1
subsidy 463.8
servant 558.2
v do a favour 134.12
aid 434.11
subsidize 463.19
do good 954.10
prevent 967.13

help to
v give 463.12

helpful
adj considerate 134.16
instrumental 369.7
useful 372.16
useful 434.21
good 954.12

helping
adj assisting 434.20
n serving 8.10
portion 462.5

hence
adv thence 179.17
therefore 843.7

her
n female 68.4
self 827.5

here
adv everywhere 149.10
aboard 150.23
now 800.3
adv there 210.16

heritage
n inheritance 464.2

hero
n victor 396.2
heroine 477.6
god 639.5
celebrity 642.8
demigod 658.3
role 682.7
lead 685.5
ideal 748.4

herself
n self 827.5

hidden
adj invisible 31.5
secret 330.11
concealed 331.11
latent 504.5
implied 504.7
abstract 507.14

hide
n fur 4.2
sheet 282.2
v conceal 331.6
conceal oneself 331.8
store up 371.10

hiding
adj concealing 331.15
n covering 281.1
concealment 331.1
hiding place 331.4
leathering 585.5

high
adj high-pitched 49.13
nasty 55.6
strong 59.8
fetid 62.4
smashed 78.7
excited 96.20
cheerful 100.11
spacious 149.8
eminent 233.9
lofty 258.11
tainted 378.34
eminent 642.16
raised 867.8
adv on high 258.15
n weather map 302.3
price 715.3
gear 986.5

High Court
adj Judicial Committee
of the Privy Council
576.9

higher
adj superior 235.12
superior 258.14

highest

hello – historic

adj top 189.8
superlative 235.13
almighty 657.9
paramount 952.23
n supremacy 235.3

highlights
n lighting 977.19

highly
adv greatly 233.14

hill
n plateau 258.8
bulge 269.2
pile 732.10

him
n male 67.4
self 827.5

himself
n self 827.5

hint
n soupçon 53.3
suspicion 234.4
remainder 242.1
warning 384.1
tip 407.2
indication 502.3
clue 502.9
implication 504.2
gentle hint 532.4
tinge 759.6
suggestion 906.5
reminder 944.5
v betoken 124.11
promise 124.12
signify 502.17
imply 504.4
intimate 532.9

hip
n side 209.1
joint 762.3

hire
n rental 595.5
v employ 595.12
rent 595.13

his
n male 67.4

historic
adj historical 697.6

historical
adj historic 697.6
fictional 700.7
real 723.11
true 928.13

history
n record 530.1
historical research
697.1
the past 799.1

hit
n kick 96.3
smash 394.4
score 394.4
stage show 682.2
popular music 686.6
blow 857.4
v impress 84.13
go 168.15
arrive 177.6
contact 212.10
waste 294.11
attack 444.12
collide 857.12
strike 857.13
shoot 859.11
impress 886.15
discover 896.2

hold
n cellar 188.14
store 371.6
custody 414.5
stronghold 445.6
possession 454.1
purchase 459.2
seizure 465.2
influence 849.1
footing 856.4
leverage 861.1
v extend 149.6
affirm 319.5
store up 371.10
confine 414.12
possess 454.4
grip 459.6
keep 459.7
exist 723.5

include 734.3
adhere 765.6
endure 789.5
remain 815.4
sustain 818.4
support 856.8
obsess 881.21
judge 901.8
conclude 901.10
think 908.11
be true 928.8
suffice 946.3

holding
adj possessing 454.9
supporting 856.10
n possession 454.1
estate 456.4
retention 459.1

hole
n compartment 188.2
cellar 188.14
crack 213.2
hovel 217.10
lair 217.23
pit 261.2
cavity 270.2
cave 270.4
opening 278.1
penetration 278.3
hiding place 331.4
deficiency 757.2

holiday
adj comfortable 20.10
n vacation 20.3
day off 20.4
absence 211.4
celebration 472.1
interim 788.1
pause 819.3
v go on holiday 20.9

holy
adj almighty 657.9
sacred 664.7
God-fearing 671.9

home
adj residential 217.28
n fireside 217.2

habitat 217.16
fatherland 221.2
asylum 964.4

homeless
adj unsettled 151.9
destitute 599.9

honest
adj natural 484.7
upright 624.9
truthful 624.12
virtuous 633.5
genuine 928.15

honey
n sweets 10.36
sweetener 57.2
baby 95.10
darling 543.6
doll 971.8
v butter up 496.4

honour
n respect 146.1
praise 494.5
probity 624.1
distinction 626.1
title 628.1
esteem 642.3
prestige 642.4
chastity 644.1
attribution 843.1
prominence 952.2
v respect 146.4
execute 422.9
celebrate 472.2
do honour 626.8
dignify 624.7
worship 675.10

hook
n angle 264.1
curve 265.2
point 269.6
v angle 264.2
curve 265.4
grab 457.9
catch 465.17
hitch 762.7

hope
n ambition 91.10

hopes 115.1
optimism 121.2
prudence 633.3
belief 908.1
possibility 921.1
recourse 964.2
v look for 115.6
expect 121.5

hopefully
adv cheerfully 100.17
expectantly 115.13
expectantly 121.14
later 801.8

hopes
n hope 115.1
expectations 121.4

hoping
adj desiring 91.20
hopeful 115.10

horrible
adj horrid 89.19
terrible 118.29
terrible 955.9
hideous 970.9

horror
n torment 87.7
hostility 90.2
fear 118.1
frightfulness 118.2
bogeyman 118.9
abomination 618.2
eyesore 970.3

horse
n parallel bars 702.7

hospital
n clinic 82.9

host
n army 446.19
mine host 566.5
master of ceremonies
720.19
throng 732.4
flock 732.5
multitude 839.3
broadcaster 983.18
v entertain 566.8

hostage

n pledge 423.2

hostile
adj dark 37.8
unpleasant 89.17
averse 90.8
opposing 436.7
warlike 443.17
antagonistic 570.10
contrary 741.5
disagreeing 751.6
counteracting 855.8
adverse 966.13

hot
adj nippy 59.7
lustful 66.25
in heat 66.26
feverish 76.23
fervent 84.16
zealous 92.9
heated 96.22
passionate 101.25
stolen 467.21
brand-new 803.10
heated 971.44
heated 972.29
charged 982.30

hotel
n inn 217.14

hour
n period 786.1
moment 786.2
time 794.2

house
n audience 39.6
dwelling 217.5
structure 252.2
council 408.1
race 540.4
family 540.5
lineage 541.4
company 597.9
theatre 682.11
market 713.1
workplace 716.1
audience 873.2
astrology 114.17
v shelter 214.9

accommodate 370.10

household
adj residential 217.28
simple 484.6
usual 831.7
well-known 883.22
n home 217.2

housing
adj structural 847.15
n lodging 214.3
abode 217.1
quarters 217.4
cover 281.2

how
adv thus 369.8

however
adv anyhow 369.9

huge
adj gigantic 15.16
large 233.7
immense 243.19

hull
n ship 171.1
shell 281.15
v husk 6.9

human
adj kind 134.13
pitying 136.6
frail 297.7
n person 297.3

human rights
n right 415.2
rights of man 622.3

humanitarian
adj benevolent 134.15
n philanthropist 134.8

humour
n serum 2.17
whim 349.1
wit 474.1
mood 933.4
v indulge 412.5

hung
adj suspended 193.9

hunger
n eating 8.1
craving 91.6

appetite 91.7
tendency 851.1
v hunger for 91.18

hungry
  adj craving 91.23
  empty 91.24

hunt
  n hunting 367.2
  search 893.14
  v pursue 367.8
  go hunting 367.9
  persecute 374.6
  seek 893.28
  search 893.29

hunter
  n pursuer 367.4
  sportsman 367.5
  shot 859.8
  seeker 893.17

hunting
  adj pursuing 367.11
  n pursuit 367.1
  shooting 367.2

hurt
  adj pained 26.9
  pained 87.23
  impaired 378.23
  n pain 26.1
  damage 378.1
  disadvantage 951.2
  evil 955.3
  v pain 26.7
  suffer 26.8
  pain 87.17
  suffer 87.19
  offend 143.21
  impair 378.9
  injure 378.12
  harm 955.6

husband
  n married man 544.6
  v reserve 371.11

I
  n self 827.5
  one 834.3

ice
  n smooth 273.3

frozen water 975.4
v top 189.7
waste 294.11

idea
  n intention 365.1
  plan 366.1
  advice 407.1
  meaning 503.1
  thought 887.1
  suggestion 906.5
  opinion 908.6

ideal
  adj model 748.8
  normal 831.6
  conceptual 887.7
  theoretical 906.10
  idealized 941.17
  perfect 957.5
  n motive 360.1
  paragon 639.4
  idol 748.4
  rule 831.4
  archetype 887.2
  idealism 941.6
  archetype 957.3

identify
  v signify 502.17
  name 512.10
  relate 737.6
  make one 740.5
  detect 896.5
  recognize 944.9

identity
  n accord 440.1
  sameness 740.1
  similarity 746.1
  equality 752.1
  particularity 827.1
  unity 834.1

ignore
  v take 125.7
  condone 139.4
  slight 148.6
  disobey 312.5
  neglect 325.6
  reject 357.2
  exclude 735.4

exclude 735.4
keep an open mind
  934.7
be inattentive 939.2

ignored
  adj unrecognized
    142.4
  neglected 325.14
  rejected 357.3
  excluded 735.7

ill
  adj ailing 76.21
  ominous 124.16
  bad 955.7
  adv badly 955.12
  n evil 955.3

illegal
  adj prohibited 429.7
  wrong 618.3
  unjust 630.8
  unlawful 654.5

illness
  n disease 76.1

illustration
  n explanation 326.4
  representation 334.1
  picture 690.9
  example 748.2
  citation 912.5

image
  n appearance 32.2
  aspect 32.3
  apparition 32.5
  unconscious memory
    83.18
  description 334.2
  likeness 334.5
  image 334.5
  affectation 485.1
  sign 502.1
  figure of speech 518.1
  picture 690.9
  copy 747.1
  picture 941.5
  picture 984.4

imagination
  n fancy 931.3

imagining 941.1
whim 941.4

imagine
v contemplate 886.13
suppose 906.7
think 908.11
fancy 941.9

immediate
adj present 210.12
adjacent 212.16
nearest 212.19
hasty 386.5
instantaneous 792.4
present 800.2
imminent 802.3
prompt 807.9

immediately
adv hastily 386.8
instantly 792.6
promptly 807.15

immigration
n wandering 168.3
incoming population
  180.3

immune
adj resistant 74.14
exempt 415.27
safe 962.4

impact
n power 18.1
meaning 503.1
force 842.2
collision 857.3
v cause 841.10
collide 857.12

imperial
adj sovereign 402.16

importance
n prestige 402.4
distinction 642.5
influence 849.1
significance 952.1

important
adj authoritative
  402.14
prominent 642.15
influential 849.13

impose
v intrude 205.5
prescribe 405.8
demand 406.5
oblige 409.5
compose 529.14
charge 610.12
impose on 623.4

imposed
adj mandatory 405.10
inflicted 623.8

impossible
adj unacceptable 99.10
out of the question
  116.12
fantastic 832.12
not possible 922.4
n impossibility 922.1

impressed
adj affected 84.21
engraved 691.8

impression
n aspect 32.3
feeling 84.1
form 248.1
indentation 270.5
imitation 321.1
description 334.2
print 502.7
print 529.3
edition 535.5
print 691.3
characteristic 827.4
impact 842.2
idea 887.1
hunch 889.3
suggestion 906.5
opinion 908.6

impressive
adj exciting 96.30
grandiose 486.17
vigorous 525.10
convincing 908.24

improve
v turn to advantage
  372.13

grow better 377.7
better 377.9
recuperate 381.17
train 549.13
be changed 814.6
change 814.7
perfect 957.4

improved
adj advanced 377.13
changed 814.10

improvement
n progression 153.1
betterment 377.1
restoration 381.1
training 549.3
change 814.1
new start 820.2

improving
adj progressive 377.15

in
adj entering 180.11
modern 803.13
adv inward 180.12
inside 198.9
n entry 178.3

in addition
adv additionally 239.10

in advance
adv before 156.4
before 207.11
on loan 600.7
early 807.11

in bed
adv at rest 20.11

in charge
adv in authority
  402.19

in fact
adv really 723.12
truly 928.18

in favour
adj on speaking terms
  568.17

in front
adj front 207.9
adv before 156.4
before 207.11

in full
adv at length 520.15
fully 728.13
completely 756.13

in general
adv generally 826.16

in hand
adj unused 375.10
undertaken 389.4
possessed 454.8
restrained 650.10
happening 793.9
operating 844.11
adv under control 593.18
in production 847.20

in hospital
adj laid up 76.24

in line
adj conformist 829.6
adv in step 750.11

in love
adj head over heels in love 95.28

in love with
adj fond of 95.29

in order
adj in shape 769.7
adv in turn 769.10

in particular
adv fully 728.13
particularly 827.15

in place
adj located 150.18
present 210.12
established 817.13
adv in position 150.20

in public
adv openly 333.15
publicly 337.18

in response
adv in answer 894.6

in return
adv in compensation 323.6
in retaliation 491.7
interchangeably 825.5

in answer 894.6

in short
adv in brief 519.7

in spite
adv meanly 135.26

in the morning
adv before noon 299.6

in time
adj synchronized 798.6
adv in tempo 687.18
eventually 831.7
in good time 807.12
periodically 812.10

in turn
adv in order 769.10
progressively 774.11
interchangeably 825.5

in two
adv separately 764.24
in half 837.7

incident
n plot 704.4
circumstance 728.1
event 793.2

include
v put in 198.5
enclose 203.5
comprise 734.3
put together 762.4
combine 767.3

included
adj embraced 734.5
involved 853.4

including
adj inclusive 734.6
composed of 758.4

income
n entrance 180.1
gain 457.3
pay 604.4
receipts 607.1

increase
n worsening 110.1
ascent 184.1
gain 237.1
addition 239.1
adjunct 240.1

expansion 245.1
improvement 377.1
multiplication 838.3
elevation 867.1
v grow 14.2
aggravate 110.2
count 230.4
graduate 231.4
enlarge 237.4
grow 237.6
add to 239.5
enlarge 245.4
enlarge 245.5
grow 245.7
multiply 838.4

increased
adj aggravated 110.4
heightened 237.7
expanded 245.10
multiple 838.6

increasing
adj rising 237.8

increasingly
adv more 237.9

incredible
adj wonderful 113.6
remarkable 233.10
fantastic 832.12
absurd 878.9
unbelievable 910.10
improbable 924.3

indeed
adv decidedly 233.18
chiefly 235.17
certainly 925.17
truly 928.18

independence
n pride 127.1
nationhood 221.3
volunteering 309.2
self-control 344.5
self-government 415.5
self-help 434.6
battle flag 443.11
neutrality 452.1
irrelevance 738.1

independent

adj proud 127.8
voluntary 309.6
strong-willed 344.13
individualistic 415.20
neutral 452.6
neutral 590.35
unrelated 738.4
separate 764.18
n free agent 415.11
neutral 452.4
neutral 590.23

index
adv bibliography 539.4
n contents 187.1
sign 502.1
pointer 502.4
hint 532.4
reference book 535.9
design 535.12
directory 555.10
outline 763.4
table 770.4
characteristic 827.4
listing 833.7
v record 530.12
classify 771.5
list 833.8

indicate
v hint 124.11
manifest 333.5
signify 502.17
mean 503.5
hint 532.9
specify 827.11
evidence 912.7

indicated
adj foreshadowed 124.14
implied 504.7
requisite 918.11

indication
n omen 124.3
manifestation 333.1
identification 502.3
hint 532.4
evidence 912.1

individual

adj personal 297.8
indicative 502.23
particular 827.12
one 834.7
n organism 291.2
person 297.3
something 725.3
entity 834.4

industrial
adj occupational 701.13
commercial 708.19
manufacturing 847.14

industry
n diligence 315.5
pains 324.2
perseverance 345.1
company 597.9
work 702.4
commerce 708.1
mass production 847.3

inevitable
adj obligatory 409.11
unavoidable 918.13
destined 919.6
certain 925.9

inevitably
adv in consequence 842.7
necessarily 918.16

infected
adj unclean 71.17
diseased 76.25

infection
n defilement 71.4
contagion 76.4
infectious disease 76.10
corruption 378.2
evil 955.3

inflation
n stretching 245.2
exaggeration 340.1
style 514.2
price index 610.4
high price 612.3
business cycle 708.9

stretching 948.7

influence
n power 18.1
supremacy 235.3
motivation 360.2
machination 400.4
prestige 402.4
power 849.1
v induce 360.21
cause 841.10
induce 841.11
determine 841.12
operate on 844.6
affect 849.7
prejudice 935.9

influenced
adj partial 630.10
prejudiced 935.12

influential
adj authoritative 402.14
powerful 849.13

information
n communication 328.1
info 532.1
news 533.1
knowledge 883.1
data 988.14

informed
adj prepared 390.13
informed of 532.16
knowing 883.12
enlightened 883.14

ingredients
n contents 187.1
substance 725.2

initial
adj beginning 780.13
v ratify 317.11
letter 527.6

initially
adv first 780.15

initiative
n vim 17.2
act 313.3
enterprise 315.6

undertaking 389.1
process 844.2

injured
  adj pained 87.23
  impaired 378.23

injury
  n pain 87.5
  indignity 147.2
  abuse 374.2
  damage 378.1
  loss 458.1
  injustice 630.4
  misdeed 635.2
  disadvantage 951.2
  evil 955.3

inner
  adj interior 198.6
  intrinsic 729.4
  particular 827.12
  n interior 198.2

innings
  n turn 787.2

innocent
  adj immature 287.9
  artless 401.4
  natural 484.7
  chaste 633.6
  not guilty 637.4
  chaste 644.4
  ignorant 885.10
  trusting 908.21
  harmless 954.20
  n child 288.3
  dupe 343.1
  ingenue 401.3
  babe 637.2

inquiry
  n trial 579.5
  inquiring 893.1
  question 893.9
  survey 893.13

inside
  adj interior 198.6
  confidential 330.14
  jailed 414.20
  adv in 198.9
  n interior 198.2

insides 729.3

insider
  n inside information 532.2
  member 597.11

insist
  v affirm 319.5
  urge 360.13
  stick to 406.8
  urge upon 424.9

inspector
  n examiner 893.16
  policeman 963.15

inspiration
  n breathing 2.14
  suction 178.5
  impulse 350.1
  motive 360.1
  fire 360.9
  encouragement 477.7
  revelation 663.4
  Muse 698.10
  genius 875.8
  good idea 887.5
  intuition 889.1
  creative thought 941.2

inspired
  adj fired 360.30
  appropriate 515.5
  imaginative 941.12

instance
  n particular 728.3
  example 748.2
  sample 748.3
  citation 912.5
  v cite 912.12

instant
  adj hasty 386.5
  instantaneous 792.4
  imminent 802.3
  prompt 807.9
  urgent 952.21
  n period 786.1
  short time 790.3
  moment 792.3

instead
  adv rather 824.8

institute
  n school 548.1
  organization 597.8
  v inaugurate 780.11
  cause 841.10
  establish 847.10

institution
  n organization 597.8
  holy orders 677.5
  workplace 716.1
  beginning 780.1
  establishment 847.4

instructions
  n directions 549.6

insurance
  n security 423.1
  precaution 479.3
  assurance 963.4

intellectual
  adj mental 874.6
  intelligent 875.10
  highbrow 883.19
  ideal 887.7
  temperamental 933.7
  n wise man 876.1
  scientist 883.9
  intellect 884.1

intelligence
  n information 532.1
  news 533.1
  aptitude 551.5
  secret service 557.12
  spirit 658.4
  intellect 874.1
  understanding 875.1
  knowledge 883.1
  understanding 883.3
  surveillance 893.8

intelligent
  adj apt 551.18
  mental 874.6
  intellectual 875.10
  knowing 883.12

intend
  v plan 365.4
  plan 366.7

intended

adj intentional 365.8
promised 421.7
meant 503.7
n betrothed 95.16

intense
adj penetrating 15.21
energetic 17.12
exquisite 24.13
colourful 34.17
fervent 84.16
zealous 92.9
great 233.6
violent 651.15
attentive 938.14

intensive
adj laborious 702.18
thorough 756.9

intention
n will 308.1
motive 362.1
intent 365.1
plan 366.1
intent 503.2

interest
n allure 362.1
benefit 372.4
undertaking 389.1
patronage 434.4
estate 456.4
gain 457.3
portion 462.5
party 597.4
lending 600.1
premium 603.3
prerogative 622.1
partiality 630.3
occupation 701.1
dividend 715.2
relevance 737.4
affair 793.3
principle 841.9
favour 849.2
curiosity 936.1
concern 938.2
importance 952.1
good 954.4
v attract 362.6

relate to 737.5
involve 853.2
concern 938.12

interested
adj partial 630.10
involved 853.4
curious 936.5
concerned 938.15

interesting
adj alluring 362.8
stimulating 938.18

interim
adj temporary 788.4
n interval 213.1
interruption 775.1
interval 788.1
delay 808.2
pause 819.3

interior
adj internal 198.6
inland 198.7
middle 781.3
n inside 198.2
inland 198.3
scene 690.10
middle 781.1

internal
adj interior 198.6
intrinsic 729.4
mental 874.6
n interior 198.2

international
adj public 297.9
universal 826.13

interpretation
n construction 326.1
explanation 503.3
solution 895.1

intervention
n intrusion 204.1
intrusion 205.1
mediation 451.1

interview
n audition 39.2
talk 523.2
conference 523.5
press conference

893.10
v interrogate 893.19

introduce
v insert 182.3
propose 424.5
initiate 549.14
present 568.13
prefix 776.3
go before 778.3
inaugurate 780.11
innovate 814.9

introduction
n import 178.7
entrance 180.1
injection 182.1
interjection 204.2
design 535.12
elementary education
549.5
acquaintance 568.4
first reading 594.4
act 682.4
overture 686.20
section 755.2
countdown 778.2
inauguration 780.5
basics 780.6
innovation 814.4

invasion
n intrusion 205.1
raid 443.3
seizure 620.3
swarming 865.2

investigate
v discuss 523.10
sift 893.21

investigation
n discussion 523.6
research 893.4

investment
n provision 370.1
endowment 463.9
commission 595.1
venture 706.3

invitation
n incentive 360.7
allure 362.1

offer 424.1
bidding 425.4

involve
v surround 200.5
signify 502.17
imply 504.4
incriminate 580.10
implicate 734.4
relate to 737.5
complicate 761.3
implicate 853.2
evidence 912.7
absorb 983.13
hamper 967.10
embarrass 968.15

involved
adj participating 461.7
partial 630.10
guilty 636.3
included 734.5
related 737.9
complex 761.4
implicated 853.4
engrossed 938.16

involved in
adj implicated in 853.5

involvement
n sympathy 84.5
surrounding 200.4
mediation 451.1
participation 461.1
incrimination 580.2
partiality 630.3
guilt 636.1
implication 734.2
implication 853.1
absorption 938.3

iron
adj brass 12.15
n stone 991.5
v press 273.6

Islamic
adj Muslim 655.26

isolated
adj quiet 164.10
private 330.13
quarantined 414.19

secluded 565.8
segregated 735.8
unrelated 738.4
separate 764.18
separated 764.19
alone 834.8

isolation
n privacy 330.2
quarantine 414.2
seclusion 565.1
xenophobia 735.3
separation 764.1
loneliness 834.2

issue
n emergence 181.1
amount 230.2
publication 337.1
escape 354.1
edition 535.5
posterity 542.1
platform 590.7
event 793.1
principle 841.9
effect 842.1
product 848.1
topic 892.1
question 893.9
solution 895.1
important thing 952.5
v emerge 181.8
flow 224.15
count 230.4
bring out 337.14
come out 337.16
come forth 354.10
parcel out 462.8
give 463.12
print 529.13
circulate 705.18
float 715.4
disperse 733.3
originate 780.12
follow 797.3
result 842.4

issued
adj published 337.17

it

n self 827.5
what's what 928.4

item
n memorandum 530.4
entry 608.5
commodity 712.2
particular 728.3
part 755.1
component 758.2
individual 834.4
citation 912.5

items
n contents 187.1
merchandise 712.1
list 833.1
knowledge 883.1

itself
n self 827.5

ivory
adj light 36.6
n smooth 273.3

jack
n seaman 174.1
flag 627.5
base 856.7
crane 867.2

jacket
n coat 5.10
skin 281.3
hull 281.15
wrapper 281.17
binding 535.14
v cloak 5.29

jail
n prison 414.8
v enclose 203.5
imprison 414.14

jailed
adj enclosed 203.9
imprisoned 414.20

jam
n sweets 10.36
obstruction 279.2
throng 732.4
barrier 967.5
pickle 968.5
v stop 279.6

fill 756.7
hook 762.7
secure 817.8
stop 819.5
teem with 839.5
overload 948.13
obstruct 967.11
densify 990.8

jazz
n traditional jazz 686.8

jet
n jet plane 172.3
spout 224.9
expulsion 864.7
heater 972.10
v fly 175.12
run out 181.10
discharge 864.23

Jewish
adj Hebrew 655.25

job
n act 313.3
heist 467.4
occupation 701.1
task 701.2
function 701.3
position 701.5
affair 793.3

jockey
n rider 169.7
v manoeuvre 400.10
compete 442.14

join
n joint 762.3
v adjoin 212.9
adjoin 212.13
flow 224.15
cooperate 435.3
side with 435.4
marry 544.12
join up 597.14
gather 732.18
identify 740.5
compose 758.3
put together 762.4
connect 762.10
be consistent 765.7

combine 767.3
continue 774.4
concur 854.2

joined
adj adjacent 212.16
accompanying 731.8
assembled 732.21
related 737.9
joint 762.11
united 762.12
consistent 765.10
combined 767.5

joining
adj connecting 762.15
n addition 253.1
junction 762.1

joint
adj cooperative 435.5
communal 461.8
accompanying 731.8
assembled 732.21
mutual 739.10
combined 762.11
combined 767.5
concurrent 854.3
n meat 10.12
crack 213.2
nick 414.9
join 762.3

joke
n jest 474.3
laughing stock 493.7
trifle 953.5
v jest 474.7
banter 475.4

journal
n notebook 530.9
periodical 536.1
account book 608.4
history 697.1
chronicle 794.6

journalist
n reporter 536.4

journey
n trip 168.4
v travel 168.17

joy

n happiness 86.2
merriment 100.5
v be pleased 86.11

judge
n arbiter 451.4
connoisseur 481.4
magistrate 577.1
justice 901.6
v mediate 451.6
administer justice 575.4
try 579.17
classify 763.8
adjudicate 901.8
think 908.11

judgment
n decision 579.9
condemnation 583.1
classification 763.3
prudence 875.7
solution 895.1
penetration 899.2
judging 901.1
opinion 908.6

juice
n current 982.2
fluid 15.2

jump
n progression 153.1
step 168.9
ascent 184.1
interval 213.1
increase 237.1
leap 351.1
promotion 431.1
v start 118.12
be startled 122.4
stroll 168.24
parachute 175.19
leave undone 325.7
leap 351.5
promote 431.2
attack 442.11
pitch into 444.13
shake 872.8

jumping
adj leaping 351.7

n leaping 351.3

junior
  adj inferior 236.6
  younger 287.13
  subsequent 797.4
  n inferior 236.2
  youngster 288.1
  subordinate 417.4

jury
  n panel 577.3

just
  adj rightful 619.8
  honest 624.9
  fair 629.6
  virtuous 653.10
  legal 653.10
  almighty 657.9
  valid 928.14
  accurate 928.16
  unprejudiced 978.12
  adv simply 760.10
  exactly 928.21

just about
  adv nearly 212.22

justice
  n judiciary 575.2
  judge 577.1
  probity 624.1
  justness 629.1
  prudence 633.3
  legality 653.1
  equality 752.1
  judge 901.6
  impartiality 934.5

justified
  adj warranted 619.9
  just 629.6

keen
  adj energetic 17.12
  acrimonious 17.13
  exquisite 24.13
  fervent 84.16
  heartfelt 84.22
  eager 92.8
  penetrating 96.31
  caustic 135.21
  sharp 271.7

willing 309.5
active 315.13
alert 324.14
enterprising 389.5
prepared 390.13
witty 474.9
violent 651.15
smart 875.12
cold 975.13
v screech 49.8

keep
  n nourishment 10.3
  accommodation 370.3
  support 434.3
  stronghold 445.6
  v obey 311.2
  provide 370.7
  store up 371.10
  reserve 371.11
  preserve 382.7
  observe 419.2
  support 434.12
  retain 459.5
  hold 459.7
  celebrate 472.2
  celebrate 680.9
  stabilize 817.7
  sustain 818.4
  bear in mind 944.10
  protect 963.18
  raise 113.5

keeper
  n saviour 382.4
  jailer 414.10
  possessor 455.1
  protector 963.5
  guardian 963.6

keeping
  adj preservative 382.9
  n symmetry 250.1
  preservation 382.1
  observance 419.1
  retention 459.1
  care 963.2

kept
  adj reserved 371.13
  preserved 382.10

key
  adj central 199.9
  n translation 326.3
  clue 502.9
  pitch 687.3
  key signature 687.9

key to
  v harmonize 750.7

khan
  n prince 589.7
  Sir 628.3

kick
  n pep 17.3
  zest 59.2
  charge 96.3
  signal 502.15
  boot 857.8
  v signal 502.22
  boot 857.18
  fire 864.18

kid
  n fledgling 288.9
  v jolly 475.5

kids
  n family 540.5
  posterity 542.1

kill
  n quarry 367.7
  v make laugh 107.9
  excise 241.9
  slay 294.10
  cover up 330.8
  end 380.12
  obliterate 380.16
  veto 429.5
  legislate 594.8
  end 782.4
  turn off 819.10

killer
  n butcher 294.8
  ruffian 574.3
  devil 651.8

killing
  adj fatiguing 21.11
  deadly 294.20
  laborious 702.18
  n violent death 293.5

slaying 294.1
rioting 651.3

kind
adj kindly 134.13
forgiving 139.6
indulgent 412.7
favourable 434.22
good 954.12
n race 540.4
nature 729.2
sort 771.3

kind of
adv somewhat 231.7

king
n sovereign 556.8
prince 589.7
man 720.16
chief 952.9

kingdom
n country 221.1
hierarchy 771.4

kiss
n touch 64.1
contact 212.5
smack 543.4
greeting 566.4
v brush 64.7
contact 212.10
smooch 543.19
greet 566.10

kit
n equipment 370.4
luggage 456.3

kitchen
adj cooking 11.5
n scullery 11.3

knee
n member 2.4
leg 168.11
angle 264.1
joint 762.3
v kick 857.18

knife
n sword 447.5
cutlery 986.2
v stab 444.20

knock

n report 47.1
hit 857.4
v crack 47.6
collide 857.12
hit 857.13
pound 857.14

know
v understand 506.7
be told 532.14
be friends 568.8
experience 793.8
perceive 883.10
be certain 925.6
recognize 944.9

know-how
n knowledge 883.1

knowing
adj intentional 365.8
experienced 398.26
cunning 400.12
intelligent 875.10
shrewd 875.13
wise 875.15
knowledgeable 883.12
n knowledge 883.1

knowledge
n information 532.1
learning 551.1
intelligence 875.1
knowing 883.1

known
adj recognized 883.21

known as
adj named 512.13

kohl
n makeup 971.10

L

L
n angle 264.1

label
n tag 502.13
name 527.3
kind 771.3
v tag 502.20
name 512.10
generalize 826.8

labour
n birth 1.1

occupation 701.1
task 701.2
work 702.4
v give birth 1.3
be busy 315.8
endeavour 388.4
work 701.10
work 702.12
insist upon 811.9

Labour Party
adj 590.36

lack
n absence 211.1
deficiency 757.2
want 947.4
imperfection 958.1
v want 757.3
fall short 866.2
want 947.7
be insufficient 947.8

lad
n guy 67.5
boy 288.5

lady
n mistress 95.13

Lady
n Excellency 628.2

lake
n landlocked water 227.1

lamb
n mutton 10.15
child 288.3
fledgling 288.9
ingenue 401.3
darling 543.6
innocent 637.2

land
n region 220.1
country 221.1
ground 223.1
real estate 456.5
v alight 175.18
get down 185.7
grab 457.9

landed
adj possessing 454.9

propertied 456.7

landing
n coming in 175.6
docking 177.2
harbour 964.6

landscape
n view 32.6
scene 690.10

lane
n passageway 368.3

language
adj speech 509.22
n speech 508.1
speech 509.1
diction 514.1
programming language 988.12

lap
n front 207.1
wash 224.8
overlap 281.4
sheet 282.2
race 442.9
circuit 869.2
v clothe 5.28
lap up 8.29
ripple 43.9
lick 64.9
lead 156.2
overtake 165.10
surround 200.5
border 202.9
overflow 224.16
fold 277.5
wrap 281.19
lie over 281.27
circle 869.5

large
adj immense 233.7
sizable 243.15
liberal 470.3

largely
adv greatly 233.14

last
adj departing 179.15
completing 392.8
final 782.10

eventual 793.11
foregoing 799.9
newest 803.14
adv finally 782.11
n end 782.1
v keep alive 292.8
persevere 345.2
live on 723.6
elapse 783.3
remain 815.4

lasting
adj persevering 345.8
sturdy 725.7
chronological 783.5
durable 789.9
protracted 789.10
permanent 815.6
unchanging 817.17
remembered 944.18
tough 994.3

late
adj retarded 166.11
dead 293.22
anachronistic 795.3
former 799.8
recent 803.12
inconvenient 806.6
belated 808.12
adv behind 808.15

later
adj subsequent 797.4
future 801.7
recent 803.12
last-minute 808.14
adv subsequently 797.5
anon 801.8

latest
adj present 800.2
newest 803.14

latter
adj foregoing 799.9
recent 803.12

laugh
n laughter 107.4
joke 474.3
v be pleased 86.11

exude cheerfulness 100.6
burst out laughing 107.8

laughing
adj happy 86.15
cheerful 100.11

laughter
n merriment 100.5
hilarity 107.4

launch
n beginning 780.1
v propose 424.5
inaugurate 780.11
throw 859.10
start 859.12

law
n rule 404.2
decree 405.4
prohibition 429.1
statute 653.3
legal system 653.4
jurisprudence 653.7
rule 831.4
axiom 929.2

lawyer
n attorney 578.1
professional 703.4

lay
adj nonordained 679.3
n direction 152.1
song 686.13
v deposit 69.9
place 150.12
deposit 150.14
level 192.6
smooth 273.5
impose 623.4

layer
n thickness 282.1
v lay down 282.4

lead
adj brass 12.15
n superiority 235.1
weight 283.4
shackle 413.4
pointer 502.4

clue 502.9
role 682.7
script 684.2
leading man or lady
685.5
chief 952.9
v head 152.6
head 156.2
head 207.6
lead 207.6
rule 235.11
rule 235.11
gravitate 283.11
induce 360.21
direct 554.8
govern 593.10
conduct 686.36
escort 731.7
precede 776.3
go before 778.3
initiate 780.10
induce 841.11
influence 849.7

lead in
v go before 778.3

lead to
v extend to 247.6
determine 841.12

leader
n vanguard 207.2
superior 235.4
born leader 555.6
conductor 688.13
precursor 778.1
special 828.2

leadership
n supremacy 235.3
mastery 402.7
statesmanship 590.3
influence 849.1
n directorship 554.4

leading
adj heading 156.3
front 207.9
chief 235.14
authoritative 402.14
directing 554.12

governing 593.16
preceding 776.4
first 780.14
paramount 952.23
n direction 554.1

leaf
n Cuban 80.2
sheet 282.2
frond 296.16
design 535.12
paper 999.5
v vegetate 296.26

league
n treaty 422.2
affiliation 435.2
association 597.1
combination 767.1
v ally 767.4

learn
v understand 506.7
awaken to 532.13
get 551.6
discover 896.2

learned
adj educated 551.16
undergraduate 553.11
wise 875.15
erudite 883.17

learning
n mental cultivation
551.1
enlightenment 883.4

least
adj humble 128.9
smallest 236.8
minority 840.7
n minority 840.3

leather
n fur 4.2
v beat up 585.14

leave
n holiday 20.3
parting 179.4
absence 211.4
consent 426.1
permission 428.1
v depart 179.6

leave behind 242.6
leave undone 325.7
abandon 355.5
resign 433.2
bequeath 463.18
separate 764.7

leaving
adj departing 179.15
n departure 179.1
absence 211.4
abandonment 355.1

left
adj departed 179.16
remaining 242.7
abandoned 355.8

left-wing
adj socialist 592.22

leg
n member 2.4
breast 10.22
limb 168.11
stake 259.6
member 755.4

legal
adj permissible 428.14
recorded 530.13
just 629.6
legitimate 653.10
valid 928.14

legend
n memory 642.7
mythology 658.13
history 697.1
tradition 804.2
caption 892.2

legislation
n lawmaking 594.3
law 653.3

legs
n member 2.4

leisure
adj idle 387.3
n idleness 316.2
ease 387.1
pause 819.3

lemon
n vinegar 58.2

length
n size 243.1
distance 247.1
overall length 253.1
extent 286.3

lens
n eye 2.6

lesbian
adj homosexual 66.28
n homosexual 66.14
amazon 67.9

less
adj inferior 236.6
fewer 840.6
adv decreasingly 238.12

lesson
n warning 384.1
reproof 495.5
teaching 549.7

let
adj employed 595.17
n rental 595.5
v draw off 183.11
permit 428.9
rent 595.13

letter
n representation 334.1
character 527.1
writing 528.8
type 529.6
message 533.4
message 534.2
v initial 527.6

letters
n writing system 527.3
literature 528.9
record 530.1
scholarship 883.5

level
adj horizontal 192.7
straight 263.6
smooth 273.9
uniform 743.5
equal 752.7
adv horizontally 192.9
n horizontal 192.3

degree 231.1
rank 231.2
smooth 273.3
layer 282.1
class 588.1
class 771.2
v flatten 192.6
smooth 273.5
raze 380.19
make uniform 743.4
equate 752.6
fell 868.5

liberal
adj permissive 415.23
charitable 463.22
free 470.3
hospitable 566.11
moderate 592.19
magnanimous 632.5
extensive 826.12
libertarian 934.9
plentiful 946.6
n free agent 415.11
moderate 592.11
bleeding heart 934.6

liberation
n escape 354.1
rescue 383.1
liberalism 415.10
freeing 416.1

liberty
n freedom 415.1
right 415.2
exemption 415.8
permission 428.1
grant 428.5
privilege 622.2
opportunity 805.2

library
adv reading room 539.1
n study 188.6
store 371.6
preserve 382.6
collection 732.11
retreat 964.5

licence

n lawlessness 403.1
freedom 415.1
exemption 415.8
permission 428.1
permit 428.6
commission 595.1
presumption 620.2
v commission 595.8

lie
n navigation 150.3
direction 152.1
falsehood 339.8
v extend 149.6
be found 150.10
lie down 192.5
be present 210.6
tell lies 339.13
shirk 353.9

Lieutenant
n Field Marshal 556.19
Admiral of the Fleet 556.20

life
n animation 17.4
stimulus 17.6
eagerness 92.1
gaiety 100.4
living 292.1
person 297.3
animation 315.2
history 697.1
existence 723.1
something 725.3
lifetime 789.4
affairs 793.4

lifestyle
n behaviour 306.1
custom 358.1
speciality 828.1

lifetime
adj lifelong 789.11
n life 292.1
life 789.4

lift
adv moving pavement 167.4
n height 258.2

helping hand 434.2
crane 867.2
elevator 867.3
v elate 100.8
transport 167.8
imitate 321.5
improve 377.9
swipe 467.15
elevate 867.4

lifted
adj raised 867.8

lifting
adj elevating 867.9
n elevation 867.1

light
adj frail 16.12
soft 34.20
fair 35.9
fair 36.6
thin 256.13
dieting 256.16
shallow 262.5
weightless 284.8
gentle 284.10
airy 302.10
fickle 349.5
tragic 682.26
superficial 877.18
trivial 953.16
lucid 977.30
n lightning 165.5
window 278.6
dawn 299.2
explanation 326.4
wave 871.4
outlook 931.2
lighter 973.4
radiant energy 977.1
light source 978.1
v land 175.18
get down 185.7
ignite 972.22
illuminate 977.27
strike a light 977.28

lighting
adj illuminating 977.39

n ignition 972.4
illumination 977.19

lightly
adv hardly 234.9
negligently 325.16
arbitrarily 349.6
unimportantly 953.20
easily 969.16

lights
n lungs 2.15
floodlights 682.14

like
adj approximate 737.8
identical 740.7
similar 746.6
equal 752.7
adv how 369.8
similarly 746.12
n love 95.1
likeness 746.3
equal 752.4
v enjoy 86.12
desire 91.13
love 95.18

like to
v want to 91.14

likely
adj apt 750.10
liable 852.5
possible 921.5
probable 923.3
disposed 933.8
expedient 950.5
adv probably 923.5

likely to
adj liable to 852.6

limit
n summit 189.2
limitation 201.2
boundary 203.3
capacity 243.2
end 756.5
extremity 782.2
v restrict 201.5
bound 202.7
narrow 256.9
restrict 413.8

limited
adj restricted 201.7
local 220.8
little 244.9
narrow 256.12
restricted 413.14
restrained 650.10
specialized 828.5
qualified 914.10
meagre 947.10

limits
n environment 200.1
bounds 202.1

line
n direction 152.1
ships 171.8
strip 253.3
cord 257.2
telephone line 332.10
policy 364.4
route 368.1
railway 368.7
manner 369.1
battlefield 448.2
score 502.6
track 502.8
letter 534.2
race 540.4
lineage 541.4
policy 590.4
air 686.3
part 686.18
staff 686.23
treatment 690.7
engraving 691.2
measure 698.9
vocation 701.6
merchandise 712.1
series 774.2
procession 774.3
sequence 777.1
sequel 797.2
speciality 828.1
trend 851.2
v fill 187.6

specialize 828.4
qualify 914.3

plaster 281.24
mark 502.19
engrave 691.6

lined
adj engraved 691.8

lines
n outline 202.2
manner 369.1
script 682.16

link
n intermediary 204.3
relation 737.1
joint 762.3
torch 978.3
v come together 732.16
relate 737.6
put together 762.4
combine 767.3
league 767.4
continue 774.4

linked
adj related 737.9
joined 762.12
allied 767.6
continuous 774.8

links
n playground 720.10

lip
n bulge 269.2

lips
n mouth 278.4
tongue 509.12

liquid
adj convertible 705.23
fluid 15.3
watery 19.14
n beverage 10.44
fluid 15.2

list
n contents 187.1
inclination 195.2
record 530.1
items 833.1
v heel 173.17
tumble 185.8
record 530.12

classify 771.5
enumerate 833.8

listed
adj enumerated 833.9

listen
v hark 39.9
hark 938.7

listen to
v listen 39.9

listening
adj attentive 39.13
n hearing 39.1
audition 39.2

lit
adj illuminated 977.38

literally
adv exactly 928.21

literary
adj bookish 883.18

literature
n writing 528.8
letters 528.9
work 696.1
lore 883.7

little
adj insignificant 234.6
inadequate 236.7
small 244.9
short 254.6
base 641.12
narrow-minded 935.10
insignificant 953.15
adv hardly 234.9
small 244.14
n modicum 234.2
short time 790.3

live
adj living 292.9
active 315.13
burning 971.46
charged 982.30
v inhabit 214.6
have life 292.5
exist 723.5
endure 789.5

live in
v inhabit 214.6

live-in
adj resident 214.12

lived-in
adj comfortable 112.11

liver
n internal organs 2.10
digestion 2.11
digestion 7.7
kidney 10.19

living
adj resident 214.12
organic 291.11
alive 292.9
existing 723.10
burning 971.46
n habitation 214.1
life 292.1
support 434.3
benefice 677.4

load
adv freight 167.5
n cargo 187.2
quantity 233.3
burden 283.5
charge 447.15
portion 462.5
charge 623.3
full measure 756.3
impediment 967.6
v burden 150.15
fill 187.6
burden 283.10
prime 390.9
fill 756.7
shoot 859.11
oppress 966.8
program 988.17

loan
n advance 600.2
v lend 600.5

local
adj localized 220.8
idiomatic 508.14

located
adj placed 150.18

location
n situation 150.1

placement 150.6
movie studio 684.3
state 727.1
discovery 896.1
farm 112.7

lock
n flowing locks 3.4
gate 225.10
bolt 413.5
half-nelson 459.3
v close 279.5
hook 762.7
obstruct 967.11

lodge
n house 217.5
cottage 217.7
lair 217.23
branch 597.10
v deposit 150.14
inhabit 214.6
house 214.9
accommodate 370.10
store 371.9
fix 817.9
root 817.10

logic
n dialectics 890.2
reasonableness 890.7

lonely
adj solitary 565.11
alone 834.8

long
adj lengthy 253.7
wordy 520.11
protracted 789.10
adv for long 789.12

long time
n length 253.1
long while 789.3

long way
n great distance 247.2

long-term
adj durable 789.9

look
n sight 27.3
appearance 33.3
looks 32.4

hint 532.4
v peer 27.12
gaze 27.14
appear 32.10
beware 479.6
heed 938.6

look after
v nurture 324.9
serve 558.12
care for 963.19

look at
v witness 873.5
examine 893.22

look for
v hope 115.6
look forward to 121.6
solicit 425.14
come 801.6
seek 893.28

look like
v hint 124.11
resemble 746.5

looking
n observation 27.2

looking for
adj expectant 121.10

looks
n features 32.4

loose
adj adrift 173.27
drooping 193.10
negligent 325.10
escaped 354.11
lax 411.3
free 415.19
uninhibited 415.22
discursive 520.12
wanton 645.23
unfastened 764.20
slack 766.4
slovenly 772.13
illogical 891.8
vague 926.13
flaccid 992.11
v loosen 416.6
detach 764.9
loosen 766.2

facilitate 969.7

lord
n proprietor 455.2
master 556.1
nobleman 589.4

lose
v fail 395.8
lose out 397.11
incur loss 458.4
waste 471.4

losing
adj speculative 722.23
n loss 458.1

loss
n disappearance 33.1
waste 238.3
damage 378.1
losing 458.1
disadvantage 951.2

losses
n net loss 458.3

lost
adj gone 33.4
past hope 116.13
lost 397.12
gone 458.7
wasted 471.7
godless 674.14
bewildered 926.15
bemused 940.11
forgotten 945.7

lot
n plot 220.4
amount 230.2
lots 233.4
real estate 456.5
portion 462.5
movie studio 684.3
state 727.1
bunch 732.7
fate 919.2
chance 927.1

lots
n lot 233.4
multitude 839.3
plenty 946.2

loud

adj intense 15.21
garish 34.18
resounding 44.11
demanding 406.9
coarse 482.9
gaudy 486.16

love
n sexuality 66.2
liking 91.2
affection 95.1
sweetheart 95.9
benevolence 134.4
accord 440.1
regards 489.7
darling 543.6
friendship 568.1
ardour 971.24
v respond 84.11
enjoy 86.12
desire 91.13
be fond of 95.18

love to
v want to 91.14

loved
adj beloved 95.23

lovely
adj delightful 88.6
endearing 95.24
beautiful 971.14

lover
n fancier 91.11
admirer 95.11
darling 543.6
friend 569.1
supporter 596.8

loving
adj fond 95.26
kind 134.13
careful 324.10
almighty 657.9

low
adj faint 43.14
deep 45.9
humble 128.9
inferior 236.6
short 254.6
flat 260.7

base 482.13
disapproving 495.19
inelegant 516.2
demographic 587.8
cheap 613.7
wicked 634.15
base 641.12
vulgar 646.8
depressed 868.12
adv below 260.9
n weather map 302.3
business cycle 708.9
price 715.3
gear 986.5
v cry 51.2

lower
adj inferior 236.6
reduced 238.10
inferior 260.8
n scowl 101.9
v look sullen 101.15
sadden 103.18
bode 124.10
debase 128.5
sink 185.6
reduce 238.7
debase 260.6
deepen 261.7
excavate 270.12
demote 432.3
cheapen 613.6
be imminent 802.2
depress 868.4

lowest
adj humble 128.9
bottom 190.7
least 236.8
lower 260.8

loyal
adj zealous 92.9
obedient 311.3
firm 344.11
persevering 345.8
observant 419.4
partisan 590.34
faithful 624.16

Luck

n Chance 927.2

lucky
adj favourable 124.17
speculative 722.23
timely 805.8
chance 927.9
fortunate 965.14

lunch
n breakfast 8.6
v dine 8.20

luxury
n pleasure 86.1
grandeur 486.5
sensuality 643.1
fat 948.4
prosperity 965.1

lying
adj prostrate 192.8
dishonest 339.22
n lowness 260.1
dishonesty 339.5

machine
n melting pot 820.10
machinery 986.3
computer 988.2
v tool 986.7

mad
adj frenzied 96.25
sore 143.29
reckless 478.7
turbulent 651.16
foolish 878.7
insane 881.22
rabid 881.26

made
adj formative 248.8
produced 847.17
man-made 847.18

made of
adj composed of 758.4

made-up
adj decorative 971.19

magazine
n store 371.6
armoury 447.2
periodical 536.1

maggot

n larva 288.11

magic
  adj illustrious 642.17
  magical 669.8
  n lustre 642.6
  sorcery 669.1

magnificent
  adj eminent 233.9
  grandiose 486.17
  superb 954.15

mail
  n shell 281.14
  armour 445.3
  post 534.4
  v send 167.9
  post 534.12

main
  adj chief 235.14
  first 780.14
  paramount 952.23
  n water main 225.6

mainly
  adv chiefly 235.17
  on the whole 754.13
  first 780.15
  generally 826.16
  normally 831.8

maintain
  v affirm 319.5
  provide 370.7
  preserve 382.7
  insist 406.8
  support 434.12
  retain 459.5
  endure 789.5
  sustain 818.4
  support 856.8
  think 908.11

maintained
  adj supported 856.11

maintaining
  adj supporting 856.10

maintenance
  n repair 381.6
  preservation 382.1
  support 434.3
  retention 459.1

support 604.8
  durability 789.1
  preservation 815.2
  continuance 818.1
  support 856.1

Major
  n Field Marshal 556.19

majority
  adj most 838.7
  n maturity 289.2
  major part 754.6
  most 838.2

make
  n structure 252.1
  yield 457.5
  composition 758.1
  kind 771.3
  disposition 933.3
  v go 168.15
  arrive 177.6
  flow 224.15
  act 313.4
  do 313.6
  perform 313.9
  make up 390.7
  accomplish 392.4
  compel 409.4
  execute 422.9
  acquire 457.8
  compose 758.3
  convert 820.11
  cause 841.10
  produce 847.8
  imagine 941.9

make it
  v arrive 177.6
  make good 394.7
  manage 394.9

make sure
  v take precautions
    479.5
  make certain 925.7
  play safe 962.3

make up
  v fabricate 339.12
  improvise 350.7
  get up 390.7

arrange 422.8
  gather 732.18
  complete 756.6
  compose 758.3
  produce 847.8
  originate 847.12
  beautify 971.12

make-up
  n mode 727.3

maker
  n artist 694.1
  agent 703.1
  author 841.4
  producer 847.7

making
  n reproduction 69.1
  forming 248.5
  structure 252.1
  acquisition 457.1
  production 847.2

male
  adj masculine 67.10
  n masculine 67.4

man
  n mankind 67.3
  male 67.4
  adult 290.1
  mankind 297.1
  person 297.3
  husband 544.6
  manservant 558.4
  piece 720.16
  v equip 370.8
  fortify 445.9

manage
  v pilot 173.10
  perform 313.9
  support oneself 370.12
  use 372.8
  treat 372.10
  accomplish 392.4
  contrive 394.9
  direct 554.8
  govern 593.10
  fare 727.4
  persist 818.5
  operate 844.5

make do 950.4
tend 113.6

management
n supremacy 235.3
performance 313.2
usage 372.2
utilization 372.6
directorate 555.11
government 593.1
operation 844.1
care 963.2
n direction 554.1

manager
n director 555.1
governor 556.6
businessman 707.1
operator 844.4

managing
adj directing 554.12
n direction 554.1

managing director
n executive 555.3

manner
n aspect 32.3
appearance 197.1
behaviour 306.1
custom 358.1
way 369.1
style 514.2
mode 727.3
kind 771.3
speciality 828.1

manufacturing
adj industrial 847.14

many
adj much 233.8
different 742.6
varied 745.4
frequent 809.4
plural 838.5
numerous 839.6
plentiful 946.6

map
n chart 150.5
representation 334.1
diagram 366.3
v locate 150.11

represent 334.8
plot 366.9

march
n progression 153.1
walk 168.8
boundary 202.3
frontier 202.5
sphere 220.2
objection 318.2
quick march 686.11
v tramp 168.26
border 202.9
object 318.5

marine
adj nautical 173.24
maritime 226.5
n navy man 174.2
navy 446.22

mark
n degree 231.1
sign 502.1
marking 502.5
marker 502.10
distinction 642.5
notation 687.6
kind 771.3
characteristic 827.4
impact 842.2
evidence 912.1
importance 952.1
stain 959.3
v celebrate 472.2
signify 502.17
pencil 502.19
letter 527.6
engrave 691.6
characterize 827.10
specify 827.11
estimate 901.9
evidence 912.7
necessitate 919.4
heed 938.6
stain 959.6

marked
adj designated 502.24
engraved 691.8
characteristic 827.13

destined 919.6
notable 952.18

market
adj sales 711.10
n square 219.6
commerce 708.1
public 710.3
sale 711.1
store 713.1
open market 713.2
workplace 716.1
v deal in 708.15
sell 711.6

marketing
adj sales 711.10
n commerce 708.1
purchase 710.1
selling 711.2

marriage
n matrimony 544.1
wedding 544.2
compound 759.4
joining 762.1
combination 767.1

married
adj matrimonial 544.16
wedded 544.19
joined 762.12
allied 767.6

marry
v wed 544.12
wed 544.13
put together 762.4
combine 767.3
league 767.4

marvellous
adj wonderful 113.6
remarkable 233.10
extraordinary 832.14
superb 954.15

mass
adj gravitational 283.15
demographic 587.8
n quantity 230.1
quantity 233.3

size 243.1
lump 243.10
thickness 255.2
gravity 283.3
store 371.1

Mass
n the Liturgy 680.6

mass
n substance 725.1
throng 732.4
accumulation 732.9
major part 754.6
conglomeration 765.5
majority 838.2
solid 990.6
v load 150.15
come together 732.16
put together 762.4
adhere 765.6

massive
adj large 233.7
bulky 243.18
thick 255.7
heavy 283.12
onerous 283.13
sturdy 725.7

Master
n Mister 67.7

master
n past master 398.13
lord 556.1

Master
n Sir 628.3

master
v become adept in
551.9

match
n image 334.5
contest 442.3
marriage 544.1
game 720.8
equal 752.4
two 835.2
safety match 973.5
light source 978.1
v parallel 194.3
line up 194.4

oppose 206.4
marry 544.12
gather 732.18
coincide 740.4
resemble 746.5
agree 750.6
equal 752.5
coincide 798.4
double 835.4
compare 898.4
be comparable 898.6

mate
n skipper 174.5
image 334.5
spouse 544.5
pal 569.4
accompanist 731.3
v copulate 66.20
marry 544.13
double 835.4

material
adj carnal 643.6
worldly 674.12
substantial 725.6
essential 729.6
relevant 737.11
evidential 912.14
important 952.16
vital 952.22
substantial 997.9
inorganic 1.3
n fabric 4.1
material 4.1
substance 187.4
store 371.1
substance 725.2
matter 997.2

materials
n store 371.1
lore 883.7
substances 999.1

mates
n two 835.2

matter
n humour 2.17
pus 12.6
substance 187.4

quantity 230.1
motive 360.1
undertaking 389.1
writing 528.8
occupation 701.1
substance 725.2
particular 728.3
affair 793.3
topic 952.1
material 997.2
v signify 952.11

matters
n affairs 793.4

mature
adj grown 14.3
grown 245.12
adult 289.9
ripe 289.10
middle-aged 290.6
prepared 390.13
ripe 392.12
experienced 398.26
complete 756.8
perfected 957.8
v grow 14.2
grow 245.7
grow up 289.7
grow old 290.5
develop 377.10
ripen 392.7
complete 756.6
evolve 823.4
originate 847.12
perfect 957.4

maximum
adj top 198.8
great 233.6
superlative 235.13
n summit 189.2
supremacy 235.3
limit 756.5
plenty 946.2

may
v be able 18.6
can 428.12

maybe
adv possibly 921.8

mayor
  n secretary of state
    556.17
  legislator 591.3

ME
  n fatigue 21.1

meal
  n mess 8.5
  feed 10.4
  cereal 10.31
  powder 996.5

meals
  n rations 10.6

mean
  adj humble 128.9
  servile 129.11
  envious 145.3
  medium 232.3
  insignificant 234.6
  inadequate 236.7
  niggardly 469.8
  low 482.13
  demographic 587.8
  small 631.6
  base 641.12
  middle 781.3
  narrow-minded 935.10
  meagre 947.10
  paltry 953.18
  n middle 232.1
  middle ground 452.3
  v manifest 333.5
  intend 365.4
  signify 502.17
  signify 503.5
  imply 504.4

meaning
  n portent 124.7
  interpretation 326.1
  intention 365.1
  significance 503.1
  lexicology 511.12

means
  n manner 369.1
  ways 369.2
  supply 371.2
  assets 456.6

funds 705.11
expedient 950.2
tool 986.1

meant
  adj intentional 365.8
  implied 503.7
  implied 504.7

meanwhile
  adv in the meantime
    783.8
  meantime 788.1
  n meantime 788.2

measure
  n space 149.1
  quantity 230.1
  amount 230.2
  degree 231.1
  size 243.1
  capacity 243.2
  length 253.1
  measurement 286.1
  measuring instrument
    286.2
  act 313.3
  portion 462.5
  sign 502.1
  harmony 515.2
  law 653.3
  air 686.3
  metre 698.7
  strain 698.9
  process 844.2
  expedient 950.2
  v count 230.4
  size 243.14
  gauge 286.7
  harmonize 750.7
  estimate 901.9

measures
  n layer 282.1
  precaution 479.3

meat
  n meal 8.5
  food 10.1
  red meat 10.12
  substance 187.4
  summary 538.2

essence 729.1
major part 754.6

mechanism
  n agency 369.3
  instrument 369.4
  art 398.7
  machinery 986.3
  machinery 986.4

medal
  n military honour
    626.6
  insignia 627.1
  relief 693.3

media
  n communications
    328.4
  communications 332.1

medical
  adj health 81.11

medicine
  n medicament 77.4
  medical practice 81.1

medieval
  adj antiquated 804.12

medium
  adj done 11.7
  mean 232.3
  middle 781.3
  mediocre 960.7
  n colour 34.8
  substance 187.4
  intermediary 204.3
  mean 232.1
  instrument 369.4
  mediator 451.3
  psychic 668.8
  agent 703.1
  idealist 998.3

meet
  adj decorous 481.7
  conventional 560.5
  timely 805.8
  n contest 442.3
  v converge 160.2
  confront 207.7
  encounter 212.11
  concur 317.8

observe 419.2
confront 436.5
brave 477.9
come together 732.16
convene 732.17
join 762.10
experience 793.8
conform 829.3
collide 857.12
suffice 946.3

meeting
adj converging 160.3
in contact 212.17
assembled 732.21
joining 762.15
n convergence 160.1
joining up 212.4
contest 442.3
conference 523.5
rendezvous 563.9
assembly 732.2
joining 762.1
impact 857.3

member
n external organ 2.4
affiliate 597.11
organ 755.4

members
n membership 597.12

membership
n association 563.6
members 597.12
inclusion 734.1

memorial
adj celebrating 472.3
n record 530.1
memorandum 530.4
monument 530.10
history 697.1
memento 944.6

memory
n celebration 472.1
notice board 530.8
remembrance 642.7
remembrance 799.4
remembrance 944.1
storage 988.7

men
n work force 18.4
mankind 67.3
staff 558.10

mental
adj intellectual 874.6
crazy 881.23
cognitive 886.17
temperamental 933.7

mention
n remark 509.3
citation 626.4
v remark 509.18
specify 827.11
touch on 938.10
mention 938.10

merchant
n supplier 370.6
trader 707.2

Mercury
n messenger 338.1
planet 114.9

mere
adj sheer 234.8
simple 760.5
n lake 227.1

merely
adv moderately 234.10
simply 760.10
solely 834.14

mess
n meal 8.5
rations 10.6
filth 71.7
chaos 249.1
fiasco 395.6
conglomeration 759.5
complex 761.2
jumble 772.3
pickle 968.5
eyesore 970.3
v feed 8.17

message
n communication
328.1
information 532.1
dispatch 533.4

letter 534.2

metal
adj metallic 12.14
n elementary metal
12.3

method
n behaviour 306.1
plan 366.1
manner 369.1
means 369.2
art 398.7
orderliness 769.3

methods
n behaviour 306.1

mid
adj middle 781.3

middle
adj central 199.9
intervening 204.7
mediating 451.8
mediocre 781.3
n centre 199.1
mean 232.1
midst 781.1
v centralize 199.7

middle class
n bourgeoisie 588.5
mediocrity 960.5

middle-class
adj upper-class 588.10
ordinary 960.8

midnight
adj nocturnal 300.9
n dead of night 300.6

might
n strength 15.1
power 18.1
greatness 233.1
authority 402.2

might be
v be possible 921.3

mike
n microphone 41.8

mild
adj insipid 56.2
bright 88.10
good-natured 134.14

lenient 412.6
meek 418.13
moderate 650.9
warm 971.43
soft 992.8
military
adj warlike 443.17
milk
n humour 2.17
fluid 15.2
v draw off 183.11
exploit 372.14
take from 465.21
strip 465.24
tend 113.6
mill
n plant 716.2
machinery 986.3
crusher 996.7
v notch 275.2
come together 732.16
tool 986.7
pulverize 996.8
million
adj numerous 839.6
mind
n psyche 83.17
will 308.1
intention 365.1
intellect 874.1
psyche 874.4
opinion 908.6
disposition 933.3
mood 933.4
attention 938.1
memory 944.1
v take amiss 143.13
refuse 310.3
obey 311.2
care 324.6
beware 479.6
heed 938.6
care for 963.19
minded
adj disposed 933.8
mine
n pit 270.3

trap 341.12
source 371.4
trench 445.5
bomb 447.19
gold mine 598.4
well 841.6
pit 12.6
v extract 183.9
deepen 261.7
excavate 270.12
blow up 380.18
fortify 445.9
take from 465.21
process 847.9
quarry 12.12
mini
adj miniature 244.11
minimum
adj least 236.8
sufficient 946.5
n modicum 234.2
minister
n secretary of state
556.17
clergyman 678.2
v officiate 680.10
ministry
n aid 434.1
service 558.11
bureau 575.3
clergy 678.1
care 963.2
minor
adj inferior 236.6
immature 287.9
insignificant 953.15
n youngster 288.1
minority
adj least 840.7
n immaturity 287.3
least 840.3
minute
adj tiny 244.10
meticulous 324.12
detailed 728.9
particular 827.12
insignificant 953.15

n entry 608.5
period 786.1
moment 786.2
instant 792.3
time 794.2
v record 530.12
keep accounts 608.8
minutes
n memorandum 530.4
report 530.7
mirror
n furniture 218.1
v imitate 321.5
reflect 334.10
resemble 746.5
miss
n girl 288.6
slip 395.4
mistake 930.3
v leave undone 325.7
slip 395.12
lose 458.4
miscarry 866.4
be inattentive 939.2
want 947.7
fall short 958.3
missed
adj neglected 325.14
missing
adj gone 33.4
absent 211.10
without being 724.7
incomplete 757.4
wanting 947.13
mission
n flight operation
175.5
adventure 389.2
operation 443.4
foreign office 557.7
delegation 557.13
commission 595.1
duty 621.1
church 681.1
task 701.2
vocation 701.6
mistake

n miss 395.4
bungle 399.5
fault 930.3
v misinterpret 327.2
misunderstand 930.11

mix
n film editing 684.5
conglomeration 759.5
v make up 390.7
compose 758.3
mingle 759.9
combine 767.3
confound 900.3

mixed
adj ambiguous 521.4
mingled 759.12
combined 767.5

mixture
n medicine 77.4
concoction 390.3
assortment 732.13
difference 742.1
composition 758.1
mixing 759.1
compound 759.4
compound 767.2

mobile
adj moving 163.6
upper-class 588.10
changeable 816.6
n work of art 690.8
sculpture 693.2

mode
n form 248.1
manner 369.1
style 514.2
state 727.1
manner 727.3

model
adj praiseworthy 494.18
exemplary 748.8
normal 831.6
perfected 957.8
n form 248.1
measure 286.2
reproduction 321.3

original 322.2
image 334.5
figure 334.6
essence 729.1
duplicate 747.3
pattern 748.1
ideal 748.4
rule 831.4
archetype 887.2
beauty 971.7
v form 248.6
sculpture 693.5

moderate
adj sedate 97.14
slow 166.9
medium 232.3
lenient 412.6
neutral 452.6
middle-of-the-road 592.19
cheap 613.7
temperate 648.7
temperate 650.9
middle 781.3
tolerable 954.19
mediocre 960.7
n wet 592.11
neutral 650.4
v slow 166.8
limit 201.5
mediate 451.6
restrain 650.5
qualify 914.3

modern
adj fashionable 559.11
present 800.2
contemporary 803.13
n modern man 803.4

modest
adj humble 128.9
meek 130.9
inferior 236.6
demurring 310.7
reticent 329.8
unselfish 632.4
decent 644.5
mediocre 960.7

moment
n prestige 402.4
period 786.1
second 786.2
short time 790.3
instant 792.3
importance 952.1

monetary
adj financial 705.22

money
n wealth 598.1
currency 705.1

monitoring
n vigilance 324.4

month
n moment 786.2

monthly
adj recurrent 811.13
momentary 812.8

mood
n plot 700.4
humour 933.4

moon
n moment 786.2
light source 978.1
satellite 1114.11
v idle 316.10
muse 940.9

moral
adj ethical 616.6
dutiful 621.11
honest 624.9
virtuous 633.5
n warning 384.1
rule 404.2
maxim 929.1

more
adj additional 239.9
plural 838.5
adv increasingly 237.9
n several 838.1

moreover
adv additionally 239.10

morning
adj dawn 294.4
adv long 789.12
n morn 299.1

mortgage
n lien 423.4
v pledge 423.8

most
adj greatest 233.13
superlative 235.13
majority 838.7
adv utterly 233.21
n supremacy 235.3
major part 754.6
majority 838.2

mostly
adv chiefly 235.17
on the whole 754.13
generally 826.16
normally 831.8

mother
adj native 215.4
n brother 540.3
maternal ancestor 541.11
author 841.4
producer 847.7
v generate 69.8
foster 434.16
care for 963.19

motion
n exercise 75.2
movement 163.1
travel 168.1
activity 315.1
proposal 424.2
gesture 502.14
trend 851.2
mechanism 986.4
v gesture 502.21

motor
n automobile 170.7
melting pot 820.10
machinery 986.3
v drive 168.29

mount
n ascent 184.1
v copulate 66.20
move 163.4
go on horseback 168.30

ascend 175.15
ascend 184.7
climb 184.10
get on 184.11
rise 191.7
grow 237.6
tower 258.7
grow 258.9
dramatize 682.20
help up 867.6

mountain
n quantity 233.3
plateau 258.4
bulge 269.2

mounted
adv on horseback 168.38

mouth
n gullet 2.12
eater 8.15
inlet 228.1
muzzle 278.4
v chew 8.26
grimace 251.8
speak 509.13
mumble 510.8

move
n act 313.3
attempt 388.2
stratagem 400.3
process 844.2
expedient 950.2
v affect 84.12
touch 136.5
settle 150.17
progress 153.2
budge 163.4
set in motion 163.5
remove 167.7
travel 168.14
behave 306.3
act 313.4
motivate 360.11
admonish 407.5
propose 424.5
sell 711.6
influence 849.7

impel 857.10
push 859.9

moved
adj affected 84.21
excited 96.20
motivated 360.29

movement
adv moving 167.3
n defecation 12.2
faeces 12.4
exercise 75.2
motion 163.1
travel 168.1
act 313.3
activity 315.1
gesture 502.14
front 590.27
passage 686.19
style 690.6
company 732.3
principle 841.9
trend 851.2
mechanism 986.4

movements
n behaviour 306.1

moves
n behaviour 306.1

movie
n motion pictures 684.1

movies
n motion pictures 684.1

moving
adj affecting 84.20
exciting 96.30
pitiful 136.7
stirring 163.6
travelling 168.32
motivating 360.24
lofty 525.13
impelling 857.20
adv removal 167.3

Mr
n Mister 67.7

Mrs
n Ms 68.7

Ms
n Mistress 68.7

much
adj many 233.8
plentiful 946.6
adv greatly 233.14
n quantity 233.3
plenty 946.2

mud
n dirt 71.6
marsh 229.1
muck 16.7

mum
adj mute 42.11
taciturn 329.7
n mummy 541.12

murder
n homicide 294.2
v assassinate 294.13
bungle 399.9

murdered
adj botched 399.18

muscle
adj skeleton 2.19
n muscularity 15.2
exertion 702.1
v thrust 857.11

museum
n gallery 371.8
preserve 382.6
collection 732.11

music
n score 686.22
harmony 687.1

musical
adj music-loving 686.38
n musical theatre 686.28

Muslim
adj Islamic 655.26
n Sunni 655.19

must
n requirement 918.2
v be necessary 918.9

mutual
adj cooperative 435.5

communal 461.8
accompanying 731.8
common 739.10
interchangeable 825.4

myself
n self 827.5
self 827.5

mystery
n secret 330.5
inexplicability 507.6
enigma 507.7
rite 680.1
the supernatural 832.7
the unknown 885.6

myth
n fabrication 339.7
memory 642.7
whim 941.4

naked
adj nude 6.14
open 333.10
unadorned 484.8
unadulterated 760.6
exposed 961.15

name
n denomination 512.3
repute 642.1
personage 952.7
v nominate 356.18
designate 502.18
nominate 512.10
appoint 595.9
specify 827.11
cite 912.11

named
adj chosen 356.25
called 512.13
former 776.5

narrow
adj limited 201.7
slender 256.12
meticulous 324.12
exclusive 735.9
narrow-minded 935.10
n narrows 256.3
v limit 201.5
contract 246.5

constrict 256.9
simplify 760.3
specialize 828.4
qualify 914.3

nasty
adj offensive 55.6
offensive 89.18
malicious 135.18
terrible 955.9

nation
n population 216.1
country 221.1
mankind 297.1
race 540.4

national
adj public 297.9
racial 540.7
demographic 587.8
universal 826.13
n citizen 216.4

nationalist
n patriot 572.3

native
adj indigenous 215.4
virgin 391.11
innate 729.5
n earliest inhabitant 216.3

natural
adj typical 334.14
unspoiled 401.5
unaffected 484.7
elegant 515.4
plain-speaking 517.3
related 540.6
informal 562.3
innate 729.5
lifelike 746.11
normal 831.6
instinctive 889.6
genuine 928.15
n talented person 398.12
note 687.8

naturally
adv artlessly 401.6
directly 484.11

plainly 517.4
informally 562.4
intrinsically 729.7
normally 831.8
in consequence 842.7
genuinely 928.19

nature
n natural state 391.2

Nature
n Mother Nature 657.5

nature
n kind 771.3
characteristic 827.4
disposition 933.3
universe 114.1

naval
adj nautical 173.24

Navy
n branch 446.17

navy
n naval forces 446.22

near
adj approaching 158.4
close 212.14
narrow 256.12
approximate 737.8
approximating 746.9
imminent 802.3
adv close 212.20
nearly 212.22
v approach 158.3
come near 212.7
come 801.6
be imminent 802.2

nearby
adj handy 212.15
adv near 212.20

nearest
adj closest 212.19

nearly
adv near 212.22
approximately 230.6
narrowly 256.17
on the whole 754.13

neat
adj shapely 250.5
elegant 515.4

chic 559.13
unadulterated 760.6
tidy 769.8
great 954.13

necessarily
adv in consequence 842.7
of necessity 918.14
inevitably 918.16

necessary
adj obligatory 409.11
obligatory 621.13
obligatory 918.10
requisite 918.11
inevitable 918.13
certain 925.9

neck
n contraction 246.1
narrow 256.3
joint 762.3
supporter 856.2
v snog 543.15

need
n desire 91.1
indigence 599.2
deficiency 757.2
requirement 918.2
want 947.4
v be poor 599.5
require 918.8
be necessary 918.9
want 947.7

need for
n requirement 918.2

need to
v be necessary 918.9

needed
adj requisite 918.11

negative
adj pessimistic 116.14
denying 320.5
unwilling 427.6
opposing 436.7
without being 724.7
contrary 741.5
disagreeing 751.6
positive 982.31

n minus sign 241.5
negation 320.1
refusal 427.1
print 691.3
film 692.8
print 747.5
mould 748.6

negotiate
v leap 351.5
manage 394.9
bargain 422.6
mediate 451.6
confer 523.9
bargain 708.17

negotiations
n conference 523.5

neighbour
adj adjacent 212.16
n bystander 212.6
friend 587.3
v adjoin 212.9
join 212.13

neighbouring
adj surrounding 200.7
nearby 212.15
adjacent 212.16

nerve
adj skeleton 2.19
n nervous system 2.9
cheek 133.3
courage 477.1
stability 817.1
v strengthen 15.12
encourage 477.12

nervous
adj neural 24.10
sensitive 24.12
excitable 96.28
anxious 117.6
fearful 118.22
highly strung 119.11
agitated 872.13

nest
n abode 217.1
beehive 217.22
fledgling 288.9
birthplace 841.8

net
n network 161.3
difference 241.7
screen 278.7
weight 283.1
snare 341.13
production 848.2
v web 161.7
trap 341.20
acquire 457.8
profit 457.12
catch 465.17

network
n weaving 161.3
informant 532.5
company 732.3
network 983.6
computer network
988.15

never
adv not ever 784.3

nevertheless
adv anyhow 369.9

new
adj additional 239.9
original 322.4
unaccustomed 359.4
unused 375.10
fashionable 559.11
present 800.2
young 803.7
adv newly 803.15

newly
adv freshly 803.15
again 836.7

news
n tidings 533.1
newspaper 536.2

news conference
n conference 523.5

newspaper
n news 533.1
news 536.2

next
adj adjacent 212.16
nearest 212.19
succeeding 777.3

adv subsequently
797.5

nice
adj tasty 54.7
pleasant 88.5
kind 134.13
meticulous 324.12
dainty 480.8
exact 928.17
good 954.12

nick
n notch 275.1
slammer 414.9
mark 502.5
v notch 275.2
bust 414.16
swipe 467.15
mark 502.19

night
adj nocturnal 300.9
n night-time 300.4
darkness 979.1

nightmare
n torment 87.7
bogeyman 118.9
dream 941.7

nights
adv nightly 300.10

no
n negation 320.1
refusal 427.1

no doubt
adv probably 923.5
unquestionably 925.19

no more
adj gone 33.4
extinct 724.9
past 799.6

no other
n one 834.3

nobody
n mediocrity 960.5

noise
n sound 41.1
blast 44.3
clash 52.2
meaninglessness 505.1

signal 532.7
pandemonium 772.5

none
n not any 724.3

nonsense
n rubbish 505.2
foolishness 878.1
absurdity 878.3

normal
adj medium 232.3
typical 334.14
customary 358.12
orderly 769.6
prevalent 826.11
natural 831.6
sane 880.2
ordinary 960.8
n vertical 191.2
straight line 263.2

normally
adv customarily 358.18
generally 826.16
naturally 831.8

north
adj northern 152.13
adv northward 152.14
n points of the
compass 152.2

northern
adj north 152.13

nose
n nostrils 60.4
bow 207.3
nozzle 225.8
snout 269.5

not have
v refuse 427.3
not endure 429.4

not know
v wonder 885.9

not like
adj different 742.6

not much
adv not nearly 234.11

not quite
adv nearly 212.22

notably

adv acutely 233.19
  conspicuously 333.16
  famously 642.19
  importantly 952.24
note
n observation 27.2
  ambience 200.3
  postscript 240.2
  comment 326.5
  sign 502.1
  memorandum 530.4
  letter 534.2
  piece 537.1
  entry 608.5
  distinction 642.5
  air 686.3
  pitch 687.3
  musical note 687.8
  interval 687.11
  paper money 705.4
  recognition 883.2
  mood 933.4
  importance 952.1
v remark 509.18
  record 530.12
  keep accounts 608.8
  heed 938.6
noted
adj distinguished
  642.14
nothing
n void 211.3
  nil 724.2
  zero 726.2
notice
n observation 27.2
  announcement 337.2
  press release 337.3
  publicity 337.4
  advertisement 337.6
  warning 384.1
  demand 406.1
  information 532.1
  commentary 537.2
  recognition 883.2
  criticism 901.2
  attention 938.1

v see 27.11
  detect 896.5
  heed 938.6
notion
n whim 349.1
  intention 365.1
  plan 366.1
  idea 887.1
  suggestion 906.5
  opinion 908.6
novel
adj original 322.4
  original 803.11
n book 535.1
  story 700.3
novice
n beginner 553.8
  nun 678.10
  beginner 780.2
now
adj modern 803.13
adv at once 792.7
  at present 800.3
  recently 803.16
n the present 800.1
nowadays
adv now 800.3
  n the present 800.1
nowhere
n the back of beyond
  247.4
nuclear
adj chromosomal
  291.14
  thermonuclear 985.14
nuclear weapons
n arms 447.1
number
n amount 230.2
  edition 535.5
  section 755.2
v count 230.4
  total 754.8
  enumerate 763.7
number one
adj paramount 952.23
n urine 12.5

  self 827.5
numbers
n quantity 230.1
  multitude 839.3
numerous
adj much 233.8
  large 243.15
  plural 838.5
  many 839.6
  plentiful 946.6
nurse
n physician 81.7
  nanny 963.8
v nourish 8.18
  treat 82.11
  foster 434.16
  hold 459.7
  care for 963.19
nursery
n bedroom 188.7
  hospital room 188.21
  infant school 548.2
  birthplace 841.8
  conservatory 112.10
O
n circle 266.1
o'clock
adv half past 794.12
object
n objective 365.2
  intent 503.2
  something 725.3
  article 997.4
v protest 318.5
  offer resistance 438.3
  disagree 751.5
objective
adj unfeeling 85.9
  unflappable 97.10
  impartial 629.8
  real 723.11
  external 730.2
  true 928.13
  unprejudiced 934.12
n will 308.1
  object 365.2
observer

n military pilot 176.2 ·
spectator 873.1
examiner 893.16

obtain
v fetch 167.10
acquire 457.8
receive 464.6
exist 723.5
induce 841.11

obvious
adj distinct 30.7
manifest 333.8
patent 925.10

obviously
adv visibly 30.8
decidedly 233.18
manifestly 333.14
really 723.12

occasion
n pretext 361.1
circumstance 728.1
event 793.2
opportunity 805.2
cause 841.1
requirement 918.2
v cause 841.10

occasional
adj circumstantial 728.7
happening 793.9
incidental 805.10
casual 810.3

occasionally
adv at intervals 775.4
on occasion 810.5

occupation
n habitation 214.1
action 313.1
possession 454.1
appropriation 465.4
work 701.1
vocation 701.6
operation 844.1

occupied
adj inhabited 214.11
busy 315.17
busy 701.12

engrossed 938.16

occur
v be present 210.6
exist 723.5
happen 793.5

ocean
n sea 226.1
sea 226.2
quantity 233.3

odd
adj dissimilar 749.4
occasional 810.3
queer 832.11
sole 834.9
insane 881.22
eccentric 882.5

odds
n gambling odds 722.5
probability 923.1

of course
adv in consequence 842.7
certainly 925.17

of interest
adj of importance 952.17

of old
adj old 804.9
adv long ago 119.14

off
adj discordant 52.4
idle 316.16
tainted 378.34
insane 881.22
delirious 881.27
erroneous 930.14
adv hence 179.17
away 247.14

offence
n pique 143.2
provocation 143.11
indignity 147.2
violation 420.2
attack 444.1
misdeed 655.2
wrong 654.3

offensive

adj nasty 55.6
fetid 62.4
objectionable 89.18
insulting 147.8
warlike 443.17
aggressive 444.24
vulgar 482.8
vulgar 490.6
terrible 955.9
hideous 970.9
n attack 444.1

offer
n attempt 388.2
offering 424.1
giving 463.1
v attempt 388.5
proffer 424.4
give 463.12
bid 710.8
answer 894.3
produce 912.11

offered
adj voluntary 309.6

offering
n offer 424.1
gift 463.4
donation 463.6
sacrifice 675.7

office
n library 188.6
bureau 575.3
commission 595.1
function 701.3
position 701.5
shop 716.6

officer
n executive 555.3
official 556.16
policeman 963.15

offices
n aid 434.1

official
adj authoritative 402.14
prescriptive 404.4
recorded 530.13
governmental 593.15

executive 593.17
occupational 701.13
authoritative 925.13
n executive 555.3
officer 556.16
agent 557.3
officially
adv authoritatively
402.17
often
adv frequently 809.6
repeatedly 811.16
oil
n balm 77.10
painting 690.12
electricity gas 977.20
fat 11.1
v smooth 273.5
provision 370.9
facilitate 969.7
grease 11.7
OK
adj great 954.13
n approval 494.1
v approve 494.7
okay
adj great 954.13
old
adj aged 289.11
disused 375.8
former 799.8
age-old 804.9
antiquated 804.12
old man
n elder 290.2
husband 544.6
has-been 804.7
old-fashioned
adj disused 375.8
gallant 489.12
dated 804.11
conservative 815.7
older
adj mature 290.6
previous 796.4
senior 804.18
oldest

adj older 804.18
Olympics
n contest 442.3
omitted
adj absent 211.10
neglected 325.14
on
adj addicted 78.8
happening 793.9
adv forward 163.8
after which 797.6
across 856.12
on behalf of
adv by proxy 557.17
on board
adv here 150.23
on board ship 173.28
on earth
adv under the sun
223.7
on one
adv on the house
463.27
on the road
adv on the way 167.14
on the move or go
168.36
on the way
adv along the way
167.14
on top
adv at or on the top
189.11
once
adj former 799.8
adv whenever 783.10
one day 799.12
one-time 810.6
singly 834.13
once again
adv again 836.7
once more
adv newly 803.15
again 811.17
again 836.7
one

adj quantitative 230.5
almighty 657.9
identical 740.7
whole 754.9
combined 767.5
single 834.7
n person 297.3
I 834.3
one another
n correspondent 739.3
one day
adv once 799.12
one-time
adj infrequent 810.2
adv once 810.6
one-way
adj direct 152.11
only
adj sole 834.9
adv moderately 234.10
simply 760.10
solely 834.14
open
adj accessible 158.5
exterior 197.6
available 211.13
spreading 245.11
communicative 328.9
overt 333.10
published 337.17
leisure 387.3
artless 401.4
outspoken 415.21
unrestricted 415.25
plain-speaking 517.3
hospitable 566.11
candid 624.13
incoherent 766.3
liable 852.5
accessible 921.7
undecided 971.2
open-minded 934.10
exposed 961.15
v crack 213.4
disclose 336.4
opening
n in 178.3

entrance 180.5
outlet 181.7
vacancy 211.2
crack 213.2
aperture 278.1
display 333.2
passageway 368.3
position 701.5
beginning 780.1
opportunity 805.2

opera
n musical theatre
686.28

operate
v treat 82.11
pilot 173.10
act 313.4
use 372.8
trade 714.11
function 844.5
function 844.7

operating
adj acting 313.10
operational 844.11

operation
n surgery 81.2
surgery 82.8
motion 163.1
action 313.1
act 313.3
function 372.5
utilization 372.6
undertaking 389.1
action 443.4
transaction 708.4
functioning 844.1
performance 847.5

operations
n action 313.1
operation 443.4

opinion
n advice 407.1
idea 887.1
estimate 901.3
sentiment 908.6
attitude 933.1

opportunity

n turn 787.2
chance 805.2
chance 927.1

opposed
adj opposite 206.5
opposing 436.7
disapproving 495.19
contrary 741.5
adverse 966.13

opposite
adj opposite 206.5
fronting 207.10
opposing 436.7
contrary 741.5
adverse 966.13
adv poles apart 206.6
n inverse 196.3
the opposite 741.2

opposition
n antithesis 206.1
refusal 310.1
dissent 318.1
opposing 436.1
resistance 438.1
disapproval 495.1
antithesis 741.1
difference 742.1
disagreement 751.1
contradiction 855.1
comparison 898.1
hindrance 967.1

optimism
n cheerfulness 100.1
rose-coloured
spectacles 115.2
eager expectation
121.2

optimistic
adj cheerful 100.11
bright 115.11
expectant 121.10

option
n discretion 356.2
free will 415.6
first refusal 710.2

orchestra
n band 688.8

order
n rank 231.2
manner 369.1
precept 404.1
command 405.1
demand 406.1
peacefulness 449.2
nomenclature 512.1
harmony 515.2
class 588.1
community 597.2
fellowship 597.3
school 597.5
decoration 626.5
medal 626.6
sect 655.2
good condition 727.2
arrangement 770.1
class 771.2
sequence 777.1
normality 831.1
verdict 901.5
v outfit 5.30
command 405.7
demand 406.5
request 425.9
arrange 770.6
classify 771.5
govern 849.8
pass judgment 901.13

ordered
adj harmonious 515.6
uniform 743.5
orderly 769.6
arranged 770.12
regular 812.6

orders
n instructions 549.6

ordinary
adj medium 232.3
inferior 236.6
customary 358.12
common 482.12
simple 484.6
demographic 587.8
prosaic 699.3
frequent 809.4

prevalent 826.11
usual 831.7
average 960.8

organic
adj structural 252.5
organized 291.11
innate 729.5

organization
n contour 248.2
structure 252.1
organism 291.2
plan 366.1
unit 446.18
establishment 597.8
workplace 716.1
composition 758.1
order 769.1
ordering 770.2
establishment 847.4

origin
n eymology 511.13
beginning 780.1
inception 780.4
source 841.5

original
adj basic 190.8
native 215.4
novel 322.4
unused 375.10
essential 729.6
preceding 778.4
beginning 780.13
new 803.7
novel 803.11
unconventional 830.6
primary 841.14
genuine 928.15
imaginative 941.12
n model 322.2
model 748.1
the specific 827.3
nonconformist 830.3

originally
adv intrinsically 729.7
first 780.15

Orthodox
adj Jewish 655.25

orthodox
adj traditional 666.5

other
adj additional 239.9
another 742.7
fresh 803.8
substitute 824.7

other side
n opposite side 206.3

otherwise
adj other 742.7
adv counter 741.7
else 742.10

ought to
v should 621.3

ourselves
n self 827.5

out
adj dislocated 151.8
old-fashioned 804.15
erroneous 930.14
extinguished 974.10
adv hence 179.17
forth 181.18
externally 197.9

out of
adj escaped 354.11
bereft 458.8
wanting 947.13

outcome
n event 793.1
effect 842.1
product 848.1
solution 895.1

outer
adj exterior 197.6

output
n yield 457.5
production 848.2

outside
adj exterior 197.6
outdoor 197.7
external 730.2
extraneous 736.4
adv externally 197.9
outdoors 197.10
n appearance 32.2

exterior 197.2
outdoors 197.3

outstanding
adj eminent 233.9
remarkable 233.10
superior 235.12
superlative 235.13
remaining 242.7
protruding 269.11
conspicuous 333.12
due 603.8
prominent 642.15
notable 952.18

oven
n wheel 719.3
furnace 971.32

over
adj superior 235.12
higher 258.14
ended 782.7
past 799.6
surplus 948.16
adv vice versa 196.7
additionally 239.10
on high 258.15
again 811.17
excessively 948.19

overall
adj cumulative 732.23
comprehensive 734.7
adv throughout 756.16
generally 826.16

overcome
adj overwhelmed 96.26
crushed 103.29
unnerved 119.14
defeated 397.13
v unnerve 119.10
excel 235.6
defeat 396.5
surmount 397.6

overnight
adv nightly 300.10

overseas
adj away from home
211.11
transatlantic 247.11

adv beyond seas 226.7
  abroad 736.5
overwhelming
  adj impregnable 15.18
  exciting 96.30
  astonishing 113.8
  irresistible 397.16
  evidential 912.11
  n penetration 210.3
own
  adj possessed 454.8
  v acknowledge 317.10
  confess 336.7
  have title to 454.5
owned
  adj possessed 454.8
owner
  n proprietor 455.2
ownership
  n title 454.2
pace
  n velocity 163.3
  step 168.9
  gait 168.10
  v lead 156.2
  walk 168.23
  go on horseback
  168.30
  measure 286.7
pack
  adv freight 167.5
  n amount 230.2
  wadding 279.4
  film 692.8
  company 732.3
  flock 732.5
  bundle 732.8
  multitude 839.3
  impediment 967.6
  v load 150.15
  fill 187.6
  package 203.8
  stop 279.6
  wrap 281.19
  tamper with 339.11
  gather 732.18
  package 732.20

fill 756.7
teem with 839.5
fix 920.4
overload 948.13
obstruct 967.11
package
  n bundle 732.8
  all 754.3
  combination 767.1
  v pack 203.8
  wrap 281.19
  parcel up 732.20
packed
  adj packaged 203.11
  stopped 279.9
  crowded 732.22
  full 756.10
  stuck 817.16
  teeming 839.9
  fixed 920.7
  overloaded 948.18
  dense 990.11
pact
  n compact 422.1
page
  n design 535.12
  attendant 558.5
  section 755.2
  paper 999.5
  v summon 405.9
paid
  adj employed 595.17
  paid-up 604.20
pain
  n suffering 26.1
  anaemia 76.9
  annoyance 87.2
  distress 87.5
  tormentor 87.10
  distress 89.5
  v hurt 26.7
  grieve 87.17
painful
  adj hurtful 26.10
  distressing 89.20
  laborious 702.18
  troublesome 968.18

paint
  n colour 34.8
  blanket 281.11
  easel 690.16
  v colour 34.12
  represent 334.8
  describe 334.9
  ornament 483.7
  spangle 483.8
  portray 690.17
painted
  adj coloured 34.15
painting
  n paintwork 34.11
  colouring 690.3
  canvas 690.12
  graphic arts 691.1
pair
  n set 746.4
  two 835.2
  v gather 732.18
  put together 762.4
  double 835.4
palace
  n estate 217.6
pale
  adj inconspicuous 31.6
  soft 34.20
  colourless 35.7
  light 36.6
  unhealthy 76.19
  dull 108.6
  deathly 293.21
  n bounds 202.1
  sphere 220.2
  plot 220.4
  leg 259.6
  v blur 31.4
  discolour 35.5
  lose colour 35.6
  take fright 118.11
Pan
  n forest god 658.10
panel
  n sheet 282.2
  forum 408.3
  discussion 523.6

jury 577.3
assembly 732.2

panic
n fear 118.1
nervousness 119.1
v start 118.12
overwhelm 397.7

paper
n wafer 256.6
printing 528.4
writing 528.8
document 530.5
newspaper 536.2
piece 537.1
sheet 999.5
v face 281.22

papers
n naturalized
citizenship 215.2
archives 530.2
document 530.5

par
adj equal 752.7
n equality 752.1

parallel
adj equidistant 194.5
side 209.4
accompanying 731.8
related 737.9
analogous 746.7
comparative 898.7
n parallel line 194.2
zone 220.3
likeness 746.3
equal 752.4
v be parallel 194.3
relate 737.6
resemble 746.5
agree 750.6
equal 752.5
compare 898.4
be comparable 898.6

parent
n ancestor 541.8
author 841.4

park
n enclosure 203.3

green 296.7
preserve 382.6
public park 720.13
v place 150.12

parliament
n legislature 594.1

parliamentary
adj governmental
593.15
legislative 594.9

part
adj partial 755.7
incomplete 757.4
half 837.5
adv partly 755.8
n region 220.1
a length 253.2
function 372.5
estate 456.4
portion 462.5
section 535.13
role 682.7
line 686.18
passage 686.19
function 701.3
mode 727.3
particular 728.3
portion 755.1
component 758.2
v space 213.3
apportion 462.6
divorce 547.5
disband 733.6
separate 764.7
part company 764.17

particular
adj meticulous 324.12
selective 356.22
proportionate 462.13
fastidious 480.6
detailed 728.9
typical 771.6
special 827.12
n instance 728.3
part 755.1
event 793.2
citation 912.5

particularly
adv acutely 233.19
chiefly 235.17
fully 728.13
specially 827.15
singly 834.13

partly
adj half 837.5
adv moderately 234.10
partially 755.8

partner
n participant 461.3
spouse 544.5
friend 569.1
companion 569.3
business partner 596.2
accompanist 731.3
v cooperate 435.3
gather 732.18
league 767.4

partnership
n affiliation 435.2
participation 461.1
bar 578.4
association 597.1
company 731.1

parts
n contents 187.1
region 220.1
substance 725.2

party
n guy 67.5
subscriber 317.6
participant 461.3
entertainment 563.11
litigant 579.11
accuser 580.5
political party 590.21
interest 597.4
festival 720.4
revel 720.6
assembly 732.2
company 732.3
company 732.3
support 856.1
v enjoy oneself 86.13
have fun 563.20

eat 649.6

pass
n narrow 256.3
valley 270.7
passageway 368.3
proposal 424.2
passport 428.7
thrust 444.2
state 727.1
crisis 805.4
throw 859.3
v disappear 33.2
overtake 165.10
transfer 167.6
travel 168.14
average 232.2
distance 235.10
die 293.14
ratify 317.11
adopt 356.14
spend 372.11
perish 380.23
succeed 394.6
promote 431.2
deliver 463.13
not understand 507.9
legislate 594.8
be annihilated 724.5
elapse 783.3
flit 790.6
occur 793.5
be past 799.5
throw 859.10
bypass 865.7
not know 885.9
stand up 897.10
suffice 946.3
exceed 948.9
excel 954.11

passage
adv transfer 167.1
n duct 2.16
progression 153.1
course 163.2
travel 168.1
wandering 168.3
voyage 173.2

entrance 180.5
corridor 188.15
channel 225.1
passageway 368.3
part 535.13
excerpt 538.3
legislation 594.3
phrase 686.19
section 755.2
conversion 820.1

passed
adj chosen 356.25
past 799.6

passenger
n traveller 169.1

passing
adj vanishing 33.3
flowing 163.7
travelling 168.32
hasty 386.5
transient 790.7
happening 793.9
n disappearance 33.1
departure 179.1
death 293.1

passion
n lust 66.5
strong feeling 84.2
desire 91.1
liking 91.2
zeal 93.1
love 95.1
ecstasy 96.8
rage 143.10
will 308.1
vehemence 525.5
turbulence 651.2
principle 841.9
mania 881.10
interest 938.2

past
adj gone 799.6
former 799.8
obsolete 804.14

pat
n pad 43.2
lump 243.10

tap 857.6
v patter 43.13
tap 857.16

path
n route 368.1
track 368.2
track 502.8
circuit 982.4

patient
adj tolerant 125.8
forgiving 139.6
persevering 345.8
lenient 412.6
tolerant 934.11
n sufferer 76.12
subject 897.7

pattern
n form 248.1
structure 252.1
measure 286.2
original 322.2
habit 358.3
diagram 366.3
motif 483.6
essence 729.1
model 748.1

pause
n respite 20.2
demur 310.2
rest 687.12
interruption 775.1
interim 788.1
delay 808.2
rest 819.3
v demur 310.4
hesitate 347.7
intervene 788.3
rest 819.7
v take a rest 20.8

pay
n payment 604.4
v do 313.6
be profitable 457.13
render 604.10
experience 793.8

pay for
v bear the expense

604.17
finance 706.14
paying
adj gainful 457.16
remunerative 604.19
payment
n incentive 360.7
paying off 604.1
pay 604.4
expenditure 606.1
payments
n outgoings 606.2
peace
n silence 42.1
peacefulness 112.2
stillness 164.1
accord 440.1
peacetime 449.1
truce 450.5
agreement 750.1
order 769.1
peaceful
adj calm 97.12
comfortable 112.11
quiet 164.10
homely 217.29
in accord 440.3
tranquil 449.7
moderate 650.9
peak
n summit 189.2
wave 224.14
plateau 258.4
projection 271.3
business cycle 708.9
limit 756.5
height 957.2
v top 189.7
peg
n degree 231.1
leg 259.6
bulge 269.2
stopper 279.3
v stroll 168.24
hook 762.7
pen
n enclosure 203.3

close quarters 414.7
writing 528.1
farm 112.7
v enclose 203.5
confine 414.12
write 528.14
write 696.5
penalty
n penance 584.1
impediment 967.6
penny
n pence 705.5
pension
n subsidy 463.8
people
n population 216.1
kindred 540.2
race 540.4
family 540.5
the laity 699.1
v settle 150.17
populate 214.8
pepper
v variegate 38.6
flavour 54.6
fire at 444.19
mark 502.19
sprinkle 733.5
shoot 859.11
percentage
n estate 456.4
gain 457.3
portion 462.5
discount 611.1
part 755.1
perfect
adj downright 233.12
complete 392.11
unrestricted 415.25
thorough 756.9
unqualified 915.1
accurate 928.16
ideal 957.5
v excel 235.6
touch up 377.11
complete 392.6
complete 782.6

develop 957.4
perfectly
adv utterly 233.21
absolutely 756.14
accurately 928.20
ideally 957.9
perform
v execute 313.9
manifest 333.5
impersonate 334.11
accomplish 392.4
practise 419.3
act 682.21
play 686.32
operate 844.5
operate 844.7
do 847.11
performance
n execution 313.2
act 333.3
display 333.2
impersonation 334.4
accomplishment 392.1
observance 419.1
acting 682.5
show 682.9
execution 686.24
musical performance 686.27
operation 844.1
execution 847.5
performed
adj produced 847.17
perhaps
adv possibly 921.8
n guess 906.4
period
n menstruation 12.9
degree 231.1
season 298.1
time 783.1
point 786.1
wave 871.4
orbit 114.14
permanent
adj persevering 345.8
almighty 657.9

durable 789.9
perpetual 791.6
unchanging 815.6
unchanging 817.17
permission
 n ratification 317.4
exemption 415.8
consent 426.1
leave 428.1
person
 n human 297.3
something 725.3
individual 834.4
body 997.3
personal
 adj individual 297.8
private 330.13
marked 502.24
particular 827.12
personality
 n psyche 83.17
person 297.3
something 725.3
particularity 827.1
influence 849.1
personage 952.7
personally
 adv privately 827.16
adv in person 210.17
personnel
 n work force 18.4
staff 558.10
perspective
 n field of view 30.3
view 32.6
station 150.2
distance 247.1
treatment 690.7
outlook 933.2
persuade
 v prevail on or upon
 360.22
admonish 407.5
convince 820.16
influence 849.7
convince 908.17
seem true 928.9

persuaded
 adj consenting 426.4
believing 908.20
confident 925.15
pet
 v stroke 64.8
snog 543.15
caress 543.16
rub 989.4
petrol
 v fuels 973.8
phase
 n aspect 32.3
phenomenon
 n apparition 32.5
event 793.2
philosophy
 n policy 590.4
ideology 887.6
reasoning 890.1
philosophical
 speculation 907.1
phone
 n telephone 332.4
speech sound 509.10
v telephone 332.11
photo
 n photograph 692.3
photograph
 n description 334.2
image 334.5
picture 690.9
photo 692.3
print 747.5
v shoot 692.10
photographer
 n journalist 536.4
press photographer
 692.2
cameraman 694.5
phrase
 n remark 509.3
part 535.13
passage 686.19
section 755.2
maxim 929.1
v say 509.16

express 514.3
physical
 adj carnal 643.6
innate 729.5
material 997.9
n checkup 893.5
piano
 n harpsichord 689.4
pick
 n choice 356.1
the best 954.8
v nibble 8.25
choose 356.12
select 356.13
collect 457.11
strum 686.33
harvest 112.18
pick up
 v fetch 167.10
recuperate 381.17
arrest 414.15
grab 457.9
collect 457.11
take up 867.7
detect 896.5
picked
 adj chosen 356.25
picture
 n description 334.2
image 334.5
image 334.5
sign 502.1
motion pictures 684.1
image 690.9
photograph 692.3
copy 747.1
vision 941.5
vision 971.6
image 984.4
v represent 334.8
describe 334.9
portray 690.17
visualize 941.10
piece
 n lump 243.10
a length 253.2
portion 462.5

writing 528.8
news item 533.3
treatment 537.1
stage show 682.2
composition 686.4
work of art 690.8
coin 705.3
man 720.16
sample 748.3
part 755.1
particle 755.3

pile
n hair 3.1
feather 3.11
lot 233.4
structure 252.2
texture 280.1
store 371.1
bundle 598.3
heap 732.10
v pile on 732.19

pilot
adj experimental 897.11
n air pilot 176.1
guide 555.7
v steer 173.10
control 175.13
guide 554.9

pin
n stopper 279.3
jewel 483.5
axle 870.5
v hook 762.7

pink
adj fresh 74.13
v notch 275.2

pipe
n tobacco pipe 80.5
tube 225.5
cylinder 268.2
horn 689.3
v blare 44.10
screech 49.8
channel 225.14
sing 686.31
sound 686.34

pit
n deep 261.2
cavity 270.2
well 270.3
indentation 270.5
tomb 295.15
seed 296.24
arena 448.1
stock exchange 714.4
mine 12.6
v dent 270.11

pitch
n tone 41.2
summit 189.2
inclination 195.2
incline 195.4
degree 231.1
plunge 352.1
intonation 509.6
tuning 687.3
throw 859.3
v establish 150.16
toss 173.22
descend 185.5
tumble 185.8
erect 191.8
incline 195.9
camp 214.10
plunge 352.5
throw 859.10

pity
n kindness 134.1
sympathy 136.1
leniency 412.1
v feel sorry for 136.3
commiserate 138.2

place
n serving 8.10
location 150.1
stead 150.4
abode 217.1
region 220.1
rank 231.2
arena 448.1
class 588.1
duty 621.1
function 701.3

position 701.5
state 727.1
continuity 769.2
turn 787.2
opportunity 805.2
v locate 150.11
put 150.12
impose 623.4
invest 706.15
distribute 770.7
classify 771.5
attribute 843.3
recognize 944.9

placed
adj located 150.18
arranged 770.12
classified 771.7

plain
adj distinct 30.7
audible 41.15
prosaic 108.8
humble 128.9
homely 217.29
mere 234.8
manifest 333.8
simple 484.6
clear 506.10
elegant 515.4
plain-speaking 517.3
informal 562.3
demographic 587.8
prosaic 699.3
thorough 756.9
simple 760.5
easy 969.13
ugly 970.5
adv absolutely 756.14
n open space 149.4
horizontal 192.3

plan
n structure 252.1
representation 334.1
intention 365.1
scheme 366.1
undertaking 389.1
intent 503.2
plot 700.4

outline 763.4
v intend 365.4
plan on 365.6
calculate 365.7
devise 366.7
prepare 390.6
organize 770.8
come 801.6
originate 847.12
prearrange 920.3

plane
adj horizontal 192.7
smooth 273.9
n aircraft 172.1
horizontal 192.3
degree 231.1
smooth 273.3
v smooth 273.5

planet
n inferior planet 114.9

planned
adj intentional 365.8
devised 366.11
prepared 390.13
future 801.7
cut out 920.6

planning
n plan 366.1
preparation 390.1
design 695.3
organization 770.2
plotting 920.1

plant
n vegetable 296.3
equipment 370.4
factory 716.2
v establish 150.16
secrete 331.7
fix 817.9
set 112.17

planted
adj located 150.18

plants
n vegetation 296.1

plastic
adj formative 248.8
changeable 816.6

pliable 992.9
n credit card 602.3
thermoplastic 999.6

plate
n serving 8.10
plating 281.12
shell 281.14
sheet 282.2
printing surface 529.8
printing plate 691.4
film 692.8
v electroplate 281.25

platform
n horizontal 192.3
policy 366.4
arena 448.1
marker 502.10
programme 590.7

play
n action 313.1
joke 474.3
writing 528.8
stage show 682.2
fun 720.2
frolic 720.5
game 720.8
sport 721.1
gambling 722.1
flicker 977.9
v act 313.4
impersonate 334.11
sham 339.14
use 372.8
affect 485.8
act 682.21
perform 686.32
sport 720.22
compete 721.2
gamble 722.19
trifle 953.12
flicker 977.24

player
n competitor 437.2
participant 461.3
movie studio 684.3
actor 685.2
instrumentalist 688.2

playboy 720.17
athlete 720.18
gambler 722.17

playing
n impersonation 334.4
acting 682.5
dalliance 953.7

pleasant
adj pleasing 88.5
cheerful 100.11
friendly 568.14
melodic 686.39
good 954.12
fine 110.6

please
v pleasure 86.5
indulge 412.5

pleased
adj delighted 86.14
content 98.7

pleasure
n enjoyment 86.1
bliss 88.1
will 308.1
option 356.2
command 405.1
amusement 720.1
v please 86.5

plenty
adj sufficient 946.5
adv greatly 233.14
n quantity 233.3
store 371.1
multiplicity 839.1
plenitude 946.2

plot
n patch 220.4
diagram 366.3
intrigue 366.5
stratagem 400.3
real estate 456.5
fable 700.4
field 112.8
v calculate 365.7
scheme 366.8
map 366.9
manoeuvre 400.10

come 801.6
prearrange 920.3

plus
adv additionally 239.10
n plus sign 239.2
surplus 948.5

PM
n afternoon 300.1

pocket
adj miniature 244.11
n bag 186.2
cavity 270.2
funds 705.11
purse 706.13
v take 125.7
load 150.15
enclose 203.5
take 465.13
receive 607.3

poem
n writing 528.8
verse 698.4

poet
n author 528.12
author 696.3
ballad maker 698.11
inventor 941.8

poetry
n fluency 525.2
verse 698.1

point
n acrimony 17.5
location 150.1
direction 152.1
the lead 156.1
summit 189.2
vanguard 207.2
degree 231.1
drop 244.6
angle 264.1
hook 269.6
tip 271.2
intention 365.1
benefit 372.4
joke 474.3
mark 502.5
meaning 503.1

engraving tool 691.5
chisel 693.4
particular 728.3
extremity 782.2
period 786.1
individual 834.4
topic 892.1
v direct 152.4
head 152.6
sharpen 271.6
gravitate 283.11
mark 502.19

point of view
n viewpoint 27.7
outlook 933.2

pointed
adj angular 264.3
acute 271.8
witty 474.9
meaningful 503.6
concise 519.5
proverbial 973.6
emphatic 952.20

pointing
n indication 502.3

pole
n timber 171.11
oar 171.13
summit 189.2
tower 258.5
shaft 259.1
beam 259.3
extremity 782.2
base 856.7
magnetic pole 982.8
wood lumber 999.3

police
n police force 963.17
v protect 963.18
watch 963.20

policeman
n constable 963.15

policy
n principles 366.4
line 590.4

polish
n gloss 273.2

smoother 273.4
cultivation 377.3
taste 481.1
good breeding 489.4
elegance 515.1
v shine 273.7
perfect 377.11
perfect 377.11
buff 989.6

political
adj governmental
590.33
governmental 593.15

politician
n expert 398.11
diplomat 400.8
politico 591.1

politics
n diplomacy 400.2
polity 590.1
political science 590.2

poll
n head 189.5
vote 356.6
returns 590.18
roll 833.6
survey 893.13
v shorten 254.4
canvass 893.27

poll tax
n tax 610.9

polls
n polling station
590.17

pollution
n defilement 71.4
unhealthiness 73.1
misuse 374.1
corruption 378.2
corruption 759.3
evil 955.3
environmental
destruction 115.2

pool
n lake 227.1
funds 705.11
swimming pool 720.11

pot 722.4

poor
adj humble 128.9
haggard 256.15
inexpert 399.12
disapproving 495.19
badly off 599.7
base 641.12
sparse 840.5
unsound 891.9
meagre 947.10
ill-equipped 947.12
paltry 953.18
inferior 960.9

pop
n beverage 10.44
pad 43.2
detonation 47.3
v patter 43.13
blast 47.8
bulge 269.8

popular
adj desired 91.28
customary 358.12
communal 461.8
common 482.12
approved 494.17
fashionable 578.11
demographic 587.8
distinguished 642.14
lay 679.3
prevalent 826.11
usual 831.7

popularity
n fashionableness 559.2
repute 642.1

population
n establishment 150.7
peopling 214.2
inhabitants 216.1

port
n airport 175.8
destination 177.5
outlet 181.7
refuge 964.1
harbour 964.6

circuit 988.3

portrait
n description 334.2
image 334.5
portrayal 690.13
photograph 692.3
copy 747.1

position
n location 150.1
navigation 150.3
rank 231.2
affirmation 319.1
class 588.1
policy 590.4
prestige 642.4
function 701.3
job 701.5
state 727.1
class 771.2
premise 890.6
opinion 908.6
attitude 933.1
outlook 933.2
v locate 150.11

positive
adj downright 233.12
affirmative 319.7
dogmatic 346.12
helpful 434.21
real 723.11
agreeing 750.9
believing 908.20
unqualified 915.1
certain 925.9
confident 925.15
dogmatic 925.16
emphatic 952.20
negative 982.31
n print 692.4

possession
n country 221.1
self-control 344.5
owning 454.1
taking 465.1
bewitchment 670.2
insanity 881.1
obsession 881.11

possibility
n latency 504.1
liability 852.1
probability 921.1
probability 923.1
good chance 927.4

possible
adj latent 504.5
probable 921.5

possibly
adv conceivably 921.8

post
adj postal 534.14
n station 150.2
standard 259.4
pillar 259.5
stronghold 445.6
mail 534.4
position 701.5
base 856.7
wood lumber 999.3
v place 150.12
send 167.9
publicize 337.15
pledge 423.8
mail 534.12
commission 595.8
list 833.8

pot
n container 186.1
ceramic ware 719.2
jackpot 722.4
v preserve 382.8
shape 719.4
plant 112.17

potential
adj latent 504.5
possible 921.5
n talent 398.4
possibility 921.1

potentially
adv latently 504.11

pound
n kennel 217.19
ounce 283.6
close quarters 414.7
penny 705.5

v hit 857.4
v suffer 26.8
drum 46.4
attack 444.12
beat time 686.35
drum 811.10
beat 857.14
pulverize 996.8

pour

v ladle 167.11
run out 181.10
flow 224.15
rain 301.4
give 463.12
discharge 864.23

poverty

n straits 599.1
scarcity 947.3

powder

n medicine 77.4
explosive 447.13
makeup 971.10
dust 996.5
v pulverize 996.8
crumble 996.9

power

adj mechanical 986.8
n strength 15.1
energy 17.1
force 18.1
country 221.1
greatness 233.4
supremacy 235.3
will power 344.4
means 369.2
talent 398.4
authority 402.1
authority 402.2
governance 402.5
vigour 525.3
control 593.2
prerogative 622.1
influence 849.1
impulse 857.1
personage 952.7
current 982.2
wattage 982.16

powerful

adj strong 15.14
potent 18.7
great 233.6
authoritative 402.14
vigorous 525.10
influential 849.13

powers

n talent 398.4

practical

adj useful 372.16
usable 372.21
occupied 701.11
operative 844.9
workable 844.10
sensible 875.16
sophisticated 911.4
practicable 921.6
realistic 942.5
practicable 950.6
handy 969.15

practice

n behaviour 306.1
action 313.1
custom 358.1
habit 358.3
manner 369.1
experience 398.9
observance 419.1
training 549.3
study 551.3
bar 578.4
vocation 701.6
exercise 702.6
operation 844.1
workout 857.7
v train 549.13
rehearse 682.24
do 701.9
reiterate 811.8

praise

n congratulation 140.1
thanks 141.2
laudation 494.5
flattery 496.1
citation 626.4

glorification 675.2
v congratulate 140.2
eulogize 494.10
flatter 496.3
glorify 675.11

precious

adj beloved 95.23
mincing 485.12
affected 515.7
dear 612.10
n darling 543.6

precise

adj meticulous 324.12
fastidious 480.6
punctilious 561.10
detailed 728.9
particular 827.12
discriminating 899.7
exact 928.17

precisely

adv meticulously 324.16
thus 728.10
punctually 807.14
particularly 827.15
exactly 928.21

predicted

adj expected 121.12
foreshadowed 124.14
future 801.7
prophesied 917.8

prefer

v desire 91.13
favour 356.16
favour 630.7
view 933.6

preferred

adj preferable 356.24

pregnancy

n gestation 69.5
meaningfulness 503.4
timeliness 805.1
productivity 845.1

pregnant

adj knocked up 69.18
meaningful 503.6
critical 805.9

original 841.14
productive 845.7
imaginative 941.12
premier
adj first 780.14
paramount 952.23
n head of state 556.7
preparation
n medicine 77.4
provision 370.1
preparing 390.1
training 549.3
early hour 807.1
foresight 916.1
prepare
v cook 11.4
provide 370.7
equip 370.8
ready 390.6
train 549.13
write 696.5
produce 847.8
prepared
adj expectant 121.10
provided 370.13
ready 390.13
skilled 398.24
foreseeing 916.4
preparing
n preparation 390.1
presence
n looks 32.4
apparition 32.5
immediacy 210.1
behaviour 306.1
existence 723.1
phantom 931.1
spectre 943.1
present
adj attendant 210.12
existing 723.10
immediate 800.2
n gift 464.3
v manifest 333.5
provide 370.7
offer 424.4
give 463.12

say 509.16
phrase 514.3
introduce 568.13
give 614.3
dramatize 682.20
produce 912.11
presented
adj phrased 514.4
preserve
n sweets 10.36
reserve 382.6
refuge 964.1
v reserve 371.11
conserve 382.7
cure 382.8
retain 459.5
perpetuate 791.5
be conservative 815.5
sustain 818.4
care for 963.19
presidency
n supremacy 235.3
mastery 402.7
leadership 554.4
president
n principal 552.7
executive 555.3
head of state 556.7
press
n extractor 183.8
squeezing 246.2
publicity 337.4
printing press 529.9
print shop 529.10
publisher 535.2
throng 732.4
thrust 857.2
v squeeze 246.6
iron 273.6
weigh 283.8
urge 360.13
hasten 386.3
insist 406.8
put pressure on 409.6
urge upon 424.9
urge 425.12
confiscate 465.20

embrace 543.18
strain 702.10
thrust 857.11
densify 990.8
pressed
adj hurried 386.7
pressing
adj motivating 360.24
demanding 406.9
compulsory 409.10
urgent 952.21
n squeezing 183.6
urgency 425.3
pressure
n touching 64.2
tension 119.3
squeezing 246.2
burden 283.5
urging 360.5
urge 360.6
insistence 406.4
coercion 409.3
urgency 425.3
influence 849.1
thrust 857.2
urgent need 918.3
urgency 952.4
adversity 966.1
v urge 360.13
twist one's arm 409.8
urge 425.12
presumably
adv supposedly 906.13
probably 923.5
pretty
adj beautiful 971.14
adv somewhat 231.7
very 233.17
tolerably 954.23
prevent
v prohibit 429.3
prohibit 967.13
previous
adj prior 796.4
former 799.8
earlier 807.10
previously

adv hitherto 796.5
   formerly 799.11
price
   n interest 603.3
   recompense 604.3
   cost 610.1
   quotation 715.3
   gambling odds 722.5
   v value 610.11
pride
   n self-esteem 127.1
   arrogance 131.2
   arrogance 132.1
   good thing 994.5
priest
   n celibate 546.2
   father 678.3
primarily
   adv chiefly 235.17
   essentially 729.8
   first 780.15
primary
   adj basic 190.8
   front 207.9
   chief 235.14
   unprecedented 322.5
   essential 729.6
   simple 760.5
   beginning 780.13
   original 841.14
   paramount 952.23
   n election 590.13
prime
   adj front 207.9
   chief 235.14
   unprecedented 322.5
   simple 760.5
   beginning 780.13
   previous 796.4
   paramount 952.23
   best 954.16
   n maturity 289.2
   v colour 34.12
   coat 281.23
   load 390.9
   shoot 899.11
prime minister

n head of state 556.7
prince
   n sovereign 556.8
   heir apparent 589.7
princess
   n queen 556.11
   infanta 589.8
principal
   adj chief 235.14
   first 780.14
   paramount 952.23
   n superior 235.4
   headmaster 552.7
   chief 556.3
   lead 685.5
   chief 952.9
principle
   n motive 360.1
   rule 404.2
   essence 729.1
   rule 831.4
   cause 841.1
   interest 841.9
   foundation 856.5
   a belief 908.2
   axiom 929.2
principles
   n policy 366.4
   ethics 616.1
   probity 624.1
   basics 780.6
print
   n indentation 270.5
   imprint 502.7
   imprint 529.3
   type 529.6
   picture 690.9
   imprint 691.3
   positive 692.4
   reprint 747.5
   print 747.5
   v represent 334.8
   mark 502.19
   imprint 529.13
   engrave 691.6
   process 692.11
   fix 817.9

printed
   adj written 528.17
   in print 529.16
   engraved 691.8
prior
   adj leading 156.3
   preceding 776.4
   previous 796.4
   former 799.8
   n monk 678.9
priority
   n the lead 156.1
   front 207.1
   superiority 235.1
   prestige 402.4
   the lead 776.1
   sequence 777.1
   previousness 796.1
   importance 952.1
prison
   n penitentiary 414.8
prisoner
   n captive 414.11
   accused 580.6
private
   adj interior 198.6
   closed 279.8
   personal 297.8
   privy 330.13
   taking 465.25
   reclusive 565.9
   intrinsic 729.4
   particular 827.12
   alone 834.8
   n enlisted man 446.6
prize
   adj best 954.16
   n ambition 91.10
   booty 467.10
   monument 530.10
   award 626.2
   good thing 954.5
   the best 954.8
   v respect 146.4
   measure 286.7
   estimate 901.9
   value 952.12

pro
adj approving 494.15
occupational 701.13
n expert 398.11

probably
adv later 801.8
likely 923.5

problem
n annoyance 87.2
enigma 507.7
topic 892.1
question 893.9
bewilderment 926.2
fault 958.2
trouble 968.3

procedure
n behaviour 306.1
rule 358.4
plan 366.1
policy 366.4
manner 369.1
process 844.2

proceedings
n activity 315.1
report 530.7
affairs 793.4

process
n manner 369.1
procedure 844.2
v prepare 390.6
develop 692.11
convert 847.9
store 999.7

produce
n vegetables 10.32
fruit 10.34
yield 457.5
groceries 712.7
production 848.2
v secrete 13.4
lengthen 253.6
do 313.6
manifest 333.5
accomplish 392.4
write 528.16
dramatize 682.20
write 696.5

cause 841.10
be productive 845.5
create 847.8
bear 847.13
advance 912.11
imagine 941.9

produced
adj formative 248.8
made 847.17

producer
n director 555.1
showman 682.18
movie studio 684.3
agent 703.1
author 841.4
maker 847.7

producing
adj bearing 845.8

product
n yield 457.5
commodity 712.2
effect 842.1
end product 848.1

production
n structure 252.1
act 313.3
display 333.2
accomplishment 392.1
yield 457.5
writing 528.8
book 535.1
performance 682.9
mounting 682.10
piece 686.4
proliferation 845.2
creation 847.1
making 847.2
produce 848.2

productive
adj able 18.9
gainful 457.16
diffuse 540.10
fruitful 845.7
creative 847.16
imaginative 941.12

profession
n acknowledgment

317.3
claim 361.2
sphere 701.4
vocation 701.6
confession 908.7
testimony 912.2

professional
adj skilful 398.20
skilled 398.24
occupational 701.13
n expert 398.11
seasoned professional
703.4

professor
n expert 398.11
teacher 552.1
reader 552.3

profile
n outline 202.2
side 209.1
contour 248.2
description 334.2
diagram 366.3
portrait 690.13
history 697.1
v outline 202.8

profit
n benefit 372.4
gain 457.3
expedience or
expediency 950.1
good 954.4
v avail 372.15
make money 457.12
come in handy 950.3
do good 954.10

profits
n gains 237.3
gain 457.3
receipts 607.1

programme
n announcement 337.2
undertaking 389.1
platform 590.7
performance 686.27
schedule 920.2
broadcast 983.13

show 984.2
v schedule 920.5
progress
n progression 153.1
course 163.2
travel 168.1
journey 168.4
way 173.5
improvement 377.1
continuance 818.1
conversion 820.1
evolution 823.1
v advance 153.2
move 163.4
travel 168.1
improve 377.7
make good 394.7
evolve 823.4
prosper 965.7
project
n intention 365.1
scheme 366.2
undertaking 389.1
task 701.2
v overhang 193.7
bring out 197.5
protrude 269.7
be manifest 333.7
mirror 334.10
plan 366.7
come 801.6
push 859.9
prominent
adj distinct 30.7
eminent 233.9
high 258.11
protruding 269.11
conspicuous 333.12
authoritative 402.14
conspicuous 642.15
notable 952.18
promise
n hope 115.1
omen 124.3
word 421.1
compact 422.1
prediction 961.1

v give hope 115.9
suggest 124.12
pledge 421.4
contract 422.5
be probable 923.2
promised
adj expected 121.12
foreshadowed 124.14
pledged 421.7
contracted 422.11
promising
adj of promise 115.12
favourable 124.17
probable 923.3
promote
v advance 153.5
publicize 337.15
motivate 360.11
be instrumental 369.6
improve 377.9
advance 431.2
be useful 434.17
commend 494.9
come in handy 950.3
promotion
n progression 153.1
publicizing 337.5
improvement 377.1
advancement 431.1
furtherance 434.5
commendation 494.3
selling 711.2
proof
adj resistant 15.19
n manifestation 333.1
trial impression 529.5
information 532.1
reasoning 890.1
test 897.2
evidence 912.1
demonstration 912.3
confirmation 912.4
v insulate 15.13
proper
adj useful 372.16
fastidious 480.6
decorous 481.7

appropriate 515.5
conventional 560.5
right 617.3
rightful 619.8
just 629.6
decent 644.5
characteristic 827.13
accurate 928.16
expedient 950.5
properly
adv tastefully 481.8
conventionally 560.6
rightly 617.4
justly 629.9
accurately 928.20
appropriately 950.8
property
n supply 371.2
possession 454.1
possessions 456.1
real estate 456.5
sign 502.1
wealth 598.1
nature 729.2
characteristic 827.4
proportion
n space 149.1
degree 231.1
symmetry 250.1
portion 462.5
harmony 515.2
equality 752.1
order 769.1
comparability 898.3
v size 243.14
balance 250.3
divide pro rata 462.7
proposal
n nomination 356.8
intention 365.1
project 366.2
advice 407.1
proposition 424.2
popping the question 543.8
theory 906.2
proposed

adj intentional 365.8
prosecution
  n lawsuit 579.1
  accusation 580.1
prospect
  n field of view 30.3
  view 32.6
  hope 115.1
  hope 115.1
  expectation 121.1
  the future 801.1
  foresight 916.1
  possibility 921.1
  probability 923.1
  v mine 12.12
prospects
  n expectations 121.4
  entitlement 619.1
protect
  v preserve 382.7
  aid 434.11
  defend 445.8
  play safe 962.3
  guard 963.18
protected
  adj limited 201.7
  private 330.13
  preserved 382.10
  safe 962.4
  guarded 963.21
protection
  n bribe 363.2
  preservation 382.1
  restraint 413.1
  custody 414.5
  pass 428.7
  aid 434.1
  defence 445.1
  precaution 479.3
  safety 962.1
  guard 963.1
protein
  n amino acid 7.5
protest
  n complaint 106.4
  demur 310.2
  objection 318.2

affirmation 319.1
resistance 438.1
disapproval 495.1
nonconformity 830.1
  v object 318.5
  affirm 319.5
  oppose 436.3
  offer resistance 438.3
  disapprove 495.9
  break step 830.4
proud
  adj self-confident
    127.8
  arrogant 131.8
  arrogant 132.8
prove
  v result 842.4
  experiment 897.8
  demonstrate 912.9
  confirm 912.10
  verify 925.8
proved
  adj tried 897.12
  proven 912.17
  true 928.13
provide
  v supply 370.7
  furnish 463.15
provided
  adj supplied 370.13
  prepared 390.13
  adv conditionally
    728.12
providing
  n provision 370.1
province
  n sphere 220.2
  state 220.5
  country 221.1
  duty 621.1
  diocese 677.3
  function 701.3
  sphere 701.4
  science 883.8
provincial
  adj local 220.8
  rustic 222.4

idiomatic 508.14
narrow-minded 935.10
provision
  n food 10.1
  providing 370.1
  preparation 390.1
  stipulation 406.2
  support 434.3
  giving 463.1
  precaution 479.3
  substitution 824.1
  condition 914.2
  foresight 916.1
  expedient 950.2
  v cater 370.9
psychological
  adj psychiatric 83.21
  mental 874.6
pub
  n restaurant 8.16
public
  adj exterior 197.6
  general 297.9
  published 337.17
  communal 461.8
  common 482.12
  demographic 587.8
  well-known 883.22
  n follower 157.2
  population 216.1
  market 710.3
publication
  n informing 328.2
  manifestation 333.1
  publishing 337.1
  information 532.1
  book 535.1
  dispersion 733.1
publicity
  n information 532.1
  repute 642.1
publicly
  adv externally 197.9
  openly 333.15
  in public 337.18
published
  adj public 337.17

publishing
  n publication 337.1
  printing 529.1

pull
  n power 18.1
  drink 79.5
  strain 702.2
  pulling 860.1
  draw 860.2
  attraction 862.1
  v smoke 80.7
  row 173.20
  extract 183.9
  lengthen 253.6
  strain 702.10
  draw 860.4
  attract 862.4

pulled
  adj lengthened 253.8

pulling
  adj drawing 860.6
  attracting 862.5
  n drawing 860.1

punishment
  n reprisal 491.2
  penalty 584.1
  chastening 585.1

purchase
  n hold 459.2
  buying 710.1
  influence 849.1
  leverage 861.1
  v bribe 363.3
  buy 710.6

pure
  adj clean 70.25
  tasteful 481.5
  simple 484.6
  elegant 515.4
  plain-speaking 517.3
  chaste 633.6
  spotless 637.5
  chaste 644.4
  God-fearing 671.9
  thorough 756.9
  simple 760.5
  genuine 972.15

perfect 957.5

purely
  adv utterly 233.21
  moderately 234.10
  simply 760.10
  solely 834.14

purpose
  n resolution 344.1
  intention 365.1
  function 372.5
  intent 503.2

pursuit
  n following 157.1
  intention 365.1
  pursuing 367.1
  vocation 701.6
  speciality 828.1

push
  n pep 17.3
  power 18.1
  enterprise 315.6
  attack 444.1
  thrust 857.2
  pushing 859.1
  v set in motion 163.5
  hustle 315.11
  urge 360.13
  hasten 386.3
  urge 425.12
  thrust 444.15
  thrust 857.11
  propel 859.9

pushed
  adj hurried 386.7

pushing
  adj propelling 859.13
  n propelling 859.1

put
  adj phrased 514.4
  n throw 859.3
  v place 150.12
  phrase 514.3
  impose 623.4
  invest 706.15
  attribute 843.3
  throw 859.10

put in

v establish 150.16
  insert 182.3
  keep within 198.5
  interrupt 205.6
  spend 372.11
  plant 112.17

put on
  v don 5.32
  cover 281.18
  sham 339.14
  affect 485.8
  put on airs 486.12
  impose 623.4
  dramatize 682.20
  help up 867.6

putting
  n placement 150.6

qualified
  adj limited 201.7
  eligible 636.23
  fitted 390.14
  competent 398.22
  restricted 413.14
  justified 619.9
  apt 750.10
  changed 814.10
  modified 914.10

qualifying
  adj modifying 914.7

quality
  n ambience 200.3
  taste 481.1
  aristocracy 588.3
  nobility 589.2
  nature 729.2
  characteristic 827.4
  goodness 954.1

quarter
  n pity 136.1
  direction 152.1
  side 209.1
  region 220.1
  part 755.1
  moment 786.2
  v house 214.9

quarters
  n living quarters 217.4

queen
 n homo 66.15
 princess 556.11
 princess 589.8
 man 720.16
 the best 954.8

question
 n enigma 507.7
 remark 509.3
 topic 892.1
 query 893.9
 doubt 910.2
 gamble 926.4
 v communicate with 328.7
 inquire 893.18
 interrogate 893.19
 doubt 910.6
 be uncertain 926.5
 be curious 936.3

questioned
 adj doubted 910.11

quick
 adj passionate 101.25
 fast 165.12
 willing 309.5
 swift 315.14
 alert 324.14
 impulsive 350.8
 hasty 386.5
 skilful 398.20
 apt 551.18
 brief 790.8
 sudden 792.5
 prompt 807.9
 smart 875.12
 adv swiftly 165.13

quickly
 adv swiftly 165.13
 swiftly 315.22
 impulsively 350.12
 hastily 386.8
 fleetingly 790.10
 instantly 792.6
 promptly 807.15

quiet
 adj holiday 20.10

silent 42.9
 calm 97.12
 reserved 130.11
 still 164.10
 taciturn 329.7
 covert 330.12
 meek 418.13
 peaceful 449.7
 tasteful 481.5
 n silence 42.1
 stillness 164.1
 peacefulness 449.2
 order 769.1
 v fall silent 42.6
 silence 42.7
 quieten 164.7
 calm 650.6

quietly
 adv silently 42.12
 dispassionately 97.16
 modestly 130.14
 still 164.14
 meekly 418.16
 tastefully 481.8

quite
 adv somewhat 231.7
 very 233.17
 absolutely 756.14

quoted
 adj repeated 811.12

race
 n run 165.3
 flow 224.4
 waterway 225.2
 mankind 297.1
 haste 386.1
 horse race 442.9
 people 540.4
 lineage 541.4
 game 720.8
 class 771.2
 v speed 165.6
 make haste 386.4
 race with 442.15

racial
 adj ethnic 540.7

racing

n track 442.8

racism
 n hate 94.1
 discrimination 935.4

racist
 adj prejudiced 935.12
 n misanthrope 94.4
 bigot 935.5

radical
 adj basic 190.8
 corrective 377.16
 extremist 592.20
 innate 729.5
 thorough 756.9
 revolutionary 822.5
 original 841.14
 n reformer 377.6
 extremist 592.12
 foundation 856.5

radio
 adj wireless 983.23
 n wireless 332.3
 informant 532.5
 news 533.1
 wireless 983.1
 radio receiver 983.2
 v wire 332.12
 broadcast 983.20

rage
 n ecstasy 96.8
 fit of temper 143.8
 passion 143.10
 fad 559.5
 violence 651.1
 turbulence 651.2
 frenzy 881.6
 mania 881.10
 v be excitable 96.16
 burn 143.15
 blow 303.14
 bluster 488.3
 storm 651.10
 be insane 881.17

raid
 n foray 444.3
 plundering 467.6
 v foray 444.18

plunder 467.16
rail
  n railway 368.7
railway
  n railroad 368.7
rain
  n rainfall 301.1
  v descend 185.5
  precipitate 301.4
  give 463.12
  flood 19.12
raise
  n poker 722.9
  v erect 191.8
  increase 237.4
  enlarge 245.4
  emboss 269.9
  ferment 288.7
  rouse 360.18
  improve 377.9
  promote 431.2
  say 509.16
  conjure 669.6
  gather 732.18
  inaugurate 780.11
  produce 847.6
  process 847.9
  elevate 867.4
  farm 1112.15
  breed 113.5
raised
  adj increased 237.7
  expanded 245.10
  studded 269.13
  produced 847.17
  made 847.18
  lifted 867.8
raising
  n erection 191.4
  training 549.3
  production 847.2
  elevation 867.1
  growing 1112.11
rally
  n objection 318.2
  recovery 381.8
  contest 442.3

call-up 443.7
electioneering 590.11
price 715.3
tournament 720.9
assembly 732.2
  v object 318.5
incite 360.16
come round 377.8
recuperate 381.17
recover 381.18
aid 434.11
call up 443.5
banter 475.4
come together 732.16
gather 732.18
produce 912.11
range
  n field of view 30.3
earshot 39.4
scope 149.2
direction 152.1
habitat 217.16
degree 231.1
size 243.1
distance 247.1
grassland 296.8
arena 448.1
scale 687.5
  v extend 149.6
wander 168.19
rank
  adj nasty 55.6
strong 59.8
fetid 62.4
filthy 71.20
rough 274.6
luxuriant 296.32
tainted 378.34
wicked 634.15
base 641.12
terrible 955.9
  n standing 231.2
prestige 402.4
class 588.1
class 588.1
nobility 589.2
prestige 642.4

state 727.1
continuity 769.2
class 771.2
  v rule 235.11
size 243.14
order 769.4
classify 770.9
classify 771.5
estimate 901.9
rate 901.15
ranks
  n army 446.19
rap
  n report 47.1
hit 857.4
tap 857.6
  v crack 47.6
pound 857.14
tap 857.16
rape
  n violation 465.3
seduction 645.6
  v ravish 465.15
seduce 645.19
rapid
  adj fast 165.12
constant 845.9
  n rapids 224.10
rapidly
  adv swiftly 165.13
constantly 809.7
rare
  adj underdone 11.8
wonderful 113.6
rarefied 284.4
raw 391.8
other 742.7
infrequent 810.2
unusual 832.10
sparse 840.5
scarce 947.11
notable 952.18
rarely
  adv infrequently 810.4
unusually 832.17
sparsely 840.8
scarcely 947.16

rate
  n velocity 163.3
  rank 232.1
  interest 603.3
  price 610.1
  worth 610.2
  v count 230.4
  measure 286.7
  price 610.11
  classify 771.5
  estimate 901.9
  rank 901.15
rather
  adv somewhat 231.7
  preferably 356.27
  counter 741.7
  instead 824.8
  tolerably 954.23
rather than
  adv preferably 356.27
rating
  n rank 232.1
  measurement 286.1
  valuation 610.3
  classification 771.1
  class 771.2
  estimate 901.3
raw
  adj sore 26.11
  immature 287.9
  windblown 303.18
  crude 391.8
  immature 391.9
  vulgar 646.8
  new 803.7
  ignorant 885.10
  cold 975.13
ray
  n radiation 162.2
  wave 871.4
  radiation 977.5
reach
  n earshot 39.4
  range 149.2
  inlet 228.1
  degree 231.1
  size 243.1

distance 247.1
  length 253.1
  knowledge 883.1
  v move 136.5
  extend 149.6
  go 168.15
  arrive 177.6
  arrive at 177.7
  communicate with
    328.7
  deliver 463.13
  equal 752.5
  suffice 946.3
reaction
  n mental disorder 83.6
  feeling 84.1
  resistance 438.1
  conservatism 592.1
  impact 842.2
  opposition 855.1
  response 858.1
  answer 894.1
  opinion 908.6
read
  v orate 524.8
  copy-edit 529.15
  study 551.12
  study for 551.15
  sound out 897.9
reader
  n lecturer 524.5
  proofreader 529.12
  textbook 535.10
  professor 552.3
  input device 988.4
reading
  n measure 286.2
  interpretation 326.1
  speech 524.2
  elementary education
    549.5
  study 551.3
  scholarship 883.5
ready
  adj expectant 121.10
  willing 309.5
  quick 315.14

alert 324.14
  handy 372.18
  prepared 390.13
  skilful 398.20
  consenting 426.4
  apt 551.18
  prompt 807.9
  foreseeing 916.4
  v repair 381.12
  prepare 390.6
ready for
  adj prepared for
    390.15
  liable to 852.6
real
  adj feudal 456.8
  actual 723.11
  substantial 725.6
  obvious 925.10
  true 928.13
  genuine 928.15
realistic
  adj descriptive 334.13
  typical 334.14
  occupied 701.12
  lifelike 746.11
  normal 831.6
  sophisticated 911.4
  genuine 928.15
  practical 942.5
reality
  n truth 723.2
  event 793.2
  truth 928.1
realize
  v bring out 197.5
  do 313.6
  mirror 334.10
  accomplish 392.4
  profit 457.12
  understand 506.7
  be sold 711.9
  cause 841.10
  establish 847.10
  perform 847.11
  know 883.10
  visualize 941.10

recognize 944.9

realized
   adj accomplished
      392.9
   known 883.21

really
   adv very 233.17
   decidedly 233.18
   actually 723.12
   truly 928.18
   genuinely 928.19

rear
   adj back 208.9
   n setting 200.2
   rear end 208.1
   rear guard 208.2
   arse 208.5
   v ascend 184.7
   rise 191.7
   erect 191.8
   loom 233.5
   tower 258.7
   foster 434.16
   train 549.13
   produce 847.8
   process 847.9
   elevate 867.4
   farm 112.15
   raise 113.5

reason
   n motive 360.1
   cause 581.5
   rationale 841.2
   intellect 874.1
   reasonableness 875.6
   sanity 880.1
   reasoning 890.1
   argument 890.5
   reasonableness 890.7
   solution 895.1
   v discuss 523.10
   think 886.6
   rationalize 890.11
   conclude 901.10
   philosophize 907.6

reasonable
   adj justifiable 581.13

cheap 613.7
intelligent 875.10
sensible 875.16
sane 880.2
logical 890.16
plausible 923.4
realistic 942.5

reasonably
   adv intelligently 875.18
   logically 890.19

rebel
   adj rebellious 312.10
   n malcontent 99.3
   maverick 312.4
   anarchist 403.3
   revolutionary 822.3
   v revolt 312.6
   object 318.5

recall
   n repeal 430.1
   remembering 944.3
   v summon 405.9
   repeal 430.2
   remember 944.8
   remind 944.16

recalled
   adj remembered
      944.18

receive
   v take in 178.9
   assent 317.7
   get 464.6
   take 465.13
   admit 566.7
   pocket 607.3
   include 734.3
   believe 908.10

received
   adj accepted 317.13
   approved 494.17
   conventional 560.5
   orthodox 666.5
   traditional 804.11
   believed 908.22
   authoritative 925.13

receiving
   adj receptive 464.9

n reception 178.1
reception 464.1

recent
   adj former 799.8
   late 803.12

reception
   n taking in 178.1
   entrance 180.1
   receiving 464.1
   taking 465.1
   welcome 566.2
   assembly 732.2
   inclusion 734.1
   belief 908.1
   fading 983.16

recession
   n regression 154.1
   retreat 159.1
   business cycle 708.9
   hard times 966.6

recognition
   n thanks 141.2
   acknowledgment 317.3
   commendation 494.3
   due 619.2
   repute 642.1
   realization 883.2
   discovery 896.1
   identification 944.4

recognized
   adj accepted 317.13
   conventional 560.5
   traditional 804.11
   known 883.21

recommend
   v urge 360.13
   advise 407.4
   propose 424.5
   commend 494.9

recommended
   adj approved 494.17

record
   n disc 41.11
   supremacy 235.3
   readiness 390.4
   recording 530.1
   history 697.1

chronicle 794.6
data 988.14
v sound 41.13
write 528.14
inscribe 530.12
record 530.12
chronicle 697.4
video 984.15

recorded
adj registered 530.13

recording
n record 41.11
record 530.1
registration 530.11
transcript 747.4

recover
v get well 74.7
rally 377.8
redeem 381.10
rally 381.18
rescue 383.3
regain 466.6
rehabilitate 820.14

recovery
n improvement 377.1
reclamation 381.2
rally 381.8
rescue 383.1
regaining 466.3
business cycle 708.9
rehabilitation 820.4

Red
n revolutionary 822.3

reduce
v relieve 111.5
debase 128.5
count 230.4
decrease 238.7
subtract 241.8
contract 246.5
shorten 254.4
count calories 256.11
demote 432.3
cheapen 613.6
moderate 650.5
simplify 760.3
depress 868.4

qualify 914.3
chemicalize 14.7
v make small 244.8

reduced
adj decreased 238.10
low 260.7
cut-price 613.9
depressed 868.12

reducing
adj dieting 256.16
mitigating 650.12
n slimming 256.8

reduction
n relief 111.1
decrease 238.1
decrease 241.2
contraction 246.1
shortening 254.2
demotion 432.1
discount 611.1
cheapening 613.4
abatement 650.2
conversion 820.1
depression 868.1

reed
n tube 225.5
grass 296.5
stem 296.18

reel
n winch 861.5
whirl 870.2
swing 871.6
v pitch 173.22
reel in 861.7
whirl 870.9
oscillate 871.8
flounder 872.12

refer
v attribute 843.3

referee
n arbiter 451.4
judge 577.1
judge 901.6
v mediate 451.6
hold court 901.12

reference
n aspect 32.3

recommendation 494.4
meaning 503.1
relevance 737.4
citation 843.2
citation 912.5

referendum
n vote 356.6
election 590.13
mandate 594.6

reflect
v curve 265.6
imitate 321.5
mirror 334.10
remark 509.18
consider 886.9
remember 944.8

Reform
adj Jewish 655.25

reform
n reformation 377.5

Reform
n Protestantism 655.9

refugee
n fugitive 353.5
alien 736.2

refusal
n unwillingness 310.1
dissent 318.1
rejection 357.1
rejection 427.1
prohibition 429.1
opposition 436.1
rebuff 863.2

refuse
n offal 71.9
remainder 242.1
derelict 355.4
discarding 375.3
waste 376.3
v be unwilling 310.3
reject 357.2
decline 427.3
prohibit 429.3
repel 863.3

refused
adj rejected 357.3

regard

n observation 27.2
aspect 32.3
love 95.1
consideration 134.3
respect 146.1
carefulness 324.1
good terms 568.3
esteem 642.3
particular 728.3
relevance 737.4
outlook 933.2
v look 27.12
cherish 95.20
be considerate 134.10
respect 146.4
care 324.6
relate to 737.5
contemplate 886.13
judge 901.8
think 908.11
heed 938.6

regime
n diet 7.9
treatment 82.5
government 593.1

region
n location 150.1
area 220.1
state 220.5

regional
adj geographic 150.19
territorial 220.7
idiomatic 508.14

register
n range 149.2
record 530.1
notebook 530.9
registration 530.11
recorder 531.1
account book 608.4
pitch 687.3
scale 687.5
chronicle 794.6
list 833.1
v be heard 39.11
limit 201.5
represent 334.8

get over or across
506.5
record 530.12
be taught 551.11
agree 750.6
list 833.1

registered
adj limited 201.7
recorded 530.13

regret
n regrets 104.1
v deplore 104.6

regular
adj gradual 231.5
symmetrical 250.4
smooth 273.9
habitual 358.13
uniform 743.5
thorough 756.9
orderly 769.6
constant 809.5
methodical 812.6
usual 831.7
ordinary 960.8
n customer 710.4

regularly
adv smoothly 273.12
habitually 358.19
constantly 743.8
methodically 769.9
constantly 809.7
systematically 812.9
normally 831.8

rejected
adj unloved 90.10
repudiated 357.3
discarded 375.9
outcast 567.9
doubted 910.11
disproved 913.6

relate
v state 509.17
report 533.11
narrate 537.11
narrate 700.6
associate 737.6
compare 898.4

related
adj kindred 540.6
connected 737.9
kindred 737.10

relation
n meaning 503.1
blood relationship
540.1
fiction 700.1
narration 700.2
story 700.3
relationship 737.1
comparison 898.1

relations
n kindred 540.2
relation 737.1
affairs 793.4

relationship
n blood relationship
540.1
relation 737.1

relative
adj indeterminate
737.7
comparative 898.7

relatively
adv moderately 234.10
comparatively 737.12
comparatively 898.9

relatives
n kindred 540.2

relax
v compose oneself
97.7
relieve 111.5
be at ease 112.8
have pity 136.4
slow 166.8
let one's hair down
562.2
ease up 650.8
amuse 720.20
amuse oneself 720.21
loosen 766.2
pause 819.7
allow for 914.5
soften 992.6

yield 992.7
v unwind 20.7

relaxation
n debilitation 16.5
rest 20.1
relief 111.1
decrease 252.1
idleness 316.2
laxness 411.1
abatement 650.2
amusement 720.1
flaccidity 992.3
softening 992.5

relaxed
adj nonchalant 97.15
at ease 112.12
nerveless 120.2
quiet 164.10
slow 166.9
negligent 325.10
leisurely 387.4
lax 411.3
informal 562.3
loose 766.4
thoughtless 888.2
flaccid 992.10

release
n freeing 111.2
death 293.1
press release 337.3
escape 354.1
rescue 383.1
exemption 415.8
freeing 416.2
permission 428.1
relinquishment 460.1
information 532.1
message 533.4
acquittal 582.1
dispersal 733.2
v free 111.6
rescue 383.3
exempt 415.13
let go 416.5
extricate 416.7
permit 428.9
let go 460.3

acquit 582.4
disband 733.6
detach 764.9
dismiss 864.17

released
adj free 415.19
exempt 415.27
liberated 416.10
relinquished 460.4

relevant
adj pertinent 737.11
apt 750.10

reliable
adj trustworthy 624.15
stable 817.12
believable 908.23
evidential 912.14
dependable 925.12
trouble-free 962.5

relief
n remedy 77.1
easing 111.1
social services 134.5
pity 136.1
projection 269.1
lightening 284.3
aid 434.1
reinforcements 434.8
welfarism 592.7
medallion 693.3
turn 787.2
interim 788.1
substitute 824.2

religion
n belief 655.1
theology 656.1
piety 671.1
faith 908.3

religious
adj theistic 655.20
theological 656.4
sacred 664.7
pious 671.8

reluctant
adj slow 166.9
grudging 310.6
resistant 438.5

remain
v be still 164.6
be present 210.6
inhabit 214.6
survive 242.5
endure 789.5
endure 815.4
continue 818.3

remaining
adj surviving 242.7
durable 789.9
permanent 815.6
continuing 818.7
surplus 948.16

remains
n remainder 242.1
corpse 293.12
record 530.1
antiquity 804.5

remarkable
adj wonderful 113.6
outstanding 233.10
extraordinary 832.14
notable 952.18

remember
v recall 944.8

remembered
adj reminiscent 799.7
recollected 944.18

remote
adj aloof 132.11
distant 247.8
reticent 329.8
aloof 564.6
secluded 565.8
selfish 631.5
far-fetched 738.6

removal
adv moving 167.3
n release 111.2
displacement 151.1
departure 179.1
extraction 183.1
subtraction 241.1
discarding 375.3
deposition 432.2
elimination 735.2

separation 764.1
throwing out 864.1
dismissal 864.5
evacuation 864.6

remove
v divest 6.5
take off 6.6
move 167.7
quit 179.9
extract 183.9
subtract 241.8
murder 294.13
discard 375.7
exterminate 380.14
depose 432.4
eliminate 773.5
detach 764.9
eject 864.11
dismiss 864.17
evacuate 864.20

removed
adj distant 247.8
secluded 565.8
unrelated 738.4
separated 764.19
alone 834.8

renewed
adj refreshed 9.4
fresh 803.8
changed 814.10
continuing 818.7
converted 820.19

rent
adj cleft 213.6
impaired 378.23
severed 764.12
n crack 213.2
rental 595.5
rental 610.8
v crack 213.4
inhabit 214.6
lease 595.13

repair
n repairing 381.6
good condition 727.2
v perfect 377.11
mend 381.12

atone 638.4

repeat
n ditto 811.5
encore 811.6
encore 836.2
v reproduce 69.7
imitate 321.5
publish 337.10
do again 811.7
recur 811.11
recur 812.5
duplicate 836.3
memorize 944.13

repeated
adj constant 809.5
reproduced 811.12

repeatedly
adv continuously 774.10
frequently 809.6
often 816.11

replace
v restore 381.9
depose 432.4
follow 797.3
substitute for 824.5
dismiss 864.17

replacement
n restoration 381.1
deposition 432.2
successor 779.4
sequel 797.2
substitution 824.1
substitute 824.2

reply
n communication 328.1
retaliation 491.1
letter 534.2
defence 600.1
reaction 858.1
answer 894.1
v answer 534.11
react 858.4
answer 894.3

report
n crash 47.1

account 334.3
announcement 337.2
publicity 337.4
bulletin 530.7
information 532.1
rumour 533.6
commentary 537.2
repute 642.1
criticism 901.2
v present oneself 210.11
communicate 328.6
announce 337.12
inform 532.8
tell 533.11
narrate 697.5
narrate 700.6
pass judgment 901.13

reported
adj published 337.17
rumoured 533.14

reporter
n informant 532.5
journalist 536.4

represent
v lead 207.6
depict 334.8
describe 334.9
mediate 451.6
act for 557.14
enact 682.22
substitute for 824.5
visualize 941.10

representation
n reproduction 321.3
display 333.2
drawing 334.1
description 334.2
representative 334.7
sign 502.1
bar 578.4
picture 690.9
copy 747.1
duplicate 747.3
substitution 824.1

representative
adj pictorial 334.12

descriptive 334.13
indicative 502.23
model 748.8
n representation 334.7
deputy 557.1
example 748.2
substitute 824.2

representing
adj representative
334.12

republic
n country 221.1
federal government
593.4

reputation
n repute 642.1
prominence 952.2

request
n proposal 424.2
asking 425.1
v ask 425.9

require
v prescribe 405.8
demand 406.5
oblige 409.5
charge 610.12
obligate 621.10
involve 734.4
determine 841.12
need 918.8
want 947.7

required
adj mandatory 405.10
obligatory 409.11
obligatory 621.13
resultant 842.6
requisite 918.11

rescue
n escape 354.1
delivery 383.1
liberation 416.1
aid 434.1
v redeem 381.10
deliver 383.3
liberate 416.4
aid 434.11

research

n investigation 893.4
v search 893.29
experiment 897.8

reserve
adj unused 391.10
substitute 824.7
n restraint 130.3
reticence 329.2
reserves 371.3
preserve 382.6
conciseness 519.1
v save 371.11
not use 375.5
allot 462.9
postpone 808.9
prearrange 920.3

reserves
n reserve 371.3
reinforcements 434.8
territorial army 446.21
team 597.7
funds 705.11
substitute 824.2

resign
v give up 355.7
abdicate 375.4
quit 433.2
relinquish 460.2

resignation
n apathy 85.4
composure 97.2
contentment 98.1
humility 125.2
surrender 355.3
cessation 375.2
submission 418.1
withdrawal 433.1
relinquishment 460.1

resigned
adj apathetic 85.13
content 98.7
reconciled 125.9
submissive 418.11

resist
v oppose 436.3
contend against 436.4
withstand 438.2

counteract 855.6
hinder 967.9

resistance
n immunity 74.4
suppression 83.14
refusal 310.1
defiance 346.4
opposition 436.1
withstanding 438.1
defence 445.1
irregular 446.12
opposition 855.1
hindrance 967.1
resistance 982.12
hardness 991.1
toughness 994.1

resolution
n distinctness 30.2
will 308.1
resolve 344.1
perseverance 345.1
intention 380.1
endeavour 388.1
proposal 424.2
adjustment 450.4
fortitude 477.4
end 782.1
conversion 820.1
solution 895.1
judgment 901.1

resolve
n resolution 344.1
intention 365.1
v will 308.2
determine 344.6
intend 365.4
endeavour 388.4
reconcile 450.8
end 782.4
solve 895.2
decide 901.11

resolved
adj resolute 344.10

resort
n haunt 217.24
agency 369.3
entertainment 720.12

expedient 950.2
recourse 964.2

resources
n means 369.2
supply 371.2
assets 456.6
funds 705.11

respect
n aspect 32.3
regard 146.1
observance 419.1
courtesy 489.1
approval 494.1
good terms 568.3
duty 621.1
esteem 642.3
particular 728.3
relevance 737.4
outlook 933.2
v be considerate 134.10
regard 146.4
observe 419.2
approve 494.7

respected
adj revered 146.11
reputable 642.13

respond
v react 84.11
interchange 825.3
react 858.4
answer 894.3

response
n feeling 84.1
sympathy 84.5
communication 328.1
meaning 503.1
defence 581.2
impact 842.2
reaction 858.1
answer 894.1

responsibility
n commission 595.1
incumbency 621.2
trustworthiness 624.5
attribution 843.1
operation 844.1

liability 852.1
n supervision 554.2

responsible
adj answerable 621.15
trustworthy 624.15
liable 852.5

rest
n repose 20.1
respite 20.2
silence 42.1
stillness 164.1
step 184.4
remainder 242.1
death 293.1
leisure 387.1
pause 687.12
pause 819.3
fulcrum 861.2
v lie 150.10
deposit 150.14
be still 164.6
do nothing 314.2
calm 650.6
pause 819.7
depend 914.6
v take it easy 20.6

restaurant
n dining room 8.16
dining room 188.9
workplace 716.1

restoration
n fortification 7.10
reproduction 69.1
improvement 377.1
replacement 381.1
restitution 466.1
recovery 466.3
rehabilitation 820.4
reversion 821.1

restore
v fortify 7.16
reproduce 69.7
put back 381.9
aid 434.11
return 466.4
rehabilitate 820.14

restored

adj refreshed 9.4
reminiscent 799.7

restricted
adj limited 201.7
out of bounds 201.8
narrow 256.12
secret 330.11
limited 413.14
confined 414.18
specialized 828.5
qualified 914.10

result
n event 793.1
effect 842.1
product 848.1
solution 895.1
v turn out 793.7
follow 797.3
ensue 842.4

retail
adj commercial 708.19
sales 711.10
n sale 711.1
v publish 337.10
deal in 708.15
sell 711.6
disperse 733.3

retain
v reserve 371.11
keep 459.5
stabilize 817.7
sustain 818.4
bear in mind 944.10

retained
adj reserved 371.13

retired
adj private 330.13
leisure 387.3
in retirement 433.3

retirement
n retreat 154.2
recession 159.1
departure 179.1
disuse 375.1
leisure 387.2
deposition 432.2
resignation 433.1

seclusion 565.1
dismissal 864.5
return
  n regression 154.1
  homecoming 177.3
  relapse 379.1
  recovery 381.8
  gain 457.3
  restitution 466.1
  retaliation 491.1
  recompense 604.3
  dividend 715.2
  repetition 811.1
  cyclical motion 812.2
  reversion 821.1
  production 848.2
  reaction 858.1
  answer 894.1
  v regress 154.4
  turn back 154.7
  restore 381.9
  restore 466.4
  repeat 811.11
  recur 812.5
  revert 821.3
  interchange 825.3
  answer 894.3
return to
  v revisit 210.9
  relapse 379.2
  resume 818.6
  revert to 821.5
returning
  adj recurrent 811.13
  answering 894.5
returns
  n gain 457.3
  election returns 590.18
  receipts 607.1
  roll 833.6
reveal
  v manifest 333.5
  disclose 336.4
  divulge 336.5
  signify 502.17
  unfold 823.6
  uncover 896.4

revealed
  adj visible 30.6
  open 333.10
  disclosed 336.9
  scriptural 663.5
revenge
  n compensation 323.1
  reprisal 491.2
  vengeance 492.1
  v avenge 492.3
revenue
  n receipts 607.1
reverse
  adj backward 154.10
  opposite 206.5
  contrary 741.5
  n inverse 196.3
  opposite side 206.3
  reversal 348.1
  relapse 379.1
  reversion 821.1
  reversal 966.3
  gear 986.5
  v back 154.6
  misinterpret 327.2
  repeal 430.2
  convert 820.11
  revert 821.3
review
  n discussion 523.6
  periodical 536.1
  commentary 537.2
  condensation 538.1
  fiction 700.1
  narration 700.2
  recounting 811.2
  afterthought 886.5
  examination 893.3
  re-examination 893.6
  criticism 901.2
  remembering 944.3
  v discuss 523.10
  write upon 537.5
  reiterate 811.8
  reconsider 886.11
  examine 893.22
  re-examine 893.25

criticize 901.14
remember 944.8
brush up 944.15
revival
  n refreshment 9.1
  animation 17.8
  reproduction 69.1
  improvement 377.1
  renewal 381.3
  memory 797.1
  change 814.1
  resumption 818.2
  new start 820.2
revolution
  n overturn 196.2
  revolt 312.3
  reform 377.5
  anarchy 403.2
  disruption 764.3
  round 812.3
  break 814.2
  violent change 822.1
  revolution 822.1
  circuit 869.2
  rotation 870.1
revolutionary
  adj rebellious 312.10
  original 322.4
  corrective 377.16
  radical 592.20
  unruly 651.17
  changed 814.10
  cataclysmic 822.5
  Marxist 822.6
  counteracting 855.8
  n rebel 312.4
  reformer 377.6
  radical 592.12
  rebel 822.3
reward
  n incentive 360.7
  reprisal 491.2
  award 626.2
  v requite 491.4
  pay 604.10
rhythm
  n accent 509.9

harmony 515.2
beat 687.13
metre 698.7
cyclical motion 812.2
pulse 871.3

rich
adj colourful 34.17
resonant 45.8
nutty 54.8
humorous 473.2
ornate 483.11
wealthy 598.8
melodic 686.39
productive 845.7
plentiful 946.6
oily 11.8

rid
adj quit 415.28

ride
n drive 168.6
merry-go-round 720.14
v go on horseback 168.30
rest on 856.9

rider
n equestrian 169.7

ridiculous
adj humorous 473.2
absurd 878.9
unbelievable 910.10
impossible 922.4

riding
n driving 168.5
state 220.5

right
adj straight 263.6
decorous 481.7
conventional 560.5
rightful 617.3
just 629.6
apt 750.10
sane 880.2
accurate 928.16
expedient 950.5
adv rightly 617.4
absolutely 756.14
exactly 928.21

excellently 954.21
n authority 402.1
rights 415.2
estate 456.4
reason 581.5
rightness 617.1
prerogative 622.1
justice 629.1
v harmonize 750.7
arrange 770.6

right now
adv at once 792.7
now 803.16

right-wing
adj conservative
592.18
conservative 815.7

rights
n right 415.2

ring
n ringing 45.3
circle 266.1
band 266.2
bulge 269.2
arena 448.1
jewel 483.5
association 597.1
clique 597.6
tiara 627.3
halo 977.15
v din 44.7
peal 45.7
encircle 200.6
telephone 332.11

rings
n parallel bars 702.7

riot
n revolt 312.3
brawl 442.5
joke 474.3
commotion 772.4
plenty 946.2
v vegetate 296.26
revolt 312.6
contend 442.10
rage 651.10
make trouble 772.9

rise
n appearance 32.1
ascent 184.1
rising 191.5
ascent 195.6
height 258.2
improvement 377.1
promotion 431.1
evolution 823.1
source 841.5
v get up 23.6
appear 32.8
din 44.7
move 163.4
ascend 184.7
arise 191.7
incline 195.9
grow 237.6
tower 258.7
ascend 284.7
make good 394.7

rising
adj flowing 163.7
ascending 184.13
uphill 195.16
increasing 237.8
n course 163.2
ascent 184.1
uprising 191.5
ascent 195.6
swelling 269.3

risk
n investment 706.3
gamble 722.2
insecurity 926.3
chance 927.1
danger 961.1
v invest 706.15
chance 722.20
gamble 927.8
endanger 961.6
take chances 961.7

rival
adj opposing 436.7
competitive 442.19
n competitor 437.2
combatant 446.1

v contend against
436.4
compete 442.14
equal 752.5
be comparable 898.6
excel 954.11

river
n stream 224.1
torrent 224.5

road
n waterway 173.6
route 368.1
highway 368.5
harbour 964.6

roads
n harbour 964.6

rob
v pick pockets 467.13

rock
adj stone 13.6
n missile 447.17
rock'n'roll 686.9
bedrock 817.6
swing 871.6
stone 991.5
stone 13.1
v impress 84.13
agitate 96.14
pitch 173.22
oscillate 871.8
flounder 872.12

rocks
n reefs 961.5

rod
n shaft 259.1
sceptre 402.9
stick 586.2
regalia 627.2

role
n function 372.5
part 682.7
script 684.2
function 701.3
mode 727.3

roll
n bun 10.28
staccato 46.1

boom 47.4
a length 253.2
coil 267.2
cylinder 268.2
record 530.1
document 530.5
film 692.8
throw 722.8
roster 833.6
rotation 870.1
swing 871.6
v perform aerobatics
175.16
ball 268.4
smooth 273.5
press 273.6
push 859.9
trundle 870.8
flounder 872.12

rolled
adj horizontal 192.7

rolling
adj highland 258.13
coiled 267.7
rotating 870.10
swinging 871.14
n throwing 859.2
rotation 870.1

rolls
n record 530.1

romance
n love affair 95.5
fabrication 339.7
whim 941.4

romantic
adj sentimental 84.19
loving 95.26
fictional 700.7
visionary 941.18
n inventor 941.8

roof
n top 189.1
abode 217.1
rooftop 281.6
v top 281.20

room
n latitude 149.3

chamber 188.1
interval 213.1
quarters 217.4
capacity 243.2
latitude 415.4
opportunity 805.2
v inhabit 214.6

rooms
n quarters 217.4
apartment 217.12

root
n taproot 296.19
primitive 511.2
morpheme 511.3
source 841.5
foundation 856.5
v vegetate 296.26
fix 817.9
take root 817.10
search 893.29

rose
n insignia 627.1

rouge
n makeup 971.10

rough
adj acrimonious 17.13
raucous 49.15
harsh 135.22
uneven 274.6
coarse 280.5
undeveloped 391.10
coarse 482.9
gruff 490.7
violent 651.15
boisterous 651.18
uneven 744.3
irregular 813.3
jolting 872.17
adv roughly 274.10
n broken ground 274.2
diagram 366.3
v rough up 274.4
maltreat 374.5

roughly
adv harshly 135.29
approximately 212.23
rough 274.10

vulgarly 482.14
irregularly 813.4
generally 826.16
round
adj circular 266.5
rounded 268.5
elegant 515.4
full 756.10
circuitous 869.7
adv around 200.11
around 870.12
n drink 79.5
step 184.4
sphere 220.2
degree 231.1
circle 266.1
route 368.1
catch 686.17
sphere 701.4
series 774.2
turn 787.2
revolution 812.3
circuit 869.2
whirl 870.2
v curve 265.6
circle 266.4
round out 268.3
circle 869.6
turn 869.6
rotate 870.7
rounds
n circuit 869.2
route
n path 368.1
routine
adj medium 232.3
habitual 358.13
orderly 769.6
frequent 809.4
prevalent 826.11
n exercise 75.2
beat 358.5
manner 369.1
act 682.4
order 769.1
series 774.2
software 988.10

row
n hullabaloo 44.4
rumpus 441.6
turbulence 651.2
series 774.2
agitation 872.1
v navigate 173.9
paddle 173.20
scrap 441.11
royal
adj dignified 127.12
sovereign 402.16
good 954.12
rubber
n eraser 380.9
elastic 993.3
rubbish
n remainder 242.1
derelict 355.4
refuse 376.3
nonsense 505.2
bull 505.3
trivia 953.4
v put down 147.6
rule
n mean 232.1
supremacy 235.3
ruler 263.3
measure 286.2
norm 358.4
governance 402.5
law 404.2
direction 405.3
decree 405.4
government 593.1
law 653.3
law 831.4
influence 849.1
axiom 929.2
v command 235.11
have power 402.12
command 405.7
sway 593.12
prevail 826.9
govern 849.8
pass judgment 901.13
ruling

adj powerful 18.7
chief 235.14
authoritative 402.14
governing 593.16
prevalent 826.11
dominant 849.14
n decree 405.4
law 653.3
verdict 901.5

run
n course 163.2
sprint 165.3
journey 168.4
voyage 173.2
flight 175.3
lair 217.23
flow 224.4
a length 253.2
race 442.9
engagement 682.8
impromptu 686.21
ornament 687.10
series 774.2
continuance 818.1
trend 851.2
v fester 12.15
exercise 75.3
extend 149.6
move 163.4
speed 165.6
travel 168.14
navigate 173.9
pilot 173.10
flow 224.15
flee 353.10
nominate 356.18
make haste 386.4
print 529.13
direct 554.8
go into politics 591.8
smuggle 709.6
elapse 783.3
endure 789.5
operate 844.5
operate 844.7
thrust 857.11
melt 972.21

program 988.17
liquefy 18.4
raise 113.5

runner
 n acceleration 165.4
branch 296.17
messenger 338.1
member 755.4

running
 adj flowing 163.7
fast 165.12
present 800.2
operating 844.11
 n pus 12.6
exercise 75.2
operation 891.1
liquefaction 18.1
 n direction 554.1
supervision 554.2

rural
 adj rustic 222.4
agricultural 112.19

rush
 n kick 96.3
course 163.2
velocity 165.1
run 165.3
flow 224.4
jet 224.9
grass 296.5
haste 386.1
demand 406.1
attack 444.1
haste 807.2
 v speed 165.6
flow 224.15
hasten 386.3
make haste 386.4
charge 444.16

rushed
 adj hurried 386.7
premature 807.8

Russian
 n Cuban 80.2

S
 adj crescent-shaped
265.9

sacred
 adj almighty 657.9
holy 664.7

sad
 adj dark 37.8
joyless 87.20
saddened 103.20
disgraceful 641.11
paltry 953.18
terrible 955.9
unfortunate 966.14

sadly
 adv horribly 89.27
gloomily 103.31
unfortunately 966.17

safe
 adj cautious 479.7
secure 962.4
protected 963.21
 n treasury 706.11

safely
 adv securely 962.8

safety
 n security 962.1
protection 963.1

said
 adj speech 509.22
former 776.5

sail
 n canvas 171.12
voyage 173.2
 v glide 168.31
navigate 173.9
get under way 173.13
float 173.21

sailing
 n gliding 168.12
water travel 173.1
aviation 175.1

saint
 n holy man 639.6
angel 659.1
 v ordain 677.7

sake
 n motive 360.1
intention 365.1

salad

 n greens 10.33

salary
 n pay 604.4

sale
 n transfer 609.1
wholesale 711.1
bazaar 711.3

sales
 adj market 711.10

sally
 n attack 444.1

salmon
 n fish 10.23

salt
 adj flavoured 53.8
salty 59.9
witty 474.9
 n seaman 174.1
preservative 382.3
wit 474.1
 v flavour 54.6
preserve 382.8

same
 adj identical 740.7
monotonous 743.6
former 776.5

sample
 adj typical 334.14
 n specimen 53.4
specimen 748.3
part 755.1
probe 897.4
subject 897.7
 v taste 53.7
canvass 893.27
experiment 897.8

sanctions
 n penalty 584.1

sand
 n grain 996.6
sand dune 13.2
 v grind 273.8
buff 989.6

satellite
 n country 221.1
television 984.1
moon 114.11

satisfaction
 n pleasure 86.1
 contentment 98.1
 compensation 323.1
 repair 381.6
 observance 419.1
 recompense 604.3
 fullness 949.1
satisfied
 adj pleased 86.14
 content 98.7
 believing 908.20
 satiated 949.5
sauce
 n cooking 11.1
save
 adj excluding 735.10
 v store up 371.10
 reserve 371.11
 not use 375.5
 preserve 382.7
 rescue 383.3
 aid 434.11
 retain 459.5
 economize 615.3
 redeem 664.6
 be conservative 815.5
 play safe 962.3
 prevent 967.13
saved
 adj reserved 371.13
 unused 375.10
 preserved 382.10
 redeemed 664.9
 converted 671.10
saving
 adj preservative 382.9
 aiding 573.4
 excluding 735.10
 n preservation 382.1
 rescue 383.1
 economizing 615.2
savings
 n reserve 371.3
 funds 705.11
saw
 n maxim 929.1

platitude 929.3
 v notch 275.2
 sever 764.10
say
 adv approximately
  212.23
 n affirmation 319.1
 vote 356.6
 free will 415.6
 remark 509.3
 speech 524.2
 turn 787.2
 influence 849.1
 v affirm 319.5
 announce 337.12
 utter 509.16
 state 509.17
 answer 894.3
 suppose 906.7
saying
 n affirmation 319.1
 maxim 929.1
scale
 n range 149.2
 map 150.5
 ladder 184.3
 step 184.4
 degree 231.1
 size 243.1
 blanket 281.11
 crust 281.13
 flake 282.3
 weighing 283.7
 measure 286.2
 register 687.5
 series 742.2
 v flake 6.11
 climb 184.10
 layer 282.4
 raid 444.18
scandal
 n slander 497.3
 dirt 533.8
 abomination 618.2
 iniquity 634.3
 disgrace 641.5
scared

adj afraid 118.21
scene
 n view 32.6
 outburst 143.9
 setting 200.2
 arena 448.1
 act 682.4
 view 690.10
schedule
 n plan 366.1
 chronicle 794.6
 list 833.1
 programme 920.2
 v plan 366.7
 allot 462.9
 spend 606.4
 list 833.8
 line up 920.5
scheduled
 adj planned 366.11
 listed 833.9
 booked 920.8
scheme
 n trick 341.6
 plan 366.1
 project 366.2
 intrigue 366.5
 stratagem 400.3
 outline 763.4
 v calculate 365.7
 plot 366.8
 manoeuvre 400.10
 come 801.6
 prearrange 920.3
schemes
 n intrigues 849.3
school
 adj scholastic 548.13
 n institute 548.1
 sect 597.5
 sect 655.2
 style 690.6
 religion 908.3
 v teach 549.10
science
 n art 398.7
 art 883.8

scientific
adj technical 883.23
realistic 942.5

score
n crack 213.2
notch 275.1
furrow 276.1
representation 334.1
hit 394.4
mark 502.5
line 502.6
account 608.2
script 682.16
piece 686.4
music 686.22
engraving 691.2
v notch 275.2
furrow 276.3
succeed 394.6
acquire 457.8
mark 502.19
engrave 691.6

scored
adj nicked 275.3
furrowed 276.4

scores
n multitude 839.3

scoring
n engraving 691.2

screaming
adj garish 34.18
vociferous 50.7
gaudy 486.16

screen
n furniture 218.1
sieve 278.7
cover 281.2
veil 331.2
pretext 361.1
movie theatre 684.6
safeguard 963.3
shade 980.1
v cover 281.18
defend 445.8
segregate 735.6
protect 963.18
shade 980.5

script
n representation 334.1
writing system 527.3
handwriting 528.3
writing 528.8
document 530.5
text 682.16
screenplay 684.2

sea
n wave 224.14
ocean 226.1
ocean 226.2
quantity 233.3

search
n quest 893.14
v pursue 367.8
hunt 893.29

search for
v seek 893.28

searching
adj pursuing 367.11
probing 893.36
n pursuit 367.1

season
n time of year 298.1
period 786.1
v flavour 54.6
mature 289.7
accustom 358.8
develop 377.10
preserve 382.8
imbue 759.10
qualify 914.3

seat
n station 150.2
headquarters or HQ 199.4
abode 217.1
capital 219.3
foundation 856.5
v place 150.12
establish 150.16
fix 817.9

second
adv secondly 836.6
n assistant 596.5
interval 687.11

moment 786.2
instant 792.3
gear 986.5
v ratify 317.11
back 434.13

secondary
adj inferior 236.6
unnecessary 730.3
eventual 793.11
substitute 824.7
unimportant 953.14
n inferior 236.2
accessory 730.1

seconds
n commodity 712.2

secret
adj invisible 31.5
closed 330.11
concealed 331.11
abstract 507.14
intrinsic 729.4
n confidence 330.5

secretary
n writer 528.10
recorder 531.1
executive 555.3
agent 557.3

secretary of state
n minister 556.17

section
n region 220.1
plot 220.4
unit 446.18
part 535.13
passage 686.19
part 755.1
prologue 755.2
class 771.2

sector
n oval 266.3
part 755.1

secure
adj fast 762.13
stable 817.12
believing 908.20
reliable 925.12
assured 925.14

confident 925.15
safe 962.4
v fetch 167.10
close 279.5
bind 413.9
guarantee 423.7
defend 445.8
acquire 457.8
receive 464.6
fasten 762.6
tie 817.8
protect 963.18
security
n hope 115.1
veil 330.3
guarantee 423.1
stability 817.1
reliability 925.3
confidence 925.4
safety 962.1
protection 963.1
prosperity 965.1
see
n diocese 677.3
v sense 24.6
behold 27.11
attend 210.8
perceive 506.8
make sure 543.14
visit 563.18
bet 722.21
witness 873.5
know 883.10
contemplate 886.13
heed 938.6
visualize 941.10
seed
n sperm 291.7
stone 296.24
lineage 541.4
posterity 542.1
egg 841.7
v plant 112.17
seeing
adj visual 27.19
n observation 27.2

observatory 114.15
seek
v pursue 367.8
endeavour 388.4
solicit 425.14
hunt 893.28
be curious 936.3
seeking
adj pursuing 367.11
n pursuit 367.1
seem
v appear 32.10
seized
adj known 883.21
select
adj chosen 356.25
exclusive 480.10
exclusive 735.9
best 954.16
v pick 356.13
designate 502.18
appoint 595.9
specify 827.11
discriminate 899.4
selected
adj chosen 356.25
selection
n choice 356.1
indication 502.3
excerpt 538.3
appointment 595.2
grouping 770.3
specification 827.6
self
n psyche 83.17
ego 827.5
sell
v publicize 337.15
provision 370.9
transfer 609.3
deal in 708.15
merchandise 711.6
be sold 711.9
convert 714.12
selling
n marketing 711.2
senate

n council 408.1
school board 548.12
send
v send off or away
167.9
communicate 328.6
mail 534.12
start 859.12
broadcast 983.20
sending
n informing 328.2
senior
adj authoritative
402.14
previous 796.4
older 804.18
n superior 235.4
elder 290.4
chief 556.3
sense
n sensation 24.1
feeling 84.1
ambience 200.3
meaning 503.1
intelligence 875.1
reasonableness 875.6
recognition 883.2
idea 887.1
hunch 889.3
reasonableness 890.7
discrimination 899.1
suggestion 906.5
opinion 908.6
v feel 24.6
feel 84.10
feel 889.4
detect 896.5
sensible
adj susceptible 24.11
sensitive 84.18
substantial 725.6
intelligent 875.10
reasonable 875.16
sane 880.2
logical 890.16
realistic 942.5
sensitive

adj sensory 24.9
responsive 24.12
sore 26.11
sensible 84.18
excitable 96.28
touchy 101.21
confidential 330.14
fastidious 480.6
discriminating 899.7
tolerant 934.11
pliable 992.9

sentence
n remark 509.3
judgment 579.9
condemnation 583.1
section 755.2
verdict 901.5
v condemn 583.2
pass judgment 901.13

separate
adj secluded 565.8
different 742.6
distinct 764.18
alone 834.8
v refine 70.22
diverge 162.4
bound 202.7
partition 204.6
space 213.3
quarantine 414.13
fall out 441.9
sow dissension 441.12
divorce 547.5
disband 733.6
segregate 735.6
differentiate 742.5
share 755.6
analyse 763.6
divide 764.7
part company 764.17
classify 770.9
discriminate 899.4

separated
adj spaced 213.5
quarantined 414.19
widowed 547.7
secluded 565.8

alienated 570.11
segregated 735.8
unrelated 738.4
disjointed 764.19

Sergeant
n Marshall of the RAF
556.18
Field Marshal 556.19

series
n following 157.1
edition 535.5
set 732.12
succession 774.2
sequence 777.1
round 812.3
broadcast 983.13

serious
adj zealous 92.9
sedate 97.14
solemn 102.3
great 233.6
resolute 344.10
lofty 525.13
cognitive 886.17
weighty 962.19
dangerous 961.9

seriously
adv ardently 92.14
sedately 97.17
solemnly 102.4
decidedly 233.18
resolutely 344.15

serve
n throw 859.3
v be inferior 236.4
act 313.4
be instrumental 369.6
avail 372.15
summon 405.9
work for 434.18
soldier 443.14
give 463.12
work for 558.12
function 701.11
suit 750.8
throw 859.10
suffice 946.3

come in handy 950.3
do good 954.10

service
n table service 8.11
kindness 134.7
obedience 311.1
agency 369.3
benefit 372.4
aid 434.1
military service 443.8
branch 446.17
servitude 558.11
worship 675.8
rite 680.1
task 701.2
throw 859.3
v repair 381.12

services
n defence forces
446.16

serving
adj acting 313.10
helping 434.20
ministering 558.13
n portion 8.10

session
n chapter 408.4
conference 523.5
assembly 732.2
moment 786.2

set
adj located 150.18
circumscribed 201.6
sharp 271.7
obstinate 346.7
customary 358.12
fast 762.13
cohesive 765.9
established 817.13
fixed 817.14
assured 925.14
hardened 991.12
n course 163.2
flow 224.4
form 248.1
arena 448.1
edition 535.5

social circle 563.5
clique 597.6
movie studio 684.3
company 732.3
suite 732.12
group 746.4
all 754.3
class 771.2
trend 851.2
disposition 933.3
v place 150.12
establish 150.16
direct 152.4
head 152.6
sink 185.6
flow 224.15
form 248.6
sharpen 271.6
heal 381.19
prime 390.9
prescribe 405.8
allot 462.9
compose 529.14
impose 623.4
compose 686.37
harmonize 750.7
fasten 762.6
adhere 765.6
fix 817.9
specify 827.11
tend 851.3
thicken 990.9
solidify 991.7
plant 112.17

set in
v dent 270.11
fix 817.9

set out
v set forth 179.8
plot 366.9
phrase 514.3
distribute 770.7
begin 780.7
start up 780.8

set to
v undertake 389.3
quarrel 441.10

set up
v refresh 9.2
establish 150.16
erect 191.8
plan 366.7
finance 706.14
order 769.4
inaugurate 780.11
cause 841.10
establish 847.10
fix 920.4

set-to
n row 441.6

set-up
adj fixed 920.7

setting
adj descending 185.11
n background 200.2
closeness 212.1
arena 448.1
motif 483.6
composition 529.2
piece 684.4
arrangement 687.2
plot 700.4
circumstances 728.2
thickening 990.4
hardening 991.4
planting 112.13

settle
v settle down 150.17
arrive 177.6
sink 185.6
get down 185.7
people 214.8
gravitate 283.11
waste 294.11
resolve 344.6
do for 380.11
clobber 397.8
arrange 422.8
pacify 450.7
reconcile 450.8
arrange 451.7
compromise 453.2
pay in full 604.13
organize 770.8

fix 817.9
interchange 825.3
conform 829.3
decide 901.11
prove 912.9
make sure 925.7

settled
adj located 150.18
firm 344.11
confirmed 358.17
clobbered 397.14
contracted 422.11
paid 604.20
ended 782.7
established 817.13
fixed 817.14
proved 912.17
assured 925.14

settlement
n establishment 150.7
peopling 214.2
country 221.1
compact 422.1
adjustment 450.4
compromise 453.1
estate 456.4
endowment 463.9
community 597.2
payment 604.1
proof 912.3

seventh
n interval 687.11

several
adj different 742.6
varied 745.4
plural 838.5
sundry 839.7
n some 838.2
a number 839.2

severe
adj acrimonious 17.13
painful 26.10
harsh 135.22
imperious 402.15
strict 410.5
unelaborate 484.9
gruff 490.7

violent 651.15
simple 760.5
exact 928.17
difficult 968.17
cold 975.13
severely
  adv harshly 135.29
  strictly 410.7
  violently 651.23
sex
  adj sexual 66.23
  n gender 66.1
  copulation 66.7
  love 95.1
  v sex 66.18
sexual
  adj sex 66.23
  amorous 95.25
  lascivious 645.26
sexuality
  n love life 66.2
  lasciviousness 645.5
sexy
  adj sexual 66.23
  lustful 66.25
  delightful 88.6
  fun 88.7
  desirable 91.29
  alluring 362.8
  lascivious 645.26
shade
  n colour 34.1
  degree 231.1
  hint 234.4
  tinge 759.6
  phantom 931.4
  protection 963.1
  shadow 979.3
  screen 980.1
  v colour 34.12
  blacken 37.6
  cloud 304.3
  conceal 331.6
  portray 690.17
  screen 980.5
shadow
  n omen 124.3

degree 231.1
hint 234.4
remainder 242.1
paper 256.6
slim 256.7
image 334.5
treatment 690.7
spirit 726.3
reflection 747.7
phantom 931.4
spectre 943.1
shade 979.3
v blacken 37.6
presage 124.9
cloud 304.3
lurk 331.9
shake
  n beverage 10.44
  speech defect 510.1
  quake 872.3
  v tremble 16.7
  weaken 16.9
  thrill 96.18
  tremble 118.14
  frighten 118.15
  daunt 118.17
  unnerve 119.10
  startle 122.7
  age 289.8
  speak poorly 510.6
  dance 683.5
  thrust 857.11
  oscillate 871.8
  wave 871.9
  agitate 872.7
  quake 872.8
  freeze 975.9
shame
  n chagrin 87.4
  regret 104.1
  humiliation 128.2
  abomination 618.2
  iniquity 634.3
  disgrace 641.5
  v humiliate 128.4
  disgrace 641.8
shape

n aspect 32.3
apparition 32.5
fitness 75.1
form 248.1
figure 248.4
structure 252.1
good condition 727.2
mode 727.3
kind 771.3
characteristic 827.4
phantom 931.4
spectre 943.1
v form 248.6
form 248.7
plan 366.7
pot 719.4
compose 758.3
conform 829.3
conform 829.3
produce 847.8
imagine 941.9
shaped
  adj formative 248.8
  structural 252.5
  made 847.18
share
  v share in 461.5
shared
  adj mutual 739.10
shares
  n stock 715.1
sharing
  adj participating 461.7
  mutual 739.10
  n sympathy 84.5
  informing 328.2
  accord 440.1
  participation 461.1
  apportionment 462.1
  association 563.6
sharp
  adj acrimonious 17.13
  exquisite 24.13
  painful 26.10
  shrill 49.14
  discordant 52.4
  bitter 55.5

pungent 59.6
heartfelt 84.22
penetrating 96.31
caustic 135.21
steep 195.17
angular 246.3
keen 271.7
quick 315.14
alert 324.14
deceitful 341.22
cunning 400.12
witty 474.9
violent 651.15
smart 875.12
cold 975.13
adv suddenly 792.8
punctually 807.14
n cheat 342.3
note 687.8
gambler 722.17

sharply
adv bitterly 135.28
gruffly 490.9

she
n female 68.4
self 827.5

shed
n hut 217.8
v cast 6.10
waste 458.5

sheep
n impostor 321.4
the laity 679.1
conformist 829.2

sheer
adj perpendicular
191.10
steep 195.17
mere 234.8
thorough 756.9
unadulterated 760.6
transparent 981.2
adv absolutely 756.14
n bias 195.3
v deviate 195.8

sheet
n blanket 281.10

leaf 282.2
section 755.2
paper 999.5

shell
n ship 171.1
exterior 197.2
frame 252.3
cavity 270.2
crust 281.13
armour 281.14
hull 281.15
armour 443.5
cartridge 447.16
shot 447.18
atom nuclide 985.3
v husk 6.9
fire at 444.19

shift
adv moving 167.3
n displacement 151.1
deviation 155.1
tour 787.3
change 814.1
conversion 820.1
expedient 950.2
v deviate 155.3
remove 167.7
vacillate 347.8
be changed 814.6
change 816.5
convert 820.11
quibble 891.6

ship
n cargo ship 171.1
aircraft 172.1
airship 172.7
v send 167.9

ships
n shipping 171.8

shirt
n waistcoat 5.11
v cloak 5.29

shit
n bastard 640.5

shock
n head of hair 3.3
pain 87.5

start 122.2
impact 857.3
shake 872.3
misfortune 966.2
discharge 982.6
v offend 89.11
agitate 96.14
terrify 118.16
startle 122.7
electrify 982.24

shocked
adj startled 122.12

shoes
n footwear 5.21

shoot
n sprout 288.10
branch 296.17
offset 542.4
v speed 165.6
strike dead 294.15
vegetate 296.26
hunt 367.9
fire at 444.19
execute 585.16
explode 651.13
film 684.7
photograph 692.10
fire 859.11

shooting
adj painful 26.10
n killing 294.1
hunting 367.2
gunfire 444.7
capital punishment
585.6
throwing 859.2

shop
n market 713.1
workplace 716.1
office 716.6
v tell on 532.12
go shopping 710.7

shopping
n purchase 710.1

shore
adj aquatic 173.25
coastal 223.5

n border 202.4
side 209.1
coast 223.2
v support 856.8

short
adj insignificant 234.6
little 244.9
brief 254.6
low 260.7
taciturn 329.7
gruff 490.7
concise 519.5
incomplete 757.4
brief 790.8
wanting 947.13
imperfect 958.4
adv abruptly 254.10
n motion pictures 684.1
v electrify 982.24

short of
adj deficient 866.5
wanting 947.13

short-term
adj brief 790.8

shortage
n deficiency 757.2
shortcoming 866.1
want 947.4
imperfection 958.1

shortly
adv briefly 254.9
concisely 519.6
fleetingly 790.10
soon 807.16

shot
adj variegated 38.7
n detonation 47.3
dose 77.6
dose 78.3
drink 79.5
put-down 147.3
lightning 165.5
try 388.3
cannonball 447.18
photography 684.4
photograph 692.3

take 692.6
bet 723.2
discharge 859.4
gunner 859.8

should
v ought to 621.3
be necessary 918.9

shoulder
n joint 762.3
v support 856.8
thrust 857.11

shouting
adj vociferous 50.7

show
n spectacle 32.7
display 197.4
display 333.2
sham 339.2
pretext 361.1
affectation 485.1
display 486.4
indication 502.3
stage show 682.2
performance 682.9
market 713.2
semblance 931.2
broadcast 983.13
programme 984.2
v show up 30.4
appear 32.8
direct to 152.5
bring out 197.5
explain 326.8
manifest 333.5
disclose 336.4
signify 502.17
teach 549.10
evidence 912.7
prove 912.9

showing
adj visible 30.6
manifesting 333.9
n appearance 32.1
display 333.2

shown
adj manifested 333.13
proved 912.17

shut
adj closed 279.8
v close 279.5
turn off 819.10

shy
adj fearful 118.22
timid 130.12
receding 159.4
demurring 310.7
wary 479.8
alone 834.8
v recoil 858.3
throw 859.3
v start 118.12
flinch 118.13
be startled 122.4
demur 310.4
hesitate 347.7
dodge 353.8
retreat 858.6
throw 859.10

sick
adj ill 76.21
insane 881.22

side
adj oblique 195.12
lateral 209.4
occasional 810.3
n aspect 33.2
conceit 131.4
incline 195.4
flank 209.1
straight line 263.2
party 597.4
outlook 933.2
v flank 209.2

sight
n senses 24.5
vision 27.1
look 27.3
field of view 30.3
view 32.6
spectacle 32.7
marvel 113.2
opinion 908.6
outlook 933.2
eyesore 970.3

v see 27.11

sign
n prognosis 82.4
omen 124.3
poster 337.7
telltale sign 502.1
signal 502.15
letter 527.1
hint 532.4
notation 687.6
substitute 824.2
miracle 832.8
evidence 912.1
v ratify 317.11
seal 422.7
secure 423.7
signal 502.22
letter 527.6

signal
n sign 502.15
hint 532.4
noise 532.7
radio signal 983.7
v communicate 328.6
sign 502.22

signed
adj accepted 317.13
completed 392.10
contracted 422.11
marked 502.24

significance
n portent 124.7
meaning 503.1
meaningfulness 503.4
distinction 642.5
importance 952.1

significant
adj forewarning 124.15
indicative 502.23
meaningful 503.6
prominent 642.15
evidential 912.14
important 952.16

significantly
adv ominously 124.18
meaningfully 503.9
importantly 952.24

signing
n sign language 40.3
signature 423.2

signs
n disease 76.1
track 502.8

silence
n stillness 42.1
stillness 164.1
taciturnity 329.1
v paralyse 19.10
hush 42.7
strike dead 294.15
extinguish 380.15
overcome 397.6
suppress 413.7
refute 913.4

silent
adj still 42.9
taciturn 329.7
unspoken 504.9

silk
n material 4.1
smooth 273.3
smoothness 280.3
putty 992.4

silly
adj nonsensical 505.7
foolish 878.7
dazed 940.14
trivial 953.16

silver
adj brass 12.15
n silver plate 8.12
whiteness 36.1
money 705.1
precious metals 705.16

similar
adj approximate 737.8
like 746.6
comparative 898.7

similarly
adv additionally 239.10
thus 728.10
correspondingly 746.12

simple
adj soft 34.20

humble 128.9
homely 217.29
mere 234.8
artless 401.4
tasteful 481.5
plain 484.6
clear 506.10
elegant 515.4
plain-speaking 517.3
informal 562.3
real 723.11
essential 729.6
plain 760.5
one 834.7
mentally deficient 877.20
ignorant 885.10
gullible 909.6
genuine 928.15
easy 969.13

simply
adv moderately 234.10
artlessly 401.6
tastefully 481.8
plainly 484.10
intelligibly 506.12
plainly 517.4
informally 562.4
plainly 760.10
solely 834.10
easily 969.16

since
adv subsequently 797.5
ago 799.13
ever since 799.15

sing
n singing 686.26
v warble 51.5
exude cheerfulness 100.6
sigh 303.15
murmur 509.19
tell on 532.12
warble 686.31

singer
n entertainer 685.1

lead 685.5
vocalist 688.9

singing
adj vocal 686.41
n vocal music 686.12
sing 686.26

single
adj unmarried 546.7
simple 760.5
characteristic 827.13
one 834.7

sir
n Mister 67.7

Sir
n sire 628.3

sister
n brother 540.3
member 597.11
nun 678.10
layman 679.2
likeness 746.3

sisters
n the laity 679.1

sit
v sit down 164.9
convene 732.17

site
n location 150.1
arena 448.1
v locate 150.11
place 150.12
establish 150.16

sitting
adv in conference
408.6
n conference 523.5
assembly 732.2

situation
n location 150.1
placement 150.6
environment 200.1
position 701.5
state 727.1
predicament 968.4

sixth
n interval 687.11

size

n greatness 243.1
extent 286.3
semiliquid 16.5
v adjust 243.14

skill
n superiority 235.1
expertise 398.1
art 398.7
production 847.2

skills
n learning 883.4

skin
n the muscles 2.3
fur 4.2
exterior 197.2
shallowness 262.1
rind 281.3
blanket 281.11
sheet 282.2
v peel 6.8
injure 378.12
tear apart 764.13
abrade 989.5

skipper
n commander 174.5
v direct 554.8

sky
n summit 189.2
the heavens 114.2

sleep
n slumber 22.2
stillness 164.1
death 293.1
v slumber 22.11
stagnate 164.8

sleeping
adj asleep 22.19
inert 164.12
latent 504.5
unwary 939.8

slice
n sheet 282.2
piece 755.3
break 764.4
v apportion 462.6
separate 755.6
sever 764.10

slide
n gliding 168.12
slip 185.4
smooth 273.3
photograph 692.3
print 692.4
merry-go-round 720.14
v glide 168.31
slip 185.9
decline 378.15
elapse 783.3

slight
adj frail 16.12
little 244.9
thin 256.13
shallow 262.5
rare 285.4
meagre 947.10
trivial 953.16
n snub 148.2
indifference 420.1
v ignore 148.6
turn one's back on
325.8
flout 439.4
disparage 497.7

slightly
adv somewhat 231.7
hardly 234.9
small 244.14
poorly 947.15

slim
adj thin 256.13
sparse 840.5
meagre 947.10
n lanky 256.7
v reduce 256.11

slip
n anchor 171.14
slide 185.4
runt 244.3
paper 256.6
blanket 281.10
avoidance 353.1
miss 395.4
bungle 399.5
notice board 530.8

lapse 930.4
harbour 964.6
mud 16.7
v glide 168.31
float 173.21
slide 185.9
decline 378.15
sink 395.9
miss 395.12
bungle 399.9
give 463.12
go wrong 634.9
elapse 783.3
err 930.8
come down in the
world 966.11
slow
adj dull 108.6
leisurely 166.9
reluctant 310.6
indolent 316.17
languid 316.18
leisurely 387.4
late 808.12
delaying 808.13
dull 877.15
adv slowly 166.12
late 808.15
slowly 808.16
v slow down or up
166.8
slowly
adv slow 166.12
by degrees 231.6
slow 808.16
small
adj humble 128.9
insignificant 231.6
inadequate 236.7
little 244.9
mean 631.6
base 641.12
narrow-minded 935.10
meagre 947.10
insignificant 953.15
adv little 244.14
smart

adj quick 315.14
alert 324.11
witty 474.9
chic 559.13
tidy 769.8
brainy 875.12
v suffer 26.8
affect 84.12
resent 143.12
smell
n senses 24.5
odour 60.1
hint 234.4
v sense 24.6
reek 60.5
scent 60.7
stink 62.3
sniff 896.6
smile
n grin 107.3
greeting 566.4
v be pleased 86.11
exude cheerfulness
100.6
crack a smile 107.7
smiling
adj happy 86.15
cheerful 100.11
smoke
n tobacco 80.1
smoking 80.6
spirit 726.3
bubble 790.5
slag 717.4
vapour 111.1
v use 78.5
inhale 80.7
cloud 304.3
preserve 382.8
let out 864.22
fume 971.42
dry 110.4
evaporate 111.7
smoking
adj burning 971.46
vaporous 111.8
n substance abuse

78.1
smoking habit 80.6
curing 382.2
evaporation 111.4
smooth
adj hairless 6.16
quiet 164.10
horizontal 192.7
straight 263.6
even 273.9
fine 280.7
cunning 400.12
suave 489.15
harmonious 515.6
eloquent 525.7
fluent 525.8
uniform 743.5
easy 969.13
oily 11.8
n plane 273.3
v straighten 263.5
flatten 273.5
coarsen 280.4
pacify 450.7
calm 650.6
facilitate 969.7
buff 989.6
snow
n powder snow 975.7
picture 984.4
v give 463.12
hail 975.11
so
adj suchlike 746.8
true 928.13
adv greatly 233.14
very 233.17
how 369.8
thus 728.10
similarly 746.12
equally 752.10
accurately 928.20
so far
adv until now 800.4
so-called
adj spurious 339.17
pretended 361.5

nominal 512.14

soap
n cleanser 70.17
broadcast 983.13
v wash 70.19

social
adj public 297.9
communal 461.8
sociable 563.21
communal 597.17

socialism
n communion 461.2
collectivization 592.6
federal government 593.4
democracy 593.6

socialist
adj left-wing 592.22
n Fabian 592.14

society
n population 216.1
mankind 297.1
culture 358.2
high society 559.6
association 563.6
the people 587.1
association 597.1
community 597.2
fellowship 597.3
company 731.1

soft
adj weak 16.11
impotent 19.13
subdued 34.20
faint 43.14
sensitive 84.18
sentimental 84.19
comfortable 112.11
pitying 136.6
light 284.10
undemanding 411.4
lenient 412.6
peaceful 449.7
cowardly 491.6
nonalcoholic 501.4
phonetic 509.23
moderate 650.9

weak 877.19
gullible 909.6
mild 992.8
pulpy 17.4

soil
n smudge 71.5
region 220.1
land 223.1
v blacken 71.14
vilify 497.9
corrupt 634.10
stigmatize 641.9
seduce 645.19
stain 959.6

soldier
n serviceman 446.5
v serve 443.14

sole
adj one 834.7
unique 834.9
n fish 10.23
base 190.2
foot 190.5

solid
adj firm 15.17
unanimous 317.14
faithful 624.16
solvent 706.16
substantial 725.6
sturdy 725.7
crowded 732.22
complete 756.8
permanent 815.6
stable 817.12
one 834.7
reliable 925.12
valid 928.14
great 954.13
dense 990.11
hard 991.9
n body 990.6

solidarity
n cooperation 435.1
accord 440.1
totality 756.1
unity 834.1

solo

adj alone 834.8
alone 834.8
adv singly 834.13
n air 686.3
aria 686.14

solution
n explanation 326.4
resolution 895.1
expedient 950.2
liquefaction 18.1
suspension 18.2

solve
v explain 326.8
resolve 895.2

some
adj quantitative 230.5
plural 838.5
adv approximately 230.6
n somewhat 230.3
several 838.1

somebody
n person 297.3
personage 952.7

somehow
adv anyhow 369.9
by chance 927.12

someone
n person 297.3

something
n some 230.3
thing 725.3
big shot 952.8
object 997.4

sometimes
adv occasionally 810.5

somewhat
adv kind of 231.7
moderately 234.10
n some 230.3

somewhere
adv someplace 150.26

son
n brother 540.3
descendant 542.3

song
n air 686.3

vocal music 686.12
lay 686.13
poetry 698.1

sons
n posterity 542.1

soon
adv later 801.8
presently 807.16

sooner
adv preferably 356.27

sophisticated
adj experienced 398.26
elegant 481.6
chic 559.13
wise 911.4

sorry
adj regretful 104.8
disgraceful 641.11
paltry 953.18

sort
n nature 729.2
kind 771.3
v size 243.14
classify 763.8
classify 770.9
classify 771.5
discriminate 899.4

sort of
adv somewhat 231.7

soul
n passion 84.2
heart 84.3
substance 187.4
interior 198.2
life force 292.2
person 297.3
something 725.3
essence 729.1
inside 729.3
particularity 827.1
individual 834.4
psyche 874.4
genius 875.8

sound
adj wholesome 74.11
solvent 706.16
sturdy 725.7

stable 817.12
sensible 875.16
sane 880.2
logical 890.16
reliable 925.12
valid 928.14
good 954.12
intact 957.6
trouble-free 962.5
n acoustic 41.1
inlet 228.1
v appear 32.10
make a sound or noise
41.13
blare 44.10
fathom 261.8
measure 286.7
say 509.16
blow 686.34
investigate 893.21

sounded
adj speech 509.22

source
n head 224.2
motive 360.1
resource 371.4
informant 532.5
origin 841.5

south
adj northern 152.13
adv southward 152.15
n points of the
compass 152.2

southern
adj northern 152.13

sovereignty
n nationhood 221.3
supremacy 235.3
governance 402.5
dominance 402.6
royalty 402.8
ownership 454.2
government 593.1
n leadership 554.4

space
adj cosmic 114.20
n extent 149.1

interval 213.1
region 220.1
degree 231.1
capacity 243.2
distance 247.1
opening 278.1
latitude 415.4
spacing 529.7
time 783.1
period 786.1
opportunity 805.2
outer space 1114.3
v dot 213.3

spare
adj additional 239.9
remaining 242.7
lean 256.14
reserved 371.13
unused 375.10
leisure 387.3
plain-speaking 517.3
simple 760.5
occasional 810.3
substitute 824.7
meagre 947.10
superfluous 948.15
surplus 948.16
n surplus 948.5
v have pity 136.4
forgive 139.3
refrain 314.3
not use 375.5
preserve 382.7
exempt 415.13
relinquish 460.2
give away 463.21
abstain 648.5

speak
v sound 41.13
affirm 319.5
communicate 328.5
signal 502.22
talk 508.10
talk 509.13
make a speech 524.7

speaker
n loudspeaker 41.7

talker 509.11
public speaker 524.4
speaking
  adj forewarning 124.15
  talking 509.24
  n communication
    328.1
  speech 509.1
  utterance 509.2
  public speaking 524.1
special
  adj undergraduate
    553.11
  detailed 728.9
  other 742.7
  typical 771.6
  particular 827.12
  notable 952.18
  n newspaper 536.2
  commodity 712.2
  feature 828.2
specialist
  adj specialized 828.5
  n doctor 81.4
  expert 828.3
specially
  adv particularly 827.15
species
  n nomenclature 512.1
  kind 771.3
specific
  adj circumscribed
    201.6
  detailed 728.9
  typical 771.6
  particular 827.12
  n remedy 77.1
specifically
  adv fully 728.13
  particularly 827.15
spectacular
  adj gaudy 486.16
  theatrical 486.20
speculation
  n investment 706.3
  trading 714.9
  gambling 722.2

gamble 722.2
consideration 886.2
theory 906.1
guess 906.4
prediction 917.1
speech
  adj language 509.22
  n communication
    328.1
  language 508.1
  talk 509.1
  diction 514.1
  talk 523.2
  talk 524.2
speed
  n velocity 165.1
  swiftness 386.2
  v move 163.4
  fly 165.6
  hasten 386.3
  facilitate 969.7
spell
  n sorcery 669.1
  magic spell 670.1
  period 786.1
  term 786.3
  stretch 787.1
  turn 787.2
  round 812.3
  superstition 909.3
  bad influence 955.4
  v mean 503.5
  spell out 527.7
spend
  v consume 372.11
  consume 373.2
  waste 473.4
  pay out 606.4
  occupy 701.8
  experience 793.8
spending
  n consumption 373.1
  expenditure 606.1
spirit
  n animation 17.4
  passion 84.2
  heart 84.3

eagerness 92.1
zeal 92.2
gaiety 100.4
extract 183.7
substance 187.4
ambience 200.3
life force 292.2
animation 315.2
enterprise 315.6
pluck 344.3
fortitude 477.4
meaning 503.1
liveliness 525.4
intelligence 658.4
air 726.3
essence 729.1
nature 729.2
inside 729.3
psyche 874.4
genius 875.8
spectre 943.1
spirits
  n the gods 658.1
spiritual
  adj sacred 664.7
  psychic 668.13
  God-fearing 671.9
  supernatural 832.15
  mental 874.6
  temperamental 933.7
  spectral 943.5
  immaterial 998.6
spite
  n hate 94.1
  spitefulness 135.5
  hostility 570.3
splendid
  adj grandiose 486.17
  illustrious 642.17
  good 954.12
  superb 954.15
  gorgeous 971.17
  bright 977.31
split
  adj cleft 213.6
  impaired 378.23
  severed 764.21

halved 837.6
n crack 213.2
opening 278.1
falling-out 441.4
break 764.4
v beat it 179.7
make tracks 211.9
crack 213.4
break 378.20
demolish 380.17
fall out 441.9
apportion 462.6
sever 764.10
break 764.11
partition 764.16
disintegrate 768.2

spoke
n step 184.4

spoken
adj vernacular 508.12
speech 509.22

spokesman
n mediator 451.3
speaker 524.4
informant 532.5
spokeswoman 557.5

spokeswoman
n mediator 451.3
speaker 524.4
informant 532.5
spokesman 557.5

sport
n hunting 367.2
joke 474.3
banter 475.1
fun 720.2
athletics 720.7
toy 720.15
sports 721.1
v wear 5.33
play 720.22

sporting
adj sportsmanlike 629.7
sports 720.29

sports
adj sporting 720.29

n sport 721.1

spot
n fleck 38.3
soil 71.5
drink 79.5
location 150.1
location 150.1
modicum 234.2
mark 502.5
state 727.1
intruder 736.1
crisis 805.4
stain 959.3
pickle 968.5
v see 27.11
variegate 38.6
soil 71.14
spatter 71.16
mark 502.19
detect 896.5
blot 959.5

spotted
adj dotted 38.10
soiled 71.18
located 150.18
sprinkled 733.8
spotty 959.8

spread
adj prostrate 192.8
increased 237.7
published 337.17
dispersed 733.7
adv transfer 167.1
n space 149.1
aberration 162.1
increase 237.1
size 243.1
expansion 245.1
breadth 255.1
publication 337.1
advertisement 337.6
dispersion 733.1
v extend 149.6
diverge 162.4
radiate 162.5
transfer 167.6
grow 237.6

broaden 255.4
publish 337.10
come out 337.16
report 533.11
disperse 733.3
generalize 826.8

spring
adj seasonal 298.8
n progression 153.1
ascent 184.1
lake 227.1
springtime 298.2
leap 351.1
source 371.4
well 841.6
recoil 858.2
elasticity 993.1
elastic 993.3
v speed 165.6
leap 351.5
recoil 858.5
give 993.5

squad
n unit 446.18
team 597.7
company 732.3
company 732.3

square
adj symmetrical 250.4
rectangular 264.4
equal 752.1
exact 928.17
adv exactly 928.21
n enclosure 203.3
market 219.6
plot 220.4
rule 263.3
v offset 323.4
pay in full 604.13
agree 750.6
equate 752.6

stability
n firmness 15.3
firmness 344.2
perseverance 345.1
moderation 650.1
substance 725.1

uniformity 743.1
continuity 774.1
durability 789.1
perpetuity 791.1
permanence 815.1
firmness 817.1
reliability 925.3
stable
adj firm 15.17
persevering 345.8
faithful 624.16
restrained 650.10
sturdy 725.7
uniform 743.3
continuous 774.8
durable 789.9
permanent 815.6
substantial 817.12
reliable 925.12
trouble-free 962.5
n barn 217.18
farm 113.4
stadium
n hall 188.4
arena 448.1
staff
n stave 259.2
sceptre 402.9
faculty 552.8
personnel 558.10
insignia 627.1
stave 686.23
supporter 856.2
base 856.7
v equip 370.8

estate 456.4
portion 462.5
scaffold 586.5
bet 722.3
v pledge 423.8
bet 722.21
stakes
n pot 722.4
stamp
n ratification 317.4
sign 502.1
print 502.7
label 502.13
print 529.3
type 529.6
postage 534.5
engraving tool 691.5
nature 729.2
mould 748.6
kind 771.3
characteristic 827.4
stomp 857.9
disposition 933.3
v impress upon 84.14
stroll 168.24
form 248.6
dent 270.11
mark 502.19
label 502.20
print 529.3
fix 817.9
stomp 857.19
instil 944.14
stance
n looks 32.4
affirmation 319.1
gesture 502.14
opinion 908.6
attitude 933.1
stand
n station 150.2
affirmation 319.1
resistance 438.1
engagement 682.8
booth 713.3
stop 819.2
footing 856.4

base 856.7
outlook 933.2
impasse 968.6
v endure 125.4
lie 150.10
settle 150.17
be still 164.6
stand erect 191.6
be present 210.6
resist 438.2
afford 606.5
exist 723.5
endure 789.5
remain 815.4
suffice 946.3
standard
adj medium 232.3
customary 358.12
prescriptive 404.4
orthodox 666.5
model 748.8
interchangeable 825.4
prevalent 826.11
usual 831.7
indistinguishable 900.5
authoritative 925.13
n degree 231.1
post 259.4
measure 286.2
rule 404.2
flag 627.5
model 748.1
rule 831.4
base 856.7
test 897.2
standards
n ethics 616.1
standing
n station 150.2
rank 232.1
class 588.1
prestige 642.4
state 727.1
state 727.1
durability 789.1
star
adj chief 235.14

stairs
n stairway 184.2
stake
n leg 259.6
collateral 423.3
stage
n setting 200.2
layer 282.1
arena 448.1
the boards 682.12
period 786.1
v dramatize 682.20

n superior 235.4
winner 394.5
ace 398.14
decoration 626.5
celebrity 642.8
movie studio 684.3
lead 685.5
chief 952.9
wonder 954.6
pulsating star 114.8
v rule 235.11
dramatize 682.20
act 682.21
matter 952.11
emphasize 952.13
feature 952.14

staring
adj conspicuous
333.12

stars
n fate 919.2
light source 978.1
fixed stars 114.4

start
n shock 122.2
starting 179.2
point of departure
179.5
boundary 202.3
advantage 235.2
beginning 780.1
v startle 118.12
be startled 122.4
set out 179.8
leap 351.5
propose 424.5
begin 780.7
start up 859.12

starting
n start 179.2

state
adj public 297.9
n territory 220.5
country 221.1
mode 721.1
v affirm 319.5
announce 337.12

declare 509.17
phrase 514.3
specify 827.11
assert 908.12

stated
adj circumscribed
201.6
affirmed 319.8
published 337.17
conditional 914.8
assured 925.14

statement
n affirmation 319.1
account 334.3
announcement 337.2
remark 509.3
report 530.7
information 532.1
declaration 579.7
bill 608.3
bill 833.5
premise 890.6
testimony 912.2

station
n status 150.2
rank 231.2
class 588.1
prestige 642.4
position 701.5
state 727.1
class 771.2
channel 983.10
channel 984.3
farm 113.4
v place 150.12

status
n station 150.2
rank 231.2
class 588.1
prestige 642.4
state 727.1
class 771.2

stay
n temporary stay 214.5
exemption 582.2
delay 808.2
supporter 856.2

prevention 967.2
v be still 164.6
slow 166.8
inhabit 214.6
stop 214.7
stop 279.6
adhere 765.6
endure 789.5
delay 808.8
postpone 808.9
wait 808.11
remain 815.4
continue 818.3
stop 819.9
support 856.8
stop 967.12

staying
adj resident 214.12
continuing 818.7
n habitation 214.1
prevention 967.2

steady
adj nerveless 120.2
firm 344.11
persevering 345.8
faithful 624.16
sturdy 725.7
uniform 743.5
orderly 769.6
continuous 774.8
perpetual 791.6
constant 809.5
seasonal 812.7
stable 817.12
continuing 818.7
reliable 925.12
trouble-free 962.5
v calm 650.6
stabilize 817.7

steam
n hot water 971.31
water 19.3
vapour 111.1
v cook 11.4
burn 143.15
navigate 173.9
let out 864.22

burn 971.41
heat 972.17
evaporate 111.7
steel
adj brass 12.15
n sword 447.5
cutlery 986.2
stone 991.5
v strengthen 15.12
harden 991.6
step
n velocity 163.3
pace 168.9
gait 168.10
stair 184.4
short distance 212.2
degree 231.1
layer 282.1
act 313.3
attempt 388.2
process 844.2
expedient 950.2
v walk 168.23
measure 286.7
steps
n stairs 184.2
precaution 479.3
sterling
adj honest 624.9
genuine 928.15
superb 954.15
n money 705.1
stick
n slim 256.7
shaft 259.1
staff 259.2
rod 586.2
v take it 125.5
place 150.12
prick 271.5
remain firm 344.8
injure 378.12
stall 395.14
stab 444.20
adhere 765.6
root 817.10
stop 819.5

stiff
adj dull 108.6
inflexible 346.8
out of practice 399.15
bungling 399.17
firm 410.6
stilted 516.3
stilted 561.9
rigid 991.10
tough 994.3
n corpse 293.12
still
adj silent 42.9
quiet 164.10
motionless 164.11
adv quietly 164.14
until now 800.4
n silence 42.1
photograph 692.3
stir
n activity 315.1
bustle 315.4
nick 414.9
v awake 23.4
make sensitive 24.7
affect 84.12
move 163.4
take hold 315.9
bustle 315.10
rouse 360.18
agitate 872.7
stock
adj trite 108.9
usual 831.7
n stem 296.18
mankind 297.1
means 369.2
store 371.1
assets 456.6
portion 462.5
race 540.4
lineage 541.4
merchandise 712.1
shares 715.1
source 841.5
materials 999.1
v provide 370.7

store 999.7
stocks
n shackle 413.4
pillory 586.3
stolen
adj pirated 467.21
stomach
n mouth 2.12
appetite 91.7
v take 125.7
suffer 428.10
stone
adj rock 13.6
n seed 296.24
pavement 368.6
missile 447.17
monument 530.10
rock 991.5
bricks and mortar 999.2
rock 13.1
v pelt 444.21
execute 585.16
stop
n standstill 164.3
destination 177.5
temporary stay 214.5
obstruction 279.2
stopper 279.3
delay 802.2
stoppage 819.2
prevention 967.2
impasse 968.6
v muffle 42.8
daunt 118.17
quiet 164.7
stay 214.7
stop up 279.6
cure 359.2
break the habit 359.3
abdicate 375.4
fend off 445.10
beware 479.6
renounce 648.6
end 782.4
delay 808.8
cease 819.4

halt 819.5
stay 819.9
stay 967.12
stopped
adj obstructed 279.9
late 808.12
stopping
n habitation 214.1
prevention 967.2
store
n hoard 371.1
storage 371.6
preserve 382.6
gain 457.3
market 713.1
workplace 716.1
materials 999.1
v load 150.15
provide 370.7
stow 371.9
put away 375.6
stock 999.7
stores
n provisions 10.5
store 371.1
storm
n outburst 143.9
strong or stiff or high
  or howling wind
  303.9
storming 444.5
tempest 651.4
v burn 143.15
blow 303.14
raid 444.18
bluster 488.3
rage 651.10
story
n lie 339.8
joke 474.3
record 530.1
news item 533.3
gossip 533.7
history 697.1
tale 697.2
short story 700.3
plot 700.4

straight
adj direct 152.11
dead straight 263.6
above-board 624.10
thorough 756.9
unadulterated 760.6
unqualified 915.1
accurate 928.16
adv directly 152.18
directly 263.7
accurately 928.20
exactly 928.21
n heterosexual 66.13
straight line 263.2
strain
n fatigue 21.1
anxiety 117.1
tension 119.3
mankind 297.1
endeavour 388.1
race 540.4
lineage 541.4
enmity 570.1
air 686.3
measure 698.9
straining 702.2
pull 860.2
disposition 933.3
overdoing 948.6
stretching 948.7
stretching 993.2
v refine 70.22
exude 181.12
pervert 251.6
demur 310.4
falsify 339.10
injure 378.12
endeavour 388.4
tense 702.10
overstretch 948.11
strange
adj extraneous 736.4
unrelated 738.4
novel 803.11
odd 832.11
insane 881.22
eccentric 882.5

unknown 885.14
strategic
adj planned 366.11
cunning 400.12
strategy
n plan 366.1
stratagem 400.3
operation 443.4
stream
n course 163.2
waterway 224.1
flow 224.4
channel 225.1
procession 774.3
trend 851.2
ray 977.5
v move 163.4
travel 168.14
flow 224.15
come together 732.16
street
n road 368.5
strength
n might 15.1
energy 17.1
power 18.1
rankness 59.3
vitality 74.3
quantity 230.1
greatness 233.1
will power 344.4
authority 402.2
vigour 525.3
substance 725.1
hardness 991.1
toughness 994.1
stress
n fatigue 21.1
psychological stress
  83.7
pain 87.5
anxiety 117.1
tension 119.3
urge 360.6
accent 509.9
metre 698.7
strain 702.2

thrust 857.2
urgency 952.4
adversity 966.1
v strain 702.10
thrust 857.11
emphasize 952.13

stressed
adj neurotic 83.22
phonetic 509.23
emphatic 952.20

stretch
n range 149.2
distance 247.1
length 253.1
strain 702.2
exercise 702.6
period 786.1
spell 787.1
term 787.4
stretching 948.7
elasticity 993.1
stretching 993.2
v exercise 75.3
extend 149.6
enlarge 245.4
enlarge 245.5
be long 253.5
lengthen 253.6
exaggerate 340.2
strain 702.10
suffice 946.3
overstretch 948.11
extend 993.4

stretched
adj lengthened 253.8
exaggerated 340.3

strict
adj meticulous 324.12
imperious 402.15
exacting 410.5
fastidious 480.6
conscientious 624.11
bigoted 666.6
exact 928.17

strictly
adv meticulously
324.16

severely 410.7
truly 928.18
exactly 928.21

strike
n revolt 312.3
objection 318.2
score 394.4
attack 444.1
walkout 704.4
stop 819.2
discovery 896.1
v impress 84.13
revolt 312.6
object 318.5
attack 444.12
push 444.15
go out 704.5
lay off 819.6
collide 857.12
hit 857.13
shoot 859.11
impress 886.15
discover 896.2

striking
adj powerful 18.7
exciting 96.30
wonderful 113.6
conspicuous 333.12
vigorous 525.10
notable 952.18

string
n step 184.4
line 253.3
cord 257.2
company 732.3
series 774.2
procession 774.3

strip
n runway 175.9
a length 253.2
line 253.3
strap 527.4
line 502.6
v divest 6.5
undress 6.7
peel 6.8
excise 241.9

fleece 465.24
simplify 760.3
tear apart 764.13

stroke
n touch 64.1
seizure 76.6
act 313.3
line 502.6
work 702.4
instant 792.3
hit 857.4
spasm 872.6
v pet 64.8
rub 989.4

strong
adj forceful 15.14
energetic 17.12
powerful 18.7
high 59.8
pungent 60.9
hearty 74.12
great 233.6
vigorous 525.10
sturdy 725.7
influential 849.13
tough 994.3

strongly
adv stoutly 15.22

structure
n house 217.5
form 248.1
construction 252.1
building 252.2
texture 280.1
clarity 506.2
plot 700.4
composition 758.1
order 769.1
v construct 252.4

struggle
n endeavour 388.1
contention 442.1
fight 442.4
fight 702.3
v endeavour 388.4
contend 442.10
strive 702.11

have difficulty 968.11

struggling
adj contending 442.18
labouring 702.17

stuck
adj fast 762.13
cohesive 765.9
fast 817.16
beat 926.17
stranded 968.27

student
n pupil 553.1
scholar 884.2

studied
adj intentional 365.8
affected 515.7
reasoned 890.17

studio
n library 188.6
gallery 690.15
workplace 716.1
radio station 983.5

study
n diagnosis 82.3
library 188.6
discussion 523.6
discipline 549.8
studying 551.3
work of art 690.8
drawing 690.11
office 716.6
science 883.8
consideration 886.2
thoughtfulness 886.3
examination 893.3
absorption 938.3
retreat 964.5
v discuss 523.10
apply oneself 551.12
consider 886.9
examine 893.3
pay attention 938.8
memorize 944.13

studying
adj engrossed 938.16
n study 551.3

stuff

n material 4.1
substance 187.4
equipment 370.4
substance 725.2
essence 729.1
matter 997.2
materials 999.1
v nourish 8.18
gorge 8.24
fill 187.6
stop 279.6
preserve 382.8
gorge 652.3
fill 756.7
overload 948.13
satisfy 949.3

stupid
adj dumb 877.14
foolish 878.7

style
n clothing 5.1
aspect 32.3
form 248.1
behaviour 306.1
preference 356.5
manner 369.1
skill 398.1
motif 483.6
mode 514.2
fashion 559.1
genre 690.6
mode 727.3
kind 771.3
speciality 828.1
v phrase 514.3

subject
adj inferior 236.6
dependent 417.10
n citizen 216.4
captive 417.6
study 549.8
plot 700.4
topic 892.1
patient 897.7

subject to
adj liable to 852.6
contingent 914.9

v impose 623.4

subsequent
adj succeeding 777.3
after 797.4

subsequently
adv after 797.5

substance
n sum and substance
187.4
quantity 230.1
meaning 503.1
summary 538.2
reason 581.5
wealth 598.1
body 725.1
stuff 725.2
essence 729.1
major part 754.6
topic 892.1
matter 997.2

substantial
adj large 243.15
meaningful 503.6
solvent 706.16
real 723.11
solid 725.6
essential 729.6
stable 817.12
influential 849.13
reliable 925.12
valid 928.14
sufficient 946.5
important 952.16
dense 990.11
material 997.9

substitute
adj alternate 824.7
n surrogate 83.19
supporting actor or
actress 685.6
successor 779.4
substitution 824.2
v exchange 824.4

subtle
adj soft 34.20
dainty 234.7
rare 285.4

meticulous 324.12
cunning 400.12
nice 480.8
elegant 481.6
thin 726.5
complex 761.4
shrewd 875.13
discriminating 899.7
exact 928.17

succeed
v accomplish 392.4
prevail 394.6
triumph 396.3
dramatize 682.20
follow 777.2
follow 779.5
follow 797.3
substitute for 824.5
prosper 965.7

success
n superiority 235.1
accomplishment 392.1
prosperity 394.1
winner 394.5
victory 396.1
stage show 682.2
prosperity 965.1

successful
adj succeeding 394.11
victorious 396.6
prosperous 965.12

successfully
adv well 394.12

succession
n accession 402.11
inheritance 464.2
posterity 542.1
devolution 609.2
series 774.2
sequence 777.1
following 797.1

successive
adj consecutive 774.9
succeeding 394.11
subsequent 797.4

sudden
adj unexpected 122.9

impulsive 350.8
precipitate 386.6
abrupt 792.5
adv suddenly 792.8

suddenly
adv unexpectedly
122.13
short 254.10
impulsively 350.12
abruptly 386.9
sudden 792.8

sue
v petition 425.10
prosecute 579.12

suffer
v hurt 26.8
ail 76.14
hurt 87.19
endure 125.4
submit 418.5
countenance 428.10
experience 793.8

suffering
adj pained 26.9
n pain 26.1
pain 87.5

sufficient
adj satisfactory 98.11
enough 946.5
tolerable 954.19

sugar
n carbohydrate 7.4
sweetener 57.2
honey 95.10
darling 543.6
v sweeten 57.3

suggest
v promise 124.12
advise 407.4
propose 424.5
signify 502.17
mean 503.5
imply 504.4
hint 532.9
resemble 746.5
evidence 912.7
remind 944.16

suggested
adj implied 504.7

suggestion
n hint 234.4
advice 422.1
proposal 424.2
aspersion 497.4
indication 502.3
clue 502.9
implication 504.2
hint 532.4
tinge 759.6
influence 849.1
suspicion 906.5

suicide
n hara-kiri 294.5

suit
n suit of clothes 5.5
appeal 425.2
canvass 425.5
lawsuit 579.1
accusation 580.1
v outfit 5.30
please 86.5
be satisfactory 98.6
fit 390.8
fit 750.8
conform 829.3
suffice 946.3

suitable
adj eligible 356.23
decorous 481.7
right 617.3
apt 750.10
timely 805.8
sufficient 946.5
expedient 950.5

sum
n quantity 230.1
amount 230.2
plus sign 239.2
meaning 503.1
summary 538.2
lump sum 705.10
total 754.2

summer
adj seasonal 298.8

n summertime 298.3
hot weather 971.28
v spend time 783.4
summit
n top 189.2
supremacy 235.3
conference 523.5
limit 756.5
height 957.2
sun
n light source 978.1
solar flare 114.12
v bask 972.19
Sunday
n holy day 680.8
super
adj superior 235.12
great 954.13
superb 954.15
superb
adj eminent 233.9
grandiose 486.17
super 954.15
superior
adj arrogant 132.8
remarkable 233.10
greater 235.12
higher 258.14
authoritative 402.14
important 952.16
above par 954.14
n chief 235.4
chief 556.3
supplied
adj provided 370.13
supplies
n provisions 10.5
provisions 370.2
store 371.1
supply
n means 369.2
provision 370.1
fund 371.2
materials 999.1
v provide 370.7
furnish 463.15
support

n nourishment 10.3
consolation 112.4
assent 317.1
means 369.2
preservation 382.1
aid 434.1
maintenance 434.3
reinforcements 434.8
subsidy 463.8
maintenance 604.8
supporting actor or
actress 685.6
financing 706.2
backing 856.1
supporter 856.2
confirmation 912.4
v strengthen 15.12
comfort 112.6
give hope 115.9
endure 125.4
ratify 317.11
provide 370.7
preserve 382.7
maintain 434.12
subsidize 463.19
encourage 477.12
commend 494.9
benefit 573.3
defend 581.9
back 590.31
afford 606.5
enact 682.22
finance 706.14
bear 856.8
confirm 912.10
care for 963.19
supported
adj approved 494.17
borne 856.11
supporting
adj approving 494.15
aiding 573.4
supportive 856.10
confirming 912.15
suppose
v imply 504.4
judge 901.8

assume 906.7
think 908.11
be probable 923.2
imagine 941.9
supposed
adj implied 504.7
assumed 906.11
supreme
adj omnipotent 18.8
top 189.8
superlative 235.13
authoritative 402.14
governing 593.16
almighty 657.9
paramount 952.23
best 954.16
sure
adj expectant 121.10
secured 423.9
believing 908.20
evidential 912.14
inevitable 918.13
certain 925.9
reliable 925.12
confident 925.15
adv surely 925.18
surely
adv inevitably 918.16
certainly 925.17
sure 925.18
surface
adj apparent 32.11
exterior 197.6
shallow 262.5
n space 149.1
top 189.1
exterior 197.2
shallowness 262.1
texture 280.1
v show 30.4
break water 173.19
arrive 177.6
emerge 181.8
shoot up 184.8
floor 281.21
come out 333.6
be manifest 333.7

be revealed 336.8

surgery
n operation 81.2
surgical treatment 82.8
hospital room 188.21

surplus
adj additional 239.9
remaining 242.7
remaining 948.16
n excess 242.4
overrunning 865.1
leftovers 948.5

surprise
n wonder 113.1
blow 122.1
v astonish 113.4
catch unawares 122.6
attack 444.12

surprised
adj wondering 113.5
astonished 122.11
unprepared 391.6

surprising
adj astonishing 113.8
astonishing 122.10
sudden 792.5

surprisingly
adv astonishingly
113.12
astonishingly 122.14
suddenly 792.8

surrounded
adj enclosed 200.9
circumscribed 201.6

surrounding
adj encompassing
200.7
enclosing 203.10
environmental 728.8
n environment 200.4

survey
n scrutiny 27.6
measurement 286.1
piece 537.1
condensation 538.1
assembly 732.1
examination 893.3

inquiry 893.13
v scrutinize 27.13
measure 286.7
write upon 537.5
examine 893.22
canvass 893.27

survival
n durability 789.1
antiquity 804.5
continuance 818.1

survive
v remain 242.5
keep alive 292.8
support oneself 370.12
recover 381.18
endure 789.5
outlast 789.7
sustain 818.4
persist 818.5

suspect
adj unbelievable
910.10
doubted 910.11
doubtful 926.11
n accused 580.6
v distrust 144.3
suppose 906.7
think 908.11
doubt 910.6

suspended
adj inert 164.12
hung 193.9
unused 375.10
incoherent 775.3

suspension
n release 111.2
pendency 193.1
inactivity 316.1
cessation 375.2
repeal 430.1
deposition 432.2
elimination 735.2
interruption 775.1
delay 802.8
pause 819.3
dismissal 864.5
solution 18.2

suspicion
n doubt 144.2
hint 234.4
distrust 479.2
hint 532.4
tinge 759.6
hunch 889.3
suggestion 906.5
doubt 910.2
incredulity 911.1

sustained
adj constant 809.5
permanent 815.6
continuing 818.7
supported 856.11

sweet
adj flavoured 53.8
sweetened 57.4
fragrant 61.8
endearing 95.24
good-natured 134.14
harmonious 515.6
melodic 686.39
n sweets 10.36
darling 543.6

swimming
adj aquatic 173.25
dazed 940.14
n exercise 75.2
bathing 173.7

swing
n thrust 444.2
jazz 686.8
rhythm 687.13
merry-go-round 720.14
trend 851.2
hit 857.4
sway 851.6
pendulum 871.7
v hang 193.6
manage 394.9
be promiscuous 645.18
change 816.5
oscillate 871.8
wave 871.9
alternate 871.11
flounder 872.12

switch
  n false hair 3.9
  change 814.1
  substitution 824.1
  trading 825.2
  v transfer 167.6
  go over 348.7
  trade 708.14
  substitute 824.4
  interchange 825.3
symbol
  n representation 334.1
  emblem 502.2
  letter 527.1
  insignia 627.1
  notation 687.6
  example 748.2
  substitute 824.2
sympathetic
  adj sensitive 24.12
  sensitive 84.18
  comforting 112.13
  kind 134.13
  pitying 136.6
  comforting 138.3
  in accord 440.3
  related 737.9
  attracting 862.5
  tolerant 934.11
sympathy
  n sensitivity 24.3
  fellow feeling 84.5
  inclination 91.3
  consolation 112.4
  kindness 134.1
  pity 136.1
  condolence 138.1
  patronage 434.4
  accord 440.1
  good terms 568.3
  relation 737.1
  attraction 862.1
  tolerance 934.4
symptoms
  n disease 76.1
system
  n plan 366.1

manner 369.1
  nature 729.2
  order 769.1
  orderliness 769.3
  network 988.15
  universe 114.1
table
  n meal 8.5
  horizontal 192.3
  furniture 228.1
  plateau 258.4
  record 530.1
  outline 763.4
  code 770.4
  contents 833.2
  v legislate 594.8
tackle
  n rigging 171.10
  tack 257.3
  equipment 370.4
  harness 370.5
  luggage 456.1
  crane 867.2
  v practise 313.8
  treat 372.10
  attempt 388.5
  undertake 389.3
  get rolling 702.15
tactics
  n behaviour 306.1
  plan 366.1
  machination 400.4
  operation 443.4
tail
  adj rear 208.9
  n rear 208.1
  rear 208.1
  scut 208.6
  member 755.4
  wake 779.2
  extremity 782.2
  v look 27.12
  trace 893.33
take
  n photography 684.4
  shot 692.6
  v eat 8.19

take ill 76.15
  pocket 125.7
  transport 167.8
  submit 418.5
  acquire 457.8
  receive 464.6
  possess 465.13
  rape 465.15
  catch 465.17
  steal 467.12
  adopt 601.4
  think 908.11
  catch fire 972.23
take it
  v take it on the chin
    125.5
  suppose 906.7
  think 908.11
  suffice 946.3
take on
  v treat 372.10
  attempt 388.5
  undertake 389.3
  contend against 436.4
  engage 442.12
  receive 464.6
  employ 595.12
  get rolling 702.15
take over
  v take command
    402.13
  take possession 457.10
  receive 464.6
  appropriate 465.19
  usurp 620.8
  succeed 777.2
take part
  v participate 461.4
take place
  v occur 793.5
take up
  v practise 313.8
  adopt 356.14
  undertake 389.3
  undertake 389.3
  patronize 434.15
  take possession 457.10

collect 457.11
espouse 494.11
discuss 523.10
do 701.9
gather 732.18
include 734.3
enter 780.9
pick up 867.7

taking
adj catching 465.25
n receiving 464.1
possession 465.1
rape 465.3
adoption 601.2
overrunning 865.1

taking place
adj happening 793.9

tale
n lie 339.8
gossip 533.7
story 697.2
story 700.3

talent
n ability 18.2
flair 398.4
talented person 398.12
artistry 690.5
brightness 875.2
genius 875.8

talk
n language 508.1
speech 509.1
diction 514.1
speech 523.2
speech 524.2
report 533.6
gossip 533.7
lesson 549.7
v communicate 328.5
signify 502.17
speak 508.10
speak 509.13
discuss 523.10
make a speech 524.7

talk to
v address 509.20

talking

adj speaking 509.24
n communication 328.1
speech 509.1

tall
adj large 243.15
long 253.7
giant 258.12

tank
n lake 227.1
store 371.6

tape
n record 41.11
dressing 77.17
strip 257.4
notice board 530.8
disk 988.6
v sound 41.13
record 530.12
put together 762.4
video 984.15

target
n objective 365.2
laughing stock 493.7

task
n undertaking 389.1
lesson 549.7
commission 595.1
charge 623.3
work 701.2
work 702.4
v impose 623.4

taste
n bite 8.2
senses 24.5
flavour 53.1
sample 53.4
liking 91.2
appetite 91.7
hint 234.4
preference 356.5
fastidiousness 480.1
good taste 481.1
elegance 515.1
sample 748.3
characteristic 827.4
discrimination 899.1

v eat 8.19
sense 24.6
taste of 53.7
savour 54.4
experience 793.8
experiment 897.8

taught
adj informed 883.14

tax
n demand 406.1
taxation 610.9
charge 623.3
overdoing 948.6
v burden 283.10
charge 610.12
impose 623.4
strain 702.10
work 702.16

taxes
n tax 610.9

taxi
n commercial vehicle
170.11
v drive 168.29

tea
n breakfast 8.6
afternoon tea 563.13

teach
v instruct 549.10

teacher
n trainer 390.5
instructor 552.1
master 556.1
professional 703.4

teaching
adj educational 549.18
n precept 404.1
instruction 549.1
lesson 549.7
religion 655.1
a belief 908.2
maxim 929.1

team
n outfit 597.7
company 732.3

tears
n digestive juice 13.2

weeping 106.2
technical
adj occupational
701.13
specialized 828.5
scientific 883.23
technique
n manner 369.1
skill 398.1
art 398.7
treatment 690.7
knowledge 883.1
technology
n art 398.7
engineer 703.7
science 883.8
teenage
adj adolescent 287.12
teeth
n tooth 2.5
clutches 459.4
tongue 509.12
telegraph
n Telex 332.2
telegram 328.8
telephone
n phone 332.4
v phone 332.11
television
n radio 332.3
informant 532.5
news 533.1
TV 984.1
television or TV set
984.10
tell
v impress 84.13
communicate 328.6
communicate 328.6
divulge 556.5
say 509.16
inform 552.8
report 533.11
narrate 697.5
narrate 700.6
have influence 849.10
evidence 912.7

recognize 944.9
matter 952.11
telling
adj powerful 18.7
vigorous 525.10
influential 849.13
evidential 912.14
notable 952.18
n informing 328.2
informing 328.2
fiction 700.1
narration 700.2
temperature
n fever 76.7
boiling point 971.25
temple
n side 209.1
tabernacle 681.2
temporary
adj interim 788.4
transient 790.7
substitute 824.7
conditional 958.2
unreliable 926.14
makeshift 950.7
n worker 703.2
tend
v head 152.6
gravitate 283.11
look after 324.9
incline 851.3
heed 938.6
care for 963.19
groom 113.6
tendency
n direction 152.1
preference 356.5
aptitude 398.5
nature 729.2
inclination 851.1
probability 923.1
disposition 933.3
tender
adj sensitive 24.12
sore 26.11
sensitive 84.18
loving 95.26

kind 134.13
pitying 136.6
light 284.10
immature 287.9
careful 339.10
lenient 412.6
soft 992.8
v offer 424.4
give 463.12
pay 604.10
tense
adj restless 96.27
anxious 117.6
uptight 119.13
in suspense 121.11
unfriendly 570.9
rigid 991.10
n time 783.1
v strain 702.10
stiffen 991.8
tension
n anxiety 117.1
strain 119.3
discord 441.1
enmity 570.1
strain 702.2
stretching 948.7
urgency 952.4
voltage 992.11
rigidity 991.2
stretching 993.2
term
n word 511.1
time 783.1
moment 786.2
time 786.3
time 787.4
v name 512.10
terms
n stipulation 406.2
adjustment 450.4
condition 914.2
terrible
adj horrid 89.19
terrific 118.29
wrong 618.3
dreadful 955.9

hideous 970.9

terribly
adv horribly 89.27
frightfully 118.33
awfully 233.20
dreadfully 955.13
hideously 970.10

territory
n open space 149.4
region 220.1
state 220.5
country 221.1
land 223.1
orbit 849.4

terror
n fear 118.1
bogeyman 118.9

terrorism
n terrorizing 118.7
violence 651.1
anarchism 822.2

terrorist
n alarmist 118.8
destroyer 380.8
revolutionary 822.3

test
adj experimental 897.11
n diagnosis 82.3
measure 286.2
contest 442.3
examination 893.2
trial 897.2
v interrogate 893.19
experiment 897.8
verify 925.8

tested
adj devoted 568.20
trustworthy 624.15
tried 897.12
assured 925.14

testing
adj examining 893.35
n checkup 893.5
experiment 897.1

text
n representation 334.1

writing 528.8
literature 528.9
textbook 535.10
design 535.12
script 682.16
score 686.22
literature 696.1
section 755.2
topic 892.1
maxim 929.1

thank
v bless 141.4

thanks
n praise 141.2
prayer 675.4

that
adj this 827.14

that is
adj happening 793.9
present 800.2

that one
adj this 827.14

theatre
n house 682.11

them
n self 827.5

theme
n motif 483.6
passage 686.19
plot 700.4
topic 892.1

themselves
n self 827.5

then
adj former 799.8
adv additionally 239.10
concurrently 783.7
thereupon 783.9
subsequently 797.5
formerly 799.11
hence 843.7

theory
n idea 887.1
hypothesis 906.1
explanation 906.2
opinion 908.6

therapy

n medicine 81.1
treatment 82.1
cure 381.7
aid 434.1

there
adv everywhere 149.10
thereabouts 150.24
adv here 210.16

therefore
adv accordingly 728.11
in consequence 842.7
hence 843.7
on balance 901.17

these
adj this 827.14

these days
n the present 800.1

they
n self 827.5

thick
adj thickset 255.7
luxuriant 296.32
inarticulate 510.11
teeming 839.9
stupid 877.14
dense 990.11
viscous 16.11
adv densely 990.14
n middle 781.1
v thicken 255.5

thin
adj dainty 234.7
infinitesimal 244.13
shrunken 246.10
slender 256.13
shallow 262.5
rare 285.4
tenuous 726.5
sparse 840.5
meagre 947.10
transparent 981.2
adv thinly 256.18
v dilute 16.10
shrink 246.7
thin down 256.10
thin out 285.3
cultivate 112.16

thing
n act 313.3
something 725.3
particular 728.3
affair 793.3
object 997.4

things
n wardrobe 5.2
equipment 370.4
belongings 456.2

think
v expect 121.5
care 324.6
intend 365.4
conceive 886.6
suppose 906.7
be persuaded 908.11

think about
v concentrate 886.8

think of
v be considerate 134.10
seize on 886.12
judge 901.8
remember 944.8

thinking
adj mental 874.6
n thought 886.1
opinion 908.6

third
n interval 687.11
gear 986.5

thirteen
n team 597.7

this
adj this one 827.14

this one
adj this 827.14

this point
n the present 800.1

this way
adv thus 728.10

thoroughly
adv carefully 324.15
completely 756.13
perfectly 957.9

those

adj this 827.14

thought
n expectation 121.1
consideration 134.3
advice 407.1
remark 509.1
tinge 759.6
intellect 874.1
thinking 886.1
idea 887.1
opinion 908.6
attention 938.1

thoughts
n train of thoughts
886.4

thousand
adj numerous 839.6

threat
n warning 384.1
menace 499.1
danger 961.1

threatened
adj foreshadowed
124.14
in danger 961.13

threatening
adj ominous 124.16
menacing 499.3
imminent 802.3
dangerous 961.9

throat
n mouth 2.12
narrow 256.3
tongue 409.12

through
adj completed 392.10
ended 782.7

throughout
adv sparsely 733.10
all over 756.16

throw
n cast 722.8
toss 859.3
v clap 150.13
upset 773.4
fling 859.10
fix 920.4

stump 926.8

throwing
n projection 859.2

thrown
adj beat 926.17

thus
adv how 369.8
this way 728.10
similarly 746.12
hence 843.7
to illustrate 912.20

ticket
n permission 428.1
label 502.13
certificate 530.6
token 705.9
v label 502.20

tide
n flow 224.4
tide gate 224.13
ocean 226.1
time 783.1

tie
n intermediary 204.3
security 423.1
fidelity 624.6
insignia 627.1
notation 687.6
relation 737.1
the same 752.3
joining 762.1
dead heat 798.3
stop 819.2
v compel 409.12
bind 413.9
obligate 621.10
relate 737.6
equal 752.5
put together 762.4
bind 762.8
secure 817.8

tied
adj bound 413.15
obliged 621.14
related 737.9
equal 752.7
joined 762.12

stuck 817.16

tight
adj narrow 256.12
close 279.10
concise 519.5
fast 762.13
tidy 769.8
sparse 840.5
rigid 991.10
adv securely 762.17

till
n treasury 706.11
v cultivate 112.16

time
n leisure 387.1
tempo 687.12
duration 783.1
period 786.1
term 786.3
age 786.4
turn 787.2
shift 787.3
term 787.4
the time 794.2
date 794.3
opportunity 805.2
v keep time 794.8

timing
n chronology 794.1

tin
adj brass 12.15
n dough 705.2
v preserve 382.8

tiny
adj insignificant 234.6
minute 244.10

tip
n summit 189.2
inclination 195.2
point 271.2
hint 407.2
gratuity 463.5
bonus 604.6
extremity 782.2
tap 857.6
surplus 948.5
v list 173.17

top 189.7
incline 195.9
top 281.20
tap 857.16

tired
adj weary 21.6
weary 109.11
worn-out 378.32
proverbial 929.5

tissue
n material 4.1
structure 252.1
organic matter 291.1
weaving 717.1

title
n possession 454.1
ownership 454.2
estate 456.4
name 512.3
book 535.1
prerogative 622.1
honour 628.1
caption 892.2
v name 512.10
focus on 892.3

to come
adj future 801.7
imminent 802.3
scheduled 920.8

to date
adv until now 800.4

to keep
adv for keeps 459.9

to let
adv for hire 595.18

today
adv now 800.3
n the present 801.1

together
adj composed 97.13
in accord 440.3
adv unanimously
317.15
cooperatively 435.6
collectively 731.9
jointly 762.16
simultaneously 798.7

concurrently 854.4

tomorrow
adv later 801.8
n the future 801.1

tone
n muscularity 15.2
colour 34.1
brightness 34.6
pitch 41.2
fitness 75.1
feeling 84.1
ambience 200.3
behaviour 306.1
manner 369.1
intonation 509.6
manner of speaking
509.7
melody 686.1
pitch 687.3
note 687.8
interval 687.11
treatment 690.7
plot 700.4
nature 729.2
trend 851.2
mood 933.4

tongue
n liver 10.19
point 269.6
language 508.1
utterance 509.2
vocal cords 509.12

tonight
adv now 800.3

too
adv additionally 239.10
excessively 948.19

too much
adj excessive 948.14
adv excessively 948.19

top
adj topmost 189.8
superlative 235.13
n top side 189.1
summit 189.2
exterior 197.2
cover 281.5

toy 720.15
limit 756.5
rotor 870.4
height 957.2
v top off 189.7
excel 235.6
overshadow 235.8
rise above 258.8
cap 281.20
exceed 948.9

torn
adj affected 84.21
impaired 378.23
shabby 378.28
alienated 570.11
severed 764.21

Tory
n conservative 592.10

total
adj great 233.6
downright 233.12
cumulative 732.23
comprehensive 734.7
whole 754.9
complete 756.8
thorough 756.9
universal 826.13
unqualified 915.1
sound 957.6
n amount 230.2
plus sign 239.2
sum 754.2
v compute 239.6
amount to 754.8

totally
adv utterly 233.21
wholly 754.12
completely 756.13
solely 834.14
perfectly 957.9

touch
n senses 24.5
contact 64.1
contact 212.5
hint 234.4
communication 328.1
skill 398.1

knack 398.6
motif 483.6
signal 502.15
implication 504.2
execution 686.24
tinge 759.6
tap 857.6
v sense 24.6
feel 64.6
affect 84.12
move 136.5
contact 212.10
signal 502.22
relate to 737.5
equal 752.5
tap 857.16

touched
adj affected 84.21
insane 881.22

tough
adj firm 15.17
obdurate 346.9
strict 410.5
resolute 477.14
difficult 507.12
laborious 702.18
sturdy 725.7
durable 789.9
difficult 968.17
hard 991.9
resistant 994.3
n hunk 15.7
combatant 446.1
hooligan 574.4
bruiser 651.9

tour
n journey 168.4
route 368.1
engagement 682.8
shift 787.3
term 787.4
circuit 869.2
walking tour 873.4
v journey 168.17

tourist
n traveller 169.1
sightseer 873.3

tournament
n contest 442.3
gymkhana 720.9

tower
n observation point 27.8
estate 217.6
structure 252.2
turret 258.5
stronghold 445.6
marker 502.10
v grow 14.2
ascend 184.7
loom 233.5
grow 245.7
soar 258.7

town
adj urban 219.8
n township 219.1
state 220.5

trace
n odour 60.1
hint 234.4
remainder 242.1
drop 244.6
image 334.5
clue 502.9
record 530.1
tinge 759.6
v represent 334.8
outline 366.10
mark 502.19
write 528.14
portray 690.17
copy 747.8
stalk 893.33
discover 896.2

track
n direction 151.1
wake 173.3
routine 358.5
route 368.1
path 368.2
railway 368.7
racing 442.8
trail 502.8
hint 532.4

playground 720.10
v hunt 367.9
follow 797.3
trace 893.33

trade
adj commercial 708.19
n vocation 701.6
commerce 708.1
trading 708.2
bargain 708.5
custom 708.6
market 710.3
trading 825.2
v transfer 609.3
deal 708.14
speculate 714.11
change 816.5
interchange 825.3

trading
adj commercial 708.19
n transfer 609.1
trade 708.2
speculation 714.9
changing 816.3
trade 825.2

tradition
n custom 358.1
rule 404.2
religion 655.1
custom 804.2
superstition 909.3

traditional
adj customary 358.12
prescriptive 404.4
conventional 560.5
orthodox 666.7
historical 697.6
mythological 804.11

traditionally
adv conventionally 560.6
in conformity 829.7

traffic
n communication 328.1
commerce 708.1
v trade 708.14

tragedy
n drama 682.3
misfortune 966.2

tragic
adj horrid 89.19
heavy 682.26
disastrous 966.15

trail
n path 368.2
track 502.8
wake 779.2
aftermath 842.3
v lag behind 157.4
dawdle 166.7
hang 193.6
come last 208.8
hunt 367.9
follow 797.3
pull 860.4
trace 893.33

train
n passenger train 170.12
attendance 731.5
procession 774.3
wake 779.2
v direct 152.4
accustom 358.8
drill 549.13
be taught 551.11
play 721.2
pull 860.4
tend 113.6

trained
adj accustomed 358.14
skilled 398.24
informed 883.14

trainer
n coach 390.5
instructor 552.6
stockman 113.2

training
n accustoming 358.6
preparation 390.1
preparation 549.3

transfer
adv interchange 167.1

n informing 328.2
transference 609.1
v transmit 167.6
communicate 328.6
deliver 463.13
commission 595.8
convey 609.3

transformed
adj improved 377.13
changed 814.10
converted 820.19

transition
adv transfer 167.1
n change 814.1
conversion 820.1

transport
adv transportation 167.2
n trance 670.3
v convey 167.6
banish 864.15

trap
n ambush 331.3
gin 341.12
lure 362.3
rocks 961.5
v catch 341.20
catch 465.17

travel
adv transportation 167.2
n progression 153.1
course 163.2
travelling 168.1
v progress 153.2
move 163.4
go 168.14
journey 168.17

travelled
adj cosmopolitan 168.35

travelling
adj moving 163.6
moving 168.32
n travel 168.1

treasury
n store 371.1

store 371.6
funds 705.11
cash 705.14
repository 706.11
collection 732.11

treat
n meal 8.5
delicacy 10.8
feast 86.3
v remedy 77.19
practise medicine 81.10
doctor 82.11
use 306.5
handle 372.10
prepare 390.6
discuss 523.10
write upon 537.5

treated
adj prepared 390.13

treatment
n medicine 81.1
therapy 82.1
cure 82.5
usage 372.2
preparation 390.1
piece 537.1
technique 690.7

treaty
n entente cordiale 422.2

tree
n timber 296.10

tremendous
adj terrible 118.29
large 233.7
huge 243.19
superb 954.15

trend
n direction 152.1
course 163.2
flow 224.4
fashion 559.1
drift 851.2
v head 152.6
flow 224.4
tend 851.3

trial
adj tentative 388.8
experimental 897.11
n trials and tribulations 87.9
attempt 388.2
preparation 390.1
contest 442.3
hearing 579.5
experiment 897.1
test 897.2
adversity 966.1

tribunal
adj judicial 576.7
n council 408.1
forum 576.1

tribute
n gift 463.4
celebration 472.1
praise 494.5
tax 610.9
citation 626.4
citation 843.2

trick
n device 341.6
pretext 361.1
intrigue 366.5
knack 398.6
stratagem 400.3
prank 474.5
style 514.2
v deceive 341.14
fool 341.15
live by one's wits 400.9
play a joke or trick on 474.8

tried
adj experienced 398.26
devoted 568.20
trustworthy 624.15
tested 897.12
assured 925.14

trip
n journey 168.4
flight 175.3
tumble 185.3

bungle 399.5
v speed 165.6
stroll 168.24
tumble 185.8
trap 341.20
cavort 351.6
bungle 399.9
dance 683.5
play 720.22
err 930.8

triumph
n rejoicing 107.1
great success 394.2
victory 396.1
celebration 472.1
crowing 487.2
v beat 235.7
win through 394.10
prevail 396.3
exult 487.7

troops
n work force 18.4
army 446.19

trophy
n ambition 91.10
victory 396.1
monument 530.10
laurels 626.3
memento 946.6
good thing 954.5

trouble
n annoyance 87.2
affliction 87.8
anxiety 117.1
imposition 623.1
exertion 702.1
commotion 772.4
inconvenience 951.3
adversity 966.1
impediment 967.6
the matter 968.3
v distress 87.16
agitate 96.14
concern 117.3
take liberties 620.7
upset 773.4
agitate 872.7

inconvenience 951.4
beset 968.13

troubled
adj annoyed 87.21
distressed 87.22
agitated 96.23
anxious 117.6
agitated 872.13
beset 968.20

trousers
n pair of trousers 5.14

truck
n lorry 170.10
communication 328.1
luggage 456.3
commerce 708.1

true
adj straight 263.6
firm 344.11
observant 419.4
devoted 568.20
trustworthy 624.15
faithful 624.16
real 723.11
certain 925.9
truthful 928.13

truly
adv decidedly 233.18
truthfully 624.18
really 723.1
certainly 925.17
really 928.18

trust
n hope 115.1
estate 456.4
commission 595.1
company 597.9
credit 602.1
investment company
714.8
belief 908.1
confidence 925.4
v hope 115.6
commit 463.16
believe 908.10
confide in 908.16

truth

n reality 723.2
certainty 925.1
very truth 928.1
axiom 929.2

try
n whack 388.3
test 897.2
v attempt 388.5
give a hearing to
579.17
experiment 897.8
hold court 901.12

trying
adj debilitating 16.17
fatiguing 21.11
oppressive 89.24
examining 893.35
adverse 966.13
troublesome 968.18

tube
n train 170.12
pipe 225.5
cylinder 282.2

tune
n melody 686.1
harmony 686.2
air 686.3
pitch 687.3
v fit 390.8
harmonize 686.29
harmonize 750.7

tunnel
n lair 217.23
channel 225.1
cave 270.4
passageway 368.3
trench 445.5
v deepen 261.7
excavate 270.12

turkey
n flop 395.2
stage show 682.2

Turkish
n Cuban 80.2

turn
n start 122.2
kindness 134.7

deviation 155.1
bias 195.3
form 248.1
distortion 251.1
bend 265.3
act 313.3
act 682.4
bout 787.2
shift 787.3
round 812.3
change 814.1
reversion 821.1
tendency 851.1
deviation 869.1
circuit 869.2
whirl 870.2
disposition 933.3
v direct 152.4
head 182.5
turn round 154.8
deviate 155.3
deviate 195.8
distort 251.5
curve 265.6
wind 267.4
blunt 272.2
recur 812.5
be changed 814.6
change 816.5
tend 851.3
go around 869.6
rotate 870.7

turn to
v resort to 372.12
undertake 389.3
attend to 938.5

turned
adj tainted 378.34

turning
adj deviating 155.7
winding 267.6
rotating 870.10
n deviation 155.1
bend 265.3
winding 267.1
rotation 870.1

TV

n television 984.1
television 984.10

twice
adv doubly 836.5

twin
adj accompanying 731.8
identical 740.7
analogous 746.7
two 835.5
n image 334.5
the same 740.3
likeness 746.3
equal 752.4
v double 835.4
duplicate 836.3

two
adj dual 835.5
n couple 835.2

type
n form 248.1
measure 286.2
representative 334.7
preference 356.5
print 529.6
nature 729.2
model 748.1
example 748.2
kind 771.3
speciality 828.1
disposition 933.3
v write 528.14

typical
adj exemplary 334.1
indicative 502.23
model 748.8
special 771.6
normal 831.6

ugly
adj dangerous 961.9
unsightly 970.5

ultimate
adj top 189.8
completing 392.8
ending 782.7
final 782.10
eventual 793.11

future 801.7
n height 957.2

ultimately
adv finally 782.11
eventually 793.12
in time 801.10

unable
adj incapable 19.14
incompetent 399.16

uncertain
adj inconspicuous 31.6
irresolute 347.9
ambiguous 521.4
speculative 722.23
relative 737.7
irregular 813.3
changeable 816.7
doubting 910.9
unsure 926.10
unsafe 961.11

uncertainty
n low profile 31.2
suspense 121.3
irresolution 347.1
ambiguity 521.4
gamble 722.2
dependence 722.23
irregularity 813.1
instability 816.2
doubt 910.2
chance 926.1
chance 927.1
inaccuracy 930.2
dangerousness 961.2

uncle
n brother 540.3

under
adj lower 260.8
adv low 260.9

underground
adj subterranean 261.11
dissenting 318.6
covert 330.12
concealed 331.11
adv six feet under 295.22

n train 170.12
subversive 342.8
irregular 446.12

underlying
adj basic 190.8
latent 504.5
essential 729.6

understand
v interpret 326.7
comprehend 506.7
know 883.10
suppose 906.7

understanding
adj patient 125.8
pitying 136.6
in accord 440.3
intelligent 875.10
astute 875.14
knowing 883.12
n unanimity 317.5
obligation 421.2
compact 422.1
accord 440.1
compromise 453.1
compact 750.2
intellect 874.1
intelligence 875.1
comprehension 883.3
intuition 889.1

understood
adj tacit 504.8
traditional 804.11
known 883.21
supposed 906.11

undoubtedly
adv unquestionably 925.19
truly 928.18

unemployed
adj motionless 164.11
idle 316.16
unused 375.10

unemployment
n idleness 316.2
seasonal
unemployment 316.3

unexpected

adj unprepared for
122.9
sudden 792.5
unusual 832.10
fantastic 832.12
improbable 924.3
chance 927.9

unfair
adj not fair 630.9

unfortunately
adv unfavourably
124.19
inappropriately 951.8
unluckily 966.17

unhappy
adj cheerless 103.21
disapproving 495.19
inconvenient 806.6
undesirable 951.5
unfortunate 966.14

unification
n affiliation 435.2
identification 740.2
joining 762.1
combination 767.1
unity 834.1

uniform
adj symmetrical 250.4
smooth 256.9
equable 743.5
agreeing 750.9
simple 760.5
orderly 769.6
continuous 774.8
regular 812.6
one 834.7
indistinguishable 900.5
n civilian dress or
clothes 5.6
insignia 627.1
v outfit 5.30

union
n convergence 160.1
junction 212.3
affiliation 435.2
accord 440.1
marriage 544.1

association 597.1
relation 737.1
identification 740.2
agreement 750.1
joining 762.1
joint 762.3
combination 767.1
n collaboration 854.1

unique
adj wonderful 113.6
original 322.4
other 742.7
novel 803.11
infrequent 810.2
characteristic 827.13
unusual 832.10
one 834.7
sole 834.9

unit
n organization 446.18
something 725.3
one 834.3

united
adj in accord 440.3
joined 762.12
combined 767.5
integrated 834.10
concurrent 854.3

United Nations
n League of Nations
593.5

units
n work force 18.4

unity
n accord 440.1
sameness 777.1
uniformity 743.1
whole 754.1
wholeness 754.5
totality 756.1
simplicity 760.1
individuality 834.1
indivisibility 990.2

universal
adj comprehensive
734.7
whole 754.9

thorough 756.9
infinite 785.2
galactic 826.13
usual 831.7
cosmic 114.20

universe
n totality 756.1
world 114.1

university
adj scholastic 548.13
n college 548.5

unknown
adj concealed 331.11
anonymous 528.3
unnotable 641.14
unsuspected 885.14

unlike
adj different 742.6
dissimilar 749.4
incomparable 898.8

unlikely
adj improbable 924.3

unrest
n trepidation 96.5
motion 163.1
agitation 872.1

unusual
adj novel 803.11
infrequent 810.2
contrary 830.5
uncommon 832.10

up
adj awake 23.8
adv upward 184.14
vertically 191.11
on high 258.15
v ascend 184.7
increase 237.4

up and down
adv to and fro 871.17

up for
adj prepared for
390.15

up on
adj skilled in 398.25
informed 883.14
versed in 883.15

up to
  adj able 18.9
  prepared for 390.15
  competent 398.22
  sufficient 946.5

upon
  adv after which 797.6

upper
  adj superior 235.12
  higher 258.14
  n stimulant 77.9

upset
  adj agitated 96.23
  unnerved 119.14
  defeated 397.13
  disorderly 772.11
  agitated 872.13
  disproved 913.6
  bewildered 926.15
  confused 940.12
  n anxiety 117.1
  unseating 151.2
  overturn 196.2
  fall 380.3
  revolution 822.1
  agitation 872.1
  refutation 913.2
  confusion 940.3
  frustration 967.3
  v embarrass 87.15
  distress 87.16
  agitate 96.14
  concern 117.3
  worry 117.4
  unnerve 119.10
  capsize 182.18
  overturn 196.5
  overthrow 380.20
  overcome 397.6
  overbalance 753.2
  disorder 772.8
  disturb 773.4
  revolutionize 822.4
  agitate 872.7
  refute 913.4
  thwart 967.14

upstairs

  adv up 184.14

urban
  adj metropolitan 219.8

urgent
  adj motivating 360.24
  hasty 386.5
  demanding 406.9
  teasing 425.18
  vehement 525.12
  necessary 918.10
  imperative 952.21

use
  n employment 372.1
  utility 372.3
  benefit 372.4
  function 372.5
  wear 378.5
  estate 456.4
  v be on 78.5
  treat 306.5
  practise 313.8
  utilize 369.5
  utilize 372.8
  treat 372.10
  exploit 372.14
  exert 702.8

used
  adj employed 372.22
  wasted 471.7
  secondhand 804.17

used to
  adj accustomed 358.14
  familiar with 358.15
  in the habit of 358.16

useful
  adj instrumental 369.7
  of use 372.16
  helpful 434.21
  helpful 434.21
  expedient 950.5
  good 954.12

using
  adj addicted 78.8
  n utilization 372.6

usual
  adj medium 232.3
  typical 334.14

  customary 358.12
  same 743.6
  orderly 769.6
  frequent 809.4
  prevalent 826.11
  regular 831.7
  ordinary 960.8

usually
  adv customarily 358.18
  frequently 809.6
  generally 826.16
  normally 831.8

valley
  n crack 213.2
  pit 261.2
  vale 270.7

valuable
  adj of value 372.20
  precious 612.10

value
  n measure 286.2
  benefit 372.4
  worth 610.2
  worth 612.2
  importance 952.1
  goodness 954.1
  v respect 641.4
  measure 286.7
  price 610.11
  estimate 901.9
  esteem 952.12

van
  n wagon 170.2
  vanguard 207.2

varied
  adj different 742.6
  assorted 745.4
  mixed 759.12

variety
  n drama 682.3
  assortment 732.13
  difference 742.1
  irregularity 744.1
  diversity 745.1
  kind 771.3
  change 814.1
  several 838.1

various
 adj different 742.6
 uneven 744.3
 varied 745.4
 plural 838.5
 several 839.7

vary
 v deviate 155.3
 vacillate 347.8
 differ 742.4
 differentiate 742.5
 diversify 744.2
 diversify 745.2
 disagree 751.5
 fluctuate 813.2
 be changed 814.6
 change 814.7
 change 816.5

vast
 adj spacious 149.8
 large 233.7
 huge 243.19

vat
 n store 371.6

vegetable
 adj herbal 296.28
 passive 314.6
 n plant 296.3

vegetables
 n produce 10.32

vehicle
 n colour 34.8
 carrier 170.1
 instrument 369.4
 stage show 682.2

venture
 n undertaking 389.1
 company 597.9
 investment 706.3
 trading 714.9
 gamble 722.2
 v attempt 388.5
 dare 477.8
 presume 620.6
 invest 706.15
 trade 714.11
 chance 722.20

venue
 n station 150.2

verdict
 n judgment 579.9
 solution 895.1
 decision 901.5

version
 n reproduction 321.3
 rendering 326.2
 writing 528.8
 score 686.22
 story 700.3

very
 adv somewhat 231.7
 exceedingly 233.17

very good
 adj good 954.12

very well
 adv excellently 954.21

veteran
 adj experienced 398.26
 n old man 290.2
 vet 398.16
 vet 446.15

vice
 n misconduct 307.1
 criminality 634.1
 weakness 634.2
 wickedness 635.1
 substitute 824.2

vice-president
 n vice-chancellor 557.8
 substitute 824.2

victim
 n sufferer 76.12
 sufferer 87.11
 dupe 343.1
 quarry 367.7
 loser 397.4
 laughing stock 493.7
 cheat 722.18
 unfortunate 966.7

Victorian
 adj antiquated 804.12

victory
 n success 394.1
 triumph 396.1

video
 adj televisual 984.16
 n videorecorder 984.11
 v record 984.15

view
 n look 27.3
 field of view 30.3
 aspect 32.3
 scene 32.6
 scene 690.10
 estimate 901.3
 opinion 908.6
 outlook 933.2
 v see 27.11
 look 27.12
 contemplate 886.13
 be disposed to 933.6
 heed 938.6

villa
 n estate 217.6

village
 adj urban 219.8
 n hamlet 219.2
 state 220.5

violence
 n acrimony 17.5
 cruelty 135.10
 rage 143.10
 abuse 374.2
 coercion 409.3
 venom 651.1

violent
 adj acrimonious 17.13
 frenzied 96.25
 passionate 96.29
 forcible 409.12
 venomous 651.15
 rabid 881.26

virgin
 adj country 222.5
 native 391.11
 continent 644.6
 intact 754.10
 unadulterated 760.6
 unproductive 846.4
 unknown 885.14
 unharmed 957.7

n spinster 546.4

virtually
adv latently 504.11
on the whole 754.13

virus
n infection 76.4
germ 76.11
drop 244.6
organism 291.2
language 988.12

visible
adj visual 27.19
visual 30.6
apparent 32.11
manifest 333.8

vision
n sight 27.1
apparition 32.5
deception 341.1
phantom 931.4
whim 941.4
picture 941.5
dream 941.7
spectre 943.1
picture 971.6

visit
n social call 563.7
v go to 168.21
enter 180.7
attend 210.8
pay a visit 563.18

visitor
n traveller 169.1
entrant 180.4
patron 210.5
guest 566.6

visual
adj skeleton 2.19
eye 27.19
visible 30.6

vital
adj powerful 18.7
organic 291.11
living 292.9
vigorous 525.10
durable 789.9
requisite 918.11

all-important 952.22

vitamin
n vitamin complex 7.3

voice
n note 356.6
utterance 509.2
manner of speaking 509.7
soprano 687.4
singer 688.9
v say 509.16

volume
n loudness 44.1
space 149.1
quantity 233.3
size 243.1
capacity 243.2
book 535.1
tome 535.4
edition 535.5
part 535.13

voluntary
adj willing 308.4
gratuitous 309.6
optional 356.21
intentional 365.8

vote
n voting 356.6
approval 494.1
introduction 594.4
v cast one's vote 356.17
participate 461.4
support 590.31

voting
n vote 356.6
participation 461.1
going to the polls 590.16

vulnerable
adj helpless 19.18
open-minded 849.15
liable 852.5
weak 961.16
brittle 995.3

wage
n pay 604.4

v practise 313.8

wages
n pay 604.4

wait
n delay 808.2
v await 121.8
be patient 125.3
delay 808.11

wait for
v await 121.8

waiting
adj expectant 121.10
serving 558.13
imminent 802.3
n suspense 121.3
lingering 808.3

waiting for
adj expectant 121.10

wake
n wakefulness 23.1
track 173.3
last rites 295.4
track 502.8
social gathering 563.10
trail 779.2
aftermath 842.3
v awake 23.4
awaken 23.5

walk
n ramble 168.8
gait 168.10
sphere 220.2
route 368.1
path 368.2
race 442.9
sphere 701.4
vocation 701.6
v exercise 75.3
traipse 168.23
be free 415.16
go free 416.9

walker
n pedestrian 169.6
baby buggy 170.4

walking
adj travelling 168.32
n exercise 75.2

going on foot 168.7

wall

n precipice 191.3
fence 203.4
partition 204.4
barrier 967.5
v fence 203.7
fortify 445.9

want

n desire 91.1
absence 211.1
indigence 599.2
deficiency 757.2
requirement 918.2
lack 947.4
imperfection 958.1
v desire 91.13
be inferior 236.4
be poor 599.5
lack 757.3
fall short 866.2
require 918.8
lack 947.7
be insufficient 947.8

want to

v wish to 91.14

wanted

adj desired 91.28
welcome 566.12
requisite 918.11

wanting

adj desiring 91.20
absent 211.10
bereft 458.8
without being 724.7
incomplete 754.4
short of 866.5
insufficient 947.9
lacking 947.13
imperfect 958.4

war

n contention 442.1
warfare 443.1
campaign 443.3
military science 443.5
v contend 442.10
wage war 443.12

ward

n hospital room
   188.21
state 220.5
custody 414.5
dependent 417.5
defence 445.1
stronghold 445.6
constituency 590.14

warm

adj colouring 34.14
fervent 84.16
zealous 92.9
comfortable 112.11
kind 134.13
vehement 525.12
hospitable 566.11
cordial 568.15
thermal 971.43
v heat 972.17

warning

adj forewarning 124.15
cautioning 384.5
advisory 407.6
n forewarning 124.4
caution 364.1
caution 384.1
preparation 390.1
demand 406.1
advice 407.1
threat 499.1
clue 532.3

wash

n colour 34.8
washing 70.5
laundry 70.6
wake 173.3
lap 224.8
marsh 229.1
painting 690.12
v colour 34.12
bathe 70.19
soak 19.11

washing

n ablutions 70.5
laundry 70.6

waste

adj country 222.5
unproductive 846.4
n excrement 12.3
offal 71.9
loss 238.3
remainder 242.1
derelict 355.4
consumption 373.1
refuse 376.3
wastage 378.4
destruction 380.1
wastage 458.2
extravagance 471.1
extract 848.3
v decrease 238.6
rub out 294.11
be consumed 373.3
waste away 378.17
destroy 380.10
deplete 458.5
consume 471.4

watch

n observation 27.2
hand 174.4
vigilance 324.4
shift 787.3
timepiece 794.4
watchman 963.10
v look 27.12
await 121.8
attend 210.8
be vigilant 324.8
witness 873.5
scout 893.26
heed 938.6
care for 963.19
keep watch 963.20

watching

n observation 27.2
vigilance 324.4

water

n urine 12.5
kaleidoscope 816.4
matter 997.2
fluid 15.2
steam 19.3
v secrete 13.4

corrupt 378.11
adulterate 759.11
moisten 19.10
tend 113.6

wave
n billow 224.14
winding 267.1
greeting 566.4
waving 871.2
ray 871.4
swing 871.6
v cut or style the hair
3.13
manifest 333.5
show off 486.13
signal 502.22
oscillate 871.8
undulate 871.9
flutter 872.9

way
n direction 152.1
progression 153.1
progress 173.5
entrance 180.5
channel 225.1
behaviour 306.1
custom 358.1
habit 358.3
plan 86.1
route 368.1
manner 369.1
knack 398.6
style 514.2
mode 727.3
nature 729.2
speciality 828.1

way in
n entrance 180.5

way out
adj nothing like 749.5
modern 803.13
n outlet 188.7
loophole 354.4

ways
n behaviour 306.1
means 369.2

weak

adj feeble 16.11
impotent 19.13
tired 21.6
inconspicuous 31.6
colourless 35.7
faint 43.14
insipid 56.2
thin 256.13
decrepit 289.13
feeble 347.12
lax 411.3
cowardly 476.6
unclean 634.12
fragile 726.6
open-minded 849.15
powerless 850.3
feeble 877.19
unsound 891.9
vulnerable 961.16

weakness
n softness 16.1
weak point 16.4
impotence 19.1
fatigue 21.1
low profile 31.2
paleness 35.2
insipidness 56.1
tenderness 44.6
weak will 347.4
laxness 411.1
cowardice 476.1
vice 634.2
openness 849.5
powerlessness 850.1
tendency 851.1
feeblemindedness
877.7
gullibility 909.2
fault 958.2
vulnerability 961.4

wealth
n assets 456.6
gain 457.3
riches 598.1
plenty 946.2
prosperity 965.1

weapons

n arms 447.1

wear
n clothing 5.1
use 378.5
disintegration 768.1
abrasion 989.2
v have on 5.33
be tedious 109.6
decrease 238.6
waste 378.17
affect 485.8
endure 789.5
abrade 989.5

wearing
adj fatiguing 21.11
oppressive 89.24
wearying 109.10

weather
n weather conditions
175.10
climate 302.2
v waste 378.17
stand fast 817.11
be safe 962.2

wedding
n marriage 544.2
joining 762.1
combination 767.1

week
n moment 786.2

weekend
n holiday 20.3
v spend time 783.4

weekly
adj recurrent 811.13
momentary 812.8
n periodical 536.1

weight
n power 18.1
fitness 75.1
sadness 103.1
body weight 283.1
paperweight 283.4
extent 286.3
prestige 402.4
formality 561.1
charge 623.3

parallel bars 702.7
influence 849.1
validity 928.6
importance 952.1
impediment 967.6
v weigh 283.8
weigh or weigh down
283.9

welcome
adj wanted 566.12
n greetings 177.4
reception 178.1
welcoming 178.8
assent 317.1
liberality 470.1
welcoming 566.2
v receive 178.9
assent 317.7
make one feel at
home 566.9
incur 852.4

welfare
n subsidy 463.8
welfarism 592.7
good 954.4
prosperity 965.1

well
adj all right 74.10
adv ably 18.11
kindly 134.18
successfully 394.12
skilfully 398.29
excellently 954.21
n lake 227.1
pit 261.2
pit 270.3
source 371.4
spring 841.6
v run out 181.10

well-known
adj distinguished
642.14
real 723.11
widely known 883.22

west
adj northern 152.13
adv westward 152.17

n points of the
compass 152.2

western
adj northern 152.13

wet
adj moderate 592.19
fluid 15.3
moist 19.13
n rain 301.1
wet weather 301.3
moderate 592.11
moisture 19.1
v moisten 19.10

what
n whatever 826.5

whatever
adv at all 771.8
n whatsoever 826.5

wheel
n circle 266.1
rack 586.4
kiln 719.3
roulette 722.10
round 812.3
propeller 859.6
whirl 870.2
rotor 870.4
n helm 554.5
v recur 812.5
circle 869.5
rotate 870.7
whirl 870.9

when
adv upon which 783.6

whenever
adv when 783.6
if ever 783.10

where
adv whereabouts
150.21

wherever
adv anywhere 150.22

while
n time 783.1
period 786.1
meantime 788.2
v spend 372.11

white
adj colourless 35.7
pure white 36.5
vacant 211.12
aged 289.11
n whiteness 36.1
egg 291.10

White House
n house 217.5

whole
adj comprehensive
734.7
total 754.9
complete 756.8
one 834.7
unqualified 915.1
sound 957.6
n quantity 230.1
totality 754.1
all 826.3

why
adv how come 843.8

wide
adj spacious 149.8
voluminous 243.16
broad 255.6
extensive 826.12
broad-minded 934.8
adv widely 247.16
clear 247.18

widely
adv extensively 149.9
wide 247.16

widespread
adj spacious 149.8
spreading 245.11
broad 255.6
customary 358.12
dispersed 733.7
extensive 826.12

wife
n woman 68.5
married woman 544.7

wild
adj hectic 92.12
frenzied 96.25
passionate 96.29

infuriated 143.30
country 222.5
defiant 312.9
unmanageable 346.11
uninhibited 415.22
reckless 478.7
foolhardy 478.8
unrefined 482.10
turbulent 651.16
unruly 651.17
boisterous 651.18
savage 651.19
absurd 878.9
rabid 881.26
distracted 940.10
fanciful 941.14

will
n volition 308.1
resolution 344.1
will power 344.4
choice 356.1
intention 365.1
command 405.1
bequest 463.10
v wish 308.2
resolve 344.6
bequeath 463.18

willing
adj voluntary 308.4
ready 309.5
obedient 311.3
trial 388.8
consenting 426.4
apt 551.18

win
n victory 396.1
v beat 235.7
triumph 396.3
acquire 457.8

wind
n breathing 2.14
lightning 165.5
current 303.1
bull 505.3
belch 864.9
flatulence 111.3
v stray 155.4

curve 265.6
twine 267.4
prime 390.9
rotate 870.7

window
n window glass 278.6

wing
n breast 10.22
addition 240.3
air force 446.24
party 597.4
branch 597.10
company 732.3
member 755.4
v fly 175.12

wings
n stage 682.12

winner
n superior 235.4
star 394.5
victor 396.2

winning
adj endearing 95.24
alluring 362.8
successful 394.11
victorious 396.6
speculative 722.23
influential 849.13
n acquisition 457.1

winter
adj seasonal 298.8
n wintertime 298.6
cold weather 975.3
v spend time 784.4

wire
n cord 257.2
telegram 332.8
end 762.8
battery accumulator 982.19
v telex 332.12
bind 762.8
electrify 982.24

wisdom
n depth 875.5
understanding 883.3
maxim 929.1

expedience or
  expediency 950.1

wise
adj sage 875.15
knowing 883.12
learned 883.17
sophisticated 911.4
expedient 950.5
n manner 369.1

wish
n desire 91.1
ambition 91.10
will 308.1
request 425.1
v desire 91.13
will 308.2
request 425.9

wish to
v want to 91.14

with it
adv in step 750.11

withdraw
v use 78.5
retreat 154.5
recede 159.2
retract 159.3
quit 179.9
extract 183.9
subtract 241.8
dissent 318.4
hesitate 347.7
retract 348.8
abandon 355.5
repeal 430.2
separate 764.7
stand alone 834.6

withdrawal
n substance abuse 78.1
alienation 83.13
unfeeling 85.1
retreat 154.2
recession 159.1
departure 179.1
extraction 183.1
dissent 318.1
reticence 329.2

denial 348.3
abandonment 355.1
repeal 430.1
resignation 433.1
seclusion 565.1
elimination 735.2
separation 764.1
loneliness 834.2
disinterest 937.1
withdrawn
adj apathetic 85.13
reticent 329.8
private 330.13
aloof 564.6
secluded 565.8
alone 834.8
uninquisitive 937.3
within
adv in 198.9
without
adj excluding 735.10
adv externally 197.9
witness
n informant 532.5
party 579.11
spectator 873.1
testimony 912.2
spectator 912.6
v see 27.11
attend 210.8
testify 319.6
be pious 671.6
see 873.5
testify 912.8
woman
n womankind 68.3
lady 68.5
adult 290.1
person 297.3
wife 544.7
women
n womankind 68.3
wonder
n astonishment 113.1
marvel 113.2
miracle 832.8
prodigy 954.6

v marvel 113.3
not know 885.9
be uncertain 926.5
wonderful
adj marvellous 113.6
remarkable 233.10
extraordinary 832.14
superb 954.15
wondering
adj marvelling 113.5
wood
n woodland 296.11
firewood 973.3
wooden
adj dull 108.6
impassive 507.18
dull 877.15
woods
n hinterland 222.2
woodland 296.11
word
n affirmation 319.1
oath 319.4
account 334.3
command 405.1
promise 421.1
utterance 509.2
remark 509.3
term 511.1
information 532.1
news 533.1
message 533.4
testimony 912.2
maxim 929.1
v say 509.16
phrase 514.3
words
n quarrel 441.5
contention 442.1
speech 509.1
vocabulary 511.11
diction 531.1
talk 523.2
work
n action 313.1
act 313.3
function 372.5

undertaking 389.1
fortification 445.4
writing 528.8
book 535.1
stage show 682.2
piece 686.4
work of art 690.8
literature 696.1
occupation 701.1
occupation 701.1
task 701.2
vocation 701.6
labour 702.4
operation 844.1
product 848.1
v form 248.6
act 313.4
be busy 315.8
use 372.8
accomplish 392.4
work at 701.10
labour 702.12
busy 702.16
mix 759.9
operate 844.5
operate 844.7
perform 847.11
influence 849.7
suffice 946.3
come in handy 950.3
cultivate 112.16
work for
v serve 434.18
serve 558.12
work 701.10
work on
v operate on 844.6
lean on 849.9
work out
v exercise 75.3
carry out 313.7
plan 366.7
accomplish 392.4
arrange 422.8
amplify 520.7
play 721.2
elaborate 823.5

solve 895.2

worker
  n employee 558.3
  working man 588.9
  agent 703.1
  labourer 703.2

workers
  n lower class 588.7

working
  adj acting 313.10
  busy 315.17
  occupied 701.12
  labouring 702.17
  operating 844.11
  n motion 163.1
  action 313.1
  utilization 372.6
  operation 844.1
  cultivation 112.12

working class
  adj upper-class 588.10
  n lower class 588.7

works
  n act 313.3
  literature 696.1
  plant 716.2
  mechanism 986.4

world
  n quantity 233.3
  plot 700.4
  universe 114.1

worn
  adj haggard 21.8
  trite 108.9
  reduced 238.10
  well-worn 378.27
  decomposing 768.3
  stale 804.13
  secondhand 804.17

worried
  adj vexed 117.7
  troubled 968.20

worries
  n worry 117.2

worry
  n annoyance 87.2
  worries 117.2

trouble 968.3
  v upset 117.4
  worry oneself 117.5
  trouble 968.13

worrying
  adj troublesome 117.8
  n worry 117.2

worse
  adj aggravated 110.4
  impaired 378.23
  changed 814.10

worst
  adj terrible 955.9

worth
  adj possessing 454.9
  priced 610.14
  n benefit 372.4
  value 610.2
  value 612.2
  funds 705.11
  importance 952.1
  goodness 954.1

worthy
  adj dignified 127.12
  eligible 356.23
  competent 398.22
  praiseworthy 494.18
  justified 619.9
  honest 624.9
  reputable 642.13
  n good person 639.1
  celebrity 642.8
  personage 952.7

would-be
  adj presumptuous 132.9
  nominal 512.14

wound
  n pain 87.5
  v pain 26.7
  pain 87.17
  offend 143.21
  injure 378.12
  harm 955.6

wounded
  adj pained 26.9

pained 87.23

wrapped
  adj surrounded 200.9
  packed 203.11
  covered 281.28

write
  v represent 334.8
  describe 334.9
  pen 528.14
  compose 528.16
  record 530.12
  correspond 534.10
  compose 686.37
  author 696.5
  produce 847.8

write to
  v correspond 534.10

writer
  n scribbler 528.10
  author 528.12
  correspondent 534.8
  essayist 537.3
  author 696.5
  narrator 700.5

writing
  n representation 334.1
  letter 527.1
  inscription 528.1
  authorship 528.2
  the written word 528.8
  document 530.5
  book 535.1
  elementary education 549.5
  composition 696.2

written
  adj penned 528.17
  destined 839.7

wrong
  adj wrongful 638.3
  unjust 630.8
  wicked 634.15
  iniquitous 635.5
  inconvenient 806.6
  erroneous 930.14
  mistaken 930.16
  undesirable 951.5

bad 955.7
  adv wrongly 618.4
badly 955.12
  n wrongness 618.1
  injustice 630.1
  injustice 630.4
  iniquity 634.3
  misdeed 635.2
  offence 654.3
  error 930.1
  evil 955.3
  v do one an injustice
    630.6
  harm 955.6
yacht
  n sailing vessel 171.2
  v navigate 173.9
yard
  n enclosure 203.3
  plant 716.2
year
  n class 553.10

moment 786.2
years
  n age 289.1
  long time 789.3
yes
  adv approvingly 426.5
  n affirmative 317.2
yesterday
  adv formerly 799.11
  n the past 799.1
yet
  adv additionally 239.10
  previously 796.5
  until now 800.4
you
  n self 827.5
young
  adj juvenile 287.8
  new 803.7
  n young people
    288.2
  brood 542.2

young man
  n boy 288.5
young people
  n youth 288.2
younger
  adj junior 287.13
  subsequent 797.4
  n youngster 288.1
yourself
  n self 827.5
youth
  n tenderness 287.1
  youngster 288.1
  young people 288.2
  boy 288.5
  origin 780.4
zone
  n region 220.1
  longitude 220.3
  band 266.2
  layer 282.1
  orbit 114.14